ADVERTISING
IDENTIFICATION AND PRICE GUIDE

Other **CONFIDENT COLLECTOR** *Titles*
of Interest
from Avon Books

ART DECO
IDENTIFICATION AND PRICE GUIDE
by Tony Fusco

BOOKS
IDENTIFICATION AND PRICE GUIDE
by Nancy Wright

COLLECTIBLE MAGAZINES
IDENTIFICATION AND PRICE GUIDE
by David K. Henkel

FINE ART
IDENTIFICATION AND PRICE GUIDE
by Susan Theran

ORIGINAL COMIC ART
IDENTIFICATION AND PRICE GUIDE
by Jerry Weist

PRINTS, POSTERS & PHOTOGRAPHS
IDENTIFICATION AND PRICE GUIDE
by Susan Theran

QUILTS
IDENTIFICATION AND PRICE GUIDE
by Liz Greenbacker & Kathleen Barach

Coming Soon

WESTERN MEMORABILIA
IDENTIFICATION AND PRICE GUIDE
by William C. Ketchum

Avon Books are available at special quantity discounts for bulk purchases for sales promotions, premiums, fund raising or educational use. Special books, or book excerpts, can also be created to fit specific needs.

For details write or telephone the office of the Director of Special Markets. Avon Books, Dept. FP, 1350 Avenue of the Americas, New York, New York 10019, 1-800-238-0658.

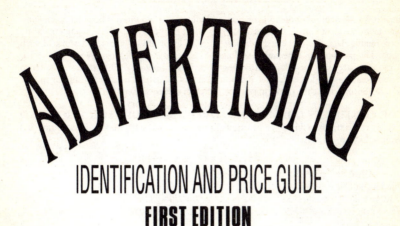

IDENTIFICATION AND PRICE GUIDE
FIRST EDITION

DAWN E. RENO

If you purchased this book without a cover, you should be aware that this book is stolen property. It was reported as "unsold and destroyed" to the publisher, and neither the author nor the publisher has received any payment for this "stripped book."

Important Notice: All of the information, including valuations, in this book has been compiled from the most reliable sources, and every effort has been made to eliminate errors and questionable data. Nevertheless, the possibility of error always exists in a work of such scope. The publisher and the author will not be held responsible for losses which may occur in the purchase, sale, or other transaction of property because of information contained herein. Readers who feel they have discovered errors are invited to *write* the author in care of Avon Books so that the errors may be corrected in subsequent editions.

THE CONFIDENT COLLECTOR: ADVERTISING IDENTIFICATION AND PRICE GUIDE (1st edition) is an original publication of Avon Books. This edition has never before appeared in book form.

AVON BOOKS
A division of
The Hearst Corporation
1350 Avenue of the Americas
New York, New York 10019

Copyright © 1993 by Dawn Reno
The Confident Collector and its logo are trademarked properties of Avon Books.
Interior design by Robin Arzt
Published by arrangement with the author
Library of Congress Catalog Card Number: 93-1872
ISBN: 0-380-76884-4

Page v acts as a continuation of this copyright page.

All rights reserved, which includes the right to reproduce this book or portions thereof in any form whatsoever except as provided by the U.S. Copyright Law. For information address Mildred Marmur Associates, Ltd., 310 Madison Avenue, Suite 607, New York, New York 10017.

Library of Congress Cataloging in Publication Data:

Reno, Dawn E.
Advertising identification and price guide / Dawn E. Reno.
   p. cm
   Includes index.
   1. Advertising specialties—Collectors and collecting—United States—Catalogs.   I. Title.
NK1125.R376   1993   93-1872
741.6'7'075—dc20   CIP

First Avon Books Trade Printing: November 1993

AVON TRADEMARK REG. U.S. PAT. OFF. AND IN OTHER COUNTRIES, MARCA REGISTRADA, HECHO EN U.S.A.

Printed in the U.S.A.

OPM 10 9 8 7 6 5 4 3 2 1

Front Cover, clockwise from top left:

Advertisement from the Sundblom Santa Series courtesy of The Coca-Cola Company.

Monarch Tea chromolithographed tin, 1923, courtesy of Irreverent Relics; photo by Donald Vogt.

Uneeda Crackers chromolithographed ad, 1901, courtesy of Irreverent Relics; photo by Donald Vogt.

Campbell Kids™ courtesy of The Campbell Soup Company.

Jell-O Desserts, 1920, courtesy of Irreverent Relics; photo by Donald Vogt.

Back Cover, counterclockwise:

Gold Dust Detergent ad, 1916, courtesy of The Marinace Collection; photo by Donald Vogt.

Page & Shaw Candy Boxes, ca. 1930s, and Nut & Fruit assortment, ca. 1930s, courtesy of Irreverent Relics; photo by Donald Vogt.

Coca-Cola framed paper sign, 1903, courtesy of The Allan Petretti Collection, photo by Donald Vogt.

Moxie Soda cardboard cutout window display, 1918, courtesy of The Allan Petretti Collection; photo by Donald Vogt.

Old Dutch Cleanser ads, ca. 1920s & 1930s, courtesy of Irreverent Relics; photo Donald Vogt.

*This one's for Dottie Harris
with appreciation for believing in me and my work*

CONTENTS

Introduction	1
Bits 'n' Pieces	5
1. Animal Products, Remedies, Feeds	15
2. Baking Products	20
3. Bread	37
4. Breweriana	40
5. Candy	64
6. Cereal	83
7. Cleaning Products	95
8. Clothing	103
9. Cocoa	114
10. Coffee	118
11. Communications Devices: Phonographs, Radios, Televisions and Telephones	125
12. Condiments, Spices	131
13. Crackers, Cookies, Biscuits	140
14. Dairy Products	154
15. Desserts	169
16. Dyes	173
17. Farm Equipment	176
18. Fruits, Vegetables	181
19. Gardening Supplies	189
20. Government, Military	195
21. Gum	199
22. Guns and Accessories	204
23. Health and Beauty Aids	209
24. Insurance Companies	223

25.	Kitchen Appliances	229
26.	Lighting	236
27.	Liquor	240
28.	Meats, Fish, Frozen Foods	251
29.	Medicines	255
30.	Miscellaneous Categories	278
31.	Movies, Concerts, Theater	303
32.	Paints, Varnishes	309
33.	Peanuts and By-Products	314
34.	Pens, Pencils, Inks	324
35.	Razors	327
36.	Restaurants	335
37.	Sewing Products	344
38.	Shoes, Boots	350
39.	Soap	355
40.	Soda	365
41.	Soups	409
42.	Store Fixtures	412
43.	Stores	416
44.	Stoves	421
45.	Tea	427
46.	Timepieces	432
47.	Tobacco	435
48.	Tourist Attractions, Travel	477
49.	Toys, Hobbies, Games, Sports	481
50.	Transportation	487

Conclusion: Some Companies to Watch in the Future	526
Appendix A: List of Contributors	530
Appendix B: Clubs	536
Appendix C: Bibliography	538
Index	547

INTRODUCTION

How to Use this Book

I have tried to design this volume of *The Confident Collector: Advertising Identification and Price Guide* with you, the reader, in mind. Being a collector of advertising myself, I know that I steer to certain fields—dairy collectibles line my kitchen walls, tobacco tins fill up one shelf of a chimney cupboard, while movie posters grace walls in my office. Thus, I've split the chapters into topic areas, placing in particular chapters the companies that produce those items—Anheuser-Busch is in the Breweriana chapter, McDonald's is in the Restaurants chapter, and Quaker Oats is in the Cereal chapter. Sometimes the companies that produce, for example, cereal items might also produce other items. In that case, I filed the company information in the chapter a collector might most easily recognize (Procter & Gamble made Ivory soap, so their company information is in the Soap chapter—though the company made quite a few health-and-beauty aids). I have made sure to indicate product names in each chapter and to direct you to where the main company information is located. If all else fails and you can't find the information you need or the company that made your item, check the index.

Items and Values

The items are listed in as full and complete descriptions as was humanly possible to collect. Some descriptions are more complete than others, but most include the condition of the item, its age, size, and approximate value.

Value was determined by many factors, primarily condition—poor, fair, good, very good, excellent, near mint, and mint. For example, if an item is described as in very good condition and the value is $50–$100, you can determine that $50 is the value of the item in poor condition and $100 in mint condition. Very good condition would make the item worth approximately $75.

My price listings are always the hardest portion of the book to put together. I searched the country for collectors, dealers, auctioneers, and other specialists. Prices come directly from them and are determined by their expert appraisals of what the market will bear. Naturally, a rare item in mint condition will often demand its own price, thus it is difficult to pin that piece of information down. A commonly found item often runs the gamut, depending on where the item is found, whether it is being sold at auction, by a dealer or collector, and what condition the item is in. I often feel the need to remind people that items sell for one price in New York City and may command a completely different price in Mobile, Alabama. Thus, I warn you that the prices are meant to be a *guide* and should never be taken literally.

Division of Areas
■ ■ ■

I have tried to cover each area with equal fairness; however, some areas of collecting are larger than others and that has been reflected in the size of my chapters. Tobacco, soda items, breweriana, and medicine advertising collectibles have received a lot of attention and there is plenty of information easily had about those items, thus those chapters are my largest. However, I have also tried to uncover information about advertising collectibles that have not, as yet, been thoroughly covered in other books on the subject, such as typewriter ribbon tins, Sunshine Biscuit tins, and several others.

Naturally when one is covering such a huge subject as advertising collectibles, there is not enough room to give everyone what they need in one volume. Should you not find the information you need here or should you have more complete histories or more accurate data than what I was able to find, please contact me in care of the publisher, and I will make every attempt to include such information in a future volume.

Contributors
■ ■ ■

I would like to thank each and every dealer, auctioneer, and contributor who took the time to answer my letters and who offered photos of their items to be included in this volume. All are listed in the index of the book, and I urge you, the reader, to contact all of them as they are open to talking to others in their fields.

I also offer my gratitude to the many companies whose archives I contacted for more specific information. Both the archivists and public relations departments of the companies listed in the index offered me the opportunity to have my information corrected by the experts so that I could present the very best, most accurate company biographies to my readers. They took the time and effort to correct my copy, to offer photographs, and to answer my questions. They made a gigantic project almost easy.

Acknowledgments

And, finally, to those who had a hand in helping me physically put together this book, I offer my utter and total gratefulness. First and foremost, my editor, Dottie Harris, who was there to answer questions and to help me put the many jumbled pieces of the puzzle together. My photographer, Donald Vogt, who not only offered his camera skills but also his knowledge of the area of collecting he knows almost as well as the professionals we met during our two "road trips." My friend and fellow writer, Jenna Bartlett, who devoted many afternoons of her time to helping me identify photographs and tie together loose ends. My part-time secretary, Jeanne Stitz, who diligently assembled my bibliography, filed the mountains of paperwork, and learned how to input information into a computer—a new feat for her. My future son-in-law, Isaac Karachepone, whose English spellings of some of the words somehow crept into the manuscript. My fellow writer and listening board, Carol Quinto, who encouraged me in the beginning when I was daunted by the project and certain I couldn't make deadline. My family—Bobby, my husband, and Jennifer, my daughter—who thought I'd turned into a mummified version of myself sitting at my computer. And, finally, my agent, Mildred Marmur, who continues to carve avenues for me in the literary world and who is putting into reality a career about which I dreamed as a child.

To all, thanks once again. This is for you.

Bits 'n' Pieces

This introductory section is designed to give you some interesting information about the different types of advertising available to collectors. However, if you need more detailed information, I suggest you investigate some of the wonderful volumes listed in my bibliography or flip to the chapter that covers the items made by the company you collect. The field of advertising is huge and would take many volumes to cover. I hope to uncover more information for you in future editions of this book. And I hope that you will let me know which areas interest you and that you will share your information with me.

General Information

Though some form of advertising has always existed, the age of advertising as we know it began during the late nineteenth century. Up until that time, advertising was done by word of mouth, by creating symbolic signs that were hung in merchants' windows or near the door (a hand would indicate a glovemaker; a figure holding cigars would designate a tobacconist; a shoe meant a cobbler conducted business inside), and by handing out trade cards that told the customer about a product and often included clever illustrations. But printed material, such as magazines or newspapers, had yet to utilize the power of advertising.

Though Ben Franklin printed illustrated ads in his *Pennsylvania Gazette* prior to 1750, there was little improvement in that form of advertising until steam-powered newspaper presses were introduced in the 1830s and 1840s, encouraging newspapers to expand their ideas about advertising.

Suddenly advertisement was attractive, easy to create, and companies discovered people *read* the ads—not to find what they needed but to see what they *wanted*. Desire, created by advertising, led manufacturers to realize larger sales. The industry grew, and by the First World War, advertisers were spending more than a billion dollars on an annual basis. Some advertisers spent a million dollars a year on magazine advertising alone. Advertising had become a science—the science of persuasion.

Ads published in the late 1800s utilized a new philosophy that reduced designs to flat color planes, introduced by Louis Prang, a printer. Prang's newly termed chromolithography, invented in the mid-1860s, had a great impact on the advertising industry and made Prang enormously successful.

After the 1876 Centennial Exhibition in Philadelphia, American advertisers began using Prang's chromolithographic process to create brochures, trade cards, handbills, flyers, and posters to advertise their products. Huge advertisements were pasted to the sides of buildings, barns, even mountain faces. Trolley car advertising became popular, and the lithography process was even adapted so that it could be used on tins.

Huntley, Boorne, and Stevens of England was the first company to succesfully use lithography on tin in 1877. Other attempts had been made, but only the simplest designs and basic colors were used. During the period between 1875 and 1885, fancier tins began to appear, and as the process developed, tin design became more interesting. By 1903, the development of a rotary offset lithograph, designed to transfer the image directly to the tin, made the process easier, faster, and more durable. Companies hired artists to create beautiful designs and the art of the tin became highly collectible.

In 1893, Mellin's Food was the first company to use full-color ads to advertise its products in American magazines. By 1920, the advertising industry, as we know and understand it, was pretty much in place. The major differences between the advertising done in 1920 as compared to what's being done today are apparent in the technological advances made by the media. For example, 1920 advertisements utilized magazines, newspapers, billboards, and some radio. Today, television plays a large part in most companies' advertising budgets. Who knows what tomorrow may hold?

Some Types of Items Used to Advertise
■ ■ ■

ALMANACS

Best are the eighteenth–century examples published in Boston and New York. Almanacs were designed to give people information about the upcoming year, its weather, tips on how to garden, and often offered homespun advice. Many companies printed them and offered them to their customers—free of charge—as an incentive to buy their products.

Customers began to collect the annual almanacs and some companies printed many thousands every year to meet the demand.

BARBER POLES

Few people who see the red-and-white pole, which indicates the existence of a barber shop, realize the origin of the pole—one of the first types of advertising. At one point in history, barbers practiced bloodletting for healing purposes. They hung the bloody towels on a pole outside to dry—thus the red-and-white pole. (Gruesome, huh?)

Barbers served as surgeons and dentists, as well as haircutters (thus the bloody band). When barbers and surgeons were split by law into two professions in the early 1300s, barber poles were white-and-blue striped. Later, when the two once again merged into one profession, the poles were red, white, and blue. One legend states that the colors represented America's patriotism, while another says the red stripe stood for arterial blood, the blue for venuous blood, and the white for purity.

For more information, read: *A History of Shaving and Razors* by Philip Krumholz (Ad Libs Publications, Bartonville, Illinois).

BLOTTERS

Blotters were given away during the days when pens were dipped into inkwells. Companies made advertising blotters in abundance from 1890 to 1920, though blotters continued to be made after that time.

BOTTLES

Before 1845, bottles were made of blown glass. According to an article by Sharon Ogan in the March 1992 issue of *The Antique Shoppe*: "When the body of the bottle had been formed, the glass blower broke it away from the blow pipe. To hold the bottle while forming the neck and lip, the glass blower dipped an iron rod, called a pontil, into molted glass and attached it to the bottom of the bottle. When complete, the pontil was broken off, leaving a hole in the bottom which was then filllled with glass. A definite 'open pontil mark' can be seen on these bottles."

By approximately 1845, the pontil rod left a round pontil mark on the bottom of a bottle because the rod had a round iron ball attached to it.

The snap case method, used after 1860, left an unmarred bottom, and by 1903 bottles were made by machines.

CALENDARS

Calendars have existed since the mid-nineteenth century as advertising tools. Nineteenth-century printers' calendars produced by lithographers in New York and Philadelphia are the most valuable, according to collectors.

CANDY BAR WRAPPERS

The first chocolate bar appeared in England in the 1840s. By the twentieth century, Europeans had started collecting candy bar wrappers. Hershey was responsible for producing the first American-made candy bars in 1894, but it wasn't until the 1920s that the industry became commercially successful. During that decade, approximately 40,000 different candy bars were invented and put on the market, most only lasting a short period of time.

CANS

(*see also* "General Information," page 5, for more information about cans)

An Englishman named Thomas Kensett brought the canning process to America in 1825—and President James Madison awarded him a patent for the process.

CIGAR LABELS

The labels attached to the outside of cigar boxes were called "outs" and usually average 4½ x 4½ inches. The fancier labels were inside the box ("ins") and average approximately 6 x 9 inches.

Because cigars were most popular during the turn of the century (1890–1910), most cigar labels collected are from in that time frame. There were approximately 350,000 brands by 1900. Obviously, I will not even come close to covering that many within this book. However, information about labels is available by contacting sources such as: Cerebro, P.O. Box 1221, Lancaster, PA 17603.

CIGARETTE ADVERTISING

An exhibit called "Smoke Signals," which traced the industry's history, was put together and shown at the Museum of Our National Heritage in Lexington, Massachusetts, in February 1991. One of the comments the show's curators made was that the cigarette industry advertising coaxed the United States into becoming one of the biggest consumer nations in the world. According to an article written by Rebecca Hanks for the February 1991 issue of *Art & Antiques:* "Americans consume some 542 billion cigarettes a year—that's $30.2 billion up in smoke."

Because of the stringent restrictions on the tobacco industry, cigarette manufacturers have had to shift gears in recent years regarding advertising. Magazine and newspaper advertising budgets have grown to fill in the void left when the products could no longer be advertised on television. Collectors should pay attention to certain characters used by cigarette advertising, such as Joe Camel, because I predict that within the next decade or so we may find the cigarette industry no longer exists—and everything made during this decade will become highly collectible.

FAST-FOOD COLLECTIBLES

All of the restaurants considered to be fast-food chains regularly promote their products with giveaway items that might be related to current events or movies. Such giveaways might be glasses, toys, figurines, or just plain ol' boxes, bags, signs, or packages—make sure they have a logo on them and keep track of *when* you got them so you'll be able to date them later on.

"HOT STUFF"

(*see also* "Conclusion: Some Companies to Watch in the Future")

Getting more expensive and more difficult to find are: peanut butter collectibles (i.e., tins, pails, buckets), chewing gum advertising items, any three-dimensional figures, and die-cut signs (even cardboard examples).

Prices are starting to go up on fruit, vegetable, can, and tobacco labels, because demand is up and supply is down. For now, these are also highly colorful, inexpensive collectibles—perfect for the beginner looking to put together an easily stored collection of advertising. The labels are extremely popular in England and Italy.

Any type of advertising that features the American West will be highly collectible—already is! However, this advertising has not risen so highly in price as the other items in that area of collecting, so get on the bandwagon quick!

LABELS

Fruit and vegetable labels began to be used in the 1880s, when railroads were used to ship these items from where they were grown to the rest of the nation. The first to be shipped were oranges and lemons from southern California, grapes from central California, then apples and pears from northern California, Oregon, and Washington. Labels were used to identify and advertise the products and were utilized until the 1950s, when wooden boxes were replaced by cardboard boxes.

Hints for care: store in acid-free paper or plastic and, when mounting, use stamp hinges and water-based glue.

Though labels are one of today's hottest collectibles, the novice may not realize that particular attention should be given to the label's condition. Trimmed edges, overall soiling, foxing (discoloration), and age fading are some of the things that lessen a label's value.

Many labels are inexpensive, though some are expensive. Collectors watch for rare labels with colorful or simply attractive graphics—in good condition! Should you decide this is your avenue, try to focus on one type of label, or better yet, one company.

MATCHBOOKS

Just about every firm, restaurant, hotel, and tourist attraction (and even some people) has printed a matchbook at one time or another. There are many associations that specialize in getting collectors of matchbook covers—people called phillumenists (lovers of light)—together. Collectors usually "shuck" matchbooks before storing them in a book, drawer, or box—which merely means removing the matches from the cover.

Matchbook collecting is one of the most pervasive forms of advertising . . . and probably the cheapest, since matches are usually free!

MEDICINE

Anyone could make patent medicines prior to 1906, when the Federal Drug Administration started to elicit control over medicine-making. Medicine-makers comprised the largest portion of advertisers in the early 1800s, probably because so many were allowed to hawk medicinal products without being "legal" doctors or pharmacists.

MIRRORS

A popular giveaway, advertising mirrors reached their peak in the 1920s. Some of the mirrors were made in the shape of their product; others simply gave the customer a bit of trivial information. The mirrors were produced in two sizes: the smaller was approximately the size of a half dollar; and the larger version was approximately half an inch bigger.

PLATES

Limited-edition collector plates, though pretty and easy to find, are difficult to sell unless you've held on to them for at least twenty to twenty-five years. Before that time, a collector is lucky to get a quarter of the original retail price of the plate.

POSTERS

Circus posters made by commercial lithographers were a sizable industry by the late nineteenth century. The Strobridge Company of

Cincinnati produced a good portion of the circus and theatrical posters used throughout the country.

Movie posters are becoming more and more popular as fewer of these delicate items are found intact. The terminology for these posters is as follows: lobby cards (11 x 14 inches), usually printed on heavy cardboard and made in sets of eight; window cards (22 x 14 inches), with blank spaces where theaters could insert ther own names; insert cards (36 x 14 inches), on heavy stock, usually with two horizontal folds; half-sheets (22 x 28 inches), usually with horizontal and vertical folds; one-sheet (41 x 27 inches), most desirable size, two horizontal folds and one vertical; three-sheet (81 x 41 inches), designed to overlap, as they were pasted on walls, rare; six-sheet (81 x 81 inches), as the three-sheet, they were designed to overlap and are even more rare; twenty-four-sheet (9 x 20 feet), extremely rare.

Posters need to be deacidified, and it is a matter of opinion whether a paper or linen background is best. For more information, read *Movie Collector's World*, a biweekly tabloid published by Brian Bukantis of Fraser, Michigan.

RADIO PREMIUMS

Listeners were lured to change their radio dials in the late 1920s when the radio stations offered premiums to measure their listenerships. By the 1930s, radio giveaways helped advertise products for companies such as Jell-O (one such giveaway: the Aldrich Family recipe booklet); Kellogg's (Pretty Kitty Kelly film viewer and films); Oxydol (flower seeds from Ma Perkins); Grape-Nuts (Burns & Allen booklet); General Foods (Young Doctor Malone locket); Chase & Sanborn (Charlie McCarthy puppet); and Morton Salt (Buck Rogers rubber band guns).

Thousands of premiums were given away—far too many to list in this volume. To think of the myriad items given away between 1920 and 1950 is a bit daunting.

It is also quite difficult to discover which articles were given as premiums or radio prizes unless one can link the item directly to a show. However, if you know which shows regularly awarded prizes to listeners, you can narrow your search.

REPRODUCTIONS

Aunt Jemima items, Luzianne coffee items, Uncle Rastus, the Quaker Oats man, and many other items have been reproduced during the years. Some collectors don't mind adding new reproductions to their collections, others are looking for the original pieces and are dismayed when a dealer—unknowingly or otherwise—sells them an advertising collectible as old when it is actually new.

Be on the lookout for the above items, as well as Jersey Coffee store bins (wooden and painted red) and newly made "anniversary" editions of old tins by companies such as Gold Medal flour, Quaker Oats, Nestlé, Hershey's, Baker's Cocoa, and many others.

Paper goods are also being reproduced. Early in 1991, a Topsy Granulated Smoking Tobacco advertising poster sold for $55,000—in 1992, copies of that poster were selling for $2,000 each. The new printing technology allows the "creator" to closely match antique styles, even to the point of mimicking aging.

Even newspapers and magazines are being "faked," reported the *Maine Antique Digest* in its April 1992 issue. Some newspapers appeared at New England auctions and were touted as eighteenth-century—one identifiable feature of the fakes was an oval stamp that read "Tontine Coffee Room, Glasglow."

Another type of reproduction is tin signs, which are being reproduced from the original paper signs. An example, reports *Kovels on Antiques and Collectibles* June 1992 newsletter, is a sign that states, "When he wears them, Shoeless Joe Jackson wears Selz Shoes," and depicts that baseball player and his two smiling bare feet. The sign, rusted and in horrible shape, was being sold for $1,000. There are other signs of this type ("bent, rusted and filled with bullet holes") being offered for sale.

I have included some prices on reproductions that are currently found in the marketplace and have marked them as such. I believe this book is the first to do so. One of the reasons I chose to include some repros is that the average collector would have a very difficult time finding some of the original items. Repros serve a purpose—they are affordable, easy to find, and attractive—as long as they are represented as reproductions!

To discover the reproduction, you must be extremely familiar with the old pieces. Do your homework, ask questions, and buyer beware!

SIGNS

In the April 1992 of *Kovels on Antiques and Collectibles*, the noted antiques authors reported that there "are no authentic baseball-related advertising signs made of tin, according to Joshua Leland Evans." However, repros of those signs would retail for about $10 each and be treated as *reproductions*. My question is: How can it be *re*produced if it was never produced?

SPOONS

Souvenir spoons, collected since the nineteenth century, were one of the first advertising giveaways, but were not given credit as collectibles until Daniel Low of Salem, Massachusetts, designed two witch spoons that became popular instantly.

Painted enamel and gilt souvenir spoons were designed to promote tourist attractions, state seals, personalities (movie stars), sports figures, and holidays. Some companies offered spoons as a premium when a customer purchased a product.

TRADE CARDS

Trade cards have existed since the 1600s, but their use was basically social—as a calling card. In the late 1800s, when chromolithography (an inexpensive form of color printing) was invented, the plain black-and-white trade cards were replaced by new, colorful ones.

American companies embraced the polychrome trade card concept and began using trade cards to advertise their porducts. Almost immediately, the cards became collectors' items. Since most weren't larger than 3 x 5 inches, thousands could be collected without taking up too much space.

Trade cards advertised everything from medicine to lawn mowers and often offered practical advice to homemakers or were issued in a series to a company's clients, who were encouraged to collect the whole set. When radio advertising became popular in the 1930s, interest in trade cards began to decline.

Collectors separate trade cards into five types: plain, mechanical, metamorphic, see-through, and die-cut. The plain ones are easiest to find, thus the least valuable. When a card was cut into the shape of an object, the tool used to do the job was a die—thus the term *die-cut*. They're easy to find and still fairly reasonably priced. Mechanical trade cards have moving parts and are rare because they were often favorite playthings. A card that has a flap that shows a different scene when opened is a metamorphic card (one example is a card designed like a barn door—when the flaps are open, you can see the animals inside). They are also rare. See-through cards were printed in such a way that when they're held up to the light, additional words or pictures can be seen.

Some of the most collectible trade cards were made by printing companies like Louis Prang & Company or Currier & Ives.

TRADEMARKS

Most companies create a trademark that is specifically associated with their logo, and most are memorable (Aunt Jemima, Betty Crocker, Nipper, Uncle Rastus, the Mobil horse, and so on). Collecting items marked with this trademark is an easy way to break into the advertising field. Some of the newer ones (Joe Camel of Camel cigarettes, the California Raisins, the McDonald's figures) are extremely easy to collect—and items made with their "faces" on them might even be free!

CHAPTER ONE
■ ANIMAL PRODUCTS, ■ REMEDIES, FEEDS

BARKER'S HORSE AND CATTLE POWDER
Barker's Horse and Cattle Powder, paper sign; rare; paper over canvas; depicts animals being startled by passing train; 30 x 24 inches excluding frame; overall 32½ x 26½ inches; fair/good condition, overall soiling; $150–300.

BEN-HUR HORSE BLANKETS
Ben-Hur Horse Blankets, self-framed tin sign; pictures horse looking into store window filled with horse products and mannequin; the line of products sold at the Geo. Worthington Co., Cleveland; frame marked "The Horse Knows"; 20 x 16½ inches; excellent condition; $750–1,500.

CHAMPION KING BULL DOG COLLAR
Champion King Bull Dog Collar, advertisement; original frame; three-dimensional relief of dog house with bulldog "inside" door wearing product; 8½ x 9 inches; excellent condition, minor discoloration on dog's chin that appears to have been done in printing process; $125–275.

CLAYTON'S DOG REMEDIES
Clayton's Dog Remedies, papier-mâché dog; 30 inches long; brown and black; gold letters on side read "Clayton's Dog Remedies"; bulldog was probably counter display piece; fair condition; $1,200–1,800.

COLGATE AND CO.
Colgate and Co. Harness and Stable Soaps, paper sign; depicts four horses drawing carriage for Sunday ride; 16½ x 21 inches; very good/excellent condition, some discoloration, trimmed borders; $400–600.

DR. DANIELS
This company was incorporated in 1899 and was out of business less than twenty years later in 1916. The original owner, Dr. Daniels, used his own face to advertise his products for animals. Out of all the companies who made animal prod-

ucts or produced veterinary needs, this seems one of the easiest to find and is highly valued by collectors because the products were made for such a short period of time. Particularly valued are the store cabinets used to display the items the company made.

DR. DANIELS

Dr. Daniels, catnip ball, box; Dr. A. C. Daniels, Inc., Webster, Massachusetts; all four sides of this box depict the cat playing with the catnip ball; ca. early 1900s; excellent condition; $6–12.

Dr. Daniels, embossed dye cabinet; depicts the Doctor and his products (worm killer, colic cure, etc.); pricing on bottom of image; 21 x 27 x 7½ inches; good/very good condition, some minor chipping to embossed images and some minor scratching to background, appears to have no in-painting; $1,250–2,500.

Dr. Daniels, embossed tin cabinet; depicts the Doctor and his products, replaced oak case; tin is 13¾ x 19¾ inches; cabinet is 17 x 23⅓ x 6¼ inches; condition of tin is fair/good, chipping overall, especially lower half around products and background; $650–950.

Dr. Daniels, pocket mirror; celluloid; pictures woman, house, and dog; 2 inches diameter; excellent condition; $80–160.

Dr. Daniels, thermometer; wood thermometer promoting multiple products; 6 x 24 inches; working; fair/good condition, general loss of background and decal; $25–100.

Dr. Daniels, tin remedies cabinet; all-tin dog and cat medicine cabinet with marquee from veterinary supplier Dr. A. C. Daniels; 13½ x 20 x 5¼ inches; very good condition, some overall wear; $3,000–5,000.

GAINES

Gaines Dog Meal, thermometer; etching of Pointer on front; ca. 1960s; very good condition; approximately 15 inches long, 3 inches wide; $20–30.

HARTZ

Hartz Mountain, Dried Shrimp Fish Food, tin, ½ ounce; ca. 1960s; excellent condition; $6–8.

Hartz Mountain, My-T-Mite Powder, tin, ¼ ounce (left is marked 25 cents; right is marked 20 cents); ca. 1950s; $8–10.

ANIMAL PRODUCTS, REMEDIES, FEEDS ■ 17

Hartz Mountain, left and right side/back—My-T-Mite Powder, ¾ ounce (left is marked 25 cents; right is marked 20 cents), ca. 1950s, $8–10; center—Song Restorer, copyright 1935, 3½ ounces, ca. 1940s, $10–15; left/front—Dried Shrimp Fish Food, ½ ounce, ca. 1960s, $6–8; Natural Gold Fish Food, ¾ ounce, ca. 1960s, $8–10, all in excellent condition. *Courtesy of Irreverent Relics. Photo by Donald Vogt.*

Hartz, Natural Gold Fish Food, tin, ¾ ounce; ca. 1960s; excellent condition; $8–10.

Hartz, Song Restorer, tin, copyright 1935, 3½ ounces; ca. 1940s; excellent condition; $10–15.

HUMPHREYS'
Humphreys' Veterinary, cabinet; embossed composition cabinet with raised horse's head on textured background; original condition; 21 x 28 x 10½ inches; excellent condition, original color, overall soiling, some discoloration to original finish of case, minor distortion to front; $1,500–2,500.

Humphreys' Veterinary, cabinet; tin-fronted version of cabinet depicting farm animals and listing products; rare; case in good condition; 22 x 27¾ x 9 inches; refinished cabinet, tin front restored; $1,000–1,750.

INTERNATIONAL STOCK FOOD
International Stock Food, paper poster; depicts sitting pig opening box of food with vignettes of horse and cow who also want the food shown above; 17½ x 28½ inches excluding frame; good condition, several small holes; $150–300.

18 ■ ADVERTISING

KENDALL'S
Kendall's Spavin Cure, paper sign; couple with horse and insert of institute; 24½ x 30½ inches; poor/fair condition, overall age darkening, tears and rips, some paper loss; $150–300.

MANSON CAMPBELL
Manson Campbell, self-framed tin sign; gold-and-gray embossed-edged advertisement with images of founder and products including carts, mill, brooder, and incubator with chicks; lettering reads "The Manson Campbell Co. Limited—Detroit, Mich.—Chatham, Ontario"; 33 x 23 inches; good condition, slight fade, overall wear, some chipping; $250–400.

MISCELLANEOUS
Thimbles; group of three thimbles that advertised farm products, as well as a coal company; *left*: Purina chicken feed, the thimble was attached to a bag of the feed and the wording on the bag stated that a thimbleful of a certain product was added to the feed to encourage better egg production; *center*: "Lay or Bust" thimble was given away by another chicken feed company; *right*: coal company thimble; good condition; ca. early 1900s; $1–3 each.

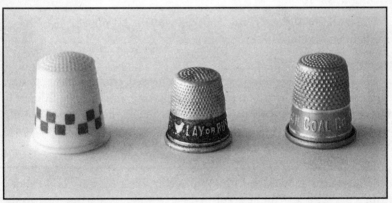

Thimbles, group of three thimbles that advertised farm products, as well as a coal company; left—Purina chicken feed, the thimble was attached to a bag of the feed and the wording on the bag stated that a thimbleful of a certain product was added to the feed to encourage better egg production; center—"Lay or Bust" thimble was given away by another chicken feed company; right—coal company thimble. Good condition; ca. early 1900s; $1–3 each. *Courtesy of Estelle Zalkin, author of* Zalkin's Handbook of Thimbles and Sewing Implements.

PARD DOG FOOD
Pard Dog Food, electric clock; Swift's dog with bobbing head eating plate of Pard food; 15¾ inches square x 3½ inches; very good/excellent condition, some soiling, slight scratches and chips, working condition; $250–450.

PUTNAM HORSESHOE NAILS
Putnam Horseshoe Nails, paper sign; illustration of carriage drawn by two prancing horses; ca. 1888; approximately 27½ x 20¾ inches excluding mat and frame; overall 32½ x 25½ inches; fair condition; $200–400.

SINGER'S GRAVEL
Singer's Gravel, paper sign; advertisement for paper "for the bottom of bird cages"; woman in diaphanous dress chases birds in Victorian garden, a bird cage is at her feet; 10 x 13 inches; very good condition, overall soiling, edge trims; $450–650.

CHAPTER TWO
▪ BAKING PRODUCTS ▪

ARM & HAMMER
Arm & Hammer, sign; depicts minstrel figure holding box of product; wears large plaid tie and what looks to be a skirt; nineteenth century; rare; mint condition; $1,500–2,000.

AUNT JEMIMA
(*see also* "Quaker Oats" in Cereal chapter)

In 1989, the Aunt Jemima trademark celebrated its one hundredth birthday, and the company decided to give the centenarian a face-lift. Gone is the head scarf, added is a stylish, gray-streaked hairdo (can't make a hundred-year-old *too* young!), a prim and proper collar, and a pair of pearl earrings. It was time for the Quaker Oats Company to bring their multimillion-dollar producer into the 1990s.

When Aunt Jemima was first presented to the American public as a registered trademark in 1889, it was the result of a search conducted by Chris L. Rutt, a reporter for the St. Joseph, Missouri, *Gazette*, and Charles G. Underwood, owner of the Pearl Milling Company. Rutt helped Underwood find a symbol the Pearl Milling Company would be able to use on a new pancake mix. He discovered the idea for Aunt Jemima when visiting a vaudeville house in New Orleans.

Baker and Farrell, a team of blackface comedians, were performing a cakewalk as part of their routine—the tune they strutted to was called "Aunt Jemima" and the costumes the vaudeville team wore consisted of aprons and red bandannas. Excited, Rutt copied that image and the song, determined to mold it into the trademark for which he and Underwood had been looking. Though the song-and-dance team inspired the idea, that was not the end of the search.

By 1893, the company had hired a real person to act as Aunt Jemima—a fifty-nine-year-old former slave from Montgomery County, Kentucky, named Nancy Green. She served as the official trademark for approximately thirty years. It was the first time in American history that a real person was used as a company's trademark.

When Green died after being hit by an automobile, Edna/Anna Robinson was hired to take her place, and later, Rosie Lee Moore Hall of Hearne, Texas, assumed the role until her death in 1967. It has been noted by various researchers that Nancy Green was a thin woman who never resembled the drawing of Aunt Jemima, but that Edna/Anna Robinson's was the face from which the modern symbol, adapted by the company in 1936, was based.

Though Aunt Jemima was represented by real women, the company continued to promote the romance of Aunt Jemima as a southern cook whose pancakes influenced the master of a large Louisiana plantation. The gentleman, Colonel Higbee, had an African-American cook who was famous for her breakfast foods, the likes of which "you'd never taste elsewhere in all the old South." In one ad, the history of the pancakes stated: "Twenty years or so after the Civil War" an old Confederate general and his orderly became separated from their troops and stopped at a cabin to ask directions. A "mammy" directed them, then insisted they stop for a snack. Naturally, this was the same "mammy" who had been the cook for Colonel Higbee. He brought others back to sample her cooking and one of them was a representative of the company that eventually bought her recipe and image. Of course, the story in the advertisement was a fallacy and the true story is as stated earlier.

The Aunt Jemima promotional campaign's influence traveled all over the world and soon Aunt Jemima became one of the most famous trademarks of all time. Aunt Jemima dolls were first made in 1896, with later versions of her husband, Uncle Moses, daughter, Diana, and son, Wade, made for collectors. Cookie jars, sugar shakers, plastic syrup pitchers, trade cards, paper dolls, and rag dolls were added as premiums. Ceramic salt and pepper shakers in the Aunt Jemima image were distributed by the millions in the 1920s and 1930s. She became so popular that other companies tried to create similar advertising slogans in the Aunt Jemima image. However, the company protected its trademark and no one has seriously challenged its rights since 1917.

In 1926, the Aunt Jemima products were acquired by the Quaker Oats Company and that company continued to bring out innovative products under the Aunt Jemima symbol, such as the first reduced-calorie syrup, called Aunt Jemima Lite, and even reduced-calorie microwaveable frozen pancakes, called Aunt Jemima Lite Buttermilk Pancakes. Today the products represented by this familiar black woman represent about $300 million of the company's $5.3 billion in sales.

AUNT JEMIMA

Aunt Jemima Flour, cardboard box; older version of Aunt Jemima; 13 x 14 x 9 inches; fair/good condition; $35–75.

Aunt Jemima, puzzle attached to flour bag; instructions say "To place the two tags or fac-similie packages on the same string without untieing, but it will NOT puzzle you to decide which is the best Pancake Flour after you have tried THE ORIGINAL Aunt Jemima Pancake Flour"; rare; near-mint condition; $50–75.

Aunt Jemima, sign for Aunt Jemima Breakfast Club; 6-inch hanging round; cardboard; mint condition; $8–12.

Aunt Jemima, trolley sign; cardboard; 1918; framed; 10 x 20½ inches; near-mint condition; $300–600.

BAKER'S COCONUT

(*see also* "Kraft General Foods" in Dairy Products chapter)

A Philadelphia flour miller, Franklin Baker, bought a small coconut business in 1895 after a Cuban merchant he had sold flour to paid him with a cargo of fresh coconuts. Actually, Baker tried to *sell* the coconuts to a coconut merchant but ended up *buying* the coconut business himself. The gamble paid off, and in 1897 Baker's Coconut was so successful that Franklin gave up his flour business to devote all his time to coconuts.

His son joined the company in 1897, and together they formed the Franklin Baker Co. By 1913 the business had moved to Brooklyn, New York, and in 1924, both the plant operations and general offices were moved to Hoboken, New Jersey. In 1927, Baker's Coconut became part of Postum Company, predecessor to General Food Corporation.

BAKER'S COCONUT

Baker's Coconut, advertisement from *Ladies' Home Journal*, February 1928; 10 x 13 inches; full color; depicts maid treating family at table with coconut cake; $4–6.

BAKING PRODUCTS ■ 23

Baker's Coconut, advertisement from *Ladies' Home Journal*, February 1928 issue; 10 x 13 inches; full color; depicts maid treating family at table w/coconut cake; $4–6. *Courtesy of Paper Lady/Bernie and Dolores Fee. Photo by Donald Vogt.*

Calumet, advertisement from *Ladies' Home Journal* illustrated by Norman Hall; depicts cook presenting maid with cake; $15–18. *Courtesy of Lester Morris. Photo by Donald Vogt.*

BISQUICK
(*see* "General Mills")

CALUMET
(*see also* "Kraft General Foods" in Dairy Products chapter)

William W. Wright developed Calumet Baking Powder in his Chicago lab/office/bedroom in 1889. He chose his product's name because there were several areas of Chicago named Calumet (i.e., Calumet Harbor, Calumet Lake, and Calumet River). His product soon became so successful that he joined with chemist George C. Rew to perfect Calumet's formula.

In 1902, he went from a three-floor plant to a new factory, and in 1912, had to enlarge once more. In 1928, Calumet Baking Powder Company was acquired by Postum Company, predecessor to General Foods Corporation.

CALUMET
Calumet, advertisement from *Ladies' Home Journal*, 1922; illustrated by Norman Hall; depicts cook presenting maid with cake; $15–18.

24 ■ ADVERTISING

Calumet, advertising regulator clock; calendar clock with reverse glass panel that says "Time to buy Calumet Baking Powder/'Best by Test'"; 16½ x 35 x 4¾ inches; good original condition, some paint loss to black background; $300–500.

Calumet Baking Powder, can; 1 pound; depicts Indian on front; ca. 1930; good condition; $18–25.

Calumet Baking Powder, can; ½ pound; depicts Indian on front; ca. 1950; good condition; $10–15.

Calumet, wood thermometer; marked "Call for Calumet Baking Powder/Trade Here and Save"; approximately 24 inches long; excellent condition; $750–1,000.

CERESOTA

Ceresota Flour, match safe; depicts boy sitting on stool; ca. 1920s; $250–300.

Ceresota Flour, match safe; die-cut and embossed tin classic of boy with round barrel; 2½ x 5½ inches; good/very good condition, minor scratches; $150–300.

Ceresota Flour, match holder; tin; die-cut and embossed; depicts the Ceresota farm boy cutting bread atop round barrel; 2½ x 5½ x 1½ inches; good condition, minor dents; $200–400.

Ceresota Flour, match safe; depicts boy sitting on stool; ca. 1920s; $250–300. *Courtesy of Marilyn & De Underwood/Tins Again Collectibles. Photo by Donald Vogt.*

Baking Products   25

Ceresota Flour, poster; approximately 20 x 24 inches; depicts mother buttering bread for son; by artist Esther Smith; very good condition; $30–85.

CLABBER'S
Clabber's, want list/grocery list; ca. 1910–1915, excellent condition; $15–25.

CREAM CITY FLOUR
Cream City Flour, bin and sifter; patented November 21, 1893; painted dark red with black lettering; approximately 24 inches tall; excellent condition; $400–600.

CRISCO
(*see* "Proctor & Gamble" in Soap chapter)

DAVIS BAKING POWDER
(*see* "R. J. Reynolds" in Tobacco chapter)

FIVE ROSES FLOUR
Five Roses Flour, porcelain sign; depicts Indian with bag of flour over his shoulder; approximately 30 x 24 inches; blue background; ca. 1920s; Ingram Richardson Manufacturing Co. of Beaver Falls, Pennsylvania; excellent condition; $3,000–4,200.

FLEISCHMANN'S YEAST
Fleischmann's Yeast, cardboard calendar; 1906; pad starts with July; 10¼ x 14¼ inches; excellent condition; $75–125.

FRANKLIN MILLS FLOUR
Franklin Mills Flour, cardboard stand-up sign; depicts little girl in pink dress; she holds Wheatlet breakfast food in left hand and Franklin Flour in right; caption reads "All the Wheat that's Fit to Eat is Contained in Franklin Mills Flour and Wheatlet"; 9 inches tall; excellent condition; $200–450.

GENERAL MILLS/Betty Crocker

Contrary to popular opinion, Betty Crocker was never a real person, though her personality and voice have been represented on radio and television, as well as through a number of advertising mediums.

The idea for a "woman's woman" to represent Gold Medal products began in November 1921, when a Gold Medal© flour promotion offered consumers a pincushion that resembled a flour sack as a gift if they completed a jigsaw puzzle of a milling scene. The promotion was an enormous success that unearthed not only thousands of responses but questions about baking problems as well. All of the mail taken in at the Washburn Crosby Company (the forerunner of General Mills, Inc.) caused a bit of concern, until advertising manager Sam Gale suggested that a woman be appointed spokesperson for the company. Thus, the fictitious Betty Crocker was created.

(It should be noted here that Washburn erected his first flour mill in 1866 and formed a partnership with John Crosby in 1877, thus the Washburn Crosby Company. They entered three brands of their flour in the 1880 Millers' International Exhibition and the winning flour was named Gold Medal because it had been awarded a gold medal.)

According to company literature, "the surname Crocker was chosen to honor a popular, recently retired director of the company, William G. Crocker. It was also the name of the first flour mill in Minneapolis, Washburn Crosby's hometown. The name Betty was chosen simply as a friendly sounding name. Women employees were invited to submit sample Betty Crocker signatures, and the one judged most distinctive continues in use today."

The name Betty Crocker was first used in correspondence by James A. Quint, advertising manager of the Washburn Crosby Company. During the next three years, little was done to build the Betty Crocker personality, largely because the Home Service Department effort was devoted to cooking school demonstrations. However, the name was used in advertisements carrying recipes, on printed recipes and on other Home Service literature, until October 1924, when Donald D. Davis, vice president and secretary, decided that a Home Service broadcasting program should be started on the company's new radio station in Minneapolis, WCCO. Ultimately, the Home Service Department became the Betty Crocker Kitchens.

During the period from October 1924 through November 1926, Betty Crocker policy was created and refined. During that same time period, Washburn Crosby was also expanding its product line and produced its first new product in 1924, a flaked cereal called Wheaties. Home economists organized and gave cooking schools and demonstrations in various parts of the country, the Betty Crocker Cooking School of the Air was broadcast on radio (and continued for twenty-four years with over one million listeners), and Betty Crocker was established as "the personal name, voice and being of Gold Medal Home Service."

In 1925–1926, a recipe box containing guide cards and 5 x 3 inch recipe cards was created and offered for $1—the recipe box succeeded the historic *Gold Medal Flour Cookbook*, and the original plan was to keep a permanent list of customers, sending them new cards from time to time. That proved to be too expensive, so it was discontinued. However, more than 350,000 boxes were distributed during the two years, and for a long period after the boxes were discontinued, mail request responses or recipes sent to cooking school registrants were printed on 5 x 3 inch cards.

Also in 1926, the company reorganized its Wheaties advertising campaign and aired its first singing commercial on WCCO, the company's radio station. Soon, sales began to rise.

In 1928, Washburn Crosby Company merged with a number of leading U.S. flour milling concerns to form General Mills, Inc. and one of the first new products was Bisquick, the nation's first prepared baking mix. In 1941, the company introduced another unique product, the world's first ready-to-eat oat cereal, Cheerios. Other General Mills consumer food products are listed below.

In 1933, a Bisquick booklet entitled "101 Tricks with Bisquick" was printed and distributed at 25 cents each (731,000 copies). Also, the "25,000 Dollar Recipe Set" was printed in Paris and featured the Famous Chefs campaign. In 1934, a book on baked goods, built around movie stars, was featured as part of the Bread Energy for Vitality campaign. In 1935,

325,000 customers bought 25 cent copies of the Bisquick booklet entitled "How to Make a Trick a Day."

The General Mills company reports that one of the earliest tests for a Betty Crocker voice was conducted in 1930 when Edna Wallace Hopper, a former actress and promoter of cosmetics, was hired. However, her fast, high-pressure style was not what the company was looking for, and within a few years Edna Wallace Hopper faded from the scene. The company's literature also states: "Betty Lutz (Mrs. Arden Buchholz) was the first network Betty Crocker broadcaster commencing in 1927 and except for five years of residence in California following her marriage (when Mrs. Adelaide Finch carried on) continued as the network voice of Betty Crocker until 1948."

The Betty Crocker Food Service was written and sent to newspaper editors beginning in 1937 and continuing for six years after that. At one time over 208 papers were buying the service.

Betty Crocker's fifteenth anniversary was officially celebrated June 1, 1936, and the high spot of the year was the unveiling of the famous Neysa McMein portrait of Betty Crocker (McMein was a prominent New York artist). In addition, a little folder with fifteen Betty Crocker recipes (the most popular during the fifteen years she had been part of the company) was distributed—in fact, approximately four million copies were sent to and distributed through grocery stores. That first portrait of Betty Crocker featured a fairly stern-faced middle-aged woman with gray streaks at her temples wearing a ruffled white

Betty Crocker, photo of the changes the famous trademark had gone through during the years. *Photo courtesy of General Mills Consumer Services.*

blouse with a darker jacket. The artist signed his work in the lower left-hand corner. Other portraits evolved through the years. Three of them were the same woman with updated hairstyles and clothes (1965, 1968, and 1980), while the 1955 version showed a matronly, friendly-looking woman with gray streaks at the temples; the 1972 version was of a Jacqueline Kennedy lookalike with a rather "mod" background; and the 1986 version showed a younger, working woman model with lighter auburn hair than the other versions.

Six well-known artists (including Norman Rockwell) competed for the right to paint the 1955 version of Betty Crocker, but illustrator Hilda Taylor's version won after being evaluated by about 1,600 women from across the country. Noted magazine illustrator Joe Bowler painted the 1965 and 1968 versions, and the 1972 version was done by Minnesota artist Jerome Ryan. The 1986 version, done by New York artist Harriet Pertchik, was unveiled on May 23, 1986, in connection with the introduction of the sixth edition of *Betty Crocker's Cookbook*.

The first Betty Crocker portrait appeared in print ads for Gold Medal® flour in 1936 and the first package to carry the image was Softasilk® cake flour in 1937. It wasn't until 1941 that Betty Crocker became a brand name when the image appeared on Betty Crocker® soups. Her face no longer appears on packages; however, the red spoon logo with her signature is carried on more than 130 products.

During the war years, restrictions governed use of paper and packaging materials, so the company looked for different ways to advertise Betty Crocker's services. It printed and dis-

Betty Crocker, photo of the contemporary Betty Crocker trademark. *Photo courtesy of General Mills Consumer Services.*

tributed nearly seven million copies of a booklet entitled "Your Share," which contained menus, wartime recipes, and other service material, and Betty Crocker was also commissioned to deliver a series of broadcasts on National Broadcasting Company called "Our Nation's Rations," which taught women how to make the most of their restricted food supplies.

After the war, the National Broadcasting Company continued to run "Betty Crocker Time," while the American Broadcasting Company began running "The Betty Crocker Magazine of the Air" (featuring Zella Layne as Betty Crocker) in mid-1947. Also during this time, Betty Crocker was chosen as the trademark for the company's new cake mixes and, later, piecrust mix, as well as being the sponsor of the new line of home appliances. And, in May 1947, a new type of Betty Crocker printed service was tested—a menu-planning and recipe service for three Sunday meals that was tied in with the full line of General Mills household products—in four-page inserts in magazines such as *Life*, *McCall's* and *Look*.

In September 1950, the *Betty Crocker Picture Cook Book*, which had been in preparation for ten years, was published and distributed by McGraw Hill, as well as directly by General Mills. In one year a million copies were sold—a new record for the publishing trade!

During the early years of television, Betty Crocker's use and development tended to slow down. Television could not take the place of the radio shows, thus a public relations study was conducted by the N. W. Ayer Agency, concluding that Betty Crocker must be the center of the company's relationship with the household consumer. A new program was launched in early 1953 covering eleven areas of concentration, which included packaging, publicity, correspondence, consumer promotions, up-to-date portraits, a continuation of Betty Crocker literature, and a strengthened use of the radio medium.

In 1963, the big *G* (already used on the company's breakfast cereals) became General Mills's corporate symbol and was applied to all product packaging, advertising, and correspondence materials. During the 1960s, General Mills concentrated on its largest-ever acquisition program, leading it into several major areas including consumer foods, toys, fashion, specialty retailing, and restaurants. Some of the brand names now owned by General Mills include Yoplait yogurt; Gorton's

BAKING PRODUCTS ■ 31

frozen seafood; Kenner Products; Parker Brothers; Monet; Izod; Ship 'n Shore; Eddie Bauer, Inc.; Red Lobster Inns; York Steak House Systems; and Vroman Foods.

During the past several decades, Betty Crocker has not lost any value with the American public, is still connected with over 130 products, and the company still continues to research her value to them.

One thing has to be said: With more than seventy years under her belt, Betty Crocker may be the only recognizable woman who not only doesn't age but actually looks better with time!

GOLD MEDAL FLOUR

Gold Medal Flour, advertisement from *Harper's Bazaar*, 1910; depicts woman covering rising loaf of bread; $4–6.

Gold Medal Flour, advertisement from *Harper's Bazaar*, ca. 1918–1919; depicts bag of Gold Medal and recipe for salad rolls; $4–6.

Gold Medal Flour, advertisement from *The Farmer's Wife*, April 1925; depicts sliced loaf of bread; $4–6.

Gold Medal Flour, advertisement from *Ladies' Home Journal*, ca. 1923; full-color, depicts farm in background, sack of flour in center; $4–6.

Gold Medal Flour, advertisement from *Needlecraft Magazine*, 1918; depicts Santa with bag of flour over his shoulder; $4–6.

Gold Medal Flour, advertisement from *The Farmer's Wife*, April 1925; depicts sliced loaf of bread; $4–6. *Courtesy of Paper Lady/Bernie and Dolores Fee. Photo by Donald Vogt.*

Gold Medal Flour, advertisement from *Needlecraft Magazine*, 1918; depicts Santa with bag of flour over his shoulder; $4–6. *Courtesy of Paper Lady/Bernie and Dolores Fee. Photo by Donald Vogt.*

Gold Medal Flour, advertisement from *Needlecraft Magazine*, ca 1917; shows woman at door waiting for delivery of Corn Flour; $4–6.

HECKER'S BUCKWHEAT

Hecker's Buckwheat, sign; printed by Giles Litho Co., New York; ca. 1893; depicts baby in high chair often used to promote products made by the Hecker-Jones-Jewell Milling Co.; 29 x 42 inches; good condition; $1,000–1,800.

HOYT'S

Hoyt's Pie and Cake Filler, tin; 10 ounces; still full; picture of cake and pie on front; company located in Newark, New Jersey; ca. 1940s; very good condition; $8–12.

MAGIC YEAST

Magic Yeast, store dispenser; unusual dispenser for Magic Yeast products; gravity fed; 27¼ x 3 inches; good condition with wear from use; $150–300.

N. T. SWEZEY'S SON & CO

N. T. Swezey's Son & Co. Flour, tin sign; reproduction; depicts white boy sitting on flour barrel and black boy behind him; 12½ x 17 inches; $15 retail.

OCCIDENT

Occident Flour, advertisement from *Ladies' Home Journal*, 1915; made by Russell-Miller Milling Company; full-color "framed" ad of woman holding Japanese lantern; excellent condition; $4–8.

Hoyt's Pie and Cake Filler, tin; 10 ounces; still full; picture of cake and pie on front; company located in Newark, New Jersey; ca. 1940s; very good condition; $8–12. *Courtesy of Dawn and Bob Reno. Photo by Donald Vogt.*

Occident Flour, advertisement from *Ladies' Home Journal*, 1915; made by Russell-Miller Milling Company; full-color "framed" ad of woman holding Japanese lantern; $4–6. *Courtesy of Paper Lady/Bernie and Dolores Fee. Photo by Donald Vogt.*

OGLIVE'S

Oglive's Flour, paper sign; patriotic Canadian Victory surmounting the globe and flanked by bags of product; very colorful; original frame; 27¾ x 34¾ inches including frame; good/very good condition, colors bright, some creasing, paper loss at edges, some tears; $200–550.

PILLSBURY

Charles A. Pillsbury, owner of a flour business in Minnesota, adopted the four-X symbol in 1872. Early millers had used a XXX symbol for bread after Christ's death—each X represented one of the crosses on Cavalry. Though the original meaning was lost, millers throughout the medieval era continued to use the XXX mark—but they used it to grade their flour. When Pillsbury added the fourth X, it was to prove "Pillsbury's Best is really the best." The flour was packaged in sacks marked with the XXXX symbol, and those sacks were even considered high-fashion clothing for a while back in the late 1950s.

Pillsbury's business began in 1869 when Charles and his uncle, John Sargent Pillsbury, bought one third of a nearby mill. Charles, Wells Gardner, and George Crocker (the original owners) controlled the mill until Charles bought Crocker's share in 1870. Gardner and Pillsbury bought another mill in 1871, changed the name of the company to C. A. Pillsbury & Company, then welcomed Fred Pillsbury into the business in 1875.

The company grew, prospered, and became the Pillsbury Flour Mills Company in 1908. In 1914, the company's name was changed to Pillsbury Mills, Inc., and in 1958 to the Pillsbury Company.

They produced only Pillsbury's Best Flour for seventy-five years, then introduced a wheat cereal called Vitos in 1898, which was improved and changed to Farina in 1905. Other products were introduced through the years, but the most famous was Ann Pillsbury (1944).

The company's Grand National Recipe and Baking Contest (Pillsbury Bake-off) began in 1949 and the Poppin' Fresh Doughboy, the company's contemporary trademark, was created in the late 1960s.

The family still controls the company that makes its staple flour products, cake mixes, refrigerated biscuits, rolls, and

34 ■ ADVERTISING

cookies. They also own or control other companies such as Green Giant foods, French's potatoes, Burger King restaurants, Steak 'n Ale restaurants, and Häagen-Dazs ice cream.

PILLSBURY

Pillsbury Flour, advertisement from *Ladies' Home Journal*, February 1920; full color; depicts mountain scene and loaf of bread in center; $4–6.

Pillsbury Flour, advertisement from *Ladies' Home Journal*, May 1920; depicts painting in frame of two children and Pillsbury products at bottom of ad; full color; $4–6.

Pillsbury Flour, advertisement from *Pictorial Review*, 1923; shows woman making pancakes; full color; $4–6.

Pillsbury Flour, advertisement from *Modern Priscilla*; depicts girl on phone with boy pointing to box of Pillsbury's Pancake Flour; 10 x 13 inches; full color; $4–6.

Pillsbury, Poppin' Fresh Doughboy, cookie jar; white ceramic cookie jar; ca. 1970s; excellent condition; $20–30.

Pillsbury Flour, paper sign; rare patriotic poster of eagle surmounting barrel, surrounded by activity of men loading flour onto ships in New York and Liverpool harbors, insert of factory below; only two known; 18 x 24 inches excluding original frame; overall 24 x 30 inches; printed by Comtom and Sons; very good condition, water stain; $1,000–2,000.

Pillsbury Flour, advertisement from *Pictorial Review*, 1923; shows woman making pancakes; full color; $4–6. *Courtesy of Paper Lady/Bernie and Dolores Fee. Photo by Donald Vogt.*

Pillsbury Flour, advertisement from *Modern Priscilla*; depicts girl on phone with boy pointing to box of Pillsbury's Pancake Flour; 10 x 13 inches; full color; $4–6. *Courtesy of Paper Lady/Bernie and Dolores Fee. Photo by Donald Vogt.*

QUAKER OATS
(*see* Cereal chapter)

RED-TOP FLOUR
Red-Top Flour, sign; curved porcelain; bright colors; depicts child in sailor outfit in center; approximately 24 x 36 inches; excellent condition; $5,000–6,400.

ROYAL BAKING POWDER
Royal Baking Powder spent almost half a million dollars a year to spread their slogan, "Absolutely Pure," and it worked. Soon their words and goodwill were valued at $15 million. Royal's slogan, one of the first to be widely used, was so successful that by the 1890s slogans were de rigueur.

ROYAL BAKING POWDER
Royal Baking Powder, tin; 12 ounces; red background, black-and-white lettering; 1938; very good condition; $6–12.

Royal Baking Powder, tin; 6 ounces; very good condition; $10–15.

SEA FOAM
Sea Foam, paper sign; cartoonlike figure promotes this baking powder known for its "purity/excellence/strength/healthfulness/economy"; 13 x 20½ inches; very good condition, some creasing, trimmed margins; $400–600.

SHAKER
(*see also* Gardening Supplies chapter)
Shaker, flour sack; Shaker Mills, New Gloucester; the Shakers in Maine sold this product in linen bags; ca. 1880–1890; very good condition; $600–800.

Shaker, flour sack; Shaker Mills, New Gloucester; the Shakers in Maine sold this product in linen bags; ca. 1880–1890, very good condition; $600–800. *Courtesy of Dr. M. Stephen Miller. Photo by Dr. M. Stephen Miller.*

SLEEPY EYE FLOUR

Sleepy Eye Flour, embossed tin sign; depicts "Old Sleepy Eye," the Indian, in oval insert; colorful; near-mint condition; $1,000–1,750.

SNOW WHITE FLOUR

Snow White Flour, bag; depicts the classic Walt Disney character rolling dough; mint condition; $5–20.

THE B & M MILLING & ELEVATOR CO.

The B & M Milling & Elevator Co., paperweight; ca. 1920–1945; company located in Adams, Nebraska; 2½ x 4 inches; $30–45.

THOMPSON & TAYLOR SPICE CO.

The Thompson & Taylor Spice Co., advertising card; "Dey say dis yere baking powder is the best—I'll soon tell"; ca. 1910–1920; good condition; $15–20.

WATKINS BAKING POWDER

Watkins Baking Powder, 1 pound; paper and tin; ca. 1940s; very good condition; $35–40.

WHITE ROSE

White Rose Corn Meal Mix, paper bag; 25 pounds net; full color with white rose emblem on front; made at the Midget Mills, Somerset, Kentucky; near-mint condition; $15–20.

The B & M Milling & Elevator Co., paperweight; ca. 1920–1945; company located in Adams, Nebraska; 2½ x 4 inches; $30–45. *From the collection of Stuart Kammerman. Photo by David Kammerman.*

United States Baking Co., Noah's ark; 8¾ inches long lithographed, paper-covered, ark-shaped wood box; made as container for baked goods sold by United States Baking Co.; the long-bearded Noah and all animals are realistically represented; $125–225. *Collection of and photograph by Evelyn Ackerman.*

CHAPTER THREE
▪ BREAD ▪

BOND
Bond Bread, blotter; pictures balloon; excellent condition; $20–25.

BUTTERNUT
Butternut Bread, cardboard sign; depicts Boy Scouts; mint condition; $5–15.

Butternut Bread, tin sign; depicts baker holding loaf of bread under his arm; 11½ x 17½ inches; ca. 1950s; $50–75.

COBAK CO.
Cobak Co., bread display case; multishelved oak-and-glass display case for Lone Ranger giant loaf bread with red, blue, and white decal on front; 36 x 42 x 28 inches; good original condition, general overall wear due to storage; $200–400.

GROMMES ULLRICH
Grommes Ullrich's Rye, paper sign; bold image of Pilgrims landing in Illinois and meeting costumed Indians; original frame; very good condition, some dirt speckling to print, water staining to mat, decorative loss to frame; $300–600.

H. H. KOHLSAAT & COMPANY
H. H. Kohlsaat & Company, tin sign; framed; 12 x 16 inches; black background with loaf of bread in middle; ca. 1930s; $100–125.

HOLSUM
Holsum, poster; 12 x 20 inches; wood block prints on cardboard; excellent/near-mint condition; $7–10.

MERITA
Merita Bread, cardboard sign; depicts Lone Ranger; approximately 20 x 14 inches; excellent condition; $1,475–2,000.

Merita Bread, reproduction of old tin sign featuring the Lone Ranger; new/reproduction condition; $12.

38 ■ ADVERTISING

Merita Bread, tin sign; depicts the Lone Ranger; reproduction; approximately 14½ x 9 inches; $15 retail. *Courtesy of Doc Davis/Antique-Alike. Photo by Donald Vogt.*

Mi-Te Good Bread, Columbia Baking & Mfg. Co., cardboard fan with wood handle; 16 inches height; good condition; ca. 1960s; $10–15. *Collection of and photo by Iris November.*

Merita Bread, tin sign; depicts the Lone Ranger; reproduction; approximately 14½ x 9 inches; $15 retail.

MI-TE GOOD
Mi-Te Good Bread, Columbia Baking & Mfg. Co., cardboard fan with wood handle; 16 inches height; ca. 1960s; good condition; $10–15.

OLD GRIST MILL
Old Grist Mill Dog Bread, mechanical display; clockwork animation featuring two bulldogs facing each other over package of product; inside product is pop-up cat; under dog on left is "You take the cat"; under cat in bread bag: "Gee, I'm happy"; under dog on right: "Not much! I want the bread"; approximately 36 x 26 x 4 inches; fair condition, some chips, holes, breaks, and general wear; $200–450.

PAN-DANDY
Pan-Dandy Bread, paper sign; shows slices of bread floating to table full of bread products; colorful; near-mint condition; $5–20.

SOUTHERN ENRICHED BREAD
Southern Enriched Bread, tin sign; 28 x 5½ inches; ca. 1950s; $50–75.

THOMAS
Thomas Bread, door push; porcelain; excellent condition; $75–100.

WONDER BREAD

Wonder Bread, story/two pages from *Mechanix Illustrated*, September 1948; depicts "Signboard in the Sky"; $6–8.

ZEPPELIN

Zeppelin Bread, reproduction of old tin sign featuring a zeppelin and declaring "Eat Zeppelin Bread/It's Light as Air"; new/reproduction condition; $12.

Zeppelin Bread, tin sign; reproduction; depicts the zeppelin and caption reads "It's Light as Air"; 11 x 14 inches; $15 retail.

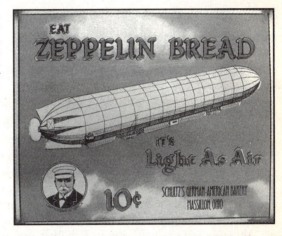

Zeppelin Bread, tin sign; reproduction; depicts the zeppelin and caption reads "It's Light as Air"; 11 x 14 inches; $15 retail.
Courtesy of Doc Davis/Antique-Alike. Photo by Donald Vogt.

CHAPTER FOUR
◼ BREWERIANA ◼

GENERAL INFORMATION

Cone-top beer can production in the United States lasted from 1935 to 1950. Though designs were changed every few years, the basic cone top remained the same. Some smaller breweries didn't replace their cone-top canning lines until well into the 1950s, however, they were the exception rather than the rule.

ANCHOR BREWING

Anchor Brewing (microbrewery owned by Fritz Maytag of the Maytag washing machine company), cardboard signs; ca. 1960s; $3–5 each.

ANHEUSER-BUSCH

Born in Germany in 1839, Adolphus Busch migrated to St. Louis in 1857. He married Lilly Anheuser there and joined her father, Eberhard Anheuser, in business. Anheuser, a wealthy businessman, manufactured soap and owned a brewery whose product was (reportedly) awful. Busch joined with his father-in-law to improve the beer—and both of their fortunes.

The Anheuser-Busch brewery grew throughout the Gay Nineties—so dramatically, in fact, that Adolphus was able to laugh at a $12 million offer for his brewery in 1892. A shrewd businessman, he reinvested his profits in other businesses, such as asphalt mines, hotels, oil fields, coal mines, real estate, livestock, and timber. He also bought out competing breweries.

Adolphus Busch had a cutthroat way of dealing with competitors. On at least one occasion, he cut prices again and again until the other companies came to him and handed him the unique opportunity to control prices for twenty-five years (in the state of Louisiana). His pit-bull-like attitude shadowed the company's policies for over a century.

Adolphus lived the life of the wealthy, with mansions in the United States as well as in his native Germany. He built houses for his thirteen children and, in many ways, acted like his nickname, Prince Adolphus.

Four generations of the Busch family have brought the company through two world wars, an almost crippling Prohibition, and intense competition from other breweries. All four generations were devoted to the family business, though each brought its own style of management to Anheuser-Busch.

The *A* and eagle, Anheuser-Busch's trademark, showed up before the turn of the century—often in unpredictable places like Adolphus's Pasadena estate's flower bed—and continues to be the company's recognized symbol today. One of the company's earliest advertising coups occurred in 1894 when Adolphus purchased a bloody and gory painting by Cassilly Adams titled *Custer's Last Fight*. He made the painting's gory effects even more heightened, then printed lithographed copies that became the most popular advertising promotion he'd ever launched.

The company never scrimped on advertising, promoting new products with the usual newspaper and magazine ads as well as with giveaways ranging from pocketknives and diamond stickpins to automated clocks featuring the famous Clydesdales (the horses were introduced at the end of Prohibition to herald the brewery's return to business).

Like other companies, Anheuser-Busch was not above using celebrities (such as Frank Sinatra) to promote the company's beer during television broadcasts of special appearances.

The company's link with sports programs solidified when Gussie Busch ran the Cardinals baseball team as chairman of the board and president. The company sponsored twenty-three television broadcasts of twenty-four major league teams.

The beers produced by Anheuser-Busch include: Budweiser, Busch, King Cobra malt liquor, Natural Light, Michelob, LA, O'Doul's, and variations of each of those.

Collectible advertising items include serving trays, tip trays, clocks, lights, mirrors, knives, tap knobs, ashtrays, posters, signs, ads, plates, bar displays, leaded glass windows, and other items too numerous to count.

ANHEUSER-BUSCH

Anheuser-Busch, art plate; stock image of girl with long flowing hair and bared bosom; 10 inch diameter; good condition, minor chipping and rust pitting to image and edge wear; $50–100.

42 ■ Advertising

Anheuser-Busch, brewing tray; depicts Victory with cherubs holding bottles of the Busch products; oblong/oval shape; 16½ x 13½ inches; excellent condition; $400–700.

Anheuser-Busch, glass shade; advertises Barley malt syrup; colored milk glass; 4¾ x 6¾ inches; very good condition; $125–225.

Anheuser-Busch, paper sign; one of a series of five frontier images by August A. Busch; this one called "The Father of Waters"; depicts Indians with product on river raft; 17 x 8½ inches excluding frame; very good condition; $75–150.

Anheuser-Busch, paper sign; another of a series that depicts five frontier images; this one titled "Attack on an Emigrant Train"; Indians attack wagonload of frontiersmen and product; 17 x 8½ inches excluding frame; very good condition; $75–150.

Anheuser-Busch, salt and pepper shakers; celebrating centennial; mint condition; one of a kind; $300–400.

Anheuser-Busch, stein; Sea World dolphin; dolphin on 7 ½ inch tall pewter lidded stein; ceramic insert; only 5,000 made; mint condition; $75–100.

Anheuser-Busch, tray; large and colorful factory scene with hops and eagle border; 19 x 15½ inch oval; very good/excellent condition; $600–1,000.

Anheuser-Busch, tray; lithograph on tin; depicts factory scene; 15½ x 18½ inches; printed by Standard Adv. Co., Coshocton, Ohio; excellent condition; $1,250–1,850.

ARROW
Arrow Beer, paper poster; late reissue of nude; 14 x 28 inches excluding frame; very good condition, some overall wear, overstrips top and bottom; $35–75.

BALLANTINE
Ballantine Beer, New York/New Jersey, tap knob (swivels to indicate keg is empty); ca. 1940; $10–15.

Ballantine, mini neon sign (four colors); 1 x 2 feet; ca. 1940s; $100–175.

Ballantine, tin on cardboard sign; ca. 1935–1936; $90–100.

BREWERIANA ■ 43

Ballantine, mini neon sign (four colors); 1 x 2 feet; ca. 1940s; $100–175. *Collection of Matthew E. Hunt. Photo by Donald Vogt.*

Ballantine, tin on cardboard sign; ca. 1935–1936; $90–100. *Courtesy of Paul Brady. Photo by Donald Vogt.*

BARTEL'S
Bartel's Malt Extract, Wilkes-Barre, Pennsylvania, tin framed sign; ca. 1906; $125–150.

Bartel's Brewery, tray; depicts "Jim with Stein," a Viking-like fellow holding spear in one hand, stein in other; 12 inch diameter; good overall condition, wear and white spotting; $30–100.

BARTHOLOMAY
Bartholomay Beer, change tray; girl on winged wheel; 4¼ inch diameter; good/very good condition, minor chipping especially to rim; $25–100.

BERGHOFF
Berghoff Brewing Co., tray; depicts beer and sandwich; 13 x 10½ inch rectangle; fair/good condition; $75–125.

BILLY BEER
Billy Beer, carton of cans; 24-can case; unopened; mint condition; $35–50.

BILOW
Bilow Beer, commemorative cans (the company packaged beer for other breweries); cans were produced 1979–1982; approximately $1 each.

BUDWEISER BEER
(*see also* "Anheuser-Busch")
Budweiser/Anheuser-Busch, reunion cup; Princeton University; excellent condition; contemporary; $7–10.

Budweiser, charger; "Say When"; man on right is adding beer to Anheuser-Busch fondue pot; 16 inch diameter; excellent condition; $150–350.

Budweiser, Christmas ornament; 1991; ceramic; mint condition; $15–20.

Budweiser, collector plate, 1989; "Winter Day" by Bud Kemper; 8½ inch diameter; trimmed in 24-karat gold; made in USA; Holiday Plate I, N2295; mint in-box condition; $75–100.

Budweiser, Field & Stream set of steins; CS 95; four steins with display shelf and all original packaging; mint condition; $250–350.

Budweiser, stein; depicts Bud Man; 1989; mint condition; ceramic; $30–40.

Budweiser, stein; limited-edition collector stein made in 1985; lidded; "Brewing and Fermenting"; numbered and gift-boxed; made in Brazil; mint in-box condition; $250–300.

Budweiser, tray; depicts crew loading the *Robert E. Lee* at the "St. Louis Levee in the Early Seventies"; 17½ x 13 inch rectangle; near-mint condition; $50–125.

Budweiser, truck bank, 1926; Mack truck; Anheuser-Busch graphics, rubber tires, detailed cab interior, chrome-plated accessories, coin slot and lock and key for easy coin removal; mint condition; $25–35.

BUFFALO BREWING CO.

Buffalo Brewing Co., tip tray; colorful image of girls from all nations at the 1915 San Francisco Exposition; 4¼ inch diameter; near-mint condition; $150–300.

BUNKER HILL

Bunker Hill Brewery, cardboard sign; fur-coated girl in 1908 auto; Boston brewery; 14 inch diameter; good to very good condition, some creasing, hole in upper left, minor wear; $150–250.

BURGERMEISTER

Burgermeister Beer, six-pack; soft aluminum tops; ca. 1961–1962; $25–35.

E & J BURKE

E & J Burke Ale, paper sign; depicts Chicago and New York World Series baseball team captains toasting each other with glass of ale and ball players in background; presumably portrait of Chicago's Captain Anson and New York's Captain Buck Ewing; one of two known; approximately 20 x 26 inches excluding frame; good condition, some wood and water staining, general overall soiling; $25,000–35,000.

BUSCH BEER
(*see* "Anheuser-Busch")

CLAUSEN BEER
Clausen Beer, paper poster; Tutonian king drinking flagon of beer flanked by Gothic structure; 17¾ x 22 inches; good/very good condition, bottom cropped, borders trimmed, some staining and overall soiling; $150–300.

COLUMBIA BREWING CO.
Columbia Brewing Co., tray; depicts Columbia with shield; three colors; 12 inch diameter; good condition, overall checking and paint loss to rim; $75–125.

COORS
In 1868, Adolph Herman Joseph Coors came to the United States. He started his Colorado brewery in 1873, then died mysteriously in 1929. His son, Adolph Jr., took over the business, and *his* sons, Adolph III, William, and Joseph, succeeded him. Adolph III was kidnapped and killed in 1959, before the company achieved popularity as a cult beer in the 1960s and 1970s.

As with many other products, Coors's success was partially due to celebrity endorsements (i.e., President Gerald Ford, Henry Kissinger, Paul Newman, and Clint Eastwood).

In 1990, Coors took over the Stroh's brewery in Memphis and began brewing Coors there. Prior to 1990, Coors had two brands; by the time that decade began, the company was producing nine.

The Coors family-controlled company is also involved in ceramics, natural gas, coal, aluminum technology, and recycling.

COORS
Coors Light, stein; Tappa-Kega-Bru; promotional stein for college; gray; 5 inches tall; mint condition; $10–15.

Coors, stein; 1989 Winterfest I—outdoor skating; ceramic; mint condition; $75–90.

Coors, stein; made for employees; white background with colorful scene; 3,000 made by Coors Ceramic Co.; 7 inches tall; mint condition; $150–175.

CROWN
Crown Beer, paper calendar, 1915; rolls down; depicts beautiful woman holding rose; Bartells Brewing Company; 10 x 34 inches; excellent condition, minor soiling; $200–400.

DAUKES ALE
Daukes Ale, paper sign; early colorful advertisement set in double registers—gentleman holding foaming glass in the top register, ale kegs in the bottom, and the two are intertwined by bottles and curlicue banner; printed by Major & Knapp Co.; 18 x 24 inches excluding frame; very good/excellent condition, overall darkening due to age; $300–500.

DIAMOND STATE
Diamond State Brewery, tray; rare; from Wilmington, Delaware; shows satisfied customer with stein of beer and spaniel at his feet; 12 inch diameter; excellent condition; $200–300.

DIEHL
Diehl Brewing Co., tray; depicts an alluring maiden with erect bottle of Diehl Centennial beer; 12 inch diameter; very good condition; $35–100.

DOBLER
Dobler Brewing Co., tray; shows Asti profiled girl with cleavage; 13 inch diameter; excellent condition; $50–100.

DOELGER
Doelger Brewing Co., serving tray; intricate factory scene with biplanes overhead flanked by bottles of Peter Doelger beer; 16½ x 13½ inch oval; fair condition, general overall wear, scratches and chipping, slight fade to color; $300–600.

Doelger's Beer, tin sign; die-cut top; graphic; vibrant colors; Hofbrau gnome with foaming beer stein on early hops-decorated store signs; 19½ x 28 inches; printed by Kaufmann & Strauss; excellent condition, minor chipping at corners and edges; $500–1,500.

DUQUESNE
Duquesne Can-o-Beer, cone-top can; made in Pittsburgh, Pennsylvania; ca. 1935–1950; $40–50.

EDELWEISS
Edelweiss Beer, tin die-cut hanger; 23 inch total height; 1909 copyright; collector only knows of one other for this company and it depicts a different woman; excellent condition; $4,000–5,000.

EMMERLING'S
Emmerling's Beer, tin sign; elderly couple quaffing mugs of Grassvader lager while enjoying bratwurst dinner; printed by Kaufmann & Strauss Co., New York; ca. 1913; 27½ x 19¾ inches excluding frame; near-mint condition, great sheen to colors, minor rubs, slight dirt spots; $1,500–2,500.

EMPIRE
Empire Brewing Co., self-framed tin sign; five potential customers including storekeeper, cowboy, trainmen, and workers with factory in background, admiring labeled bottle; 28½ x 22½ inches; fair/good condition, darkening of color, overall wear, some touch-up; $250–450.

ENCORE BEER
(*see* "Schlitz")

ENTERPRISE
Enterprise Brewing Company, tin tray; image of Victorian lady in bright yellow fancy dress holding a red corsage on a dark green background; 13½ inch diameter; good/very good condition, some scratches and chipping; $175–275.

FEIGENSPAN
Christian Feigenspan Brewing Co., cone-top can; made in Newark, New Jersey (P.O.N. = Pride of Newark); ca. 1940; $20-30.

Feigenspan's Ale, porcelain sign; die-cut corner sign with red, blue, and white lettering; 18 x 24 inches; fair/good condition, some chipping overall, some soiling; $150–300.

Feigenspan Breweries, tray; stock image of girl with long flowing hair in profile; 1910; 13 inch diameter; good condition, lacquer loss to image, spotting discoloration and chipping to image and rim; $25–75.

FIDELIO
Fidelio Brewery, tray; pictures men at tavern table; ca. 1936; 12 inch diameter; very good condition, some image wear with rim chipping; $35–75.

FRONTENAC
Frontenac Beer, tray; colorful view of factory with street scene; made in Montreal, Canada; 12 inch diameter; very good/excellent condition, minor chipping; $50–150.

GEO. EHRET'S
Geo. Ehret's Brewery, tray; depicts company trademark; 13½ x 16½ inch oval; good condition with overall touch-up; $25–75.

GOLD MEDAL
Gold Medal Beer, Stegmaier Brewing Co.; Wilkes-Barre, Pennsylvania, 1935–1950; $40–50.

GOLDENROD
Goldenrod Beer, bottle caps; Brooklyn, New York; set of six (out of a set of eight); ca. 1935; Katzenjammer Kids (different characters); $60–90 (if set is complete, $80–110).

GREENWAY'S
Greenway's Ales, tin sign; Griffith trademark on this early Tuchfarber sign in original frame; 20 x 27 inches including frame; fair condition, general overall flaking; $700–1,000.

Gold Medal Beer, Stegmaier Brewing Co.; Wilkes-Barre, Pennsylvania; 1935–1950; $40–50. *Collection of Jay Herbein. Photo by Donald Vogt.*

Goldenrod Beer, bottle caps; Brooklyn, New York; set of six (out of a set of eight); ca. 1935, Katzenjammer Kids (different characters); $60–90 (if set is complete, $80–110). *Collection of George Arnold. Photo by Donald Vogt.*

HAMM

Hamm, stein; depicts bear; 1972 decanter; 11 inches tall; ceramic; mint condition; $65–75.

HAMPDEN

Hampden Brewing Co., tray; "The Handsome Waiter"; ca. 1934; 13 inch diameter; good condition with chipping and whiting spots to image; $35–100.

Hampden Ale-Beer, tray; made at Hampden Brewing Co., Willimansett, Massachusetts; 12 inches; ca. late 1940s–early 1950s; $30–50.

HARVARD

Harvard Ale, die-cut tin sign; unusual mug-shaped sign picturing costumed characters enjoying mugs of Harvard beer; 9 x 12½ inches; good condition, general overall fading, slight denting, scratches and chipping; $50–150.

Harvard Brewing Co., paper sign; interesting and rare image of vignetted views through ivy-covered walls; a portholed image of the collegiate regatta including Harvard, Yale, and Cornell crews with factory through lower window in this 1901 poster; 23 x 33 inches; excellent/near-mint condition, very slight staining primarily to edges, some wrinkling, minor creasing; $500–1,000.

Harvard Brewing Co., tin sign; large, colorful image of elaborate Moroccan interior with well-dressed woman pouring a glass of Harvard beer; classic image; 28 x 37 inches excluding frame; excellent condition, minor hairline scratches, slight chipping primarily to background, general soiling; $1,000–2,000.

HELLMAN BOCK

Hellman Bock Beer, paper poster; black-and-white image of ram exiting broken beer keg with frothy mug in paw; 18 x 24 inches; very good condition, overall general wear, some creasing, two thumbtack holes at top; $25–75.

Hellman Brewing Company, paper sign; depicts a bighorn sheep breaking through the end of a barrel holding a glass of beer in its paw; 17½ x 23½ inches excluding frame; good overall condition with some staining around edges; $100–300.

Hensler's Light Beer, bottle (1860-1957); late 1940s; half gallon (called picnic bottle); $10–25. Also cans (1955); $55–75; and bottle made during Prohibition; light green; $5–10. *Collection of Frank Baranco. Photo by Donald Vogt.*

Holihan's Ale, cardboard stand-up sign; Diamond Spring Brewery, Inc., Lawrence, Massachusetts, Holly-7; 15 cents; ca. 1940s; $15–20. *Collection of Matthew E. Hunt. Photo by Donald Vogt.*

HENSLER'S

Hensler's Light Beer, bottle (1860–1957); late 1940s; half gallon (called picnic bottle); very good condition; $10–25.

Hensler's Light Beer, can; 1955; very good condition; $55–75.

Hensler's Light Beer, bottle; made during Prohibition, light green; $5–10.

HOLIHAN'S

Holihan's Ale, cardboard stand-up sign; Diamond Spring Brewery, Inc., Lawrence, Massachusetts, Holly-7; 15 cents; ca. 1940s; $15–20.

HOSTER

Hoster Brewing Co., tin sign; drunken monk among beer barrels; 20 x 16 inch oval excluding frame; good/very good condition, slight wear overall, minor scratching; $50–150.

IMPERIAL

Imperial Ale, tap knob; North American Brewing Co., New York City; ca. 1940; $40–50.

IRON CITY

Iron City Beer, cone-top can; made at Pittsburgh Brewing Co.; ca. 1935–1950; $70–80.

JONES

Jones Brewing Company, tray; stock image of "Geannette" (Victorian woman glancing sideways at viewer); 13 inch diameter; fair condition, two holes in center of tray, overall fading and scratches throughout; $50–100.

KING COBRA BEER

(*see* "Anheuser-Busch")

KING'S BEER

King's Beer, tin sign; gold background, red-and-black lettering; in business 1933–1938; Brooklyn, New York; approximately 8 x 30 inches; very good condition; $75–150.

KNICKERBOCKER

(*see also* "Ruppert Knickerbocker Beer")
Kickerbocker Beer, sign; reverse on glass; framed; ca. 1955; $125–150.

Knickerbocker grouping; can $8–25, coasters $1–2 each, menu insert $2–3, cooler bag (six-pack went inside and the bag hung over the boat) $5–7, Ruppert Knickerbocker tray $15–25.

KRUEGER

Krueger, tap knobs; ca. 1939–1951; $15–30.

LA BEER

(*see* "Anheuser-Busch")

MCSORLEY'S

McSorley's Famous Lager Beer, bottle; put out by Fidelio Breweries, later by Rheingold; New York; ca. 1935; $35–50.

MICHELOB BEER

(*see* "Anheuser-Busch")

MILLER

Miller Lite, stein; 1983; world series of tavern pool at Caesar's Palace; 6 inches tall; mint condition; $8–10.

Miller, stein; 1991; Birth of a Nation—Paul Revere on horseback; first in series of five; 7 inches tall; mint condition; $10–15.

Coasters; assorted companies; late 1950s–current; .50–$1 each. *Courtesy of Alan E. Paschedag. Photo by Donald Vogt.*

MISCELLANEOUS

Coasters; assorted companies; late 1950s–current, .50–$1 each.

Foam scrapers; Trommer's, Ambassador, Ballantine, Rheingold, Mt. Carbon; ca. 1940s; average $15–25.

MOERLEIN

Moerlein's Beer, tin sign; depicts attractive, scantily dressed woman holding tray of beer in one hand and raised beer glass in the other; 20 x 28 inches excluding frame; very good/excellent condition, minor background inpainting, slight soiling overall, minor scuffing; $1,000–2,500.

NARRAGANSETT

Narragansett Beer, roll-down poster; depicts a woman sitting at a table with a beer stein full of beer; 17 x 23 inches; vivid and bright colors; good overall condition with some creasing and minor chipping to edges; $100–300.

Narragansett Brewing, tray; lettered logo; 16½ x 13½ inch oval; good condition with touch-up to background and rim chipping; $75–150.

National Bohemian Pale Beer, cone-top can; ca. 1935–1950, the National Brewing Company; Baltimore, Maryland; $40–50. *Collection of Jay Herbein. Photo by Donald Vogt.*

Newman Brothers, Inc., paperweight; depicts factory in Pittsburgh, Pennsylvania; company sells "Everything for your Brewery"; ca. 1890–1910; 3 inch diameter dome; $100–165. *From the collection of Stuart Kammerman. Photo by David Kammerman.*

BREWERIANA ■ 53

NATIONAL BOHEMIAN
National Bohemian Pale Beer, cone-top can; ca. 1935–1950; the National Brewing Company; Baltimore, Maryland; excellent condition; $40–50.

NATURAL LIGHT BEER
(*see* "Anheuser Busch")

NEWMAN BROTHERS, INC.
Newman Brothers, Inc., paperweight; depicts factory in Pittsburgh, Pennsylvania; company sells "Everything for your Brewery"; ca. 1890–1910; 3 inch diameter dome; $100–165.

O'DOUL'S NON-ALCOHOLIC BEER
(*see* "Anheuser-Busch")

OLD BOSTON BREWERY
Old Boston Brewery, paper sign; interesting early image of suited man toasting the oval image of beer factory in background; early piece; 20 x 18 inches excluding frame; fair/good condition, appears trimmed; $200–400.

OLD COPPER
Old Copper Snapper, ale containers (2); 5½ x 3 inch diameter; good overall condition; $65–125.

OLD GERMAN
Old German Premium Beer, plastic signs; four in set–1910 Stanley Steamer, 1911 Ford T-Touring, 1912 Maxwell Roadster, 1928 Packard Roadster; ca. late 1950s; $60–75 for all four.

Old German Premium Beer, plastic signs; four in set–1910 Stanley Steamer, 1911 Ford T-Touring, 1912 Maxwell Roadster, 1928 Packard Roadster; ca. late 1950s; $60–75 for all four. *Courtesy of Alan E. Paschedag. Photo by Donald Vogt.*

Old German Premium Lager Beer, cone-top can; the Queen City Brewing Co.; Cumberland, Maryland; ca. 1935–1950; $40–45. *Collection of Jay Herbein. Photo by Donald Vogt.*

Old German Premium Lager Beer, cone-top can; the Queen City Brewing Co.; Cumberland, Maryland, ca. 1935–1950; $40–45.

OLD MILWAUKEE BEER
(*see* "Schlitz")

PABST

Founded in 1844 in Milwaukee by Jacob Best and his four sons, the Pabst Brewing Company was originally called the Best Brewing Company. When Frederick Pabst married one of Jacob's granddaughters in 1862, he didn't realize he was marrying into the company that would make him one of the most important figures in brewing history.

By 1866, Pabst had bought the brewery from his father-in-law. Brother-in-law Emil Schandein shared the brewery with Pabst, but Pabst soon became the dominant partner. In 1873, the company became a corporation and was named the Best Brewing Company; it was called that until the stockholders voted to change the name to the Pabst Brewing Company in 1879.

Pabst was selected as America's best beer at the 1893 Columbian Exposition in Chicago. Captain Pabst died in 1904, and his sons, Gustav and Fred Jr., took over the brewery.

After Prohibition (1934), Pabst acquired a brewery in Peoria Heights, Illinois, and in 1945, expanded once again, buying a third brewery in Natick, New Jersey; he added a fourth in Los Angeles in 1948.

Pabst's directors and shareholders bought the Blatz Brewing Co. in 1958. Though Pabst had, at one time, ranked right up with the best American breweries, it dropped to thirteenth in the industry in the 1970s.

PABST

Pabst Blue Ribbon Beer, paper sign; factory framed dual bottled image with glass of beer and oysters; 18½ x 14½ inches excluding frames, 30 x 26½ inches overall; good/very good condition, minor paper loss lower left corner, vertical tear in opened bottle, puncture tear in closed bottle, otherwise image is near mint; $400–600.

Pabst Blue Ribbon Beer, tray; depicts traditional smiling gent pouring beer; 10½ x 13½ inch rectangle; excellent condition, horizontal scratch in man's chest, minor damage to background and rim; $100–150.

BREWERIANA ■ 55

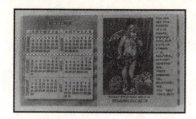

Pabst, half-year calendar; 1896–1897; $12–15. *Collection of Dennis McEvoy. Photo by Donald Vogt.*

Pabst, matchbooks (one of the first advertised beers on a matchbook cover was Pabst); $1–5. *Collection of Dennis McEvoy. Photo by Donald Vogt.*

Pabst Brewing Company, cardboard sign; 1936; depicts Colonial gentlemen in library drinking steins of Pabst beer; 41½ x 29½ inches excluding frame, overall 46 x 34 inches; very good condition, some wrinkling, minor scratching and overall wear; $50–125.

Pabst, half-year calendar; 1896–1897; fair condition; $12–15.

Pabst, postcard; entrance to brewery; ca. 1913; good condition; $5–10.

Pabst, pamphlets; giveaway booklets at brewery; ca. late 1800s; good condition; $20–30 each.

Pabst, ink blotters; one with gentleman, 1933; other is older; good condition; $10–20.

Pabst Malt Extract, poster; illustrated image of knight astride a swan; 14 x 22 inches; excellent condition; $75–150.

Pabst, matchbooks (one of the first advertised beers on a matchbook cover was Pabst); $1–5 each.

Pabst, paper poster; depicts team pulling a wagonload of Wilbur's Tonic with running dog in foreground—"Blue Ribbon Winners"; 34 x 17 inches including frame; very good condition, overall soiling; $50–100.

Pabst, postcard; depicts brewery; ca. 1920; good condition; $5–10.

Pabst, postcard; depicts brewery in Milwaukee, Wisconsin; ca. 1915–1918; good condition, $5–10.

56 ■ ADVERTISING

Pabst, postcard; depicts brewery in Milwaukee, Wisconsin; ca. 1915–1918; $5–10. *Collection of Dennis McEvoy. Photo by Donald Vogt.*

Pabst, postcard; depicts the Beautiful Blue Ribbon Hall; early 1920s; $5–10. *Collection of Dennis McEvoy. Photo by Donald Vogt.*

Pabst, postcard; depicts the Beautiful Blue Ribbon Hall; early 1920s; very good condition; $5–10.

Pabst, songbook; ca. 1933; $12–15.

Pabst, stein; 1988 King Gambrinus holiday stein; ceramic; mint condition; $20–25.

Pabst, Wilbur's Stock Tonic, paper sign; a Pabst product portrayed by the loaded Pabst wagon pulled by six dappled horses accompanied by a running dog; 32 x 15 inches; fair/good condition, image primarily in excellent shape, paper loss at edges and border, some tears; $50–125.

PFAFF'S

Pfaff's Lager, thermometer; rare wooden beer thermometer for a Boston brewery; working; 5 x 21 inches; fair/good condition, general wear to background color and lettering; $25–100.

Philadelphia Old Stock, cooler keg tap knob (used for picnic barrels of beer); ca. 1940; $15–20. *Courtesy of Paul Brady. Photo by Donald Vogt.*

PHILADELPHIA OLD STOCK
Philadelphia Old Stock, cooler keg tap knob (used for picnic barrels of beer); ca. 1940; excellent condition; $15–20.

PICKWICK
Pickwick Ale, self-framed tin sign; three dapper gents toasting with mugs of ale; printed by Chas. W. Shonk Co. Litho., Chicago; 22¼ x 28¼ inches; very good/excellent condition, bright sheen to bold image, minor scuffing, slight chipping, dark green overpaint to raised border covering Harvard Brewing Co. label at bottom; $500–1,200.

PIEL BROS. BEER
Piel Bros. Beer, self-framed tin sign; very unusual and rare New York brewery sign of two elves with beer bottles; 13 inch diameter; excellent/near-mint condition, minor chipping primarily at edge, slight overall soiling; $350–550.

PREMIER
Premier Beer, tray; still life depicting lobster and beer; 13 x 10 inch rectangle; fair condition, overall wear to image, chipping to background and rim, some overpaint drips; $25–75.

PRIMO BEER
(see "Schlitz")

PUNXY
Punxy Special Beer, tray; swashbucklers at play and at sport; 17 x 12 inch rectangular; good condition, apparent residual shaped shadow discoloration and whiting to image, rim chips; $25–75.

RAINIER
Rainier Beer, Washington State, mirror; reverse painting on glass; framed and matted; $400–500.

Rainier Beer, Washington State, mirror; reverse painting on glass; framed and matted; $400–500.
Courtesy of Leo's Quality Cans. Photo by Donald Vogt.

Rainier Beer, rolled-edge tin sign; image of girl resting on growling bear's head for this Seattle Brewing Co. tin sign; ca. 1913; 15 x 15 inches; very good/excellent condition, strong colors, minor chipping primarily to background; $250–450.

Rainier Beer, die-cut tin hanger; 23 inches total height; H. D. Beach Co.; ca. 1909; extremely rare (only one known by collector); excellent condition; $6,000–8,000.

RAM'S HEAD
Ram's Head Ale, tap knob; Valley Forge Brewery; Philadelphia, Pennsylvania; ca. 1950; excellent condition; $10–20.

REID'S
Reid's Stout, sign; gold griffith image; surrounded by black background and white milk glass backing in metal frame; 12 x 30 inches; near-mint condition; $100–300.

RHEINGOLD
Rheingold, cardboard display pieces (slipped over neck of bottle of beer); ca. 1935; excellent condition; $35–40 each.

Rheingold Scotch Ale, reverse on glass sign backed with cardboard; Liebmann Breweries; Brooklyn, New York, and Orange, New Jersey; ca. 1955 (Liebmann 1920–1964; Rheingold brewery out of business 1976); mint condition; $25–50.

ROESSLE
Roessle Brewery Co., paper sign; three images of this Boston brewery, encircled by hops; rare; lithographed by Taber-Prang; 28 x 20 inches excluding frame; near-mint condition; $500–800.

ROLLING ROCK
Rolling Rock Premium Beer, chalkware bar piece; made in mid-1960s; approximately 10½ inches high; Latrobe, Pennsylvania; very good condition; $15–25.

RUBSAM & HORRMANN
Rubsam & Horrmann Brewing Co., tip tray; Stapleton, New York; Chrysanthemum Girl, Copyright 1910 (1870–1953); near-mint condition; $200–300.

RUPPERT KNICKERBOCKER
Ruppert Knickerbocker, can; (1940); in mint shape, $125; as is, $15.

Rolling Rock Premium Beer (1933–present), chalkware bar piece; made in mid-1960s; approximately 10½ inches high; Latrobe, Pennsylvania; $15–25. *Courtesy of Alan E. Paschedag. Photo by Donald Vogt.*

Rubsam & Horrmann Brewing Co., tip tray; Stapleton, New York; Chrysanthemum Girl, Copyright 1910 (1870–1953); almost-mint condition; $200–300. *Collection of George Arnold. Photo by Donald Vogt.*

Ruppert Knickerbocker, can; (1951); very good condition; $35–50.

Ruppert Knickerbocker, can; (1948); very good condition; $35–50.

Ruppert Knickerbocker, tip trays (set of four originally); made in late 1950s; $5–7 each.

Ruppert Knickerbocker, coasters; ca. 1940–1941; $5–7 each.

Ruppert Knickerbocker, tip tray; ca. 1939; very good condition; $25–35.

SCHLITZ BEER

August Krug started the Schlitz company in 1849, but when Krug passed away in 1856, his bookkeeper, Joseph Schlitz, took over—completely! He even went so far as to marry Krug's widow, then changed the name of the company to Jos. Schlitz Brewing Co. in 1874.

Ruppert Knickerbocker grouping; Jacob R. can (1940) in mint shape $125, as is $15; Ruppert (1951) $35–50; Ruppert Knickerbocker can (1948) $35–50; tip trays (set of four originally), (late 1950s) $5–7 each; coasters, (ca. 1940–1941) $5–7 each; tray, Jacob Ruppert, (ca. 1939) $25–35. *Collection of Joe Radman. Photo by Donald Vogt.*

In 1875, both Schlitz and his bride died in an accident while on their way to vacation in Germany. Krug's nephews, August, Henry, Alfred, and Edward Uihlein, then took over the brewery and the company has been family managed ever since.

"The Beer that Made Milwaukee Famous" slogan goes back to the Chicago fire, when the city's residents were waterless and Schlitz came to the rescue by sending beer. Schlitz's "Beer that Made Milwaukee Famous" is nearing its century birthday, a fact that will stimulate collectors to scoop up every available piece of advertising memorabilia. The slogan began appearing on beer bottle labels in 1895.

Among the promotions Schlitz has done through the years were a "Schlitz Milwaukee Dictionary" (copyrighted in 1899) and ads telling women"how to pamper a husband" in 1951; salt and pepper shakers were made, as were trays, tumblers, postcards, signs, patches, and all the usual bar memorabilia.

Competition is fierce within the beer industry. Where there was once 750 breweries, there is now only approximately fifty. Battles with the "big boys" (Anheuser-Busch and Miller) have often pushed Schlitz into a dark corner. In fact, one of Schlitz's distributors once said, "We are overwhelmed by Anheuser advertising. It keeps our brands out of the consumer's mind" (quote taken from Eric Clark, *The Want Makers*, Viking Publishers, New York).

Some of the beers made by the company today include Schlitz, Schlitz Malt Liquor, Encore, Primo, and Old Milwaukee (including light versions of some of the above).

SCHLITZ

Schlitz, cardboard advertisement; depicts factory scene with angel in top left and nymph sitting on the world in lower right corner; framed; 33 x 45 inches; near-mint condition; $1,800–2,400.

Joseph Schlitz Brewing Company, paper litho; nice image of husband and wife with children looking up at parents; factory with horse-drawn streetcars and trolley cars in the road; 21¾ x 26½ inches excluding mat and frame; very good overall condition with some minor staining; $750–1,150.

Schlitz/Schlitz Lite, tap handles; ca. 1960s–1970s; excellent condition; $4–8.

Schlitz/Schlitz Lite, tap handles; ca. 1960s–1970s; $4–8. *Courtesy of Paul Brady. Photo by Donald Vogt.*

SCHMIDT'S

Schmidt's (Philadelphia), foam scraper holder, pot metal; ca. 1940–1950; excellent condition; $5–25.

Schmidt's Beer, tray; shows "Mayflower Passengers" in shades of blue; 12½ x 15½ inch oval; excellent condition; $50–100.

SEITZ

Seitz Brewing Co., tray; depicts winged eagle logo; 13 inch diameter; good condition, overall scratches to image and border, some color loss to rim; $75–125.

STEGMAIER BREWING CO.

Stegmaier Brewing Co., plates (2); Limoges giveaway plates from Pennsylvania brewery; one pictures a Victorian lady with green feathered hat; the other depicts pink flower blossoms and lily of the valley; both are 9¼ inches in diameter; excellent condition, minor color loss due to age; $75–150.

Stegmaier Brewing Co., tip tray; factory scene; 4¼ inch diameter; excellent condition, slight wear, minor scratch in border, slight edge chipping; $75–150.

Stegmaier Brewing Co., tray; factory scene; 13 inch diameter; very good condition, scratches to image and edge; $50–100.

STROH'S

Stroh, stein; 1984 holiday; "Our family's 200-year brewing heritage assures you of consistently superior quality beer"; 7½ inches tall; ceramic; mint condition; $20–25.

Stroh, stein; Audubon Society IV; Humpback whale; ceramic; mint condition; $100–125.

Stroh's Bohemian Beer, tray; shows waiter with tray of beer bottles and glasses; 12 inch diameter; fair condition; $35–75.

TERRE HAUTE
Terre Haute Brewing Co., tray; depicts angels passing beer to group of ladies and men in powdered wigs; 12½ x 15 inch oval; good condition, overall scratching; $75–150.

TROMMER'S
Trommer's Beer, wall plaque; Brooklyn, New York (1897–1951), and East Orange, New Jersey (1934–1950); wooden veneer; "Good Luck Enjoy Trommer's"; excellent condition; $25–40.

Trommer's Beer, fork and spoon; from the Beer Garden in Brooklyn; ca. 1930s; excellent condition; $10–20.

UNION BEER
Union Beer, tray; depicts colorful "Heine" Dutch boy serving beer and sausage; 10½ x 13 inch rectangle; good/very good condition with background and rim chipping; $35–75.

UTICA CLUB
Utica Club, reunion cups; Princeton University; 1958; excellent condition; $20–25.

Trommer's Beer, fork and spoon; from the Beer Garden in Brooklyn; ca. 1930s; $10–20. *Collection of Mark Oleske. Photo by Donald Vogt.*

BREWERIANA 63

VALLEY FORGE
Valley Forge Beer, tray; shows "Washington's Headquarters" with enlisted men raising the flag and Washington standing in foreground; rim of tray marked "Sheidt's"; 13 inch diameter; very good condition; $75–125.

Valley Forge Beer, tray; shows "Washington's Headquarters" with house in background, Washington on horse surrounded by soldiers; 13 x 10½ inch rectangular; very good/excellent condition; $50–125.

VX
Vx Beer, tap knob; Greater New York Brewery; ca. 1940; excellent condition; $40–50.

WATNEY'S
Watney's Ale, glass sign; elk pictured on white milk glass reverse sign with metal-cased frame; 12 x 30 inches overall; near-mint condition; $200–400.

WEST END
West End Brewing Company, paper calendar; 1907; pretty girl with bottle of beer and factory out window; elaborate Victorian interior setting; calendar has full pad; 16 x 21 inches excluding mat and frame; excellent condition, colors bright and rich, minor tear lower left corner, minor staining; $300–600.

ZANG BREWING
Zang Brewing, paper poster; a trio of monks surrounds another of the order who appears inebriated; Denver, Colorado, brewery; approximately 20 x 15 inches excluding multiple mats and frame; excellent/near-mint condition, minor tears lower right and slight water staining; $350–500.

CHAPTER FIVE
■ CANDY ■

ALLENBURYS

Allenburys, Glycerine & Black Currant Pastilles, tin; 4 ounces; gold, blue, and black design; made by Allen & Hanburys Ltd., London; excellent condition; $5–10.

BABY RUTH

The candy bar, named for President and Mrs. Grover Cleveland's eldest daughter (Ruth), is now owned by Standard Brands and has been its top-selling nut roll bar for years. Originally called Kandy Kake, the candy bar was named by an employee of the Curtiss Candy Company. The company had run a naming contest for the candy bar several years after Curtiss Candy Company was organized by its founder, Otto Schnering. The trademark's lettering imitated the engraved words on a medallion that depicted the president, Mrs. Cleveland, and "Baby Ruth" and that was introduced at the 1893 Chicago World's Columbian Exposition.

To advertise the new candy, Curtiss gave away thousands of samples in a unique marketing program, even hiring airplanes to drop the candy via tiny parachutes over Pittsburgh in 1924. They also used a circus, hockey and bowling teams, a six-pony team, and a Scottish Kiltie band to market Baby Ruth candy.

BABY RUTH

Baby Ruth, advertisement from *Boys' Life*, 1944; depicts sailors on

Allenburys, Glycerine & Black Currant Pastilles, tin; 4 ounces; gold, blue, and black design; made by Allen & Hanburys Ltd., London; excellent condition; $5–10. *Courtesy of Dawn and Bob Reno. Photo by Donald Vogt.*

CANDY ■ 65

Baby Ruth, advertisement from *Boys' Life*, 1943; depicts zeppelin; two-color ad; $4–7. *Courtesy of Paper Lady/Bernie and Dolores Fee. Photo by Donald Vogt.*

Brach's Fine Candies, advertisement from *Life* magazine, 1946; depicts Mint Twins bar; $4–7. *Courtesy of Paper Lady/Bernie and Dolores Fee. Photo by Donald Vogt.*

phone; caption reads "... and she's got Cookies made with Baby Ruth"; $4–7.

Baby Ruth, advertisement from *Boys' Life*, 1943; depicts zeppelin; two-color ad; $4–7.

Baby Ruth, advertisement from *Boys' Life*, 1944; depicts men coming off boat; $4–7.

BEECH-NUT

Beech-Nut Candy, tin display; three-tiered package display; 9¾ x 11½ x 15 inches; fair condition, scratches, chips, fading; $75–150.

Beech-Nut Mints, tin display box; hinged marquee shows packages of flavored mints in five-cent packages, as do sides; 9½ x 7½ x 8½ inches; excellent overall condition; $75–150.

BIT-O-HONEY
(*see* "Nestlé")

BLUE BIRD

Blue Bird Marshmallows, tins (3); 1 pound triangular can with colorful image of birds in tree; 5 pound tin with birds and contents; and 1 pound round can with blue bird in flight; sizes as previously stated; very good/excellent condition, minor scratches; $400–600.

BRACH'S FINE CANDIES

Brach's Fine Candies, advertisement from *Life* magazine, 1946; depicts Mint Twins bar; $4–7.

BUTTERNUT
(*see* "Leaf, Inc.")

CHUNKY
(*see* "Nestlé")

CIRCUS CLUB
Circus Club Mallows Candy, tin; colorful cartoon image of bear in yellow sports jacket; made in Toronto, Canada; 3 inch diameter x 7 inches overall (hat, 4 inch diameter); good condition, some scratching and paint loss due to overall wear, slight denting, hole in bottom and hat; $50–150.

Circus Club Mallows Candy, tin; colorful cartoon image of cat in bow tie; made in Toronto, Canada; 3 inch diameter x 7 inches overall (hat, 4 inch diameter); excellent/near-mint condition, minor chipping; $150–300.

Circus Club Mallows Candy, tin; colorful cartoon image of magnificently dressed monkey with red hat; made in Toronto Canada; 3 inch diameter x 7 inches overall (hat, 4 inch diameter); very good/excellent condition, minor chipping; $150–300.

CRACKER JACK
F. W. Rueckheim, a German immigrant, came to Chicago after the Great Fire of 1871 and, with only $200 in his pocket, opened a popcorn stand on what is now Federal Street. His brother, Louis, soon joined him in the successful venture, and they later added marshmallows and other confections to their popcorn.

F. W. Rueckheim and Brother changed locations five times between 1875 and 1884. They doubled and quadrupled their space as the demand for their product increased. In 1885, they moved their factory to a brick building at 266 South Clinton Street, but the building was destroyed by fire two years later. It took only six months for the brothers to rebuild their company.

A combination popcorn-peanuts-molasses confection was sold in 1893 at the Columbian Exposition, Chicago's first world's fair, and that confection was a forerunner to the Cracker Jack brand. The name Cracker Jack was coined by a salesman in 1896, and the first slogan—"The more you eat, the more you want"—was provided by a customer. By 1899, Henry Eckstein had joined the brothers, and he invented the packaging that kept the confection fresh.

In 1908, the song "Take Me Out to the Ballgame" (composed by Albert Von Tilizer and written by Jack Norworth) immortalized the confection with the words "Buy me some peanuts and Cracker Jack."

Most collectors like the coupons and novelties produced by the company from the early 1900s. The 1910–1911 packages carried coupons that could be redeemed for premiums, but the most valuable collectible Cracker Jack produced is a 116-page catalog that was issued in 1912. The post card-size catalog showed hundreds of items that could be obtained with coupons printed on the sides of Cracker Jack boxes. The coupons were discontinued in 1912 when Rueckheim introduced prizes that were to be included in each and every package (see a detailed list of types of prizes on page *68*).

The Cracker Jack logo, Sailor Jack and dog Bingo, was added to the box after World War I. The package was redesigned at that time, adding a patriotic flair with red, white, and blue stripes. F. W.'s grandson, Robert, who died of pneumonia shortly after the character first appeared on packages, was the model for the original Sailor Jack. Though the figures have been slightly modified through the years, Sailor Jack and Bingo have remained the Cracker Jack logo for over seventy years.

During the 1930s, the Cracker Jack Mystery Club provided members with a chance to collect a set of U.S. Presidential Medals. Later, a set of movie star cards would be added. The first prizes to be included in the Cracker Jack box were made in Japan, however, these prizes were discontinued shortly before World War II.

Like other companies in business during World War II, Cracker Jack provided emergency rations for the Allies and was recognized for its achievements by both the army and the navy.

The toys were wrapped individually in 1948 to provide better protection.

In 1964, Borden, Inc. purchased the Cracker Jack Company and introduced changes in automation and packaging. By 1978, Cracker Jack was packaged in foil, and in 1985–1986, the company introduced larger package sizes.

Many of the toys produced by Cracker Jack are on display at the Center of Science and Industry, located in Columbus, Ohio.

For more information about the many types of Cracker Jack prizes, see *Cracker Jack Prizes* by Alex Jaramillo, published by Abbeville Press, New York, in 1989. Mr. Jaramillo is the world's best-known Cracker Jack collector and once served as the company's official spokesperson.

Types of Toys Found in Cracker Jack Boxes Through the Years

1912–1930	Metal whistles, brooches, pins, spin tops, puzzles, yo-yos, paper games
1930–1940	Hand-painted metal, wooden, and porcelain toys; a complete train set; lead charms and trinkets
1940–1950	World War II pilots, commanders, artillery equipment
1950–1960	Television and space-age toys; molded plastic whistles, cars, and animals
1960–1970	Mini-sized storybooks, riddles, fun books, tattoos, and encyclopedias
1970–1980	Mini pinball games, superhero stick-ons, plastic prisms, fun books, and rub-off maze games
1980	Super Surprise promotion with prizes worth up to $10,000; Mattel toys
1984	Series of wiggle pictures to commemorate Olympics
1985	Stickers depicting endangered wild animals

CRACKER JACK

Cracker Jack, doll; 14 inches tall; made by Vogue dolls; 1979; mint in-box condition; $75–100.

Cracker Jack, miniature comb; excellent condition; $22–25.

Cracker Jack, miniature sundial; excellent condition; $22–25.

Cracker Jack, miniature tray; depicts Cracker Jack box; ca. 1930s; very good condition, some chips and scratches; $20–35.

Cracker Jack, pocket mirror; tin-rimmed mirror depicts package; giveaway; 1⅛ inch die; very good condition; $25–50.

Cracker Jack, tin top; excellent condition; $38–45.

Cracker Jack, top; depicts Cracker Jack box and words "Always on Top/World's Famous Confection"; ca. 1930s; excellent condition; $20–35.

Cracker Jack, toy; 1930s; 1½ inch long train engine; excellent condition; $6–8.

Cracker Jack, toy; 1930s cast-iron gun; excellent condition; $1–3.

DONRUSS BASEBALL CARDS AND GUM
(*see* "Leaf, Inc.")

DRUM MAJOR
Drum Major Marshmallows, tin; depicts drum major; colorful; made in Toronto, Canada; 10½ inch diameter x 5 inches; very good/excellent condition, slight overall wear, minor denting; $35–75.

EMPRESS
Empress Chocolates, celluloid sign; depicts empress in regal robes and crown; 14 x 18 inches; printed by Whitehead and Hoag Co.; ca. 1906; very good condition; $200–400.

FANNY FARMER
Fanny Farmer Easter Candies, 4 ounce cardboard boxes; decorated with bunny and chickie designs; excellent condition; $25–30 each.

J. S. FRY & SONS
J. S. Fry & Sons, tin candy container and bank; pictorial and figural reusable toy bank; made in Montreal, Canada; 4 x 4½ x 3 inches; very good condition, minor fading to left side, overall slight scratching and chipping, minor denting, primarily to roof; $100–300.

GOOBERS
(*see* "Nestlé")

GOOD 'N PLENTY
(*see also* "Leaf, Inc.")
Good 'N Plenty, figure; depicts Good 'N Plenty children and their "choo-choo"; vinyl and paper-mâché, extremely rare; 5 inches; late 1960s; $500–600.

Good 'N Plenty, figure; vinyl and papier-mâché; extremely rare; 5 inches; late 1960s; $500–600.
Courtesy of Neil and Nancy Berliner. Photo by Donald Vogt.

HEATH BARS
(*see* "Leaf, Inc.")

HERSHEY'S

Hershey is one company that was quite capable of becoming a success without the benefit of an enormous advertising budget. Milton Hershey, founder of the company, was the person responsible for the no-advertising policy, because he believed a good product, package display, and value sold an item rather than its advertising.

Hershey had originally worked for a confectioner in Lancaster, Pennsylvania, then started his own candy store in Philadelphia in 1876 with a $150 loan from his aunt. He distributed his business cards at the Centennial Exposition that year, but the business did not boom as he had expected it to.

After several more tries (and failures), he moved to New York in 1883 and began work for a well-known candy maker, Heyler's. An enterprising man, he used his off hours to produce caramels in his landlady's kitchen. Still, he could not succeed, and he returned to Lancaster, Pennsylvania, penniless.

An 1893 visit to the World's Columbian Exposition in Chicago introduced him to chocolate-making machines. Determined to succeed somehow in the candy business, he bought the machines once the fair closed and used them to make chocolate to cover his caramels. In 1903, he finally became successful enough to build his own factory in Derry Church (renamed Hershey in 1906).

Hershey designed his original red-and-black milk chocolate bar wrappings, and they quickly gained public acceptance. However, Hershey switched to maroon-and-silver labels printed on imported flint-coated stock around the time of his move to the new factory (1903).

The company trademark at one time included an angelic child seated atop a cocoa bean and holding either a bar of candy or a cup of hot cocoa aloft in one hand. The trademark, though not used on packaging, was still used on company letterhead in 1971.

Hershey quit the business when he made his first million at the age of forty-three, but soon became bored, came back to the business, and made one hundred times as much as he had before. He built one of the first community-oriented/employee-oriented factories in the United States in Hershey, Pennsylvania, and the "community" grew until it housed one of the most visited amusement parks/factory complexes in the nation.

CANDY ■ 71

Hershey's, bank; ceramic; ca. 1983; made in Taiwan; 6½ inches, $50–75.
Courtesy of Neil and Nancy Berliner. Photo by Donald Vogt.

Hershey's, ceramic figure; "Sharing the Good Things"; depicts boy and girl holding on to Hershey's pot; made by Hershey Foods Corp., J. M. Schuler Co. Licensee; ca. 1960s; extremely rare; $275–350. *Courtesy of Neil and Nancy Berliner. Photo by Neil Berliner.*

In 1945, at the ripe old age of eighty-eight, Hershey died, leaving 70 percent of his fortune to a school for orphaned boys.

Reproductions of the old Hershey labels are available from the Hershey Foods Corporation, as well as during special supermarket promotions.

HERSHEY'S

Hershey's, bank; ceramic; ca. 1983; made in Taiwan; 6½ inches; excellent condition; $50–75.

Hershey's, ceramic figure; "Sharing the Good Things"; depicts boy and girl holding on to Hershey's pot; made by Hershey Foods Corp., J. M. Schuler Co. Licensee; ca. 1960s; extremely rare; excellent condition; $275–350.

Hershey's, tin; made for Hershey's Hometown Series (Hershey's Kisses); canister #4; 1990; near-mint condition; $3–5.

HOYT'S

Hoyt's, figural candy box; railroad-shaped candy box; used as store display for But-A-Kiss; toy inside; 18½ x 10½ x 8 inches; very good condition, minor chipping and scuffing; $300–650.

HOLLYWOOD BRANDS

(*see* "Leaf, Inc.")

JOLLY RANCHER

(*see* "Leaf, Inc.")

Hershey's, gum ball gaming machine; insert a penny and pull a plunger, which results in getting a gum ball; at the same time, the wheel in the middle spins (if the product on the wheel lined up with the same product in the arrow, the merchant would give you a candy bar for free); bottom of machine reads "For Advertising Purposes Only" to avoid classification as gambling device; very colorful; 12 x 7 x 4 inches; ca. 1940s; $350–500. *From the collection of Leonard A. Calabrese. Photo by Adalbert Krei.*

KRAFT

(*see also* "Kraft General Foods" in Dairy Products chapter)

Kraft Chocolate Fudgies, advertisement from *Life* magazine, 1956; depicts life-size pieces; done by Whitney Darrow, Jr.; $4-7.

LEAF, INC.

In December 1983, Huhtamaki Oy, a Finnish conglomerate, purchased Beatrice Foods's confectionary division (Leaf Confectionary), as well as General Mills's Donruss division. The company is an interesting conglomeration of several "parts" of other well-known companies, such as Heath Brothers, Hollywood Brands, the Jolly Rancher Candy Company, Leaf Brands, Warner Lambert, Switzer, and Donruss. Some of the products produced by Leaf, Inc. include Heath Bars, Whoppers, Milk Duds, Zero and Pay Day candy

Kraft Chocolate Fudgies, advertisement from *Life* magazine, 1956; depicts life-size pieces; done by Whitney Darrow, Jr.; $4–7. *Courtesy of Paper Lady/Bernie and Dolores Fee. Photo by Donald Vogt.*

bars, Switzer licorice, Good 'N Plenty candy, and Donruss baseball cards.

Heath Bars originated in Robinson, Illinois, in 1914 when the Heath brothers dubbed their candy "America's Finest English Toffee." In 1928, the candy's name was Heath English Toffee. Heath was acquired by Leaf, Inc. in 1989.

Frank Martoccio of the F. A. Martoccio Macaroni Company began focusing his full attentions on the part of his company that produced candy in 1933. Soon after the decision to do so, he also decided a name change was due, thus Hollywood Brands, Inc. was born. In 1936, his son, Clayton, sold the macaroni factory and joined his father in the candy business.

Together, they produced such candy bars as Butternut (1916), Polar (1924), Pay Day (1932), and Milkshake and Zero (1933).

The company was second in the country in volume produced in the 1960s, and in 1967, was sold to Consolidated Foods, Inc. (which later became Sara Lee Corporation). In 1988, Leaf North America acquired Hollywood Brands.

Bill and Dorothy Harmsen founded the Jolly Rancher Candy Company in Golden, Colorado, in 1949. They sold soft ice cream and chocolate candy under the copyrighted Jolly Rancher name until 1966, when the company was sold to Beatrice Foods. Jolly Rancher's line of candy (which includes its Stix Bar line) was acquired by Leaf, Inc., confectionary division to Leaf.

Overland Candy Company made the malted milk candy called Whoppers, but the candy was not known by that name until 1949, two years after Leaf acquired the company. RainBlo gum balls were introduced by Leaf in 1940, while Milk Duds, originally owned by F. Hoffman & Company of Chicago (bought from Milton J. Holloway in 1920), were created in 1926. Good 'N Plenty, introduced in 1883 by Quaker City Confectionary, ranks as one of the oldest American candies. The candy became part of Leaf, Inc. in 1983. Another well-known candy, Switzer licorice (created in 1916), was also acquired during Leaf's merger with Beatrice Foods's confectionary division. Leaf acquired Donruss, the baseball card business, and now produces over 800 cards, including Rated Rookies, Diamond Kings, and the Highlights Series.

LIFESAVERS

The popular candy with the hole in the middle was developed and marketed by Clarence Crane, father of the well-known American poet, Hart Crane. Clarence was a chocolate candy manufacturer based in Cleveland, Ohio. He sold Life Savers in 1913.

LIFESAVERS

Lifesavers, advertisement from *Life* magazine, 1946; depicts carousel made of Life Savers; full color; $4–7.

Lifesavers, trade sign; 23 inches; depicts package of product; excellent condition; $375–450.

Lifesavers, trade sign; 4 feet; depicts form of mint package; excellent condition; $475-550.

MAR-O-BAR

(*see* "M & M/Mars")

M & M/MARS

The Mars family has controlled the company since Frank and his wife, Ethel, created buttercream candy in their Tacoma, Washington, kitchen in 1911. They are extremely secretive, withholding all the usual company information—except for the fact that they spend approximately $400 million a year to advertise.

Frank and Ethel decided to go public with their popular candy in 1920 when they moved to Minneapolis and opened a candy factory. Mar-O-Bar was their first candy bar, but it was not successful. Snickers, their second bar, was *very successful*.

Lifesavers, advertisement from *Life* magazine, 1946; depicts carousel made of Life Savers; full color; $4–7. *Courtesy of Paper Lady/Bernie and Dolores Fee. Photo by Donald Vogt.*

CANDY

Mars/Marsettes Candies, advertisement from *Life* magazine, 1959; depicts Christmas tree made out of the candies; $4–7. *Courtesy of Paper Lady/Bernie and Dolores Fee. Photo by Donald Vogt.*

Then came Milky Way, Forrest Mars's (Frank and Ethel's son) creation. Frank gave Forrest $50,000 to go to Europe to produce Mars candy there. Forrest's sweeter Milky Way and packaged pet foods were so successful that he returned to the United States in 1940 to open his own company: M & M. The two companies were separate entities until their 1964 merger.

When Forrest retired in 1973, he went into seclusion and refused to have his (or any of the company's executives') pictures taken for publication. Forrest's twin sons (Forrest Jr. and John) took over the company as copresidents.

In addition to their famous candy products, the company also sells pet food and Uncle Ben's Rice.

MARS
Mars/Marsettes Candies, advertisement from *Life* magazine, 1959; depicts Christmas tree made out of the candies; $4–7.

MELLO MINTS
Mello Mints, oval tin; 2½ ounces; all-tin; ca. 1940s; very good condition; $30–35.

MELROSE MARSHMALLOWS
Melrose Marshmallows, tin; 4 ounces; all-tin; ca. 1940s; very good condition; $35–40.

MILK DUDS
(*see* "Leaf, Inc.")

MILKSHAKE
(*see* "Leaf, Inc.")

MILKY WAY
(*see also* "M & M/Mars")

Milky Way, advertisement from *Life* magazine, 1943–1944; depicts infantryman holding bar of Milky Way; $4–7.

Milky Way, advertisement from *Life* magazine, 1948; depicts little girl feeding teddy bear; full color; $4–7.

Milky Way, advertisement from *Life* magazine, 1953; record album eating bar of Milky Way; caption reads "Heavenly Harmony"; $4–7.

MISCELLANEOUS
Lollipop scale, 1 cent; approximately 70 inches tall; good condition; $250–500.

Candy jar display rack; wire rack with 13 covered glass jars; good condition overall; $200–400.

Marshmallow tins (2); varied sizes; good/very good condition, some chipping and general soiling overall; $25–75.

MONARCH
Monarch Toffies, store bin; large tin depicts "Teenie Weenies" defending a plate of packaged candies; 12 x 14½ inches; very good condition, some dents and scratches; $150–300.

MOONLIGHT MELLOS
Moonlight Mellos, tin; large candy container with winged angel on

Milky Way, advertisement from *Life* magazine, 1943–1944; depicts infantryman holding bar of Milky Way; $4–7. *Courtesy of Paper Lady/Bernie and Dolores Fee. Photo by Donald Vogt.*

Milky Way, advertisement from *Life* magazine, 1948; depicts little girl feeding teddy bear; full color; $4–7. *Courtesy of Paper Lady/Bernie and Dolores Fee. Photo by Donald Vogt.*

CANDY

Necco, advertisement from *Life* magazine, 1954; Halloween ad showing children feeding pumpkin; full color; $4–7. *Courtesy of Paper Lady/Bernie and Dolores Fee. Photo by Donald Vogt.*

stringed decoration; made in Toronto, Canada; 10½ inch diameter x 5 inches; excellent condition, slight scratching and denting; $35–100.

NATIONAL MINTS AND GUM

National Mints and Gum, vending machine; five-cent glass-and-metal vending machine; ca. 1925; 8 x 15½ x 6 inches; excellent original condition, with key and workings; $150–300.

NECCO WAFERS

Necco, advertisement from *Life* magazine, 1954; Halloween ad showing children feeding pumpkin; full color; $4–7.

Necco Wafers, tin display; four-column five-cent tin candy display with Necco trademark on panels; 7 x 19 x 7 inches; good condition, original, some chipping and soiling overall, includes swivel base; $75–150.

NESTLÉ

The company, founded in Switzerland, didn't actually start making chocolate until 1904. Though it had European beginnings, one of the founders was Charles A. Page, an American consul who was sent to Zurich after the Civil War. Page and his brother, George, organized the Anglo-Swiss Condensed Milk Company in 1866. Meanwhile, German-born Henry Nestlé began making a milk-product substitute. Eventually, the two companies became rivals, then they joined forces in 1905 to become the Nestlé and Anglo-Swiss Condensed Milk Company.

The company's first non-milk-related product (instant coffee) was put on the market in 1938.

78 ■ ADVERTISING

Some of the brands Nestlé owns are:

Candy: Goobers, Bit-O-Honey, Chunky, O'Henry!, Nestlé candy bars, Raisinets

Coffee/Tea: Taster's Choice (coffee), Hills Bros. (coffee), Chase & Sanborn (coffee), Nestea (tea), Nescafé (coffee)

Milk Products: Carnation

Cocoa: Quik

Cosmetics: L'Oreal, Lancôme, Cosmair

They also make seasonings, soups, frozen foods, wines, and pet foods.

NESTLÉ
Nestlé's Chocolate, glass display case; etched glass tiered store case; missing back door; 12 x 10¾ x 15½ inches; excellent overall condition; $150–300.

O'HENRY
(*see* "Nestlé")

PAGE & SHAW
Page & Shaw, candy boxes; Cambridge, Massachusetts; 1 pound net; assorted; ca. 1930s; very good condition; $15–18.

Page & Shaw, candy boxes; Cambridge, Massachusetts; 14 ounces; nut and fruit assortment; ca. 1930s; very good condition; $15–18.

PAY DAY
(*see* "Leaf, Inc.")

PETER PAUL MOUNDS
Peter Paul Mounds Bar, advertisement from *Life* magazine; full color; depicts candy bar coming out of coconut; ca. 1958; $4–7.

PEZ
Pez, head of display piece; plastic; 20 inches tall; ca. 1990; $100–125.

POLAR
(*see* "Leaf, Inc.")

RAINBLO GUM BALLS
(*see* "Leaf, Inc.")

RAISINETS
(*see* "Nestlé")

Pez, head of display piece; plastic; 20 inches tall; ca. 1990; $100–125. *Courtesy of Neil and Nancy Berliner. Photo by Donald Vogt.*

RINGED LICORICE

Ringed Licorice, paper sign; dual image—one shows child trying to break "old-style" licorice, while the other shows baby in basket eating sectioned licorice with ease; 13 x 9¾ inches; excellent condition, trimmed borders, minor soiling; $400–600.

SAMOSET

Samoset Chocolate, plaster sign; three-dimensional Indian in canoe (the Samoset logo); 20 inch diameter x 4 inches; good original condition, some flaking to surface, minor inpainting or repair; $100–300.

Samoset Chocolates, tin sign; "Chief of Them All"; lithographed in gold, blue, red, and black on silvery background; 3½ x 21 inches long; very good condition; $35–80.

SCHRAFFT'S

The company, founded in 1861 by W. F. Schrafft and sons, was originally called the Boston Candy Company. One of Schrafft's salesmen, an enterprising chap named Frank Shattuck, was responsible for creating the first Schrafft's Candy and Ice Cream Shop in New York in 1898. This was the first of a chain of food and ice cream restaurants with shops from coast to coast.

A 1931 ad mentions the candy's ability to replace the tired feeling one gets when overworked. At that time, the candy was sold for .60 to $2 a pound.

Schrafft's was sold to Pet Incorporated in 1968, then the ice cream division was acquired by Restauranteur, Inc. in 1973. The original building still stands in Charlestown, Massachusetts, but the company offices are now located in Pelham, New York.

SCHRAFFT'S

Schrafft's, pail; "The old woman who lived in a shoe"; 4 x 3¾ inches with bail; excellent condition (pail), fair condition (lid); $200–400.

Schrafft's, paper-on-canvas-sign; depicts attractive woman with red ribbon in her hair; "The Chocolate Girl"; 18 x 24 inches excluding frame; overall 23¼ x 29¼ inches; fair/good condition, minor wear and chipping; $100–300.

Schrafft's, paper-on-canvas sign; depicts pretty girl with red ribbon in hair; "The Chocolate Girl; 18 x 24 inches excluding frame; overall 23¼ x 29¼ inches; fair/good condition; $125–275.

Schrafft's, sign; "Chocolate Girl"; 22½ x 32 inches including original frame; fair/good condition, tears and creasing, overall soiling; $50–150.

SHARP'S TOFFEE

Sharp's Toffee, tin; barrel-shaped and embossed, with lid and handle; depicts trademarked image of monocled man (looks like Charlie Chaplin as The Little Tramp) and leering parrot; made in Maidstone, England; 7 inch diameter x 8½ inches; good condition, some rusting, chipping, slight denting; $100–150.

SNICKERS

(*see* "M & M/Mars")

STOLLWERCK

Stollwerck, glass vending machine insert; etched and beveled glass sign for door of L-shaped chocolate vender; 5 inch diameter; good condition, some paint loss to background; $25–75.

SWITZER LICORICE

(*see* "Leaf, Inc.")

TOOTSIE ROLL

Leo Hirshfield, a candymaker, came to New York City in 1896 from Vienna. He brought with him the memory of his childhood sweetheart, Tootsie, and a formula for a rolled, chewy, chocolaty candy. He made the candy, selling it for a penny apiece, and decided to name it after his former sweetheart. The candy's success was immediate, and millions of pieces of the candy were soon produced daily.

Many collectible items, such as banks and tin replicas of the candy, have been produced and reproduced over the years, and

CANDY 81

W. G. Dean & Son, paperweight; "the only firm ever awarded a medal for the best Spanish licorice by the American Institute Fair"; company located in New York; ca. 1890–1910; 2½ x 4 inches; $50–75. *From the collection of Stuart Kammerman. Photo by David Kammerman.*

one would imagine that since Tootsie Roll's hundredth anniversary is coming up soon, we can expect much more.

TOOTSIE ROLL

Tootsie Roll, rocket game; includes the game board, target, and plastic rocket; given as premium in 1962; 17 x 20 inches; excellent condition; $20–30.

Tootsie Roll, rocket; 1962 premium; rare; paper game board; plastic rocket; in original mailer; near-mint condition; $26–32.

W. G. DEAN & SON

W. G. Dean & Son, paperweight; "the only firm ever awarded a medal for the best Spanish licorice by the American Institute Fair"; company located in New York; ca. 1890–1910; 2½ x 4 inches; $50–75.

WHITMAN'S

In 1912, Whitman introduced the sampler device to sell its chocolates in boxes—"samples" of each kind of chocolate they made. The company, in business since Stephen F. Whitman sold candy out of his Philadelphia store in 1842, needed a way to announce this innovation. Whitman designed a needlework-type design called the "sampler." Whitman had kept notes of his customers' preferences in candy and would make up a box with their favorites.

When his son, Horace, joined the firm in 1869, Stephen F. Whitman & Son was born. They exhibited at the 1876

Philadelphia Centennial and won a bronze medal. In 1907, the candy was distributed nationally, and in 1909, the first ad appeared in the *Saturday Evening Post*. The Whitman's messenger was added to the design in 1915, and was registered as a companion trademark. In 1932, the sampler box's paper cover was changed to linen and special gift boxes were made from 1924 to 1926. In 1939, the slogan "A Woman Never Forgets a Man Who Remembers" was introduced.

The company was the first to utilize a four-color ad in the *Saturday Evening Post*, and collectors prize Whitman's ads for their beauty and artistic images. Whitman's maintains a permanent display of over 600 exquisite samplers dating from 1790 to 1840 as a tribute to the golden age of samplery and the president's unique advertising idea.

Whitman's was acquired by Pet Incorporated in 1963 and is now part of IC Industries Company.

WHITMAN'S

Whitman's, chocolate cigarettes; paper container in two pieces; very good condition; ca. 1950s; $3–8.

Whitman's Chocolates, folder; ca. 1920s; nice colors; excellent condition; $16–20.

WHOLE-SUM MINTS

Whole-Sum Mints, tin; circus parade graphics; 2½ ounces; all-tin; ca.1930s; $30–35.

WHOPPERS

(*see* "Leaf, Inc.")

WYLER'S

Wyler's Mint Leaves, tin; ¾ ounce; ca. 1950s; very good condition; $18–22.

ZERO

(*see* "Leaf, Inc.")

ZINGO

Zingo Sweets, tin; black-and-gold; unusual 10 pound candy can picturing a two-seater open race car; 10 inch diameter x 8½ inches; fair/good condition, some denting, chipping, gold discoloration overall; $75–125.

CHAPTER SIX
■ CEREAL ■

AMERIKORN
Amerikorn—The Nation's Breakfast Food, advertisement from the *Saturday Evening Post*, 1919; rare three-color ad; Penny Ross, illustrator; depicts girl in flowered dress and hat saying "Come on Over! Amerikorn for Supper!"; $4–10.

CHEERIOS
(*see* "General Mills" in Baking Products chapter)

CREAM OF WHEAT
(*see also* "Nabisco" in Crackers/Cookies/Biscuits chapter)

Another item produced by the Nabisco Company is the Cream of Wheat cereal products. A real person was used in ads for Cream of Wheat cereals, but the general manager of the company and discoverer of its trademark, Colonel Mapes, never identified the original man named Rastus (though it was rumored he knew who he was).

Legend has it that as Mapes was lunching in Kohlsaat's Restaurant in Chicago in the early 1900s, a very handsome and jovial black waiter served him. Mapes, struck by the man's affability, paid the waiter $5, secured the man's photograph, and got a release to use it in advertisements. He not only used it, he made it into an instantly recognizable symbol of good food. However, when they wanted more pictures later, they could not find the original waiter.

"Rastus's" image promoted a new porridge developed by Mrs. Thomas Amidon, wife of a miller at the Diamond Mill in Grand Forks, Iowa, in 1894. At that time, the owners of the company, Emery Mapes and George Bull, used an old woodcut of a black chef on the box and the product soon sold by the carloads. Once the photo of the waiter was used, Cream of Wheat became even more popular.

Collectors of this trademark love the ads that appeared in magazines and newspapers. Some simply showed the Cream of Wheat man feeding his special cereal to children; others utilized old nursery rhymes, such as "Old King Cole," to sell the product. A printed and stuffed 18-inch Rastus doll was produced in 1936 and sold for ten cents by the company. A wooden jigsaw puzzle and trade cards are also available.

In 1981, several oil paintings done by illustrators from 1900 to 1950 and featuring the Cream of Wheat man were found by the company. The paintings were assembled into a traveling exhibition and sent around the country to further promote the popularity of this familiar face in advertising.

Today the Cream of Wheat logo is owned by Nabisco Brands. More information about collecting advertising materials featuring the Cream of Wheat man can be found by writing the archivist at Nabisco Brands, East Hanover, New Jersey 07936.

CREAM OF WHEAT

Cream of Wheat, advertisement from *Collier's*, 1906; depicts chef in field with scythe; full color; $15–25.

Cream of Wheat, advertisement from *Collier's*, 1907; N. C. Wyeth series; depicts cowboy putting letter in wooden mailbox; full color; $15–25.

Cream of Wheat, advertisement from *Collier's*; 1906; depicts children holding hands, chef coming in with steaming bowls of product; full color; $15–25.

Cream of Wheat, advertisement from *Collier's*, 1906; depicts children holding hands, chef coming in with steaming bowls of product; full color; $15–25. *Courtesy of Paper Lady/Bernie and Dolores Fee. Photo by Donald Vogt.*

Cream of Wheat, advertisement from *Modern Priscilla*, 1920; depicts child eating product; "Little Indian—Sioux or Crow . . ." $15–25. *Courtesy of Paper Lady/Bernie and Dolores Fee. Photo by Donald Vogt.*

CEREAL ■ 85

Cream of Wheat, advertisement from *McCall's*, 1902; rare; depicts Colonial couple skipping down the walk; "To Market, to market . . ."; full color; $15–25.

Cream of Wheat, advertisement from *Modern Priscilla*, 1920; depicts child eating product; "Little Indian—Sioux or Crow . . ."; $15–25.

EGG-O-SEE
Egg-O-See Cereal Company, advertisement from *Pictorial Review*, 1914; depicts boy in wheat field; full color; $4–10.

FARINA
(*see* "Pillsbury" in Baking Products chapter)

FLAKED RICE
Flaked Rice, cloth giveaway doll; ca. 1890; Canadian; 12 x 25 x 3½ inches; very good condition, some slight staining overall, light wear; includes separate dress and skirt; $200–400.

GRAPE-NUTS CEREAL
(*see also* "Post")
Grape-Nuts, advertisement from *Etude Magazine*, 1910; depicts farmer with oxen; full color; $4–10.

Grape-Nuts, advertisement from *Literary Digest*, 1916; depicts nurse feeding baby in wicker chair; $4–10.

Grape-Nuts, advertisement from *Modern Priscilla*, ca. 1921; back cover; depicts circle of children; $4–10.

Grape-Nuts, self-framed tin sign; titled "To School Well Fed"; depicts red-caped child with St. Bernard dog; 20½ x 30¼ inches; very good condition; $900–1,400.

Grape-Nuts, tin sign; depicts girl in red cape going to school with St. Bernard dog; 30½ x 20 inches; near-mint condition; $1,500–2,500.

Grape-Nuts, tin sign; embossed; schoolgirl and St. Bernard dog; 20 x 30 inches; good, slight overall fade, some chipping and scratching, minor soiling; $500–750.

HONEY COMB
Honey Comb, cel; unusual storyboard-type cel advertising Honey Comb cereal with boy holding box of cereal and science-fiction "man/moose"; drawn; pastel background; line and colored cel overlay;

approximately 12 x 9½ inches excluding mat and frame; near-mint condition; $100–400.

KELLOGG'S

Dr. John Harvey Kellogg and Will Keith Kellogg, his younger brother, invented flaked cereal by accident in 1894 at the Battle Creek Sanitarium where John was sanatarium superintendent and his brother was his business manager. The two Kellogg brothers invented many grain-based foods besides the flaked cereal, though that cereal became one of the most popular in the world.

The accident occurred when the two men were trying to develop tasty substitutes for the sanitarium's hard and tasteless bread. After cooking and rolling the wheat into long sheets of dough, the men were called away, and when they returned, the wheat was stale. Rather than waste it, the Kelloggs experimented with forcing the tempered grain through the rollers and the result was a small, thin flake. After baking, the flakes tasted light and crisp.

Because the patients wanted to enjoy their wheat flakes at home, Dr. Kellogg started the Sanitas Nut Food Company and put his brother in charge of the business end of producing the cereal. W. K. Kellogg began developing the process for flaking corn in 1898, and, believing the product to have a promising future, expanded the business himself. His brother did not have any interest in doing so, thus Will Keith continued alone. By 1902, the flaked cereal business had become a success, with more than forty factories near the sanitarium, all copying and retailing the Kelloggs' flaked wheat cereal. By 1906, Will Keith formed the Battle Creek Toasted Corn Flake Company (renamed Kellogg Company in 1922).

Kellogg's idea of advertising was to emphasize the flavor, freshness, value, and convenience of their foods, rather than its obvious nutritional value, because he reasoned that people ate food because they *liked* it rather than because it made them healthy. The idea worked: a full-page ad in the July 1906 issue of the *Ladies' Home Journal* boosted sales from 33 to 2,900 cases per day. Additional sales promotions pushed the company's annual sales past a million cases by 1909. Other promotions included the "Give the Grocer a Wink" promotion, which won shoppers free samples of Kellogg's Toasted Corn Flakes, and

"The Jungleland Funny Moving Pictures" book of 1910, which was the first of thousands of premiums Kellogg's customers enjoyed. The slogan, "The Original Bears This Signature" (W. K. Kellogg's), was included in every ad, no matter how large or small.

In 1914, the company introduced a new type of packaging called Waxtite®, designed to keep products fresh, and in 1923, W. K. hired Mary Barber to establish a professional home economics department that would create recipes utilizing Kellogg products.

Other Kellogg products added to the company's success, among them All-Bran (1916) and Rice Krispies (1928). Today, more than forty different cereals are sold in more than 130 countries.

Like many other companies, Kellogg supported the United States's war effort during the 1940s by packaging the military's K-rations; after the war, Kellogg began supplying elementary school teachers with nutrition information in game formats. It continues to do so today, supplying educational computer programs and fitness videos.

In 1951, W. K. Kellogg died at ninety-one years of age. But the company continued to produce throughout that decade, developing cereals that appealed to children, such as Kellogg's Corn Pops® (1950), Kellogg's Frosted Flakes® (1952), and Kellogg's Honey Smacks® (1953). With the introduction of Kellogg's Frosted Flakes® came the emergence of another recognizable face in advertising—Tony the Tiger®—and his statement: "They're g-r-r-eat!" However, Kellogg's did not forget the premise on which the company began and continued to look for new products that were also healthful, such as their 1955 introduction of Kellogg's Special K® cereal.

The advent of television gave the company a new area in which to advertise, so Kellogg began sponsoring family shows such as "Superman" and "Wild Bill Hickock." Even personalities such as Howdy Doody endorsed products like Kellogg's Rice Krispies®.

The company was one of the first to voluntarily list sugar on its labels in 1976 and included amounts of sodium and dietary fiber by 1979. Labels included cholesterol and potassium levels by the mid-1980s, and the company continues to pay close attention to communicating good messages about nutrition on all its packaging.

During the 1980s, the Kellogg's company, through advanced technology, produced several new products such as Kellogg's Nutri-Grain® (1981), a flaked whole-grain cereal that was the first produced with no sugar added; Kellogg's Crispix Cereal® (1983); Kellogg's Just Right Cereal® (1985); and Kellogg's Mueslix Cereal® (1987).

The company continues to use familiar faces in advertising some of its cereals—Tony the Tiger® for Kellogg's Frosted Flakes®; and Snap!®, Crackle!®, and Pop!® for Kellogg's Rice Krispies®. Tony, introduced in 1952, shared the package with Katy the Kangaroo® for a while, but he was more popular than his kangaroo friend, so the company retired her after the first year. Tony continued to be used, to the point of obtaining star status. Though he has changed several times throughout the years, the scarf around his neck remains a constant, and most of the artwork on the character is done by Hanna-Barbera, the cartoon people.

The three gnomelike characters who represent Kellogg's Rice Krispies were born in the 1930s. Before that time (until 1936), a single gnome who wore a baker's hat (Snap!®) had appeared solo on the packages, but the other two gnomes (Crackle!®, with his red or striped stocking hat, and Pop!®, in his military hat) had joined him in print ads. By the 1940s, all three were pictured on side and back package panels and were even featured in World War II ads to urge customers to "Save time, save fuel, save energy." Though the characters have evolved from gnomes to more humanlike beings, their hats have always remained the same.

KELLOGG'S

Kellogg's Corn Flakes, advertisement from *Life* magazine, 1940; "Switch to something you'll like"; picture of two freckled kids; some collectors will purchase this ad because of the dish in which the cereal is being served (Fiestaware); $7–10.

Kellogg's Frosted Flakes, advertisement from *Life* magazine; double-page spread; full color; depicts full-bodied Tony; $12–15.

Kellogg's Raisin Bran, cardboard store display; 8 x 24 x 35 inches; contemporary; $60–100.

Kellogg's Corn Flakes, advertisement from *Life* magazine, 1940; "Switch to something you'll like"; picture of two freckled kids; some collectors will purchase this ad because of the dish in which the cereal is being served (Fiestaware); $7–10. *Courtesy of Lester Morris. Photo by Donald Vogt.*

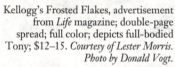

Kellogg's Frosted Flakes, advertisement from *Life* magazine; double-page spread; full color; depicts full-bodied Tony; $12–15. *Courtesy of Lester Morris. Photo by Donald Vogt.*

Kellogg's Rice Krispies, advertisement from *Life* magazine, 1940; "Speaking of lasting Crispies/Snap! Crackle! Pop!"; this ad came with poem "Sailing, Sailing..."; $7–10.

Kellogg's Shredded Krumbles, advertisement, 1920; $15–20.

Kellogg's Toasted Corn Flakes, advertisement from *Ladies' Home Journal*, June 1909; full color; depicts woman floating above cornfield in box of product; $4–10.

Kellogg's Raisin Bran, cardboard store display; 8 x 24 x 35 inches; contemporary; $60–100; advertisement for Kellogg's Shredded Krumbles, 1920, $15–20. *Courtesy of Biggar's Antiques. Photo by Donald Vogt.*

Rice Krispies, advertisement from *Life* magazine, 1940; "Speaking of lasting Crispness/Snap! Crackle! Pop!" this ad came with poem "Sailing, Sailing ..."; $7–10. *Courtesy of Lester Morris. Photo by Donald Vogt.*

90 ■ ADVERTISING

Kellogg's, "Papa Bear" doll from the Goldilocks group; has red-and-yellow-striped trousers and blue jacket; 14 inches; first advertising dolls made by Kellogg's; premium/giveaway, uncut; 1925; $15–25. *Photograph copyrighted courtesy of Evelyn Ackerman, collection of Evelyn Ackerman.*

Maypo, vinyl Marky Maypo figure; 8¾ inches high; ca. early 1960s; $125–175. *Courtesy of Neil and Nancy Berliner. Photo by Neil Berliner.*

Kellogg's Toasted Corn Flakes, advertisement from *Youth's Companion*, 1912; depicts child pulling cover off table to get box of cereal; full color; $4–10.

Kellogg's Toasted Corn Flakes, advertisement from *Youth's Companion*, 1910; child saying "I love my jam—but O You Toasted Corn Flakes"; full color; $4–10.

Kellogg's Toasted Corn Flakes, advertisement from *Ladies' Home Journal*, 1912; depicts Indian tying box of Toasted Corn Flakes on donkey in pueblo scene; rare; full color; $4–10.

Kellogg's Toasted Corn Flakes, advertisement from *Country Life in America*, 1904; strawberries; $4–10.

Kellogg's cardboard display with cloth dolls; includes twelve cloth patterns (three of each) for Dinkey the Dog, Crinkle the Cat, Dandy the Duck, and Freckles the Frog; varied sizes; excellent condition, some minor seam wrinkling to display and light overall soiling; $75–150.

Kellogg's, "Papa Bear" doll from the Goldilocks group; has red-and-yellow-striped trousers and blue jacket; 14 inches; first advertising dolls made by Kellogg's; premium giveaway, uncut, 1925; $15–25.

Kellogg's Rice Krispies, slide puzzle; depicts Snap, Crackle, and Pop; 1979; very colorful; near-mint condition; $4–8.

MAYPO

Maypo, vinyl Marky Maypo figure; 8 ¾ inches high; ca. early 1960s; $125–175.

MOTHER HUBBARD ENERGY
Mother Hubbard Energy, wheat cereal box; 1940s; depicts Mother Hubbard in center; 5 pound package; excellent condition; $130–175.

PETTIJOHN'S
Pettijohn's Breakfast Food, advertisement from *Collier's*, 1905; depicts boy saying "Now I'm Ready for Anything"; full color; $4–10.

Pettijohn's Breakfast Food/Rolled Wheat with all the Bran, paper/cardboard round container; has registered trademark brown bear on label; ca. 1880s; good condition (both top and bottom are off); $10–20.

Pettijohn's Breakfast Food, paper lithograph; depicts Little Red Riding Hood having breakfast food cooked for her by a bear in chef's hat; framed; 10⅛ x 13 inches; excellent condition; $200–400.

POST
C. W. Post, of Fort Worth, Texas, spent some time at the Battle Creek Sanitarium when Dr. Kellogg was testing his cold breakfast cereal in 1891. Post believed so strongly in the idea that eating healthy food was the secret to being physically healthy that he became one of Kellogg's strongest competitors.

He opened a home called the LaVita Inn (close to Battle Creek) and began spreading his newfound nutrition knowledge to his customers. Knowing that Kellogg and the sanitarium denied their customers a cup of morning coffee, Post invented a substitute, which he dubbed Postum, and stated that it "was not a substitute for anything . . ." but was a "pure food drink" that stood "on its own basis as a separate and distinct article." The coffee had no caffeine and became extremely popular—soon Post was selling thousands of dollars worth of Postum every month.

When other products began competing with his, Post turned the tables in a most unusual fashion by creating his own competition: Monk's Brew—and he sold it for one fifth the price of Postum! The ploy worked; he wiped out the competition and turned to creating other products.

Grape-Nuts cereal, invented in 1897, went on the market in 1898. The cereal's name came from the process C. W. Post used in creating the breakfast food. The repetitive baking process reduced the whole-wheat, malted barley flour, and yeast to grape-sugar, and the mixture tasted like nuts—thus the name:

92 ■ ADVERTISING

Postum, tin; 8 ounces; red lettering, light gray background, and blue trim; "makes 100 cups"; ca. 1940s; $15–25. *Courtesy of Marilyn and De Underwood/Tins Again Collectibles. Photo by Donald Vogt.*

Grape-Nuts. He marketed the cereal as a health food rather than a breakfast cereal and sales were soon double that of Postum's. The Grape-Nut ads are some of the most desirable advertising memorabilia, yet few know that Norman Rockwell illustrated a 1919 ad for the food.

Post's empire grew with the introduction of his own corn flakes, dubbed Elijah's Manna, in 1906 and changed (because of religious infuriation) to Post Toasties in 1908.

Though Post's ads touted his products' healthy aspects, Post never saw the total culmination of his own "healthy" success because of a slip into an unhealthy depression that resulted in his suicide in 1914.

POST

Post Toasties, advertisement from *Ladies' Home Journal*, 1926; depicts rag doll sitting next to bowl of cereal; $4–10.

Post Toasties, advertisement from *Youth's Companion*, 1913; depicts child holding boxes of cereal with one spilled on sidewalk; full color; $4–10.

Postum, tin; 8 ounces; red lettering; light gray background, and blue trim; "makes 100 cups"; ca. 1940s; $15–25.

PUFFED WHEAT

Puffed Wheat, pinback; pictures movie/television star William Bendix; ca. 1950s; good condition; $8–15.

QUAKER OATS

In 1850 a German immigrant named Ferdinand Schumacher opened a grocery store in Akron, Ohio. He found a way to prepare oatmeal so that it would take less time to cook and packaged his product in glass jars, suggesting that his customers try his oatmeal with syrup, molasses, butter, cream, or sugar. Soon Schumacher's product became so popular that he was dubbed the "Oatmeal King of America."

The Quaker Oats Co. evolved after a series of consolidations among the principal oatmeal millers, but the company name was not used until 1877. Henry D. Seymour, one of the company's founders, was responsible for the famous Quaker man trademark, believing that the Quakers' purity, honesty, and strength were exactly the images he wanted associated with his product. William Heston, Seymour's partner, also claimed to be responsible for the trademark, reporting that he borrowed the image after seeing a picture of William Penn. The Society of Friends was not happy that the Quakers were associated with the product and even brought an unsuccessful lawsuit against the company.

By the end of the nineteenth century, the Quaker Oats product was produced in a carton to be placed on grocery shelves. Prior to that time, oatmeal was bought from grocery store barrels. Henry Crowell, president of the American Cereal Co., was responsible for changing the industry's view of selling in bulk to selling a packaged product and was also one of the visionaries who understood the value of advertising. When his company acquired the Quaker Oats brand, Crowell launched an unprecedented ad campaign, including international personal appearances by the trademarked Quaker Oats man.

Some of the advertising promotions the company used over the years included a Quaker Cooker offer, which resulted in 700,000 giveaways in 1909; a silverware giveaway in 1907; a land deed giveaway in 1955 that was tied in to the "Sgt. Preston of the Yukon" television show; free aviation gifts tied in with Pat O'Brien's starring role in *China Clipper*; a Quaker Oats radio ($5) in 1921; and 16-page Quaker comic books distributed in 1894.

QUAKER OATS

Quaker Puffed Wheat, advertisement from *Pictorial Review*, August 1926; depicts girl with hand in box; full color; $4–10.

Quaker Oats, paper sign; depicts Jimmy Cagney offering free airplane models; colorful; near-mint condition; $5–20.

Quisp, bank; very rare; 7 inches, papier-mâché; made in Taiwan; ca. early 1980s; $500–650. *Courtesy of Neil and Nancy Berliner. Photo by Donald Vogt..*

QUISP

Quisp, bank; very rare; 7 inches, papier-mâché; made in Taiwan; ca. early 1980s; $500–650.

RALSTON PURINA

Ralston Purina, advertisement from *Ladies' Home Journal*, 1919; depicts little girl and little boy acting like their elders (war effort); full color; $4–10.

Ralston Purina, advertisement from *Ladies' Home Journal*, 1911; fuschia tones; depicts miller with group of children holding products; $4–10.

WHEATIES

(*see also* "General Mills" in Baking Products chapter)

Wheaties, ten-package cereal trays (3); illustrations of buildings and stores on individual packages; interesting presentation for collectible boxes; overall package size 14½ x 4¼ x 4 inches each; good/very good condition, general age soiling, some minor edge tears to exterior boxes; $50–150.

CHAPTER SEVEN
■ CLEANING PRODUCTS ■

BLUMERS
Blumers Shirt Waist Starch, box; 5 cent box of the starch; in red and blue; ca. 1910; near-mint condition; $5–10.

BON AMI
Bon Ami soap "hatched" in 1890, the creation of J. T. Robertson Soap Co. of Manchester, Connecticut. The chick that "hasn't scratched yet" was the creation of the company's promotion man, Louis H. Soule, in 1901. Though the chick was only meant to be used for one advertising promotion, it ended up being the company's well-known logo for what is now over a century.

BON AMI
Bon Ami, advertisement from *Ladies' Home Journal*, 1929; "The Easiest Way to Keep Bathrooms Spotless"; $17-20.

Bon Ami, paper and tin container; 12 ounces; ca. 1950s; very good condition; $20–25.

BORAX
Borax, cardboard die-cut display; panoramic three-dimensional store display for 20-mule-team Borax picturing people using the product and a theatrical depiction of the team; approximately 54 x 33 x 24 inches; excellent/near-mint condition, minor creasing, in original packing box, slight soiling; $800–1,200.

BROWNIE
Brownie Laundry Wax, display box; glass-fronted slant-lid cardboard container and display with Palmer Cox Brownies on paper label; 9½ x 5¾ x 7 inches; good condition, some discoloration, wear and chipping; $25–100.

96 ■ Advertising

Bon Ami, advertisement from *Ladies' Home Journal*, 1929; "The Easiest Way to Keep Bathrooms Spotless"; $17–20. *Courtesy of Lester Morris. Photo by Donald Vogt.*

DIAMOND GLOSS STARCH

Diamond Gloss Starch, poster; depicts a bonneted baby; 17 x 22 inches; fair condition; $25–100.

DUTCH CLEANSER
(*see also* "Old Dutch Cleanser")

The cleanser with the Dutch lady dressed in blue as its trademark was introduced in 1906 as a cleansing powder designed to remove stubborn stains from kitchen utensils. Though the artist who created Dutch Cleanser's trademark remains nameless, the product was soon recognized by most leaders of America's households. The Dutch lady even appeared on World War I bond posters (even though her symbol has been used on labels printed in many languages, it has never been produced in Dutch, however).

The Purex Corporation shortened its product's name, originally "Old Dutch Cleanser," to simply "Dutch Cleanser" when they bought the product from the Cudahy Packing Company. The modern version of the trademark shows the Dutch girl's face and blond hair, her hood updated to a perky white cap, and her dress brightened with a white collar and cuffs.

ELECTRIC-LUSTRE-STARCH

Electric-Lustre-Starch, paper sign; unusual advertisement of four ladies advertising a starch product; 18 x 9 inches; good condition, showing wear with small nail holes; $50–150.

FAB

Fab Flakes, advertisement from *Ladies' Home Journal*, August 1923;

"made by Colgate & Co."; depicts children digging sand castles; full color (pastels); $4–8.

Fab Flakes, advertisement from *Pictorial Review*, April 1923; "made by Colgate & Co."; depicts mother with one child on her lap, another sitting at her feet; full color (pastels); $4–8.

Fab Flakes, advertisement from *McCall's*, October 1923; "made by Colgate & Co."; depicts mother and children cleaning baby; full color (pastels); $4–8.

Fab Flakes, advertisement from *Modern Priscilla*, 1928; "made by Colgate & Co."; 'Babes in Woods"; full color (pastels); $4–8.

N. K. FAIRBANKS SOAP COMPANY/GOLD DUST/ FAIRY SOAP/SILVER DUST

The N. K. Fairbanks Soap Company, in business from 1897 to 1930, produced many different types of soap products, some of which were Fairy Soap, Gold Dust products, and Silver Dust products. The company's original owner, Nathanial K. Fairbank, a former grain agent, opened a lard-rendering plant before 1880 in Chicago. Later, he had two partners, Armour and Morris, made their fortune in the cottonseed market when they formed the American Cotton Oil Trust. American Cotton Oil Trust metamorphosed into Best Foods, Inc. in 1941. The company merged with Corn Products Refining of New Jersey in 1958.

Fairy Soap was oval in shape, at a time when all the products of the competition were rectangular. Fairbanks advertised the new product heavily from the beginning (1897), when they first marketed the soap with an ad depicting a child sitting on a cake of Fairy Soap. Through the years, Fairy Soap produced many types of memorabilia/ephemera, such as magazine ads, a doll (1912), boxes, pocket mirrors, and beverage trays. The slogan used by the company, "Have You a Little Fairy in Your House?" was one most collectors easily recognize, but like so many things, it would not work in today's world.

Gold Dust products were represented by a pair of twin African children who became one of the most well-known of all nineteenth-century trademarks. The twins were found on all packaging, tin signs, advertising, buttons, boxes, fans, calendars, World's Fair items, trade cards, and other memorabilia.

One of the original models for the Gold Dust Twins was David H. Snipe of New York City. Snipe had been adopted by a vaudeville husband-and-wife team when he was only six years old. The couple (Harvey and DeVore) had seen young Snipe tap-dancing on a street in New York City and wanted him to become part of their act. They made a deal with Snipe's parents, promising that they would educate and care for him. The dancing team was with Snipe when, at a trade convention in Chicago in 1902, he was picked to pose as one of the Gold Dust Twins. It was the first time manufacturers had registered their trademarks.

The artist who sketched the Gold Dust Twins was a leading artist of the time. Edward Windsor Kemble died in 1933, but his pen-and-ink drawings still fetch a respectable price when they're put on the auction block. Any original illustrations of the Gold Dust Twins are obviously worth more to the collector; however, they are very rare.

Though Gold Dust washing powder had been manufactured by the Fairbank Company since the early 1880s, it was not until the twins started appearing on their advertisements that the cleaner met its full success. Some of the slogans used during the years were "Let the Twins Do Your Work" and "Fast Colors Warranted to Wash Clean and Not to Fade."

The Gold Dust Twins appeared as radio personalities starting in 1925. Two white performers, Harvey Hindermyer and Earl Tuckerman, were the voices used to represent the twins. The program and Gold Dust's popularity lasted until the 1930s, when the company was sold.

A new product, called Silver Twins, was introduced when interest in Gold Dust waned. The idea of having twins represent the product continued and two blond-haired girls appeared as the Silver Twins logo. Again, all types of packaging and memorabilia were made with the twins logo, but interest in the Silver Twins was not as high as it had been for the Gold Dust Twins and the item was not on the market long.

FAIRY SOAP
(*see* "Fairy" in Soap chapter)

GLOREX
Glorex Cleanser, tin shaker; 14 ounces; blue-and-white-checked

CLEANING PRODUCTS ■ 99

Glorex Cleanser, tin shaker; 14 ounces; blue-and-white-checked design; distributed by Jewel Tea Co., Inc.; ca. 1940s; very good condition, some rust; $6–10. *Courtesy of Dawn and Bob Reno. Photo by Donald Vogt.*

design; distributed by Jewel Tea Co., Inc.; ca. 1940s; very good condition, some rust; $6–10.

GOLD DUST

Gold Dust, advertisement; 5 x 6 inches; ca. 1920s; very good condition; $20–25.

Gold Dust, advertisement; copyright 1916; 10 x 14 inches; good condition; $100–125.

Gold Dust, boxes (15); 3½ x 4¾ x 1½ inches each; very good condition overall; $75–125.

Gold Dust, cardboard box; full of detergent; Spanish directions; $30–40.

Gold Dust, cardboard cans (4); classic image of black twins and piles of coin; 3 inch diameter x 4¾ inches each; very good condition overall; $50–125.

Gold Dust and Fairy Soap, round cardboard hand fan; depicts Gold Dust Twins overlooking scene of St. Louis World's Fair (1904); flip side shows children's heads; 7½ inch diameter x 12 inches; excellent condition; $50–100.

Gold Dust, die-cut two-sided cardboard strung display; depicts the trademark twins and lettering superimposed above boxes; one of two known examples; 1912; when outstretched, sign reaches approximately 7 feet; very good/excellent condition; $8,000–12,000.

Gold Dust, paper poster; depicts Uncle Sam and President Roosevelt welcoming the Gold Dust Twins with the Statue of Liberty in the background; 20 x 10½ inches excluding frame; very good condition, three vertical creases, strong colors; $800–1,500.

Gold Dust, cardboard shipping box; multiple images of twins; rare; 19½ x 12 x 13½ inches; fair/good condition, some surface damage due to wear, chipping and rubbing; $75–150.

HURD'S
Hurd's Washing Mixture, paper sign; early image of housewife washing clothes with miraculous appearance of Hurd's magical mixture; ca. 1870s; interior kitchen scene with iron coal cookstove and washing tub; 13¼ x 10½ inches; good/very good condition, borders appear trimmed, minor paper loss; $500–1,000.

LILY WHITE
Lily White Starch, containers (2); child's wooden trunk with exterior and interior paper labels; shows child, keyed lock, and embossed tin with hinged-lid container; varied sizes; good condition overall, some paper loss to paper labels, overall wear to both pieces, minor fading to tin can; $75–200.

LISK
Lisk Wash Boiler, front-of-boiler label; illustration is of a woman holding boiler; 26 x 16 x 12 inches; fair/good condition, some paper loss to label, overall soiling and fading; $50–100.

LYSOL
Lysol, booklet "Protecting the Dionnes," 1936; excellent condition; $14–20.

O-CEDAR
O-Cedar, display items (lot); die-cut topped tin shelved display holder for mop polish with original can; 10 x 17½ x 4 inches; very good condition, some chipping primarily to edges, minor scratches; Housewife with O-Cedar dust mop cardboard die-cut display; 24 x 44½ inches; good condition, some minor holes, overall soiling and foxing; $250–500.

OLD DUTCH CLEANSER
Old Dutch Cleanser, advertisements; depict the Dutch woman in various cleaning chores; ca. 1920s–1930s, excellent condition; $10–24.

CLEANING PRODUCTS ■ 101

Old Dutch Cleanser, advertisement from *Ladies' Home Journal*, 1915; depicts woman with graniteware cooking utensils; $4–10.

Old Dutch Cleanser, advertisement from *Ladies' Home Journal*, 1914–1915; depicts "Doc Scrubbing Brush"; full color; $4–10.

PROCTER & GAMBLE
(*see also* "Procter & Gamble" in Soap chapter)
Procter & Gamble, Tide, boxes; 7⅛ ounces; ca. 1950s; mint/unused condition; $10–18 each.

SILVER DUST
(*see also* "N. K. Fairbanks")
Silver Dust, box; "A White Sudsy Soap for Dishes and Laundry"; Gold Dust Corporation; New York, Baltimore, St. Louis, Montreal; copyright 1931, G. D. Corp.; "New Weight" 16 ounces; good condition; $15–30.

SNOWBOY
Snowboy Washing Powder, canvas poster; depicts child on sled holding box of product; caption reads "Snow Boy Washing Powder/Will make clothes whiter, work easier and kitchen cleaner/Newest and Best/Use a tablespoonful in your dishwater/For Sale by all Principal Grocers/Lautz Bros. & Co., Buffalo, N.Y."; 42 x 28 inches; excellent condition; $4,500–5,500.

Old Dutch Cleanser, advertisement from *Ladies' Home Journal*, 1915; depicts woman with graniteware cooking utensils; $4–10. *Courtesy of Paper Lady/Bernie and Dolores Fee. Photo by Donald Vogt.*

Silver Dust, box; "A White Sudsy Soap for Dishes and Laundry"; Gold Dust Corporation; New York, Baltimore, St. Louis, Montreal; copyright 1931, G. D. Corp.; "New Weight" 16 ounces; good condition; $15–30. *Courtesy of Irreverent Relics. Photo by Donald Vogt.*

Swift's Pride Washing Powder, sign; approximately 12 x 9 inches; depicts little maid with brush in her hand; reproduction; $15 retail. *Courtesy of Doc Davis/Antique-Alike. Photo by Donald Vogt.*

S.O.S. SOAP PADS
(*see* "Miles Laboratories" in Medicines chapter)

SWIFT'S PRIDE
Swift's Pride Washing Powder, sign; approximately 12 x 9 inches; depicts little maid with brush in her hand; reproduction; $15 retail.

CHAPTER EIGHT
■ CLOTHING ■

ARROW SHIRTS

The Arrow Man, as created by illustrator J. C. Leyendecker, was strong-jawed, his features chiseled, his attitude sophisticated and worldly. Though the physical features have changed, the Arrow Man is still represented by illustrators (such as LeRoy Neiman in 1986) as sophisticated and worldly.

Originally, Arrow shirts were simply collars—and from 1851 through 1921, starched collars were the only thing the company made. George B. Cluett bought the company in 1885, and the company took his name until Frederick F. Peabody joined him four years later.

Peabody's trademark "Arrow" and his innate advertising sense helped him create the "Arrow Collar Man." Though many artists illustrated for the line, the aforementioned Leyendecker Arrow Man served as the image that best represented the turn-of-the-century male. The first J. C. Lyendecker *Saturday Evening Post* cover was sold in 1899.

Cluett-Peabody's business changed at the end of World War I—the need for collars diminished when doughboys came home from the war in one-piece shirts. In 1921, Arrow produced its first attached-collar shirt. Unfortunately, it was not a great success (it shrank). Eventually, the company devised the "Sanforizing Process," which controlled shrinkage, and the company still thrives, though today's sales are higher for sports shirts than for the tucked-bodice tuxedo shirts seen in those early, elegant ads.

ARROW

Arrow Collars and Shirts, advertisement from the *Saturday Evening Post*, April 12, 1913; double-page spread; Leyendecker illustration; depicts men sitting and standing (one with tennis racket, one with dog); $8–12.

Arrow Shirts, advertisement from the *Saturday Evening Post*,

104 ■ ADVERTISING

Arrow Collars and Shirts; advertisement; from the *Saturday Evening Post*, April 12, 1913; double-page spread; Leyendecker illustration; depicts men sitting and standing (one with tennis racket, one with dog); $8–12 *Courtesy of Paper Lady/Bernie and Dolores Fee. Photo by Donald Vogt.*

September 19, 1931; Leyendecker Illustration; depicts teacher/coach with football players; full color; $8–12.

BLUE JEANS

Blue Jeans, paper poster; vignetted scenes of blue jeans and their wearers done when the product was first invented; ca. late 1800s; 42½ x 28½ inches; excellent condition, minor creasing and edge tears; $100–200.

BLUE MOON

Blue Moon Silk Stockings, sign; depicts woman in diaphanous clothing showing her stockings, sitting on crescent moon; 12 x 14 inches; reproduction; $15 retail.

BOSTON GARTER

Boston Garter, tin display cabinet; depicts man demonstrating product; 14½ x 13 x 5 inches; good condition, overall wear; $125–225.

CELLULOID CORSETS

Celluloid Corsets, paper sign; depicts two women wearing corsets standing in front of oval bedroom mirror; lettering reads "Celluloid Corset Clasps Side & Dress Steels—Manufactured by F. Lee Egbert—Warranted not to rust any under any circumstances—Need not be taken out when the corsets are washed"; 15 x 21¼ inches; very good/excellent condition, borders trimmed, minor wrinkling due to shrinkage, slight overall soiling; $2,500–3,750.

DETMER WOOLEN

Detmer Woolen, heavy cardboard display box; when opened reveals pictures of stores and customers wearing this company's woolens; 29 x 21 x 21 inches when open; very good condition; $25–100.

DR. JAEGER'S WOOLENS

Dr. Jaeger's Woolens, tin sign; black, silver, and gold stenciled sign for sanitary woolens; early Tuchfarber sign; 20 x 13½ inches excluding frame; very good condition; $100–250.

DUCHESS TROUSERS

Duchess Trousers, tin sign; large bold factory image on this original framed piece; 34½ x 24½ inches overall; good condition, slight fade overall; $50–200.

FERRIS

Ferris Corsets, metal two-sided display; depicts woman wearing corset; H. D. Black Co. Litho.; approximately 45 inches tall; very rare (only four or five in existence); ca. 1910; excellent condition; $4,000–5,000.

Ferris Waists, self-framed tin sign; depicts two young girls in dressing room with corsets reflected in mirror of dressing table; 16½ x 22½ inches; fair overall condition; $250–500.

Ferris Corsets, metal two-sided display; depicts woman wearing corset; H. D. Black Co. Litho.; approximately 45 inches tall; very rare (only four or five in existence); ca. 1910; excellent condition; $4,000–5,000. *Collection of and photo by Grant Smith.*

Ferris Waists, self-framed tin sign; oval image of two girls in corsets; by Beach Art Display Company; 16½ x 22½ inch oval; fair/good condition, general fading overall, scratches and rubs; $50–150.

FINCK'S
Finck's Overalls, embossed tin sign; slogan reads "They wear like a Pig's Nose"; depicts two hefty hogs; 23½ x 11¾ inches excluding frame; very good condition, slight overall wear, some scratching; $100–200.

FOSTER HOSE
Foster Hose, celluloid sign; classic image of woman and corset; 9 x 17 inches; very good/excellent condition, minor crack, slight edge wear, some general wear overall; $100–300.

HANES HOSIERY

Pleasant Henderson Hanes began his career as a businessman by selling tobacco during the mid-1880s and was soon selling close to a million pounds of plug tobacco a year. Some of the brand names included Greek Slave, Man's Pride, and Missing Link. He competed with R. J. Reynolds and the other tobacco manufacturers of the day, but eventually took the money he made and put it into a new business: selling men's underwear. His new business promptly took off, and Hanes succeeded in selling shorts, long johns, and eventually, knit hosiery.

The slogan "Gentlemen prefer Hanes" began when the company manufactured only men's underwear, but was kept even after it began making women's stockings.

HANES HOSIERY
Hanes Hosiery, advertisement from *Life* magazine, ca. 1958; illustration of frog in pond; caption reads "she's irresistible"; $6–8.

HATHAWAY SHIRTS

David Oglivy, one of the first to break advertising tradition and to treat the potential customer as an intelligent peer, was responsible for the device that hooked the readers' attention, making them remember Hathaway Shirts—the Hathaway Man's eye patch. Actually, there was nothing wrong with the male model's eye—he was a displaced White Russian baron named George Wrangell. The device was introduced many years after Hathaway began selling shirts in 1837 and was used for almost forty years. Originally, the ads ran exclusively in *The*

Clothing ■ 107

Hanes Hosiery, advertisement from *Life* magazine, ca. 1958; illustration of frog in pond; caption reads "she's irresistible"; $6–8. *Courtesy of Lester Morris. Photo by Donald Vogt.*

Jantzen, advertisement from *Esquire* magazine, 1941; illustrated by Varga; depicts girl in orange suit with hat, and man standing above her; $25–30. *Courtesy of Lester Morris. Photo by Donald Vogt.*

New Yorker, but the mysterious man in the eye patch soon caused Hathaway's sales to escalate, and he became a recognizable "folk" hero.

HATHAWAY SHIRTS

Hathaway Shirts, paper sign; interior view of Victorian dressing room ca. 1874; depicts a child holding a box of Hathaway shirts for father while mother looks on; border illustrations of shirts; 17½ x 23½ inches excluding mat; very good condition, piece has been deacidified and cleaned, several repaired tears, some roughness and loss in margins; $1,250–2,500.

JANTZEN

Jantzen, advertisement from *Esquire* magazine, 1941; illustrated by Varga; depicts girl in orange suit with hat, and man standing above her; very good condition; $25–30.

J. L. TAYLOR

J. L. Taylor, sample book; large; 1912; 83-page catalog with pictorial images of clothing styles and material samples; 16½ x 23 inches; good condition overall, some samples missing, general age wear to interior illustrations; $25–100.

KNOX HATS

Knox Hats, oval cardboard hatbox with leather strap; red with company trademark; company located in New York; $65–85.

108 ■ ADVERTISING

KNOX KNIT HOSIERY
Knox Knit Hosiery, paper bag; mint condition; $3–5.

KUPPENHEIMER
Kuppenheimer Men's Wear, window display; 6 inches; ceramic; ca. late 1940s; $275–350.

LEE RIDERS
Lee Riders, vertical banner; silk-screened paint on denim; depicts cowboy on bucking bronco; approximately 2 x 4 feet; good condition; $500–800.

Lee Riders, two-sided metal sign; 19 inch diameter; depicts cowboy on bucking horse; very good condition; $250–350.

LEVI'S
On the way to the Gold Rush, a twenty-four-year-old Easterner named Levi Strauss found his fortune in San Francisco—but not in gold, in durable pants. The denim pants, dubbed Levi's, are one of the few pieces of clothing that haven't changed at all in over a hundred years. We won't even count

Kuppenheimer Men's Wear, window display; 6 inches; ceramic; ca. late 1940s; $275–350. *Courtesy of Neil and Nancy Berliner. Photo by Neil Berliner.*

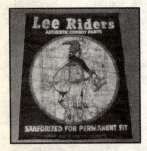

Lee Riders, vertical banner; silk-screened paint on denim; depict cowboy on bucking bronco; approximately 2 x 4 feet; good condition; $500–800. *Collection of Jim Ed Garrett. Photo by Jenny Garrett.*

Lee Riders, two-sided metal sign; 19 inch diameter; depicts cowboy on bucking horse; very good condition; $250–350. *Collection of Jim Ed Garrett. Photo by Jenny Garrett.*

how many million pairs of tough work pants ol' Levi Strauss's company has manufactured . . . and how his distribution centers exist in over seventy countries.

Though the first Levi's customers were gold diggers who needed the strength of Strauss's copper-riveted seams to withstand tough working and washing conditions (the oldest known pair dates from the 1890s and was found in a Mojave Desert silver mine), his 1930s clientele were Easterners who had visited western dude ranches and liked the jeans so much they began to wear them as sports and leisure clothing. This opened up a whole new market.

The first pants were made out of brown tent canvas, but when the tent material ran out, Levi switched to blue serge material made in Nimes, France—its full name was "serge de nimes," later shortened to "denim." The term "jeans" came from the French work *genes*, which was used to describe cotton trousers.

The red tag that has traditionally been sewn on the back right pants pocket and the right edge of the left breast jacket pocket has existed since 1936. However, the logo changed in 1971 (the pre-1971 tag spelled LEVI'S with a capital *E*—after that time, the *e* is lower-case).

Zippers were not put in until 1955, and the pants did not truly become part of popular culture until the 1960s. Jimmy Carter gave Levi's presidential approval and high-fashion designers started to put their own touches on jeans in the 1970s.

Some of the advertising collectibles the company made include banners, figures, Buddy Lee dolls, and posters.

Even though other companies have manufactured denim blue jeans, Levi Strauss & Co. still sells more pairs than anyone else in the world. The Levi Strauss & Co. Museum is located at 250 Valencia Street, San Francisco, California. It is housed in the company's oldest factory and is open by appointment only (call 415-565-9153).

LEVI'S

Levi's, banner; advertises "the finest overalls since 1850"; approximately 2½ x 6 feet; excellent condition; $200–400.

Levi's, banner; silk-screened paint over denim; depicts cowboy lying on his side looking at full moon; approximately 2 x 6 feet (trimmed); very good condition; $1,500–1,750.

Levi's, banner; silk-screened paint over denim; depicts cowboy lying on his side looking at full moon; approximately 2 x 6 feet (trimmed); very good condition; $1,500–1,750. *Collection of Jim Ed Garrett. Photo by Jenny Garrett.*

Levi's, banner; silk-screened paint over denim; depicts a couple on horseback, backs to the viewer, reaching over to hug each other; approximately 2 x 8 feet; excellent condition; $1,500–2,000. *Collection of Jim Ed Garrett. Photo by Jenny Garrett.*

Levi's, banner; silk-screened paint over denim; depicts a couple on horseback, backs to the viewer, reaching over to hug each other; approximately 2 x 8 feet; excellent condition; $1,500–2,000.

Levi's, Buddy Lee doll; 12 inches tall; excellent condition; $100–200.

Levi's, figural composition display; blue-jeaned cowboy carrying saddle and branding iron and wearing ten-gallon hat; approximately 15 x 31 x 10 inches; good condition, some paint loss, thumb missing on left hand, paint crazing, primarily on hat; $800–1,200.

Levi's, corrugated backed paper sign; silk-screened in vibrant colors; features comical barber scene in old western town (Levi's did a number of different scenes that were in keeping with this style, size, and material makeup); 8 feet wide; very good condition; $600–800.

Levi's, corrugated backed paper sign; silk-screened; depicts young cowboy leading his pony past older cowboys; vibrant colors; 8 feet wide; very good condition; $600–800.

Levi's, corrugated backed paper sign; silk-screened in vibrant colors; features comical barber scene in old western town (Levi's did a number of different scenes that were in keeping with this style, size, and material makeup); 8 feet wide; very good condition; $600–800. *Collection of Jim Ed Garrett. Photo by Jenny Garrett.*

CLOTHING ■ 111

Levi's, corrugated backed paper sign; silk-screened; depicts young cowboy leading his pony past older cowboys; vibrant colors; 8 feet wide; very good condition; $600–800. *Collection of Jim Ed Garrett. Photo by Jenny Garrett.*

MISCELLANEOUS

Figural clothing display; wooden man with hand in pocket; 8 x 24 x 4 inches; good condition, general overall wear, end of nose chipped; $250–450.

Thimbles, group of three advertising thimbles to promote "Hosiery," "Brassieres," and "Millinery"; ca. early 1900s; very good condition; $1–3 each.

MUNSING WEAR

Munsing Wear, die-cut tin sign; two children in their "union suits" are depicted on this teeter-totter; store display unit set up on a pivotal base; 21 x 22 inches; excellent condition, minor edge chipping, good sheen; $3,500–5,000.

Munsing Wear, tin sign; depicts woman with red tasseled hat and white sweater within holly-and-berry wreath; 11 x 16 inches; $15 retail.

MURPHY HATTER

Murphy Hatter, cloth banner; pictures a top hat; 17¾ x 26 inches; good condition, general aging; $400–700.

P. N. CORSETS

P. N. Corsets, form; store display for practical front corsets with sample corset attached; approximately 8 inch diameter x 30 inches; good/excellent condition; $100–300.

Thimbles, group of advertising thimbles to promote "Hosiery," "Brassieres," and "Millinery"; ca. early 1900s; very good condition; $1–3 each. *Courtesy of Estelle Zalkin, author of* Zalkin's Handbook of Thimbles and Sewing Implements.

R & G CORSETS
R & G Corsets, cardboard sign; red silhouette of a corset on black background with red lettering on bottom right; 20 x 29 inches overall; cardboard is in generally very good condition overall, had a wood frame with a shiny varnished finish and the words "Tapering Waist" engraved at the bottom and "R & G" engraved at the top; $275–475.

SAWYER'S SLICKERS
Sawyer's Slickers, cardboard sign; 29½ x 17⅓ inches; little girl in orange slicker and hat, going to school; caption on bottom third of sign reads "Sawyer's genuine oiled Slickers/In Colors for Men, Women and Children"; ca. 1930s; excellent condition; $1,000–1,500.

SILAS KING
Silas King Dry Goods, broadside; early black and white on heavy stock with insert of horse-drawn express wagon loaded with boxes; 12 x 13½ inches excluding frame; good condition, some spotting to paper, creasing; $10–50.

STAG TROUSERS
Stag Trousers, tin sign with curled corners; depicts elk's majestic head; 15 inch square; excellent condition; $100–300.

SUN GARTER
Sun Garter, display case; small curved-glass-and-oak display case for men's sock garters; original apparatus displayed; ca. 1902; 5¼ x 10¾ x 6½ inches; very good original condition; $100–200.

TOM SAWYER
Tom Sawyer Apparel for Real Boys, wood freestanding counter sign; depicts Tom Sawyer painting his name on fence; 22 x 6 inches; $150–175.

TOWN TALK
Town Talk Caps, cardboard hatbox; white and red; depicts various sports and the hats worn for them around perimeter; 11 inch diameter; ca. 1920s–1930s; $95–125.

VINDEX SHIRTS
Vindex Shirts, cardboard cutout; depicts man wearing one of the shirts, lighting cigarette; near-mint condition; $15–40.

WARD'S COLLARS
Ward's Collars, paper sign; depicts circus act in middle with various members of the circus utilizing Ward's Paper Collars; approximately

20½ x 15¾ inches; very good/excellent condition, some wrinkling and paper loss, creasing, margins trimmed; $700–1,000.

WRANGLER

Wrangler, banner; silk-screened paint on denim; "Wrangler Worn by Champion Cowboys/for comfort fit and long wear"; depicts rodeo acts in all four corners; excellent condition; $750–1,000.

Wrangler, banner; silk-screened paint on denim; depicts the word *Wrangler* written so that it makes the design of a bucking horse's body; very good condition; $350–500.

Wrangler, tin lithographed coasters; set of four; excellent condition; $60–75.

Wrangler, plastic vacuum-form sign; for Authentic Dress Western Shirts; ca. 1970s; excellent condition; $75–125.

Wrangler, banner; silk-screened paint on denim; "Wrangler Worn by Champion Cowboys/for comfort fit and long wear"; depicts rodeo acts in all four corners; excellent condition; $750–1,000. *Collection of Jim Ed Garrett. Photo by Jenny Garrett.*

Wrangler, banner; silk-screened paint on denim; depicts the word *Wrangler* written so that it makes the design of a bucking horse's body; very good condition; $350–500. *Collection of Jim Ed Garrett. Photo by Jenny Garrett.*

Wrangler, plastic vacuum-form sign; for Authentic Dress Western Shirts; ca. 1970s; $75–125. *Collection of Jim Ed Garrett. Photo by Jenny Garrett.*

CHAPTER NINE
■ COCOA ■

BAKER'S CHOCOLATE

When Anna Baltaug, a former Viennese waitress, married her prince in 1745, her new husband presented her with a portrait of herself in her waitress's uniform. Well-known Swiss artist Jean-Etienne Liotard created the portrait, which was later placed in the Dresden Art Gallery. The portrait, titled *La Belle Chocolatiere*, was adopted by Walter Baker as the trademark for his chocolate and cocoa products in 1764. His mill was located in Dorchester, Massachusetts, and though it became part of the General Foods Corporation in 1927, cocoa and other chocolate products are still produced in Dorchester. The original painting was hidden during World War II, but returned to the Dresden Collection afterward.

BAKER'S

Baker's Cocoa, die-cut tin display; Baker Cocoa urn-shaped counter display with oval product tray on top picturing four varieties of company products with portrait trademark on urn; 16½ x 23½ x 13½ inches including the original tray; very good condition; $1,000–2,000.

Baker's Cocoa, paper sign; early J. Mayer litho for the W. Baker Cocoa Company of Massachusetts; center medallion flanked by vignettes of factory and transportation; ca. 1860s; deaccessioned by Strawberry Banke of Portsmouth, New Hampshire; 22 x 17½ inches; good condition, general overall darkening due to foxing and water and wood staining; $100–300.

Baker's Cocoa, items (3); large store card, photographed flyer, and factory-labeled wooden box; varied sizes; good condition; $50–100.

Baker's Cocoa, tin; ½ pound; paper and tin; ca. 1950s; very good condition; $35–40.

Baker's Cocoa, tin sign; depicts famed "Cocoa Girl" carrying tray with cup of cocoa on it; framed; near-mint condition; $300–500.

Baker's Cocoa, tin; ornately patterned with colorful trademark insert on two sides and cap; 3¼ inch square x 5¾ inches; excellent condition; $50–100.

W. H. Baker's Best Cocoa, tin; paper label; side view of woman with bonnet drinking cocoa; excellent condition; $30–50.

Walter Baker & Co., cardboard advertising sign; interior image of Colonial people savoring cocoa; early ad; 27 x 23½ inches excluding frame; fair/good condition, some water staining and damage to surface, general soiling; $200–400.

Walter Baker & Co. Ltd., tip tray; 6 inches; ca. 1910; shows trademark cocoa lady above vignette of New England homestead; excellent/near-mint condition; $225–300.

Walter Baker & Co., paper sign; factory and street scene in the 1870s; surrounded by medallions of notable exhibitions and awards; printed by Hatch Litho. Co.; 32 x 24 inches excluding original frame; overall 35¼ x 27¼ inches; good/very good condition, some minor paper loss, minor inpainting; $2,000–4,000.

Walter Baker & Co., sign; cloth backed with board framed in wood; 79 x 46 inches; printed by Forbes Co.; ca. 1900–1910; said to have come from company's headquarters; excellent condition; $1,750–2,250.

Walter Baker Co., tin art plate; depicts chocolate girl in center; jeweled border; 10 inch diameter; good/very good condition; $50–150.

FRY'S
Fry's Pure Cocoa, tin; 1 pound; mustard-colored label with red lettering; made by House of Fry/Cadbury Schweppes; label is printed in both English and French; ca. 1910; excellent condition; $3–10.

LIPTON'S
Lipton's Cocoa, self-framed tin sign; woman with cocoa pot at table plus labeled package; 9 x 13¼ inches; fair condition, overall rust speckling, some denting; $25–100.

Lipton's Instant Cocoa, tin lithographed sign; depicts woman holding cocoa pot and cup of cocoa; ca. 1920s; dark blue background; 13 x 9 inches; excellent condition; $300–500.

LOWNEY'S
Lowney's Cocoa, tin; paper label depicts woman with Gibson Girl–type hairdo drinking cup of cocoa; colorful; excellent condition; $40–75.

MONARCH
Monarch Cocoa, tin; 16 ounces, chromolithographed, excellent condition; $35–50.

PRESTON COCOA
Preston Cocoa, paper sign; early 1860s display depicts central image of piled cocoa boxes with vignettes of factory, store, and people using cocoa and chocolate; early Ch. Crosby lithograph from Boston; deaccessioned from Strawberry Banke Museum; one of only two known; 18 x 23½ inches excluding frame; good condition; $700–900.

PULVER'S
Pulver's Cocoa, tip tray; depicts a little girl on a container of cocoa drinking out of a dainty little cup; 4½ inch diameter; good condition with some scratches and chipping and minor rust spots on edges; $150–250.

QUIK
(*see also* "Nestlé" in Candy chapter)
Nestlé's Quik, Chocolate Milk; counter display; 29 x 9 x 9 inches; $12–15.

RUNKEL BROTHERS
Runkel Brothers Cocoa and Chocolates, self-framed tin sign; 28½ x 22¼ inches; tray made by Chas. W. Shonk Co.; ca. 1904; caption reads "Drinking Cocoa at the Court of Louis XV"; fine/excellent condition; $800–1,100.

STOLLWERCK
Stollwerck Cocoa, tin tip tray; 5 inch diameter; very good condition; $25–100.

SUCHARD
Suchard Cocoa and Chocolate, toy truck; lithograph on tin; 7½ x 4½ x 3 inches; ca. 1915; truck pictures boy holding a can on each side; excellent condition; $500–1,000.

VAN HOUTEN

Van Houten's, framed cardboard sign; depicts a woman in bonnet and shawl pouring cocoa into cup; nice Dresden plates around the molding by the tops of the doors; 33½ x 22 inches; very good condition; $250–500.

Van Houten's Cocoa, paper sign; depicts big sister lifting baby to table for cup of cocoa; children's toys on floor; 21 x 27 inches excluding original jessoed frame; fair condition, overall age discoloration, tears in paper, darkened surface; $700–1,000.

CHAPTER TEN
■ COFFEE ■

AMERICAN ACE
American Ace Coffee, can; 1 pound, pictures famous flyer; 5 inch diameter x 3¼ inches; excellent condition, minor scratches, colors bright, good sheen; $75–150.

AURORA
Aurora Coffee, pail; 1 pound; early paper-labeled tin with original lid and bail; 5 inch diameter x 4¾ inches; good condition, front label darkened with age, minor wear on back label, overall chipping; $100–175.

AVON
Avon Club Coffee, can; 1 pound; paper label; shows couple on horseback with clubhouse in background; 4¼ diameter x 5¼ inches; fair/good condition, some paper loss to label, general overall wear, chipping and age discoloration; $175–250.

BAGDAD
Bagdad Coffee, cans (2); 5 pounds, Middle Eastern scene; colorful can depicts Iraqi sultan being served coffee; 7½ inch diameter x 8¾ inches each with lids and bails; good condition, slight fading to one with overall wear, scratches and chipping to both; $125–250.

CAMPBELL
Campbell Coffee, can; 4 pounds; depicts camels in the country; 8 inch diameter x 8 inches; excellent condition, slight chipping, minor rubs, slight dents; $100–200.

CASTLE BLEND
Castle Blend Coffee, can; oval image of Windsor Castle on colorful can; 4¼ inch diameter x 5 inches; made in Montreal, Quebec, St. John (New Brunswick), Canada; good condition, overall scratching, some denting; $200–400.

CHASE & SANBORN COFFEE
(*see also* "Nestlé" in Candy chapter)
Caleb Chase and James Sanborn, tea and coffee merchants from Boston, formed Chase & Sanborn Coffee in 1861 and

were the first to sell coffee in sealed tin cans in 1879. The company advertised its product in every manner possible, including trade cards, magazine and newspaper ads, and radio advertising. It even sponsored a show called "The Chase & Sanborn Hour with Edgar Bergen and Charlie McCarthy." As a result of the onslaught of media hype, the company's sales were number one in the nation up until World War II.

When Maxwell House came on the market, it created stiff competition for Chase & Sanborn, so stiff that Chase turned away from selling its product to the household consumer and turned to the more stable outlet of selling to restaurants and fast-food chains.

Standard Brands bought the company in 1929, and it passed through several other hands until Hills Brothers bought it in 1984.

CHASE & SANBORN

Chase & Sanborn, paper poster; 1897 view of "an old-fashioned New England grocery"; 23 x 20 inches including mat but excluding frame; good condition, some tears, minor holes; $150–300.

Chase & Sanborn, tin; 5 pounds; red background, white letters; milk-can-type tin with bail; excellent condition; $225–325.

Chase & Sanborn, tin; 1 pound; ca. 1950s; $5–10.

CONDOR

Condor Coffee, can; 1 pound; rare condor-imaged can with palm trees; 4¼ inch diameter x 6¾ inches; good condition, overall wear, some denting, age darkening; $350–500.

DALLEY'S

Dalley's Prime Coffee, can; 1 pound; pastoral scene with extract and jelly containers on back; made in Hamilton, Toronto, Canada; original wood-knobbed slip lid; 4¼ inch diameter x 7½ inches; fair/good condition, general overall wear, scratches and chipping, minor dents; $50–150.

DAUNTLESS

Dauntless Coffee, cardboard sign; depicts soldier and dog; mint condition; $5–20.

DRAKO

Drako Coffee, can; 1 pound; rare coffee can pictures colorful duck in water; 4 inch diameter x 6 inches with original screw lid; good condition, general light overall wear, some minor chipping, slight scratching; $100–300.

ENTERPRISE
Enterprise, cast-iron coffee grinder; no. 3 coffee mill with original drawer; 15 x 16 x 11 inches; good condition, original paint, age and soil darkening, some paint loss; $350–500.

FLAROMA
Flaroma, tin; 1 pound; trademark on red background; 4 inch diameter x 6 inches; very good/excellent condition, some minor chipping, scratch about the size of a dime just to upper left of word *Coffee*; $75–150.

FORT PITT
Fort Pitt Coffee, can; 3 pounds; fort pictured on insert; 6 inch diameter x 8 inches; very good condition, some chipping, slight denting, light wear; $300–450.

GOLDEN GRAINS
Golden Grains, tin coffee bin; slant lid; packed for Gateway Grocery Company; 6½ x 8 x 9¼ inches; good condition, with scratching, paint chipping, and overall wear from use; $150–200.

GOLDEN ROD
Golden Rod Coffee, can; 1 pound; paper-labeled can with store building on label; 4¼ inch diameter x 5 inches; fair/good condition, some nicks and chips to paper, wrinkles, spotting; $50–150.

HILLA
Hilla Coffee, can; 5 pounds; coffee field inset; 8¼ inch diameter x 8½ inches with original lid and bail; good condition, some scratching and chipping, dents; $50–125.

HILLS BROS.
(*see also* "Chase & Sanborn"; "Nestlé" in Candy chapter)
Hills & Sons Coffee, paper sign; "Remember the Maine" 1898 display of United States Navy ships; 26 x 28 inches excluding frame; printed by C. A. Musselman; good condition, some creasing and minor edge chips; $75–150.

HY-QUALITY
Hy-Quality, die-cut cardboard sign; 39 inches tall; depicts woman sitting on swing, sipping coffee; excellent condition; $1,000–1,500.

Luzianne, Wm. B. Reily & Company, Inc., New Orleans; 1 pound size; white label; "15 cents off"; ca. 1930s; $20–30. *Courtesy of Irreverent Relics. Photo by Donald Vogt.*

KING COLE

King Cole, can; ½ pound; classic image of the Merry Old Soul being served coffee; made in St. John, New Brunswick, Canada; 4½ inch diameter x 3 inches; good/very good condition, slight overall fade, light wear, minor scratches and dents; $100–150.

LILY OF THE VALLEY

Lily of the Valley Coffee, can; 1 pound; depicts lilies in bloom as product logo; 4 inch diameter x 6¼ inches; excellent condition, minor scratching; $150–300.

LINCOLN CLUB

Lincoln Club Coffee, can; 5 pounds; paper-labeled tin with portrait of Abe Lincoln; 7½ inch diameter x 9 inches including lid and bail; very good/excellent condition, minor scratching, slight wear, minor denting to lid; $100–175.

LION

Lion Coffee, paper sign; child at window with colorful package surrounded by Easter lilies; approximately 18 x 20 inches excluding frame; good condition, appears trimmed, horizontal crease in middle; $100–300.

LUZIANNE

Luzianne, can; Wm. B. Reily & Company, Inc., New Orleans; 1 pound size; white label; "15 cents off"; ca. 1930s; $20–30.

MAXWELL HOUSE

In 1874, Joel Cheek, a twenty-two-year-old former Kentucky farm boy, made his living selling coffee in the Nashville area. By

1892, one of his customers was the Maxwell House, a plush hotel. The hotel's customers loved Cheek's coffee, so he took the opportunity to call his brew "Maxwell House Coffee."

Theodore Roosevelt actually was responsible for coining the coffee's memorable slogan: "Good to the last drop." He had tasted the coffee while visiting the Hermitage House in Nashville. When offered a second cup, he replied, "Will I have another? Delighted! It's good to the last drop!"

The coffee, produced at first by Joel Cheek & Sons; then Cheek & Norton (1897); Cheek, Norton & Neal (1902); and later by Cheek-Neal Company (1905), was sold to General Foods in 1928 for a multimillion-dollar sum, and in 1985, was acquired by Philip Morris, Inc.

Though the coffee has changed a bit, its original trademark (the tilted cup) and Roosevelt's slogan have been the same as they were in the beginning.

MAXWELL HOUSE

Maxwell House, advertisement from *Ladies' Home Journal*, August 1924; depicts distinguished white-haired gentleman drinking a cup of coffee; excellent condition; $12–15.

Maxwell House, tin; 1 pound; blue with orange lettering; ca. 1950s; $5–10.

MONADNOCK

Monadnock Coffee, tin; 1 pound; 4 inch diameter x 6 inches high; very good/excellent condition, minor scratches; $100–150.

Maxwell House, advertisement from *Ladies' Home Journal*, August 1924; depicts distinguished white-haired gentleman drinking a cup of coffee; excellent condition; $12–15. *Courtesy of Lester Morris. Photo by Donald Vogt.*

NASH'S
Nash's Coffee, can; 5 pounds; two trumpeters herald "Fathers of Confederation"; 7½ inch diameter x 8¾ inches with original lid and bail; very good condition, minor scratches, primarily at top, some wear, minor denting; $200–400.

NESCAFÉ
(*see* "Nestlé" in Candy chapter)

OUR JEWEL
Our Jewel Coffee, can; 1 pound; wistful portrait of child in diamond medallion; 4¼ inch diameter x 6 inches with original slip lid and wooden knob; good condition, slight overall fade, general wear, some chipping; $50–125.

PILOT-KNOB
Pilot-Knob Coffee, can; 5 pounds; rare can picturing Pilot Mountain, North Carolina; 7½ inch diameter x 8¾ inches including original lid and bail; very good condition, some soiling, chipping, color discrepancy between lid and can; $250–450.

RADIO
Radio Coffee, can; 3 pounds; extremely rare; shows early radio with large speaker horn; fair condition, surface rust; $150–250.

RED WOLF
Red Wolf Coffee, can; 6 pounds; rare tin with red wolf on label; original slip lid and bail; 8 inch diameter x 9¼ inches; good condition, overall wear, some scratches and chipping, slight denting; $400–550.

SWANSDOWN
Swansdown Coffee, can; 1 pound; white swan on oval insert; 4¼ inch diameter x 6¼ inches; very good condition, some light wear, minor scratches and chipping, slight dents; $250–500.

TASTER'S CHOICE
(*see* "Nestlé" in Candy chapter)

VELVET
Velvet Coffee, can; 5 pounds; W. H. Mailkin store front and steaming cup of coffee on opposite sides; 8¼ inch diameter x 8½ inches with original lid and wood-handled bail; made in Vancouver, Canada; good/very good condition; $175–250.

VETERAN BRAND
Veteran Brand Coffee, can; 1 pound; logoed portrait depicts side view of white-haired soldier; 4¼ inch diameter x 5½ inches; good condition, some minor wear, darkened discoloration on lid and top edge, minor fade to bottom, some scratching; $100–150.

WASHINGTON'S
Washington's Coffee, display case; made of wood and glass; ca. 1920–1930; caption reads "Better Coffee that will Never Disturb You"; 15 x 15 x 10½ inches; near-mint condition; $200–350.

WEDDING BELL
Wedding Bell Coffee, die-cut cardboard display; seasonal display utilizing country cottage to frame package; on left of the "door" is a summer scene with caption "Serve Cold When Hot"; on right, a winter scene and caption "Serve Hot When Cold"; 27½ x 16½ inches; good condition; $200–400.

WHITE SWAN
White Swan Coffee, cans (4); different name logos on cans even though each depicts white swan logo; 5 x 4 x 3½ inches, 5 x 4¼ x 3½ inches, 5 x 4¼ x 3½ inches, 5 x 3¾ x 3½ inches; good overall condition, general wear; $100–200.

White Swan Coffee, carton; 25 pounds; rare cardboard carton with paper label of swan in pond; 11 x 17 x 11 inches; fair condition, overall wear, paper loss, creases and tears; $25–75.

CHAPTER ELEVEN

■ COMMUNICATIONS ■ DEVICES: PHONOGRAPHS, RADIOS, TELEVISIONS AND TELEPHONES

BELL TELEPHONE/AT&T
(AMERICAN TELEPHONE & TELEGRAPH CO.)

The blue bell has always been the symbol of the United States's largest phone company. Even now that the company has faced its first competitors, Americans automatically recognize the bell, which indicates a phone is nearby. AT&T's first general superintendent created the trademark to indicate the fact that Alexander Graham Bell invented the phone; inside the bell's outline were the words "Long Distance Telephone." The symbol (or service mark) was approved on January 5, 1889.

In 1895, local equipment connected with long-distance stations, thus the wording on the symbol changed to "Local and Long Distance Telephone." At first, a rectangle framed the bell, but a double circle replaced the rectangle in 1900. In 1939, the words "American Telephone & Telegraph Co. and Associated Companies," appeared within the double circle and "Bell System" was inscribed on the bell. The double circle disappeared in 1964, and in 1969, all wording was deleted from the bell symbol.

The AT&T symbol was not a registered trademark until 1953.

AT&T/BELL TELEPHONE

Bell Telephone Co. of Pennsylvania, milk glass hanging glass shade; 11½ x 4 inches (fitter ring); canteen-shaped shade; enamel Bell System roped image surrounded by wording on both sides; excellent condition; $400–600.

California Interstate Telephone Company, aluminum sign; 16 x 22 inches; blue background, white letters; ca. 1960; very good condition; $150–250.

California Interstate Telephone Company, aluminum sign; 16 x 22 inches; blue background, white letters; ca. 1960; very good condition. $150–250. *Collection of and photo by Michael Bruner.*

Interstate Telegraph Company, gas globe, 15 inch diameter; blue on white milk glass; ca. 1930; excellent condition, $750–850. *Collection of and photo by Michael Bruner.*

The Mountain States Tel. & Tel. Co./American Telephone & Telegraph Co., tin public telephone sign; 5½ x 19 inches; blue and white; ca. 1930; excellent condition; $250–400.

Ohio Associated Telephone Co., tin public pay station sign; 11 x 11 inches; blue and white; ca. 1920; very good condition; $700–800.

Ossipee Valley Tel & Tel, porcelain flange sign; early local and long-distance bell logo; 17½ x 22½ inches; fair condition, some bending; $175–350.

Wisconsin Telephone Company/AT&T, tin sign; 18 x 18 inches; blue and white; ca. 1910; very good condition, $450–550.

BALTIMORE TELEGRAM

Baltimore Telegram, lithograph on paper; 10 x 13 inches; printed by A. Hoen & Co., Baltimore; ca. 1890; colorful; multiple vignettes of people reading *The Great Southern Weekly*; very good condition; $1,400–1,800.

The Mountain States Tel. & Tel. Co./American Telephone & Telegraph Co., tin public telephone sign; 5½ x 19 inches; blue and white; ca. 1930; excellent condition; $250–400. *Collection of and photo by Michael Bruner.*

COMMUNICATIONS DEVICES ■ 127

Ohio Associated Telephone Co., tin public pay station sign; 11 x 11 inches; blue and white; ca. 1920; very good condition; $700–800. *Collection of and photo by Michael Bruner.*

Wisconsin Telephone Company/AT&T, tin sign; 18 x 18 inches; blue and white; ca. 1910; very good condition; $450–550. *Collection of and photo by Michael Bruner.*

INDEPENDENT TELEPHONE

Independent Telephone, glass hanging shade; 8 inch globe; 4 inch fitter ring; milk glass with red, white, and blue patriotic emblem for local and long-distance independent telephones; excellent condition; $950–1,300.

KELLOGG TELEPHONE

Kellogg Telephone, paper sign; depicts little girl holding telephone to puppy's ear; ca. 1902; approximately 12 x 19 inches excluding mat and frame; excellent condition; $200–400.

MISCELLANEOUS

Stained-glass "Telephone" sign; made of glass and lead; 7 x 18⅝ inches; ca. 1915; off-white and green stained glass; excellent condition; $300–500.

VICTOR TALKING MACHINE CO.

The Victor Company metamorphosed from various mergers and licenses. The original product, a Gramophone, was sold by Victor Berliner, a German in competition with Edison's Phonograph and Alexander Graham Bell's Columbia Photograph.

The trademark dog listening to "His Master's Voice" was born in 1900 and has not changed since. Nipper, an obese fox terrier, belonged to an English artist named Francis Barraud. When Barraud spotted his dog peering into an early gramophone's trumpet, he painted him and titled the picture *His Master's Voice*. In 1901, the Victor Talking Machine Company acquired the United States rights to using the portrait. Its first appearance (in the April 25, 1903, edition of the *Saturday Evening Post*) caused quite a stir.

Because the device was a new and complicated one, so were the ads explaining it. In 1904, the company advertised (and explained) how it was recording on both sides of the disk, and in 1908, returned to the task—this time to explain what "records" were.

Victor eventually surpassed all competition and maintained "exclusive" artists who endorsed the product (such as Enrico Caruso, the opera star, and Sousa, the "March King").

For years, the gramophone kept its cheerleaderlike megaphone, then electric speakers took over in the 1930s.

VICTOR BERLINER

The Victor Berliner Gram-o-phone Co., tip tray; "The Victor and Berliner" record machine; trademarked image of dog and gramophone; 4 inch diameter; fair/good condition, overall wear, crazing of color, rim chips; $45–100.

The Victor Berliner Gram-o-phone Co., tip tray; pictures trademarked image "His Master's Voice" for the Berliner; 4 inch diameter; good condition, overall fading, chipping, general wear; $45–100.

RCA

RCA, display piece; 35 inch papier-mâché three-dimensional figure of Nipper, the RCA dog; excellent condition; $300–500.

RCA, figural; hard rubber figural of Nipper, the trademark; approximately 14 x 32 x 32 inches; good condition, several breaks, some retouching; $50–150.

RCA, figurine/award; person holding medallion; 14 inches; dated March 1955; given to employees in recognition of their work for National Television Servicemen's Week; $150–250.

RCA, figurine/award; hand holding RCA medallion; 13 inches; $150–250.

RCA, papier-mâché figural; depicts Nipper, the company's trademark; three-dimensional; approximately 18 x 36 x 36 inches; good condition, some overpainting, cracks and chips; $200–400.

RCA, Radiotrons figure; "the sellin' fool," designed by Maxfield

COMMUNICATIONS DEVICES ■ 129

RCA, figurine/award, person holding medallion; 14 inches; dated "March 1955"; given to employees in recognition of their work for National Television Servicemen's Week, $150–250; figurine/award, hand holding RCA medallion; 13 inches; $150–250. *Courtesy of Neil and Nancy Berliner. Photo by Donald Vogt.*

RCA, Radiotrons figure; "the sellin' fool," designed by Maxfield Parrish; 16 inches; ca. 1926; point-of-sale piece; composition; $1,000–1,500. *Courtesy of Neil and Nancy Berliner. Photo by Donald Vogt.*

Parrish; 16 inches; ca. 1926; point-of-sale piece; composition; $1,000–1,500.

WESTERN UNION

Western Union, sign; says "Telephone Your Telegrams from here/Ask Operator for Western Union"; 16 x 17 inches; black, yellow, blue, and white; very good condition; $400–500.

Western Union, sign; says "Telephone Your Telegrams from here/Ask Operator for Western Union"; 16 x 17 inches; black, yellow, blue, and white; very good condition; $400–500. *Collection of and photo by Michael Bruner.*

Western Union Telegraph and Cable, porcelain sign; 36 inch oval; blue and white; ca. 1900; excellent condition; $800–1,000. *Collection of and photo by Michael Bruner.*

Western Union, tin sign; 36 inch oval; blue and white; ca. 1910; very good condition; $400–500. *Collection of and photo by Michael Bruner.*

Western Union, tin sign; 36 inch oval; blue and white; ca. 1910; very good condition; $400–500.

Western Union Telegraph and Cable, porcelain sign; 36 inch oval; blue and white; ca. 1900; excellent condition; $800–1,000.

CHAPTER TWELVE
◼ CONDIMENTS, SPICES ◼

BEARD
Beard Cinnamon, wooden keg; 10 pounds; colorful paper label with camel scene; unusual and early; 8½ inch diameter x 10¼ inches; fair/good condition, label creased, minor paper loss, tears, age soiling; $200–400.

BROOKSIDE
Brookside Vinegar, bottle; 1 quart; John T. Connor Company; Boston, Massachusetts (distributors); paper label; ca. 1910–1920; excellent condition; $20–25.

C. J. FELL & BROTHER
C. J. Fell & Brother Spice Co., paper sign; made by Herline & Co., Philadelphia; ca. 1857; vignetted display of natural spices framed by Victorian border of flowers and birds; lists available products; from an 1857–1858 business atlas printed by Herline; 18⅜ x 15¾ inches; excellent condition; $500–1,000.

COLMAN'S
Colman's Mustard, paper sign; trademarked image in medallion insert; colorful; 16 x 22 inches; good/very good condition, overall soiling; $150–300.

Colman's Mustard, porcelain sign; large blue-and-yellow sign; 38 x 36 inches; very good condition, some chipping in edges, slight overall wear, strong colors; $50–150.

Colman's Mustard, tin display cabinet; red and black on yellow background; small tin three-shelved display cabinet; 10 x 16 x 7¼ inches; fair condition, rust spotting overall, some chipping; $50–100.

Colman's Mustard, tin; ¼ pound; made in England; bull on label; ca. 1930s; very good condition; $6–10.

CORBIN, SONS & CO.
Corbin, Sons & Co., cinnamon flavoring extract bottle; extremely colorful lithographed label for this Chicago Co. product; approximately

Brookside Vinegar, bottle; 1 quart; John T. Connor Company; Boston, Massachusetts (distributors); paper label; ca. 1910–1920; excellent condition; $20–25. *Courtesy of Irreverent Relics. Photo by Donald Vogt.*

Colman's Mustard, tin; ¼ pound; made in England; bull on label; ca. 1930s; $6–10. *Courtesy of Dawn and Bob Reno. Photo by Donald Vogt.*

6 inches tall; label in excellent condition, bottle still darkened with residue; ca. 1870s; $12–20.

CORN PRODUCTS

Corn Products Refining Co. (now Best Foods), the Indian Princess doll; composition; dated 1925; extremely rare; 11 inches; excellent condition; $1,250–1,500.

DR. PRICE'S

Dr. Price's Flavoring Extracts, bottles (3); imitation maple, orange; imitation banana; imitation raspberry; ½ fluid ounce size; very good condition; $4–6 each.

Corn Products Refining Co. (now Best Foods), the Indian Princess doll; composition; dated 1925; extremely rare; 11 inches; $1,250–1,500. *Courtesy of Neil and Nancy Berliner. Photo by Donald Vogt.*

Dr. Price's Flavoring Extracts, bottles (3); imitation maple, orange; imitation banana; imitation raspberry; ½ fluid ounce size; very good condition; $4–6 each. *Courtesy of Irreverent Relics. Photo by Donald Vogt.*

CONDIMENTS, SPICES ■ 133

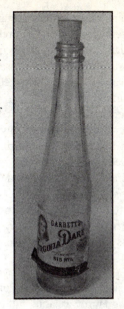

Garrett's Virginia Dare Red Wine, bottle; embossed on back; paper label on front has picture of "Virginia Dare" in full color; ca. 1940s; very good condition; $15–25. *Courtesy of Dawn and Bob Reno. Photo by Donald Vogt.*

GARRETT'S

Garrett's Virginia Dare Red Wine, bottle; embossed on back; paper label on front has picture of "Virginia Dare" in full color; ca. 1940s; very good condition; $15–25.

HEINZ

The company that boasted "57 Varieties" actually had more than 1,250 on its roster in 1969 when it celebrated its hundredth anniversary. Thus, the logo was changed and "57 Varieties" was dropped on most products (it does, however, continue to be seen on selected items).

H. J. Heinz began his first business in 1869 at the age of twenty-five. Together with partner L. C. Noble, he sold horseradish; later, he added sauerkraut, pickles, and vinegar to his list of products. (The Heinz 57 Varieties didn't come into existence until 1896.) Unfortunately, the panic of 1875 pushed him out of business for over a year. Determined to make another go of it, he paid off all his bills and began again, gaining a reputation as "the pickle king." Relishes, condiments, sauces, beans, and tomato soup were added to his product line, and by 1893, Heinz's exhibit was the largest of any American food company at the Chicago World's Columbian Exposition.

Henry Heinz designed the company's logo after spotting a train car advertisement that touted a brand of shoes in "21 styles" and adapted that idea to his own needs. New York's first electric sign was a six-story advertisement that depicted a Heinz pickle. Norman Rockwell illustrated for Heinz Baked Beans—"The Best Lunch for a Hike."

By the twentieth century, the company produced the most pickles, vinegar, and catsup of any American food company. The company was run by the Heinz family for 117 years—until Jack Heinz died in 1987.

Some of the brand names under the Heinz aegis include: StarKist (tuna), Weight Watchers (diet products), Ore-Ida (frozen potatoes), 9-Lives (cat food), Alba (milk products), Steak-umm (frozen meat), Skippy Premium (peanut butter), Glamour Puss (cat food), and Cardio-Fitness Centers.

HEINZ

Heinz Oven Baked Beans, advertisement from *Pictorial Review*, 1923; shows maid feeding family at table; full color; $4–6.

Heinz, clock radio; approximately 8 inches; ca. 1980s; given only to employees; excellent condition; $200–250.

Heinz Oven Baked Beans, advertisement from *Pictorial Review*, 1923; shows maid feeding family at table; full color; $4–6. *Courtesy of Paper Lady/Bernie and Dolores Fee. Photo by Donald Vogt.*

Heinz, clock/radio; approximately 8 inches; ca. 1980s; given only to employees; $200–250; molded rubber paperweight; ca. 1940s; $300–400; molded rubber miniature paperweight; ca. 1940s; $35–50. *Courtesy of Neil and Nancy Berliner. Photo by Donald Vogt.*

Heinz Pickling Distilled Vinegar, cruet; all-glass stopper; marked "Greenfield Village" in raised letters on base, Heinz imprint and "Pittsburgh, U.S.A." on back; mint condition; probably an employee gift; contemporary; $40–50. *Courtesy of Irreverent Relics. Photo by Donald Vogt.*

Heinz, circular paper cutout; depicts pickle with company name on it in center; near-mint condition; $5–20.

Heinz, molded rubber paperweight; ca. 1940s; excellent condition; $300–400.

Heinz Pickling Distilled Vinegar, cruet; all-glass stopper; marked "Greenfield Village" in raised letters on base; Heinz imprint and "Pittsburgh, U.S.A." on back; mint condition; probably an employee gift; contemporary; $40–50.

Heinz Pickling Vinegar, die-cut cardboard display; woman holding 1 gallon pickling solution sitting on barrel of H. J. Heinz Co. pickling vinegar; rare; 40 x 57 inches; fair condition, some loss to cardboard edges, some small holes, soiling overall; $600–1,200.

Heinz, molded rubber miniature paperweight; ca. 1940s; excellent condition; $35–50.

Heinz, pin; in the shape of a pickle; ca. 1950s; excellent condition; $5–10.

Heinz Pork and Beans, sign; depicts giant-size display can; Heinz logo in pickle; approximately 4 feet tall; 1906; excellent condition; $1,250–1,600.

Heinz Vinegar, sign; original embossed frame; depicts lady in kitchen with products; excellent condition; $775–1,000.

MCCORMICK

McCormick is number one in producing spices and seasonings, and has been so for over a hundred years. Willoughby McCormick founded the company in 1889. At first, he sold root beer flavoring extract and fruit syrups under the Bee Brand and Silver Medal product names. McCormick also sold other items from door to door, such as Iron Glue and Uncle Sam's Nerve and Bone Liniment.

In 1896, McCormick's business expanded when he bought the F. G. Emmett Spice Company of Philadelphia. He opened an export office in New York, and four years later added such brands as Reliable (1900), Banquet Brand (1902), and Tea House Tea (1937).

McCormick's and Company, Inc. now sells approximately one third of its products to supermarkets and the other two thirds to restaurants and big food packagers. They import spices, seasonings, and flavorings from all over the world and are based in Baltimore.

MCCORMICK

McCormick Paprika, tin; approximately 2½ x 1¼ inches; printed in red, white, and green; excellent condition; $4–8.

McCormick Pepper, tin; approximately 2½ x 1¼ inches; printed in red, white, and black; excellent condition; $4–8.

MIRACLE WHIP

(*see also* "Kraft General Foods" in Dairy Products chapter)

Miracle Whip salad dressing was introduced by Kraft at the 1933 Century of Progress Chicago World's Fair and became the largest selling brand in the country. Kraft launched its new product with an unsurpassed advertising campaign that emphasized the quality of Miracle Whip, using radio and print to advertise that Miracle Whip was: ". . . not too bland, not too tart. Not too oily. Just perfect." After only twenty-seven weeks on the market, the salad dressing was number one.

Through the years, some of the innovative advertising promotions Kraft has used have included ads with simple recipes, "before and after" ads showing homemakers how to improve their culinary skills by using Miracle Whip, and a fiftieth anniversary recipe book (distributed in 1983).

CONDIMENTS, SPICES ■ 137

MIRACLE WHIP

Miracle Whip, advertisement from *Ladies' Home Journal*, 1939; depicts a housewife saying "What a difference it makes in my salads" and includes vignettes on how she discovered the difference; full color; excellent condition; $5–8.

Miracle Whip, advertisement from *Saturday Evening Post*, ca. 1950s; full page, full color; "Health Giving Salads . . . they always taste better with Miracle Whip"; tells readers to "tune in Bing Crosby, with star cast and famous guests. Every Thursday night, NBC Red Network"; excellent condition; $6–10.

MISCELLANEOUS

Multidrawer tin spice cabinet; eight-drawer mirrored-front tin store cabinet; 32 x 16 x 13 inches; good condition, general soiling overall, discoloration due to age, some chipping to paint and mirror corner; $150–350.

MORTON SALT

The Morton Salt Girl began to be used in 1914, but has undergone many changes over the years (every ten to twelve, to be exact). The first girl was a curly-haired blonde, then a straight-haired brunette was introduced, and today's version is a pageboy'd blonde.

Sterling Morton was head of the company when the ad logo was chosen. It struck him that the umbrella, indicating damp weather, and the free-flowing salt under the girl's arm, presented the whole picture of what he wanted his customers to believe Morton Salt would give them. Nineteen years later, the company copyrighted its slogan, "When it rains, it pours"—though it had been used from the moment Morton and his co-workers decided to use the girl with the umbrella.

Morton Salt, advertisement from *Time* magazine, 1969; shows all six phases Morton Salt went through; $4–7. *Courtesy of Lester Morris. Photo by Donald Vogt.*

138 ■ ADVERTISING

MORTON SALT

Morton Salt, advertisement from *Time* magazine, 1969; shows all six phases Morton Salt went through; excellent condition; $4–7.

Morton Salt, advertisement from *Woman's Day*, ca. 1965; depicts pumpkin with carrot nose, filled with popcorn; excellent condition; $4–7.

Morton Salt, advertisement from *Family Circle*, ca. 1965; depicts two girls with Morton Salt umbrellas; excellent condition; $4–7.

Morton Salt, advertisement from *Family Circle*, ca. 1970s; depicts sepia-toned photo of salt pouring on counter; excellent condition; $4–7.

Morton Salt, advertisement from *Time* magazine, ca. 1975; old-fashioned photo of group of women with Teddy Roosevelt photo on wall in background; excellent condition; $4–7.

Morton Salt, advertisement from *Life*, 1948; depicts grapefruit; full color; excellent condition; $3–5.

Morton Salt, advertisement from *Life*, 1956; depicts people putting salt on fruit; full color; excellent condition; $3–5.

Morton Salt, advertisement from *Life*, 1956; depicts grapefruit; full color; excellent condition; $3–5.

Morton Salt, advertisement from *Family Circle*, ca. 1970s; depicts sepia-toned photo of salt pouring on counter; $4–7. *Courtesy of Lester Morris. Photo by Donald Vogt.*

Morton Salt, advertisement from *Life*, 1958; depicts yellow-and-red tomatoes; full color; $3–5. *Courtesy of Paper Lady/Bernie and Dolores Fee. Photo by Donald Vogt.*

CONDIMENTS, SPICES ■ 139

Watkins, salesman's door-to-door rack full of samples of all the items the company sold; ca. 1920s–1940s; samples $5–40 each, display rack $100–150. *Courtesy of Marilyn & De Underwood/Tins Again Collectibles. Photo by Donald Vogt.*

Morton Salt, advertisement from *Life*, 1958; depicts yellow-and-red tomatoes; full color; excellent condition; $3–5.

QUINCY
Quincy Brand Allspice, tin; 1½ ounces; ca. 1940s; very good condition; $25–28.

SANFORD'S GINGER
Sanford's Ginger, paper poster; depicts graphic image of black boy with watermelon and large bottle; 21½ x 28½ inches excluding frame; printed by Forbes Co., very good/excellent condition, minor edge tear, some water staining; $2,500–3,500.

WATKINS
Watkins, salesman's door-to-door rack full of samples of all the items the company sold; ca. 1920s–1940s; samples $5–40 each, display rack $100–150.

WINDSOR COCONUT
Windsor Coconut, can; paper label depicts palm tree scene; excellent condition; $20–40.

WORCESTER SALT
Worcester Salt, framed chromolithograph ad; depicts "Worcester Salt Special," train of 162 cars with largest single shipment of manufactured commodity ever made to date (1897); very good condition; $75–150.

CHAPTER THIRTEEN
CRACKERS, COOKIES, BISCUITS

ANIMAL CRACKERS
(*see* "Nabisco")

BROWNIES LOG CABIN
Brownies Log Cabin, cardboard box; log cabin–shaped biscuit box with Palmer Cox Brownies all around; 3½ x 2¾ x 3 inches; very good/excellent condition; $25–75.

EDUCATOR CRACKERS
Educator Crackers, ark tin; lithograph on tin; 5 x 10½ x 3½ inches; printed by Chas. Shonk Co., Litho., Chicago; figural American food tin shaped like Noah's ark with animals looking out windows on four sides; one side of roof opens; one of three known; excellent condition; $1,500–2,500.

Educator, tin; 1 pound; blue and brown; ca. 1950s; $25–50.

Educator, lunchbox tin; nursery rhyme animals; ca. 1920s; 3 x 6 inches; very good condition; $175–225.

Educator, tin; mustard background with black lettering; ca. 1910–1920, 6 x 5½ x 5½ inches; very good condition; $50–100.

MICKEY MOUSE ANIMAL CRACKERS
Mickey Mouse Animal Crackers, box; 1933; printed in full color; excellent condition; $750–1,500.

NABISCO
In the heyday of the general store, customers would fill a paper bag with crackers. Many of the bankers who created these crackers soon discovered it was difficult to make a living on their own, so they consolidated. Soon, only three large companies (New York Biscuit, American Biscuit, and United States

Baking) ruled the market. They decided to merge, thus the National Biscuit Company was launched in 1898.

Chaired by Adolphus W. Green, the company adopted as its trademark an ancient symbol the early Christians used to demonstrate the triumph of spiritual over worldly things. The fifteenth-century colophon, used at the end of a book or manuscript, originally had been used by the Society of Printers in Venice.

At first, "IN-ER-SEAL" was printed inside the circle, but in 1918, NBC was added, and five years later "Uneeda" was added below the seal. In 1935, the company dropped "Uneeda" from the trademark, and in 1941, Nabisco (the corporate contraction) replaced "NBC." In 1952, the symbol/trademark was placed in a red triangle in order to draw customer attention to Nabisco products.

The Uneeda Biscuit Boy, dressed in his yellow slicker and rain hat, was Gordon Stille, the five-year-old nephew of one of N. W. Ayer's copywriters (Ayer was the advertising agency hired to name the National Biscuit Company's crackers and to give them an image that would advertise the product in a positive manner). The box and its watertight liner, invented by an NBC lawyer, were produced before the logo was created—thus the idea of a boy carrying a watertight package in the rain.

Today, the National Biscuit Company is responsible for a wide variety of products such as Oreo Cookies (introduced in 1912), Fig Newtons (introduced in 1891 and named after the wealthy area, Newton, near Boston), Oysterette Crackers (first sold in 1900), Premium Saltines, Animal Crackers (which were introduced in 1902 and had been produced in a tin container), and Milk Bone dog biscuits. (*See also* information about Planters Peanuts products, also manufactured by Nabisco, in the Peanuts and By-Products chapter of this book, as well as information about Cream of Wheat, manufactured by Nabisco, in the Cereal chapter.)

NABISCO

Nabisco, Saltine Crackers, tin; 14 ounces; ca. 1960s; excellent condition; $6–12.

Nabisco, Saltine Crackers, tin; ca. 1940s; printed in English and Spanish; very good condition; $10–15.

OYSTERETTE CRACKERS
(see "Nabisco")

OREO COOKIES
(see "Nabisco")

PEEK FREAN'S
Peek Frean's Biscuits, oval tin; Christmas design; made in Canada; ca. 1930s; fair condition; $20–40.

PREMIUM SALTINES
(see "Nabisco")

SUNSHINE BISCUITS

In 1902, J. L. and J. S. Loose of Kansas founded a baking company based on the premise that they'd produce quality cookies and crackers in a bakery filled with sunshine. Prior to that time, bakeshops were located in dark, dank basements.

The Loose-Wiles Biscuit Company arose out of the partnership formed by the Loose brothers and a leading industrialist, John A. Wiles. They called their product Sunshine Biscuits and immediately became a success.

The popularity of their soda biscuits, sugar wafers, and Hydrox® creme-filled chocolate sandwich cookies soon spread throughout the Northeast, and by 1912, the company moved to Long Island City (by 1955, the New York landmark became the world's largest bakery).

A 1915 ad for Sunshine Biscuits shows a stylishly dressed woman entering a shop where Sunshine products are stacked on a rack right inside the door. Many varieties (fourteen, at that point) were sold by the company, Loose-Wiles Biscuit Company of New York. Sunshine's unique advertising campaign included magazines offering customers sample packets of Sunshine products. As grocers started to jump on the bandwagon, more and more Sunshine racks showed up in neighborhood stores. Sunshine grew, and it began producing new products such as Krispy Crackers, Hi Hos, and Cheez-Its.

As did many other companies, Sunshine contributed to the war effort in World War II. Once the war was over it changed its corporate name to Sunshine Biscuits, Inc. It expanded, opening a bakery in Oakland, California, in 1949, then another in Columbus, Georgia.

CRACKERS, COOKIES, BISCUITS ■ 143

During the early 1960s, modern baking technology and an expanding market convinced Sunshine to call the Long Island City "Thousand Window Bakery" obsolete. It replaced that bakery with a new, bigger version in Sayreville, New Jersey. In 1966, Sunshine Biscuits, Inc. became part of what is now American Brands, Inc.

The company has made a habit of producing one special-edition tin for collectors on a yearly basis and still produces colorful and highly collectible tins during the holiday season for the holiday cookie assortment, endeavoring to produce new and notable designs annually. During at least five years of the company's history, its tins were produced without being marked "Sunshine."

SUNSHINE BISCUITS

Sunshine Biscuits, tin display shelf; 29 x 52 inches; ca. 1915; loaded with examples of the tins; good condition; $150–250.

Sunshine Biscuits, Martini Butter Crackers, tin; 13 ounces; red, blue, and white design; ca. 1940s; very good condition; $15–18.

Sunshine Biscuits, Martini Crackers, tin; 13 ounces; Manhattan scene; yellow, aqua, and deep blue; excellent condition; $18–24.

Sunshine Biscuits, tin; Currier & Ives "American Express Train"; 14 x 11 inch oval; 1982; excellent condition; $3–12.

Sunshine Biscuits, tin; Niagara Falls; 14 x 11 inch oval; 1986; excellent condition; $3–10.

Sunshine Biscuits, tin display shelf; 29 x 52 inches; ca. 1915; loaded with examples of the tins; $150–250. *Collection of Diana Perry. Photo by Laura Garner.*

Sunshine Biscuits, tin; U.S. Military Academy at West Point; 14 x 11 inch oval; 1983; excellent condition; $3–10.

Sunshine Biscuits, tin; 75th anniversary tin; "Shopping on Main Street"; 14 x 11 inch oval; 1977; excellent condition; $5–12.

Sunshine Biscuits, tin; Currier & Ives "The Morning Ride"; 14 x 11 inch oval; 1976; excellent condition; $5–12.

Sunshine Biscuits, tin; American folk art 75th anniversary tin; "Holiday Parade"; 14 x 11 inch oval; 1977; excellent condition; $5–12.

Sunshine Biscuits, tin; Mississippi steamboats; Mississippi in time of peace; 14 x 11 inch oval; 1978; excellent condition; $5–12.

Sunshine Biscuits, tin; Currier & Ives "Mount Vernon—The Home of Washington"; 14 x 11 inch oval; 1983; excellent condition; $3–10.

Sunshine Biscuits, tin; Currier & Ives "America as It Was—Winter Pastimes"; 14 x 11 inch oval; 1980; excellent condition; $3–12.

Sunshine Biscuits, tin; "Washington Crossing the Delaware"; 14 x 11 inch oval; 1984; excellent condition; $3–10.

Sunshine Biscuits, tin; Currier & Ives "Clipperships & Fabulous Trips," Clippership *Red Jacket*; 14 x 11 inch oval; 1981; excellent condition; $3–12.

Sunshine Biscuits, tin; Currier & Ives "Clipperships & Fabulous Trips," Clippership *Flying Cloud*; 14 x 11 inch oval; 1981; excellent condition; $3–12.

Sunshine Biscuits, tin; Statue of Liberty; 14 x 11 inch oval; 1985; excellent condition; $5–15.

Sunshine Biscuits, tin; the Liberty Bell; 14 x 11 inch oval; 1985; excellent condition; $5–15.

Sunshine Biscuits, tin; "Signing of the Declaration of Independence"; 14 x 11 inch oval; 1984; excellent condition; $3–10.

Sunshine Biscuits, tin; Mt. Rushmore; 14 x 11 inch oval; 1986; excellent condition; $3–10.

Sunshine Biscuits, tin; Currier & Ives "Across the Continent"; 14 x 11 inch; 1982; excellent condition; $3–12.

Sunshine Biscuits, tin; Paris street scenes by Utrillo; twin trays; 3 x 14 x 11 inches; oval; excellent condition; $5–15.

CRACKERS, COOKIES, BISCUITS ■ 145

Sunshine Biscuits, tin; Currier & Ives "Winter"; wall plaque design; snap-on lid; 14 x 11 inch oval; 1971; excellent condition; $5–15.

Sunshine Biscuits, tin; "Blue Boy"; snap-on lid; 3 x 12 inches; round; 7 inch cardboard center; 1959; excellent condition; $15–20.

Sunshine Biscuits, tin; "Age of Innocence"; snap-on lid; 3 x 12 inches; round; 7 inch cardboard center; 1960; very good condition; $15–20.

Sunshine Biscuits, tin; "Miss Murray"; snap-on lid; 3 x 12 inches; round; cardboard center; 1961; very good condition; $15–20.

Sunshine Biscuits, tin; Currier & Ives "Summer"; wall plaque design; snap-on lid; 14 x 11 inch oval; 1971; excellent condition; $5–15.

Sunshine Biscuits, tin; "T'ang Dynasty"; twin trays; 4 x 13 inches round; 1973; excellent condition; $3–10 each.

Sunshine Biscuits, tin; Audubon's "Birds of America"; twin trays; 4 x 13 inches; round; 1972; excellent condition; $12–20.

Sunshine Biscuits, tin; Currier & Ives "Spring"; wall plaque design; snap-on lid; 14 x 11 inch oval; 1972; excellent condition; $5–15.

Sunshine Biscuits, tin; depicts battleships; octagon shape with handle; U.S.S. *Idaho* on lid and other U.S.S. ships around sides; 3½ x 9¼ inches; 1937; very good condition; $30–50.

Sunshine Biscuits, tin; depicts 1939 World's Fair; octagon shape with handle; famous places in New York on sides—Times Square, Radio City Music Hall, Statue of Liberty, etc.; 3½ x 9¼ inches; 1939; very good condition; $35–65.

Sunshine Biscuits, tin; "Hiawatha's Wedding Journey"; octagon shape with handle; story of the journey on sides; 3½ x 9¼ inches; 1936; very good condition; $35–85.

Sunshine Biscuits, tin; "All American"; octagon shape with handle; Statue of Liberty on lid, historic events on sides—Gold Rush, signing of Constitution, pioneers moving west, etc.; 3½ x 9¼ inches; 1940 (this tin was the last one with "Loose Wiles—Bakers of Sunshine" embossed on the bottom); very good condition; $25–35.

Sunshine Biscuits, tin; "Famous Paintings"; octagon shape with handle; Homer Winslow, Degas, *The Horse Fair*, etc., on sides; 3½ x 9¼ inches; 1948 (the first tin with the new Sunshine logo; i.e., "Loose Wiles" dropped); very good condition; $20–30.

146 ■ ADVERTISING

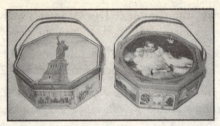

Sunshine Biscuits, tins; (left) "All American"; octagon shape with handle; Statue of Liberty on lid, historic events on sides—Gold Rush, signing of Constitution, pioneers moving west, etc.; 3½ by 9¼ inches; 1940 (this tin was the last one with "Loose Wiles—Bakers of Sunshine" embossed on the bottom); $25–35. (Right) "Famous Paintings"; octagon shape with handle; Homer Winslow, Degas, *The Horse Fair*, etc. on sides; 3½ x 9¼ inches; 1948 (the first tin with the new Sunshine logo; i.e., "Loose Wiles" dropped); $20–30. *Collection of Diana Perry. Photo by Laura Garner.*

Sunshine Biscuits, tin; depicts Grand Canyon; octagon shape with handle; other famous American sites around sides—Mt. Rainier, Washington Monument, etc.; 3½ x 9¼ inches; 1935; very good condition; $30–50.

Sunshine Biscuits, tin; depicts the White House; octagon shape with handle; Presidents George Washington to Franklin D. Roosevelt around sides; 3½ x 9¼ inches; 1933; very good condition; $30–75.

Sunshine Biscuits, tin; George Washington portrait on lid; octagon shape with handle; Washington at Valley Forge, inaugural, Mt. Vernon, family, etc. on sides; 3½ x 9¼ inches; 1939; very good condition; $30–50.

Sunshine Biscuits, tin; octagon shape with handle; *Niña, Pinta, Santa Maria* on lid, famous sailing ships on sides; 3½ x 9¼ inches; 1937; very good condition; $30–50.

Sunshine Biscuits, tin; "Robin Hood"; octagon shape with handle; Robin Hood meets Maid Marion in Sherwood Forest; 3½ x 9¼ inches; 1937; very good condition; $30–65.

Sunshine Biscuits, tin; depicts the White House; octagon shape with handle; Presidents George Washington to Franklin D. Roosevelt around sides; 3½ x 9¼ inches; 1933; $30–$75. *Collection of Diana Perry. Photo by Laura Garner.*

CRACKERS, COOKIES, BISCUITS ■ 147

Sunshine Biscuits, tin; Currier & Ives "Summer"; wall plaque design; snap-on lid; 14 x 11 inch oval; 1972; excellent condition; $5–15.

Sunshine Biscuits, tin; depicts Van Gogh's *Bridge Scene*; twin trays; 4 x 13 inches; round; 1969; excellent condition; $5–15.

Sunshine Biscuits, Krispy Crackers, tin; 2 pounds; hinged lid; 7½ x 9 x 7½ inches, red, white, and blue; good condition; $20–45.

Sunshine Biscuits, Sunshine Toy Cookies, cardboard tin; 11 ounces, with handle; 5 x 5½ inches, tin lid; very good condition; $25–45.

Sunshine Biscuits, Sunshine Thin Pretzel Stix, tin; 14 ounces; 6 x 8 inches; round; very good condition; $20–45.

Sunshine Biscuits, Sunshine Whole Wheat Crackers, tin; 11 ounces; 5 x 6 inches; round; very good condition; $20–40.

Sunshine Biscuits, tin; Currier & Ives "The Road Winter"; 14 x 11 inch oval; 1976; near-mint condition; $5–12.

Sunshine Biscuits, Sunshine Krispy Crackers Biscuits, tin; paper label; 10 x 10 x 11 inches; lift-off lid; good condition; $35–50.

Sunshine Biscuits, tin; octagon shape with handle; 9½ x 7¾ inches, woven cane design; very good condition; $15–25.

Sunshine Biscuits, Clover Leaf Sugar Wafers, tin; 8 x 10 x 8 inches, hinged lid; black; very good condition; $40–55.

Sunshine Biscuits, tin store display; glass front; hinged lid; good condition; $30–65.

Sunshine Biscuits, Sunshine Martini Crackers, tin; 13 ounces, 6 x 6 inches; good condition; $25–45.

Sunshine Biscuits, tins (3); Clover Leaf Sugar Wafers, 8 x 10 x 8 inches, hinged lid, black, $40–55; octagon shape with handle, 9½ x 7¾ inches, brown and beige wood grain, $15–25; octagon shape with handle, 9½ x 7¾ inches woven cane design, $15–25. *Collection of Diana Perry. Photo by Laura Garner.*

Sunshine Biscuits, tins; (top left) "Charms of Country Living;" octagon shape with snap-on lid, wall plaque design, 4 x 12 inches; October 1967; $15–18; (bottom left) "The Nest;" octagon shape with snap-on lid, wall plaque design, 4 x 12 inches; $15–18; (top and bottom right) "Twin Bouquets" by Redon and Renoir; twin trays 4 x 13 inches; round; 1968; $8–12. *Collection of Diana Perry. Photo by Laura Garner.*

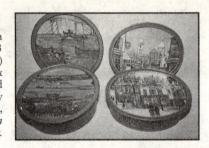

Sunshine Biscuits, tins; (top left) Van Gogh's *Bridge Scene*, twin trays, 4 x 13 inches, round, 1969, $5–15; (bottom left) Van Gogh's *Farm Scene*, twin trays, 4 x 13 inches, round, 1969, $5–15; (top and bottom right) Paris street scenes by Utrillo, twin trays, 3 x 14 x 11 inches, oval, 1970, $5–15. *Collection of Diana Perry. Photo by Laura Garner.*

Sunshine Biscuits, tin; "Charms of Country Living"; octagon shape with snap-on lid; wall plaque design; 4 x 12 inches; October 1967; excellent condition; $15–18.

Sunshine Biscuits, tin; "Blue Rose"; 14 x 11 x 3 inches; oval; 1963; excellent condition; $3–10.

Sunshine Biscuits, tin; "Twin Bouquets" by Redon and Renoir; twin trays; 4 x 13 inches; round; 1968; excellent condition $8–12.

Sunshine Biscuits, tin; Van Gogh's *Farm Scene*; twin trays; 4 x 13 inches; round; 1969; excellent condition; $5–15.

Sunshine Biscuits, tin; "White Rose"; 14 x 11 x 3 inch oval; 1962; excellent condition; $3–10.

Sunshine Biscuits, tin; "Old Masters"; octagon; 4 x 12 inches; wall plaque design; 1966; excellent condition; $13–20.

Sunshine Biscuits, tin; "The Nest"; octagon with snap-on lid; wall plaque design; 4 x 12 inches; excellent condition; $15–18.

Sunshine Biscuits, tin; "Grecian"; octagon shape; wall plaque design; 4 x 12 inches; 1965; excellent condition; $10–15.

Sunshine Biscuits, tin; "Gold Rose"; 14 x 11 x 3 inches; oval; 1964; excellent condition, $3–10.

CRACKERS, COOKIES, BISCUITS ■ 149

Sunshine Biscuits, tin; Wedgewood design; round with snap-on lid; raised, molded material to look like Wedgewood; 3½ x 10 inches; 1956; very good condition; $14–20.

Sunshine Biscuits, tin; octagon with handle, 9½ x 7¾ inches; brown and beige wood grain; very good condition; $15–25.

Sunshine Biscuits, Sunshine Whole Wheat Wafers, tin; oblong; glass topped; 7 x 5½ x 5½ inches; good condition; $20–40.

Sunshine Biscuits, tin; "Red Boy"; round with snap-on lid; 3 x 12 inches; 7 inch cardboard center; 1958; good condition; $15–20.

Sunshine Biscuits, fruit cake tin; 2 pounds; 7½ inches; round; very good condition; $8–15.

Sunshine Biscuits, fruit cake tin; 4 pounds; 9¼ inches; round; very good condition; $8–15.

Sunshine Biscuits, Spur Biscuits, tin; 9 ounces; cylinder; 3 x 8 inches; very good condition; $25–47.

Sunshine Biscuits, tins; (top left) "Red Boy," round with snap-on lid, 3 x 12 inches, 7 inch cardboard center, 1958, $15–20; (top right) "Blue Boy," round with snap-on lid, 3 x 12 inches, 7 inch cardboard center, 1959, $15–20; (bottom left) "Age of Innocence," round with snap-on lid, 3 x 12 inches, 7 inch cardboard center, 1960, $15–20; (bottom right) "Miss Murray," round with snap-on lid, 3 x 12 inches, 7 inch cardboard center, 1961, $15–20. All in this series were the round wall-type plaque cover of famous paintings. The centers are cardboard prints glued to the center of the lid. These were the last tins with "Sunshine" embossed on the tin and on the lid inside. *Collection of Diana Perry. Photo by Laura Garner.*

Sunshine Biscuits, tins; (top far left) Spur Biscuits, 9 ounces, cylinder, 3 x 8 inches, $25–47; (top middle left) Chocolate Wafers, 9 ounces, cylinder, 3 x 8 inches, $25–47; (middle right) Pilot Wafers, 12 ounces, cylinder, 5 x 8 inches, round paper label, $35–75; (right) Cheese Wafers, 10 ounces, cylinder, 5 x 7 inches, $18–40; (bottom left) fruit cake, 1 pound, orange/fruit trim, oblong, 3 x 6 inches, $15–25. *Collection of Diana Perry. Photo by Laura Garner.*

150 ■ ADVERTISING

Sunshine Biscuits, fruit cake tin; 1 pound; orange/fruit trim; 3 x 6 inches; oblong; very good condition; $15–25.

Sunshine Biscuits, Chocolate Wafers, tin; 9 ounces; cylinder; 3 x 8 inches; very good condition; $25–47.

Sunshine Biscuits, Pilot Wafter, tin; 12 ounces; cylinder; 5 x 8 inches; round paper label; very good condition; $35–75.

Sunshine Biscuits, Cheese Wafers; tin; 10 ounces; cylinder; 5 x 7 inches; good condition; $18–40.

Sunshine Biscuits, Oxford Fruit Cake, tin; Loose-Wiles Biscuit Co.; oblong; 4 x 9½ inches; early 1900s; good condition; $30–50.

Sunshine Biscuits, tin; Art Deco; round with handle; 10 inches; very good condition; $20–35.

Sunshine Biscuits, tin; Currier & Ives "America as It Was—The Village Blacksmith"; 14 x 11 inch oval; 1979; near-mint condition; $3–12.

Sunshine Biscuits, tin; American Folk Art 75th anniversary tin; "Holiday Parade"; 14 x 11 inch oval; 1977; excellent condition; $5–12.

Sunshine Biscuits, tins; (top left) Art Deco, round with handle, 10 inches, $20–35; (middle) Oxford Fruit Cake, Loose-Wiles Biscuit Co., oblong, 4 x 9½ inches; early 1900s, $30–50; (right) Sunshine Whole Wheat Wafers, oblong, glass topped, 7 x 5½ x 5½ inches, $20–40. *Collection of Diana Perry. Photo by Laura Garner.*

Sunshine Biscuits, tins; (top left) American Folk Art, 75th anniversary tin, "Holiday Parade," 14 x 11 inch oval, 1977, $5–12; (bottom left) 75th anniversary tin, "Shopping on Main Street," 14 x 11 inch oval, 1977, $5–12; (top right) Mississippi Steamboats, (Mississippi in time of peace), 14 x 11 inch oval, 1978, $5–12; (bottom right) "Rounding a Bend" (on the Mississippi), 14 x 11 inch oval, $5–12. *Collection of Diana Perry. Photo by Laura Garner.*

CRACKERS, COOKIES, BISCUITS ■ 151

Sunshine Biscuits, tins; (left) fruit cake, 1 pound, 3 x 6 inches, oblong, $15–30; (middle) fruit cake, 2 pounds, 7½ inches, round, $8–15; (right) fruit cake, 4 pounds, 9½ inches, round, $8–15. *Collection of Diana Perry. Photo by Laura Garner.*

Sunshine Biscuits, tin; "Rounding a Bend" (on the Mississippi); 14 x 11 inch oval; 1978; excellent condition; $5–12.

Sunshine Biscuits, tin; "The Jerk Line," oval, 14 x 11 inches; 1988; excellent condition; $3–10.

Sunshine Biscuits, tin; Currier & Ives "America as It Was"—The Season of Blossoms"; 14 x 11 inch oval; 1980; excellent condition; $3–12.

Sunshine Biscuits, tin; 75th anniversary tin; "Shopping on Main Street"; 14 x 11 inch oval; 1977; excellent condition; $5–12.

Sunshine Biscuits, tin; beachside painting by Frank Benson; 14 x 11 inch oval; 1991; near-mint condition; $3–10.

Sunshine Biscuits, fruit cake tin; 1 pound; 3 x 6 inches; oblong; good condition; $15–30.

Sunshine Biscuits, tin; "Capitol Building"; rectangular shape with hinge (only rectangular tin with hinged lid ever made); 3 x 11 x 12½ inches; 1953; very good condition; $35–65.

Sunshine Biscuits, tin; Currier & Ives "America as it was—The Mill Dam at Sleepy Hollow"; 14 x 11 inch oval; 1979; excellent condition; $3–12.

Sunshine Biscuits, tin; "Signing the Constitution"; 14 x 11 inch oval; 1987; near-mint condition; $3–10.

Sunshine Biscuits, tin; "Grand Canyon"; 14 x 11 inch oval; 1989; near-mint condition; $3–10.

Sunshine Biscuits, tin; "America the Beautiful"; octagon shape with handle; scenes depicting phrases from the song "America the Beautiful" on sides; 3½ x 9¼ inches; 1952; very good condition; $20–30.

Sunshine Biscuits, tin; "American Heritage"; octagon shape with handle; "The Liberty Bell's First Note" on lid, events from U.S. history on sides—Paul Revere's ride, discovering gold in California, signing the Constitution; 3½ x 9¼ inches; 1950; very good condition; $20–30.

Sunshine Biscuits, tin; "U.S. Constellation"; 14 x 11 inch oval; 1975; very good condition; $10–15.

Sunshine Biscuits, tin; petit point floral, round with snap-on lid; molded material to look and feel like needlepoint; 3¼ x 10¼ inches; 1955; very good condition; $15–25.

Sunshine Biscuits, tin; "Magnolias"; 14 x 11 inch oval; 1991; near-mint condition; $3–10.

Sunshine Biscuits, tin; "Breezing Up"; 14 x 11 inch oval; 1989; near-mint condition; $3–10.

Sunshine Biscuits, tin; "Mayflower"; round with snap-on lid; *Mayflower* in molded raised metal on lid; wall plaque design; 3 x 12 inches; 1957; very good condition; $20–35.

Sunshine Biscuits, tin; "Signing the Constitution"; 14 x 11 inch oval; 1987; near-mint condition; $3–10.

Sunshine Biscuits, tin; Currier & Ives "Early Winter"; "Sunshine" on front; 8 inches; round #2; 1987; near-mint condition; $5–8.

Sunshine Biscuits, tin; "Independence Hall"; 14 x 11 inch oval; 1987; near-mint condition; $3–10.

Sunshine Biscuits, tin; "Flowers and Fruit"; 14 x 11 inch oval; 1990; near-mint condition; $3–10.

Sunshine Biscuits, tins; (top left) "Flowers and Fruit," 14 x 11 inch oval, 1990, $3–10; (bottom) "Fruit," 14 x 11 inch oval, 1990, $3–10; (top right) "Magnolias," 14 x 11 inch oval, 1991, $3–10; (bottom right) beachside painting by Frank Benson, 14 x 11 inch oval, 1991, $3–10. *Collection of Diana Perry. Photo by Laura Garner.*

Crackers, Cookies, Biscuits

Sunshine Biscuits, tin; "U.S. Constitution"; 14 x 11 inch oval; 1975; excellent condition; $10–15.

Sunshine Biscuits, tin; "Fruit"; 14 x 11 inch oval; 1990; near-mint condition; $3–10.

Sunshine Biscuits, tin; "Looking Up Yosemite Valley"; 14 x 11 inch oval; 1988; near-mint condition; $3–10.

Sunshine Biscuits, Sunshine Trumps Cookies, tin; 16 ounces, 5 x 6 inches; round; very good condition; $25–45.

Sunshine Biscuits, Krispy Crackers, tin; yellow; 8 x 9 x 7 inches; hinged lid; good condition; $20–45.

Sunshine Biscuits, tin; "White House"; octagon shape with handle; Presidents Washington to Franklin D. Roosevelt around sides; 3½ x 9¼ inches; 1933; very good condition; $30–75.

UNEEDA
(*see also* "Nabisco")

Uneeda Butter Wafers, tin; 12½ ounces; yellow and blue; poor condition; $20–45.

Uneeda Butter Wafers, tins; 12½ ounces; by the National Biscuit Company; good condition; $15–25 each.

Uneeda Biscuit, cardboard children's alphabet blocks; not complete set; approximately six blocks; fair condition; $75–200.

Uneeda, chowder mug; with Uneeda Biscuit Boy logo; marked "Semi-Vitreous China" on base; J & B Mayer; average condition; turn of the century; fair condition; $75–175.

Uneeda, chromo lithograph advertisement; features boy reaching for biscuits in cupboard; copyright 1901 by N. W. Ayer & Son; very good condition; $100–175.

Uneeda, Graham Wafers, tin; 1 pound, 3 ounces; good condition; $15–25.

WELSH RABBIT BISCUIT

Welsh Rabbit Biscuit, box; flower patterned tin with domestic interior scene of family at dining room table; 10 x 2 x 4¼ inches; good condition; $25–75.

CHAPTER FOURTEEN
■ DAIRY PRODUCTS ■

ALBA
(*see* "Heinz" in Condiments/Spices chapter)

ALFA De LAVAL

Dr. Gustaf De Laval's first cream-separating machine was introduced on January 14, 1879, in Stockholm, Sweden. The device was invented to replace the slow sedimentation methods for creaming with centrifugal separation.

The De Laval separator could be mass-produced cheaply, but it was not capable of producing more than 130 liters per hour. Thus, De Laval began putting together sketches for a larger separator in the spring of 1879.

The separator was manually operated by a farmer's wife and/or his children. Milk was fed into the cream separator at the top of the machine (a supply can). From there, the milk would travel to a lower bowl, then through disks (which looked like upside-down funnels) that distributed the milk. Via centrifugal force, the cream was then separated from the milk as it was forced from the distributor's center. Collected there, the cream was then forced upward, separated from the milk, which flowed out through the skim milk outfit.

The new machine was not ready to be introduced until 1884. By 1885, the separator's capacity was 450 liters per hour, and a year later, it had risen to 650 liters. In 1882, the turbine-driven separator was invented, and in 1886, the company sold thirty-five direct-driven turbine separators.

The first Alfa separators came on the market in the spring of 1890: they were the Alfa A1 and A2 (the dairy-size models) and the Alfa Baby (the hand-driven separator). The Alfa Baby sold extremely well—44,000 during the twenty years it was on the market. Ads for the machines showed women in traditional Swedish dress demonstrating the machines. The company also made a number of different advertising promotion items that collectors prize, including large and colorful tin signs, match holders, hand-held mirrors, watch fobs, tip trays, serving trays, postcards, pins, calendars, trade cards, and much more.

Before the end of the century, milk pumps, butter churns, preheaters, heaters, coolers, pasteurizes, and emulsifiers were added to the line of machines produced.

The dairy separator began to change shape, and problems were corrected during the 1890s. Alfa Laval continued to produce hand-driven separators until 1914. They also produced industrial separators, which became more important to the company after the turn of the century.

Many changes have taken place over the years. For a full history, read the quite detailed book about the company, written by Borje Magnusson (*see* the Bibliography).

ALFA De LAVAL

De Laval Co., die-cut advertising card; with cow and calf cutouts and words "De Laval presents the ideal Ayrshire Cow and Calf; near-mint condition; $10–30.

De Laval, advertising card; contains picture of barn with "John Brown Dairy" on barn, two men and a boy peering in, and words "The Secret of Farmer Brown's Success" at bottom; opens to show picture of girl operating separator watched by a man and words "nearly 600,000 in use" at bottom with John Brown's testimony on top and words on side; rare; ca. 1903; near-mint condition; $35–75+.

De Laval Co., advertising card; with picture of girl in colorful dress standing next to a separator and the words "Separator, Alpha B—Aktiebolaget Separators Patent"; words on back of card include "World's Fair, Chicago 1893"; near-mint condition; $10–20.

De Laval, 1901 almanac; "A Cyclopedia of Statistics and General Information"; 5¾ x 8½ inches; good condition, mold spots and edge/binding wear; $30–40.

De Laval Co., die-cut advertising card; with cow and calf cutouts and words "De Laval presents the ideal Ayrshire Cow and Calf"; near-mint condition; $10–30. *Collection of Sam Stephens. Photo by Dawn Reno.*

156 ■ ADVERTISING

Alpha De Laval, book; with words "Farm and Dairy—The Alpha De Laval Baby Cream Separators. A practical education—in the varied advantages of centrifugal separation. What users have to say, 1894"; 5¾ x 9 inches; excellent condition, minor edge/binding wear, some sticker damage lower right corner, $30–60. *Collection of Sam Stephens. Photo by Dawn Reno.*

De Laval Separator Works, postcard; with picture of the works and lettering on the bottom; excellent condition, some wear around edges; $5–15. *Collection of Sam Stephens. Photo by Dawn Reno.*

Alpha De Laval, book; with words "Farm and Dairy—The Alpha De Laval Baby Cream Separators. A practical education—in the varied advantages of centrifugal separation. What users have to say, 1894"; 5¾ x 9 inches; excellent condition, minor edge/binding wear, some sticker damage lower right corner; $30–60.

Alpha De Laval, Baby Cream Separators, book; no. 279; copyright March 1899; with additional words "See supplemental sheet for new century capacities and improvements"; 5¾ x 9 inches; very good condition, some staining on cover, minor edge wear; $35–50.

De Laval Co., book; "Illustrated Patent History of the Centrifugal Cream Separator"; copyright 1913; no. 92-13; 6¼ x 9 inches; very good condition, edge wear; $30–50.

De Laval, card; with lettering written backwards—"Buy De Laval Cream Separator"; "W. H. Preston Agent Springwater" on back; nice colors; near-mint condition; very rare; only one known to collector; $20–50+.

De Laval Cream Separator, cloth banner; a large store banner with oval insert of woman using machine; 10 x 3 feet; good condition, general overall soiling and wear, some staining, minor holes; $200–500.

De Laval Cream Separator; original yellow cast-iron cream separator; 14 x 48 x 32 inches; good original condition; $150–250.

De Laval, tin counter display figure; Jersey cow; lithographed; 5 inches long; excellent condition; $75–100.

De Laval, match safe; depicts woman with separator; made by the De Laval Separator Co.; Winnipeg/Toronto/Montreal, Canada; 4¼ x 5½ x 1 inch; fair condition, some paint loss, overall rust haze, denting; $100–200.

De Laval Cream Separator Co., postcard; with picture of a separator; bright colors; near-mint condition; $5–10.

De Laval Separator Works, postcard; with picture of the works and lettering on the bottom; excellent condition, some wear around edges; $5–15.

De Laval, porcelain agency sign; in white, blue, and yellow; 30 x 20 inches; very good condition, some chipping along edges, minor paint dribbles on background; $75–150.

De Laval, tin sign; green background, bonneted baby with Bessie and four vignettes of cows and creamers; original frame; ca. 1907; 30 x 41 inches including frame; very good/excellent condition, pinpoint rust spotting and chipping, some decorative loss and touch-up to frame; $1,500–3,000.

De Laval, tin sign; bonneted baby holding Bessie; women of various countries in vignettes; red background and original frame; 29 x 40 inches including frame; good to very good condition, some fading, scratching, some paint loss due to white drips of paint; $2,000–3,000.

De Laval, round tin sign; depicts Homespun Honey with double nozzled cream separator and child carrying cream into barnyard; 26 inch diameter with rolled and embossed border; printed by H. D. Beach; good/very good condition, some minor scratching, minor discoloration to border, some rubbing especially to raised rim; $1,500–3,000.

BORDEN'S

Elsie the Cow debuted in 1937, designed as a cartoon character who was used to convince doctors of the healthy qualities of milk. Within a year, her bright-eyed Jersey face smiled from a daisy's center in four-color ads everywhere. In 1939, Borden produced a real Elsie at the New York World's Fair, and the bovine beauty soon moved on to stage, screen, and television.

Borden celebrated its hundredth anniversary in 1975, and Elsie produced twin (fictional) calves to celebrate the event. The company ran a contest to name the twins, awarding the $25,000 prize to a woman from Anaheim, California, who christened the calves Latabee and Lobelia.

Elsie appears on all of Broden's milk products and has not aged over the years, as other recognizable faces in advertising have.

BORDEN'S

Borden's Cheese Spreads, advertisement from *Ladies' Home Journal*, 1946; depicts different types of cheeses and what can be made with them; $4–7.

Borden's Milk, flanged tin sign; depicts Elsie the Cow on left and Borden's Milk on right; approximately 24 x 14 inches; ca. 1950s; excellent condition; $195–245.

Borden's Milk, trade card; 1886; depicts baby playing with spoons atop can; excellent condition; $5–8.

Borden's, sign; shows Elsie the Cow's face in middle of daisy; approximately 24 inch diameter; ca. 1950s; mint condition; $250–300.

BOSSIE'S BEST BRAND

Bossie's Best Brand Butter, waxed cardboard box; 1 pound; ca. 1940s; excellent condition; $3–6.

CARNATION

(*see* "Nestlé" in Candy chapter)

Borden's Cheese Spreads, advertisement from *Ladies' Home Journal*, 1946; depicts different types of cheeses and what can be made with them; $4–7. *Courtesy of Paper Lady/Bernie and Dolores Fee. Photo by Donald Vogt.*

Hood, vinyl Harry Hood figurine; 8 inches tall; ca. 1981; $100–175. *Courtesy of Neil and Nancy Berliner. Photo by Neil Berliner.*

CHASE'S

Chase's Ice Cream, box; ½ pint; 1923; girl on skis; near-mint condition; $5–15.

FULTON'S

Fulton's Ice Cream Parlor, leaded glass shade; 17½ x 23½ x 23½ inches; green, red, and white with "Fulton's" on the side and "Soda" on other side, plus letter "F" on two remaining sides; aluminum framework; excellent condition; $500–750.

H. P. HOOD

Hood's Ice Cream, wood advertising ruler; 12 inches long; excellent condition; $25–35.

Hood, vinyl Harry Hood figurine; 8 inches tall; ca. 1981; excellent condition; $100–175.

Hood's reverse glass sign; pictures bottle and cow on this unusual and seldom seen piece; 16 x 9 inches excluding frame; good/very good condition, minor lifting in background, small loss to Hood bottle; $100–200.

H. P. Hood Milk, toy wagon; horse-drawn milk wagon with doll; retaining wagon marquee and cow pictured side transfers; approximately 26 x 14 x 9 inches; fair/good condition; $1,000–1,500.

KRAFT GENERAL FOODS

The Kraft General Foods corporation recently revised its history and has stated: "Although Kraft General Foods was not formed as a company until 1989, its history goes back centuries. It is a company with many different roots and founders . . . a history of the company is almost a history of the food industry. Perhaps the simplest way to recount the company's beginnings is to review the history of four predecessor companies: Kraft (established 1903), National Dairy Products Corporation (established 1923), General Foods (established 1895), and Oscar Mayer (established 1883)." I have covered several of these companies in other parts of this text, to satisfy the need to clarify how the companies came into being and what they produced. However, it is not necessary to go into explicit detail for this type of book, so I have tried to stick to the basics.

History of Kraft

James Lewis Kraft, born in Ontario, Canada, on December 11, 1874, the son of Canadian pioneer settlers, eventually became president of one of the largest American corporations because of hard work and determination.

He began peddling eggs across the United States border at sixteen in order to earn money to help his family pay the mortgage on their farm. At the age of eighteen, he tried an ice business, but the winter was too warm, so he abandoned that idea and worked other jobs in order to save enough money to invest in a cheese company in Buffalo. However, that business also failed when his partners left him high and dry while he was in Chicago to monitor that branch of the company.

In 1903, stuck in Chicago with only $65 in his pocket, he rented a horse and wagon and sold a variety of cheeses to small stores in the city. The business grew, and Kraft soon hired some of his brothers to help him.

In 1909, Kraft incorporated to become J. L. Kraft & Bros. Co. The Company packaged and distributed thirty varieties of cheese under the brand named Kraft and Elkhorn. By 1914, the brands were available throughout the United States. Most of the company's cheeses were packaged in glass jars or foil-wrapped packages. By 1916, Kraft had patented his processed cheese.

During World War I, Kraft's tins of cheese were sent to soldiers fighting overseas. After the war, wooden boxes replaced the tins as receptacles for Kraft's 5-pound, foil-wrapped cheese loaves.

In 1928, Kraft bought the Phenix Corp., makers of Philadelphia Brand cream cheese and merged the two companies to form Kraft-Phenix Cheese Corporation. In 1930, National Dairy Products Corporation acquired Kraft, and in 1969, the corporate name was changed to Kraftco Corporation; in 1976, it was changed again, to Kraft, Inc.

Kraft used all kinds of methods to advertise his products, including ads on Chicago's elevated trains, billboards, mailing circulars, magazines/newspapers, radio, and television. The "Kraft Musical Review" started on radio in 1933, then became the weekly "Kraft Music Hall." The show promoted such Kraft products as Velveeta pasteurized process cheese spread (originally introduced in 1928), Kraft French dressing (1928), Miracle Whip salad dressing (1933), Kraft caramels (1933) Kraft macaroni and cheese dinners (1937), and Parkay margarine (1940).

As did other companies, Kraft sent its products overseas in World War II, shipping four million pounds of cheese each week to feed England's war-torn population. Once the war was over and business went back to normal, Kraft introduced sliced processed cheese (1950) and Cheez Whiz pasteurized processed cheese spread (1953).

In the 1950s and 1960s, Kraft introduced its jellies and preserves (1956), Kraft Jet-puffed marshmallows (1959), Kraft Barbeque Sauce (1960), Light 'N Lively low-fat yogurt and ice milk (1969). The company also introduced a lot of its American-made products in international markets, such as Austrialia, Spain, Ireland, Belgium, Switzerland, and England.

In 1976, Kraftco Corporation became Kraft, Inc., and in 1980, the company merged with Dart Industries, Inc. to form Dart & Kraft, Inc. Then, in 1986, Dart & Kraft, Inc. split to form Premark International, Inc. (which included most of the company's nonfood business) and Kraft, Inc. (which included the Kraft food and Duracell battery businesses, with the latter being sold off in 1988). However, the most important business merger in Kraft's history was when it became part of the Philip Morris Companies, Inc., in 1988, a move that created the world's largest consumer products company. In 1989, Philip Morris combined Kraft, Inc. with General Foods Corporation to make Kraft General Foods, Inc., America's largest food company.

Other Kraft General Foods companies included in this book include Birds Eye, Velveeta, Sealtest, Miracle Whip, Log Cabin, Jell-O, Calumet, Baker's Coconut, Philadelphia Cream Cheese, and Oscar Mayer & Co.

KRAFT

Kraft, Kay Cheese, advertisement from *Saturday Evening Post*, March 24, 1928; shows hostess with tray of cheese sandwiches; full color; excellent condition; $4–7.

LEE LEWIS ICE CREAM

Lee Lewis Ice Cream, round tin sign; 13 inches; red, white, and black; ca. 1920; excellent condition; $175–275.

LITTLETON CREAMERY COMPANY

The Littleton Creamery Company, paperweight; ca. 1900–1920; depicts the company "3 blocks from Colorado's best market" in Denver; 2½ x 4 inches; $50–75.

Kraft, Kay Cheese, advertisement from *Saturday Evening Post*, March 24, 1928; shows hostess with tray of cheese sandwiches; full color; $4–7. *Courtesy of Paper Lady/Bernie and Dolores Fee. Photo by Donald Vogt.*

The Littleton Creamery Company, paperweight, ca. 1900–1920; depicts the company "3 blocks from Colorado's best market" in Denver; 2½ x 4 inches; $50–75. *From the collection of Stuart Kammerman. Photo by David Kammerman.*

MCCORMICK'S

McCormick's Jersey Cream, Cardboard container; great transformable container into child's toy drum enhanced by pictorial image of boy w/drum; drum image is superimposed over advertising; paper label over cardboard; 9¼ inch diameter x 6 inches; good condition, overall soiling, slight creasing and edge chips; $40–100.

MERIT

Merit Separator Co., embossed tip tray; pictures cream separator; 3¼ x 4⅞ inches; excellent condition, minor wear, overall soiling; $75–175.

MISCELLANEOUS

Advertising card; in German; with picture of cream separator and a man and a woman on left and a machine on the right corner; the name "Carl Kratzig" appears on the left bottom; color copy; only one known; original owned by collector; excellent condition; $40–50.

Bottle; marked "Drink Milk/Buy War Bonds"; ca. World War II years; excellent condition; $30–50.

Box; 1 dozen eggs cardboard box; ca. 1940s; excellent condition; $3–6.

Copper ice cream hanging rack; brass and copper with glass insert; for early ice cream parlor; 18 inch diameter x 18 inches; excellent condition; $500–800.

Figural ice cream cone; large, bejeweled, embossed copper figural trade sign; unusual soda fountain item; 12 inch diameter x 33 inches; very good condition, minor dent to top, discoloration to copper, general wear; $700–1,000.

Figural ice cream cones (2); pair of embossed copper 5-cent ice cream displays in diminishing sizes; 6 inch diameter x 13½ inches and 5 inch diameter x 12½ inches; very good/excellent condition, minor age discoloration, overall wear; $300–500.

Dairy Products ■ 163

Glass ice cream cone dispenser; 6½ x 14½ inches; original interior and lid; very good condition, dent in lip top; $150–250.

Ice cream parlor display cabinet; copper, brass, and glass inset; 22 x 25 x 5 inches; excellent condition; $300–500.

Squared ice cream scoop; Automatic Cone Company; rare; marked "ICYPI"; 3½ x 10 x 1 inch; very good condition; $100–200.

PHILADELPHIA CREAM CHEESE
(*see also* "Kraft General Foods")

A dairyman named William Lawrence invented a cream cheese made from cream and milk in 1872. In 1880, a cheese distributor named Reynolds started purchasing Lawrence's supply of cream cheese. At the same time, Lawrence acquired a production facility (the Empire Cheese Company in South Edmeston, New York) and took the Philadelphia Brand trademark.

When the plant was destroyed by fire, the new company, which was the result of a rebuilding of the original Empire Cheese Company, was named the Phenix Cheese Company, unintentionally misspelling the phoenix of mythology. Kraft Cheese Company merged with Phenix Cheese Corporation in 1928 to form Kraft-Phenix Cheese Corporation.

PHILADELPHIA/PHENIX

Phenix Cheese (Philadelphia Cream Cheese), advertisement from *Ladies' Home Journal*, January 1927; depicts different meals made with the cheeses; $4–7.

Phenix Cheese (Philadelphia Cream Cheese); advertisement from *Ladies' Home Journal*, January 1927; depicts different meals made with cheeses; $4–7. *Courtesy of Paper Lady/Bernie and Dolores Fee. Photo by Donald Vogt.*

PRIMROSE

Primrose Ice Cream, die-cut hanging sign; depicts woman on swing eating bowl of ice cream; 39 inches tall; ca. 1915; very good condition; $1,200–1,750.

PURITY

Purity Ice Cream, tin tray; depicts two children with plenty of vanilla and chocolate ice cream in front of them; 1915; 13¼ inches square; very good condition, some soiling, minor chipping; $275–425.

ST. CHARLES

St. Charles Evaporated Cream, cast-iron clock frame; 9 x 15 x 2½ inches; ca. 1890; made in the shape of a standing cow (hole in cow's belly is where clock should have been); excellent condition; $200–350.

SAWYER FARMS

Sawyer Farms Butter, waxed cardboard box; 1 pound; ca. 1940s; excellent condition; $3–6.

SEALTEST
(*see also* "Kraft General Foods")

The Sealtest name first appeared in 1935 as the Sealtest System of Laboratory Protection, National Dairy Product Corporation's system of assuring quality control for its fluid milk and other dairy products. Within a few years, the Sealtest name evolved into a national brand name that replaced hundreds of regional brands acquired by National Dairy Products Corporation in the 1920s and 1930s. Today's Sealtest products include ice cream, frozen yogurt, sherbert, sour cream, cottage cheese, and dips.

SEALTEST

Sealtest Ice Cream, hanging clock; octagon; lights up; company name over 12 ("Southern Dairies"); excellent condition; $250–400.

Sealtest Ice Cream, tin sign; marked "Lake Shore Sealtest Ice Cream" and below with the Sealtest seal; approximately 20 x 30 inches; excellent condition; $130–175.

7-ELEVEN

7-Eleven Ice Cream, paper sign; depicts product and dairy complete with Holsteins; 1958; near-mint condition; $5–20.

SHARPLES

Sharples Separator Co., advertising card; shows cows with mechanical milkers on top and cows with pails under them with words ending in "Dreams Come True"; excellent condition; $20–35.

Sharples Separator Co., advertising card; shows boy, a girl, a separator, and a calf with the words "Who's Afraid?"; color copy; $15–25.

Sharples Separator Co., advertising card; shows farm girl with pail and a separator in the background; the words "The Beauties of the Farm" appear on the bottom of the card; full color; excellent condition; $5–15.

Sharples Separator Co., advertising sewing kit; with picture of a woman sewing little boys' shorts with words "Compliments of The Sharples Separator Co., Westchester, Pa" on top, and "A Stitch in Time—Try a Tubular Now" at the bottom; bright colors; near-mint condition; $25–50.

Sharples Cream Separator, advertising cards; with picture of three boys on farm with words "Preparedness on the farm includes a Sharples Cream Separator" on the bottom of the card; color copy; $10–20.

Sharples Tubular Cream Separator, advertising card; with the agent's name—C. W. Marshall, Smiths Basin, New York; very good condition, small tear in right corner. $10–20.

Sharples Tubular Separator, advertising card; shows one of the others on the left and the Tubular Sharples on the right; bright colors; excellent condition, some wear around edges. $20–50+.

The Sharples Tubular Cheese Separator, advertising card; depicts woman working separator; with the agent's name—C. W. Marshall, Smiths Basin, N.Y."; very good condition, small tear in right corner; $10–20. *Collection of Sam Stephens. Photo by Dawn Reno.*

166 ■ ADVERTISING

Sharples Co., book; with picture of two little girls working the separator and the cows in the background; with words "A Little Helper"; the name "Deere and Webber Co., Minneapolis, Minn." appears on the bottom (Deere and Webber was a distributor for Sharples); 6 x 8¼ inches; bright colors; near-mint condition; 1905; only illustration with the artist style seen in Sharples material; extremely rare; $75–100+. *Collection of Sam Stephens. Photo by Dawn Reno.*

Sharples Separator, calendar; shows Tubular and Jersey cream separators; image of lady with bonnet and white apron standing next to the separator machine with cow looking through the window; 7¼ x 14 inches; very good condition, starts with month of February; $75–150.

P. M. Sharples Co., book; with words "Cream by Machinery—How Fine Butter is Made" together with a description of the celebrated Darlington Farm Herd and diary and the De Laval Cream Separator from the De Laval Separator Co.; printed by the Jersey City Printing Co.; 1884; 5½ x 7¾ inches; excellent condition, minor edge wear, extremely rare; from when Sharples sold De Laval and manufactured in U.S.; $100–200+.

Sharples Co., book; with picture of two little girls working the separator and the cows in the background; with words "A Little Helper"; the name "Deere and Webber Co., Minneapolis, Minn." appears on the bottom (Deere and Webber was a distributor for Sharples); 6 x 8¼ inches; bright colors; near-mint condition; 1905; only illustration with the artist style seen in Sharples material; extremely rare; excellent condition; $75–100+.

Sharples Co., book; with words "Sharples Tubular Cream Separators—The World's Best" on top, picture of machine in room with a cow looking in and a farm couple at a window and words "The Sharples Separator Company" at bottom; 6 x 8¼ inches; bright colors; very rare; ca. 1912; near-mint condition; $35–75.

Sharples Separator Co., letter; dated December 14, 1908; addressed to "Messrs. A. C. Reid and Co., Upperville, Va."; near-mint condition; $5–15.

P. M. Sharples "The Russian Cream Separators," letter; dated F 31, 1895;

addressed to "L. J. Follett and Sons, Adams, Mass"; excellent condition, some smudging (may be original); $10–25.

Sharples Tubular Separator, paper sign; bold promotional poster with great graphics of frustrated farmer and wife dealing with inferior machine, while woman on right side of poster has no such problems with Sharples machine; 42 x 29 inches; very good condition, strong color, some water staining at bottom, soiling primarily on right edge; $300–600.

Sharples, paper sign; milking maid with cows in field; approximately 19 x 12 inches excluding mat and frame; excellent condition, water stain to mat, vague shadow of Sharples image in sky to right; $100–300.

Sharples Separator Co., pinback; full color; 1¼ inch diameter; "The W & H Co. Patented July '84", excellent condition, normal wear around edges; $10–35.

Sharples Tubular Cream Separator, pocket-size mirror; depicts woman using separator with child at her side; 3 x 1¾ inch oval; excellent condition, some rust around mirror edge, some age discoloration on advertising side; $75–175+.

Sharples Co., postcard; in German; with picture and words "Harburg-Hamburg" on left; color copy; only one known; collector has original; $60–75+.

Sharples Tubular Cream Separator, pot and pan scraper; 2½ x approximately 2½ inches; depicts woman climbing steps with cream bucket in hand; ca. 1909; excellent condition, small stain on lower left front side; $75–170.

THOMAS MILLS & BRO.
Thomas Mills & Bro. Ice Cream Mfg. Co., equipment catalog; 1931; near-mint condition; $5–20.

T. S. TOWNSEND CREAMERY CO.
T. S. Townsend Creamery Co., paperweight; ca. 1890–1920; 2½ x 4 inches; excellent condition; $50–75.

VALLEY FARM
Valley Farm's Bing Crosby Ice Cream, cardboard box; 1 pint; has Crosby's picture on front; full color; excellent condition; $20–25.

TUBULAR CREAM SEPARATORS
Tubular Cream Separators, match safe; depicts the cream separator operated by mother and child with cow scene in background; 2 x 7 inches; good condition with some minor scratching and staining; $75–150.

Kraft Velveeta, advertisement from *Ladies' Home Journal*, June 1930; depicts woman dishing out food to her children; $4–7. *Courtesy of Paper Lady/Bernie and Dolores Fee. Photo by Donald Vogt.*

VELVEETA
(*see also* "Kraft General Foods")

Velveeta pasteurized processed cheese spread, introduced by Kraft in 1928, was first mentioned in a *Saturday Evening Post* advertisement during the same year, and was in its first exclusive advertisement in *Good Housekeeping*'s, February 1930 issue. In 1942, the slogan "Eat the Foods That Make America Stronger" began appearing in ads, and twenty years later (1962), the Velveeta oval logo was introduced. In 1986, the American Dairy Association's "Real Seal" appeared on the Velveeta box.

VELVEETA
Kraft Velveeta, advertisement from *Ladies' Home Journal*, June 1930; depicts woman dishing out food to her children; excellent condition; $4–7.

WILLIAM ELLIOT/FIRST NATIONAL STORES
William Elliot/ First National Stores, corrugated paper egg box; ca. 1940s; excellent condition; $3–6.

CHAPTER FIFTEEN
■ DESSERTS ■

DRAKE BAKERIES

In 1888, Newman E. Drake developed a pound cake at home that became so popular with friends and family that, in 1896, he opened Drake Baking, a bakery in which he could make more of his successful pound cakes. Though the company that eventually became Nabisco bought Drake's in 1899, Newman still ran the bakery. His sons formed Drake Brothers Bakery in 1900 and made a slab pound cake in Brooklyn. By 1913, the company had entered the million-dollar-a-year sales bracket.

Devil Dogs were introduced in 1923, and in 1929, Drake's bought the Yankee Cake Co. of Providence, Rhode Island, taking over its popular Yankee Doodles cupcakes. In 1961, the company introduced Ring-Dings, and in 1964, Fruit Doodles.

Newman Drake died in 1930, before the Depression pulled company sales down and prior to Borden's purchasing Drake in 1946. In 1954, the last Drake to work for the bakery, Newman's son, Arthur, retired. Borden sold Drake to Continental Baking in 1986, and in 1989, for the first time in company history, Drake's cakes were distributed on the West Coast.

DRAKE'S

Drake's, plastic head-of-display piece; 23 inches tall; ca. 1992; excellent condition; $100–125.

Drakes, magazine advertisement; for Devil Dogs; ca. 1950s; $4–6.

GORTON'S

Gorton's, paper poster; depicts white woman in hammock being attended by black maid and fanned by black boy; they're surrounded by puddings, pies, and pastries; 26½ x 20½ inches; good/very good condition, vertical crease borders trimmed, some edge tears, slight wear to clay-coated stock; $250–500.

JELL-O
(*see also* "Kraft General Foods" in Dairy Products chapter)
Jell-O Brand Gelatin—one of the best-known American brand

Drake's, plastic head-of-display piece; 23 inches tall; ca. 1992; $100–125. *Courtesy of Neil and Nancy Berliner. Photo by Donald Vogt.*

names—was coined by the maker's wife, May Davis Wait. May's husband, Pearl B. Wait, a cough medicine manufacturer, adapted a version of Peter Cooper's patented gelatin dessert in 1895. Wait did not have much success with his new product and, in 1899, he sold the Jell-O business to his neighbor, Orator Francis Woodward.

Woodward didn't have much luck with Jell-O either, and tried unsuccessfully to sell the whole business for $35. When the buyer refused, Woodward had no choice but to keep the dessert and work on improving it. In 1902, he was pleasantly surprised when Jell-O finally caught on with the public. By 1902, sales were up to a quarter of a million dollars, and by 1906, sales reached just under one million.

Woodward began advertising Jell-O Brand Gelatin in 1902, claiming the product was "America's most famous dessert." In 1904, the Jell-O Girl debuted. She appeared on packages of Jell-O until 1950. In real life, the child was Elizabeth King, the English daughter of Franklin King, an artist who worked for the advertising agency for Jell-O Brand Gelatin. In 1908, the creator of Kewpie dolls, Rose O'Neill, started to draw the Jell-O Girl for print ads and store displays. It is that drawing that remained part of the package's design.

The manufacturers of Jell-O began distributing recipe books around 1904, and some of them were illustrated by famous artists such as Norman Rockwell and Maxfield Parrish. F. L. Baum (*The Wizard of Oz*) wrote books featuring Jell-O to appeal to children.

In 1925, the Jell-O Company was acquired by the Postum Cereal Company of Battle Creek, Michican. Postum eventually grew into General Foods Corporation.

JELL-O

Jell-O; advertisement; designed by Maxfield Parrish; depicts woman serving tea in kettle to husband and daughter seated at table; framed; good color; excellent condition; $60–90.

Jell-O, advertisement; designed by Maxfield Parrish; "Polly Put the Kettle on, We'll All Make Jell-O"; copyrighted by Genesee Food Co., 1923; framed; excellent condition; $50–100.

Jell-O, booklet; illustrated by Maxfield Parrish on front and back; 1920s–1930s; excellent condition; $50–85.

Jell-O, magazine advertisement; 1955; nursery rhyme series—"Jack Be Nimble, Jack Be Quick"; full color; excellent condition; $8–10.

Jell-O, magazine advertisement; 1956; nursery rhyme series—"Pat-a-Cake, Pat-a-Cake"; full color; excellent condition; $8–10.

Jell-O, magazine advertisement; 1957; nursery rhyme series—"Baa Baa Black Sheep"; full color; excellent condition; $8–10.

Jell-O, recipe booklet; designed by Maxfield Parrish; printed in 1924 by Genesee Food Co.; color covers front and back; very good condition; $20–45.

Jell-O recipe booklet; depicts girl with ice cream on cover, copyright 1925 by the Jell-O Co., Inc.; excellent condition; $18–24.

Jell-O, recipe booklet; girl with fruit basket; copyright 1920 by the Genesee Pure Food Company; excellent condition; $20–25.

Jell-O, Sebastian Miniatures figurine; made in Marblehead, Massachusetts; Scottish girl; ca. 1950s; excellent condition; $35–75.

Jell-O, Sebastian Miniatures figurine; made in Marblehead, Massachusetts; man with cookbook; ca. 1950s; excellent condition; $35–75.

Jell-O, Sebastian Miniatures figurines; made in Marblehead, Massachusetts; (left) man with cookbook, $35–75; (right) Scottish girl, $35–75. *Courtesy of Neil and Nancy Berliner. Photo by Donald Vogt.*

Jell-O, tin sign; reproduction; 16 x 11½ inches; copy of Maxfield Parrish picture; depicts family at fireplace; $15 retail. *Courtesy of Doc Davis/Antique-Alike. Photo by Donald Vogt.*

Jell-O, tin sign; reproduction; 16 x 11½ inches; copy of Maxfield Parrish picture; depicts family at fireplace; new/reproduction condition; $15 retail.

KNOX
Knox Unflavored Gelatin, all-paper container; 1 ounce; ca. 1950s; very good condition; $15–18.

MILLINS
Millins Taystee Lemon Flavored Dessert, paper and tin container; 8 ounces; very good condition; $25–28.

WARD'S
Ward's Cake, tin display box; classic country store display bin having four tin signs inserted with glass display area; 12¾ x 20½ x 17 inches; fair/good condition, some fading, spotting, general overall wear; $1,250–2,000.

CHAPTER SIXTEEN
■ DYES ■

DIAMOND DYES

This company started in Burlington, Vermont, in 1872. Owners Edward Wells, W. J. Van Patten, and A. E. Richardson, wholesale druggists, were joined in 1873 by Henry Wells and in 1881 by F. H. Wells.

The company did extensive advertising to promote its dyes, as well as other products such as Kidney-Wort (a medicinal remedy), Lactated Food, and Paine's Celery Compound. In fact, by 1881 their advertising budget totaled $150,000 a year.

In 1881, the druggists started Diamond Dyes and began making thirty-six different colors of dye that could be used for fabrics as well as feathers. Soon, they sold their product worldwide.

The cabinets were defined and illustrated in the October/November 1992 issue of *Tin Type* magazine, published by the Tin Container Collectors Association. Listed are the "Red Headed Fairy with Wand" (difficult to find), "Blonde Fairy" (similar to Red-Headed, same dimensions and markings), "Court Jester," "Cycles of Life" or "Evolution of Woman," several different examples of "Washer Woman," "Children with Balloon," "Maypole," "Governess," and "Children Skipping Rope." The colorful cabinets are highly collectible and desirable, but the company also made other forms of advertising, including a lithograph by Bessie Pease Guttman, sample cards, printed catalogs, almanacs, and even a rare hanging store cardboard parrot.

The company closed in 1943.

DIAMOND DYES

Diamond Dyes, cabinet; embossed tin children with balloons; 15 x 24½ x 9 inches; excellent condition, strong color, minor denting, slight scratches and chipping to background; $500–800.

Diamond Dyes, cabinet; children skipping rope on embossed tin sign on both sides of this double-doored cabinet; 15 x 24½ x 8½ inches; one side is in good condition, some denting, chipping, minor spotting, fading of color, some creasing; other side is poor, overall loss of color, chipping, fading; $500–800.

Diamond Dyes, cabinet; girls with ribbons on embossed tin front; 23 x 30 x 10 inches; fair/good condition, tin front has overall rust specks, some minor denting and chipping; $600–800.

Diamond Dyes, die-cut cardboard hanging sign; two pieces; depicts the rare parrot; 16 inches tall; very good condition; $800–1,300.

Diamond Dyes, lithographed tin sign; illustrated by Bessie Pease Guttman; titled "A Busy Day in Dollville"; depicts blond little girl dying clothes for her dolls; 25¾ x 17¼ inches; very good condition; $1,500–3,000.

GLOBE DYES

Globe Dyes, cabinet; paper color swatched insert on wooden case; 16 x 24½ x 9½ inches; good condition, replaced back, gallery top missing, some loss of color patches; $100–300.

HANDY

Handy Dyes, paper-labeled sign; depicts cherubs carrying colored cloths; 16¾ x 11½ inches; excellent condition; $35–95.

HAZARD'S

Hazard's, paper sign; woman looking at and using ultramarine blue for dying clothing and draperies; approximately 18 x 22 inches; good condition, borders trimmed, overall soiling; $100–300.

PEERLESS

Peerless Dyes, cabinet; lithograph on tin; wood trim; 25½ x 19 x 10 inches; front measures 20 x 14 inches; lithograph done by Harris, Campbell & Harris, Lith., New York; ca. 1888; depicts pretty Gypsy woman in center and camel caravan at bottom; rare; very good condition; $2,000–2,800.

Peerless Dyes, wood cabinet ; lithograph on tin; 30¾ x 23 x 10½ inches; ca. 1890; rare; lithograph is scene of train and camels; cabinet has sliding doors and pigeon-holed interior, as well as original package of dyes; good/very good condition; $5,000–8,500.

Peerless Dyes, cabinet; tin front; depicts train and camel caravan; rare; 23 x 31 x 10½ inches; fair condition; $1,500–3,000.

Peerless Dyes, cabinet; tin front; depicts woman with peacock and butterflies; 18 x 25½ x 10 inches; tin front is 14 x 20 inches; rare; fair condition, missing rear doors; $600–850.

PERFECTION
Perfection Dyes, sign; lithograph on tin; originally made for a small dye cabinet; 13¼ x 9¼ inches; made by "F. Tuckfarber Co., Cin., O."; ca. 1885; near-mint condition; $300–600.

PUTNAM
Putnam Dyes, metal cabinet; 18¾ x 7¾ x 15 inches; fair condition, faded, rust spotting and some color loss; $50–100.

Putnam Dyes, metal cabinet; 19¼ x 5¾ x 15 inches; fair/good condition, missing back cover; $50–100.

Putnam Dyes, tin cabinet; trademarked image of Washington and British; interior contains multiple packages of product; 18¾ x 14½ x 7¾ inches; fair/good condition, slight overall fade, general wear, scratches and denting; $75–125.

Putnam Dyes, tin display unit; chromo design on front includes trademark general leading charge; interior is cubbyholed and still full of dyes; excellent condition; 6 x 15 x 11 inches; $265–300.

SAWYER'S CRYSTAL BLUE
Sawyer's Crystal Blue Dyes, paper sign; made by "H. Sawyer, Boston, Massachusetts"; depicts elaborately dressed woman as the admiral of the fleet; she holds boxes of blue dye; 17½ x 22 inches; good condition, borders trimmed; vertical tears, general overall wear to coated surface, soiling; $275–475.

TURKISH
Turkish Dyes, display cabinet; paper front; camel caravan beneath Turkish shield promoting these dyes; 23 x 34 x 11 inches; good overall condition, general soiling, cabinet overpainted; $500–800.

CHAPTER SEVENTEEN
■ FARM EQUIPMENT ■

ADRIANCE BUCKEYE
Adriance Buckeye Farm Machinery, paper poster; barefoot farm girl with inserts of horse-drawn farm equipment; 1897; 20½ x 28 inches; good condition, some creasing, wrinkling, slight chipping; $300–500.

Adriance Buckeye Farm Machinery, paper poster; panoramic view of Hudson River with paddle wheelers; vignettes of scenes of horse-drawn equipment; 22 x 28 inches; excluding frame; very good condition, some spotting; $150–350.

AMERICAN STEEL FARM FENCES
American Steel Farm Fences, tin match holder; depicts wire fence "Made in All Heights"; 3½ x 5 x 1¼ inches; good condition; color fading and overall scratches; $25–100.

AUBURN WAGON CO.
Auburn Wagon, paper sign; amusing scene of husband and wife on Auburn wagon mistakenly outpacing racing trotters; lettering says "The Auburn Takes the Lead"; 26 x 19¾ inches; very good condition, paper tear near top border, slight tears in upper border, slight abrasion at middle bottom of picture with in-painting; $200–400.

CASE TRACTORS
Case Tractors, embossed tin sign; depicts steam threshing machine; printed by Tuscarora Advertising Company; 19½ x 13½ inches; excluding frame; very good condition, overall darkening of color, minor denting, some soiling; $2,500–3,500.

Case Tractors, tin sign; 11½ x 17 inches; depicts the tractor in full color; reproduction; $15 retail.

FARM EQUIPMENT ■ 177

DAFT BROS.
Daft Bros., brass sign; hay and grain display building sign; 28 x 28 inches; good condition; $175–350.

JOHN DEERE
Originally a Vermont blacksmith, John Deere moved to Grand Detour, Illinois, in 1836, He designed a new, more efficient plow blade in the late 1830s and had sold hundreds of them by 1846. His steel-blade plow was so popular that he soon started making other types of farm equipment. The green-painted equipment with the leaping stag trademark (registered in 1876) can still be seen in any rural American area today.

The company maintains offices in Moline, Illinois, where John Deere moved in 1848.

JOHN DEERE
John Deere, iron holder; hangs on wall with pocket for papers or whatever; 16 x 11 inches; green and yellow; reproduction; $25 retail.

John Deere, tin sign; depicts the Deere tractor; caption reads "Quality... for over 100 years"; reproduction; 12 x 16 inches; $15 retail.

John Deere, tin sign; green and yellow; depicts two-cylinder tractor; reproduction; 11 x 15 inches; $15 retail.

John Deere, tin sign; green and yellow; depicts the Deere deer; reproduction; 12 x 15 inches; $15 retail.

DEERING
Deering, paper poster; depicts a whole town out to see a man's new horse-drawn grass-cutting machine; two small circular inserts of other mowing equipment; colorful; printed by the Milwaukee Litho Company; 28½ x 22½ inches excluding mat and frame; excellent condition; $2,250–3,250.

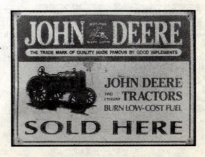

John Deere, tin sign; green and yellow; depicts two-cylinder tractor; reproduction; 11 x 15 inches; $15 retail. *Courtesy of Doc Davis/Antique-Alike. Photo by Donald Vogt.*

GIBBS

Gibbs Plows, embossed tin sign; large factory scene with store insert, trains in foreground, and billowing factory chimneys; 38 x 25½ inches; very good condition, some overall scratching, primarily in border; $100–250.

GOOD ROADS

Good Roads Farm Machinery, paper sign; colorful factory scene with horse-drawn and steam equipment on street 11½ x 11¾ inches excluding mat and frame; excellent condition, some creasing, colors bright; $175–275.

HAPGOOD'S

Hapgood's Wooden Wagon, sign; shadowed lettering on green background; 37½ x 14 inches; good condition, some overall paint loss primarily on background green; $25–100.

HARTLEY GRAIN CO.

The Hartley Grain Co., paperweight; 1901; depicts the grain company's buildings 2½ x 4 inches; excellent condition; $50–75.

J. I. CASE THRESHING MACHINE CO.

J. I. Case Threshing Machine Co., embossed tin sign; wood frame; 13¾ x 20 inches; marked "The Tuscarora Adv. Co."; ca. 1880–1890; deeply embossed and colorful image of the threshing machine; sign was voted Best of Show at 1989 convention; only three known; excellent condition; $3,000–5,000.

KALAMAZOO

Kalamazoo, paper sign; depicts half-moon insert image of farmer with horse-drawn harrowing equipment; printed by Kreds Litho Company;

The Hartley Grain Co., paperweight; 1901; depicts the grain company's buildings; 2½ x 4 inches; $50–75. *From the collection of Stuart Kammerman. Photo by David Kammerman.*

FARM EQUIPMENT   ■ 179

Pacific Grain Co., paperweight; depicts company's buildings in Portland, Oregon; ca. 1900–1930; 2½ x 4 inches; $35–50. *From the collection of Stuart Kammerman. Photo by David Kammerman.*

28 x 22 inches excluding frame; excellent/near-mint condition; $1,500–3,000.

MCCORMICK REAPER

McCormick Reaper, paper poster; "Testing of the first reaping machine near Steele's Tavern, Va."; 35 x 24 inches excluding frame; very good condition, some creasing, overall soiling, minor staining; $475–675.

NATIONAL HAY RAKE

National Hay Rake, paper sign; graphics of hay rake machine; printed by Milton Bradley Co. Lith.; approximately 15½ x 12½ inches excluding mat and frame; overall size 21 x 17 inches; very good condition; $100–250.

OLIVER PLOWS

Oliver Plows, embossed tin sign; 27½ x 10 inches excluding frame; very good condition, minor denting, overall wear; $150–300.

PACIFIC GRAIN CO.

Pacific Grain Co., paperweight; depicts company's buildings in Portland, Oregon; ca. 1900–1930; 2½ x 4 inches; very good condition; $35–50.

SANDWICH MANUFACTURING COMPANY

Sandwich Manufacturing Company, hay press, paper sign; made by "Sandwich Manufacturing Company, Sandwich, Illinois"; illustrates the "new way" large bale hay press; approximately 24 x 18 inches excluding mat and frame; overall 29 x 23 inches; good condition; $125–250.

180 ■ ADVERTISING

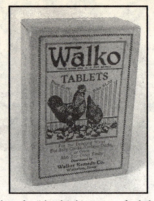

Walko Tablets, box; for "the drinking water for baby chicks, turkeys, ducks or geese, also for older fowls"; ca. 1930s; excellent condition; $6–8. *Courtesy of Dawn and Bob Reno. Photo by Donald Vogt.*

WALKO

Walko Tablets, box; for "the drinking water for baby chicks, turkeys, ducks or geese, also for older fowls"; ca. 1930s; excellent condition; $6–8.

WOOD, TABER & MORSE

Wood, Taber & Morse's Steam Engine Works, paper poster; depicts horse-drawn steam farm equipment including vignettes with stationary engines; early leafed and wooded borders; colorful; printed by Cosack & Co.; 28 x 22 inches; near-mint condition; $4,000–7,000.

CHAPTER EIGHTEEN
■ FRUITS, VEGETABLES ■

BIRDS EYE

(*see also* "Kraft General Foods" in Dairy Products chapter)

Clarence Birdseye discovered that he could freeze/preserve vegetables by dropping them in barrels of freezing water when he was living in Labrador in the winder of 1916. He worked on a fish and wildlife survey there for the United States government and had grown tired of seeing his wife and baby go without fresh foods. Soon, he not only froze the vegetables that came in on the supply ship but fish and caribou meat as well.

Birdseye took his new "quick frozen" invention back to New York, planning to get rich, but his company, Birdseye Seafoods, lasted only a couple of months. Determined, he moved to a laboratory-type setting on the Fort Wharf in Gloucester, Massachusetts. Marjorie Merriweather Post, head of the Postum Company (which eventually became General Foods), became one of his supporters.

In 1929, General Foods bought Birdseye's patents and trademarks for $22 million.

Birdseye died in 1951, claiming never to have minded when his name was chopped in half to make the now-famous trademark.

BIRDS EYE

Birds Eye, advertisement; features frozen pear; full color; ca. 1940s; excellent condition; $4–6.

Birds Eye, advertisement; features woman stocking freezer with frozen Birdseye products; ca. 1950s; excellent condition; $4–6.

Birds Eye, Mike, Merry, and Minx cloth cut-out dolls; used to promote Birdseye frozen orange juice; ca. 1950s; $15–25 each.

CALIFORNIA RAISINS

California Raisins, box; pictures cowboy with lasso on horseback on interior label; California packer; unusual 20 x 9 x 2½ inches; (box); 8 x 17 inches (label); good, original condition (box); fair/good condition (label);

large vertical stain, some other generalized staining with creases and edge losses to paper; $50–150.

California Raisins, figurines; raisinlike stars of television commercial; purple in color; one wears sunglasses; rubber and plastic; contemporary; $8–15 each.

CHIQUITA BRAND BANANAS
(see also "United Fruit and Vegetable Association")

The United Fruit Company originally produced Chiquita Bananas and hired two songwriters (Len MacKenzie and Garth Montgomery) to produce a jingle to advertise the bananas in 1944.

> I'm Chiquita Banana and I've come to say
> Bananas have to ripen in a certain way . . .
> Bananas like the climate of the very, very
>   tropical equator
> So you should never put bananas in the
>   refrigerator . . .

Unlike the copyrighted trademarks, the calypso-oriented blue seal did not appear until *after* the song.

In 1970, United Fruit changed its marketing subsidiary's name to Chiquita Brands, Inc.

Various women have been the Chiquita Banana Girl. The first was singer Patti Clayton, then came Elsa Miranda, a Puerto Rican. The Chiquita girls starred on radio, with the Boston Symphony, in movies, commercials, and television.

CHIQUITA

Chiquita Bananas, rubber doll squeak toy; 1950s premium; excellent condition; $15–25.

Chiquita Bananas, cloth doll; 16 inches; wears red dress, hat, and ballerina shoes; marked with blue trademark on dress; 1974; excellent condition; $10–20.

CAPE COD CRANBERRIES

Cape Cod Cranberries, boxes; 1 pound; full-color decoration on front shows cranberries and map of Massachusetts (Cape Cod); very good condition; $15–22 each.

FRUITS, VEGETABLES ■ 183

Defender Brand Tomatoes, can label, one side depicts red tomato, the other is a sailboat on the sea; ca. 1920s; 9 x 3¼ inches; $2–4. *Courtesy of Cerebro Lithographs. Photo by Dawn Reno.*

DEFENDER BRAND
Defender Brand Tomatoes, can label; one side depicts red tomato, the other is a sailboat on the sea; ca. 1920s; 9 x 3¼ inches; mint condition; $2–4.

DEKALB CORN
DeKalb Corn, wooden sign; depicts flying corn; 17 x 32 inches; ca. 1940s; very good condition; $45–65.

EXETER LILY
Exeter Lily, grapes label; depicts one lily; made in Exeter, California; mint condition; $3–5.

FRUITS OF CALIFORNIA
Fruits of California, lithograph on heavy paper; 13¼ x 10 inches; printed by Bosqui Engraving & Printing Co., S.F.; depicts patriotic eagle trying to steal canned fruit from bears; colorful; mint condition; $1,000–1,500.

KILTIE
Kiltie, grapefruit label; depicts serving of grapefruit in plaid; from Corona, California; mint condition; $2–4.

KING'S CADETS
King's Cadets, asparagus label; depicts marching cadets; from Clarksburg, California; mint condition; $3–5.

KING PELICAN
King Pelican Lettuce, tin sign; reproduction; depicts green pelican with crown on his head; approximately 13 x 16 inches; $15 retail.

184 ■ ADVERTISING

King Pelican Lettuce, tin sign; reproduction; depicts green pelican with crown on his head; approximately 13 x 16 inches; $15 retail. *Courtesy of Doc Davis/Antique-Alike. Photo by Donald Vogt.*

Kraft, vinyl salad figure, 6 inches, ca. 1970s, $150–200; cameraman, from "Kraft Television Theater," 4 inches, ca. 1950s, $125–200. *Courtesy of Neil and Nancy Berliner. Photo by Donald Vogt.*

KRAFT

(*see also* "Kraft General Foods" in Dairy Products chapter)

Kraft, cameraman; from "Kraft Television Theatre"; 4 inches; ca. 1950s; very good condition; $125–200.

Kraft, vinyl salad figure; 6 inches; ca. 1970s; very good condition; $150–200.

LIBBY'S

Libby's, advertisement from *Saturday Evening Post*; 1928; depicts white asparagus; excellent condition; $15–20.

MISCELLANEOUS

Apple label, baby on red background; made in Seattle, Washington; mint condition; $3–5.

Libby's, advertisement from *Saturday Evening Post*, 1928; depicts white asparagus; $15–20. *Courtesy of Lester Morris. Photo by Donald Vogt.*

Lemon label; Arab on horse, made in San Dimas, California; mint condition; $40–60.

Melon label; "Buxom"; depicts 1940s girlie art; made in Firebraugh, California; mint condition; $6–10.

Orange label; "Bronco"; depicts cowboy on horse; made in Redlands, California; mint condition; $5–8.

Orange label; "California Dream"; depicts two peacocks and castle; made in Placentia, California; mint condition; $30–40.

Orange label; "Golden Gate"; depicts oranges and vase; from Lemon Cove, California; mint condition; $20–25.

Orange label; "Hummingbird"; depicts oranges and hummingbird; from Santa Susana, California; mint condition; $40–50.

Pear label; "Blazing Star"; depicts framed flower; from Kelseyville, California; mint condition; $3–5.

Pear label; "Lake Wenatchee"; depicts cabin and lake; from Cashmere, California; mint condition; $2–4.

Tomato label; "Texas"; depicts Texan in hat; made in Weslaco, California; mint condition; $2–4.

Vegetable label; "Challenger"; depicts cowboy on Bronco; made in Guadalupe; mint condition; $2–4.

MORNING CHEER
Morning Cheer, lemon label; depicts lemons and mountains; from Porterville, California; mint condition; $3–5.

NUCHIEF
NuChief, apple label; depicts Indian boy and apple; from Wenatchee, California; mint condition; $4–6.

ORE-IDA FROZEN POTATOES
(*see* "Heinz" in Condiments/Spices chapter)

PURE GOLD
Pure Gold California Oranges, Lemons, Grapefruits; cardboard stand-up sign; depicts baby in diaper crawling, wears hat with product name on it; 16¼ inches tall; very good condition; $400–600.

SHAKER

(*see also* "Shaker" in Gardening Supplies chapter)

Shaker, applesauce firkin, manufactured by the Canterbury Shakers; East Canterbury, New Hampshire (applesauce was one of the Shakers's most popular products, put up by all of their communities); ca. 1900–1910; very good condition; $1,200–1,400.

SQUAW BRAND

Squaw Brand Early June Peas, can label; distributed by Centerville Canning Co.; Centerville, Maryland; peas on one side, squaw with papoose on the other; 11 x 4¼ inches; ca. 1920s; mint condition; $2–4.

SUNKIST

(*see also* "R. J. Reynolds Tobacco Company" in the Tobacco chapter)

Sunkist Growers annually spends $15 million to advertise its fresh fruit. Seventy-six percent of its advertising budget is spent on various forms of television advertising, especially for the summer season. It also promotes the Sunkist Fiesta Bowl on network television in January and produces and sponsors a half-hour cable program on ESPN sports cable network called "Sunkist Kids," as well as airing "Sunkist Classic" commercials on the Nickelodeon cable channel.

Shaker, applesauce firkin; manufactured by the Canterbury Shakers; East Canterbury, New Hampshire; (applesauce was one of the Shakers' most popular products, put up by all of their communities); ca. 1900–1910; $1,200–1,400. *Courtesy of Dr. M. Stephen Miller. Photo by Dr. M. Stephen Miller.*

FRUITS, VEGETABLES ■ 187

Squaw Brand Early June Peas, can label, distributed by Centerville Canning Co.; Centerville, Maryland; peas on one side, squaw with papoose on the other; 11 x 4¼ inches; ca. 1920s; $2–4. *Courtesy of Cerebro Lithographs. Photo by Dawn Reno.*

Sunkist products have advertised since 1908, and the company (Sunkist Growers, Inc.) is headquartered in Sherman Oaks, California.

SUNKIST
Sunkist, milk glass reamer; excellent condition; $8–15.

SYRUP OF FIGS
Syrup of Figs, self-framed celluloid sign; image of woman reaching for figs; unusually large; 7¾ x 11 inches; excellent condition, slight overall soiling; $200–400.

Syrup of Figs, paper poster; large unusual California company multi-sheet billboard depicting woman picking figs by Pacific ocean; bold image and vivid colors; 80½ x 52 inches excluding oversized linen borders; good/very good condition, backed on linen, some inpainting primarily to background; $2,000–4,000.

UNITED FRESH FRUIT AND VEGETABLE ASSOCIATION
The United Fresh Fruit and Vegetable Association promotes its healthy products with a program originally called "Fresh for Health." The Fresh Approach Program was the nation's only generic promotional program designed to advertise the different flavors, colors, excitement, and nutritional value of all fresh fruits and vegetables and has been supported through voluntary investments since it began in 1953. A recent offshoot of the campaign includes a point-of-purchase video series called "Fresh Tip Tapes." The association has also initiated a program designed specifically for food editors who work in the industry.

The Fresh Approach has been supported for more than forty years by the government and reports are produced yearly to support nutritional values, offering customers dietary guidelines, new cooking ideas, produce industry news, agricultural trends, news about new produce varieties, and other educational materials.

June has been designated National Fresh Fruit and Vegetable Month because that is the time of year when most fruits and vegetables are at their peak. The event is promoted through commercials, point-of-sale advertising, and articles in major publications throughout the United States.

There are hundreds of commissions, growing associations that focus on particular types of fruits and vegetables such as apples, apricots, artichokes, asparagus, avocados, bananas, blueberries, broccoli, celery, cherries, citrus, corn, cranberries, dates, dried fruits, grapes, herbs, kiwifruit, lettuce, mushrooms, nectarines, nuts, onions, papayas, peaches, pears, pineapples, plums, prunes, potatoes, specialties, strawberries, sweet potatoes, tomatoes, watermelon, and other miscellaneous fruits and vegetables. For a complete list, contact the United Fresh Fruit and Vegetable Association, 727 North Washington Street, Alexandria, VA 22314-1977.

WAYNE'S

Wayne's, cans; full of tomatoes and wax beans; full-color lithographed labels; near-mint condition; $10–15 each.

WINCHESTER POTATOES

Winchester Potatoes, burlap sack; three-color overprint of Conestoga wagon with Winchester rifle superimposed in red, yellow, and blue on this Washington State potato sack; 22 x 36 inches; very good condition, some dirt discolorations and mildew spotting; $10–50.

CHAPTER NINETEEN
■ GARDENING SUPPLIES ■

DIXIE BOY
Dixie Boy Vegetable Seeds, tin sign; full color; depicts black boy sitting on log eating watermelon; reproduction; 11 x 16 inches; $15 retail.

DUNLAP'S SEEDS
Dunlap's Seeds, paper poster; image of child holding large cabbage and surrounded by the vegetables produced from this New Hampshire company's seeds; lithographed by J. Ottmann; 16 x 23½ inches; excluding mat and frame; very good/excellent condition; tear left side, colors bright; $475–675.

D. M. FERRY & CO.
D. M. Ferry & Co. Seeds, reproduction of old tin sign; features abundant crop; 11 x 15 inches; new/reproduction condition; $12.

Ferry Seeds, advertisement; full sheet; "Peter Piper Picked a Peck of Peppers"; Maxfield Parrish illustration; two colors; excellent condition; $45–65.

Ferry Seeds, advertising print; illustrated by Maxfield Parrish; depicts Peter Piper; great color quality; very good condition; $40–75.

GRIFFITH & BOYD CO.
Griffith & Boyd Co. Fertilizers, paper sign; fur-wrapped pretty girl holding snowball; appears to be calendar top; 15 x 19½ inches excluding mat and frame; overall 20 x 24½ inches; excellent condition, slight wear; $200–400.

Griffith & Boyd Co. Fertilizers, paper poster; stock image of Asti girl (calendar top); approximately 15 x 19 inches excluding mat and frame; overall 20 x 24¼ inches; very good/excellent condition, minor creasing; $150–300.

LAKE SHORE
Lake Shore Seed Co. of Dunkirk, New York; paper seed packages;

190 ■ ADVERTISING

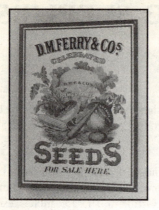

D. M. Ferry & Co. Seeds, reproduction of old tin sign; features abundant crop; 11 x 15 inches; new/reproduction condition; $12. *Courtesy of and photo by Castle Antiques & Reproductions.*

chromolithograph; late 1940s–early 1950s; very good condition; $8–10 per pack.

MANDEVILLE & KING

Mandeville & King Superior Flower Seeds, box; inside cover label depicts salpiglossis flowers; full color; lists types of seeds on right side of cover label; 12 x 9 x 3 inches; refinished; ca. 1920s; $100–125.

NEW ENGLAND FERTILIZER

New England Fertilizer, 1925 calendar; farm scene; entire calendar pad intact; near-mint condition; $10–30.

RICE'S SEEDS

Rice Seeds, advertisement; muskmelon seeds; color lithographed; ca. late 1800s; good condition; $50–75.

Rice's Seeds, advertising card; printed in blue, red, and black on gray stock; printed by Cosack & Co., Buffalo & Chicago; ca. 1900; original black wood frame; frame imprinted with "Cambridge Valley Seed Gardens, New York"; shows man trying to lift cabbage grown with Rice's Seeds; very good condition; $55–95.

Rice's Seeds, paper poster; depicts happy man holding giant cabbage; "The true early winningstadt"; early poster printed by Cosack & Co.; approximately 20 x 27 inches excluding mat and frame; excellent condition; $700–1,000.

Rice's Seeds, sign; printed by Cosack Co., Buffalo & Chicago; ca. 1900; advertises "Jerome B. Rice's True Early Winningstadt, The Best

Cabbage in the World"; depicts man trying to lift huge cabbage from the ground; framed; 15 x 11 inches; excellent condition; $50–100.

SHAKER

The Shaker community was one of the first religious sects to support itself by selling items it produced. It was also one of the first organizations to effectively advertise those products, and labels, containers, and ads that were used to sell Shaker-made products are in much demand.

Shakers used many different styles of text, illustration, and size of product wrappers, according to the item. Text on an herb wrapper or cloak display card could be short in order to call the customer's attention to the product for sale. However, other items needed longer text in order to persuade the customer that the Shaker version of the product was the only one they should purchase.

Some labels are very colorful (such as the "Lemon Syrup" broadside and most seed packages), and often the typeface will help to identify the date of a piece. The more ornate styles date after 1840, products of commercial presses. Around the turn of the century simpler type was used; spare, modern type was developed during the Arts and Crafts movement. Before the 1830s, printing shops run by the Shakers themselves provided simple letterpress broadsides, seed envelopes, herb wrappers, and labels. However, after that time, the Shaker community farmed the printing out to commercial printers.

Although the Shakers did endeavor to advertise their products diversely, the wording on their packages was not as overblown as that advertising their "worldly" counterparts. While Shaker seeds might be described as "splendid seeds," the ones sold by commercial growers would be called "the world's finest."

The words "genuine Shaker" began to appear after about 1870 (see *A Century of Shaker Ephemera* by Dr. M. Stephen Miller, published by Dr. M. Stephen Miller, Six Park Place, New Britain, CT 06052), when imitations of Shaker furniture began to come onto the market. Often the label also included the name of the maker or his or her initials as an "assurance of quality" (again, see *A Century of Shaker Ephemera*). Some of these highly regarded individuals included: Nathaniel Draper

(N.D.) from Enfield, New Hampshire; Francis Winkley (F.W.) from Canterbury, New Hampshire; David Meacham (D.M.) from New Lebanon and Watervliet, New York; and Daniel Goodrich (D.G.) from Hancock, Massachusetts.

The Shakers' industries survived during the years between the Civil War and the beginning of the new century through their genius for organization, but they never succumbed to the temptation of letting their quality suffer by mass-producing their items. They continued to hand-produce their products and gave the customers quality, fairness, and honest value.

The first Shaker garden seeds were produced in New Lebanon, New York, as early as 1789. It was the first major industry for the group and within a little more than a decade all the eastern societies were raising and selling seeds. They were the first to sell seeds in packages and the industry was active until the 1890s.

At first, the envelopes were printed on community letterpresses, but beginning in 1836 at New Lebanon, New York, gardeners' manuals were commercially printed and sold for six cents each. Other ephemera related to the seed industry was also printed commercially throughout the 1890s.

The Shakers began to sell food products in New Lebanon, New York, in 1828, when they began their dried sweet corn industry, they continually produced until about 1910. Sometimes business was so good for the Shaker community that they had to buy corn from "worldly" farms.

Other communities started producing certain foods at the same time as New Lebanon. For instance, Sabbathday Lake Shakers produced pickles and sold their goods to Edward D. Pettengill of Portland, Maine, who opened a retail grocery store in 1867. Pickles weren't the only thing the Shakers supplied for Pettengill—they also made catsup, horseradish, and apple cider. The Pettengill Company grew, but changed its name twice during its twenty-seven-year history (from 1880 to 1892 it was called E. D. Pettengill & Co.; from 1893 to 1904 it was E. D. Pettengill Co.; and from 1905 to 1908 the company was E. D. Pettengill Sons Co.).

Some of the other food products made by the Shakers included applesauce, fresh produce (such as apples, peaches, pears, cherries, tomatoes, and quinces), vegetables, butter, cheeses, jellies, preserves, and marmalades. Surprisingly, they also made at least fourteen types of wine, and distilled and marketed harder spirits as well.

One of the best-known Shaker cottage industries was the medicinal herb industry, which began in New Lebanon, New York, early in the nineteenth century. By the 1820s, printed labels and catalogs appeared and by mid-century the community was producing "between three and four tons of plant extracts annually" (see *A Century of Shaker Ephemera*). The industry prospered as the nation grew and the people became more aware of personal health and home remedies.

Large packages of dried herbs were sold by the brick, wrapped in printed papers "which contained the common name, Latin name and community or origin"; other preparations were sold in glass bottles and vials, ceramic jars, cardboard boxes, and tin or cardboard cylindrical containers (see *A Century of Shaker Ephemera*).

Some of the Shakers known to produce items in this category were: Thomas J. Corbett (1780–1857), a degreed doctor responsible for the following preparations: Compound Syrup of Sarsaparilla, Compound of Wild Cherry Pectoral Syrup, Vegetable Family Pills, and Dyspepsia Cure; and James V. Calver (1839–1913), a dentist who was responsible for Shaker Tooth-Ache Pellets (and who really wasn't part of the Shaker community when be began producing the pellets, though his sister—whose face he used as his trademark—was).

Other items the Shakers produced and sold to consumers include the Improved Washing Machine, women's cloaks, and poplarware.

SHAKER

Shaker, almanacs; issued annually to advertise the medicines the Shakers made for a "worldly" wholesaler, A. J. White; ca. 1880–1898; very good condition; $75–125.

Shaker, seed box; such boxes were filled with seed envelopes each spring and left with merchants on a commission basis; ca. 1860–1890; very good condition; $800–1,200 (double if inside label is present).

Shaker, seed box; lid labels were bought separately and married together; colorful; "Shakers' Genuine Vegetable & Flower Seeds/Mount Lebanon" and illustrations on top half of label; bottom half lists contents of the box; good condition; if all original, $5,000+; in as-is "married" condition, $2,000–3,000.

Shaker, seed envelopes; the Shakers made these small (2 x 2¾ inches) packages of flower seeds in different colors to attract attention; ca. 1840–1860; excellent condition; $50–75 each.

CHAPTER TWENTY

GOVERNMENT, MILITARY

GENERAL INFORMATION

The World War I recruiting posters feature Uncle Sam and patriotism pretty prominently. James Montgomery Flagg (1877–1960), the illustrator who created many of the posters of that era, was also responsible for creating the face of the fictional Uncle Sam. He didn't have to look very far—his own mirror reflected the image of the stern-faced figure demanding "I want YOU for U.S. Army." Flagg never charged a fee for creating this image, used in both world wars, but he created many other distinctive war posters.

Other well-known illustrators lent their talents to helping the war effort, such as J. C. Leyendecker (1874–1951), well-known for his Arrow Shirts Man. He created the same type of chisel-faced characters for his navy posters—in fact, his flag-draped Lady Liberty figure looks like a close relation of the navy hero she's sending off to war.

Howard Chandler Christy's women were the most recognizable turn-of-the-century images in America. More romantic and softer figures than Leyendecker's, Christy's Statue of Liberty was an ethereal type, scantily clad, rather than a strong-jawed, patriotic type. Even his woman dressed in a sailor suit ("Gee! I wish I were a man—I'd join the navy") has that soft, romantic Christy feel. Christy's 30 x 20 foot well-researched painting, *Signing of the U.S. Constitution*, hangs in the Capitol in Washington.

Norman Rockwell (1894–1979), known for his realistic American faces, studied Leyendecker's style—even though he didn't strictly imitate it. He created many World War II posters that graphically depicted the previously glamorized military man.

One of the illustrators who created World War II posters actually became part of the war and was declared lost at sea when the boat he was on sank. McLelland Barclay (1891–1943) painted beautiful post-flapper-period people and was known for delicately clothed women dubbed "Barclay women."

In World War II, women played an important role at home, working as machinists and laborers, like the Rosie the Riveter character depicted by J. Howard Miller in War Production Coordinating Committee posters of the era.

Americans were urged, via colorful posters, to fight for their freedoms in World War II and not to talk about their country's secrets; in World War I, they were urged to knit socks for the troops or to defeat the Kaiser; and during the Vietnam era, posters to end the war depicted men in uniform holding doves, urging people to oppose the unpopular conflict.

American Red Cross, cardboard free-standing poster; 17 x 22 inches; full color; depicts nurse in cap and cape with background of newspaper headlines; illustration by Lawrence Wilbur; ca. 1940s; very good condition; $65–80.

American Red Cross, cardboard free-standing poster; 21 x 18 inches; illustrations by Hayden Hayden; depicts nurse in cap and cape taking over the helm; ca. 1940s; very good condition; $65–80.

American Red Cross, poster; "Join the Red Cross—Work Must Go On"; 35 x 54 inches; red background and illustration of nurse designed by Dexter; very good condition; $20–35.

American Red Cross/World War I, poster; "The Greatest Mother in the World"; designed by A. E. Foringer; depicts nurse caring for wounded; good condition; $35–75.

Board of Elections, cardboard sign; "You're Right to Vote"; 10 x 20 inches; holds voter registration forms; 1992; near-mint condition; $5–10.

"Fight or Buy Bonds" poster; depicts woman holding flag in foreground and troops in background; illustrated by Howard Chandler Christy; 40 x 30 inches; attached to cloth; very good condition; $250–350.

Armed Forces, poster; "Keep 'Em Smiling"; lithographed in blue on white stock; depicts sailor, soldier, and airman; 1918; designed by M. Leone Bracker; good condition; $25–60.

Civil War, broadside; 1861; Maine call for volunteers; caption reads "Volunteers Wanted for the Thirteenth Regiment . . . "; printed by R. Thurston; Portland, Maine; 35 x 24 inches; original folds; very good condition; $1,500–2,000.

GOVERNMENT, MILITARY ■ 197

American Red Cross, cardboard freestanding poster; 17 x 22 inches; full color; depicts nurse in cap and cape with background of newspaper headlines; illustration by Lawrence Wilbur; ca. 1940s; $65–85. *Courtesy of Biggar's Antiques. Photo by Donald Vogt.*

Board of Elections, cardboard sign; "You're Right to Vote"; 10 x 20 inches; holds voter registration forms; 1991; $5–10. *Collection of and photo by Iris November.*

Defense Plant, porcelain sign; approximately 3 x 4 feet; states "Defense Plant/Part of the Arsenal of Democracy" and depicts flying bird symbol; very good condition; $350–450.

The United Nations, poster; "The United Nations Fight for Freedom"; designed by Broder; 1942; depicts Liberty holding the torch; flags of all UN member nations are in color against black background; full sheet; excellent condition; $25–60.

United States Fuel Administration, poster; "Order Coal Now"; designed by J. C. Leyendecker; color lithograph by Edwards & Deutsch Lith. Co., Chicago; depicts team of draft horses with coal wagon and worker shoveling coal; 29 x 20 inches; near-mint condition; $350–550.

War Bonds, poster; Norman Rockwell's rendition of one of the "Four Freedoms" (this one is Freedom of Worship); folded and in fair condition; $15–75.

World War I/Army, poster; "Men Wanted for the Army"; designed by B. Hazelton; 1914; color litho; depicts soldiers with rifles charging; 40 x 30 inches; good condition; $75–125.

World War I/Library Association, poster; "Hey Fellows"; color; shows soldier with armful of books and sailor reading books; 30 x 20 inches; excellent condition; $50–150.

World War I/Navy, poster; "Enlist in the Navy"; illustrated by

Milton Bancroft; lithograph of sailor blowing a bugle "To Arms"; 40 x 30 inches; excellent condition; $80–150.

World War I, poster; "Fight or Buy Bonds"; color lithograph illustrated by Howard Chandler Christy; shows woman representing American Liberty holding flag; troops in background; 30 x 20 inches; excellent condition; $60–110.

World War I, poster; "I Want YOU for U.S. Army/Nearest Recruiting Station"; with James Montgomery Flagg's Uncle Sam; approximately 24 x 20 inches; excellent condition; $200–400.

World War I, poster for bonds; depicts Joan of Arc and states "Joan of Arc saved France/Women of America/Save Your Country/Buy War Savings Stamps"; 30 x 40 inches; excellent condition; $40–75.

World War I, posters, "They Did Their Part" and "Make Yours a Victory Home"; 22 x 28 inches each; good condition; $25–100.

World War II/Navy, poster; "Don't Give Up the Ship/Swing It Brother"; depicts shipworkers; designed by Paul Hesse; 40 x 30 inches; excellent condition; $20–40.

World War II, poster; "A Good Soldier Sticks to His Post"; depicts soldier firing machine gun; published by U.S. Government in 1943; 40 x 30 inches; near-mint condition; $30–60.

World War II, poster; "Freedom from Fear"; illustrated by Norman Rockwell; depicts mother and father tucking in sleeping children; double sheet; 56 x 40 inches; original folds; published in the *Saturday Evening Post* as part of a series printed by U.S. Government in 1943; near-mint condition; $30–75.

World War II, poster; "Short Cuts can Shorten the War"; 1943; War Production Board poster that depicts defense worker crew saving time while doing their jobs; designed by Koerner; 40 x 30 inches; excellent condition; $30–60.

World War II, poster; "Work to Keep Free"; 1943; depicts worker holding sledgehammer casting shadow of Liberty holding torch; 40 x 30 inches; excellent condition; $30–75.

CHAPTER TWENTY-ONE
■ GUM ■

ADAMS

Adams Gum, tin display and change tray; pepsin gum counter display for packages of 5 cent Chiclets and stick gum; 16 x 2½ x 12¼ inches; good/very good condition, some chipping and scratches; $150–350.

Adams Gum, tin display box; green hinged lid; pictures packages of gum; 6¼ x 6 x 4¾ inches; good condition, some chipping and rusting; $100–250.

Adams Silver Roll Gum, tin; lithographed; 8¼ x 4¾ inches; spool-shaped with unusual decoration; domed cover with second interior lid seal; pedestal base; early and rare; very good/excellent condition; $400–600.

Adams Spearmint Gum, tin; striped; hinged lid; pictures packages of gum; 6¼ x 6 x 4¾ inches; good condition, some bubbling to surface and rust overall; $100–300.

BABY RUTH

Baby Ruth Gum, advertisement from *Country Gentleman*, 1929; depicts red-striped package, real mint; rare; full color; excellent condition; $4–7.

BEECH-NUT

Beech-Nut Chewing Gum, tin display and stand; original marquee displays bust of little girl with bow in her hair; she's holding pack of advertised Peppermint-flavored chewing gum; packages cost 5 cents; approximately 9½ x 15 x 9½ inches; very good condition; minor scratches and chips; $300–500.

CARNATION

Carnation Gum, lithograph on self-framed tin; 13¾ inches square; made by Meeks Co.; depicts pretty girl holding carnations; very good condition; $500–$1,000.

CLARK'S

Clark's Peppermint Gum, wrapper; excellent condition; $5–20.

Baby Ruth Gum, advertisement from *Country Gentlemen*, 1929; depicts red-striped package, real mint; rare; full color; $4–7. *Courtesy of Paper Lady/Bernie and Dolores Fee. Photo by Donald Vogt.*

Clark's Teaberry Gum, glass display; etched-glass shelf display for packages of gum; 16 x 5 x 4¼ inches; very good/excellent condition, minor chip edge upper right, slight discoloration to plating on brackets; $50–125.

DAVAL

Daval Gum, vendor trade stimulator; pot metal embossed cased three-reeled trade stimulator and gum ball vendor; 9 x 9 x 12 inches; very good condition (restored), back door and lock replaced, some age discoloration and chipping to reel strips; $250–450.

DIETZ

Dietz, 5 cent trade stimulator and gum vendor; ca. 1930; nickel flip and package gum vendor in pressed steel case; 9½ x 14½ x 6½ inches; good original condition, some surface rusting and paint loss to case, Bozo decal and flip track peeling, back door missing, appears to be working; $75–150.

FLEER'S

Fleer's Gum, tin sign; rare; with oval portrait of maker promoting "Guru-Kola Gum"; printed by Sentenne & Green; 13¾ x 9¾ inches; good/very good condition, some bends, chips, wear; $5,000–7,000.

HOADLEY'S

Hoadley's Gum, tin and bank; lithographed on tin; 11 x 15 inches; printed by "Somers Bros., N.Y."; green and yellow multi-tiered tin; slit in top for entry; rare; very good condition; $200–400.

Hoadley's Tolu Chewing Gum, tin; Somers Bros. Chicle tin promoting medicinal benefits; 2¼ x ¾ x 1 inch; very good condition; $200–400.

JUICY FRUIT
Juicy Fruit, tin match safe; pictures the "Man who Made Famous" Juicy Fruit; 3½ x 5 x 1¼ inches; excellent condition; $150–250.

KIS-ME
Kis-Me Gum, die-cut and embossed cardboard sign; depicts attractive woman with red bow in hair in center; she's encircled by red flowered border; approximately 13½ x 17½ inches excluding frame; good condition, some water staining; $150–300.

LARSON'S
Larson's Spearmint Gum, wrapper; excellent condition; $5–20.

LISTERATED
Listerated Gum, mechanical card; nice piece and colorful; near-mint condition; $5–20.

MANSFIELD
Mansfield Pepsin Gum, glass display case; depicts woman holding package of gum in "wintergreen, blood orange, peppermint"; on oak base; 6½ x 11½ x 4¾ inches; very good original condition, top piece missing; $1,250–2,000.

MELLOW FRUIT
Mellow Fruit Gum, cardboard display sign; depicts a black woman smiling and holding pack of gum next to her face; ca. 1950s; super colors; near-mint condition; $20–50.

MISCELLANEOUS
Store chewing gum dispenser, five-sided gum vendor with Zeno, Beech-Nut brand, and Sen-Sen decals on glass; revolving pressed steel case with cast base; 8 inch diameter x 14½ inches; very good condition, original, some chipping to paint, minor discoloration to mirrors; $100–200.

Zeno 1 cent gum machine; plain oak cased machine with embossed tin front; locked; deaccessioned from Strawberry Banke Museum; 10½ x 16½ x 9¼ inches; very good original condition; $500–700.

MY FAVORITE CHOCOLATE
My Favorite Chocolate Chewing Gum, lead foil wrapper; unusual; near-mint condition; $5–20.

PRIMLEY'S
Primley's California Fruit Gum, cardboard sign; depicts bear holding

package of gum and ignoring the beehive at his side; one of only two known; approximately 14 x 22 inches excluding mat and frame; overall 18½ x 26½ inches; very good condition; $2,500–5,000.

Primley's Pepsin Sticks Chewing Gum, lithographed and embossed tin sign; 19¼ x 13¼ inches; printed by Townsend Hostetter & Co., Chicago; ca. 1890; depicts woman reaching over man's shoulder for package of Primley's California Fruit Pepsin Sticks gum; rare; very colorful; excellent condition; $15,000–20,000.

PULVER

Pulver Gum, machine; a red-and-white "Two Choos" and "Joy Mint" gum on red-and-white porcelain rounded-corner case; mechanism has yellow kid with cloth clothing; 9 x 20 x 4½ inches; excellent/near-mint condition, some minor dirt, slight wear at upper right corner of window, key included; $400–600.

Pulver Gum, 1 cent vendor; yellow enameled case with mechanical clown interior; 9 x 20½ x 4½ inches; excellent condition, general overall soiling, some scratches to enamel, locked case; $300–500.

SEN-SEN

Sen-Sen Gum, die-cut cardboard display sign; 1902; depicts Japanese woman with fan and box for 5 cent chewing gum; 20 x 40 inches; good condition, some restoration; $275–400.

SHORT'S

Short's Skotchemint Chewing Gum, stick and wrapper; near-mint condition; $5–20.

STERLING

Sterling Pepsin Gum, cardboard sign; girl's face and gum package; original frame; 24½ x 34½ inches overall; good/very good condition, some water stains, some background in-painting, minor chipping due to overall wear; $100–250.

WALLA-WALLA

Walla-Walla Pepsin Gum, jar; paper label; trademarked Indian on label; from Knoxville, Tennessee; 5 x 11 inches including (replaced) lid; excellent condition, some minor fading and wear; $300–500.

WRIGLEY'S GUM

William Wrigley, Jr., originally sold soap; chewing gum was strictly given as a premium to advertise his soap products. Soon, he noticed the gum seemed more popular than his soap, so he turned to gum and made millions of dollars on his five-cent product. His three famous flavors—spearmint, doublemint, and juicy fruit—were all made by 1914 and were Wrigley's *only* flavors until competition stirred the company to make new flavors fifty-nine years later.

Wrigley advertised his foil-wrapped individual sticks in the print medium as well as on streetcar and subway ads, billboards, radio, and television. One of his ad campaigns—the female Doublemint Twins—was successful for over four decades (1940s–1980s). The ads continue to run today, but the people are not all female.

Wrigley bought office buildings, hotels, an island (Catalina), and a baseball team (the Chicago Cubs), but never added any other products to his line other than gum.

Wrigley's corporation became public in 1919, and in 1923 it was listed on the New York Stock Exchange.

WRIGLEY'S

Wrigley's cardboard cutout of spearmint gum package; 3½ x 10½ inches; excellent condition; $20–50.

Wrigley's Spearmint Gum, cardboard display box; early; excellent condition; $20–50.

Wrigley's Spearmint Pepsin Gum, display box; large; early; excellent condition; $75–150.

Wrigley's, glass change tray; large chewing gum tray with decaled image of "Double Mint, Spearmint, Juicy Fruit" gum packages in change depression; 16¾ x 18 inches; very good condition; $250–500.

Wrigley's Licorice Gum, wrapper; rough; good condition; $5–20.

Wrigley's Gum, die-cut tin display; vertical variety of Wrigley's Man (arrowhead) atop a slant–front case designed to hold packages of the chewing gum; 13¼ x 19 x 6¼ inches; very good condition, minor bends and chips; $600–900.

Wrigley's Gum, die-cut display; trademarked Wrigley Man holds four boxes of chewing gum; complete with four different boxes of gum; celluloid head intact; approximately 14 x 13½ x 7 inches; very good condition, original label on back; $400–600.

Wrigley's, wax paper box wrap; near-mint condition; $10–20.

CHAPTER TWENTY-TWO
■ GUNS AND ACCESSORIES ■

COLT

Colt, paper sign; depicts sheriff on horseback; 19½ x 33 inches; very good condition slight soiling and creasing; $600–1,000.

DuPONT

The DuPont family's genealogy is an impressive one, stretching back to the late 1700s and early 1800s, when Pierre-Samuel duPont de Nemours was patriarch. His son Victor spied on American naval vessels during the Revolution, thus beginning the legend of one of America's most fascinating dynasties. Thirteen duPonts arrived in America in December 1799, headed by Pierre–Samuel, and were important enough to be welcomed to their new home via a warm letter from Vice President Thomas Jefferson.

The duPonts, having been trained as clockmakers in their native France, were anxious to start some kind of business in their new homeland. They got their chance in 1800 when they decided to go into gunpowder manufacturing. Eleuthère Irénée, Pierre-Samuel's other son, had learned how to make gunpowder in France and was quite sure that he could make millions doing so in America.

In July 1803, after producing his first batch of saltpeter, Eleuthère Irénée informed President Jefferson, who promptly gave the duPonts a small order for gunpowder for the U.S. Army. Prior to that time (in 1802), Pierre-Samuel had organized the duPont business affairs into three categories: Victor duPont & Co., with offices in New York; Wilmington (Delaware) Powder Co.; and DuPont de Nemours (Pere et Fils & Co.), with offices in Paris and New York. Despite many problems, the business had grown substantially by 1817, when Pierre-Samuel died. The brothers, Victor and Eleuthère-Irénée, continued to improve their business, supplying the American Army with gunpowder throughout the Revolution and the War of 1812 until their own deaths: Victor's in 1827 and Eleuthère's in 1834.

Eleuthère's oldest son, Alfred Victor Philadelphe, took over the company reins in 1834, but never felt comfortable with the business, so his brother-in-law, Antoine Bidermann, took over until 1837 and then turned the company back to Alfred Victor, who died in 1856.

Advertisements for the gunpowder depicted the American hunter amidst a plethora of beasts. The ads also noted when each of the DuPont mills had opened.

The family-owned business continued to thrive for many generations—even after the U.S. government broke up DuPont's gunpowder monopoly in 1911 (they still remained the largest explosives manufacturer in the United States). By 1920, the DuPonts controlled Detroit's major automobile company (General Motors), America's biggest explosives company, and had a solid hold on the chemicals industry, as well as a huge investment in United States Steel. The DuPont Cellophane Co. was created in 1920, and today it is the largest manufacturer of high-performance plastics, in addition to over 1,200 other products. DuPont's people invented fabrics such as Duco, neoprene, and nylon during the 1930s, adding to the company's already incredible wealth.

DuPONT

DuPont, Superfine Fg Gunpowder, tin; Wilmington, Delaware; paper label over red tin; never opened; excellent condition; ca. 1870s; $65–85.

DuPont Powders, self-framed tin sign; depicts father and son with dogs in field; "Generations have Used It"; 23 x 33 inches; good condition, some scratches and chips; $200–400.

DuPont Smokeless Powders, paper sign; depicts cavalry image of soldier on horseback shooting buffalo and separate image of two setters pointing at prey; original advertising mat; approximately 31 x 12 inches excluding frame; overall 33½ x 14½ inches; very good/excellent condition, some staining and age discoloration; $50–150.

DuPont Gunpowder, tins (2); paper-labeled cans for "FF" and "F"; 4 x 6 x 1½ inches each; good condition, slight fade in paper, minor rust spotting and scratching; $100–200.

HERCULES

Hercules Powder, World War I anniversary calendar; pictures soldier and dog; 13 x 30½ inches; very good condition, some minor edge loss, minor staining and wrinkling; $75–150.

Hercules Powder, paper sign; winter scene of black boy hunting with muzzle–loading rifle; 1920; 15½ x 25 inches; including metal strips; excellent condition, minor horizontal creases, edge chipping; $750–1,000.

Hercules Powder, paper sign; two black boys with muzzle-loading rifle; 1924; 15½ x 25 inches including metal strips; very good/excellent condition, some horizontal creases, edge chipping, tear lower right bottom; $400–600.

INFALLIBLE

Infallible Smokeless Shotgun Powder, reproduction of old tin sign; features woman carrying gun and accompanied by setter; 10 x 15 inches; new/reproduction condition; $12.

LAFLIN & RAND

Laflin & Rand Powder Company, cardboard sign; four images of men and boys with rifles; approximately 35½ x 15½ inches excluding mat and frame; overall 45 x 24 inches; good/very good condition; $200–400.

Infallible Smokeless Shotgun Powder, reproduction of old tin sign; features woman carrying gun and accompanied by setter; 10 x 15 inches; new/reproduction condition, $12. *Courtesy of and photo by Castle Antiques & Reproductions.*

Remington UMC, tin sign; 10 x 16 inches; reproduction; depicts partridges flying out of brush; $15 retail. *Courtesy of Doc Davis/Antique-Alike. Photo by Donald Vogt.*

PETERS

Peters, die-cut cardboard sign; depicts a man holding Peters ammunition boxes; bright and vivid colors; very good overall condition; $200–400.

Peters, die-cut cardboard display; hunter with gun and shotgun for "Victor High Velocity" loads; 26 x 46 inches; good/very good condition, horizontal crease at fold, some minor loss at edges, minor tears, strong colors; $475–675.

Peters, die-cut cardboard display; depicts hunter with display of cartridges; 25 x 42 inches; good/very good condition, horizontal crease at fold, minor damage to edges, strong colors; $250–500.

Peters, die-cut cardboard display; depicts two springer spaniels with a shotgun and "Victor" shotgun shells; 26 x 20 inches; good/very good condition; $225–425.

Peters, die-cut cardboard display; depicts sitting setter with crate of shotgun shells; 22 x 25 inches; very good/excellent condition, minor chipping, slight creasing, primarily to edges; $250–450.

REMINGTON

Remington, canvas banner; colorful image of big game hunter shooting attacking lion with Kleanbore 22s; 55½ x 50¼ inches; good condition overall, general soiling, chipping to overblacking on top half; $50–150.

Remington UMC, die-cut cardboard display; large image of double guns with birds and loads; 29 x 39 inches; good/very good condition, horizontal crease at fold; $350–600.

Remington UMC, paper poster; elaborate design with animals, bullets and guns; 20 x 24 inches; good condition, overall soiling, some trimming; $100–300.

Remington Game Load, paper poster; multiple animal images with numbered index; ca. 1923; 18½ x 26 inches; excellent condition, some creasing overall, generalized soiling; $40–125.

Remington UMC, tin sign; 10 x 16 inches; reproduction; depicts partridges flying out of brush; $15 retail.

SMITH & WESSON

Smith & Wesson Revolvers, poster; printed in full color halftone;

original painting by Dan Smith; trademark in lower left 22 x 18 inches; very good condition; minor foxing; $250–350.

UMC

UMC, Nitro Club Shells, cardboard sign; depicts black-and-white pointer; 25 x 20 inches excluding frame; excellent condition, some overall soiling, minor water stain; $300–500.

U.S. AMMUNITION

U.S. Ammunition, self-framed tin sign; pictures military meeting "At Bisley" with bullets pictured on border; 28½ x 22 inches; good/very good condition, some wear primarily on border, slight fade to image, overall soiling, small dents; $450–750.

WINCHESTER

Winchester Big Game Rifles, lithograph on paper; printed by Forbes Co., Boston; ca. 1904; colorful image of hunter with foot atop a mountain goat and rifle in hand; 26 x 15¼ inches; excellent condition; $500–1,000.

Winchester, 1889 paper calendar; rare poster version; vignettes of hunters stalking, shooting, and carrying home the kill; surrounded by birch tree motif; missing calendar overpad; approximately 15 x 23 inches excluding mat and frame; overall 19¾ x 28¼ inches; excellent condition; $1,000–1,500.

Winchester, cardboard window display; triptych design; features cowboy on horse in center panel and woodland animals on outside panels; excellent condition; $600–800.

CHAPTER TWENTY-THREE
■ HEALTH AND ■
BEAUTY AIDS

ANAMI
Anami, powder tin; pictures a Victorian woman on front; good condition; $60–80.

AYER'S
Ayer's Hair Vigor, glass sign; early sepia photograph adhered to hand-lettered glass with color-enhanced imaging; approximately 11¼ x 13 inches excluding frame; fair/good condition, touch-up to photo image, lettering, and background; $150–300.

Ayer's Hair Vigor, paper sign; bare-chested nymph rising from lily (her long hair covers chest); 10¾ x 13¾ inches; excellent condition, borders trimmed, minor surface wear; $1,200–1,800.

Ayer's Hair Vigor, tin sign; original composition over wood frame; ca. 1880–1885; features long-haired girl; 25½ x 11¼ inches; very good condition; $2,000–2,600.

Ayer's Hair Vigor, sign; depicts woman with long hair standing beside occasional table; good condition, some wear; $250–650.

Ayer's Hair Vigor, tin sign; depicts woman with especially long hair feeding horse, dogs at her feet; reproduction; 10 x 16 inches; $15 retail.

BAND-AID
(*see also* "Band-Aid" in Medicines chapter)
Band-Aid, tin; made by Johnson & Johnson; ca. 1950s; excellent condition; $2–5.

BONNIE-B
Bonnie-B Hair Net, tin display case; six-sided cabinet on wooden base with mirror front and images of Priscilla Dean on panels; revolving back door with shelves; ca. 1921; 13¾ x 14 x 11 inches; good condition, overall dirt and rust hazing, some pinpoint spotting of overpaint, general wear; $150–300.

BRICKMORE
Brickmore Easy Shave Cream, cardboard display piece; 35 cents;

210 ■ ADVERTISING

Ayer's Hair Vigor, tin sign; depicts woman with especially long hair feeding horse, dogs at her feet; reproduction; 10 x 16 inches; $15 retail. *Courtesy of Doc Davis/Antique-Alike. Photo by Donald Vogt.*

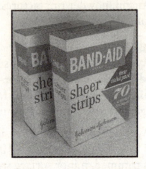

Band-Aid, store display; box of 70 sheer strips; 15 x 22 x 5 inches; contemporary; $35–50. *Courtesy of Biggar's Antiques. Photo by Donald Vogt.*

depicts man in T-shirt getting ready to shave; near-mint condition; $35–85.

Brickmore Easy Shave Cream, lithographed cardboard point-of-sale advertising sign; very good condition; $100–300.

BURMA-SHAVE

Burma-Shave's roadside signs date back to 1926, when the first grouping was planted on U.S. Highway 65 near Lakeville, Minnesota. In the beginning, the manufacturer wrote all the jingles, but by the end of the 1920s, contests were held annually to determine the new jingles, with prizes ranging from $2 to $100. The signs marched along America's highways until 1963, when Burma-Shave sold out to Philip Morris.

A Minneapolis manufacturing family, the Odells, started the Burma-Shave business by introducing a liniment called Burma-Vita, which meant "life [or vigor] from Burma." The family had seen a series of signs attached to fenceposts along a southern Minnesota highway that advertised a filling station. They decided to try the idea of multiple signs themselves. Soon, almost every state in the United States sported a road with Burma-Shave signs—that is, except Arizona, Nevada, and New Mexico, because there was too little traffic; and Massachusetts, because the roads took too many twists and turns.

The Odells' Burma-Shave was produced in either a tube or jar and had to be spread across the face with the user's fingers. By the time the cream was accepted, the electric shaver was invented, creating competition for the creamy product. Sales rose until 1947, then started sinking. The reason? Cars were driving by too quickly to read the signs.

Some of the classics are:

(The original, from 1925) SHAVE THE MODERN WAY/FINE FOR THE SKIN/DRUGGISTS HAVE IT / BURMA-SHAVE

(end of the 1930s) PAST / SCHOOLHOUSES / TAKE IT SLOW / LET THE LITTLE / SHAVERS GROW / BURMA-SHAVE

(1947) ALTHO / WE'VE SOLD / SIX MILLION OTHERS/WE STILL CAN'T SELL / THOSE COUGHDROP BROTHERS / BURMA-SHAVE

(1955) SLOW DOWN, PA / SAKES ALIVE / MA MISSED SIGNS / FOUR / AND FIVE / BURMA-SHAVE

Sets of the Burma-Shave boards hang in the Smithsonian Institution; the American Advertising Museum in Portland, Oregon; and the Ford Museum in Dearborn, Michigan.

BURMA-SHAVE
Burma-Shave, tool box; made out of four signs cut up to make box; unique piece of folk art; 40 x 21 x 13 inches; $375–450.

CALIFORNIA PERFUME
California Perfume, tin container; suitcase shape; Jack and Jill motif; 5¾ x 1¼ x 3¾ inches; very good condition; $35–75.

CHEVALIER'S
Chevalier's Hair Restorer, paper sign; "strengthening and preserving hair vigor"; depicts Lady Godiva on horse riding through factory town; 13 x 10 inches; very good condition, minor paper loss at ringed top, soiling overall; $275–475.

COLGATE-PALMOLIVE
William Colgate began the company in 1806 in New York. He sold "Soap, Mould & Dypt Candles." In 1877, Colgate began selling toothpaste in jars, then introduced Colgate Ribbon Dental Cream, its first toothpaste in a tube in 1908.

Palmolive soap was introduced in 1898. Colgate penetrated the overseas market in 1913 and has consistently done better there than in the United States. During the 1970s, Colgate-Palmolive bought more than twenty companies, but turned around and sold them during the 1980s.

Colgate-Palmolive spends much of its advertising energy competing with Procter & Gamble products. However, Colgate is the number-one manufacturer of liquid soap and liquid dishwasher detergent. They are global merchants who, nevertheless, maintain a seventy-five acre research center in New Jersey.

One of the most controversial products Colgate has ever produced was Darkie toothpaste. The product came to the company through its purchase of Hawley & Hazel, a Hong Kong–based company. At first, Colgate continued to market the product overseas, despite strong protest. In 1989, the company changed the toothpaste's name to Darlie and the portrait of an Al Jolson–type man used to promote the product was changed to a man of "ambiguous race."

COLGATE

Colgate Co., advertisement; 100th anniversary (1806–1906); designed by Maxfield Parrish; 16 x 10 inches; depicts servants with trays and soup kettle serving a man and two women; excellent condition; $35–60.

Colgate's Cold Cream, advertisement from *Life*, September 19, 1912; full-color illustration of the product; excellent condition; $4–8.

Colgate's Baby Talc Powder, tin; baby in insert holding Baby Talc in arms (etc.); 6 inches; ca. 1910; excellent condition; $125–175.

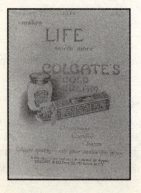

Colgate's Cold Cream, advertisement from *Life*, September 19, 1912; full-color illustration of the product; $4–8. *Courtesy of Paper Lady/Bernie and Dolores Fee. Photo by Donald Vogt.*

HEALTH AND BEAUTY AIDS ■ 213

Colgate's Dactylis Talc Powder, tins; (left rear) 6 inches, ca. 1910, $25–50; (center) Dactylis Talc Powder, 4½ inches, ca. 1920s, $50–75; (right) Colgate's Baby Talc, baby in insert holding baby talc in arms (etc.), 6 inches, ca. 1910, $125–175; (front) Colgate's Dental Powder, sample tin, ca. 1900–1910, $25–50. *Courtesy of Marilyn and De Underwood/Tins Again Collectibles. Photo by Donald Vogt.*

Colgate's Dactylis Talc Powder, tin; 4½ inches; ca. 1920s; excellent condition; $50–75.

Colgate's Dactylis Talc Powder, tin; 6 inches; ca. 1910; excellent condition; $25–50.

Colgate's Dental Powder, sample tin; ca. 1900–1910; excellent condition; $25–50.

Colgate's Soaps and Perfumes, advertisement from *Ladies' Home Journal*, ca. 1925; depicts all of Colgate's products and asks readers to "Find the Mis-spelled Word"; excellent condition; $15–18.

COLUMBIA HERP
Columbia Herp C. Hair Tonic, blue bottle; with paper label and cork stopper; label depicts almost bare-breasted woman; made by Columbia Perfume Co.; Pittsburgh, Pennsylvania; chips on lip; excellent condition; $75–150.

CREST
(*see* "Procter & Gamble" in Soap chapter)

COMFORT
Comfort Powder, tin; depicts chubby child's face; 2½ inch diameter x 4 inches; good condition, slight overall fade, general wear, some chipping, minor denting; $100–300.

CURLOX
Curlox Hair Net, display and case; glass-fronted wood case with display of product and label decaled sides; 19 x 12½ x 10½ inches; very good condition, age cracks to decal and staining to original finish; $75–150.

DARKIE/DARLIE
(*see also* "Colgate-Palmolive")

Darlie Toothpaste, sheet of uncut boxes; produced when Darkie Toothpaste was changed to Darlie; contemporary; excellent condition; $40–50.

DJER-KISS

Djer-Kiss, advertisement from *Ladies' Home Journal*, December 1916; illustrated by Maxfield Parrish; shows woman on swing amid many flowers; very good condition; $50–100.

Djer-Kiss, advertisement from *Ladies' Home Journal*, April 1918; illustrated by Maxfield Parrish; depicts woman in woods with elves offering a container of the scent; very good condition; $95–135.

Djer-Kiss, advertisement from *Ladies' Home Journal*, April 1921; illustrated by Maxfield Parrish; depicts woman on a swing surrounded by flowers; excellent condition; $60–90.

ESPELL

Espell Perfumes Spring Blossom Talcum, tin; 16 ounces, very good condition; ca. 1940s; $40–60.

EVER-READY

Ever-Ready, advertising clock; depicts man with foam on his face shaving; 18 x 22 x 4½ inches; good original condition, general overall wear and fading, pendulum missing; $300–600.

GLEEM TOOTHPASTE

(*see* "Procter & Gamble" in Soap chapter)

GODLEY BROS., INC.

Godley Bros., Inc., Hair Rinse, box; original; still full; blonde; blue-and-red design; made in Cincinnati, Ohio; ca. 1940s; near-mint condition; $3–6.

Goldey Bros., Inc., Hair Rinse, box; original; still full; blonde; blue-and-red design; made in Cincinnati, Ohio; ca. 1940s; near-mint condition; $3–6. *Courtesy of Dawn and Bob Reno. Photo by Donald Vogt.*

HEALTH AND BEAUTY AIDS ■ 215

GOODMAN CHEMICAL
Goodman Chemical Co., tin; 6 ounces; Brooklyn, New York; floral fragrance—"Gardenia"; all tin; ca. 1940s; excellent condition; $40–45.

HALL'S
Hall's Hair Renewer, paper sign; depicts beautiful woman with hair extending to floor and child hiding behind hair; 10½ x 13¼ inches excluding mat and frame; good/excellent condition, nice colors; $600–900.

HINDS HONEY & ALMOND CREAM
The company originated in Livermore, Maine, as a drug business started by Auerlius S. Hinds, a Maine native. However, in 1862, Hinds moved to the H. H. Hay drugstore in Portland, then started his own store in 1869. His Hinds Honey & Almond Cream hand lotion sold so well that he opened a factory and began to advertise nationally in 1904.

Hinds advertised in 1918 that his cream would "keep the skin soft and free from the irritating effects of the sun and the wind." His company also made cold cream, disappearing cream, soap, face powder, and talcum. Hinds offered samples of his products and mailed them directly from the laboratory.

In 1925, the company was sold to a New York firm, and it has been a division of Sterling Drug, Inc. since approximately 1966.

HINDS HONEY & ALMOND CREAM
Hinds Honey & Almond Cream, advertisement from *McCall's*, 1916; full color; large letters with children sitting on letters; $4–8.

Hinds Honey & Almond Cream, advertisement from *McCall's*, 1916; full color; large letters with children sitting on letters; $4–8. *Courtesy of Paper Lady/Bernie and Dolores Fee. Photo by Donald Vogt.*

216 ■ ADVERTISING

Hinds Honey & Almond Cream, advertisement from *Ladies' Home Journal*, December 1926; full color; woman and child in snow feeding birds; $4–8. *Courtesy of Paper Lady/Bernie and Dolores Fee. Photo by Donald Vogt.*

Johnson's Baby Powder, tins; (left) 4⅛ ounces, ca. 1940s, $25–50; (right) sample tin, ca. 1940s, $50–75. *Courtesy of Marilyn and De Underwood/Tins Again Collectibles. Photo by Donald Vogt.*

Hinds Honey & Almond Cream, advertisement from *Ladies' Home Journal*, December 1926; full color; woman and child in snow feeding birds; $4–8.

HOYT'S

Hoyt's Cologne, reverse glass sign; mother-of-pearl and glass sign for "Hoyt's German Cologne"; 26 x 20½ inches excluding frame; good condition, some lifting to paint; $400–650.

Hoyt's Cologne, tin sign; early Wells & Hope perfume advertisement; depicts girl's head in rosebud; 25½ x 31½ inches overall, includes original frame; good condition, light overall flaking; $1,000–2,000.

Hoyt's German Cologne, paper poster; child surrounded by flowers; "The Most Fragrant and Lasting of all Perfumes"; approximately 16½ x 22½ inches excluding mat and frame; overall 21¼ x 27¾ inches; printed by J. Ottmann; very good condition; $275–475.

JOHNSON'S

Johnson's Baby Powder, tin; 4⅛ ounces; ca. 1940s; $25–50.

Johnson's Baby Powder, sample tin; ca. 1940s; $50–75.

KHUSH-AMADI

Khush-Amadi Talcum Powder, tin; butterfly-winged maid in lily pond surrounded by flowers; 2¾ x 5 x 1½ inches; excellent/near-mint condition, slight crazing to colors; $100–300.

LANDER

Lander Gardenia and Sweet Pea Talc, tin; 5 ounces; all tin; Fifth Avenue, New York City; ca. 1940s; excellent condition; $40–45.

Lander Gardenia and Sweet Pea Talc, tin; 5 ounces; can; ca. 1920s; excellent condition; $30–40.

Lander Lilacs and Roses Talc, powder can; 1 pound; Fifth Avenue, New York; ca.1920s; very good condition; $25–45.

Lander Lilac and Roses Talc, can; 1 pound; all tin; Fifth Avenue, New York City; ca. 1940s; very good condition; $40–45.

LILT HOME PERMANENTS
(*see* "Procter & Gamble" in Soap chapter)

L'OREAL PRODUCTS
(*see* "Nestlé" in Candy chapter)

LORIE

Lorie Gentlemen's After Shaving Powder, tin; 3 ounces; ca. 1950s; excellent/very good condition; $18–24.

MCKESSON'S

McKesson's Baby Powder, tin; two naked children warming themselves in front of fire; was pictured on cover of *Tin Type*; 2½ x 6¼ x 1½ inches; excellent/very good condition, minor chipping; $150–350.

MENNEN'S

Mennen's Sure Corn Killer, Gerhard Mennen's first product, was made in 1878 and sold in his drugstore, along with others. Wise to the ways of business, Mennen used all avenues of advertising to sell his product. In 1889, he created Mennen's Borated Talcum Infant Powder and used an extremely innovative selling tool—the Mennen's Talcum Show, a mistrel act.

Early containers were cardboard, but the company soon discovered they leaked and replaced them with the shaker-top cans. Mennen's trademark depicted a small picture of Gerhard Mennen's head, while the front of the tin showed him as a baby.

In order to sell their product during the Victorian era, Mennen's Toilet Powder ads focused on the devotion between mother and child. Ads depicted the baby center stage, with the mother off to the side, her attention focused on her child. In

1906, Mennen's ad read "Women can't do anything without Mennen (Toilet Powder)."

Famed illustrator Norman Rockwell endorsed Mennen Shaving Cream in 1929, telling Jim Henry, "I can put more chuckles in my pictures when I've had this COOL shave." By adding a coupon for two free samples of the cream, the company was able to discern how many people were reading their ads.

Mennen died in 1902, and his wife, Elma Christina, took over as president of the firm, then turned the company over to her son, William, in 1916. His sons, George S. and William Jr., took over in 1963.

Today, the company is still a privately owned, through not family-run, business. It makes over fifty health and beauty aid products.

MENNEN'S

Mennen's Violet Talcum Powder tin; pink and violet; ca. 1930s; very good condition; $15–25.

Mennen's Powder, tin; ca. 1910; baby in insert; very good condition; $75–125.

Mennen's Flesh Tint Talcum, tin; rose graphics; ca. 1940s; very good condition; $15–25.

Mennen's Borated Talcum Powder, tin; ca. 1930s; blue-and-mustard graphics; baby in insert; very good condition; $15–17.

Mennen's Talcum Powder, tins (2); Borated Talcum with babies and Sen-Yang with Oriental image; 2½ x 4½ x 1½ inches each; very good/excellent condition, minor chipping, slight wear overall; $250–350.

Mennen's Powder, tins, (from left to right): ca. 1910, depicts baby in insert, $75–125; Mennen Violet Talcum, pink and violet, ca. 1930s, $15–25; Mennen's Flesh Tint Talcum, rose graphics, ca. 1940s, $15–25; Mennen's Borated Talcum Powder, ca. 1930s, blue-and-mustard graphics, baby in insert; $50–70. *Courtesy of Marilyn and De Underwood/Tins Again Collectibles. Photo by Donald Vogt.*

HEALTH AND BEAUTY AIDS ■ 219

Murray's Superior Hair Dressing Pomade, "Copyright 1926 by Murray's Superior Products Co.; Chicago, IL; 35 cents"; mint condition, $18–24. *Courtesy of Irreverent Relics. Photo by Donalt Vogt.*

Polly Peachtree Hair Dressing, bottle in box; 1⅞ ounces; "Distributed by Cheatham Chemical Co.; Atlanta GA"; ca. 1940s, mint condition; $15–18. *Courtesy of Irreverent Relics. Photo by Donald Vogt.*

MIRADOR PERFUME
Mirador Perfume Co., tin; New York/Toronto; Talisman Rose; 13 ounces; ca. 1940s; excellent/very good condition; $40–60.

MISCELLANEOUS
Perfume vendor; ca. 1920s; fancified oak vendor with lion heads that spurt 1 cent squirts of perfume; excellent condition; $3,500–4,500.

MURRAY'S
Murray's Superior Hair Dressing Pomade, bottle; "Copyright 1926 by Murray's Superior Products Co.; Chicago, IL; 35 cents"; mint condition; $18–24.

NYSIS
Nysis Talcum Powder, tin; stylized Art Deco Egyptian portrait motif; 1¾ inch triangle x 6¼ inches; good condition, general overall wear, slight nicking; $25–75.

POLLY PEACHTREE
Polly Peachtree Hair Dressing, bottle in box, 1⅞ ounces; "Distributed by Cheatham Chemical Co.; Atlanta, GA." ca. 1940s; mint condition; $15–18.

POMPEIAN MASSAGE CREAM
Pompeian Massage Cream, advertisement from *Ladies' Home Journal*, 1914; full color; shows woman's face; excellent condition; $4–8.

Pompeian Massage Cream, advertisement from *Ladies Home Journal*, 1914; full color; shows woman's face; $4–8. *Courtesy of Paper Lady/Bernie and Dolores Fee. Photo by Donald Vogt.*

Pond's Creams, advertisement from *Ladies' Home Journal*, November 1918; depicts full-color insert of women who use the cream; $4–8. *Courtesy of Paper Lady/Bernie and Dolores Fee. Photo by Donald Vogt.*

POND'S

Pond's Creams, advertisement from *Ladies's Home Journal*, November 1918; depicts full-color inserts of women who use the cream; excellent condition; $4–8.

PRELL SHAMPOO

(*see* "Procter & Gamble" in Soap chapter)

QUEEN HAIR DRESSING

Queen Hair Dressing, tin; depicts black woman; ca. 1930s; very good condition; $14–18.

RAWLEIGH'S

Rawleigh's Talcum, cardboard tin; ca. 1950s; Mother Goose characters; excellent condition; $50–75.

Rawleigh's Talcum, tin; 4 ounces; hexagonal shape; baby in teardrop necklace; pastels; ca. 1940s; excellent condition; $25–50.

Rawleigh's Talcum, tin; ca. 1950s; red, white, and blue clown graphics; near-mint condition; $50–75.

Rawleigh's Talcum, tin; gray background with Mother Goose characters; ca. 1950s; excellent condition; $75–125.

Rawleigh's Panjang Talcum Powder tin; Oriental graphics; ca. 1940s; excellent condition; $25–50.

HEALTH AND BEAUTY AIDS ■ 221

Rawleigh's Violet Talcum Powder tin; peacock design; ca. 1950s; excellent condition; $15–25.

REEL MAN

Reed Man Talcum Powder, tin; unusual after-shave talc tin picturing trout fisherman in stream; 3 x 4¾ x 1 inch; excellent/near-mint condition, minor chipping primarily on raised rim and top; $150–250.

SCOPE MOUTHWASH

(*see* "Procter & Gamble" in Soap chapter)

SOZODONT

Sozodont Tooth Powder, paper sign; woman in pink points to her teeth with one hand and holds a can of Sozodont in the other; 8½ x 13 inches; excellent condition, trimmed margins; $50–150.

SPILTER'S

Spilter's Buttermilk Talcum Powder, tin; rare talc with baby on stork's back; very detailed graphics; 2½ x 4¼ x 1½ inches; excellent condition, some chipping primarily to embossed rim and top; $150–350.

SYKES COMFORT

Sykes Comfort Powder, tin; two girls on front and nurse on back; 2¼ x 4½ x 1¼ inches; very good/excellent condition, minor scratching and chipping, slight color distortion between lid and can; $100–300.

Rawleigh's Talcum, tins; (back row left) gray background with Mother Goose characters, ca. 1950s, $75–125; (center) ca. 1950s, cardboard, Mother Goose characters, $50–75; (right) ca. 1950s, red, white, and blue clown graphics, $50–75; (front left) Violet Talcum Powder, peacock design, ca. 1950s, $15–25; (center) hexagonal shape, baby in teardrop necklace, 4 ounces, pastels, ca. 1940s, $25–50; (right) Panjang Talcum Powder, Oriental graphics, ca. 1940s, $25–50. *Courtesy of Marilyn and De Underwood/Tins Again Collectibles. Photo by Donald Vogt.*

Sykes Comfort Powder, tin; deep blue in color; front image in pale yellow of two little girls nearly cheek to cheek; 2¼ x 2 x 4½ inches; good/very good condition, some minor chipping and scratching; $75–150.

TETLOWS
Tetlows Face Powder, die-cut cardboard display; little girl trying to powder face of Union officer; 14 x 19 inches; good condition, minor paper loss at edges, some wear, overall minor spotting, $200–400.

VASELINE
Vaseline, tin ledger marker; 12 x 3 inches; ca. 1880–1890; "The Best Family Remedy in Use"; red and black on one side, black and beige on reverse; lists treatments and products made by "Colgate & Co."; fine/excellent condition; $100–200.

Vaseline, tin display box; hinged front door displays varieties of petroleum jelly tubes; 7½ x 16 x 6½ inches; good condition; $75–150.

WEST ELECTRIC HAIR CURLERS
West Electric Hair Curlers, tin display; shows product on lid and front with hinged slant lid; 4½ x 9 x 9½ iches; good condition; $75–100.

WEST HAIR NET
West Hair Net, tin display cabinet; unusual revolving tin display with sliding back doors picturing bare-bottomed nymphs in background and inserts of woman with automobile and women washing their hair and using product; ca. 1921; 13 x 20 x 11½ inches; good condition, overall soiling, some rust spotting, original condition; $150–400.

WITOL'S VAMPIRE SHAMPOO
Witol's Vampire Shampoo, paper-and-cardboard container; 2 inch diameter round box for dry shampoo "for Brunette Hair"; made by Marvo Beauty Laboratories, 1700 Broadway, New York"; still full; near-mint condition; $8–15.

CHAPTER TWENTY-FOUR
■ INSURANCE COMPANIES ■

AETNA INSURANCE
Aetna Insurance Company, calendar; dated 1891; depicts a port scene with mountain in background; 6½ x 9½ inches excluding mat and frame; fair condition; $25–100.

Aetna Insurance, tin letter folder; depicts Mt. Vesuvius erupting logo; Kellogg & Bulkeley rule; 3 x 12½ inches; good condition, some fading; $50–150.

CITY OF NEW YORK INSURANCE
City of New York Insurance, embossed tin sign; oval insert with Manhattan skyline; 27 x 19 inches excluding frame; very good/excellent condition, some hairline scratches, minor chipping and rubbing, slight dents; $450–650.

CONNECTICUT GENERAL FIRE INSURANCE
Connecticut General Fire Insurance Company, calendar, depicts a general on his horse carrying an important document; 13½ x 19½ inches; fair/good condition with some staining, creasing, and fading; $50–150.

CONNECTICUT MUTUAL INSURANCE
Connecticut Mutual Insurance, tin sign; elaborate Victorian building in round insert on this early Wells & Hope tin sign; ca. 1882; 18 x 24 inches excluding frame (which appears to be original); excellent condition; $500–1,000.

CONTINENTAL INSURANCE
Continental Insurance, self-framed tin sign; depicts the trademarked image of Continental soldier at the ready; 20 x 30 inches; very good condition, some scraping, minor fading, some rust spotting primarily to border, chipping; $350–600.

JOHN HANCOCK
In the original incorporation papers sent to the governor of Massachusetts in 1861, the name of this firm was to have been the Benjamin Franklin Protective Life Insurance Company.

Albert L. Murdock led a group of two hundred Boston merchants and bankers to petition the governor for incorporation, but the governor turned him down.

Murdock didn't give up. In 1862, he was back with a new charter, $104,000, one hundred subscribers, and a new name for the corporation: John Hancock Mutual Life Insurance Co. Murdock believed the John Hancock name would create instant stature and that Hancock's signature would make a recognizable trademark. He was right. Through the years, the company has become one of the best known in the insurance business, as well as one of the most respected.

JOHN HANCOCK INSURANCE

John Hancock Insurance Company, calendar; dated 1893, depicts a scene of that period with horse-drawn carriage; 15¾ x 12½ inches excluding mat and frame; very good condition with some minor staining; $25–100.

HARTFORD INSURANCE

The Hartford Insurance Group's stag (called a hart) trademark came from the citizens of seventeenth-century Hertford, England. Their official seal showed a stag (they called it a hert, which they pronounced "hart") crossing a ford. Those Hertfordites took their seal with them when they migrated to America and settled along the banks of the Connecticut River. The city's spelling was soon changed to Hartford to agree with its pronunciation.

Soon Hartford became the capital of Connecticut, as well as capital of the nation's insurance industry. The Hartford Fire Insurance Company, the first insurance company in town, adopted the seventeenth-century Hertford seal as its trademark. That company is the parent of the Hartford Insurance Group, and both are still in existence today.

Sir Edwin Landseer, a British artist, created the stag portrait ("Monarch of the Glen") in 1851. The portrait was reproduced many times after Westminster Palace refused to hang it (because the House of Commons had not been consulted about the artist's fee). Copies eventually showed up in saloons across America's frontier, helping the trademark become even more recognizable.

HARTFORD

Hartford, advertisement from *Fortune Magazine*, 1935; double-page spread; "A Promise that Has been Kept"; black and white; excellent condition; $16–20.

HINGHAM MUTUAL FIRE INSURANCE

Hingham Mutual Fire Insurance Company, calendar; unusual black-and-white calendar dated 1905; depicts a township scene with trees on both sides of road and a large home with white picket fence; 15 x 14¼ inches; very good/excellent condition; $100–200.

LIBERTY NATIONAL LIFE

Liberty National Life, metal sign; 20 x 30 inches; ca. 1950s; fair condition; $50–75.

MASSACHUSETTS BONDING AND INSURANCE

Massachusetts Bonding and Insurance, wood sign; logoed image of Massasoit Indian for Boston insurance company; 30½ x 17 inches excluding frame; very good condition, some wear to background and lettering decals; $150–350.

MIDDLESEX MUTUAL FIRE INSURANCE

Middlesex Mutual Fire Insurance Company, calendar; colorful scene depicting nice house and church in old country setting; 8¼ x 11¾ inches

Hartford, advertisement from *Fortune Magazine*, 1935; double-page spread; "A Promise that Has been Kept"; black and white; $16–20. *Courtesy of Lester Morris. Photo by Donald Vogt.*

Liberty National Life, metal sign; 20 x 30 inches; ca. 1950s; fair condition; $50–75. *Collection of and photo by Iris November.*

excluding mat and frame; very good condition with minor paper loss and creasing on edges; $50–150.

MUTUAL LIFE OF NEW YORK
Mutual Life of New York Insurance, cardboard sign; fair/good condition; $50–100.

NATIONAL INSURANCE
National Insurance, tin letter folder; depicts Lady Liberty and the flag; Kellogg & Bulkeley folder; rare variety; 3 x 12¾ inches; good condition, some rusting and chipping; $50–150.

NEW YORK LIFE INSURANCE
New York Life Insurance Company, paper poster; depicts a man and boy on bicycle with flag dating 1897; 15¼ x 20¾ iches; good overall condition; $100–300.

NIAGARA FIRE INSURANCE
Niagara Fire Insurance Company, paper sign; depicts a scene of Niagara Falls with $1 million mark; 21½ x 16 inches; very good condition overall with some staining; $150–300.

PROVIDENCE INSURANCE
Providence Insurance Co., tin sign; oval portrait of George Washington; 17½ x 24 inches; good/very good condition, overall dirt haze, some small rust spots, minor scratching; $150–250.

PRUDENTIAL INSURANCE

Prudential was founded in 1875 by John F. Dryden. The slogan this company had used since 1896 ("The Prudential has the Strength of Gibraltar") is so closely associated with the company's solidity that, over the years, some people have been surprised that the actual Rock of Gibraltar does not have the slogan written across its face. Mortimer Remington, an account executive, coined the phrase when the president of Prudential requested his advertising agency to create "a symbol of lasting, enduring strength."

The company's contemporary slogan—"Get a Piece of the Rock"—was introduced in 1970 and has been used ever since.

PRUDENTIAL
Prudential, rotogravure advertisement from the *New York Times*,

INSURANCE COMPANIES ■ 227

Prudential, rotogravure advertisement from the *New York Times*, 1918; sepia ad depicts warships set against the Rock; $20–25. *Courtesy of Lester Morris. Photo by Donald Vogt.*

Prudential, advertisement from *National Geographic*, 1931; "Look—Before you lapse"; family scene; black and white; $9–12.

Prudential Insurance Co. of America, paperweight; ca. 1890–1920; depicts home office in Newark, New Jersey; 2½ x 4¼ inches; $50–75. *From the collection of Stuart Kammerman. Photo by Donald Vogt.*

1918; sepia ad depicts warships set against the Rock; excellent condition; $20–25.

Prudential, advertisement from *National Geographic*, 1931; "Look—Before you lapse"; family scene; black and white; excellent condition; $9–12.

Prudential, advertisement from *Sunday News Coloroto Magazine*, 1956; color photo depicts little girl and boy walking down forest path; excellent condition; $8–10.

Prudential, advertisement from *Sunday News*, June 17, 1956; red background with child wearing mortarboard and tassel; excellent condition; $8–10.

Prudential Insurance Co. of America, paperweight; ca. 1890–1920; depicts home office in Newark, New Jersey; 2½ x 4¼ inches; excellent condition; $50–75.

UNION CENTRAL LIFE

Union Central Life Insurance, self-framed tin sign; large image of Union Central Life home office; 25½ x 37½ inches; very good/excellent condition, light overall soiling, some minor rubs, old small scratch in sky; $500–700.

VERMONT MUTUAL FIRE INSURANCE

Vermont Mutual Fire Insurance Company, calendar; dated 1902; depicts a green concrete background with spread-winged eagle flying out of the background; 11½ x 16¼ inches; fair/good condition with some tears and creasing; $25–100.

WILLIAM G. LORD INSURANCE

William G. Lord Insurance Company, calendar; colorful scene of mother and son looking into the port awaiting the return of the man of the house; 9¾ x 16½ inches; good overall condition with some minor edge loss, good colors; $25–100.

CHAPTER TWENTY-FIVE
KITCHEN APPLIANCES

DOVER

Dover Egg Beater, paper sign; maid uses Dover beater to whisk eggs in a bowl; early 1870s lithograph; approximately 9 x 12 inches; excellent condition; trimmed edges, minor soiling; $1,000–1,600.

MAYTAG

The Maytag Company was founded in 1893 by F. L. Maytag and three other men. Maytag had come to Iowa as a boy in a covered wagon. The first inventions the company produced were a threshing machine band-cutter and self-feeder attachments. By the turn of the century, the firm was also producing hay presses, hog waterers, and numerous specialized feeders and harvesting equipment. Between 1907 and 1911, the company made Maytag-Mason automobiles and produced farm tractors as late as 1916. In fact, the first Maytag clothes washer was not made until 1907 and was considered only a sideline to the farm equipment. It was at this time that F. L. Maytag became the sole owner of the firm.

Maytag's first washer, the Pastime, has a wooden tub with a hand crank. The crank turned an inside dolly with pegs, which pulled the clothes through the water and against the corrugated tub sides (see "Brief History of Maytag," published by the company). By 1911, changes to the washer were made and the first model with an electric motor was introduced. In 1914, the Multi-Motor gasoline engine washer became available to those customers who did not have electric power, and in 1919, the company cast its first aluminum washer tub.

During the first half of the 1920s, the company expanded under the supervision of L. B. Maytag, F. L. Maytag's son. L.B. served as president of the company from 1920 to 1926, and was a member of the board of directors from 1940 until he died in 1966.

Howard Snyder, a former mechanic, invented a new type of washer that Maytag introduced in 1922. The new washer forced

Hotpoint, wooden jointed doll; point-of-sale piece; designed by Maxfield Parrish; ca. 1930s; 17 inches; $1,000–1,500. *Courtesy of Neil and Nancy Berliner. Photo by Donald Vogt.*

water through the clothes with a vaned agitator mounted in the bottom of the tub, rather than dragging clothes through the water with a lid dolly. The success of the new washer put Maytag into the washer business exclusively; it discontinued the farm machinery line. By 1927, the company had produced its first million washers, and by contemporary times has produced more than forty-five million laundry and kitchen appliances.

Like many other companies, Maytag discontinued its production of washers during World War II, concentrating on helping war efforts. It resumed production of wringer washers in 1946, however, and added a clothes dryer to the product line in 1953. It also began marketing a line of ranges and refrigerators in 1946, but discontinued the ranges and refrigerators in 1960. In the late 1950s, the company expanded into the commercial laundry field and introduced many innovations, such as stacking two regular-size dryers on top of each other to save space and conserve energy. In 1968, the company unveiled a line of food waste disposals, and in 1969, added a built-in dishwasher as well as a convertible dishwasher. Today Maytag builds a complete line of dishwashers.

The company continued to grow by acquiring other companies such as Hardwick Stove Company of Cleveland, Tennessee (1981); Jenn-Air Corp. of Indianapolis, Indiana (1982); and the Hoover Group/Chicago Pacific Corporation (1989).

One of the most recognizable advertising campaigns is Maytag's "lonely repairman." Originally played by Jesse White, an actor whose career was well established by the 1940s, the role has recently been taken over by Gordon Jump, of television's "WKRP in Cincinnati." The year 1992 marked the character's twenty-fifth anniversary—the longest-running commercial campaign in television history.

The character was originally created in 1967 by Leo Burnett, the well-known advertising company that has been responsible for many of today's familiar faces in advertising. The agency contacted Hollywood casting agents and requested an individual who would not only look like a repairman but have an expressive face and the ability to speak with authority. Several actors vied for the part, including well-known comedian Phil Silvers, but Jesse White was chosen because of his sad, puppy-dog look. It was a look that certainly fit the "Ol' Lonely" trademark tag. (Though White has been replaced by Jump in Maytag's commercials, he still works for the company as a consultant.)

Some of the best-known individual commercials include: "Drill Sergeant," 1967; "Oldest Maytag Repairman," 1971; "Lighthouse," 1982; "Guitar," 1981; and "Repairman's Dream," 1983.

The Maytag corporation includes the following companies and products: Hoover/North America; Jenn-Air; Magic Chef; Admiral; Norge; Hardwick; Hoover/Europe; Hoover/Australia; and Dixie-Narco.

MAYTAG

Maytag, advertisement from *Good Housekeeping*, 1927; black and white; winter scene and Maytag washer; excellent condition; $9–12.

Maytag, advertisement from *Good Housekeeping*, 1927; depicts three wise men at bottom of ad "Christmas—The Ideal Gift" (shows washer); excellent condition; $9–12.

Maytag, advertisement from *Good Housekeeping*, 1927; depicts three wise men at bottom of ad; "Christmas—The Ideal Gift (shows washer); $9–12. *Courtesy of Lester Morris. Photo by Donald Vogt.*

232 ■ ADVERTISING

Maytag, advertisement from *Successful Farming*, 1917; depicts women outside with washer (on battlefield); black and white; $4–7. *Courtesy of Paper Lady/Bernie and Dolores Fee. Photo by Donald Vogt.*

Maytag, advertisement from *Successful Farming*, 1917; at North Dakota; black and white; $4–7. *Courtesy of Paper Lady/Bernie and Dolores Fee. Photo by Donald*

Maytag, advertisement from *The Household Magazine*, 1948; color ad depicts Millie Peterson and her reliable washer; excellent condition; $6–8.

Maytag, advertisement from *Successful Farming*, 1917; depicts women outside with washer (on battlefield); black and white; excellent condition; $4–7.

Maytag, advertisement from *Successful Farming*, 1917; depicts women in classroom at Iowa State College; excellent condition; $4–7.

Maytag, advertisement from *Successful Farming*, 1917; at North Dakota; black and white; excellent condition; $4–7.

Maytag, advertisement from *Successful Farming*, 1917; depicts washer working at Plattsburg Reserve Officers Military Training Camp; excellent condition; $4–7.

MR. CONTROL

Mr. Control (oven control settings), metal figure, 8¼ inches tall; "made by Robertshaw-Fulton Co.; Greensburg, Pa."; ca. 1960s; extremely rare; excellent condition; $350–450.

PROCESS

Process Gas Range, paper sign and calendar; 1898; depicts domestic interior with female cook holding loaf of just-baked bread; approximately 14½ x 22½ inches excluding mat and frame; overall 19½ x 27½ inches; excellent condition, full calendar pad attached; $150–250.

KITCHEN APPLICANCES ■ 233

Mr. Control (oven control settings), metal figure; 8¼ inches tall; "made by Robertshaw-Fulton Co.; Greensburg, Pa."; ca. 1960s; extremely rare; $350–450. *Courtesy of Neil and Nancy Berliner. Photo by Neil Berliner.*

Tupperware, ceramic figurine; 8 inches; woman with Tupperware products; "special edition made exclusively for Tupperware, series 1" on bottom of figure; ca. 1970s; $300–400. *Courtesy of Neil and Nancy Berliner. Photo by Donald Vogt.*

PYNX

Pynx, glass display sign; interesting backlit display pictures maid holding wash product with sink in background; mottled green background with gold letters; 28 x 21½ x 14 inches; excellent condition; $100–300.

TUPPERWARE

Tupperware, ceramic figurine; 8 inches; woman with Tupperware products; "special edition made exclusively for Tupperware, series 1" on bottom of figure; ca. 1970s; excellent condition; $300–400.

WHIRLPOOL

The Whirlpool Corporation began as Upton Machine Co. in St. Joseph, Michigan, in 1911. The company produced electric-motor-driver wringer washers and sold its first order to Sears, Roebuck and Co. in 1916, but did not become Sears' sole supplier of washers until 1924. In 1929, Upton merged with Nineteen Hundred Washer Company of Binghamton, New York, and operated plants in both Michigan and New York until the Binghamton site closed in 1939.

The first automatic washer, nicknamed the "Jeep," was introduced by Sears in 1947, but the Whirlpool brand automatic washer was not introduced until 1948—one line of products for Sears, another for Whirlpool.

In 1950, the Nineteen Hundred Washer corporation was renamed the Whirlpool Corporation and automatic dryers were added to the company's product line. By 1951, Whirlpool opened its own parts distribution center, located in LaPorte, Indiana. The company also merged with Clyde Porcelain Steel (Ohio) and converted that plant to washer production; it ultimately became the world's largest washer plant.

In 1955, a busy year for the corporation, whirlpool purchased manufacturing facilities in Marion, Ohio, and merged with Seeger Refrigeration Co. of St. Paul, Minnesota, as well as with the Estate range and air-conditioning divisions of RCA, thus establishing RCA Whirlpool as the brand name and Whirlpool-Seeger Corporation as the company name. During that year, it also acquired a refrigeration plant in Evansville, Indiana, from International Harvester.

The first full line of RCA Whirlpool home appliances was introduced in 1956, and the name was used until 1967, but in 1957, the company name was changed back to Whirlpool Corporation. The year 1957 also saw Whirlpool's entrance into the international market with its purchase of equity interest in Multibras S.A.

During the 1960s, Whirlpool purchased more manufacturing facilities, entered the Canadian market, and constructed new manufacturing plants. The trend continued throughout the 1970s and 1980s. In 1985, the company purchased Mastercraft Industries Corporation, marking its entry into the manufacture of kitchen cabinets, and in 1986, purchased KitchenAid and St. Charles Manufacturing, but sold Heil-Quaker Home Systems Inc., its central heating and cooling business.

The 1980s and early 1990s saw more mergers for Whirlpool to bring them an even larger slice of the international market. In 1988, the company acquired the Roper brand name (Roper produced a full line of value-oriented home appliances).

Currently the company is the world's leading manufacturer and marketer of major home appliances; is headquartered in Benton Harbor, Michigan; and manufactures products in ten countries, while marketing products under nine major brand names in more than forty-five countries.

WHIRLPOOL

Whirlpool, advertisement from *Ladies' Home Journal*; ca. early 1960s; shows the latest in Whirlpool's line of dishwashers; excellent condition; $4–6.

Whirlpool, advertisement from unknown magazine; shows woman with newest Whirlpool washer and dryer; ca. 1950s; excellent condition; $4–6.

CHAPTER TWENTY-SIX
◼ LIGHTING ◼

EDISON MAZDA
(*see also* "General Electric")
Edison Mazda, blotter; pictures bulbs; excellent condition; $18–24.

Edison Mazda, calendar; dated 1924; illustrated by Maxfield Parrish; calendar illustration is *The Venetian Lamplighter*; months of November and December remain on pad; calendar advertises for Higgins & Gilgore of Scotia, New York; small size; good condition; $500–750.

Edison Mazda, calendar; dated 1925; illustrated by Maxfield Parrish; calendar illustration is *Dreamlight*; rich colors; large size; December sheet on pad; excellent condition; $1,800–2,000.

Edison Mazda, calendar; dated 1932; illustrated by Maxfield Parrish; small calendar print; illustration is titled *Solitude*; print is cropped and framed; very good condition; $165–225.

Edison Mazda, calendar; dated 1923; illustrated by Maxfield Parrish; *The Lamp Seller of Baghdad*; large size; full calendar pad; mint condition, complete with original mailing tube; $2,500–3,500.

Edison Mazda, calendar; dated 1931; illustrated by Maxfield Parrish; *The Waterfall*; 40 x 21 inches; full calendar pad; framed; near-mint condition; $1,800–2,400.

Edison Mazda, countertop display; papier-mâché light bulb; approximately 3 feet tall; good condition; $80–120.

Mazda/General Electric, pressed cardboard bulb man figure; ca. 1920s; 18 inches; average condition; $1,000–1,500.

Mazda Lamps, hooded metal and glass light fixture; promotes "National Mazda Lamps"; 13¾ x 24 x 12½ inches overall; very good condition overall, operational; $200–400.

GENERAL ELECTRIC
General Electric, the number-one distributor of home appliances also is involved in broadcasting, aerospace, and plastics.

LIGHTING ■ 237

Surprisingly, the small household appliances that bear the GE logo are made by other companies that have bought the right to use the General Electric name. (All the microwave ovens bearing the GE name are made by the Korean firm Samsung.)

The company was established by Thomas A. Edison in 1878 as the Edison Light Company. In 1889, the Edison General Electric Company was established, and in 1892, these two companies merged with the Thomas-Houston Electric Company to make General Electric.

In 1948, GE introduced a garbage disposal to shred food waste and wash it down the drain.

General Electric's consumer brands include Hotpoint, RCA, and Monogram. The company has made many advertising promotional items through the years, including ashtrays, clocks, salt-and-pepper shakers, tape measures, and numerous others.

GENERAL ELECTRIC

General Electric Can-A-Rama, giveaway; unopened; back reads "Important: 1.) This can contains a prize for you! 2.) Some cans contain valuable Bonus Prize Certificates. 3.) You must open can at dealer's store listed above to qualify for top prizes."; near-mint condition; $20–30.

General Electric, doll; used to promote General Electric's line of radios; 18 inches tall; called Bandy; looks like bandleader; jointed arms and legs; excellent condition; $125–175.

Mazda/General Electric, pressed cardboard bulb man figure; ca. 1920s; 18 inches; average condition; $1,000–1,500. *Courtesy of Neil and Nancy Berliner. Photo by Donald Vogt.*

General Electric Can-A-Rama, giveaway; unopened; back reads "Important: 1.) This can contains a prize for you! 2.) Some cans contain valuable Bonus Prize Certificates. 3.) You must open can at dealer's store listed above to qualify for top prizes"; $20–30. *Courtesy of Irreverent Relics. Photo by Donald Vogt.*

238 ■ ADVERTISING

The Plume & Atwood M'f'g Co., paperweight; ca. 1890–1910; promotes "kerosene oil burners, the royal lamp, the banner heaters, the banner bicycle lanterns"; "offices in New York, Boston and Chicago"; 2½ x 4 inches; $50–75. *From the collection of Stuart Kammerman. Photo by David Kammerman.*

General Electric, salt-and-pepper shakers; resemble refrigerator; made of milk glass; approximately 3 inches tall; excellent condition; $20–35.

PLUME & ATWOOD

The Plume & Atwood M'f'g Co., paperweight; ca. 1890–1910; promotes "kerosene oil burners, the royal lamp, the banner heaters, the banner bicycle lanterns"; "offices in New York, Boston and Chicago"; 2½ x 4 inches; excellent condition; $50–75.

REDDY KILOWATT

Ashton B. Collins, of the Alabama Poser Company, created the symbolic Reddy Kilowatt figure after experiencing an incredible lightning display that appeared to resemble the body (legs and arms) of a human being. In the late 1920s, Collins organized a firm, Reddy Kilowatt, Inc., to counsel clients on advertising and public relations.

The company owned the trademark and licenses to the Reddy Kilowatt symbol and "rented" the rights to electric companies who wanted to use it. Philadelphia Electric became the

Reddy Kilowatt, two versions of Reddy Kilowatt (both glow in the dark); (left) older version, ca. late 1940s, 5½ inches, $400–500; (right) newer version, 1951, came in a postcard mailer, $200–350. *Courtesy of Neil and Nancy Berliner. Photo by Donald Vogt.*

first company to use "Reddy" in 1934. Since that time, hundreds of domestic and foreign power companies have been licensed.

REDDY KILOWATT

Reddy Kilowatt, plastic figurine; ca. late 1940s; 5½ inches; glows in the dark; excellent condition; $400–500.

Reddy Kilowatt, plastic figurine; 1951; came in postcard mailer; glows in the dark; excellent condition; $200–350.

Reddy Kilowatt, pencil; excellent condition; $8–16.

CHAPTER TWENTY-SEVEN
■ LIQUOR ■

ADAMS TAYLOR & CO.
Adams Taylor & Co. (company made whiskey), paperweight; depicts two wooden barrels; ca. 1890–1920; 2½ inch diameter; excellent condition; $50–75.

A. OVERHOLT
A. Overholt Rye, reverse glass sign; reads "Established 1810, A. Overholt & Co./Branch Office Pittsburgh, PA./Pure Rye"; portrait of elderly gentleman in center; 36 x 24 inches excluding frame; very good/excellent condition; $500–800.

BEEFEATER GIN
Founded in 1820 in Chelsea, England, the company chose its trademark, a man attired in the uniform of the Yeoman Warders of the Tower of London in the 1890s. However, the trademark was not registered until 1910. James Burrough's sons were the people responsible for making the firm a limited liability company, as well as for choosing the company's trademark.

Beefeater is distributed all over the world by James Burrough Limited, Distillers.

BEEFEATER
Beefeater, counter display figurine; depicts gentleman who represents Beefeater's Gin; approximately 10 inches tall; plastic; ca. 1950s; $65–100.

Beefeater, store display figure, life-size cardboard display of Tudor gentleman; $45–85.

BELLE OF KENTUCKY WHISKEY
Belle of Kentucky Whiskey, bottle; paper label depicts woman (belle of Kentucky?); marked "bottled expressly for family and medicinal use"; ca. turn of century; 12 inches tall; very good condition; $25–30.

BENGAL GIN
Bengal Gin, figural display; depicts a roaring tiger in yellow and black paint; 9 x 6 x 7 inches; good condition; $50–100.

Adams Taylor & Co., paperweight, company made whiskey; paperweight depicts two wooden barrels; ca. 1890–1920; 2½ inch diameter; $50–75. *From the collection of Stuart Kammerman. Photo by Donald Vogt.*

BERNARD FISCHER

Bernard Fischer Whiskey, tin tray; 12 inches; made by Chas. W. Shonk Co.; ca. 1910–1920; depicts elderly gentleman drinking a glass of Bellmore Whiskey, and his likeness is also on bottle held in his hands; excellent condition; $150–300.

BLACK & WHITE

Black & White Scotch Whiskey, cardboard sign; depicts two Scottie dogs playing tug-of-war; original frame; 24½ x 20½ inches overall; good/very good condition, minor chipping and scuffing, slight edge wear to original mat, wear to frame; $75–150.

Black & White Scotch, figural bar display; approximately 9½ inches high; papier-mâché; excellent condition; $30–40.

CALVERT EXTRA
(*see* "Seagram's")

CLUB MANHATTAN

Club Manhattan Cocktails, tin sign; original gold leaf frame; depicts gentleman sitting on wicker chair, enjoying a smoke and a cocktail; 14½ x 10½ inches; printed by Chas. W. Shonk Co.; ca. 1894; excellent/near-mint condition; $350–450.

CROWN ROYAL
(*see* "Seagrams")

DEWAR'S

Dewar's Whiskey, tin sign; depicts Santa sitting on top of boxes of the liquor making out his Christmas list; reproduction; 13 x 16 inches; new condition; $15 retail.

ECONOMY WHISKEY

Economy Whiskey Pure Rye & Malt, sign; outstanding reverse-painted on glass; promotes "Economy Whiskey Pure Rye & Malt"; "established by the Harmony Society 1827, Economy Distilling Company, Pittsburgh, Pennsylvania"; sign has wonderfully bright reverse-painted colors including silver and gold on a black background with polychromed central figure depicting men shoveling hops; framed in oak; overall 44½ x 32½ inches; generally excellent condition to near-mint; $5,000–8,000.

FRIEDMAN

Friedman, Keiler Distillers, paper sign; depicts woman reclining on a couch with a table holding a bottle of Brook Hill Whiskey (this company's product) near her hand; approximately 20 x 14 inches excluding frame; excellent condition, bright colors, minor water stain on edge, slight soiling; $1,000–2,000.

GLENLIVET

(see "Seagram's")

GOLD SEAL

Gold Seal Champagne, change trays (2); both picture the champagne bottle; good/very good condition; $75–150.

GREEN RIVER

Green River Whiskey, tin charger; disheveled black man with sway-backed donkey; 24 inch diameter; good condition, general overall fading, scratches and chipping; $250–500.

Green River Whiskey, tin sign; familiar black man and mule; 33 x 24 inches excluding frame; frame original, missing imprinted tag; very good condition, some minor overall fading, rust spotting, slight wear overall; $200–500.

Green River Whiskey, tin sign; classic image of black man and mule in original retouched frame; 40½ x 31 inches overall; fair condition, overall fading, general wear and soiling; $250–500.

I. W. HARPER

I. W. Harper Whiskey, sign; depicts hunting cabin scene with game pelts hanging on wall and lying on floor; 17½ x 23½ inches excluding frame; very good/excellent condition, vivid colors; $450–650.

I. W. Harper Whiskey, Vitrolite sign; interior of hunting lodge; 18 x 24 inches excluding frame; poor condition, several reglued breaks; $100–200.

HUNTER BALTIMORE RYE

Hunter Baltimore Rye, tin sign; dapper gent on stallion bounding over rail; brightly colored; 18 x 24 inches excluding frame; excellent condition; $1,250–1,550.

JACK DANIEL'S

Jack Daniel's Whiskey, tin sign; depicts the label in black and white; approximately 17½ x 12½ inches; reproduction; $15 retail.

JAMES HANLEY BREWING

The James Hanley Brewing Co., paperweight; ca. 1890–1920; picture of Prince Alert 1.57, "The World's Champion Harness Gelding"; 2½ x 4 inches; excellent condition; $50–75.

JAMES E. PEPPER

James E. Pepper Whiskey, reverse-painted glass sign; large factory scene of distillery with mother-of-pearl and etched highlights; rare; original frame; 43 x 31½ inches including frame; generally good condition, some paint lifting in background and some discoloration; $3,000–4,000.

Jack Daniel's Whiskey, tin sign; depicts the label in black and white; approximately 17½ x 12½ inches; reproduction; $15 retail. *Courtesy of Doc Davis/Antique-Alike. Photo by Donald Vogt.*

The James Hanley Brewing Co., paperweight; ca. 1890–1920; picture of Prince Alert 1.57, "The World's Champion Harness Gelding"; 2½ x 4 inches; $50–75. *From the collection of Stuart Kammerman. Photo by David Kammerman.*

Jim Beam, Statue of Liberty figurine bottle, 18 inches tall, made of china, ca. 1976; Kontinental Wine, Statue of Liberty figurine bottle, 14 inches tall; both in excellent condition; $35–40 each. *Collection of and photo by Iris November.*

JIM BEAM

Jim Beam, Statue of Liberty figurine bottle; 18 inches tall; made of china; ca. 1976; Kontinental Wine, Statue of Liberty figurine bottle; 14 inches tall. Both in excellent condition; $35–40 each.

Jim Beam, glasses; promote Kentucky Derby; assorted designs; 7½ inches tall; 1988, 1989, 1990; $3–5 each.

JOHN JAMISON

John Jamison & Son Whiskey, self-framed tin sign; 28 x 22 inches; good condition; $50–150.

JOHNNIE WALKER

In 1820, John Walker, a Scot, bought a grocery and liquor business in Kilmarnock and made a success of it. His son, Alexander, brought the company to international markets, and his grandson (also Alexander) was knighted in 1888. It was the younger Alexander's idea to memorialize John Walker by depicting him as a jaunty Regency figure, the trademark for the firm, and to accompany the trademark with the slogan "Johnnie Walker born 1820—still going strong." The company has used the striding figure since 1910; the original sketch survived World War II bombings and it remains with the company to this day.

JOHNNIE WALKER

Johnnie Walker Chuck-a-Luck Game; approximately 6 feet tall; dice cage twirls several pairs of fuzzy dice; rules are written below the dice cage; "Bust or 1 pair = 1 point, 2 pair or three of a kind = 2 points, Straight or full house = 3 points, 4 of a kind = 5 points, 5 of a kind = 10 points"; ca. 1960s; very good condition; $250–400.

J. W. M. FIELD'S WHISKEY

J. W. M. Field's Whiskey, tin sign; pretty hostess in gown and wearing pearls holds advertising tray with bottle and shot of Champion whiskey on top; approximately 19½ x 28 inches excluding frame; very good/excellent condition, some minor pitting of surface with apparent overall surface treatment and minor in-painting; $800–1,500.

KENTUCKY WHISKEY

Kentucky Whiskey, counter display piece; hollow plaster St. Bernard dog; approximately 3 feet tall; excellent condition; $400–800.

MAHONEY WHISKEY

Mahoney Whiskey, tip tray; pictures pillared and porticoed building (possibly the Jefferson Memorial in Arlington, Virginia); 4¼ inches; good to very good condition, some chipping and spotting, overall wear; $55–110.

McCULLOUGH'S LEAP

McCullough's Leap Rye Whiskey, tin tray; 12 inches; made by Tuscarora Adv. Co.; ca. 1890–1900; pictures frontiersman with Indians in background; fine/excellent condition; $200–400.

MONTICELLO

Monticello Distilling Company, self-framed tin sign; irregular-shaped embossed framed image of the "Home of Thomas Jefferson" with colonists preparing for hunt in foreground; 39 x 28 inches; good condition, fading primarily to building in background, overall chipping, minor rust spotting and soiling; $300–600.

Monticello Whiskey, change trays (2); hunting scene on lawn in front of Monticello; 6¼ x 4½ inch oval; good/very good overall condition; $25–100.

JAS. E. PEPPER

Jas. E. Pepper, reverse glass sign; large factory scene of distillery with abalone and etched highlights; exceedingly rare; original frame; 43 x 31½ inches including frame; fair condition, general overall lifting of background colors, some discoloration to lettering, decorative loss to original frame; $2,500–4,000.

OLD CROW

Old Crow, plastic counter display figure; depicts trademark Old Crow in top hat, with glasses and sparkle-top cane; approximately 32 inches tall to top of hat; all pieces are intact; ca. 1950s; excellent condition; $250–350.

OLD JUDSON

Old Judson/J. C. Stevens, match safe; depicts daughter handing father drink, wife helping him on with coat; ca. 1910–1920s; excellent condition; $150–200.

OLD LOG CABIN

Old Log Cabin Bourbon Whiskey, container; depicts log cabin in the woods; never opened; 4 x 8½ inches; good condition with paint chipping overall; $150–225.

OLD OVERHOLT

Old Overholt Whiskey, tin sign; two hunters and setter in field sharing bottle of whiskey; 36 x 28 inches overall including original frame; excellent condition, few small chips, slight overall soiling; $500–1,000.

OLD SCHENLEY

Old Schenley Whiskey, tin sign; depicts Daniel Boone—"I've Struck the Trail"—with canoe in background; 19½ x 28 inches excluding frame; good condition, some wear overall; $200–600.

Old Judson/J. C. Stevens, match safe; depicts daughter handing father drink, wife helping him on with coat; ca. 1910–1920s; $150–200. *Courtesy of Marilyn and De Underwood/Tins Again Collectibles. Photo by Donald Vogt.*

P. H. Hamburger Co., paperweight; ca. 1900–1930; promotes "Bridgeport Pure Rye/G.W. Jones Monongahela Rye/Bridgeport Pure Malt"; "offices in Pittsburg, PA"; 2½ x 4 inches; $40–60. *From the collection of Stuart Kammerman. Photo by Donald Vogt.*

Seagram's, advertisement from *Life* magazine, 1958; depicts silver tray holding bottle of whiskey and two full glasses; $7–9. *Courtesy of Lester Morris. Photo by Donald Vogt.*

O.V.G.

O.V.G. Whiskey, porcelain shot glass holder; approximately 3¼ inch diameter x 3½ inches including shot glass; good/very good condition, some wear to transfer, bottom is chipped, gold leaf is somewhat worn; $100–200.

PAUL JONES

Paul Jones Whiskey, tin sign; depicts large folio scene of dead game on cabin wall; 32 x 46 inches excluding original frame; overall 44 x 58 inches; good condition, some in-painting and overall surface coating; $200–500.

P. H. HAMBURGER CO.

P. H. Hamburger Co., paperweight; ca. 1900–1930; promotes "Bridgeport Pure Rye/G.W. Jones Monongahela Rye/Bridgeport Pure Malt"; "offices in Pittsburgh, PA"; 2½ x 4 inches; excellent condition; $40–60.

SEAGRAM'S

In 1889, Yechiel Bronfman fled Russia for Canada, his destiny—the liquor business. During World War I, Bronfman's sons, Samuel and Allan, sold liquor via mail order, even though all of the Canadian provinces (except Quebec) were dry. Surprisingly, liquor sales were allowed via the mail system.

When liquor was legalized in the 1920s, the brothers began a distillery and bought out Joseph E. Seagram & Sons, then adopted the name in 1927. They were opened for business in 1928 and took advantage of Prohibition, which had swept the United States. Thus Seagram's popularity was already entrenched when Prohibition ended, and in 1934 Seagram's introduced Seagram's 5 Crown (which later became 7 Crown).

By 1938, Seagram's was number one in the liquor business. However, as the decades progressed, whiskey's popularity declined, so Seagram's got into other businesses—for example, it became 19 percent owner of Conocol Oil Company in 1980.

Seagram's whiskeys include: Seagram's Five Star, 7 Crown, Seagram's V.O., Crown Royal, and Calvert Extra. The scotch whiskeys include: Glenlivet and Crown Royal. It also makes gins, rums, cognac, wines, wine coolers, and fruit juice coolers.

SEAGRAM'S
Seagram's, advertisement from *Life* magazine, 1947; Air Express goods from nonstop planes; $7–9.

Seagram's advertisement from *Life* magazine, 1958; depicts silver tray holding bottle of whiskey and two full glasses; $7–9.

Seagram's Whiskey, paper poster; depicts 1905 horse and jockey parade after the Ontario Jockey Club race; approximately 43 x 29 inches excluding mat and frame; overall 51½ x 37½ inches; F. D. M. Printers; white border folded beneath mat (not trimmed); excellent to near-mint condition, minor spotting in sky, slight chipping; $800–1,250.

SEAL OF KENTUCKY
Seal of Kentucky Whiskey, tin sign; depicts gentlemen raising a shot of whiskey to three nudes floating above him; 19½ x 27½ inches excluding frame; very good condition, some color fading, some in-painting, lettering at bottom retouched and background enhanced; $9,000–14,000.

SOCIETY
Society Rye, tin sign; curled-corner sign with stock image of girl holding carnations; 16 x 18 inches; good overall condition, darkening to surface, minor spotting and soiling; $350–650.

STONE HILL
Stone Hill Wine, tin sign; depicts the "Bacchus Festival" with nymphs feasting and drinking; 23 inch diameter; fair/good condition, overall

flaking, surface appears treated and darkened with age, border has minor age discoloration and chipping; $200–400.

SUNNY BROOK

Sunny Brook Whiskey, tin sign; large horizontal sign with image of old man and young girl sitting on bluff overlooking factory in valley below; multi-colored, unusual, and rare; original frame; 47½ x 27 inches overall; very good/excellent condition, general soiling overall, some rust spotting; $3,000–5,000.

TRINERS

Triners Bitter Wine, paper poster; depicts a heart-shaped image with husband and wife watching daughter spell out the advertisement with building blocks; 13 x 18 inches excluding mat and frame; very good overall condition; $25–125.

WELLS AND HOPE DISTILLERS

Wells and Hope Distillers, J. Pettibone Whiskey, tin sign; early advertisement; oval insert with woman wearing lace shawl; border is made up of shafts of wheat, barrels of rye and bourbon, varieties from this New York whiskey distiller; 20 x 28 inches excluding frame; excellent condition, minor in-painting, some crazing primarily in background, overall surface preservation coat; $750–1,500.

WHITE SEAL

White Seal Pure Rye, paper sign; bare-breasted woman bathing beside a Bedouin barge; unusual and provocative poster; 37 x 24 inches excluding original frame; 49½ x 36½ inches overall; fair/good condition, top irregular, some tears and discoloration due to age, some chipping, frame repainted; $4,500–6,000.

WHITE STAR

White Star Rye, tin sign; depicts cowboy, bartender, and the dude at the rail toasting "Here's oh"; double registered promotion for pure rye whiskey; one of two known in this size; 22 x 32 inches excluding frame; 27 x 37 inches overall; period Eastlake frame; very good/excellent condition; $20,000–25,000

WILSON

Wilson Whiskey, tin sign; lettering reads "A Nightcap of Wilson"; depicts two diaphanously gowned women taking shots of Wilson's whiskey; boudoir is elaborately decorated with draped bed in background; 37 x 49 inches overall in original frame; good/very good condition, some overall fading, minor denting, slight in-painting primarily to background; $7,500–12,500.

WRIGHT & TAYLOR

Wright & Taylor Whiskey, tin sign; large image of two pretty girls in stream overlooking multiple factory buildings with train; important early piece, one of only two known; "Blend and Straight" (whiskeys) has been added to sign's lettering (probably by distributor); printed by Chas. Shonk; enlarged version of tray with same design; 33½ x 23½ inches; excluding frame; very good condition, some minor color fading, minor scratches; $1,500–3,500.

CHAPTER TWENTY-EIGHT
■ MEATS, FISH, ■ FROZEN FOODS

ARMOUR AND COMPANY

The Armour and Company name began in 1867 when Philip Danforth Armour and John Plankinton moved their Milwaukee, Wisconsin, provision business to Chicago. By 1872, they moved to another plant at the Union Stock Yards, where they soon began using the natural ice and coolers developed during that year.

The Armour Star oval label, created in 1877, was used to designate the company's ham and bacon. The company began to can its meats in 1879 and used its Veribest trademark on those canned products at the turn of the century.

Other products produced by the company include pork and beans (1897), sliced bacon in jars (1902), condensed milk (1912), and a variety of other products including soda fountain supplies, peanut butter, soups, and fruits.

A 1917 Armour's ad depicts a black cook wearing an Armour's hat and holding an Armour's holiday ham. The lettering in the upper left-hand corner reads "The Ham What Am."

Armour's packagings was redesigned in 1931 and the company began using its trademarks "Armour" and "Armour Star" on every label. The company redesigned packages again in 1943, then in 1960, and modified its trademark into a star and rectangle in 1963.

ConAgra, Inc. acquired Armour in 1983. Today the canned products are produced by Armour-Dial, a division of the Greyhound Corporation.

ARMOUR

Armour, paper over cardboard puzzle; very rare; depicts interior of tent (at world's fair?) showing many people enjoying live animal displays; 20 x 28 x ¼ inch; very good/excellent condition, slight soiling; $150–350.

Armour, doll; one of thirty different styles offered by the company since 1972 as a promotional item, sometimes tied in with its advertising; 8 inches; dressed in native French costume; near-mint condition; $5–10.

Armour, trade cards; set of eight; string bound; 1892; colorful; near-mint condition; $20–50.

GORTON'S FROZEN SEAFOOD
(*see also* "General Mills" in Baking Products chapter)

Gorton's, advertising doll; resembles Gorton's fisherman in ads; 7½ inches tall; vinyl; excellent condition; $12–15.

MASON'S

Mason's Essence of Beef, paperweight; made by Mason Concentrated Food, Co., New York; depicts a jar of the "essence," which is "specially prepared for invalids"; ca. 1890–1910; 2½ x 4 inches; excellent condition; $60–85.

OSCAR MAYER & CO.
(*see also* "Kraft General Foods" in Dairy Products chapter)

Oscar F. Mayer leased a meat market in Chicago in 1883, and by 1888 it was so popular that the owner refused to renew the lease. The Mayer family started all over again by building their own store. By 1900, forty-three employees helped Oscar and his brothers deliver their meats all over the Chicago area.

The company's first major expansion occurred in 1919. Oscar F.'s son, Oscar G. Mayer, had traveled to Madison, Wisconsin, to visit his fiancée and took advantage of an opportunity to purchase a meat-packing plant while he was there.

In 1929, the company decided to distinguish its meats from other brands on the market by banding its frankfurters with a yellow paper band bearing the Oscar Mayer name and the U.S. government inspection stamp. The company developed a pack-

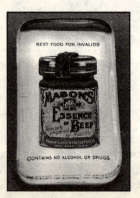

Meat, Mason's Essence of Beef, paperweight; ca. 1890–1910; made by Mason Concentrated Food Co., New York; depicts a jar of the "essence," which is "specially prepared for invalids"; 2½ x 4 inches; $60–85. *From the collection of Stuart Kammerman. Photo by David Kammerman.*

aging, merchandising, and advertising program in 1943 that stressed future needs for distribution facilities, engineering and food technology advances, and quality-control standards.

OSCAR MAYER

Oscar Mayer, advertisement from unknown newspaper, 1955; depicts Little Oscar; caption reads "Folks! For sandwich variety enjoy Oscar Mayer Bologna and Liver Sausage"; "price for the combination pack: 50 cents"; excellent condition; $5–8.

Oscar Mayer, advertisement from *Saturday Evening Post*, 1955; full color; double-page spread; depicts Little Oscar and advertises Oscar Mayer Weiners; excellent condition; $8–10.

Oscar Mayer, inflatable Little Oscar figure; available to customers as mail-in premium; approximately 30 inches tall when inflated; excellent/near-mint condition; $10–20.

MCMENAMIN & CO.

McMenamin & Co. Deviled Crabs, paper sign; depicts two women and a man in a fishing boat in background with crab crawling on shore in foreground; Virginia company; approximately 9¼ x 12½ inches; printed by A. Hoen; very good condition, borders appear trimmed, minor wrinkling and overall soiling; $1,000–2,000.

ST. LOUIS

St. Louis Beef, paper sign; depicts a man seated at a table with black butler unsheathing a tower of St. Louis Beef in front of him; 10½ x 13½ inches; printed by A. Gast & Co., St. Louis; good/very good condition, trimmed borders, some creasing to image, wrinkling, slight soiling; $300–700.

SQUIRE'S

Squire's Pig, self-framed tin sign; classic frontal sitting pig image with John P. Squire's eyes following you around the room; ca. 1906; 19¾ x 24½ inch oval; very good/excellent condition, good sheen to colors except some touch-up to background at nine o'clock, minor rubs, slight soiling; $1,800–2,500.

STARKIST TUNA

(*see* "Heinz" in Condiments/Spices chapter)
StarKist, vinyl doll; depicts Charlie the Tuna; wears glasses and a hat marked with his name; 7 inches tall; excellent condition; $7–15.

StarKist, lamp; Charlie the Tuna base; approximately 12 inches tall; excellent condition; $5–15.

StarKist, rug; depicts Charlie the Tuna; ca. 1970s; excellent condition; $8–20.

STEAK-UMM
(*see* "Heinz" in Condiment/Spices chapter)

SWIFT'S PREMIUM
Swift's Premium Ham, advertisement from *Ladies' Home Journal*, November 1921; designed by Maxfield Parrish; full spread; very good condition; $75–125.

CHAPTER TWENTY-NINE
■ MEDICINES ■

ABBOTT'S
Abbott's Angostura tin sign; reads "Aids Digestion"; depicts distinguished gentleman in tux pouring himself a glass of the product; 50 x 38 inches including frame; ca. 1899; very good condition; $4,000–5,000.

ALKA-SELTZER
(*see also* "Miles Laboratories")
Alka-Seltzer, advertisement from *Time*, ca. 1970s; "I Ate the Whole Thing"; excellent condition; $4–6.

Alka-Seltzer, hard vinyl bank; depicts Speedy figure; approximately 5½ inches tall; excellent condition; $25–45.

Alka-Seltzer, vinyl Speedy figure; 7½ inches; ca. late 1950s; very good condition; $400–500.

Alka Seltzer, cardboard box; store display; 20 x 5 x 5 inches; ca. 1970; excellent condition; $20-40.

J. C. AYER
One of the most readily recognized names in the medicine business was James C. Ayer of Lowell, Massachusetts, who invented Cherry Pectoral. He ran ads in all local newspapers that reached his customers, then branched out to include pills and sarsaparillas in his product list. He was one of the few manufacturers who could claim that a town had been named after him; Ayer, Massachusetts. (Due to Ayer's success, his hometown, Groton Junction, changed its name to his.)

Ayer started selling medicinal products around 1840 and had become a multimillionaire by 1871. By that time, his line of products included Ayer's Sarsaparilla, Ayer's Cathartic Pills, and Ayer's Cherry Pectoral, as well as a dozen or so other remedies.

Ayer advertised via almanacs, pamphlets, and newspaper ads. His shrewd business sense was revealed in the contracts he drew up between himself and the newspapers in which he advertised. He added a clause that forced the newspapers to work for patent medicine interests.

Alka-Seltzer, vinyl Speedy figure; 7½ inches; ca. late 1950s; $400–500. *Courtesy of Neil and Nancy Berliner. Photo by Donald Vogt.*

Alka-Seltzer, cardboard box store display; 20 x 5 x 5 inches; ca. 1970s; $20–40. *Courtesy of Biggar's Antiques. Photo by Donald Vogt.*

AYER'S

Ayer's Cathartic Pills, cutout Counter Display; "copyright 1883, by J. C. Ayer & Co., Lowell, MA"; 13 x 7½ inches; good condition; $400–500.

Ayer's Medicines, paper sign; winged angel distributing products for Spanish-speaking clients; 10½ x 13½ inches; excellent condition, borders trimmed, minor soiling overall; $100–300.

Ayer's Pills, tin sign; depicts cherubs holding up Cathartic pill; red background; rare; printed by Wells & Hope; 14 x 20 inches excluding frame; good/very good condition; $2,000–4,000.

Ayer's Sarsaparilla, tin sign; early Wells & Hope image of sickly girl being attended by friend and nurse in intricately decorated Victorian bedroom with patterned floor, Eastlake furniture, and clothing; 14 x 20 inches; ca. 1882–1886; good overall condition, soil spotting, some rubbing, minor chipping, hole at top and wrinkle at lower left; $1,000–3,000.

BACTINE

(see "Miles Laboratories")

BAND-AID

(*see also* "Band-Aid" in Health and Beauty Aids chapter)

Band-Aids were invented by Earle Dickson of Brunswick, New Jersey, to provide his new wife with relief from the cuts, burns, and bruises she earned in her new kitchen. Dickson worked for Johnson & Johnson, who soon heard of his ingenuity and adopted his new product. W. Johnson Kenyon, superintendent of the mill, suggested the name Band-Aid, and the product soon found a place in hospitals, pharmacies, and American homes.

The trademark was registered in 1920 and is now seen on many first aid and surgical products.

Dickson retired from Johnson & Johnson as vice president in 1957.

BAND-AID

Johnson & Johnson Band-Aids, advertisement from *Life*, 1952; full color; "Mommy always says you're safe . . ." series; near-mint condition; $4–8.

Johnson & Johnson Band-Aids, advertisement from *Saturday Evening Post*, October 22, 1949; full color; caption reads "Mommy always says you're safe when you use Johnson & Johnson"; near-mint condition; $4–8.

Band-Aid, store display box; contains seventy sheer strips; 15 x 12 x 5 inches; contemporary; near-mint condition; $35–50.

BAUER & BLACK

Bauer & Black gauzes, advertisement from *Ladies' Home Journal*, 1918; full color; depicts woman sitting in chair with child on lap; illustration by William Meade Prince; excellent condition; $4–8.

Johnson & Johnson Band-Aids, advertisement from *Life*, 1952; full color; "Mommy always says you're safe . . ." series; $4–8. *Courtesy of Paper Lady/Bernie and Dolores Fee. Photo by Donald Vogt.*

Johnson & Johnson Band-Aids, advertisement from *Saturday Evening Post*, October 22, 1949; full color; caption reads "Mommy always says you're safe when you use Johnson & Johnson"; $4–8. *Courtesy of Paper Lady/Bernie and Dolores Fee. Photo by Donald Vogt.*

Bauer & Black Sterile Surgical Dressings, advertisement from *Ladies's Home Journal*, August 1919; depicts little girl with shoe off reaching for bandages; excellent condition; $4–8.

BAYER ASPIRIN

Bayer Aspirin, tin sign; orange, navy, and white; caption reads "Safe for Aches and Pains/Bayer Aspirin/Does not depress the heart"; 18 x 15 inches; ca. 1940s; excellent condition; $75–100.

Bayer Aspirin, store display box; yellow and brown; ca. 1960s; 11 x 5 x 20 inches; near-mint condition; $65–80.

Bayer Timed-Release Aspirin, store display box; green, blue, white, and red; 11 x 5 x 20 inches; contemporary/near-mint condition; $35–50.

BEECHAM'S PILLS

Thomas Beecher, responsible for Beecham's Pills, was knighted by Queen Victoria. By 1908, he was selling a million Beecham's Pills every day. The pills claimed to cure a variety of ailments including headaches, back pains, vomiting, stomach ailments, liver complaints, nervous afflictions, kidney and urinary disorders, and menstrual problems.

BEECHAM'S

Beecham's Pills, trade card; depicts woman with pills; chromolithograph; excellent condition; $10–15.

BEECH-NUT

(*see also* "Beech-Nut" in Gum chapter)

Beech-Nut Cough Drops, tin display; vertical store dispenser for 5 cent packages; 3¼ x 10½ x 5¼ inches; excellent condition; $45–90.

Bayer Aspirin, store display box; yellow and brown; ca. 1960s; 11 x 5 x 20 inches; $65–80. *Courtesy of Biggar's Antiques. Photo by Donald Vogt.*

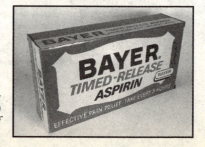

Bayer Timed-Release Aspirin, store display box; green, blue, white, and red; 11 x 5 x 20 inches; contemporary; $35–50. *Courtesy of Biggar's Antiques. Photo by Donald Vogt.*

BONE EAGLE & CO.
Bone Eagle & Co. Cough Drops, tin; pictures bone and eagle trademark for "Black" variety cough drops; 5 inch square x 7¾ inches; good condition, some overall wear; $75–150.

BOSCHEE'S AND GREEN'S
Boschee's and Green's, "Shut the Door" store card; depicts druggist mixing up potion for colds and complaints while promoting Boschee's and Green's products; 9¾ x 7¾ inches; printed by Chas. Shields; very good condition; $600–850.

CENTILIVRE
Centilivre Tonic, cardboard sign; nurse holding packaged product; 22 x 11½ inches excluding mat and frame; very good/excellent condition, minor rubbing/chipping/scratches; $40–100.

CHIEF TWO MOON
Chief Two Moon Bitter Oil, three-section cardboard display; held ointment and elixir; excellent condition, overall color spotting; $100–200.

COOK, EVERETT AND PENNELL
Cook, Everett and Pennell (wholesale druggists from Portland, Maine), Elixir of Peptic Ferments Comp., brown glass apothecary bottle approximately 13 inches tall; ca. 1870s; two large chips near cork stopper; very good condition; $55–85.

C. R. THOMAS
C. R. Thomas Eclectric Oil, tin sign; reproduction; approximately 11 x 17 inches; depicts cat climbing out of box; $15 retail.

C. R. Thomas Eclectric Oil, tin sign; reproduction; approximately 11 x 17 inches; depicts cat climbing out of box; $15 retail. *Courtesy of Doc Davis/Antique-Alike. Photo by Donald Vogt.*

CUSHING MEDICAL SUPPLY CO.
Cushing Medical Supply Co., alcohol bottle; paper label depicts Boston Gardens; full quart; ca. 1880s; excellent condition; $20–30.

DARBY'S
Darby's Swan Tolu, square-edged tin; early Somers Bros. tin for medicinal candy; black on red; 4 x 1½ x 3½ inches; very good condition, some wear; $25–75.

DAVIS'
Davis' Pain Killer, tin sign; very busy image with various types of people milling around a giant bottle of Davis' Pain Killer in Lilliputian fashion; 24 x 18 inches; good original condition, general soiling overall, some spotting; $3,000–6,000.

Perry Davis' Pain Killer, tin sign; early; depicts horse-drawn buggy loaded with bottles of the product; 23 x 18 inches excluding frame; very good condition, minor fade to colors, slight overall rubbing, soiling; $2,500–4,000.

DR. DeWITT'S REMEDIES
Dr. DeWitt's Remedies, cardboard sign; center is intricate store interior scene; around the sides are vignettes in which the product is used; 28 x 22 inches excluding frame; overall 30¼ x 24¼ inches; printed by Equitable Lith. and Eng. Co.; fair/good condition, some soiling/staining/creasing; $1,500–3,000.

DR. FROST'S
Dr. Frost's Medicinal, cabinet; blue-and-white tin front listing Dr. Frost's cures; multiple-drawer interior; wood back to case missing; 13½ x 19 x 8½ inches; very good condition, some rust spotting to front, case original, minor fade to tin; $450–750.

DR. LYNAS
Dr. Lynas Extracts, cardboard sign; no graphics; near-mint condition; $20–50.

DR. MORSE'S
Dr. Morse's Indian Root Pills, tin sign; reproduction; 10 x 16 ½ inches; depicts Indian on horse fighting bear; $15 retail.

DR. PIERCE'S

Dr. Pierce's Medicinal, paper sign; lettering reads "Pierce's Pleasant Purgative Pellets—The Little Giant Cathartic"; depicts a giant peering out a castle window at the small messenger trumpeting on the steps; printed by Clay, Cosack & Co.; ca. 1872; red and black; approximately 21½ x 27½ inches excluding frame; very good condition, minor overall soiling, some water staining, minor paper loss at edges; $2,000–4,000.

DR. SCHOLL'S

Dr. Scholl's, tin display case; features four faces; 12¼ x 15¼ x 6½ inches; very good condition, chipping and scratching, slight overall wear; $150–300.

Dr. Scholl's, tin store displays (2); one is glass-fronted, showing actual products, while other displays advertising on tin; glass-front display: 14½ x 23 x10½ inches, tin-front: 13 x 17¼ x 6½ inches; good overall, some paint loss and wear due to use; $200–300.

DR. SHOOP'S

Dr. Shoop's Restorative, embossed tin sign; framed; 9¾ x 7⅛ inches; ca. 1905; embossed portrait of Dr. Shoop and list of his cures; fine/excellent condition; $550–750.

DR. SWETT'S

Dr. Swett's, cardboard store sign; depicts trademark of boy growing to old age; 13½ x 18 inches; good condition, some staining; $35–75.

DR. THOMSON'S

Dr. Thomson's Sarsaparilla Cures, slant-front cabinet; frosted letters read "Dr. Thomson's Sarsaparilla Cures/Thomson's Flavoring Extracts are the Best"; 29 x 19½ x 17½ inches; excellent condition; $500–750.

DOUGLASS

Douglass & Sons (New Haven, Connecticut) Cough Drops, windowed store bin; early silhouette letters; oval portraits on sides; 6½ x 8 x 7 inches; fair condition, overall wear, scratches, age discoloration; $100–200.

DUKE'S PHARMACY

Duke's Pharmacy (Atlanta, Georgia), calendar drop regulator clock; 16 x 30½ x 5½ inches; good condition, case appears reconditioned, face has been retouched; $300–600.

FEHR'S

Fehr's Tonic, tin sign; scantily clad and smiling woman sits with cherubs beside her, large bottle of the tonic to her left; 22 x 29 inches; fair condition, overall fading/soiling/scratching; $50–150.

GIBLIN'S

Giblin's Liniment, display case; two-door wood case with multiple shelves; name of liniment above doors; 24 x 25¾ x 7½ inches; excellent condition; $450–850.

GIBSON'S

Gibson's Lozenges, tin; colorful floral decoration; 5¾ inches square x 8¾ inches; made in Manchester, England; very good/excellent condition, slight denting and scratches, colors bright, good sheen; $200–300.

GREEN'S MEDICINAL

Green's Medicinal, paper sign; early shot of Boschee's and Green's factory for medicinal products with Victorian building in foreground; the image is framed as if in a theater setting; 30 x 22 inches; good condition, rebacked on linen, age discoloration, some overall foxing; $500–1,000.

HENRY AND JOHNSON

Henry and Johnson Liniment, tin sign; depicts several bottles of liniment and elixir sitting on what appears to be a concrete wall; printed by Wells & Hope; 13½ x 19½ inches excluding frame; very good condition with some fading spots; $300–700.

HOOD'S

Originally from Chelsea, Vermont, Charles I. Hood moved in 1861 to Lowell, Massachusetts, where he apprenticed with a druggist. In 1866, he began working for Theodore Metcalf and Company of Boston. He opened his own drugstore in 1870, entering into partnership with a friend from Lowell. Hood wholly owned the store six years later, and soon compounded his own medicines, selling them in his store as well as in nearby towns.

Within a short period of time, he began advertising his medicines and selling them under his own label. Some of the bottled medicines and other products he sold nationally included Hood's Sarsaparilla and Hood's Pills.

He created almanacs, calendars, coupon certificates, trade cards, posters, jigsaw puzzles, and other types of advertising memorabilia to promote his products and illustrated them with cherubic children's faces or attractive female images.

HOOD'S

Hood's, calendar; 1894; full pad; excellent condition; $75–175.

Hood's calendar; 1888; full pad; small piece out of top; near-mint condition; $75–175.

Hood's calendar; 1898; full pad; near-mint condition; $75–175.

Hood's calendar; 1918; full pad with insert flyer; near-mint condition; $75–175.

Hood's Sarsaparilla, plate; lithographed on cardboard; 8¾ inches; ca. 1885; depicts farmer with gun, black man with stick, and barking dog all in pursuit of hawk swooping to catch chicken; testimonials on back regarding cures obtained by using Hood's Sarsaparilla; extremely rare; very good condition; $250–400.

Hood's, cardboard advertising plate; Sarsaparilla medicinal plate; two birds on front; testimonials on back; 9 inch diameter; excellent condition; $25–75.

HOSTETTER'S

Hostetter's Bitters, reverse glass sign; depicts St. George slaying the dragon; image is surrounded with mother-of-pearl inset letters; 22 x 28½ inches excluding frame; poor/fair condition, colors are flaking and leaf is lifting; $100–300.

HUMPHREY'S

Humphrey's Remedies, display case; double-sided tin case with lists of medicines; 18½ x 21 x 6¾ inches; fair/good condition, chipping and fading on one side, discoloration and chipping to the other; $150–300.

HUNT'S

Hunt's Health Pills and Liver Cure, tin sign; 5½ x 6¾ inches; printed by Kellogg & Bulkeley; ca. 1880–1890; inset depicts little girl in sailor outfit; excellent condition; $250–350.

IMPERIAL COUGH DROPS

Imperial Cough Drops, tin; early Ginna two-color tin; topography display; 6 x 8 x 4 inches; fair/good condition, some chipping and rust spotting; $25–75.

Jos. Fleming & Son, paperweight; "physicians prescribe Fleming's Export Rye Whiskey and Fleming's Malt Whiskey"; "company located in Pittsburg, PA"; ca. 1890–1920; 2½ x 4 inches; $50–75. *From the collection of Stuart Kammerman. Photo by David Kammerman.*

JOS. FLEMING & SON

Jos. Fleming & Son, paperweight; "physicians prescribe Fleming's Export Rye Whiskey and Fleming's Malt Whiskey"; "company located in Pittsburg, PA"; ca. 1890–1920; 2½ x 4 inches; excellent condition; $50–75.

KENNEDY'S

Kennedy's Medicine, tin sign; Winged Victory—"The Angel of Mercy"—slaying a serpent, the entwined pestilence of disease; early Kellogg & Bulkeley sign; 20 x 28 inches excluding frame; fair condition, general wear overall, surface coating, age discoloration; $450–750.

KIDNEY-WORT

(*see* "Diamond Dyes" in Dyes chapter)

KLEIN'S

Klein's Cough Drops, pocket tin; Japanese-style figural animal on front, lettered back; 3 x 3 inches; good condition, some paint loss to the sides and image; $25–75.

LASH'S

Lash's Bitters, wood sign; lithograph decal transfer on oak panel with gold leaf letters; depicts an attractive woman patting a horse's head; lettering reads "Perfect Laxative"; 14 x 20 inches; good/very good condition, overall darkening due to age, soiling, vertical age crack; $300–600.

LUDEN'S

Luden's Cough Drops, tin; 7⅞ x 6 x 3¼ inches; early version with lettering on only one side; very good/excellent condition; $50–100.

LUTTED'S
Lutted's Cough Drops, glass jar; figural log cabin cough drop container; 7½ x 5½ x 7 inches; very good condition, some chips; $200–400.

LYDIA PINKHAM
Lydia Pinkham first sold her Vegetable Compound for women's ills in 1875. Pinkham, an abolitionist and women's rights activist, lived and worked in Lynn, Massachusetts, near the little house where fugitive slave Frederick Douglass had lived. Mother of four, Pinkham kept a notebook that she filled with folk remedies while she watched her children grow up. When her husband's business failed, he became ill and the responsibility of supporting the family fell on Lydia and her sons.

One of the cures Lydia had listed in her notebook labeled "Medical Directions for Ailments" was a "female weakness cure." When women from Salem came to the Pinkham house to purchase a few bottles of Lydia's remedy one day, Dan Pinkham, Lydia's son, came up with the idea of bottling and selling the medicine.

The family worked together, creating ads and pamphlets to sell "Lydia E. Pinkham's Vegetable Compound." They brewed the first batches in the cellar, but in 1876, the Lydia E. Pinkham Medicine Company was formed.

Many thousands of pamphlets were distributed to promote Lydia's medicine, then Dan started selling the compound via horse-and-wagon sales. But sales truly picked up when the family began advertising in the *Boston Herald*. In 1879, Lydia Pinkham's photograph was added to the brochures and other advertising. Meant to convey the image of a "healthy woman," Pinkham's portrait was the first used to sell a product. She soon became a national figure and even became the focus of an 1880s song.

Subsequent generations of the Pinkham family continued to run the Lynn, Massachusetts, factory for many years, but in 1968, the physical plant moved to Puerto Rico (the original Lynn building still stands).

LYDIA PINKHAM
Lydia Pinkham's Compound, bottle; ca. late 1880s; paper label describes what the compound will do; 9 inches tall; excellent condition; $18–22.

Lydia Pinkham's Compound, trade card; chromolithograph; decorated with flowers; approximately 3 x 4 inches; excellent condition; $5–8.

MATHIEU

Mathieu Syrup for Coughs and Colds, wooden medicinal thermometer; lettering is in both English and French; made in Canada; 4 x 24 inches; good condition, some chipping primarily at edges, age darkening; $150–250.

MILES LABORATORIES

Miles Laboratories of Elkart, Indiana, was founded by Dr. Franklin L. Miles in 1884. He had been marketing and selling a product he called "Restorative Nervine," a tonic that was to have treated a number of chronic illnesses. Miles served as president of the firm from the time he founded it until his death in 1929.

When the business was incorporated in 1885, Dr. Miles had two partners: Hugh McLachlan and Norris Felt. The three joined to make the Dr. Miles Medical Company. At first, business was lean and the company seemed ready to go under, but in 1887 McLachlan and Felt sold their interests to George Compton and A. R. Burns (a druggist). After the sale, more money was put into advertising. One of the first ads was placed in the *Goshen Weekly News* in 1887 and read: "$5,000 Reward will be freely given for a better remedy for Headache, Nervousness, Sleeplessness, Etc. than Dr. Miles' Restorative Nervine, A Brain and Nerve Food. Contains no Opium or Morphine. Sold by Druggists. Sample Bottle Free." Marketing ideas included newspaper ads, free samples, eye-catching labeling, drugstore displays (which featured the use of paper dolls), oversized apothecary display jars (for Dr. Miles' Anti-Pain Pills to cure headache), Little Books, testimonials, pamphleteering (in English as well as foreign languages), premium offers of gold-framed pictures of *Sweet Sleep* and so on (see *Miles, 1884–1984, A Centennial History, Miles, Inc.*)

By the 1890s, the company's trademark was the so-called double profile—one profile being the nervous system of a man's face and the other the man's normal face. The company's first five products were all variations of the original Nervine tonic: Nervine (1882–present), Nerve and Liver Pills (1884–1949), Blood Purifier (1885–1937), Tonic (1885–1938), and Heart Cure (1888–1938).

Once the company was under way, advertising methods for the products became more creative. In 1890, Dr. Miles produced Little Books that reached almost every American household (*Dr. Miles Cook Book*, *A New Mother Goose*, and *Dr. Miles Candy Book*); in 1902, the first almanacs were published and they came out annually until 1942; in 1904, the first calendars arrived.

The company sent out quite a few calendars and almanacs. For example: In 1928, 2,500,000 almanacs and 200,000 calendars were printed, and at the peak of production, 23,000,000 almanacs and 35,000,000 Little Books were printed. But they weren't the only form of advertising used. In addition to advertisements in local and regional newspapers and magazines, even paper dolls were produced to sell Nervine, and point-of-purchase display units were used to sell Aspir-Mint in 1928.

Alka-Seltzer products took prominence in the almanac advertising in the 1930s and one of the first coupons was offered in 1931 (the regular twenty-five-cent package for ten cents). By 1935, the almanac was using the slogan that made Alka-Seltzer famous: "You won't dread the morning after if you take Alka-Seltzer the night before." Alka-Seltzer had been invented by A. H. "Hub" Beardsley to ward off the flu, but Maurice Treneer was the person who made the medication effervesce. The large white tablet's main ingredients are bicarbonate of soda, citric acid, magnesium, calcium, phosphate, and aspirin. By the time Miles began marketing Alka-Seltzer in 1931, Beardsley had already tested the product extensively, even to the point of taking samples on an ocean voyage he took with his family. The tablet cured the everyday aches and pains that went along with colds and flus.

The company promoted Alka-Seltzer in every way, shape, and form, but the real springboard for sales was the attention it received on radio programs such as "The Songs of Home Sweet Home," where the first Alka-Seltzer commercial aired on January 12, 1932. The announcer would command: "Listen to it Fizz!" By 1935, the slogans had changed somewhat, to "There's nothing quite like Alka-Seltzer" and "The morning after's what I hate; take Alka-Seltzer, it's great."

When television began to take over as the primary advertising medium, Alka-Seltzer sponsored a great variety of shows such as "One Man's Family," "Bonanza," "The Naked City," and "The Flintstones." Even though the advertising slogans were memorable and Alka-Seltzer's sales were far from poor, the product still needed new promotional ideas, so, in 1951, Robert Watkins, a commercial artist, drew the first "Mr. Alka-Seltzer."

That redheaded wooden figure with the Alka-Seltzer tablet for a stomach became Speedy Alka-Seltzer, a familiar advertising personality who made more than one hundred commercials. Speedy's voice was provided by Dick Beals—no one else was ever used. Speedy won many awards, including being voted top commercial for the 1950s, but in 1963, the Miles company turned over its advertising to another agency (Jack Tinker) and Speedy was dropped for another idea.

The new idea was funny, clever, and also won many awards. "No matter what shape your stomach is in" won the Cleo and a gold medal from the Art Director's Club of New York. The stomach montages continued through the 1960s, but in 1971 Miles again changed agencies (to Wells, Rich, Greene). This move occurred because of Mary Wells, who originally created the "stomachs."

This time the advertising slogans included "Try it, you'll like it" and "I can't believe I ate the whole thing." Again, Alka-Seltzer's commercials were memorable, even to the point that the "whole thing" quote became one of the ten best of the decade, according to *Newsweek*.

In addition to the regular Alka-Seltzer tablets, Miles introduced Alka-Seltzer Plus Cold Tablets in 1969; Alka-Seltzer Gold, for people who prefer an aspirin-free antacid; and Alka-2, an antacid tablet, in 1976. Another Miles product that became famous for its slogans was One-A-Day Vitamins. After years of inventive research, One-A-Day began being distributed to drugstores and warehouses in October 1940.

The company remembered its successful advertising campaign for Alka-Seltzer and repeated the formula to promote One-A-Day. The product was soon advertised on radio shows such as the "National Barndance," "Quiz Kids," and the "Alec Templeton Show." The tagline used to help customers remember the product was: "Look for the Big One on the Package." One-A-Day Vitamins were sold in apothecary jars until the 1960s, when a bottle with a safety cap was introduced.

In 1943, one of the One-A-Day ads was written in verse:

> *The One-A-Day vitamin twins are we,*
> *B Complex and A & D,*
> *And we're the ones, we must confess*
> *Who give you more, yet cost you less.*

Though the vitamins suffered a decline in 1941, several new products were introduced shortly afterward: B-Complex tablets, in January 1942, and One-A-Day multivitamins in 1943. Other variations were soon to follow—in 1948, sugar-coated One-A-Day multivitamins, and in 1952, an improved multiple tablet.

When One-A-Day ads were used on television in the 1960s, their slogan was often the sentence used to close a program; "The world's most trusted vitamin" and "The pill for people who don't know what they're missing" came to be recognized and trusted symbols of the vitamin.

In 1958, Miles researched a tasty vitamin tablet for children, which they named Chocks and introduced in 1960. An improved fruit-flavored version was introduced in 1963, and in 1969, the vitamins assumed cartoon character shapes.

In 1968, the company's advertising agency, J. Walter Thompson, suggested that Miles make children's vitamins in the shape of the familiar Flintstones characters. They proved extremely successful and are still being sold today. One of the advertising giveaways used to promote the Flintstone vitamin line through the years was a Flintstone mug, which was offered free with proof of purchase and fifty cents for postage.

Bugs Bunny tablets joined Mile's line of children's vitamins in 1971 and included the regular version plus Bugs Bunny Plus Iron and Bugs Bunny with Extra C. By the early 1980s, Miles vitamins were the most popular on the market. The company had added Theragran, Myadec 17, and Centrum 21, as well as several new and improved versions of its other vitamins.

In 1947, the Miles Production Research Laboratory began work on a product that was first called "XM472" (sounds like a rocket missile, doesn't it?). What the doctors on the project wanted to develop was a "household antiseptic germicide for topical application." The product, marketed nationally in May of 1950, was eventually called Bactine.

Early marketing stated that Bactine was a medicated, spray-on first-aid "for cuts, scratches, scrapes, sunburn, minor burns, acne and pimples." Advertising stressed that the product had multiple uses, but the product didn't take off until the packaging was revamped and Bactine was made available in aerosol form in 1953. By the mid-1950s, slogans advertising Bactine read "When a little helper gets a burn," "To clean away the dirt and help heal the hurt," and "Mom reaches for Bactine." In 1965, Bactine Skin Creme was introduced; however, it was discontinued within a few years. Additional Bactine products include Bactine Hydrocortisone Skin Care Cream (1981) and Bactine Skin Wound Cleanser (1982).

In September 1968, Miles acquired S.O.S, the number-one steel wool soap pad in United States and Canada. No one seems to know what S.O.S stands for, but it is one of America's best-known trademarks (and there is no period after the second "s"). The steel wool pad had been devised by a salesman named Edwin Cox in 1917, specifically to keep the aluminum cookware he was selling clean and shiny. He devised and patented the pad, which contained steel wool and soap, and the product caught on and grew until there were plants throughout the West and Midwest. In 1958, S.O.S was sold to General Foods, but there were legal problems and the opportunity for Miles to purchase the company opened up in 1968.

When Miles bought the company, there were already other items beside the original S.O.S pad, such as S.O.Ettes, which had a sponge attached to the back of the steel wool, and Tuffy, a plastic scouring ball. Also available were metal cleaners such as Copper-Kleen and Sliver-Kleen.

Some of the advertising Miles used for S.O.S includes television spots that featured such lines as "It's crazy to cook without it" and "We deserve every dirty pan we get." It also provided promotional booklets, such as the one available in 1979, the "S.O.S Outdoor/Indoor All-Purpose Cleaning Book." In addition, a character named Big Blue was used, appealing to the customer—"If You Love Me, You'll Use Me."

In addition to its medicinal and cleaning products, Miles began producing Cutter's insect repellent in 1983. When it was first introduced in 1960, marketing of the product began in sporting goods outlets, but word rapidly spread that Cutter's was "incredibly effective" and drugstores soon began to stock it.

Another of Miles's products was a line of food products named Morningstar Farms in the early 1970s. The products looked and tasted much like ham, sausage, and bacon, and Miles thought it was on to the food of the future, especially for those people watching their cholesterol intake. However, in mid-1982, the company decided to get out of the vegetable protein food business entirely and sold the Morningstar Farms brand.

In 1978, Bayer AG, the German pharmaceutical research center, acquired Miles. The merger expanded Miles's reach and its international growth and filled out the coverage Miles had of the pharmaceutical market.

Today Miles is active in pharmaceutical production all over the world and is responsible for so many products (both over-the-counter and prescription) that it would be extremely difficult to provide you with details of all of them within the covers of this book. (*See also* individual products listed by product name—i.e., Alka-Seltzer)

MINARD'S

Minard's Liniment, die-cut cardboard store display; costumed girl holding package of product; 9½ x 21 inches; very good/excellent condition, slight horizontal creasing, minor edge damage; $100–200.

MISCELLANEOUS

Apothecary globe; leaded glass; multicolored; drugstore hanging fixture; approximately 11 inch diameter x 16 inches; very good condition, some irregularity to shape; $1,000–1,500.

Optician's eye tester; unusual brass and cast-iron optical examiner manufactured by F. A. Hardy & Co., Chicago; approximately 12 x 23 x 22½ inches; excellent original condition, minor wear to gold leaf pinstriping, appears to be complete; $450–650.

Optician's viewing device; veneered wood box containing collapsible optical viewer; manufactured by E. Ziegler, Paris; approximately 16¼ x 17 x 9 inches when opened (adjustable height); apparatus in very good/excellent condition, some surface staining to wood, box in fair condition, some wood separation and veneer loss primarily to lid; $275–475.

MODOX

Modox, die-cut tip tray; Indian with full headdress; 4¾ x 5 inches; very good condition, some rust; $200–400.

MOSES COUGH DROPS
Moses Cough Drops, tin; early orange-and-black Summers Brothers tin with insert picture of can on lid; 6 x 1½ x 4 inches; good condition, some minor flaking and overall soiling; $200–400.

MRS. DINSMORE'S
Mrs. Dinsmore's Cough Drops, tin; early Somers Bros. tin; portrait inset on front shows child holding crock on sides; yellow background; 5 inch square x 8 inches; fair/good condition, some chipping and rust spotting; $125–250.

MUNYON'S
Munyon's Homeopathic, tin cabinet; slant-front store display; pictures portrait of Munyon with multiple-drawered backing; 14 x 12 x 14 inches; good/very good condition, some color distortion due to streaking on left side, some chipping and paint loss to background of top, overall light wear; $300–600.

NATURE'S REMEDY
Nature's Remedy, reverse glass lighted display box; chipped and etched reverse glass mirrored medicinal sign in copper-framed light box; promotes Nature's Remedy tablets; 26½ x 19½ x 5½ inches overall; excellent condition; $300–500.

Nature's Remedy, reverse glass hanging sign; two-sided chipped and reverse-painted mirror-backed glass sign; lighted hanging exterior wooden frame; 17 x 23½ x 11½ inches overall; good/very good condition, overall wear; $600–850.

PAINE'S CELERY COMPOUND
(*see* "Diamond Dyes" in Dyes chapter)

PAPILLON
Papillon Cure, paper sign; depicts a lady very sparsely dressed with a black man holding a large runner around her feet; 21½ x 28½ inches excluding frame; fair condition; $150–300.

PEPTO BISMOL
(*see also* "Procter & Gamble" in Soap chapter)
Pepto Bismol, cutout display; depicts bespectacled gentleman in striped pajamas holding up bottle of product; caption reads "Upset Stomach?/Take Soothing Pepto-Bismol"; ca. 1960s; colorful and amusing; excellent condition; $20–50.

MEDICINES ■ 273

Pepto Bismol, rubber doll; called "24 hour bug"; pink and green; made by Niagara Plastics; 7 inches tall; excellent condition; $7–15.

PERRY DAVIS
(*see also* "Davis")
Perry Davis' Pain Killer, lithographed tin pictorial trade sign; very good condition; $75–150.

PORTER'S
Porter's Liniment Salve, tin; 3 ounces; made by the Geo. H. Rundle Company; Piqua, Ohio; blue and gray; ca. 1920s; excellent condition; $6–12.

RADWAY'S
Radway's Medicinal, paper sign; scantily clad woman in center of sign presents Sarsaparillian Resolvent and Regulating Pills to men on one side and women on the other; 13¼ x 10¼ inches; very good condition, overall soiling; $600–1,200.

RAWLEIGH'S
(*see also* "Rawleigh's" in Health and Beauty Aids chapter)
Rawleigh's Antiseptic Powder, tin; 8 ounces; picture of Honorable W. T. Rawleigh on tin; blue and white; ca. 1920s; $5–8.

REED'S TONIC
Reed's Tonic, advertising clock; miniature grandfather clock with

Rawleigh's Antiseptic Powder, tin; 8 ounces; picture of Honorable W. T. Rawleigh on tin; blue and white; ca. 1920s; $5–8. *Courtesy of Dawn and Bob Reno. Photo by Donald Vogt.*

Porter's Liniment Salve, tin; 3 ounces; made by the Geo. H. Rundle Company; Piqua, Ohio; blue and gray, ca. 1920s; excellent condition; $6–12. *Courtest of Dawn and Bob Reno. Photo by Donald Vogt.*

impressed wood decoration, beveled glass bezel, and original advertising panels for the "Gilt Edge" tonic that read "REED'S Tonic" (on the clock face), "Reed's Tonic cures" (on the body), and "Malaria Indigestion" (on the base); 10½ x 20 x 4½ inches; excellent condition, original label back; $700–1,000.

SANATOGEN

Sanatogen, box; "made for anaemic and convalescent patients"; never opened; yellow and white with blue lettering; made by the Bauer Chemical Co., New York; ca. 1890s; near-mint condition; $10–18.

SCHENCK'S

Schenck's Medicinal, tin sign; ca. 1880; Wells & Hope sign for Mandrake Pills and Seaweed Tonic; depicts Dr. Schenck on insert with Indian in background; 28 x 22 inches excluding frame; fair/good condition, general overall soiling, left vertical margin trimmed; $700–1,000.

Schenck's Medicinal, tin sign; black, silver, and gold; early Wells & Hope ad for Pulmonic Syrup with butterfly motif; 20 x 14 inches excluding frame; good overall condition, some chipping and wear; $400–700.

Sanatogen, box; "made for anaemic and convalescent patients"; never opened; yellow and white with blue lettering; made by the Bauer Chemical Co., New York; ca. 1890s; near-mint condition; $10–18. *Courtesy of Dawn and Bob Reno. Photo by Donald Vogt.*

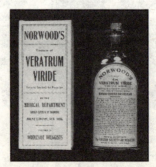

Shaker, Norwood's Veratrum Viride, wholesale druggists' bottle and box; 4 ounces; marked at bottom of bottle: "Medical Department—The United Society of Shakers, Mount Lebanon, New York" (the Shakers were renowned for their medicines—this preparation was made for eighty years); ca. 1920–1940, $600–800. *Courtesy of Dr. M. Stephen Miller. Photo by Dr. M. Stephen Miller.*

MEDICINES ■ 275

Similac, wood figurine; 5½ inches; ca. late 1950s; extremely rare; $250–350. *Courtesy of Neil and Nancy Berliner. Photo by Donald Vogt.*

Schenck's Pulmonic Syrup, Seaweed Tonic, and Mandrake Pills; tin sign; bright yellow; depicts an Indian being offered the medicines; very good condition; $15,000–19,000.

SHAKER MEDICINES
(*see also* "Shaker" in Gardening Supplies chapter)
Shaker, Norwood's Veratrum Viride, wholesale druggists" bottle and box; 4 ounces; marked at bottom of bottle: "Medical Department—The United Society of Shakers, Mount Lebanon, New York" (the Shakers were renowned for their medicines—this preparation was made for eighty years); ca. 1920–1940; excellent condition; $600–800.

SHAW'S
Shaw's Malt, self-framed tin sign; lethargic robed woman in overstuffed chair with child playing at her feet and maid carrying in a tray with bottle and shot of "medicinal" liquor; Victorian setting; 16 x 22¼ inches; good condition, some chipping, primarily in vertical sides of frame, slight fade; $1,000–2,000.

SIMILAC
Similac, wood figurine; 5½ inches; ca. late 1950s; extremely rare; excellent condition; $250–350.

SLIPPERY ELM
Slippery Elm Lozenges, tin with glass front; 7½ x 7 x 4½ inches; made by Ginna; great medicinal picture on reverse side; very good condition; $75–125.

SMITH BROTHERS

The word "trademark" was actually used as a nickname for William Smith ("Trade") and Andrew Smith ("Mark"), the Smith Brothers of Poughkeepsie, New York, familiar faces on cough drop packaging. James Smith, the boys' father, had migrated from Quebec in 1847, gave up his itinerant carpentry business, and opened a restaurant. A customer actually gave Smith a "secret" recipe for a cough candy that Smith immediately prepared on his kitchen stove. He sold the drops out of glass jars in pharmacies for a while, advertising them as a remedy for all "afflicted with hoarseness coughs or colds," and called them James Smith and Son's Compound of Wild Cherry Cough Candy. Newspaper ads touting the drops date back as early as 1852, which makes their ad campaign one of the longest running in American history.

In 1866, William and Andrew took over their father's business, set up a small plant, and began selling the drops to stores in the Hudson Valley. Other people imitated their product and sold theirs under similar names, thus the Smith Brothers realized it was time to create an identifying trademark. A picture of their own faces ended up on their packages with the words "Trade" under William's picture and "Mark" under Andrew's.

After quite a successful beginning, the Smith Brothers added other products to their line, including Menthol Cough Drops in 1922, Cough Syrup in 1926, Wild Cherry Cough Drops in 1948, and Assorted Fruit Cough Drops and Smokers' Drops in 1958.

SMITH BROTHERS

Smith Brothers Cough Drops, tin display; louvered, vertically hinged top dispenser; pictures packages of products; 4¼ x 10½ x 3½ inches; very good condition, some normal wear; $100–200.

Smith Brothers Cough Drops, die-cut figural cardboard displays; depict the brothers themselves; approximately 12 x 34 inches each; excellent condition; $100–225.

Smith Brothers, tin display; for cough drops; ca. late 1800s; very good condition; $150–250.

ST. JACOB'S

St. Jacob's Oil, paper poster; monk holding glowing bottle of product aloft; "great German remedy"; 9½ x 18 inches; very good condition, general overall soiling, borders trimmed; $100–300.

TANLAC

Tanlac, boxes (3); "splendid tonic and system purifier"; 8 ounce size is $20–25 each; larger box holds six 8 ounce bottles, $35–45.

Tanlac, die-cut cardboard display; bold Uncle Sam image holding package with world in background; lettering reads "Tanlac Covers America . . . the master medicine . . . nine million bottles sold in three years"; 20 x 30 inches excluding frame; good/very good condition, water staining, overall soiling, horizontal crease in middle due to folding, other creasing; $100–200.

TIPPECANOE

Tippecanoe, paper sign; pictures a birch canoe and the words "the best for Malaria, tired feeling"; 21 x 9¼ inches; good condition with some paper loss to edges and corners; $50–150.

TUMS

Tums, advertising fan; ca. 1920; excellent condition; $5–15.

VICKS

(see "Procter & Gamble" in Soap chapter)

VICTORY

Victory Lozenges, figural tin; hexagonal gazebo with trellised flowers and birds surrounding V windows; hinged roof opens to display product and promotion; exceedingly rare and unusual; 8½ x 9½ x 7½ inches; good/very good condition, slight wear, minor scratching and chipping, slight denting; $300–600.

Victory-V Lozenges, tin; pictures children on sled; rare; 4½ x 1 x 3 inches; very good/excellent condition, some wear; $25–75.

WINE COCA

Wine Coca, metal sidewalk sign; advertises medicinal drink that relieves headache, assists digestion, and sells for 5 cents; 19¾ x 37 inches overall; fair condition, overall soiling, heat blistering, paint chipping; $1,500–2,250.

WRIGHT'S

Wright's, tin curled-corner sign; 9¾ x 9¾ inches; printed by The Meek Company; ca. 1907; caption reads "Recommended for Curing the Cough and Liniment for Instant Relief"; excellent/near-mint condition; $400–500.

CHAPTER THIRTY
MISCELLANEOUS CATEGORIES

ADVERTISING SIGNS

Advertising, Chas. W. Shonk, tin clip; an advertising piece promoting advertising signs; early and colorful; minor stains, excellent condition; $50–100.

BABY-RELATED PRODUCTS

GERBER

In the 1920s, Mrs. Dan Gerber made baby food history when she asked her husband if his canning business could purée peas for Sally (their baby daughter) as easily as it puréed tomatoes for its customers. That simple question launched Gerber and his father, Frank, in a multimillion-dollar business.

The trademark that advertises Gerber's baby food was originally un unfinished charcoal sketch done by artist Dorothy Hope Smith. She never finished the sketch, though she offered to, but the company's judges thought the simplicity of the sketch best represented the company's determination to produce fresh baby food. Soon the slogan "Babies are our business . . . our only business" accompanied the sketch and became part of the trademark. The slogan was directed solely at Gerber's competitors: Heinz and Beech-Nut. It was dropped when Gerber expanded to include trucking, furniture, insurance, and other businesses (such as Buster Brown children's wear).

Though the Gerber family does not control the day-to-day happenings at their factory in Fremont, Michigan they still keep in touch with the board.

Gerber Baby Foods, advertisement from *Woman's Day*, ca. 1965; shows baby—"My We're Busy Blossoming Out"; $4–7.

Gerber Baby Foods, rubber doll; 18 inches; ca. 1950s; marked on back of head "Mfg by The Sun Rubber Co. Barbert, Ohio U.S.A."; near-mint condition; $30–50.

Heywood-Wakefield, uncut advertising sheet; depicts mother and baby with wicker baby buggy; 33½ x 48 inches; good condition; $25–75.

Miscellaneous Categories ■ 279

Baby-related Products, Gerber Baby Foods, advertisement from *Woman's Day*, ca. 1965; shows baby—"My We're Busy Blossoming Out"; $4–7. *Courtesy of Lester Morris. Photo by Donald Vogt.*

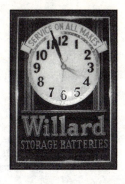

Batteries, Willard Storage Batteries, clock; marked "service on all makes" above clock's face; green, red, black, and white; glass is backlit; 14 x 24 inches; ca. 1930; excellent condition; $600–800. *Collection of and photo by Michael Bruner.*

Playtex Nursery-Pak; given to mothers as they left hospital with new baby; includes baby oil, baby powder, and baby cream; box opened but items unused and in original iron holder; late 1940s; near-mint condition; $18–24.

BARB WIRE
Glidden Steel Barb Wire, tin sign; depicts trains, factory, livestock; reproduction; 16 x 12½ inches; $15 retail.

BATTERIES
Willard Storage Batteries, clock; marked "service on all makes" above clock's face; green, red, black, and white; glass is backlit; 14 x 24 inches; ca. 1930; excellent condition; $600–800.

BOOKS
R. S. Squires, "School Books a Specialty," color lithographed advertisement; ca. 1880s; 4 x 9 inches; good condition; $75–100.

BRICKS
F. O. Pierce, paper sign; this advertisement for a brick company depicts three cats on a roof; 9 x 11¼ inches; excellent condition, borders trimmed; $250–500.

CAMERAS
DeVry Cameras and Projectors, advertisement from *American Magazine*, 1929; full color; depicts all the current models; $6–12.

Cameras, DeVry Cameras and Projectors, advertisement from *American Magazine*, 1929; full color; depicts all the current models; $6–12. *Courtesy of Paper Lady/Bernie and Dolores Fee. Photo by Donald Vogt.*

Cameras, Eastman Kodak, advertisement from *Literary Digest*, 1923; color; depicts doughboys in front of YMCA; $8–12. *Courtesy of Paper Lady/Bernie and Dolores Fee. Photo by Donald Vogt.*

EASTMAN-KODAK

George Eastman began reading up on photography in the 1870s after discovering he could not carry all the photographic equipment necessary to take photos on his Caribbean vacation. By 1880, he had done enough studying to invent dry plates, and in 1884, he presented his new product: rolls of film. In 1888, the Kodak camera, the first "disposable" camera (you sent camera *and* film to Eastman's Rochester, New York, factory in order to get your pictures developed) was created and became popular.

Eastman himself wrote the slogan "You press the button—we do the rest" in 1889. However, he had to scrap his memorable line in the mid-1890s after discovering that people thought the only place where their film could be developed was the company's factory.

Eastman also "invented" the name Kodak, figuring that a trademark needed to be short, unique, and meaningless (i.e., not actually defined as a word). He came up with a name he liked after deciding it should begin with his favorite letter (*K*) and fooling around with a number of combinations. His invention became as synonymous with "camera" as Kleenex is with "tissues."

Other products introduced by the company include a movie camera (1923), Kodachrome color film (1935), the Brownie hand-held movie camera (1951), the Instamatic camera (1963), and the Pocket Instamatic (1972).

Eastman committed suicide at the age of seventy-seven in

Group from left to right: Baker's Cocoa, 1/2 pound, paper and tin, ca. 1950s, $35-40; Watkins Baking Powder, 1 pound, paper and tin, ca. 1940s, $35-40; Bon Ami, 12 ounces, paper and tin, ca. 1950s, $20-25. *Center top:* Typewriter ribbon, "Panama," all tin, made by Manifold Supplies Co., Brooklyn, New York, reads "always a live wire," ca. 1940s, $40-45.   *Courtesy of Irreverent Relics. Photo by Donald Vogt.*

Group from left to right: Goodman Chemical Co. of Brooklyn, New York, Floral Fragrance, "Gardenia," 6 ounces, all tin, ca. 1940s, $40-45; Lander, Fifth Avenue, New York City, Lilac and Roses Talc, 1 pound, all tin, ca. 1940s, $40-45.

Courtesy of Irreverent Relics. Photo by Donald Vogt.

Shell, gas cans; 5 gallon size; restored; $95-125.

Courtesy of Past Gas. Photo by Donald Vogt.

Uncle John's Maple Syrup, cardboard display piece, depicts Uncle John and has space for tin of maple syrup; 12 inches high x 16 inches long; ca. 1880s; very good condition; $25-50.

Collection of and photo by Dawn and Robert Reno.

Tom Sawyer Apparel for Real Boys sign; wood free-standing counter sign; depicts Tom Sawyer painting his name on fence; 22 inches x 6 inches; $150-175. *Courtesy of Biggar's Antiques. Photo by Donald Vogt.*

Bulova Watches, paper poster; depicts Santa with Bulova watches at sale at Siegel's on "South Side"; "terms as low as 50¢ a week"; ca. 1950s; 28 inches x 11 inches; $40-60.

Courtesy of Biggar's Antiques. Photo by Donald Vogt.

Philip Morris, tin sign; depicts cigarette and Philip Morris bellboy; 28 inches x 10 inches; ca. 1940s; $75-110.

Courtesy of Biggar's Antiques. Photo by Donald Vogt.

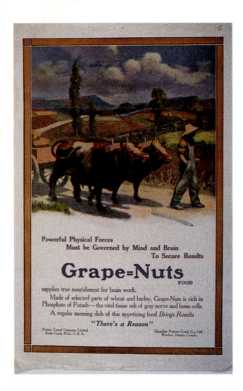

Grape-Nuts ad; *Etude Magazine*, 1910; depicts farmer with oxen; full color; $4-10. *Courtesy of Paper Lady/Bernie and Dolores Fee. Photo by Donald Vogt.*

Climax Corn, chromolithograph on paper; front shows scene with two young children, decorative border; 7 1/8 inches high x 5 1/8 inches wide. *Collection of and photo by Evelyn Ackerman.*

Kellogg's Toasted Corn Flakes ad, *Ladies' Home Journal*, 1912; depicts Indian tying box on donkey in pueblo scene; rare; full color; $4-10. *Courtesy of Paper Lady/Bernie and Dolores Fee. Photo by Donald Vogt.*

Kellogg's Toasted Corn Flakes ad; *Youth's Companion*, 1912; depicts child pulling cover off table to get box of cereal; full color; $4-10. *Courtesy of Paper Lady/Bernie and Dolores Fee. Photo by Donald Vogt.*

Valley Farm's Bing Crosby Ice Cream box; cardboard; has Crosby's picture on front; full color; one pint size; $20-25. *Courtesy of Biggar's Antiques. Photo by Donald Vogt.*

Old Crow display figure; plastic counter figure of trademark Old Crow in top hat with glasses and sparkle-top cane; approximately 32 inches tall; all pieces are intact; ca. 1950s; excellent condition; $250-350. *Collection of and photo by Dawn and Robert Reno.*

McLaughlin's XXXX Coffee: Late 19th-century (1895) man (with one extra suit included); 6 inches high. A companion woman: 5 1/2 inches high. *Collection of and photo by Evelyn Ackerman.*

Albany Grease, handled tin; No. 3 grease; late 1860s; excellent condition; $30-60. *Collection of and photo by Dawn and Robert Reno.*

Kentucky Fried Chicken, hanging lamp; milk glass type; depicts bucket with Colonel Sanders's likeness; 12 inches from bottom of bucket to top of brass "crown"; $200-250.
Courtesy of Biggar's Antiques. Photo by Donald Vogt.

Pal Double-Edge Blades counter display; ladder-type display holds 20 packages of blades that sell for 25 cents; all original; ca. 1950s; $30-40.
Courtesy of Biggar's Antiques. Photo by Donald Vogt.

Pepsi counter display; Pepsi's Norman Rockwell Santa dancing with Pepsi bottle in hand; 20 inches high; self-standing; cardboard; $45-75.

Courtesy of Biggar's Antiques. Photo by Donald Vogt.

Four gas pumps; completely restored; *from left to right:* Blue Sunoco, approximately 7 feet tall, ca. 1940s, $1,400-1,600; Esso, Sinclair, and Shell are all approximately 6 feet tall, all ca. 1950s, all have replacement globes, all priced at $1,075-1,200 each.

Courtesy of Past Gas. Photo by Donald Vogt.

Shaker almanac, issued annually to advertise the medicines that the Shakers made for a "wordly" wholesaler A.J. White; ca. 1880-1898, $75-125.   *Courtesy of Dr. M. Stephen Miller. Photo by Dr. M. Stephen Miller.*

Cameras, Eastman Kodak, advertisement from *Country Life*, ca. 1909; depicts man developing photos in outdoor camp; full color; $10–15. *Courtesy of Paper Lady/Bernie and Dolores Fee. Photo by Donald Vogt.*

Cameras, Eastman Kodak, advertisement from *Youth's Companion*, 1924; full-color photo of woman holding camera under arm and umbrella over shoulder; $9–15. *Courtesy of Paper Lady/Bernie and Dolores Fee. Photo by Donald Vogt.*

1932, leaving a note that read: "To my friends, My work is done. Why wait? G.E."

Eastman Kodak, advertisement from *Ladies' Home Journal*, December 1919; black and white; shows woman in ermine stole holding camera; excellent condition; $7–14.

Eastman Kodak, advertisement from *Literary Digest*, 1923; color; depicts doughboys in front of YMCA; excellent condition; $8–12.

Eastman Kodak, advertisement from *Country Life*, ca. 1909; depicts man developing photos in outdoor camp; full color; excellent condition; $10–15.

Eastman Kodak, advertisement from *Youth's Companion*, 1924; full-color photo of woman holding camera under arm and umbrella over shoulder; excellent condition; $9–15.

Cameras, Kodak, advertisement from *Life* magazine, 1939; full color; depicts Kodak Vigilant Six-20 camera; $5–8. *Courtesy of Paper Lady/Bernie and Dolores Fee. Photo by Donald Vogt.*

Cameras, Kodak, advertisement from *Country Life In America*, ca. 1906; full color; illustrated by Elizabeth Shippen Green; depicts children on floor, one fooling with camera, one with rolling lamb; $7–10. *Courtesy of Paper Lady/Bernie and Dolores Fee. Photo by Donald Vogt.*

Canned Goods, Monarch, advertisement from *Life* magazine, 1949; shows girl leading team of rabbits with jar of pickles on wagon; tree of Monarch's goods in background; full color; $9–12. *Courtesy of Lester Morris. Photo by Donald Vogt.*

Kodak, advertisement from *Life* magazine, 1939; full color; depicts Kodak Vigilant Six-20 camera; very good condition; $5–8.

Kodak, advertisement from *Country Life in America*, ca. 1906; full color; illustrated by Elizabeth Shippen Green; children on floor, one fooling with camera, one with rolling lamb; excellent condition; $7–10.

Kodak, advertisement from *Country Life in America*, 1907; sepia tones; illustration by Edward Penfield of women taking pictures of Dutch people; excellent condition; $10–15.

Kodak, sign; photo image of man with Kodak camera about to photograph friends holding fishing catch of day; original frame; 34½ x 28½ inches; good condition; $250–400.

CANNED GOODS

D. W. Hoegg Canned Goods, paper poster; displays canned products with paper labels surrounded by interesting topography and raw products such as corn and a lobster; Canadian company; 22 x 27½ inches excluding mat and frame; $700–1,500.

D. W. Hoegg Canned Goods, paper advertisement; lithograph; 28 x 22 inches; ad printed by "Geo. Bishop Eng & P'T'G Co., Montreal"; ca. 1885; displays food products surrounded by lobster and interesting typography; framed; near-mint condition; $500–800.

Monarch, advertisement from *Life* magazine, 1949; shows girl leading team of rabbits with jar of pickles on wagon; tree of Monarch's goods in background; full color; excellent condition; $9–12.

CATALOGS

L. C. Tiffany Studio, 1913 catalog; shows Tiffany Favrile Glass, Tiffany Windows, Tiffany Mosaics, Tiffany Monuments, etc.; 9 x 6½ inches; stamped stone-gray cover; each color plate protected by tissue guards; very good condition; $350–500.

COMPANIES/CORPORATIONS

American Exchange National Bank (Dallas), paperweight; depicts bank; ca. 1910–1920; 2½ x 4 inches; excellent condition; $40–60.

American Express Co., embossed tin sign; 27 x 19½ inches; printed by Hauesermann Co. Litho; ca. 1913; early ad for the company that tells in detail what they do for their customers; excellent condition; $600–800.

Armstrong Mfg. Co., paperweight; company made adjustable stock and dies for pipe and bolts; located in Bridgeport, Connecticut; ca. 1900–1920; 2½ x 4 inches; excellent condition; $50–75.

Bommer Spring Hinges, paperweight; ca. 1890–1920; depicts the hinges, which are claimed to be "the best, practically unbreakable"; 2½ x 4 inches; excellent condition; $50–75.

Companies/Corporations, Armstrong Mfg. Co., paperweight; company made adjustable stock and dies for pipe and bolts; located in Bridgeport, Connecticut; ca. 1900–1920; 2½ x 4 inches; $50–75. *From the collection of Stuart Kammerman. Photo by David Kammerman.*

Companies/Corporations, American Exchange National Bank (Dallas), paperweight; depicts band; ca. 1910–1920; 2½ x 4 inches; $40–60. *From the collection of Stuart Kammerman. Photo by David Kammerman.*

Companies/Corporations, Bommer Spring Hinges, paperweight; ca. 1890–1920; depicts the hinges, which are claimed to be "the best, practically unbreakable"; 2½ x 4 inches; $50–75. *From the collection of Stuart Kammerman. Photo by David Kammerman.*

Companies/Corporations, Boston Belting Company, paperweight; promotes "vulcanized rubber belting, hose packing, mechanical rubber goods"; company located in Boston, Massachusetts; ca. 1890–1910; 2½ x 4 inches; $50–75. *From the collection of Stuart Kammerman. Photo by David Kammerman.*

Companies/Corporations, Leggett & Platt, paperweight; ca. 1890–1920; company makes noiseless springs; offices in Carthage, Missouri, and Louisville Kentucky; 2½ x 4 inches; $50–75. *From the collection of Stuart Kammerman. Photo by David Kammerman.*

Boston Belting Company, paperweight; promotes "vulcanized rubber belting, hose packing, mechanical rubber goods"; company located in Boston, Massachusetts; ca. 1890–1910; 2½ x 4 inches; excellent condition; $50–75.

Leggett & Platt, paperweight; ca. 1890–1920; company makes noiseless springs; offices in Carthage, Missouri, and Louisville, Kentucky; 2½ x 4 inches; excellent condition; $50–75.

Lindsay & McCutcheon, paperweight; ca. 1890–1920; promotes "iron & steel hoops & bands, cotton ties, etc."; depicts the company's factory; 2½ x 4 inches; excellent condition; $50–75.

Macbeth-Evans Glass Company, paperweight; depicts man blowing glass; ca. 1890–1910; company located in Pittsburgh, Pennsylvania; 2½ x 4 inches; excellent condition; $50–75.

Companies/Corporations, Lindsay & McCutcheon, paperweight, ca. 1890–1920; promotes "iron & steel hoops & bands, cotton ties, etc."; depicts the company's factory; 2½ x 4 inches; $50–75. *From the collection of Stuart Kammerman. Photo by David Kammerman.*

Companies/Corporations, Macbeth-Evans Glass Company, paperweight; depicts man blowing glass; ca. 1890–1910; company located in Pittsburg, Pennsylvania; 2½ x 4 inches; $50–75. *From the collection of Stuart Kammerman. Photo by David Kammerman.*

Companies/Corporations, Robert Griffin Co., paperweight; ca. 1910–1930; promotes "wall paper for export"; office on Fifth Avenue, New York; 2½ x 4¼ inch oval; $30–50. *From the collection of Stuart Kammerman. Photo by David Kammerman.*

Companies/Corporations, Shackamaxon Worsted Co., paperweight; ca. 1890–1910; depicts the factory, which "manufactures fine fancy worsted suitings, trouserings and piece dyes for the merchant tailoring trade"; 3 inch diameter dome; $100–165. *From the collection of Stuart Kammerman. Photo by David Kammerman.*

Companies/Corporations, Stuart Bros. Company, paperweight; ca. 1890–1920; promotes "blank books"; offices in Philadelphia; 2½ x 4 inches; $50–75. *From the collection of Stuart Kammerman. Photo by David Kammerman.*

National Park Bank, self-framed tin sign; interior view of the bank's building; 31 x 41 inches including embossed border; good condition, overall color fading; $50–150.

Robert Griffin Co., paperweight; ca. 1910–1930; promotes "wall paper for export"; office on Fifth Avenue, New York; 2½ x 4¼ inch oval; very good condition; $30–50.

Shackamaxon Worsted Co., paperweight; ca. 1890–1910; depicts the factory, which "manufactures fine fancy worsted suitings, trouserings and piece dyes for the merchant tailoring trade"; 3 inch diameter dome; excellent condition; $100–165.

Stuart Bros. Company, paperweight; ca. 1890–1920; promotes "blank books"; offices in Philadelphia; 2½ x 4 inches; very good condition; $50–75.

Teachenor-Bartberger Engraving Co., paperweight; ca. 1900–1930; promotes designs, illustrations, halftone and zinc etchings; offices in Kansas City; 2¾ inch diameter octagon; very good condition; $60–85.

The Automatic Tap & Faucet Co. Ltd., paperweight; ca. 1900–1920; company made Linindoll's Celebrated Ale Taps and Faucets; located in Fort Edward, New York; 2¼ x 4 inches; very good condition; $50–75.

Companies/Corporations, Teachenor-Bartberger Engraving Co., paperweight; ca. 1900–1930; promotes designs, illustrations, halftone and zinc etchings; offices in Kansas City; 2¾ inch diameter octagon; $60–85. *From the collection of Stuart Kammerman. Photo by David Kammerman.*

Companies/Corporations, The Automatic Tap & Faucet Co. Ltd., paperweight; ca. 1900–1920; company made Linindoll's Celebrated Ale Taps and Faucets; located in Fort Edward, New York; 2¼ x 4 inches; $50–75. *From the collection of Stuart Kammerman. Photo by David Kammerman.*

Companies/Corporations, The Babcock Printing Press Mfg. Co., paperweight; ca. 1890–1910; shows the company's "Dispatch" press; company located in New London, Connecticut; 2½ x 4 inches; $50–75. *From the collection of Stuart Kammerman. Photo by David Kammerman.*

The Babcock Printing Press Mfg. Co., paperweight; ca. 1890–1910; shows the company's "Dispatch" press; company located in New London, Connecticut; 2½ x 4 inches; excellent condition; $50–75.

The Electric Storage Battery Co., paperweight; ca. 1910–1930; advertises the "Exide" battery; 2½ x 4¼ inches; excellent condition; $35–60.

The Long Beach National Bank, paperweight; ca. 1910–1930; depicts woman riding wave and marked "Queen of the Beaches"; bank located in Long Beach, California; 2½ x 4 inches; very good condition; $40–60.

Companies/Corporations, The Electric Storage Battery Co., paperweight; ca. 1910–1930; advertises the "Exide" battery; 2½ x 4¼ inches; $35–60. *From the collection of Stuart Kammerman. Photo by David Kammerman.*

Companies/Corporations, The Long Beach National Bank, paperweight; ca. 1910–1930; depicts woman riding wave and marked "Queen of the Beaches"; bank located in Long Beach, California; 2½ x 4 inches; $40–60. *From the collection of Stuart Kammerman. Photo by David Kammerman.*

MISCELLANEOUS CATEGORIES ■ 287

Timken Roller Bearing Co., paperweight; ca. 1890–1920; promotes roller bearing axles; offices in Canton, Ohio; 2½ x 4¼ inches; excellent condition; $35–60.

W. B. Fonda, paperweight; ca. 1890–1910; "manufacturer of lime"; office in St. Albans, Vermont; 2½ x 4 inches; excellent condition; $45–65.

Walt Disney, letterhead; ca. 1930s; from Hollywood lot; masthead depicts Snow White, Dwarfs, rabbit, and chipmunks; full color; 8½ x 11 inches; near-mint condition; $125–175.

CONSTRUCTION COMPANIES

Staggs-Bilt Homes, nodder; 7 inches; company from Arizona; "Happy Homer"; ca. 1970s; excellent condition; $500–700.

CURTAINS

P. K. Wilson & Son, paperweight; ca. 1890–1920; depicts the factory; company imported lace and curtains; offices in New York City; 2½ x 4 inches; $50–75.

ENGINES

Watertown Steam Engine Co., paperweight; ca 1890–1910; depicts one of the engines; offices in Watertown, New York; 2½ x 4 inches; excellent condition; $50–75.

Companies/Corporations, Timken Roller Bearing Co., paperweight; ca. 1890–1920; promotes roller bearing axles; offices in Canton, Ohio; 2½ x 4¼ inches; $35–60. *From the collection of Stuart Kammerman. Photo by David Kammerman.*

Companies/Corporations, W. B. Fonda, paperweight; ca. 1890–1910; "manufacturer of lime"; office in St. Albans, Vermont; 2½ x 4 inches; $45–65. *From the collection of Stuart Kammerman. Photo by David Kammerman.*

Construction Companies, Staggs-Bilt Homes, nodder; 7 inches; company from Arizona; "Happy Homer"; ca. 1970s; $500–700. *Courtesy of Neil and Nancy Berliner. Photo by Donald Vogt.*

288 ■ ADVERTISING

Curtains, P. K. Wilson & Son, paperweight; ca. 1890–1920; depicts the factory; company imported lace and curtains; offices in New York City; 2½ x 4 inches; $50–75. *From the collection of Stuart Kammerman. Photo by David Kammerman.*

Engines, Watertown Steam Engine Co., paperweight; ca. 1890–1910; depicts one of the engines; offices in Watertown, New York; 2½ x 4 inches; $50–75. *From the collection of Stuart Kammerman. Photo by David Kammerman.*

Fire Kegs, Hazelton's High Pressure Chemical Fire Keg, brown glass fire grenade; 13 inches tall; ca. 1910; $150–200. *Collection of and photo by Michael Bruner.*

FIRECRACKERS

Dixie Boy brand Flashlight Crackers, poster; 20 x 28 inches; ca. 1940s; with package of original firecrackers; excellent condition; poster $125–150, firecrackers $10–15.

FIRE EXTINGUISHERS

Badger's Pony, fire extinguishers (5); very good condition; $200–450.

Gold Seal, fire extinguisher, emblem is Statue of Liberty seal; 24 inch tall cylinder; ca. 1930s; poor condition; $125–200.

FIRE KEGS

Hazelton's High Pressure Chemical Fire Keg, brown glass fire grenade; 13 inches tall; ca. 1910; very good condition; $150–200.

FOOD PRESERVATION

Patterson Preserving Co., paper sign; depicts two women and a man (all dressed in Victorian clothes) having a picnic by a lake and eating lobster, lamb, olives, mixed pickles, and rum cake; printed by Clay & Richmond; 21¼ x 16¾ inches; excellent condition, margins trimmed; $2,500–4,000.

FUEL

War Eagle Fuel Co., paperweight; ca. 1910–1930; depicts Indian standing on chunk of coal; offices in Columbus, Ohio; 2½ x 4 inches; excellent condition; $40–65.

MISCELLANEOUS CATEGORIES ■ 289

GLUE
LePage's Liquid Glue, advertisement; "It Sticks Everything"; 5 x 7 inches; engraved and printed in black and red; matted; shows character drawings of cats, mice, spiders, dogs, all using LePage's glue; very good condition; $25–40.

HABERDASHERY
Haberdashery sign; mid-nineteenth century; three-dimensional; depicts top hat; hat detaches from wrought iron holder; excellent condition; $1,500–2,000.

HEATING
Lennox Heating, Lennie Lennox ceramic salt and pepper set; 4¾ inches high; ca. late 1940s; excellent condition; $250–350.

HOT FUDGE
Johnston's Instant Hot Fudge, aluminum dispenser; 11 inches tall; ca. 1950; red, black, and silver; excellent condition; $75–150.

HOUSEHOLD FURNITURE
D. R. Brown's Patent Baby Tender, paper sign; historical interior view of period front room; ca. 1860s; small children sitting in various types of baby seats—wheeled varieties, spring cribs, and high chairs; adults dine at table; printed by J. Rau, New York; 22 x 18 inches; very

Fuel, War Eagle Fuel Co., paperweight; ca. 1910–1930; depicts Indian standing on chunk of coal; offices in Columbus, Ohio; 2½ x 4 inches; $40–65. *From the collection of Stuart Kammerman. Photo by David Kammerman.*

Hot Fudge, Johnston's Instant Hot Fudge, aluminum dispenser; 11 inches tall; ca. 1950; red, black, and silver; excellent condition; $75–150. *Collection of and photo by Michael Bruner.*

Household Spray, Lucky Strike, can; ½ pint; yellow, red, and black; ca. 1940s; good condition; $10–15. *Courtesy of Dawn and Bob Reno. Photo by Donald Vogt.*

Jars, Relio Brand Jar Rubbers, box; colorful lithographed box with eagle trademark; still full of jar rubbers; near-mint condition; $10–15. *Courtesy of Dawn and Bob Reno. Photo by Donald Vogt.*

Jewelry, Jos. Linz & Bro., paperweight; ca. 1890–1910; "importers and jobbers/fine watches, diamonds & jewelry"; store in Dallas, Texas; 2½ x 4 inches; $75–100. *From the collection of Stuart Kammerman. Photo by David Kammerman.*

good condition, some water and wood staining, slight foxing, general soiling due to age; $2,500–4,500.

HOUSEHOLD SPRAY

Lucky Strike, can; ½ pint; yellow, red, and black; ca. 1940s; good condition; $10–15.

HUNTING/FISHING

Izaak Walton League of America, embossed tin sign; warns campers, hunters, and fishermen to take care of nature; 11½ x 18 inches excluding frame; excellent condition; $150–300.

JARS

Relio Brand Jar Rubbers, box; colorful lithographed box with eagle trademark; still full of jar rubbers; near-mint condition; $10–15.

JEWELRY

Jos. Linz & Bro., paperweight; ca. 1890–1910; "importers and jobbers/fine watches, diamonds & jewelry"; store in Dallas, Texas; 2½ x 4 inches; very good condition; $75–100.

J. M. Paul/Jeweler & Optician, advertising clock; encased in wood frame; ca. 1910–1920; 38½ x 15½ inches; excellent condition; $400–600.

MISCELLANEOUS CATEGORIES ■ 291

W. W. W. Ring, mechanical display; highly unusual figural clock-worked ring display; mechanical butterfly with flapping wings is an effective display for rings set with monthly birthstones; 14¼ x 20⅓ x 7 inches; fair/good condition, felt covered surface, dirt stained and mildew spotted in "as is" found condition, working; $700–1,100.

JUICES

Hawaiian Punch, telephone; 12 inches; ca. late 1970s; excellent condition; $150–250.

Hawaiian Punch, squeezable Punchy bottle; 11 inches; ca. 1989; near-mint condition; $5–7.

Winter Hill Sweet Cider, bottle; ½ gallon; paper label; four colors; ca. 1940s; excellent condition; $18–24.

KEYS/LOCKS

Independent Lock Company of Fitchburg, Massachusetts, die-cut tin store display sign; double-sided figure of a key; 32 feet; good overall condition with some scratches due to use; $125–225.

LAMP OILS

Devoe Oil, paper sign; rarely utilized night illustration promoting this lamp oil in various uses including a lighthouse and train; 17 x 13 inches; very good condition, some slight tearing, wrinkles, borders trimmed; $500–900.

MAPLE SYRUP

LOG CABIN

(*see also* "Kraft General Foods" in Dairy Products chapter)
Introduced in 1887 by a St. Paul, Minnesota, grocer named

Juices, Hawaiian Punch; telephone, 12 inches, late 1970s, $150–250; squeezable Punchy bottle, 11 inches, ca. 1989, $5–7. *Courtesy of Neil and Nancy Berliner. Photo by Donald Vogt.*

Juices, Winter Hill Sweet Cider, bottle; ½ gallon; paper label; four colors; ca. 1940s; excellent condition; $18–24. *Courtesy of Irreverent Relics. Photo by Donald Vogt.*

P. J. Towle, Log Cabin Syrup, in its small sealed container, became the most popular syrup on the market. The container, shaped like a log cabin, was designed to keep the syrup free from dirt and other impurities. The container survived until after World War II, when the war forced Log Cabin into bottles.

In 1927, Postum Company (predecessor to General Foods Corporation) purchased the Log Cabin Products Company.

Log Cabin Syrup, figural tins (3); log-cabin-shaped tins with "Frontier Inn," "Stockade School," or "Express Office" on one side each; varied sizes; very good overall condition, some scratches, minor denting; $200–300.

Lower Canada Maple Syrup, can; unusual early rare can picturing woodland scene of sugaring surrounded by maple leaves and beaver on this early red-and-black tin; early soldered seam; ca. 1870; Montreal, Canada; 5 inch diameter x 7 inches; good/very good condition, some chipping and rust spotting; $300–600.

Lower Canada Maple Syrup, can; small early yellow-and-black maple sugaring scene surrounded by leaves and portrait; Danville, Quebec, Montreal/Canada; 3 inch diameter x 3 inches; good condition; pinpoint chipping due to overall wear; $100–150.

Towle's Log Cabin Syrup, lithographed paper die-cut display; ca. 1915; "Makes Home Sweet Home"; excellent condition; $1,400–1,800.

Uncle John's Maple Syrup, cardboard display piece; depicts Uncle John and has space for tin of maple syrup; 12 x 16 inches; ca. 1880s; very good condition; $25–50.

MATCHES

Butterfly Match, tin box; butterflies and pansies on early Ginna Box; has a striker end; includes original waxed matches; 6¼ x ¾ x 1¾ inches; excellent condition, minor scratching; $50–100.

Diamond Match, tin box; black family reacts to match dispenser; caption reads "You Chillun Keep Back Deah! You want You Heads Blowed Of'n You Shouldus?"; 4½ x 1½ x 2¼ inches; very good condition; $200–300.

MUSICAL INSTRUMENTS

Hohner Harmonicas, Grand Prix Philadelphia, 1926, harmonica stand; with three harmonicas; 32 inches tall; excellent as-found condition; $600–700.

MISCELLANEOUS CATEGORIES ■ 293

Holton Band Instruments, cardboard sign; unusual piece showing the O'Brien Minstrels with various brass horns and drums for this band instrument manufacturer; 41 x 27 inches; very good condition, repaired tear in lower right, some overall wear, minor edge tears, mounted on heavy stock backing; $75–150.

NETTING

R & H Adams Netting, paper sign; depicts boy riding bee into gauzy netting; "A Protection against Insects"; 10½ x 13½ inches; excellent condition, minor edge trim; $500–1,500.

NEWSPAPERS/MAGAZINES

Boston Sunday Globe, cardboard stand-up; gentleman with large belly, across which is written "The Largest Circulation in New England"; 1895; 7½ inches tall; excellent condition; $50–100.

Collier's, cover, 1931; depicts boy riding rocking horse; mint condition; $18–24.

Forest & Stream, paper sign; unusual graphic advertisement for this rod-and-gun weekly journal with inserts of hunters, fishermen, women shooting arrows, and sportsmen; very colorful; 15½ x 10 inches; excellent condition, border appears trimmed, minor soiling overall; $700–1,000.

The World, paper poster; torch-bearing goddess promotes the "cheapest newspaper in the United States"; 11 x 14½ inches; good/very good condition, some edge tears, trimmed borders; $100–300.

Vogue, cover, 1922; depicts woman holding Japanese-style umbrella with spotted Greyhound at her side; near-mint condition; $50–100.

OYSTERS

H. McWilliams & Co., tin sign; reproduction; depicts train, ships, factory; "Baltimore Oysters for sale here"; 16 x 13 inches; $15 retail.

PAPERWEIGHTS

H. Waterbury & Sons Co., paperweight; ca. 1900–1920; company manufactured papermakers' feltings; offices in Oriskany, New York; 2½ x 4 inches; excellent condition; $50–75.

PASTA

Victor Macaroni, tin; made in North Reading, Massachusetts; handled bucket; paper label in near-mint condition, depicts the factory in early 1920s; tin is in overall excellent condition; $35–50.

294 ■ ADVERTISING

Paperweights, H. Waterbury & Sons Co., paperweight; ca. 1900–1920; company manufactured papermakers' feltings; offices in Oriskany, New York; 2½ x 4 inches; $50–75. *From the collection of Stuart Kammerman. Photo by David Kammerman.*

Paperweights, "Compliments of the Big 4" (The Eberhard Mfg. Co., Iver Johnson's Arms & Cycle Works, North Bros. Mfg. Co., and Coates Clipper Mfg. Co.); ca. 1890–1920; 2½ x 4 inches; $35–50. *From the collection of Stuart Kammerman. Photo by David Kammerman.*

PEST CONTROL

Raid, phone; in shape of bug; 8½ inches; ca. 1980s; excellent condition; $100–150.

Raid, clock radio; in shape of bug; 7 inches; ca. 1980s; excellent condition; $100–150.

Wells Co. Rough on Rats, tin sign; depicts a harried family chasing a rat who has escaped through a hole in the floor; good/very good condition, overall darkening due to age, some wear primarily to background, minor chipping, minor in-painting, primarily to background, edge holes; $1,500–3,500.

PLUMBING

Cleveland Faucet Co., cardboard display sign; unusual 1895 collage advertisement including a diminutive brass version of pump attached to sign that shows the workings of pump at a fancy bar; 16 x 22½ inches excluding frame; good condition, some overall soiling, small holes, thermometer missing from brass pump, some in-painting; $300–600.

Pest Control, Raid, phone, in shape of bug, 8½ inches, ca. 1980s, $100–150; clock/radio, in shape of bug, 7 inches, ca. 1980s, $100–150. *Courtesy of Neil and Nancy Berliner. Photo by Donald Vogt.*

MISCELLANEOUS CATEGORIES   ■   295

Popsicles, advertisement from *Life* magazine, 1953; "Caught!"; baseball mitt with orange; $7–10. *Courtesy of Lester Morris. Photo by Donald Vogt.*

Cleveland Faucet, cardboard display sign; shows workings of "Champion Pump"; overlaid as sample in brass on pictorial image; 19 x 26 inches including frame; good condition; $100–300.

POPSICLES

Popsicles, Howdy Doody Twin Pops, tin sign; 6½ x 13½ inches; reproduction; depicts Howdy and his pop; $15 retail.

Popsicles, advertisement from *Life* magazine, 1953; "Caught!"; baseball mitt with orange; excellent condition; $7–10.

ROLY POLY

Mayo's Roly Poly, "Dutchman"; 6 inch diameter x 7 inches; good condition, slight fade overall, some denting and chipping; $300–450.

Mayo's Roly Poly, "Mammy"; 6 inch diameter x 7 inches; good/very good condition, overall slight darkening from age and soiling, minor denting and chipping; $375–500.

Mayo's Roly Poly, "Man from Scotland Yard"; 6 inch diameter x 7 inches; good/very good condition, overall soiling, minor chipping and spotting; $750–1,100.

Mayo's Roly Poly, "Satisfied Customer"; 6 inch diameter x 7 inches; good/very good condition, soiling overall, minor rust spotting and chipping, slight denting; $300–500.

Mayo's Roly Poly, "Singing Waiter"; 6 inch diameter x 7 inches; good/very good condition, overall soiling, minor denting, small chips; $350–500.

Mayo's Roly Poly, "Store Keeper"; 6 inch diameter x 7 inches; good/very good condition, overall darkening due to age, slight denting and chipping; $300–450.

Snacks, Frito-Lay, advertisement from *Look* magazine, 1968; Wanted ad for the Frito Bandito; black and white; $9–12. *Courtesy of Lester Morris. Photo by Donald Vogt.*

Thimbles, group of three advertising thimbles; (left) Feed and Supplies thimble whistle, (center) Cities Service Fuel Oil Thimble, (right) celluloid advertising thimble whistle for children marked "A Rootin' Tootin' Tarnow Man. Capt. Mac says don't blow in house or school"; ca. early 1900s; $25–35 each. *Courtesy of Estelle Zalkin, author of* Zalkin's Handbook of Thimbles and Sewing Implements.

RUBBER GOODS

Boston Belting, paper sign; multiple vignettes of rubber gathering and belting factory for "Vulcanized Rubber Goods"; 14 x 18½ inches excluding frame; good condition, some tears and scratches; $200–300.

SADDLE AND TRUNK MAKERS

J. R. Hewitt Saddle & Trunk Maker, paper sign; pictures early frontier store front; 10 x 14 inches excluding frame; very good/excellent condition, minor creasing; $100–200.

SALESMAN'S SAMPLES

Cabinet door and draft eliminator; unusual wood-and-brass, bracket-footed vertical counter display; 10 x 21 x 12½ inches; excellent condition, slight joint separation due to age, minor staining to original finish; $50–200.

SNACKS

Frito-Lay, advertisement from *Look* magazine, 1968; Wanted ad for the Frito Bandito; black and white; excellent condition; $9–12.

STONEWARE

Tin sign; boy and dog both want doughnuts from stoneware crock; 13 x 19 inches; very good condition, vivid colors, some minor scratching and pitting; $50–200.

MISCELLANEOUS CATEGORIES ■ 297

Typewriters and Supplies, A. P. Little ribbon tins; (left) orange, blue, and gold—black boy in inset, ca. 1940s, $25–50; (right) gray background with red lettering, black boy in inset, ca. 1930s–1940s, $30–60. *Courtesy of Marilyn and De Underwood/Tins Again Collectibles. Photo by Donald Vogt.*

Typewriters and Supplies, Carter's ribbon tins; (left) water lily with dragonfly graphic on front (flower is pink, background is black), ca. 1950s, $8–15; (right) dragon graphics on front, blue-and-purple background, ca. 1940s–1950s, $8–15. *Courtesy of Marilyn and De Underwood/Tins Again Collectibles. Photo by Donald Vogt.*

SYRUP

Karo, tin sign; reproduction; depicts Dionne quintuplets; 14 x 11 inches; $15 retail.

THIMBLES

Group of three advertising thimbles; Feed and Supplies thimble whistle, Cities Service Fuel Oil thimble, celluloid advertising thimble whistle for children marked "A Rootin' Tootin' Tarnow Man. Capt. Mac says don't blow in house or school"; ca. early 1900s; $25–35 each.

TINSMITH

Trade sign; oversized pair of wooden tinsmith's shears; approximately 5 feet tall; excellent condition; $100–200.

TYPEWRITERS AND SUPPLIES

A. P. Little, ribbon tin; gray background with red lettering; black boy in inset; ca. 1930s–1940s; excellent condition; $30–60.

A. P. Little, ribbon tin; orange, blue, and gold; black boy in inset; ca. 1940s; excellent condition; $25–50.

Addressograph, ribbon tin; stand-up typewriter tin; 2 x 1½ inches; scenes of women at typewriters on all four sides; ca. 1910–1920s; black and orange printing; excellent condition; $15–25.

Carter's, ribbon tin; dragon graphics on front; blue-and-purple background; ca. 1940s–1950s; excellent condition; $8–15.

Carter's, ribbon tin; water lily with dragonfly graphic on front (flower is pink, background is black); ca. 1950s; excellent condition; $8–15.

Typewriters and Supplies, Eriksen Ribbon and Carbon Co./The Viking Line ribbon tins; depicts Viking sailing ship in orange and blue; ca. 1940s; $25–50. *Courtesy of Marilyn and De Underwood/Tins Again Collectibles. Photo by Donald Vogt.*

Typewriters and Supplies, F. S. Webster Co., Inc., ribbon tins; Battleship brand grouping: (left) ca. 1940s, $25–50; (center) ca. 1940s, $25–50; (right) ca. 1950s, $25–50. *Courtesy of Marilyn and De Underwood/Tins Again Collectibles. Photo by Donald Vogt.*

Eriksen Ribbon and Carbon Co./The Viking Line, ribbon tin; depicts Viking sailing ship in orange and blue; ca. 1940s; excellent condition; $25–50.

F. S. Webster Co., Inc., ribbon tin; Battleship brand; ca. 1940s; excellent condition; $25–50.

Franklin Ribbon & Carbon Co., ribbon tin; brown and beige; Benjamin Franklin graphics; ca. 1940s; excellent condition; $25–50.

H. M. Storms Co., ribbon tin; American Brand; orange background; Indian graphics; ca. 1940s; excellent condition; $40–75.

Little's Brilliant, ribbon tin; "made by A. P. Little, Rochester, New York"; beige and blue; ca. 1920s; excellent condition; $5–8.

Miller, ribbon tin; ca. 1940s; blue-and-yellow graphics; butterfly trademark; excellent condition; $8–15.

Typewriters and Supplies, Little's Brilliant, ribbon tin; "made by A.P. Little, Rochester, N.Y."; beige and blue; ca. 1920s; excellent condition; $5–8. *Courtesy of Dawn and Bob Reno. Photo by Donald Vogt.*

Miscellaneous Categories ■ 299

Typewriters and Supplies, Miller, ribbon tins; (center back) tall thin version, ca. 1920s, blue background with white-and-yellow lettering, $20–40; (front left) ca. 1950s, round, yellow-and-black graphics, $5–15; (front right) ca. 1950s, round, yellow-and-blue with elk, $5–15; (back left) square, grayish background with carnation flower, ca. 1940s, $15–25; (back right) ca. 1940s, blue-and-yellow graphics, butterfly trademark, $8–15. *Courtesy of Marilyn and De Underwood/Tins Again Collectibles. Photo by Donald Vogt.*

Typewriters and Supplies, Old Dutch Carbon & Ribbon Co./Waters & Waters, ribbon tins; (left) blue background with Dutch scene including fisherman on dock, ca. 1950s, $25–50; (right) ca. 1940s, same scene as left only more detailed and old-fashioned, map of United States on back; $25–50. *Courtesy of Marilyn and De Underwood/Tins Again Collectibles. Photo by Donald Vogt.*

Miller, ribbon tin; ca. 1950s; round; yellow-and-black graphics; excellent condition; $5–15.

Miller, ribbon tin; ca. 1950s; round; yellow-and-blue with elk; excellent condition; $5–15.

Miller, ribbon tin; square; grayish background with carnation flower; ca. 1940s; excellent condition; $15–25.

Miller, ribbon tin; tall thin version; ca. 1920s; blue background with white-and-yellow lettering; excellent condition; $20–40.

Mittag & Volger, ribbon tin; ecru background with black-and-dusty rose printing; ca. 1940s; excellent condition; $15–25.

Mittag & Volger, ribbon tin; mustard background with black printing; ca. 1930s; excellent condition; $15–25.

Old Dutch Carbon & Ribbon Co./Waters & Waters, ribbon tin; ca. 1940s; blue background with Dutch scene including fisherman on dock; map of U. S. on back; excellent condition; $25–50.

Old Dutch Carbon & Ribbon Co./Waters & Waters, ribbon tin; same scene as above but less detailed and more modern; ca. 1950s; excellent condition; $25–50.

Typewriters and Supplies, Quest Mfg. Co., ribbon tin; Old Hickory brand; orange background; set in cotton field, old black man lying in left corner; ca. 1940s; $40–75. *Courtesy of Marilyn and De Underwood/Tins Again Collectibles. Photo by Donald Vogt.*

Old Town, ribbon tin; cover depicts woman in ball gown; ca. 1920s–1930s; very good condition; $8–15.

Old Town, ribbon tin; Hermetic secretarial typewriter ribbon; silhouette of woman at typewriter; ca. 1950s; key lid with ribbon still in it; excellent condition; $8–15.

Panama, ribbon tin; made by Manifold Supplies Co., Brooklyn, New York; reads "always a live wire"; ca. 1940s; very good condition; $40–47.

Quest Mfg. Co., ribbon tin; Old Hickory brand; orange background; set in cotton field, old black man lying in left corner; ca. 1940s; excellent condition; $40–75.

REMINGTON TYPEWRITERS

During the last decade of the nineteenth century, more than half of the companies that employed advertising to sell their products were selling patent medicines. Remington typewriters was one of the few companies to advertise a product other than medicine or food and was considered one of the biggest advertisers of 1890.

Ads in the late nineteenth and early twentieth centuries extolled the virtues of typewriters and how they could help the "girls" in the office. Some even had an adding and subtracting attachment, according to a 1908 ad. In 1910, an image of a straight-backed secretary and her mustached boss graced an ad that discussed the attributes of a Remington, which was "sold in New York and Elsewhere."

In 1917, Remington ranked 182nd in the country (as a company) by virtue of its assets, yet in 1914 the company ranked 37th in what it spent on national magazine advertising.

Remington, ribbon tin; Paragon ribbon for standard Remington typewriter; ca. 1930s–1940s; excellent condition; $8–15.

MISCELLANEOUS CATEGORIES ■ 301

Typewriters and Supplies, Remington, ribbon tins; (back left) Paragon ribbon for standard Remington typewriter, ca. 1930s–1940s, $8–15; (back center) stand-up tin, ca. 1920s–1930s, $10–20; (back right) ca. 1940s, $5–15; (front left) round, cardboard, depicts woman in ball gown looking in mirror, ca. 1950s, $5–10; (front center) white and blue, ca. 1950s, $5–10; (front right) light blue, Patrician ribbon, ca. 1950s, $5–10. *Courtesy of Marilyn and De Underwood/Tins Again Collectibles. Photo by Donald Vogt.*

Typewriters and Supplies, U.S. Typewriter Ribbon Mfg. Co., ribbon tin; U.S. brand; blue stars on cream background; ca. early 1950s; $15–25. *Courtesy of Marilyn and De Underwood/Tins Again Collectibles. Photo by Donald Vogt.*

Remington, cardboard ribbon tin; round; depicts woman in ball gown looking in mirror; ca. 1950s; excellent condition; $5–10.

Remington, ribbon tin; stand-up tin; ca. 1920s–1930s; excellent condition; $10–20.

The M. B. Cook Co./Chicago, Illinois, ribbon tin; Beaver ribbon; ca. 1940s; black background; nice graphics of beaver family; excellent condition; $25–50.

U.S. Typewriter Ribbon Mfg. Co., ribbon tin; U.S. brand; blue stars on cream background; ca. early 1950s; excellent condition; $15–25.

WATER

Apollinaris Table Water, tin sign; depicts a horse and rider; 17½ x 13½ inches; good/very good condition; some chipping to paint; $100–225.

Florida Water, paper sign; 1880 image of fountain in tropical setting; printed by L. Prang; 10 x 14¼ inches; very good/excellent condition, minor rubbing, borders trimmed; $275–500.

Poland Water, reverse glass sign; green, black, and white on beveled surface; advertises Maine water product; 18 x 24 inches; poor/fair condition, general overall lifting and some discoloration; $100–200.

WOOD

Wood and iron brewer, painted trade sign; depicts bottle and keg; very good condition; $250–350.

Horlick's Wood, ruler; lithograph on tin; 9½ x 1½ inches; marked "Somers Bros., N.Y."; rolled edge; printed on cream yellow background; very good condition; $175–250.

CHAPTER THIRTY-ONE
■ MOVIES, CONCERTS ■ THEATER

MOVIES

MGM

MGM's lion, created in 1916 by Howard Dietz, was born of Dietz's association with Columbia University, a school fascinated with lions. Leo was a real lion—or, shall we say, *several* real lions; the original photograph was updated whenever the company decided it needed a "fresh [lion] face." Unfortunately, when MGM decided to take Leo back to Africa and give him his freedom, it wasn't quite sure *which* one it was returning. Animal lovers put up such a fuss that MGM sent one of the Leos to a zoo, where he spent his last days.

In 1924, three men and their companies merged to form Metro-Goldwyn-Mayer: Metro, owned by Marcus Loew; Goldwyn, for Samuel Goldwyn, who started a movie company with Cecil B. DeMille, then went on to found yet another movie company in 1916 with Edgar and Arch Selwyn; and Mayer, for Louis B. Mayer, who was production chief until 1951.

In 1949, the U.S. government ordered MGM to sell off its chain of theaters, and in the 1950s, MGM's strength was weakened by television's popularity.

Before the White Man Came, lobby cards (8); include photo prints with tinted highlights; 14 x 11 inches; excellent condition; include original paper wraps; $100–200.

Before the White Man Came, paper movie poster; colorful full headdress costumed Indian chief on horseback for this movie with an "all Indian cast"; 26½ x 40½ inches; fair/good condition, several folds and creases, some paper loss, especially at folds, dry mounted; $100–200.

Bus Stop, lobby card; depicting Marilyn Monroe and scenes from the movie; excellent condition; $75–125.

Cabin in the Sky, poster; all-black cast starring Ethel Waters; Al Hirschfeld artwork; 1943; $3,500–4,500.

Casablanca, cardboard calendar and *Casablanca* music sheets; Humphrey Bogart, Ingrid Bergman, and Paul Henreid on covers; varied sizes; very good condition; $45–75.

GI Blues, movie card; depicting Elvis Presley and scenes from the movie; excellent condition; $65–85.

Gone With the Wind, program book; reproduction (original made in 1939); full color; new; $7–10.

I Thought She Loved Me, poster; silent movie; ca. 1910; color lithograph for Independent Moving Picture Co. of America; printed by Film Dealer Litho Co., Cleveland; 40 x 27½ inches; linen backing; excellent condition; $100–200.

Jetsons—The Movie, 3-D watch; features Elroy and Astro; excellent condition; $7–10.

Nanook of the North, poster; depicts stars of film; said to be first important film documentary; 1921; one sheet; excellent condition; $5,000–7,500.

Snow White and the Seven Dwarfs, insert card; Disney classic; 1937; first full-length feature; excellent condition; $8,000–12,000.

Tarzan and His Mate, poster; depicts stars Johnny Weismuller and Maureen O'Sullivan on backs of elephants; 1934; one sheet; excellent condition; $5,000–7,500.

The Birth of a Nation, poster; 1916 D. W. Griffith film; depicts Klansman with fiery cross; excellent condition; $40,000–50,000.

The Fireman, Charlie Chaplin lobby cards (7); from Republic Pictures; all show Chaplin in this firefighting movie; early classic; 14 x 11 inches; very good condition, some soiling overall, tack holes in borders; $1,000–1,500.

The Kid, poster; depicts Charlie Chaplin and "the kid" turning to look behind them; 1921; one sheet; $25,000–30,000.

The Maltese Falcon, poster; depicts stars Humphrey Bogart and Mary Astor; 1941; three sheets; not desirable because it shows Bogart from another film and star Mary Astor's head on Ida Lupino's body; excellent condition; $6,000–8,000.

The Outlaw, poster; sexy view of star Jane Russell; 1942 Howard Hughes film; excellent condition; $5,000–10,000.

The Scarlet Empress, poster; movie starred Marlene Dietrich; though it was about Catherine the Great, the poster shows Dietrich in modern dress; 1934; half sheet; excellent condition; $3,000–4,000.

The Seven-Year Itch, poster; depicts star Marilyn Monroe; 1955; one sheet; excellent condition; $1,000–2,000.

The Son of the Sheik, poster; 1926; one sheet; restored; depicts star Rudolph Valentino baring his chest to kneeling woman; very good condition; $10,000–15,000.

The Stampede, poster; silent movie; full-color litho for Independent Moving Picture Co. of America; lithographed by Film Dealer Litho Co.; ca. 1910; 40 x 27½ inches; linen backing; excellent condition; $100–200.

The Virginian, poster; depicts stars Gary Cooper and Walter Huston on one sheet; excellent condition; $8,000–10,000.

Uncle Tom's Cabin, paper posters (3); includes "Marks the Lawyer," "Uncle Tom," and "Eliza"; 13 x 22 inches excluding frame; fair/good condition, some water staining, minor paper loss, general wrinkling; $225–350.

Wings, poster; a Paramount Picture starring Charles Rogers, Clara Bow, and Richard Arlen; stars are in silhouette looking up into sky where dogfight is happening; 1927; first film to win Oscar for Best Picture; one sheet; excellent condition; $4,500–5,500.

The Wizard of Oz, glasses; made to celebrate fiftieth anniversary of the movie; depict scenes from same; near-mint condition; $9–15.

CONCERTS/PERSONALITIES

Allen Ginsberg/Timothy Leary/Jerry Rubin/Dick Gregory, poster; 1967; Golden Gate Park "Gathering of the Tribes for a Human Be-In"; designed by Stanley Mouse and Michael Bowen; purple and gold on white stock; good condition; $250–350.

B. B. King, concert poster; presented by Bill Graham in San Francisco; designed by S. Singer; lithographed in color by Tea Lautrec Lithographs, San Francisco; 24 x 14 inches; very good condition; $35–75.

Beatles, ice cream wrapper; 1960s; mint condition; $10–15.

Beatles, tour programs; 1964 and 1965; 12 x 12 inches; near-mint condition; $16–25/pair.

Big Brother & the Holding Company/Bo Diddley/Earthquake, concert poster; designed by Stanley Mouse and Alton Kelley; concert held at Avalon Ballroom; reddish orange and blue; very good condition; $40–75.

Elvis Presley, promotional 1969 Easter postcard; color photo; excellent condition; $8–10.

Eric Burdon and the Animals/Quicksilver Messenger Service/Sons of Champlin, concert poster; 1968; Fillmore Auditorium; designed by Dana W. Johnson; yellow, black, and pink/green; good condition; $30–75.

Flintstones, comic book; "Flintstones at the World's Fair"; 1965; near-mint condition; $6–8.

Grateful Dead, concert poster; called "Skull and Roses"; designed by Stanley Mouse and Alton Kelley; 1966 Avalon Ballroom appearance; published by Family Dog Productions, San Francisco, California; printed in red, blue, and black; excellent condition; $300–500.

Hopalong Cassidy, milk container; 1 pint; flattened; unused; 1970s; mint condition; $6–8.

Howdy Doody, pencils (set of six); different full-color picture on each pencil; excellent/near-mint condition; $6–10 set.

Jefferson Airplane, concert poster; presented by Bill Graham at Fillmore; printed in red and gold; designed by Peter Bailey; 1966; good condition; $75–110.

Jefferson Airplane and the Other Half, concert poster; printed in black and white with brown star; designed by Alton Kelley; Family Dog Productions at Denver, Colorado; 20 x 14 inches; excellent condition; $35–75.

Muhammad Ali and Joe Frazier, buttons (2); 3 inch buttons that advertised the fight; fair condition; $10–15 pair.

Santana/Melanie, concert poster; 1969; Fillmore West; designed by Greg Irons; black, red, and orange on yellow stock; good condition; $45–90.

The Doors/Chuck Berry, concert poster; designed by Bill Graham (#99); red, blue, black, green, and purple; printed by Tea Lautrec Studios; titled "Six Days of Sound"; artist: Bonnie MacLean; good condition; $110–200.

The Who/Cannonball Adderly/the Vagrants, concert poster; designed by Lee Conklin for Bill Graham; yellow, reddish brown, and deep green; printed by Tea Lautrec Litho; unnumbered; concert held at Winterland and Fillmore Auditorium; very good condition; $50–100.

Willie Nelson, concert poster; 1981; Poplar Creek Music Theater; lithographed on glazed paper stock; 20 x 13 inches; very good condition; $25–50.

THEATER
Brush, King of Wizards, magician poster; paper; framed under glass; printed by Goes Litho Co.; ca. 1910; caption reads "School of Occidental and Oriental Magic"; 30½ x 23½ inches; near-mint condition; $400–550.

Eight Bells, poster; colorful image of man walking down the "human staircase" with woman in arms after rescuing her from a fire; lettering reads "The Famous Brothers Byrne in the New 8 BELLS/The Human Staircase/Great Fire Scene"; early play—ca. late 1800s; 28 x 42½ inches; excellent condition; some soiling and minor creasing; $150–250.

Si Perkins/or The Girl I Left Behind Me, poster; season of 1886–1887; stars were Frank Jones and the Pughtown Farmers Band; framed; rare; 29 x 20 inches; good condition; $75–150.

The Pirates of Penzance, poster; depicts vignetted scenes from the play; colorful; 17¾ x 23¾ inches; ca. late 1800s; very good condition, borders trimmed, lower right corner missing; $50–150.

Jack-O-V-Cudgel and *Jack-Harkaway*, theater broadsides (2); both having very nice black-and-white graphics; 18 x 23 inches and 18¼ x 23½ inches, respectively; both are in good/very good condition; $50–100.

The Inquirer, theater posters (2); depict what appears to be a woman dragging her intoxicated husband up the stairs; reads "The Comedy Drawa The New Fogg's Ferry" with a quote at the bottom of the poster saying "Don't Kill Me Mammie"; 20½ x 28½ inches; very good overall condition; $100–200.

Theater broadsides (4); multiple-imaged theater promotions including *Blue Jeans–Foggs*, *Checky Charlie*, *Dashing Duval*, and others; varied sizes; good overall condition, some chipping, minor paper loss, soiling overall, backed on cardboard; $100–200.

Theater posters (4); including *Blue Jeans* and *Fogg's Ferry*; depict various scenes from these productions; varied sizes; very good overall condition, strong colors, backed on cardboard; $100–300.

CHAPTER THIRTY-TWO
PAINTS, VARNISHES

BILLINGS-CHAPIN
　Billings-Chapin, porcelain sign; orange, blue, and white; 26 inches tall; ca. 1930; excellent condition; $500–600.

　Billings-Chapin Paints, tin match holder; shows paint with dripping brush; 3½ x 5 x 1¼ inches; good condition, some rust and chipping; $50–100.

BROOKS & CO.
　Brooks & Co., paper calendar; 1881; multipage illustrated calendar showing black people in various "comical" scenes; individual calendar sheets are 5 x 6½ inches excluding mat; overall 26 x 25¼ inches; excellent/near-mint condition; $300–450.

CAMPBELL'S
　Campbell's Varnish, display stand; multitiered wooden shelf with embossed tin signs; interior living room scene, children painting cat and woman restoring Victorian side chair; 19½ x 15 x 8 inches; good condition, overall soiling, slight crazing to tin, minor chipping; $500–1,000.

　Campbell's Varnish, embossed tin-and-wood display case; wood tiers; product name embossed in tin shelf strip below last tier; above top tier is embossed-tin depiction of children with cat in Victorian setting, as well as women admiring chair; caption reads "It is SPLENDID/Makes Old Furniture Look Just Like New"; sign printed by Chas. W. Shonk Co. Litho.; 20 x 15½ x 8 inches overall; good/very good condition; $1,500–2,500.

CARTER
　Carter White Lead, thermometer, 8 x 28 inches; red, white, and black; bottom of the thermometer shows a bucket of the paint and the slogan "Save the surface and you save all"; ca. 1930; good condition; $300–400.

DERBY
　Derby Paint, flange sign; two-sided blue-and-white enameled sign; pictures can of paint; by Charles Shonk; 12½ x 19½ inches; fair condition

Billings-Chapin, porcelain sign; orange, blue, and white; 26 inches tall; ca. 1930; excellent condition; $500–600. *Collection of and photo by Michael Bruner.*

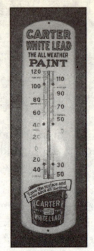

Carter White Lead, thermometer, 8 x 28 inches; red, white, and black; bottom of the thermometer shows a bucket of the paint and the slogan "Save the surface and you save all"; ca. 1930; good condition; $300–400. *Collection of and photo by Michael Bruner.*

on one side, good on the other, some wearing of color, as well as minor chipping and flaking; $75–125.

DEVOE

Devoe Varnish, cardboard poster; unusual image of cloud pouring water on touring car, which proves Devoe products "Prevent Destruction"; ca. 1925; 23½ x 34½ inches; very good/excellent condition; $250–350.

DUTCH BOY PAINTS

The registered trademark for Dutch Boy Paints is not a Dutch boy at all, but an Irishman named Michael Brady. Dutch artist Yook did the preliminary sketches of Brady, however, Lawrence Carmichael Earle completed the portrait. The portrait solved a problem for the National Lead Company, established in 1891 from the merger of twenty-five American manufacturers of white lead. They realized that they needed to appear united in order to advertise their new product, and thus they turned to O. C. Harn, their advertising manager. He came up with the Dutch Boy idea, because the Dutch had a reputation for keeping things immaculately clean and white-washed.

The Dutch Boy has been altered whenever the company needed to project a certain mood or theme—at one point he was an athlete, and on another occasion he stood on his head.

PAINTS, VARNISHES   ■ 311

DUTCH BOY

Dutch Boy, bronze statue; 5 inches; ca. late 1940s; very good condition; $125–200.

Dutch Boy, die-cut tin string holder; shows Dutch Boy painting doorway with Atlantic White Lead paint with original advertising bucket string holder; 13¾ x 30 inches including bucket; printed by American Art Sign Co.; very good/excellent condition; $1,500–2,500.

Dutch Boy, figurine; 12 inches; ca. late 1940s; very good condition; $300–400.

Dutch Boy, lamp; 15 inches; ca. early 1950s; very good condition; $150–250.

Dutch Boy Paints, die-cut embossed match holder; depicts trademark Dutch Boy with can of paint; 3 x 6½ x 1 inch; fair condition, overall fading, chips, holes; $100–200.

Dutch Boy Paints, Dutch Boy figure atop can of paint; 20 inches tall; made by National Lead Co.; ca. 1940s; $375–475.

Dutch Boy, porcelain sign; 4 x 4 feet; shows Dutch Boy in oval, stripes on bottom of sign; excellent condition; $200–300.

ELASTILITE

Elastilite Varnish, figural display case; large tin store display in shape of varnish can with shelved interior; large colorful label picturing maple leaf; 19½ x 34 x 10½ inches; very good/excellent condition, general scuffing and wear overall; $1,250–1,750.

Dutch Boy; lamp, 15 inches, ca. early 1950s, $150–250; figurine, 12 inches, ca. late 1940s, $300–400; bronze statue, 5 inches, ca. late 1940s, $125–200. *Courtesy of Neil and Nancy Berliner. Photo by Donald Vogt.*

Dutch Boy Paints, Dutch Boy figure atop can of paint; 20 inches tall; made by National Lead Co.; ca. 1940s; $375–475. *Courtesy of Neil and Nancy Berliner. Photo by Neil Berliner.*

EXCELSIOR
Excelsior Improved Varnishes/New York, price booklet; slogan: "Won't turn white"; very good condition; $15–25.

MASURY'S
Masury's Color, tin sign; man in shop filled with cans of paint pointing to emblazoned can in sky; printed by Sentenne & Green; 23 x 18 inches excluding frame; excellent/near-mint condition, minor chipping to background, minor scratches; $1,500–2,500.

NEW YORK ENAMEL
New York Enamel Paint Company, cardboard sign; rare; depicts two houses—before and after; 25¼ x 20¾ inches excluding frame; fair condition, some water staining and soiling; $400–750.

SAPOLIN
Sapolin, glass display and sign; original decal on glass sign in original display box; pictures elves in biplane painting rainbow in sky; overall 20 x 18½ x 4 inches; fair condition; $100–200.

SHERWIN-WILLIAMS PAINTS
The original "Cover-the-Earth" trademark was sketched in 1895 by George W. Ford, ad manager of the Sherwin-Williams Company, but was not adopted until 1905. The company's first trademark, created by owner Henry Sherwin, depicted a chameleon mounted on a painter's palette.

Ford had hidden his sketch so he wouldn't offend his boss, but when his work was uncovered in 1898, the boss liked it. Sherwin's general manager, Walter H. Cottingham, liked the new logo idea so much that he encouraged Sherwin to "adopt this Cover-the-Earth trademark and make it come true!"

Today, the company makes and distributes its products all over the world.

SHERWIN-WILLIAMS
Sherwin-Williams, cardboard puzzle; depicts exterior of house with four vignettes of railroad car, coach, cans, and interior; opposite side is United States map; 11¼ x 16 inches excluding frame; excellent condition; $50–150.

STANDARD
Standard Varnish Works, self-framed tin sign; painter wearing overalls stands behind lineup of products; 33 x 23 inches; good condition, overall age; $150–300.

WOOD-LAC ENAMELOID
Wood-Lac Enameloid, sign; good display piece showing product and woman using same on piece of Victorian hall furniture; 20 x 17 inches; excellent condition, minor foxing on edges and corner; $350–550.

WOOLSEY'S VARNISHES
Woolsey's Varnishes, celluloid pocket mirror; pictures can of paint; 1¼ x 2¾ inches; very good condition; $35–75.

CHAPTER THIRTY-THREE
■ PEANUTS AND ■ BY-PRODUCTS

ACORN
Acorn, 5 cent salted peanut dispenser; original decal and lighted red dome; includes key; 8 x 16 x 8 inches; good overall condition, some scratches to the label; $75–150.

BARBOUR'S
Barbour's Salted Peanuts, tin; 10 pounds; lettered red, yellow, and black can with original press lid for the "Goody-Goody Brand"; "made by G.E. Barbour Co., St. John, N.B., Canada"; 8 inch diameter x 11 inches; good/very good condition, slight fade to colors, overall wear, slight denting and chipping; $100–200.

BARRY
Barry Peanuts, roasters (3); two are copper-cased peanut roasters with original kerosene base heating units; varied sizes; fair condition; $50–150.

BEAVER BRAND PEANUT BUTTER
Beaver Brand Peanut Butter, pail; depicts beaver surmounting billboard surrounded by maple leaves; original press lid and bail; 3¾ inch diameter x 3½ inches; very good condition, slight scratches and denting; $250–450.

BOWES PEANUT BUTTER
Bowes Peanut Butter, pail; 1 pound; lettered image on can with slip lid and bail handle; 3¾ x 3¾ inches; "made by Bowes Co. Ltd., Toronto, Canada"; excellent condition, minor edge chipping, slight overall wear; $350–550.

BUNNIES
Bunnies Salted Peanuts, tin; 10 pounds; top-hatted bunny with 5 cent package on colorful tin with original press lid; 8 inch diameter x 11 inches; "made by G.E. Barbour Co., St. John, N.B., Canada"; very good condition, minor denting, overall slight scratches and chipping due to use; nice sheen to color; $300–500.

PEANUTS AND BY-PRODUCTS ■ 315

CANADA NUT CO.
(*see also* various brand names)
Canada Nut Co., peanut butter can; different version of the Squirrel brand can with press lid; 3½ inch diameter x 3½ inches; "made by Canada Nut Co., Vancouver, B.C., Canada"; very good condition with general overall rubbing and minor scratching; $75–150.

Canada Nut Co., peanut butter tin; unusual variety of Squirrel brand can with press lid; "made by Canada Nut Co., Vancouver, Canada"; 5 inch diameter x 7 inches; very good condition, slight scratching and chipping due to overall wear, minor denting, good sheen to colors; $150–250.

CLARK'S PEANUT BUTTER
Clark's Peanut Butter, pail; multiple scenes of moose hunting, Indians, beavers, and dog sled; wonderful multiple color; original slip lid and bail; 3¼ x 3½ inches; excellent condition, minor rubs to lid, slight edge chipping; $800–1,200.

DEFIANCE
Defiance, hot peanut warmer bin; tin with stenciled advertising on sides; curved glass front; 18½ x 21½ x 20 inches; good condition, some chipping and denting; $250–450.

E. F. KEMP
E. F. Kemp, tin; 1 pound mixed nuts; "made by Golden Glow Shops, Boston, Ma"; gold-and-brown design; excellent condition; $12–15.

LOUIS
Louis Brand Peanut Butter, pail; packed for the Williams-Halsell-Frasier Company; 4¾ inch diameter x 4¾ inches; good overall condition; $100–200.

E. F. Kemp, tin; 1 pound; mixed nuts; "made by Golden Glow Shops, Boston, MA"; gold-and-brown design; excellent condition; $12–15.
Courtesy of Dawn and Bob Reno. Photo by Donald Vogt.

MACLAREN'S

MacLaren's, peanut butter pail; 12 ounces; with unusual image of children playing "tea party" with pail in background being used as planter; retains original slip lid and bail; 3½ inch diameter x 3½ inches; "made by MacLaren Wright Ltd., Toronto, Canada"; very good condition, some scratching, general overall wear; $125–200.

MEADOW-SWEET

Meadow-Sweet Peanut Butter, pails (2); similarly imaged cans with rising sun over meadow and cows; bold colors; 16 ounces and larger; original lids and bails; "made by Meadow Sweet Cheese Mfg. Co., Montreal, Canada"; very good condition, some slight denting, slight overall scratching; $200–400.

OLD CITY

Old City Peanut Butter, pail; 15 ounces; rare; depicts boy fishing with can beside him (can holds worms?) and winter horse-drawn sled scene opposite; multicolored; original slip lid and bail; 3¼ inch diameter x 3¼ inches; excellent condition, slight scratching; $1,200–2,500.

PARROT PEANUT BUTTER

Parrot Peanut Butter, pail; rare; pictures parrot in circle; original press lid and bail; 3½ inch diameter x 3¼ inches; good/very good condition, scratching to image, chipping to edges; $1,250–2,500.

Parrot Peanut Butter, tin; 13 ounces; with press lid; distinctive; "made by The Westport Co. Ltd., Vancouver, B.C., Canada"; 3 inch diameter x 3¼ inches; good/very good condition, minor denting and scratches, some in-painting to logoed image, primarily lower half of bird and background; $350–500.

PETER RABBIT PEANUT BUTTER

Peter Rabbit Peanut Butter, pail; depicts Peter and his pals (by artist Harrison Cady); rare tin with original slip lid and bail; "made by Kelly Confection Co., Vancouver, B.C., Canada"; 3½ inch diameter x 3½ inches; fair/good condition, some paint loss due to chipping in image and along vertical seam, $400–600.

PLANTERS PEANUTS

(see also "Nabisco" in Crackers/Cookies/Biscuits chapter)

In 1916, a schoolboy named Antonio Gentile from Suffolk, Virginia, made a sketch of a peanut man that won a contest run by Amedeo Obici and Mario Peruzzi, cofounders of a peanut-packaging business. The sketch became Mr. Peanut, one of the most collectible figures in advertising history—and the logo for Obici and Peruzzi's peanut business.

Obici and Peruzzi, Italian fruit stand operators from Wilkes-Barre, Pennsylvania, and New York City, respectively, had begun packaging peanuts in glassine and cellophane packages, as well as in vacuum-packed cans, but it wasn't until Mr. Peanut was born that the business made the turn into a multimillion-dollar establishment. The company, organized in 1906, used the word "Planters" in its name only because Obici believed it sounded "important and dignified."

The Mr. Peanut figure has been used on all packaging for the product, and has been reproduced as toys, souvenirs, statues, and in every premium imaginable. Many of the glass jars and old cans have been reproduced, but they are clearly marked as being new.

A national club devoted to collecting Planters items has been established and publishes a newsletter called "Peanut Papers" (the address is listed in Appendix B of this book).

Planters was sold to Standard Brands in 1960.

PLANTERS

Hershey/Planters, ball gum gaming machine; insert a penny and pull plunger, which results in getting a gum ball; at the same time, the wheel in the middle spins, and if the product on the wheel lines up with the same product in arrow, the merchant would give you a candy bar for free; bottom of machine reads "For Advertising Purposes Only" to avoid classification as gambling device; very colorful; 12 x 7 x 4 inches; ca. 1940s; excellent condition; $350–500.

Planters, Mr. Peanut vender banks; plastic vender (note spelling) manufactured in three colors; although all are difficult to find in the original box, the hardest to find is the white bank, next is the yellow, and the red seems to turn up most frequently; insert coin and bank vends small amount of cocktail peanuts from a tin that is poured into Mr. Peanut's top hat; 8 x 5 inches; bank holds about $20 worth of coins; "manufactured by the Geo. S. Scott Mfg. Co. in Wallington, Ct."; ca. 1930s; all three banks in mint in-box condition with can of nuts and key; white bank $300–500, yellow $200–400, red $100–300.

Planters Peanuts, cardboard display; rare; Mr. Peanut in peanut shell canoe and girl with parasol; ca. 1920s; unusual small Planters piece; 9 x 6 x 1 inch; good condition, slight fade, creases; $400–600.

Planters, cigarette lighter assortment; (from left to right) matchbook, 2 x 2 inches, very colorful, ca. 1938, mint condition, $50–60; cocktail can lighter (large), tabletop or desktop lighter, 4 x 3½ inches, ca. 1968, mint in-box condition, $40–50; cocktail can lighter (small), same as above, but in miniature, rare and difficult to find, made in Japan, 1 inch diameter x 1½ inches, ca. 1968, $125–150; peanut-shaped composition lighter, could only be obtained by retailers by saving coupons packed with Planters merchandise sold in their store, suggested sale price .40 to customers, 2½ inches, pulls apart, ca. late 1930s–early 1940s, mint condition, $100–125; silver cigarette lighter, made by Gray Mfg. Co., U.S.A. but distributed only in Canada, 1½ x 1 x ½ inch, very rare, ca. 1940s, mint and working, $150–175. *From the collection of Leonard A. Calabrese. Photo by Adalbert Krei.*

Planters, matchbook cigarette lighter; 2 x 2 inches; very colorful; ca. 1938; mint condition; $50–60.

Planters Nuts, chopper tin; unusual nut grinder attachment for top of salted pecans can; removable Mr. Peanut top to grinder mechanism; "made by Planters Nut & Chocolate Co. Ltd., Toronto, Canada"; 3½ inch diameter x 4¼ inches; excellent condition, very minor scratching and wear; $150–300.

Planters, cocktail can lighter; tabletop or desktop lighter; 4 x 3½ inches; ca. 1968; mint in-box condition; $40–50.

Planters, cocktail can lighter (small); rare and difficult to find; made in Japan; 1 inch diameter x 1½ inches; ca. 1968; very good condition; $125–150.

Planters Salted in the Shells Nuts, counter display; store counter display for housing bags of Planters Peanuts with oval sign at the top; double sided; 18 inches tall; very good condition; $75–150.

Planters, covered jar; embossed clear jar with Mr. Peanut in a running position; 8½ inch diameter x 12 inches; good overall condition; $150–300.

Planters Peanuts, die-cut tin display; figural Mr. Peanut stands atop dispenser that holds 5 cent bars of Jumbo Peanut Block; 4¾ x 12 x 4¼ inches; very good condition, general overall wear; $1,000–1,500.

Planters, display; Mr. Peanut figural with cardboard box; papier-mâché store counter display; approximately 14 inches tall; produced by

King Cole in Ohio; ca. 1918–1919; extremely rare; mint condition; $2,500–3,500.

Planters, die-cut display; Planter Plantation cardboard box with Lady; older cardboard store counter display box contained 5 cent bags of Planters Peanuts; the die-cut increases the value of this box tremendously; ca. 1940s; unopened box is 9 x 6 x 3 inches; die-cut 6 inches; mint condition; $200–375.

Planters, square display; made of tin with distinctive litho; contained 5 cent Jumbo Peanut Block candy bars; 12 inches high, base measures 5 x 5 inches; produced by the Wilkes-Barre Can Company in Pennsylvania; ca. 1930s; very rare, especially with good litho and no rust or dents; mint condition; $500–1,000.

Planters Peanuts, composition figural peanut container; has end lid; embossed "Planter's"; 10 x 6 x 6 inches; excellent condition, some chipping along lid, rim, and container; lid fits erratically; $175–275.

Planters Peanuts, figural costume; unusual hard rubber three-dimensional Mr. Peanut and top hat; embossed "Mr. Peanut" on hat; original hat included but replacement hat on peanut; used for promotional parades and solicitations; 18 inch diameter x 47 inches; extra hat is 18 inch diameter x 13 inches; excellent condition; $500–800.

Planters, display; Mr. Peanut figural with cardboard box; papier-mâché store counter display; approximately 14 inches tall; produced by King Cole in Ohio; ca. 1918–1919; extremely rare; mint condition; $2,500–3,500. *From the collection of Leonard A. Calabrese. Photo by Adalbert Krei.*

Planters, square display; made of tin with distinctive litho; contained 5 cent Jumbo Peanut Block candy bars; 12 inches high, base measures 5 x 5 inches; produced by the Wilkes-Barre Can Company in Pennsylvania; ca. 1930s; very rare, especially with good litho and no rust or dents; mint condition; $500–1,000. *From the collection of Leonard A. Calabrese. Photo by Adalbert Krei.*

320 ■ ADVERTISING

Planters Peanuts, figural papier-mâché display stand; Mr. Peanut stands beside mottled embossed display tray; made by Old King Cole, Ohio; 11 x 14¼ x 10½ inches; good/very good condition, original paint in as-found condition, some chipping and minor cracks, slight distortion to base, tears to paper hatband; $750–2,000.

Planters, figural peanut jar; in the shape of a football with embossed peanut-handled lid; 8½ x 8 x 8½ inches; good/very good condition; $150–300.

Planters, Little Black Sambo board game; made by Funland Books and Games in New York; 12 x 16 inches; ca. 1940s; very good condition; $50–100.

Planters, jar; streamlined design with Jumbo the Elephant label; glass store display jar in slanted design with tin lid (lid comes in green, yellow, and black); held the five cent Jumbo Block, has labels on three sides (the value of the jar decreases drastically without labels); 9 x 8 x 4 inches; lid is 5 inches in diameter; ca. 1935; rare; $50 (with no labels), $500 (mint, with labels).

Planters Peanuts, jar and figural lid; octagon; embossing on six sides; 8½ inch diameter x 12½ inches; excellent condition; $75–125.

Planters Peanuts, footed jar; with original decal and lid; 9½ x 12 inches; very good condition, minor chips to lip, some discoloration to label; $100–200.

Planters Peanuts, jars (2); enameled Mr. Peanut on jar with white screw lid, and a rare glass-lidded jar with red overprint (a discontinued item by Planters due to lack of visibility when filled with peanuts); origi-

Planters Peanuts, wood display rack with assorted tins; made of plywood; distributed only in Canada; could be obtained only from Planters Nut & Chocolate Ltd. in Canada; 18 x 22 x 13 inches; ca. 1940s; mint condition (assorted tins date back to 1930s and 1940s; the lower left tin was distributed to the U.S. Armed Forces in World War II); $150–200 (rack only). *From the collection of Leonard A. Calabrese. Photo by Adalbert Krei.*

nal packing box; 6 x 8 x 6 inches and 8 x 10 x 8 inches, respectively; near-mint condition; $100–300.

Planters Peanuts, embossed jar in shape of peanut; figural lid; 9 x 14 inches including lid; excellent original condition; $100–250.

Planters Peanuts, octagonal jar with peanut figural lid; label in good original condition; 8 inch diameter x 12½ inches including lid; good condition, some paper loss and staining, jar and lid have rim chips; $150–250.

Planters Peanuts, running peanut embossed glass jar with original paper label and figural lid; 8½ inch diameter x 13 inches including lid; excellent original condition, some wear to label; $200–350.

Planters, glass store jar and cardboard salted nuts package; good/very good condition; $50–100.

Planters, composition peanut-shaped lighter; could only be obtained by retailers by saving coupons packed with Planters merchandise sold in their store; suggested sale price .40 to customers; 2½ inches; pulls apart; ca. late 1930s–early 1940s; mint condition; $100–125.

Planters, silver cigarette lighter; made by Gray Mfg. Co., USA, but distributed only in Canada; 1½ x 1 x ½ inch; very rare; ca. 1940s; mint and working; $150–175.

Planters Peanuts, embossed tin sign; unusually rare Planters sign showing Mr. Peanut, whose fingers are made of peanuts; 23½ x 9¾ inches; fair/good condition, splits in metal, minor edge loss, some denting and chipping, holes; $100–300.

Planters, Mr. Peanut figural pot metal statue (some believe this statue was meant to be a paperweight); comes in nondescript black-and-silver box; inscription on front of base reads "Mr. Peanut" and on back reads "Compliments Planters Nut & Chocolate Co."; probably given to company executives or to key account personnel; very desirable to collectors; 8 inches tall, base measures 3 x 3 inches; ca. 1930s; mint in-box condition; $500–750.

Planters Peanuts, various items; wide assortment including jars, displays, and punch boards; various sizes; very good/excellent condition; $200–500.

Planters Peanuts, battery-operated Mr. Peanut watch; man's watch; new; $25–50.

Planters Peanuts, watches (2); new-issue men's executive watches used as presents to employees, not an issued item; uncirculated condition; $200–300.

RED FEATHER PEANUT BUTTER
Red Feather Peanut Butter, pail; 1 pound; lettered logo over Red Feather image; original slip lip and bail; "made by Imperial Cocoa & Spice Co. Ltd., Hamilton, Ontario, Canada"; 3¾ inch diameter x 3¼ inches; very good condition, pinpoint imperfections overall, minor chipping; $300–600.

SMILING SAM
Smiling Sam, peanut vendor; figural head with exaggerated features; coin in head and pulling of tongue delivers handful of peanuts; 12 x 14 x 12 inches; good condition, appears repainted and metal appears repaired; $200–400.

SQUIRREL PEANUT BUTTER
(*see also* "Canada Nut Co.")
Squirrel Peanut Butter, set of three stacking cans; picture a squirrel gnawing at peanut; 48 ounces, 27 ounces, and 13 ounces; "made by Canada Nut Company Ltd., Vancouver, B.C., Canada"; good/very good condition, some scratching overall, especially on 17 ounce can, minor denting; $300–450.

Squirrel Peanut Butter, pail; 34 ounces; logoed image on orange background with original slip lid and bail; 4¼ inch diameter x 4½ inches; "made by Canada Nut Co., Vancouver, B.C., Canada"; very good/ excellent condition, minor denting, slight scratches, minor wear; $100–200.

Squirrel Peanut Butter, pail; logoed image of squirrel with nut on gold background with original slip lid and bail; 3½ inch diameter x 3½ inches; "made by Canada Nut Co., Vancouver, B.C., Canada" very good condition, slight chipping due to wear, minor denting; $200–400.

Squirrel Brand Peanut Butter, tin; 15 pound; squirrel pictured on gold background with original press lid and bail; 8¼ inch diameter x 8¼ inches; "made by Canada Nut Co., Vancouver, B.C., Canada"; very good condition, some scratches, minor denting; $175–275.

SUPREME PEANUT BUTTER
Supreme Peanut Butter, pail; depicts children playing at beach and using empty tin to carry sand; original top and bail; 3½ inch diameter x

3¾ inches; fair/good condition, some chipping, general scratches, slight fading; $150–300.

TAYLOR'S

Taylor's Homemade Peanut Butter, pail; 1 pound; interesting tin picturing Taylor's Homestead in white and blue; original slip lid and bail; 3¼ inch diameter x 3½ inches; "A. E. Taylor, Cainsville, Ontario, Canada"; good/very good condition, some background paint loss primarily under bail supports and edges; $350–550.

TEDDY BEAR PEANUT BUTTER

Teddy Bear Peanut Butter, pail; rare; pictures teddy bear; 3½ x 3½ inches; with original press lid and bail; good condition, minor overall denting, some slight chipping and background paint loss; $650–1,300.

UNCLE SAM

Uncle Sam, tin-and-glass "hot" peanut butter warmer; stenciled sides; 18 x 22 x 18 inches; fair with some chipping and general wear, soiling overall; $200–400.

WHITE SWAN

White Swan Peanut Butter, pail; 13 ounces; red, white, and blue graceful swimming swan; original slip lid and bail; "made by the White Swan Spices & Cereals Ltd., Toronto, Canada"; 3½ inch diameter x 3½ inches; very good condition, minor scratching, slight overall wear; $150–250.

CHAPTER THIRTY-FOUR
PENS, PENCILS, INKS

AULT & WIBORG, INC.
Ault & Wiborg, Inc., Co., ink paper signs (2); "The Cowgirl" and "Touching Leather"; pair of single-sheet advertising flyers with western motifs advertising this company's photochromatic colors; 8¾ x 12 inches and 9 x 12 inches, respectively; good condition; $100–200.

MacKINNON
MacKinnon Pens, paper sign; depicts gentleman sitting at rolltop desk, another man at letter box, and woman and child at home at her writing table; printed by N. Y. Liff, Co.; approximately 14½ x 18½ inches; good/very good condition, margins trimmed, minor paper loss at corners, slight ripping/soiling; $1,000–2,000.

MISCELLANEOUS
Figural camel pen display; three-dimensional resting camel with racks on saddled back; used for holding pens; 10½ x 5½ x 4½ inches; good condition, some cracking, wear of color, general soiling overall; $100–200.

PARKER PENS
Ads marketing Parker Pens in 1904 showed the pen (marked "Parker Fountain Pen" on its nib and "Geo. S. Parker" on its body) and stated: "They're Good." At that time, more than 9,000 dealers carried the pens, and they were sold with a "free accident policy insuring against breakage of rubber parts."

PARKER
Parker, advertisement from *New York Times*, 1935; "Parker was voted the College Favorite"; excellent condition; $8–10.

Parker, advertisement from *Collier's*, 1938; "3,739 Graduates of '38"; full color; excellent condition; $10–12.

Parker, advertisement from *The American Weekly*, December 6, 1942; full-page color spread depicts different sets for the holidays; excellent condition; $20–25.

Pens, Pencils, Inks ■ 325

Parker, advertisement from *New York Times*, 1935; "Parker was voted the College Favorite"; $8–10. *Courtesy of Lester Morris. Photo by Donald Vogt.*

Parker, advertisement from *Collier's*, 1938; "3,739 Graduates of '38"; full color; $10–12. *Courtesy of Lester Morris. Photo by Donald Vogt.*

Parker Pencils, 5 cent vendor; white metal case pencil vendor; "Everywhere folks write"; ca. 1930; 10 x 9 x 5 inches; very good overall condition; $25–100.

PEACOCK

Peacock Ink, tin and bottle; ink bottle with octagonal tin case; removable shoulder cap for insertion of fresh bottle; peacock motif; 2¼ inch square x 2¾ inches overall; excellent condition; $75–110.

SANFORD'S INKS

Sanford's Inks, tin flange sign; unusual variation for this popular image of bottles and jars; 20 x 13½ inches; fair condition, rust damage to bottom, general overall wear and some chipping; $500–800.

THOMAS'

Thomas' Inks, embossed tin sign; humorous and exceedingly illusive sign with black cat knocking over jar of red ink; 19½ x 13½ inches excluding frame; very good to excellent condition, minor chipping, some slight darkening of color primarily due to soiling; $13,500–16,500.

WATERMAN PENS

In a 1900 advertisement for L. E. Waterman Co., the ultimate in endorsements was made—President McKinley endorsed Waterman Pens. The advertisement stated, in McKinley's words, "I have been using one of your fountain pens for several months, and take pleasure in saying that I find it an invaluable pocket companion."

326 ■ ADVERTISING

The company was bought by the Gillette Company in 1987 (*see* "The Gillette Company" in Razors chapter).

WATERMAN'S

Waterman's, advertisement from *Pictorial Review*, ca. 1918; "The Greatest in the World"; full color; excellent condition; $20–22.

Waterman's, glass oversized figural ink bottle; with screw metal cap; 8 inch diameter x 13 inches; excellent condition; $50–200.

Waterman's Fountain Pen, cardboard sign; Christmas-wrapped packages of imaged Waterman's Ideal Fountain Pen; 20½ x 10½ inches excluding frame; fair/good condition, general overall wear and soiling, center crease appears to have been folded, tears lower left and others, margins trimmed; $50–125.

Waterman's Fountain Pen, paper poster; depicts Uncle Sam at the signing of the Treaty of Portsmouth; ca. early 1900s; approximately 41½ x 19½ inches excluding mat and frame; overall 48½ x 26 inches; excellent condition; $1,300–2,600.

Waterman's Ideal Fountain Pen, poster; French; depicts pen in foreground with Wright brothers' biplane in background; 56½ x 87 inches; has been attached to a cloth background; very good condition; $3,000–4,000.

Waterman's, advertisement from *Pictorial Review*, ca. 1918; "The Greatest in the World"; full color; $20–22. *Courtesy of Lester Morris. Photo by Donald Vogt.*

CHAPTER THIRTY-FIVE
■ RAZORS ■

DREAD-NOT
Dread-Not, razor blades dispenser; porcelain front and sides; English blade vendor; red, white and blue; depicts British battleship below product name, as well as two British flags; cast-iron mechanism; 10½ x 20 x 4½ inches; very good condition, some age discoloration to case; 350–700.

EVER-READY
Ever-Ready clock face; depicts man's face coated in shaving cream, he holds razor at the ready; fancy oak case; missing clock hands; ca. 1920; $175–275.

GEM DAMASKEENE
Gem Damaskeene Razor, advertising clock; depicts image of man shaving while holding baby in lap; lithographed wooden wall clock; 23 x 27½ inches; very good/excellent condition; in working condition and has pendulum; $1,500–2,500.

Gem Damaskeene Razor, mechanical display; cardboard with clockwork mechanism; caption reads "My! how Baby hollers, Ridding Popper's knee. Still, the shave's delightful. Pop's got a GEM you see./Gem Damaskeene Razor $1.00"; Papa rocks in chair while baby sits on knee; original instructions in back and packed in original crate; near mint condition; $3,000–5,000.

THE GILLETTE COMPANY
King Camp Gillette, born January 5, 1855, in Fond du Lac, Wisconsin, spent his early years as a frustrated inventor who had to work as a traveling salesman. Though he grew up in Chicago, Gillette moved after the Chicago Fire of 1871, then married Alanta Ella Gaines in 1890. In 1891, he began working at the Baltimore Seal Co., where he met William Painter, another inventor, and the man who encouraged Gillette not to lose sight of his dreams.

The encouragement worked, for Gillette began formulating an idea for a new safety razor with disposable blades in 1895. He

Gillette, Gillette Blue Blade, package and sample blade. *Photo courtesy of The Gillette Company, Boston, Massachusetts.*

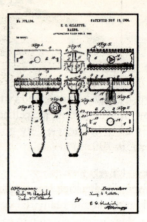

Gillette, photo of patent dated November 15, 1904, for new Gillette Razor. *Photo courtesy of The Gillette Company, Boston, Massachusetts.*

lived in Brookline, Massachusetts, at the time, so he took advantage of nearby MIT scientists (as well as experienced toolmakers) for help with his invention.

In 1901, William Nickerson, an MIT graduate, became Gillette's partner in the venture. On September 28, Gillette formed the American Safety Razor Company and began operations in an office located over a fish store at 424 Atlantic Avenue in Boston. Nickerson's genius at creating machines and processes to produce the new safety razor forged the way for the fledgling company. While he struggled with manufacturing procedures, Gillette sold stock to get financing for the company. In 1902, the company was renamed the Gillette Safety Razor Company, and production finally started in 1903, when Nickerson finished work on a second blade-sharpening machine. By the end of the year, Gillette had sold 51 razors and 168 blades. He ran his first advertisement in the October issue of *Systems Magazine*.

1904 was a better year for the company. Sales rose incredibly: 90,884 razors and 123,648 blades were sold, and the United States granted a patent for the Gillette Safety Razor on November 15. Business continued to increase in 1905, the year the company moved to a South Boston office, opened its first overseas sales office in London, and established its first overseas manufacturing operation in a Paris bicycle seat factory. A trademark, featuring King C. Gillette's portrait and signature, was

Gillette, trademark. *Photo courtesy of The Gillette Company, Boston, Massachusetts.*

adopted by the company. The trademark was used on the outer wrappings of the blades and razors.

The portrait trademark was used until 1908, when management decided the combination of portrait and signature was too elaborate in some cases. Thus they started using the now-famous "Gillette" in a diamond trademark, along with the portrait and signature mark. By this time a plant had been established in Montreal, Canada; a sales company was established in Hamburg, Germany; a small factory in Berlin began shipping blades and razors; and the company had paid its first stock dividends.

During World War I, Gillette supplied enough razors and blades for the entire U.S. Armed Forces—3.5 million razors and 36 million blades. By the end of the war, branch offices or companies had been established all over the world and worked aggressively to capitalize on the safety razor's overwhelming popularity.

Because its patent covering the original safety razor would expire in 1921 (opening the market to all kinds of imitations), Gillette prepared two new products: the New Improved Gillette Razor and the Silver Brownie Razor. The New Improved version retailed from $5 to $75, while the Silver Brownie, an old-style razor with three blades, sold for $1. The New Improved was introduced in a number of styles through a $2 million advertising campaign. By 1923, the company introduced a gold-plated razor for $1 apiece, then a feminine version (called the Debutante) for seventy-nine cents. Gillette even contracted with the Wm. Wrigley Jr. Company to provide each dealer purchasing a box of Wrigley's gum with a free Silver Brownie razor set. The promotion exceeded the total razor sales during any one of Gillette's first fifteen years.

Premiums continued to thrive. Banks offered Gillette razor sets to all new depositors (the "Shave and Save" promotion); and hotels, restaurants, service stations, and other businesses gave away razors on opening day. By its twenty-fifth anniversary (1926), millions of new customers had been attracted to Gillette products through premiums.

Gillette almost lost its hold on the razor business when Henry J. Gaisman, owner of the AutoStrop Safety Razor Company, introduced a double-edged blade to the market. He had originally offered the patent to Gillette, who had refused it. Gaisman came out with the blade on his own, Gillette followed suit with a similar blade—Gaisman's was patented; Gillette had applied for the patent. The fight was on. After a quick, but ultimately messy, battle, Gillette and AutoStrop merged in 1930—but not before Gaisman uncovered some of The Gillette Company's bookkeeping errors—notably an overstatement of earnings in 1929 of almost $3 million!

The company reorganized during 1931. King C. Gillette resigned, and died fourteen months later at age 77; Gaisman was elected chairman of the board.

Gillette factories installed the Gaisman strip processing method as soon as possible, but lost step with the industry until introducing the Gillette Blue Blade. The blade (not originally designed as blue) was colored blue and sold in a blue package so that it would be unique. The advertising campaign was designed to tell customers the truth with slogans such as "A Frank Confession" and "We Made a Mistake." The company knew it had to regain consumers' confidence and spent far more on advertising the new Blue Blade than it made in profit.

Gillette, photo of the packaging used by King C. Gillette, one of the first company owners to use his own image to sell his product. *Photo courtesy of The Gillette Company, Boston, Massachusetts.*

Competition started cutting in on the company's profits, so it tried something new: sponsoring a radio show called "The Gene and Glenn Show." The show ran through 1934, when the company introduced its first one-piece razor and the Probak Junior Blade.

In 1936, Gillette's chemists developed Brushless shaving cream and the company began distributing it nationally in 1937. In 1938, a dry shaver was introduced in the United States and Canada on a limited basis and the Gillette Thin Blade was added to the product line. A three-piece razor and the Kumpakt Dry Shaver were introduced in 1939, when Gillette started sponsoring the first radio broadcasts of the World Series ("Cavalcade of Sports"). Lather shaving cream was marketed for the first time in 1940, and during the same year, the company disposed of its inventory of dry shavers due to a sharp decline in electric razor sales.

The war years changed Gillette's outlook on the market. It began emphasizing blade quality rather than price, and was unable to introduce any new products from 1930 to 1945 due to manufacturing restrictions. In 1942, the government ordered the company to devote its production to fulfilling military needs, and Gillette contributed to the war effort in many different ways, including manufacturing fuel-control units for plane carburetors.

After the war, Gillette went into overdrive, producing new products and trying to please the consumer it'd had to ignore during wartime. It made record-breaking shipments to civilian markets, welcomed returning servicemen and women into the company, invented the Blue Blade Dispenser in 1946, and introduced the Super Speed Razor in 1947. Gillette acquired the Toni Company in 1948 and launched the new acquisition with the "Which Twin has the Toni?" ad campaign in Europe. The six sets of Toni Twins used to advertise the product toured the United States the following year, searching for other Toni Twins. Toni began television advertising on the "Arthur Godfrey Show" in 1950, introduced several new products throughout that decade (see below), and sponsored its first Miss American Pageant in 1958.

During the 1950s, products such as White Rain Lotion shampoo (1951), Prom home permanent (1951), Tonette children's home permanent (1951), Bobbi home permanent (1952), Gillette Foamy aerosol shave cream (1953), Adorn hair spray (1957), Gillette's first adjustable safety razor (1957), New Crystal Clear White Rain shampoo (1957), and Deep Magic Skin Conditioner (1959) were introduced.

The decade proved a busy one for the company, which celebrated its fiftieth anniversary in 1951; acquired all the common stock of Efdelit, S.A., a leading plastics manufacturer in Argentina, in 1952; acquired The Paper Mate Company in 1955; and opened many new markets and built warehouses, research laboratories, and manufacturing facilities in various countries throughout the world. But the most important event of the decade was changing the company's name to The Gillette Company in 1952. Now the razor, blade, and shaving cream businesses were operated as the Gillette Safety Razor Company, a division of The Gillette Company. In 1956, Paper Mate introduced its "Ninety-Eight" ball-point pen and Piggy Back refill, and in 1958, its $1.95 Mark III pen, which featured a new skip-free refill, was introduced, with the $1.79 Holiday Pen with new Jumbo Refill following in 1959.

The 1960s saw the introduction of Right Guard aerosol deodorant (1960), the Super Blue Blade (1960), the Lady Gillette razor (1963), White Rain hair spray (launched nationally in 1963), Paper Mate's Profile Trio ball-point pens, Slim, Regular, and Husky (1964), Super Stainless Steel Blades and the Techmatic Razor (1965), Heads Up grooming aids (1965), Dippity-do Setting Gel and Casual Hair Color (1965), Techmatic Razor (distributed nationally in 1966), Flair pens (1966), Shampoo-easy hair coloring and Happy Face washing cream (launched nationally in 1967), Refillable Flair pens (1967), the Hot One self-heating shaving cream (1968), Techmatic Adjustable razor (1968), Right Guard antiperspirant (1968), Gillette Super Stainless Steel Injector blade (1968), Soft & Dri antiperspirant for women (1969), the Platinum-Plus blade and Magic Moment hair coloring (launched in 1969), and Powerpoint ball-point pen refills (1969).

It was a dramatic expansion and could not be handled by one office, thus the company created the Toiletries Division to handle that business and expanded its research and manufacturing operations. By 1971, Gillette was organized into three operating groups: Gillette North America, Gillette International, and the

Diversified Companies group. Gillette North America had six major divisions: Safety Razor, Personal Care, Appliance, Paper Mate, Toiletries, and Buxton, Inc.

Meanwhile, the company continued to acquire firms like Braun AG (acquired in 1967), a large German manufacturer of electric shavers, small household appliances, and electronic and photographic equipment. Braun began distributing its Nizo Super 8 movie camera in 1969 and its Ricoh 35mm cameras and accessories in 1970.

During the past two decades The Gillette Company has expanded worldwide, acquiring new companies such as the Autopoint Company, a Chicago manufacturer of mechanical pencils, ball-point pens, and writing accessories (1970); North American Hair Goods, a New York wig manufacturer (1970); Welcome Wagon International, Inc. (1971); Jafra Cosmetics, Inc., a California-based skin-care company (1973); Hydroponic Chemical Company of Copley, Ohio, a manufacturer of home plant-care products (1973); Liquid Paper office supplies (1979); Oral-B Laboratories, Inc. (1984); Waterman Pen Company (1987), and many others.

Each division of The Gillette Company has introduced many new products, both nationally and internationally. Some of the better known are Cricket disposable lighters (1974), Daisy disposable shavers (1975), Mink Difference shampoo (1983), Good News Pivot disposable twin razor blade (1984), and many others.

The company is simply too large for this book to completely and accurately recognize each of its products, thus I have concentrated on the early years. For additional information read *King C. Gillette: The Man and His Wonderful Shaving Device: A History of The Gillette Company*, by Russell B. Adams, Jr., published by Little, Brown and Company, Boston, 1978.

GILLETTE

Gillette, advertisement from *American Magazine*, 1936; advertises Gillette one-piece razor for 98 cents each; excellent condition; $3–5.

Gillette, advertisement from *American Magazine*, ca. 1936; "How to be Generous to a man at Christmas"; excellent condition; $3–5.

Gillette, advertisement from *Review of Reviews*, ca. 1918; advertises new improved Gillette Safety Razor for Christmas; very good condition; $4–8.

334 ■ ADVERTISING

Gillette, advertisement from *American Magazine*, ca. 1936; "How to be Generous to a man at Christmas"; $3–5. *Courtesy of Paper Lady/Bernie and Dolores Fee. Photo by Donald Vogt.*

Gillette, advertisement from *Saturday Evening Post*, July 1939; blue and red; depicts couple in bathing suits, Gillette Blue Blade ("5 for 25 cents"); $3–5. *Courtesy of Paper Lady/Bernie and Dolores Fee. Photo by Donald Vogt.*

Gillette, advertisement from *Saturday Evening Post*, July 1939; blue and red; depicts couple in bathing suits, Gillette Blue Blade ("5 for 25 cents"); excellent condition; $3–5.

Gillette Blue Blade, package and sample blade; excellent condition; $30–50.

PAL
Pal Double Edge Blades, counter display; ladder-type display holds twenty packages of the blades, which sold for twenty-five cents; all original; ca. 1950s; near-mint condition; $30–40.

ROBESON
Robeson Razor, display case; wall-mount shaving razor display with several razors intact with corresponding prices; 32½ x 10½ x 2½ inches; good condition, general soiling overall; $1,000–2,000.

ROLLS RAZOR
Rolls Razor, sign; depicts all four kinds; rare; excellent condition; $275–325.

UNION
Union Razor, embossed tin sign; depicts map of North America and illustrated razor strop; 9½ x 13½ inches; fair condition; $35–90.

VULCAN
Vulcan Double Edge (Blue), hanging display; holds five packages on each side (ten total); all original; ca. 1950s; in box; near-mint condition; $15–25.

CHAPTER THIRTY-SIX
RESTAURANTS

BOB'S BIG BOY
 Big Boy, bank; 10 inches; ca. late 1960s; excellent condition; $40–75.

 Big Boy, bank; in bag; common; vinyl; ca. 1974; mint condition; $10–50.

 Big Boy, figure with hamburger in hand; 8 inches; vinyl head; made by Dakin; ca. 1974; excellent condition; $175–250.

 Big Boy, matches; excellent condition; $2–4.

 Big Boy, nodder; 8 inches; ca. 1950s; very good condition; $400–500.

 Big Boy, salt and pepper shaker; 4½ inches; Japanese made; ca. 1960s; excellent condition; $175–250.

BURGER KING
 (*see* "Pillsbury" in Baking Products chapter)
 Burger King, doll; cloth version of the Burger King; approximately 8 inches tall; ca. 1960s; good condition; $12–15.

 Burger King, doll; cloth version of the cartoon image of the Burger King; approximately 14 inches tall; ca. 1970s; good condition; $15–18.

DOMINO'S PIZZA
 Domino's Pizza, glass; 6 ounces; colorful depiction of the "Noid"; ca. 1980s; near-mint condition; $9–12.

KRYSTAL HAMBURGERS
 Krystal Hamburgers, mug; ca. 1970s; near-mint condition; $5–20.

KENTUCKY FRIED CHICKEN
 The history of one of the largest fast-food chains in the United States began in Corbin, Kentucky, when Harland Sanders, now known to millions as the Colonel, opened a small restaurant. The establishment, which had only one table and six chairs, was in front of a small service station. Soon, Sanders's reputation for excellent food encouraged him to buy a motel

336 ■ Advertising

Big Boy; nodder, 8 inches, ca. 1950s, $400–500; bank, 10 inches (two versions—see the newer/thinner version in bag), ca. late 1960s, $40–75; salt and pepper, 4½ inches, Japanese made, ca. 1960s, $175–250; figure with hamburger in hand, 8 inches, vinyl head, made by Dakin, ca. 1974, $175–250; bank, mint in bag, common, vinyl, ca. 1974, $10–50. *Courtesy of Neil and Nancy Berliner. Photo by Donald Vogt.*

and café across the street, renaming it the Harland Sanders Court & Café. The year was 1930, and the forty-year-old station operator was simply trying to make ends meet for his wife and three children.

The hot-tempered Sanders worked for himself simply because he couldn't work for anyone else; his disposition was probably due to the fact that his father had died when he was six, he'd been left to care for two younger siblings, and then was kicked out of the house at age twelve by his stepfather. He had worked hard throughout his life, even studying law via correspondence courses, then working on the railroad, in the insurance business, for a ferry service, and in the lighting business, before turning to restaurants.

Kentucky Fried Chicken, photo of Colonel Harland Sanders standing next to the sign that designates the "Birthplace of Kentucky Fried Chicken." *Photo courtesy of Kentucky Fried Chicken Department of Public Affairs.*

He did everything possible for the customers who frequented his gas station/restaurant in Corbin, from washing their windshields to making sure things were perfect in his dining room. His cooking fame grew until the state's governor recognized him in 1935 by making him a Kentucky Colonel. In 1939, his restaurant was listed in Duncan Hines's *Adventures in Good Eating*; in the same year he perfected his secret blend of eleven herbs and spices for his now famous fried chicken.

Though his business, like every other in the United States, suffered during World War II, after the war it boomed. Colonel Sanders's motel and restaurant were known throughout the region for excellent food and service.

In the mid-1950s, an interstate highway was built, bypassing Corbin by several miles. With the prospect of greatly reduced tourist traffic, Colonel Sanders sold his restaurant and motel in 1956 and began actively franchising his chicken business. He handled the franchising operation personally, traveling throughout the Midwest, calling on restaurants and cooking his chicken for the owners and their employees. If they liked it, they would pay him a few cents for every Kentucky Fried Chicken dinner they sold. The first franchisee was Pete Harman of Salt Lake City in 1952.

The Kentucky Fried Chicken trademark was copyrighted by Harland Sanders in 1954 ("Colonel Sanders' recipe Kentucky Fried Chicken"). All of the paper goods, newspaper mats, roadside signs, and other promotional aids used Colonel Sanders's image and the registered trademark "it's finger lickin' good." The paper goods included 5 and 10 pound buckets; a carryout box; a seasoned flour container; 1 quart, 1 pint, and ½ pint containers; 10, 14, and 16 ounce cold cups; a hot cup; a drinking glass; a daily menu; place mats; napkins; matches; and table tents. Plastic fluorescent signs were also used, as were Day-Glo posterboards with insets that read "Give Mom a Break! Take home . . . [barrel or bucket] Kentucky Fried Chicken." A life-size easel of the Colonel was often found in the entryway to Kentucky Fried Chicken franchises and ceiling light fixtures in the shape of KFC buckets were also made (some even revolved).

In 1955, the Colonel incorporated Kentucky Fried Chicken. By 1957, the Colonel had four hundred franchisees in the United States and Canada, and four years after that, the franchisees had grown to six hundred, including one in England.

By the early 1960s, Kentucky Fried Chicken was a tremendous success, but the Colonel discovered he had little time left for friends and family, so he sold the business to a group of investors in 1964. The investors, who included John Y. Brown, Jr., and Jack Massey, took the corporation public and listed it as an over-the-counter stock in 1966. When the stock was listed on the New York Stock Exchange in 1969, Colonel Sanders bought the first hundred shares.

The business continued to grow and Colonel Sanders continued to promote the chicken he had created, becoming the spokesperson in the company's commercials and printed advertisements. In 1971, Kentucky Fried Chicken was sold to Heublein Inc., and in 1982, it became a subsidiary of R. J. Reynolds, Inc. (now RJR-Nabisco). In 1986, RJR-Nabisco sold KFC Corp. to PepsiCo, Inc. (there is information about all of the above companies in other sections of this book).

Though Colonel Sanders died in 1980, his image lives on in KFC ads and through memorabilia collected in the Colonel Harland Sanders Museum in Louisville, Kentucky.

In 1987, KFC became the first Western-style quick-service restaurant company in China, opening a five-hundred-seat, three-story restaurant in Beijing. In 1989, KFC opened its three-thousandth international restaurant, and in 1990, its five-thousandth United States restaurant.

Kentucky Fried Chicken changed with the times in 1991, producing a new "faster, sleeker" looking logo, prominently featuring the initials "KFC." The company became the first national restaurant to place skin-free chicken, lower in fat, calories, sodium, and cholesterol, on its menu, and has added other products such as Hot Wings and chicken sandwiches. By the end of the summer of 1991, all packaging, including the traditional bucket, was changed to the new logo (making the old one much more collectible).

KENTUCKY FRIED CHICKEN

Kentucky Fried Chicken, bank; depicts the Colonel "larger than life" with restaurant at his side; 6½ inches tall; ca. 1970s; excellent condition; $50–75.

Kentucky Fried Chicken, bank; depicts the Colonel "larger than life" with restaurant at his side; 6½ inches tall; ca. 1970s; $50–75. *Courtesy of Neil and Nancy Berliner. Photo by Neil Berliner.*

Kentucky Fried Chicken, nodder; depicts the Colonel; plastic; 7 inches high; ca. 1970s; excellent condition; $150–225.

Kentucky Fried Chicken, clock; Colonel Sanders on face; plastic; square design; ca. 1960s; excellent condition; $300–425.

Kentucky Fried Chicken, hanging lamp; milk glass type; depicts bucket with Colonel Sanders's likeness; 12 inches from bottom of bucket to top of brass "crown"; $200–250.

MCDONALD'S

The first McDonald's drive-in restaurant, owned by Dick and Mac McDonald, opened in San Bernardino, California, in 1948. When Ray A. Kroc visited the restaurant in 1954, he was fascinated by the business and became their national franchising agent. On April 15, 1955, Kroc opened his first franchise. Other franchises had been granted before that time; one of the earliest was Neil Fox's of Phoenix, Arizona. Despite rumors to the contrary, the corporation still grants franchises. By 1961, the operation was going so well that Kroc bought out the McDonald brothers for $2.7 million.

The company's early forays into advertising its product included the adoption of a winking character with a hamburger face called "Speedee," who appeared on signs inviting customers to "Look for Me at McDonald's Speedy Drive-ins. Tender, Juicy, All-Beef Hamburgers Only 15c." The character had been used prior to that time by the McDonald brothers before Kroc came along.

However, that advertising figure did not stay with the company long before McDonald's astute market research revealed that customers recognized the restaurants' "Golden Arches" faster than they did Speedee. In 1961, the Golden Arches took over as McDonald's advertising symbol.

Throughout the years, McDonald's has introduced highly popular marketing campaigns and memorable characters such as Ronald McDonald, who appeared for the first time in Washington, D.C., in 1963 and went national in 1966. Today most Americans know the redheaded clown figure, who has appeared on television, participates in fund-raising events, and has lent his name to Children's Charities (founded in 1984 and dedicated to the memory of McDonald's founder, Ray Kroc) and to the Ronald McDonald House. More than 150 Houses are located throughout the United States, Europe, Canada, and Australia, housing families whose children are being hospitalized for serious illnesses. By 1966, Ronald became the company's official spokesperson, and is now known internationally, communicating in twenty-one languages.

Other characters have joined the McDonald's family, including the Hamburglar (1971), Grimace, Big Mac, the Goblins, Apple Pie Tree, Hamburger Patch (all in 1971), Uncle O' Grimacey (1975), Birdie (1980), Fry Guys (1983), the Fry Kids, the Happy Meal Guys (1987), CosMc 1988, Chicken McNuggets (1987), Mayor McCheese, the Professor, and the Captain (all 1971).

The company's influence is international, as heretofore noted, and some collectors strive to obtain promotional material in as many languages as possible. McDonald's states that its advertising "breaks the pattern" with a sound and look uniformly unique. It works with several advertising agencies to give the company insight into different cultures, types of advertising, and public relations.

It offers a yearly variety of promotions and games, including Happy Meal special giveaways. Some of the collectible promotion materials include puzzles, glasses, mugs, toys, dolls, puppets, birthday party favors, tray mats, and many more too numerous to mention.

Some notable dates in McDonald's history, other than those already mentioned, include:

1958	100 millionth hamburger sold
1959	Billboard advertising began
1961	"Look for the Golden Arches" jingle first aired
1962	"Go for Goodness at McDonald's" slogan introduced
1966	Ronald McDonald's first national television appearance in Macy's Thanksgiving Day Parade
1968	Big Mac and Hot Apple Pie introduced
1971	"You Deserve a Break Today—So Get Up and Get Away to McDonald's" slogan introduced
1973	Quarter Pounder introduced, McDonald's makes cover of *Time*, and Egg McMuffin introduced
1974	McDonald's Cookies introduced
1975	"We Do It All For You" campaign introduced, Big Mac jingle ("Twoallbeefpattiesspecialsaucelettucecheesepicklesonionsonasesameseedbun") becomes famous
1976	"You, You're the One" campaign begins
1977	Breakfast food is officially added to menu
1979	"Nobody Can Do It Like McDonald's Can" campaign, Happy Meals introduced (they had previously been in test in Missouri, Kansas, Arizona, and Colorado in 1977)
1980	Twenty-fifth anniversary
1981	"You Deserve a Break Today" campaign renewed
1983	Chicken McNuggets introduced
1984	"It's a Good Time for the Great Taste" campaign
1985	McDLT introduced, "The Hot Stays Hot and the Cool Stays Cool" jingle
1987	Salads added to menu, "McKids" clothing introduced at Sears
1990	"You Know the One, McDonald's for Food, Folks and Fun" campaign introduced
1991	McLean Deluxe sandwich introduced

MCDONALD'S

McDonald's, Ronald McDonald cup; 1960s; has picture of Ronald on side; mint condition; $4–6.

McDonald's, 1988 Mac Tonight figures; rubber; excellent condition; $3–5 each.

McDonald's, glass; depicts Charlie Brown character Lucy; says "There's no excuse for not being properly prepared"; 1983 (other

342 ■ ADVERTISING

McDonald's, group of McDonald's figures (from left to right); Ronald McDonald phone, 1985, 10 inches, plastic, $75–150; Mac Tonight vehicle, 1988, 2 inches, plastic, $5–7; wastebasket bank, 1975, 5 inches, plastic, $50–60; Ronald McDonald bank, 1980s, 7 inches, vinyl, $35–45. *Courtesy of Neil and Nancy Berliner. Photo by Neil Berliner.*

Charlie Brown character glasses were also made that year); near-mint condition; $4–6.

McDonald's, glass; features Adventureland from Disneyland and depicts Goofy; made by Libby Glass Co. in 1988; 5⅝ inches tall; near-mint condition; $5–10.

McDonald's, Hamburglar doll; approximately 17 inches tall; wears black-and-white-striped suit, orange tie with yellow dots, mask, and detachable cape; 1972; excellent condition; $15–20.

McDonald's, hand puppets; several characters were made into hand puppets of plastic and given away free at McDonald's restaurants (i.e., Mayor McCheese, Uncle O'Grimacey, and others); excellent condition; $2–4.

McDonald's, Mac Tonight vehicle; 1988; 2 inches; plastic; excellent condition; $5–7.

McDonald's, pinback buttons; 3 inches; depict Ronald, Grimace, or Hamburglar; excellent condition; $3–5 each.

McDonald's, Ronald McDonald bank; ca. 1980s; 7 inches; vinyl; excellent condition; $35–45.

McDonald's, Ronald McDonald doll; ca. 1970s; cloth; approximately 16 inches tall; originally a giveaway; marked with golden *M* on all three pockets; excellent condition; $12–18.

McDonald's, Ronald McDonald doll; produced by Remco; 1976; hard vinyl; removable clothes; shoes are molded; excellent condition; $8–12.

McDonald's, Ronald McDonald phone; 1985; 10 inches; plastic; excellent condition; $75–150.

McDonald's, wastebasket bank; 1975; 5 inches; plastic; excellent condition; $50–60.

RED LOBSTER RESTAURANTS
(*see* "General Mills" in Baking Products chapter)

STEAK 'N ALE RESTAURANTS
(*see* "Pillsbury" in Baking Products chapter)

YORK STEAK HOUSE
(*see* "General Mills" in Baking Products chapter)

CHAPTER THIRTY-SEVEN
❖ SEWING PRODUCTS ❖

BARBOUR'S
Barbour's Thread, chromolithograph trade sign; advertises the centennial of Barbour's Thread (1784–1884); some damage and repair, mounted in plexiglass; very good condition; $75–200.

BELDING
Belding Thread, cabinet; unusually large multidrawered thread cabinet with gallery top and mirrored central door; early Eastlake style with original surface; burled raised panel inserts; 35 x 45 x 17 inches; excellent condition; $2,500–3,500.

Belding Thread, display case; revolving hanging thread display in glass-and-oak cabinet; 24 x 28 x 24 inches; good original condition; $400–700.

BOYCE
Boyce, needle case; flat tin-and-oak needle dispenser; 18 x 6 x 17 inches; good (as-found) condition, general soiling overall; $50–100.

BROOK THREAD
Brook Thread, paper poster; depicts display at Paris Exhibition 1878 with people dressed appropriately; 19¼ x 13¾ inches; very good condition, minor tears, some trimming; $100–250.

BROOKS GLACÉ AND SOFT COTTON
Brooks Spool Cotton, tin sign; depicts kittens playing various musical instruments; reproduction; 16 x 11 inches; $15 retail.

Brooks Glacé and Soft Cotton, two-drawer spool cabinet; wood with two glass inserts; 6½ x 21½ x 14½ inches; ca. 1900–1910; excellent condition; $200–400.

CHADWICK'S
Chadwick's, spool drawers and desk; six-drawer lift-lid oak desk cabinet; 32 x 15 x 24 inches; very good condition, gold leaf drawers and back advertising, insert desk top missing; $350–650.

SEWING PRODUCTS ■ 345

Clark's O.N.T. Spool Cotton, sign; 11½ x 16½ inches; depicts one little girl talking in the ear of another; reproduction; $15 retail. *Courtesy of Doc Davis/Antique-Alike. Photo by Donald Vogt.*

CHICAGO TAILORING CO.

Chicago Tailoring Co., die-cut advertising card; dated from painting "Copyright 1906"; signed by A. W. Greiner; 10 x 7 inches; good condition; $150–200.

CLARK

Clark Spool Cotton, tin sign; early Kellogg & Bulkeley Co. printed lettered sign for spoolmaker; 19¾ x 13¾ inches excluding frame; very good condition, some chipping, slight wear; $100–200.

Clark's Spool Cotton, paper sign; depicts cowboy roping steer with Clark's O.N.T. spool cotton; 20½ x 16 inches; good/very good condition, margins appear trimmed, some scratching to surface coating, discoloration to coated stock; $650–900.

CLARK'S

Clark's O.N.T. Spool Cotton, sign; 11½ x 16½ inches; depicts one little girl talking in the ear of another; reproduction; $15 retail.

Clark's O.N.T., two-drawer spool cabinet; wood with reverse on glass labels; 7½ x 22 x 16 inches; ca. 1900–1910; excellent condition; $175–275.

Clark's, two-drawer spool cabinet; oak case; cased glass drawer inserts; 22 x 7½ x 15½ inches; very good condition, top drawer insert cracked; $200–300.

COATS & CLARK'S

George Clark of Newark, New Jersey, invented a six-cord thread in 1866 simply because Elias Howe's patented sewing machine could not be used without it. Clark, a thread manufacturer, called his new invention "Our New Thread." The thread—and the sewing machine—became successful, and Clark shortened his product's name to "O.N.T."

J & P Coats opened its Pawtucket, Rhode Island, mill in 1869, five years after Clark's mill opened in Newark. Coats originated in Scotland at around 1820 and had adopted a circled chain trademark. Clark merged with the Scottish thread company in 1896.

Forms of advertising include trade cards, lithographed ads, and thread cabinets—for both companies as well as for their joint venture.

The Coats & Clark company's eleven mills still make crochet cotton, yarns, embroidery floss, zippers, and thread.

J. & P. COATS

J. & P. Coats, figural spool cabinet; spool-shaped four-drawer spool cabinet; body wrapped with twine to represent giant spool of product; 18 x 22 x 19 inches; fair/good condition; general wear; $350–550.

J. & P. Coats, spool cabinet and desk; four-drawer lift-top desk and cabinet combination; oak; 29 x 14 x 21 inches; good original condition with replaced felt top; $200–400.

J. & P. Coats, six-drawer spool cabinet; embossed composition inserts on drawers and cabinet back; 26¼ x 22 x 19½ inches; fair/good condition, wear and discoloration to finish; $400–600.

J. & P. Coats, sign; paper over plaster; depicts Gulliver's Lilliputians working with "Best Six Cord Spool Cotton"; 21½ x 18½ inches excluding frame; good condition; $200–400.

J. & P. Coats' Thread, paper sign; treated paper on plaster backing; depicts fisherman and friend utilizing spools of Coats' Cotton; deaccessioned from Strawberry Banke Museum; 22 x 17½ inches excluding frame; good overall condition; $150–300.

COLUMBIA YARNS

Columbia Yarns, tin sign; fascinating image of Lady Liberty holding a skein of wool and sitting among sheep that produce Columbia Yarns; rare and early; 18 x 24½ inches excluding frame; very good condition, some chipping due to earlier flaking in background and image; $15,000–20,000.

Sewing Products ■ 347

CORTICELLI SPOOL
Corticelli Spool, display case; curved glass and drawer display case for spool silks; 21 x 18½ x 16 inches; excellent condition, several slide drawers missing; $500–750.

EUREKA SPOOL
Eureka Spool, cabinet; ten-drawer vertical case, both solid and glass-front drawers; mirrored panel sides; 23 x 25¼ x 16½ inches; very good condition, one mirrored panel cracked; $600–900.

GOLDEN FLEECE
Golden Fleece, three-drawer spool cabinet; wood cased gold metal braid cabinet; replaced knobs; 24 x 12½ x 17½ inches; excellent condition; $250–400.

HOUSEHOLD SEWING MACHINE
Household Sewing Machine, paper sign; shows small child with flowers; 14¾ x 29 inches with original metal strips; very good condition, some horizontal creases, some in-painting to mouth; $50–100.

J. R. LEESON & CO.
J. R. Leeson & Co., paperweight; ca. 1890–1910; company imported linen thread; picture of spinning wheel; 2½ x 4 inches; excellent condition; $50–75.

MERRICK'S
Merrick's, cylindrical spool cabinet; oak cased curved glass spool cabinet; 18 inch diameter x 22 inches; excellent condition; $500–750.

J.R. Leeson & Co., paperweight; ca. 1890–1910; company imported linen thread; picture of spinning wheel; 2½ x 4 inches; $50–75. *From the collection of Stuart Kammerman. Photo by David Kammerman.*

Merrick's, spool cabinet; circular oak spool cabinet with original lettered glass; 18 inch diameter x 23 inches; very good original condition; $600–1,000.

Merrick's Spool Cotton, octagonal schoolhouse clock; 16½ x 24½ x 5 inches; fair condition, glass replaced with plastic, dial appears retouched, wood octagonal bezel appears repaired and reworked, lettering in-painted; $300–500.

MISCELLANEOUS
Four-door ribbon case; countertop oak-and-glass vertical ribbon case; 26½ x 28 x 6½ inches; very good condition; $300–500.

NEW HOME SEWING MACHINE
New Home Sewing Machine, paper over cardboard poster; view of factory buildings in Orange, Massachusetts; 24¼ x 20¼ inches excluding frame; good condition, general overall staining; $25–75.

PHOENIX SEWING MACHINE
Phoenix Sewing Machine, sign; 14 inches; round; glass face with spinner; excellent condition; $175–275.

ROYAL SOCIETY
Royal Society, spool cabinet; twelve glass-front drawers; vertical case; 19 x 35½ x 19½ inches; good original condition, some wood loss to trim, surface discoloration due to age; $300–600.

SINGER SEWING MACHINE
Singer Sewing Machine, cardboard sign; three-quarter view of cos-

Phoenix Sewing Machine, sign; 14 inches; round; glass face with spinner; excellent condition; $175–275. *Collection of and photo by Michael Bruner.*

Standard Sewing Machine Sperm Oil, bottle; "made by F. C. Henderson, Boston, MA."; 5¼ inches tall; glass; paper label; marked "made in U.S.A."; ca. 1920s; $8–15. *Courtesy of Irreverent Relics. Photo by Donald Vogt.*

turned women with cape; 20½ x 29 inches excluding frame; good condition, overall soiling; $250–350.

Singer Sewing Machine, paper sign; depicts grandmother and child at machine; approximately 14 x 24 inches excluding mat and frame; overall 19½ x 20½ inches; good condition; $350–500.

Singer Sewing Machine, porcelain sign; depicts woman at sewing machine with large *S* superimposed on her; green background; 36 x 24 inches; excellent condition; $350–450.

STANDARD SEWING MACHINE
Standard Sewing Machine Sperm Oil, bottle; "made by F. C. Henderson, Boston, MA."; 5¾ inches tall; glass; paper label; marked "made in U.S.A."; ca. 1920s; very good condition; $8–15.

WHITE SEWING MACHINE
White Sewing Machine, puzzle; paper-covered wood block puzzle; depicts interior scene with Victorian furnishings; map of United States on reverse; 11 x 16 inches; good overall condition, some wear; $100–200.

WILLIMANTIC
Willimantic Spool Cotton, paper sign; depicts small children trapping a roaring elephant with this company's superior six-cord thread; 19½ x 13½ inches; very good condition, some minor wear to coated stock, slight creasing, margins trimmed; $1,250–2,500.

Willimantic, spool desk; six-drawer lift-top leather-inlaid oak desk and display case for country store; 36 x 16 x 24 inches; good, original condition; $200–500.

Willimantic, four-drawer spool cabinet; oak cased; original advertising pulls, side decals, and Eastlake decoration; 24¼ x 14¼ x 15 inches; very good condition, appears to be original finish; $400–600.

Willimantic Thread, sign; depicts expansion bridge made up of spools of cotton thread with ships below and hot-air balloon in sky; titled "The Great Willimantic Bridge"; 30½ x 24 inches excluding frame; printed by Forbes, Lith.; good condition, some age and cracks; $150–300.

CHAPTER THIRTY-EIGHT
■ SHOES, BOOTS ■

BIXBY'S

Bixby's Shoe Polish, paper sign; depicts man sitting with back to viewer, having his (very large) boots polished; humorous presentation; 17½ x 12 inches; very good condition, overall soiling, margins trimmed; $300–600.

BLACK CAT

Black Cat Shoe Polish, tin clock; rare advertising clock picturing ornate face with black cat standing upon piles of product; 17½ x 23½ x 2 inches; fair condition, overall wear to image, some in-painting; $2,000–3,500.

BROWN SHOE CO.

(*see also* "Buster Brown")

Brown Shoe Co., Buster & Tige metal sign; displays shoes in middle; approximately 40 inches tall; very rare (only three or four in existence); ca. 1910; excellent condition; $6,000–7,000.

BURT'S FINE SHOES

Burt's Fine Shoes, paper sign; early interior scene of families trying on this company's high button shoes; displays box and product; approximately 22 x 17½ inches; very good condition, margins trimmed; $500–1,000.

BUSTER BROWN

One of the nation's most familiar trademarks, Buster Brown was created in 1902 by Richard Fenton Outcault, a cartoonist who patterned the two characters (Buster and his dog, Tige) upon his own son and dog. John A. Bush, a sales executive with Brown Shoe Company (founded by George Warren Brown), persuaded his company to purchase the rights to the characters from Outcault, and Buster and Tige were introduced to the public in 1904 at the St. Louis World's Fair as the company's juvenile shoe trademark. The Brown Shoe Company won the only Double Grand Prize awarded to a shoe exhibitor at the fair.

Buster Brown; photos of the popular cartoon character Buster Brown and his dog, Tige, who appeared on an array of specialty items to help promote America's favorite brand of children's shoes—Buster Brown. The items pictured date from the 1920s and 1930s. *Photo courtesy of Brown Group, Inc., St. Louis, Missouri.*

Bush became president of the firm in 1915 and chairman of the board in 1948.

The irony of the situation was that Outcault himself set up a booth at the fair, selling the trademark rights to Buster Brown to anyone with enough money. Apparently, the cartoonist's whim helped him decide whether a fair price for the trademark rights was $5 or $1,000.

As a result, a plethora of Buster Brown products were produced, such as harmonicas, soap, a soft drink, coffee, wheat flour, apples—at least fifty products were produced bearing Buster Brown's image at one time. Today only a textile firm and the famous Buster Brown children's shoes still exist.

The Brown Shoe Company advertised and marketed the Buster Brown line of shoes nationally. Midgets, dressed like the Buster Brown image in the company's advertisements and accompanied by dogs that resembled Tige, went on tour from 1904 to 1915, playing to packed houses in theaters, department stores, and shoe stores. From 1916 to 1920, a national magazine advertising campaign promoted the shoes, then the midgets and outdoor billboards were again employed between 1921 and 1930. The company used newspapers and magazines to promote the shoes throughout the 1930s and 1940s, then introduced a radio show called "Smilin' Ed McConnell and his

Buster Brown Gang" in 1943. The show aired on the West Coast NBC radio network, a company comprised of 165 stations. Television aired the show beginning in 1951 and until McConnell died in 1954. The show continued until 1955 with Andy Devine in McConnell's spot.

Since that time, all manner of advertising/marketing mediums have been used to promote the Buster Brown shoe line. Recently, the company introduced a new logo, which shows a more modern version of Buster and Tige. The new logo's Buster is a boy in a cocked baseball hat and wearing a baseball jacket, sitting next to Tige, who sports a kerchief around his throat as in the original ad. The logo name is in lowercase letters.

BUSTER BROWN

Buster Brown, bank; made of iron; depicts Buster and Tige; approximately 5 inches tall; very good condition; $135–160.

Buster Brown, china (3 pieces); cup and saucer and small dessert plate; all with color transfer of Buster Brown and friend having cups of tea; 4¼ inch diameter x 2½ inches overall (cup and saucer) and 6¼ inch diameter (plate); very good condition, some gold leaf loss due to overall wear, minor wear to transfer; $100–200.

Buster Brown and Tige, die-cut store displays; large standing figures of silk-screened fiberboard; unusual 3-D images of these favorite characters; 31 x 68 x 31 inches for Buster and 23 x 28 x 23 inches for Tige; very good condition, some overall chipping and scratching; $400–800.

Buster Brown, doll; 13 inches; cloth; Buster Brown Shoes emblazoned on jacket; ca. 1920s; wears red hat and suit, blue bow, and matching stockings; very good condition; $100–125.

Buster Brown, paper dolls; depict Buster and Tige; Buster wears a navy suit and has several changes of clothes and hats; approximately 12 inches tall; uncut; near-mint condition; $200–250.

Buster Brown, rug; possibly unique type of advertising for Buster Brown and Tige for Brown Shoes; depicts a triple image marked "For Boys" and "For Girls"; appears to be a store runner; 9 feet x 26½ inches; fair/good condition, some overall wear, center section shows the majority of wear with a tear in middle, fading and soiling; $100–300.

CAT-TEX SOLES

Cat-Tex Soles, clock; outside rim says "we rebuild shoes like

NEW/AT LESS THAN ½ NEW COST"; black cat in center of clock; face of clock says "Cat-Tex Soles"; yellow, red, black, white; ca. 1950; excellent condition; $250–350.

EAGLE BRAND
Eagle Brand Dry Cleaner, can; made by the American Shoe Polish Co., Chicago; pictures woman with golf club and another with tennis racquet in country club setting; 2½ inch diameter x 5 inches; excellent condition, chipping primarily to raised edge; $75–150.

FRANK MILLER'S
Frank Miller's Blacking, box; interior label design depicts Uncle Sam shaving with reflection and eagle's reflection in polished boots; factory sign hangs on patriotic wallpaper; 11 x 3 x 8½ inches; excellent condition; $200–400.

HILTON'S
Hilton's Boots, tin container; early lithographed can with military portraits on each side; 4 inch square x 6 inches; very good condition, minor pinpoint blemishes, slight denting and chipping; $100–300.

LEWIS SHOEMAKER
Lewis Shoemaker, cardboard store card; early interior view of Boston shoemaker making shoes for waiting children; 13¾ x 10¾ inches; good overall condition, wear, chipping and creasing; $200–300.

REGAL BOOTS
Regal, figural boot sign; made of brass; complete with spur; very good overall condition; $1,000–3,000.

SHOE LACE SERVICE STATION
Shoe Lace Service Station, tin display box; depicts man driving shoe

Cat-Tex Soles, clock; outside rim says "we rebuild shoes like NEW/AT LESS THAN 1/2 NEW COST"; black cat in center of clock; face of clock says "Cat-Tex Soles"; yellow, red, black, white; ca. 1950; $250–350. *Collection of and photo by Michael Bruner.*

V. Schoenecker Boot & Shoe Co., paperweight; ca. 1890–1910; depicts trademark spectator boot; offices in Milwaukee; 2½ x 4 inches; $75–125. *From the collection of Stuart Kammerman. Photo by David Kammerman.*

into a station that vends laces; three-sided tin case with shelved interior; 11¼ x 11 x 11 inches; very good/excellent condition, minor denting primarily at top, marque missing, slight overall soiling; $750–1,200.

SOCIETY KING

Society King Shoes, self-framed tin sign; gentleman with high button shoes; 9¼ x 13¼ inches; very good condition; $150–250.

SOLAR TIPPED

Solar Tipped Shoes, paper sign; children climbing heights with banners proclaiming shoe name; 13 x 9 inches; very good condition, general overall soiling, minor tears, borders trimmed; $200–400.

V. SCHOENECKER

V. Schoenecker Boot & Shoe Co., paperweight; ca. 1890–1910; depicts trademark spectator boot; offices in Milwaukee; 2½ x 4 inches; excellent condition; $75–125.

WELLS SHOES

Wells Shoes, self-framed tin sign; large factory scene with store insert, trains in foreground, and billowing factory chimneys; 38 x 25½ inches; very good condition, some overall scratching, minor rust spots in sky, edge wear; $100–250.

WHITTEMORE'S

Whittemore's Bon Ton Boot Polish, store display; full of tins of the polish; tins are brown; display is orange; tins only $3–5 each.

WOODLAWN MILLS

Woodlawn Mills, Shoe Lace Service Station, tin display case; with original marque picturing man driving shoe into "Shoe Lace" station; 11½ x 14 x 11 inches; good condition, overall soiling, darkening of color, scratches and rubs, slight denting, especially to marque; $300–600.

CHAPTER THIRTY-NINE
■ SOAP ■

DAVID'S
David's Prize Soap, paper sign; comical illustration of Chinese laundryman finding gold coin in David's Prize Soap; typical of bigotry of the era; 16 x 21 inches; good/very good condition, some wear on treated surface, margins trimmed; $2,500–4,500.

DINGMAN'S
Dingman's Soap, cardboard sign; interesting variation of creeping baby display usually seen for Ivory soap; 15 x 13 inches excluding mat and frame; very good/excellent condition, some minor creases, slight edge chipping; $150–250.

D. S. BROWN
D. S. Brown Toilet Soaps, paper sign; depicts women by riverside tent in various stages of washing; vignetted bathroom and bedroom scenes; 20 x 13 inches; excellent condition; $2,000–3,000.

FAIRY
(see "N.K. Fairbanks" in Cleaning Products chapter)
Fairy Soap, box; made in Fairbanks; depicts fairy with wings on inside of lid (gingham lining is new); 17 x 16 x 8 inches; box is refinished; ca. 1920s; very good condition; $150–200.

Fairy Soap, cardboard sign; pictures logoed image of little girl sitting on letters that name the soap; 21 x 11 inches; fair condition; $50–100.

Fairy Soap, trolley sign; depicts little girl sitting atop bar of soap; framed; nice colors; near-mint condition; $250–400.

GOLD SOAP
Gold Soap, paper poster; two oval vignettes; one shows gold prospector sitting dejectedly on rock, the other depicts housewife who uses Gold Soap; approximately 22 x 17¾ inches; fair/good condition, poster trimmed, minor soiling overall, wrinkling to coated stock, some edge tears; $700–1,000.

IVORY

(*see also* "Procter & Gamble")

Ivory Soap, garment care booklet; 1925; full color; excellent condition; $15–18.

Ivory Soap, cardboard sign; interesting interior view of multiple-tiered shelves of products for the "Bath" and "Toilet"; 22 x 28 inches excluding frame; good condition, some paper loss due to scuffing, minor in-painting to chips, creases, appears to have been trimmed; $75–150.

Ivory Soap, cardboard sign; unusual Maud Humphrey image of girl washing toys with Ivory Soap and hanging them on the line to dry; "A Busy Day" (rare companion piece for its tin equivalent, "A Busy Day in Dollville"); 16¾ x 24½ inches; very good condition, minor overall soiling, slight chipping primarily to edges, two minor image repairs: one in red dress at nine o'clock, one in background at three o'clock; $1,000–1,500.

LAUTZ

Lautz Soap, paper sign; laughing man holds bar of Acme soap; approximately 21 x 17½ inches; very good condition, trimmed margins, some minor edge loss and creasing; $200–400.

LAVINE

Lavine Soap, paper sign; very colorful; ca. 1870s; image with elaborate appointed interior scene of woman bathing child, with two vignettes including factory; floral border; approximately 9 x 12 inches excluding frame; excellent condition, border appears trimmed; $350–500.

LIFEBUOY

Lifebuoy Soap, cardboard boxes (8); red background; yellow-and-white lettering; very good condition; $10–40.

Lifebuoy Soap, die-cut cardboard sign; two sided; shows old salt with lifebuoy over his arm; 16 inches tall; very good condition; $400–750.

MONKEY BRAND

Monkey Brand, box; "scours and polishes"; Lever Brothers Company, Cambridge, Massachusetts; navy-blue box with white lettering; early 1900s; very good condition; $20–32.

PALMOLIVE

Palmolive, tin truck; green; marked with maker's name; ca. 1930s; good condition; $30–40.

Monkey Brand, box; "scours and polishes"; Lever Brothers Company, Cambridge, Massachusetts; navy-blue box with white lettering; early 1900s; $20–32. *Courtesy of Irreverent Relics. Photo by Donald Vogt.*

PEARS' SOAP

One of the earliest advertisers, Pears' Soap believed that it should simply keep the product name first and foremost before the customer. (It must have worked, because Ivory Soap followed the same philosophy.) The slogan ("Have you Used PEARS' today?") was used over and over, in several variations, so that the company could meet its "new-copy-every-two-weeks" newspaper advertising rule.

The London-based firm, run by Andrew Pears after he invented a transparent mild soap in 1789, was run by his son, Francis, after 1838. Francis left the business when Thomas Barratt bought into the company in 1865, after which time Francis's son, Andrew, and Barratt spent an extraordinary $750,000 a year advertising their product. Credit goes to Barratt for beginning the advertising policy that made Pears the most widely known soap in the world.

His view of how to advertise his product was simple—he relied on repetition, proclaiming "Pears' Soap" over and over again, as if believing that if his customers saw the product name enough, that Pears' would mean soap and vice versa.

In 1886, the owners of the company paid 2,300 pounds for a Victorian portrait of an angelic boy blowing bubbles, painted by English artist Sir John E. Millais. The image was used in Pears' advertisements and opened the way for other companies to hire salon painters to create their advertising art. *Bubbles* was reproduced as a poster, depicting the original boy with a bar of Pears' Soap in the corner.

An 1886 magazine/newspaper advertisement for the product depicted a corseted woman washing at a pitcher and bowl, presumably to take advantage of the soap's power to give her "healthful skin, good complexion and soft, white beautiful hands." In an 1888 advertisement, a crying baby in a tub reaches for the soap; the wording says, "He won't be happy til he gets it!"

Pears was also one of the first companies to use celebrity endorsements in its ads. Lillie Langtry, a well-known actress of the day, stated: "Since Using Pears' Soap, I Have Discarded all Others."

The company used several successful premium promotions, including a reference book titled *Pears' Shilling Cyclopedia* (1897), Pears' Pennies (real French ten-centine pieces stamped with the company name), bookmarks, signs, posters, trays, and many other items.

Pears' still makes soap in Great Britain.

PEARS

Pears, newspaper advertisement; depicts *Bubbles*; fair condition; $10–12.

Pears, poster; approximately 20 x 24 inches; shows boy blowing bubbles and small bar of Pears Soap in corner; ca. early 1900s; very good condition; $125–175.

Pears, die-cut trade card; chromolithograph; depicts trademarked *Bubbles* portrait; very good condition; $12–18.

PROCTER & GAMBLE

The company was founded in Cincinnati in 1837 by James Gamble, soapmaker, and William Procter, candlemaker, to join together "in the art and trade of Manufacturing Soap and Candles and all things thereto belonging, and also in buying and selling all sorts of goods belonging to said trade of Soap Boiler and Candle Maker . . ." Gamble ran the factory while Procter ran the office ("store").

Originally, candles were the company's mainstay; however, by the 1880s, the company was a leader in the field of 432 national soap manufacturers.

Procter & Gamble's brochure "Memorable Years in P&G History" describes the company's emblem history as an accident—"it began about 1851 as merely a crude cross painted on boxes of

P&G Star Candles by wharf hands to help illiterate stevedores identify the boxes... sometime later... [a] wharf hand altered the cross into the form of a star and encircled it, perhaps to symbolize Star Candles, P&G's major brand of candles then. A cluster of 13 stars was added soon after that by William A. Procter, along with a quarter moon drawn as a human profile—the first standard trademark adopted by the Company." The trademark must have been thought a good one, because a Chicago soapmaker used a version of it on his soap. P&G sued and the court decided in P&G's favor. During the 1880s, the emblem was refined and became the official patented trademark. In 1902, the symbol took on some of the "gingerbread" frills typical of the period and became simple again only around 1920. Again, in the early 1930s, the trademark was redesigned, this time by Ernest Bruse Haswell, the Cincinnati sculptor who created the William Cooper Procter Memorial at Ivorydale.

In 1882, Procter launched the first advertising campaign for the company with a budget of $11,000. He had originally advertised in newspapers, such as the *Daily Gazette* in Cincinnati, but now newspaper advertising was increased and signs promoting Procter & Gamble products began showing up on storefronts, fences, and trolley buses. In fact, it is said that the company was one of the first to use large billboard posters. In addition to the advertising campaign, salespeople distributed samples of Ivory door-to-door.

Ivory was advertised in magazines as "... is $99^{44}/_{100}$ per cent pure" and "the Ivory Soap will float." The claim was substantiated with actual scientific proof, which Procter had confirmed by several chemists. The product marked a turning point for P&G, as well as for the advertising business in general.

Procter & Gamble was one of the first companies to use advertising to confirm the integrity of its products. Procter was convinced: "Advertising alone couldn't make a product successful—it was merely evidence of a manufacturer's faith in the merit of the article."

The company began to introduce other products. After putting a hydrogenation plant into operation in 1909, the company introduced Crisco in 1911. It offered several advantages over the lard products being used by the American consumer at the time, and was economical as well. The first P&G flaked soap laundry products were produced in 1919 and 1920 (Ivory Flakes and Chipso).

Several years later, the laundry products accounted for 20 percent of the company's total soap business. In 1927, P&G produced the first spray-dried soap granules, called Selox, but the detergent was not as popular as the newer, more dense Oxydol, which P&G introduced in 1929. Tide, the culmination of more than twenty years of research at Procter & Gamble, was introduced in 1947 with the radio ditty:

> *Tide gets clothes cleaner than any soap!*
> *Any soap?*
> *Yes, any soap! Tide gets clothes cleaner than any soap!*
> *T-I-D-E, Tide!*

Tide's bright orange-and-yellow bull's-eye package was easily recognized, and thus it stood out from the other products on the market. Again, P&G had developed a product that was valuable to the American homemaker. In fact, it became so popular that its sales surpassed other P&G products, such as Duz. Tide rode the wave of popularity for several years, but the product didn't meet all of its consumers' demands.

Soon other detergents were developed to meet specific laundry requirements: all-purpose, heavy duty Tide; Cheer, for cleaning in cooler water; Oxydol, which had a color-safe oxygen bleach; Dash, a low-sudsing, concentrated detergent for larger washers; for brightly colored fabrics—Bold; and for oily or greasy soils, the heavy-duty liquid detergent Era.

Procter & Gamble not only produced laundry cleaners, but in 1933 broke into the toiletries business with the introduction of Drene shampoo. However, it was Crest toothpaste, introduced in 1955, that pushed the toiletries business into success and helped other products such as Prell Concentrate shampoo (1948), Lilt Home Permanent (1949), and Gleem toothpaste (1952) become more popular. Again, the P&G laboratories had spent over five years researching ways to develop anti-tooth-decay ingredients, finally coming up with Crest. At first, the critics were skeptical, claiming the toothpaste did not provide all the benefits promised, and sales were disappointing. However, in 1960, the American Dental Association recognized the effectiveness of Crest and released a report that stated that the toothpaste could have "significant value when used in a conscientiously applied program of oral hygiene and regular professional care." The ADA also granted permission to use its name in the advertising of the product; within a year, Crest's sales nearly doubled.

During the next couple of decades, Crest's popularity opened the door for other developments, such as Scope and Head & Shoulders shampoo. In 1982, P&G acquired Norwich Eaton Pharmaceuticals and products such as Pepto Bismol, Chloraseptic, Head & Chest, and Norwich Aspirin. Then, in 1985, it acquired Richardson Vicks, Inc., which gave it such products as Clearasil and the Vicks line. Then other products, from the G. D. Searle Co., such as Metamucil, Dramamine, and Icy Hot gave Procter & Gamble the distinction of being the largest manufacturer of over-the-counter drugs in the United States.

The list below shows some of Procter & Gamble's U.S. product groups and brands, as well as the date the products were introduced.

LAUNDRY AND CLEANING PRODUCTS
  Comet (1956)
  Spic and Span (1926)
  Ivory Snow (1930)
  Tide (1946)
  Ivory Liquid (1957)
  Downy (1960)

BEAUTY CARE PRODUCTS
  Clearasil (early 1950s)
  Ivory bar soap (1879)
  Secret (1956)
  Sure (1972)
  Vidal Sassoon (1974)
  Head & Shoulders (1961)
  Noxzema skin cream (1917)
  Oil of Olay (1962)

COSMETICS FRAGRANCES
  Cover Girl (face, 1961; lips, 1964)
  Max Factor (acquired 1991)
  Navy by Cover Girl (1990)

HEALTH-CARE PRODUCTS
  Scope (1965)
  Crest (1955)
  Gleem (1952)

Metamucil (1934)
VapoRub (1905)

PAPER PRODUCTS
Luvs (1976)
Pampers (1961)
Always (1983)
Charmin (1928)
Bounty (1965)

FOOD AND BEVERAGE PRODUCTS
Crisco shortening (1911)
Duncan Hines cake mixes (1956)
Fisher Nuts (acquired 1989)
Folgers (1850)
Hawaiian Punch (1944)
Sunny Delight Florida Citrus Punch (1964)
Jif peanut butter (1956)
Pringles (1968)

The company now has fifty-six plant locations in twenty-four states and research and development facilities throughout the world.

PROCTER & GAMBLE

Procter & Gamble, advertising dolls (6); vinyl; Pogo characters; each approximately 4 to 6 inches tall; figures include Pogo, Uncle Albert Alligator, Montmingle Bugleboy III, Churchy LaFemme, Porky, and Howland Owl; premiums found in Biz, Spic & Span, Oxydol, Cascade, and Tide; 1975; $4–6 each.

Procter & Gamble Soap, paper sign; depicts a lady dressed up in a Victorian style with advertising in hairpiece and collar; 17½ x 22 inches; fair condition, some paper loss to the edges and overall soiling; $125–225.

Procter & Gamble Amber Soap, embossed tin sign; pictures man in moon with lettering and story; 19 x 12½ inches excluding frame; printed by Chas. E. Chunk Co. Litho.; fair condition, some dirt staining; $50–150.

SANTA CLAUS

Santa Claus Soap, paper sign; depicts St. Nick carrying Christmas tree loaded with presents for small child and doll sitting on floor; 20 x 36 inches including original frame; fair/good condition, strong color and intact image, several tears; $1,000–2,000.

Santa Claus Soap, tin sign; depicts Santa with bag over shoulder, child sitting on floor with doll and unwrapped bar of soap next to her; reproduction; 9½ x 16 inches; $15 retail.

STAR

Star Soap, cardboard die-cut hanging sign; two babies on swing, one holds star with company name ("Schultz & Co., Zanesville, Ohio"); 9 x 6 inches; near-mint condition; $1,400–2,000.

SWEETHEART SOAP

Sweetheart Soap, electric motorized store display; papier-mâché and composition baby in wooden basket; arms and legs move; approximately 33 x 20 x 16 inches; good condition, some paint loss to baby, paper marquee torn, worn; $350–500.

WELCOME SOAP

Welcome Soap, paper sign; three-dimensional collage depicting two women for this Curtis Davis product; original frame; uncut version; 16½ x 31½ inches including frame; excellent condition, some minor staining along edges; $800–1,400.

Santa Claus Soap, tin sign; depicts Santa with bag over shoulder, child sitting on floor with doll and unwrapped bar of soap next to her; reproduction; 9½ x 16 inches; $15 retail. *Courtesy of Doc Davis/Antique-Alike. Photo by Donald Vogt.*

WILD WEST

Wild West Soap, box; on underside of lid, colorful depiction of cowboys lassoing longhorn steers; box label depicts chapped cowboy; label printed by Henry Seibert Bro. Co. Litho; 16 x 3¼ x 12½ inches (box); 16 x 11¾ inches (label); good overall condition, some age and soiling; $1,000–2,000.

WRIGLEY'S

Wrigley's Soap, embossed tin sign; shows large package of the product; 19½ x 14 inches excluding frame; good condition, some denting and overall wear; $80–180.

Wrigley's Soap, tin tip tray; 3½ inches; "made by Chas. W. Shonk Co."; ca. 1905–1910; depicts Wrigley's black cat sitting atop bars of mineral scouring soap; near-mint condition; $100–225.

CHAPTER FORTY
■ SODA ■

A & W ROOT BEER
A & W Root Beer, mug; near-mint condition; $5–20.

BUCKEYE ROOT BEER
Buckeye Root Beer, syrup dispenser; rare porcelain ovoid and footed dispenser with foaming soap soda glass on transfer insert to sides and nut buds decoration; pump appears to be a replacement; 7½ inch diameter x 17 inches overall; good/very good condition, chip in neck, general overall soiling; $300–600.

CANADA DRY
J. J. McLaughlin, a Toronto pharmacist, concocted a carbonated beverage in 1906 that he dubbed "Canada Dry Pale Ginger Ale." His trademark included a crown because he wanted his product to symbolize superiority—a "kinglike quality." The trademark also depicts a maplike outline of Canada. The early trademark for the company included emblems of the Canadian provinces, a crouching beaver, and a maple leaf, Canada's national emblem. As the company grew, the emblems, beaver, and leaf disappeared from the trademark.

The beverage became immediately popular in the United States, and McLaughlin grew wealthy. In 1923, his heirs sold the company to P. D. Saylor and J. M. Mathes, founders of the present Canada Dry Corporation, for $1 million.

CANADA DRY
Canada Dry Ginger Ale, fountain glass; early; mint condition; $30–70.

CAWY BOTTLING CO.
Cawy Bottling Co. WaterMelon Soda, can; made in Miami, Florida; one side shows white boy, the other shows black girl; contemporary; excellent condition; $5–8.

Cherry Blossoms, bottle with tin litho—bottle display; 1921; excellent to near-mint condition; $1,000 ($600 for average/good condition). *Collection of Allan Petretti, author of Petretti's Coca-Cola Collectibles Price Guide. Photo by Donald Vogt.*

CHERRY BLOSSOMS

Cherry Blossoms, blotter; lettering reads "drink Cherry Blossoms a blooming good drink"; near-mint condition; $5–20.

Cherry Blossoms, bottle with tin litho—bottle display; 1921; excellent to near-mint condition; $1,000 ($600 for average/good condition).

Cherry Blossoms, cardboard cutout sign; depicts woman in center of cherry blossom with bottle of soda; colorful; excellent condition; $10–30.

CHERRY SMASH

Cherry Smash, syrup dispenser; classic three-cherries image on footed dispenser with original pump; 8½ x 14½ inches; excellent/near-mint condition, some discoloration under lip of pump, discoloration to pump; $1,000–1,500.

CLEO COLA

Cleo Cola, fountain glass; white; near-mint condition; $10–20.

CLICQUOT CLUB

Clicquot Club, bottle; Eskimo on paper label; excellent condition; $5–20.

Clicquot Club Ginger Ale, die-cut tin stand-up display; Standard Adv. Co. Litho.; extremely rare (only one known by collector); excellent condition; $6,000–8,000.

COCA-COLA

There are more stories generating from the Coca-Cola products than from most other American products combined. Many books have been written about the legacy Dr. Pemberton left to this country that will give you more details than will be included in this concise volume (such as Allan Petretti's *Coca-Cola*

Coca-Cola, photo of Dr. John S. Pemberton, inventor of Coca-Cola. *Courtesy of Coca-Cola Company Archives.*

Collectibles Price Guide; Mr. Petretti also runs auctions of soda items throughout the year and was quite helpful to me when putting together this chapter). The Coca-Cola company itself has an extensive archives library and museum devoted to Coca-Cola memorabilia.

The drink originated on May 8, 1886, in Atlanta, Georgia, when a pharmacist named Dr. John Styth Pemberton first produced the syrup for Coca-Cola in a three-legged brass pot in his backyard. Little did he realize when he began selling the soda for five cents a glass that he had invented the drink that would change a nation—and influence the world.

The name Coca-Cola came about because Pemberton's partner and bookkeeper, Frank M. Robinson, thought the "two Cs would look well in advertising." He was right, as proven by the first advertisement, which appeared in *The Atlanta Journal*. That first piece of advertising launched a campaign the likes of which the American public had never seen, but would imitate through the years. Oilcloth signs announced the new drink, and clocks, calendars, festoons, trays, glasses, lamps, signs, cartons, dispensing machines, mirrors, posters, billboards, playing cards, freezers, and many other items soon wore the Coca-Cola label.

Unfortunately, Dr. Pemberton didn't realize the potential of his new business, and soon sold portions to various partners until he turned over his remaining interests to Asa G. Candler shortly before his death in 1888. Candler, an Atlanta businessman, eventually acquired complete control of the company. It was under Candler's ownership that the drink flourished. By 1892, sales had increased nearly tenfold, and by 1893, the trademark "Coca-Cola" was registered in the United States Patent Office. That was the same year the first dividend was paid to Coca-Cola stockholders—and they've been paid ever since.

Starting before the turn of the century, Candler distributed thousands of coupons for a complimentary glass of Coca-Cola and continued to promote the product with countless novelties, which have been collected by aficionados ever since.

The first person to help distribute the Coca-Cola products was Joseph A. Biedenharn of Vicksburg, Mississippi. He set up bottling machinery in the rear of his store and began taking bottles up and down the Mississippi River, distributing the product to plantations and lumber camps. But the large-scale bottling network was begun by Benjamin F. Thomas and Joseph B. Whitehead of Chattanooga, Tennessee, when they secured the exclusive rights to bottle and sell Coca-Cola throughout almost all of the United States. Candler sold them the rights in 1899 and the partners began developing what we now know as Coke's worldwide bottling network.

The bottles that held Coca-Cola in the early days were straight-sided containers, but Coca-Cola wanted a more distinctive package than its competitors, so in 1916 the contour bottle was designed by the Root Glass Company of Terre Haute, Indiana.

The company's first overseas exposure began when Candler's

Coca-Cola, photo of Hutchinson bottle marked "Chattanooga, Tennessee" (1899–1902). *Photo courtesy of the Coca-Cola Company Archives.*

Coca-Cola, photo of the 1890s sampling coupon used to promote the product. *Photo courtesy of the Coca-Cola Company Archives.*

Coca-Cola, photo of 6½-ounce contour bottle with embossed lettering (1915–1957). The shape of this bottle was eventually copyrighted by the company (*see* Coca-Cola's company history). *Photo courtesy of the Coca-Cola Company Archives.*

Coca-Cola, photo of leaded-glass soda fountain lampshade with beaded trim. *Photo courtesy of the Coca-Cola Company Archives.*

son, Charles Howard, took a jug of Coca-Cola syrup with him on a trip to England—and brought back an order for five gallons. Soon the drink was distributed in Cuba, Puerto Rico, Panama, the Philippines, and Guam, where bottling operations were built in the early 1900s. By 1920, Coca-Cola was being bottled and sold in Europe when a bottling operation opened in France. By 1928, Coca-Cola became associated with the Olympics, and vendors sold the drink to fans inside the stadium while Amsterdam's cafés, refreshment stands, and restaurants served Coca-Cola to their customers.

Ernest Woodruff and his investors bought the Candler interests in the Coca-Cola company in 1919 for $25 million, and after he was elected president, he established a "Quality Drink" campaign. His sales staff aggressively sold the soda, advertising and market support were increased, and he defined quality standards for the bottling operation.

In the early 1920s, the company introduced the six-bottle carton that made it easier for customers to bring Coca-Cola into their homes, and in 1929, the open-top cooler was introduced in retail outlets. For the first time, Coke would be introduced into factories, offices, and other institutions—where it could be enjoyed cold on the spot. In the same year the Coca-Cola fountain glass was adopted and used as yet another way to advertise the soft drink.

The 1920s saw a dramatic increase in sales, probably due to Woodruff's influence and the new types of advertising used to market Coca-Cola. The company used large cardboard cutouts in store windows and employed a staff to change them to reflect seasonal themes; chic flappers posed with their favorite drink in posters and countertop displays, and the festoon was produced in 1926 to be hung behind bars and fountains. Slogans became increasingly important to the company. One of the best-remembered was introduced to the American public in 1929: "The Pause that Refreshes." Earlier slogans included the first—"Delicious and Refreshing" (1886), as well as "Thirst Knows No Season"(1922), "It Had to Be Good to Get Where It Is" (1925), and "Around the Corner from Anywhere" (1927).

In 1933, at the Chicago World's Fair, the company introduced the automatic fountain dispensers that mixed syrup and carbonated water to produce the drink, and by 1937, the dispenser was used at most fountains. "It's the Refreshing Thing to Do" became Coca-Cola's slogan in 1936.

When World War II broke out, the company made sure that "every man in uniform gets a bottle of Coca-Cola for 5 cents wherever he is and whatever it costs the Company." The soda was so popular that even General Dwight Eisenhower, in a cablegram dated June 29, 1943, got into the act by asking for shipment of machinery for operating ten bottling plants and for three million filled bottles of Coca-Cola, as well as equipment and supplies for producing the same quantity twice monthly. All kinds of novelty items were produced during the war years, such as playing cards, notebooks, bridge pads, sewing kits, and games, and raffles were held for Coca-Cola when the soda was in short supply on the battlefield—one raised more than $4,000 in Italy! The slogan for 1942 was "It's the Real Thing" (one of the most popular of all Coke's slogans, it was revived in 1969), and in 1944 it was "Global High Sign." Other slogans included: "Sign of Good Taste" (1957), "Be Really Refreshed" (1959), "Things Go Better With Coke" (1963), "Coke Adds Life" (1976), "Have a Coke and a Smile" (1979); "Coke is it!" (1982), and "Catch the wave" (1986).

In 1977 the U.S. Patent Office allowed the bottle to be registered as a Coca-Cola trademark ("Coca-Cola" was registered in 1893 and "Coke" in 1945). Steel cans were introduced to

Coca-Cola, photo of the changes the Coca-Cola bottle has gone through over the years. *Photo courtesy of the Coca-Cola Company Archives.*

domestic markets in 1960, and the diamond design that featured the famous contour bottle decorated cans from 1963 to 1966. In the late 1960s, the company first marketed no-deposit, no-return bottles, and it led the industry with PET (polyethylene terephthalate) bottles. Now, the soft drinks are sold in a variety of packages and sizes, offering consumers a choice for their particular needs. Coca-Cola even boasts being the first carbonated soft drink to be enjoyed in outer space—the company actually developed a "space can" in 1985 that allowed astronauts on shuttle flights to enjoy the drink even during the time they orbited the earth.

During the years, the company has used many illustrators to decorate its products, such as Norman Rockwell, Hamilton King, N. C. Wyeth, Haddon Sundblom (the creator of the Coke Santa), and many others. Certain collectors focus just on products decorated by their favorite illustrators or on those illustrations of particular personages. During the turn of the century a little-known actress named Hilda Clark was used as a model to advertise Coca-Cola products. Her face was immortalized on trays, calendars, and posters. From 1903 to 1905, opera singer Lillian Nordica was featured on posters, trays, coupons, metal signs, menus, bookmarks, calendars, and magazine advertising. Hamilton King's women looked like many others during the Gibson era, but he preferred doing faces rather than full-bodied figures. In the late 1920s, hostess Ida Bailey Allen "offered helpful hints for successful parties in booklets and magazine advertisements." N. C. Wyeth created calendars for Coca-Cola during 1935 and 1936, and Haddon Sundblom's Santa Claus first appeared in the 1930s.

Nowadays the Coca-Cola company is also a major producer

and distributor of motion pictures and television programming. It bought Columbia Pictures Industries, Inc. in 1982, which included the television and movie groups Embassy Telecommunications, Embassy Television, and a substantial portion of Tri-Star Pictures. Films such as *Ghostbusters*, *The Natural*, and *The Big Chill* were produced by Columbia.

In addition, Coca-Cola is one of the world's largest citrus marketers. It purchased the Minute Maid Corporation in 1960 and is now responsible for producing frozen concentrated orange juice, as well as all of Minute Maid's juices, ades, crystals, and other products, such as Five Alive, Hi-C, and Bright & Early brands, as well as Maryland Club and Butter-Nut coffees.

Other products introduced by Coca-Cola include: Fanta soft drinks (1960); Sprite (1961); TAB (1963), the company's first low-calorie beverage; Fresca (1966); Mello Yello (1979); Ramblin' Root Beer (1979); and diet versions of some of these brands. Diet Coke was introduced in 1982, and has become the most successful soft drink since Coke itself. "Just for the Taste of It" has become one of the most popular slogans, and many well-known celebrities have touted the drink.

One of the most controversial issues to surround Coke in its history was the introduction of a new version in 1985. Though taste tests proved consumers liked the new Coke over the original, the company had to keep Classic Coke on the market for those loyal customers who were deeply attached to the original taste.

Today Coca-Cola continues to make strides with new products, and its red-and-white logo is recognized in most countries on the Earth—as well as in space.

COCA-COLA

Coca-Cola, advertisement from *Old Farmer's Almanac*, 1900; nice ad on inside back cover; excellent condition; $20–50.

Coca-Cola, advertisement, 1903; Hilda Clark; black and white; matted; mint condition; $35–75.

Coca-Cola, advertisement from *Christian Herald*, 1905; complete magazine; full-color Coke soda fountain ad on back cover; beautiful and rare; near-mint condition; $250–400.

Coca-Cola, advertisement from *World* magazine, 1914; complete magazine; color; framed; near-mint condition; $50–100.

Coca-Cola, advertisement, 1938; Coke/International truck; color; mint condition; $15–25.

Coca-Cola, ashtray; depicts Coca-Cola in bottles; Bakelite; some wear, very good condition; $20–40.

Coca-Cola, plastic vending bank; with bottle; original and near-mint condition; $100–250.

Coca-Cola, canvas banner; ca. 1908; depicts straight-sided bottle; "From the bottle through a straw"; 6 feet; minor edge wear, excellent condition; $1,200–2,750.

Coca-Cola, baseball scorecard; early piece; double sided; Coca-Cola ad at top center on one side; Dr. Pepper, 7Up, and RC Cola on reverse; from Beaumont, Texas; stains, excellent condition; $20–50.

Coca-Cola, bathtub card; ca. 1907; rare piece; super condition; shows waitress delivering Coke to two gentlemen; near-mint condition; $500–1,000.

Coca-Cola, bingo board; excellent condition; $20–50.

Coca-Cola, blotter; 1906; "Restores energy . . . strengthens the nerves"; near-mint condition, minor edge wear, slight printing color difference; $100–175.

Coca-Cola, blotter; 1929; shows man holding bottle; lettering reads "One little minute for a big rest"; excellent condition, light pinhead stains; $100–250.

Coca-Cola, blotter; 1934; shows girl sitting on a picnic blanket; lettering reads "And one for you"; mint condition; $100–200.

Coca-Cola, blotter; 1942; shows two Boy Scouts taking bottles from a cooler; lettering reads "Wholesome refreshment"; near-mint condition; $20–50.

Coca-Cola, book (first edition); 1923; *The Coca-Cola Company*; hardcover; opinions, orders, injunctions relating to unfair competitions and trademark infringement; a great book explaining all such cases; also full-color art of logos, labels for Coke-ola, Co-Kola, Kola, Coca-Cola Chewing Gum, showing wrapper; rare; near-mint condition; $400–750.

Coca-Cola, book (second edition of above); 1923–1930; "Volume 2"; loaded with hundreds of cases and showing hundreds of different logos; near-mint condition; $300–500.

Coca-Cola, book; *Coca-Cola: An Illustrated Profile*; hardcover; near-mint condition; $30–60.

Coca-Cola, bottles; six-pack; Cape Cod, 50th anniversary, 1989; near-mint condition; $10–25.

Coca-Cola, bottle; light amber; Indiana, Pennsylvania; excellent condition; $75–150.

Coca-Cola, bottle; amber; New York; some case wear, scratches, good condition; $60–100.

Coca-Cola, bottle; light green; logo two times at neck; Boise, Idaho; case wear, excellent condition; $20–60.

Coca-Cola, bottle; early 1900s; Birmingham, Alabama; "Hutchinson Bottle"; near-mint condition; $650–1,000.

Coca-Cola, bottle; December 23, 1923; Spokane, Washington; clean; near-mint condition; $10–25.

Coca-Cola, bottle; November 16, 1915; East Boston, Massachusetts; case wear, chip on base, good condition; $20–40.

Coca-Cola, bottle; script; Chicago; green; near-mint condition; $60–90.

Coca-Cola, cardboard cutout bottle display; 1927; near-mint condition; $225–250.

Coca-Cola, bottle opener; lion; a beauty and rare; excellent condition; $75–150.

Coca-Cola, bottle opener and metal catch; original box; near-mint condition; $50–100.

Coca-Cola, brick; Coca-Cola script logo on top and around edges; "Help Build Lamar Community House"; rare and unusual piece; near-mint condition; $250–500.

Coca-Cola, calendar; 1908; full pad; beautiful brilliant colors and great detail; top (January) sheet has some tears; beautifully matted and framed; near-mint condition; $3,300–4,500.

Coca-Cola, calendar; 1930; full pad; December 1929 cover sheet; beautiful colors; minor mouse chew upper right corner and corner of pad, excellent condition; $950–1,300.

Coca-Cola, calendar; 1931; Norman Rockwell art; full pad with poem; beautifully framed; very minor edge tear, near-mint condition; $300–700.

Coca-Cola, calendar; 1937; N. C. Wyeth art; full pad with cover sheet; crease and mouse chew, edge wear lower left border, nicely framed, excellent condition; $175–400.

Coca-Cola, calendar; 1969; complete; excellent condition; $75–125.

Coca-Cola, can; 1989 Canada Games; near-mint condition; $5–20.

Coca-Cola, can; 1988 Olympic Games; near-mint condition; $5–20.

Coca-Cola, can; 1980 New England grand opening; full; near-mint condition; $5–20.

Coca-Cola, carton stuffer; depicts Coke Santa; excellent condition; $1–5.

Coca-Cola, director's chair; canvas and wood; never used; mint condition; $50–100.

Coca-Cola Chewing Gum, jar with original lid; a beauty; chips on inside bottom of lid, otherwise perfect; near-mint condition; $600–750.

Coca-Cola, Christmas card; New England scene; mint condition; $1–5.

Coca-Cola, Christmas card; Waltham plant; mint condition; $1–5.

Coca-Cola, clock; ca. 1896; Baird; early; difficult to find; face dark, has been repainted, runs perfect; excellent condition; $3,000–5,000.

Coca-Cola, clock; glass front lights up; works great; some hairline cracks, some touch-up to outside rim, some wear; excellent condition; $150–300.

Coca-Cola, T-shirt; near-mint condition; $5–20.

Coca-Cola, knit ski cap; near-mint condition; $5–20.

Coca-Cola, windbreaker; large; near-mint condition; $5–20.

Coca-Cola, 3-D cardboard cutout counter display piece; 1944; Niagra Lithographers; 15 x 20 inches; near-mint condition; $250–1,000.

Coca-Cola, cutout; depicts a circus scene; 1932; edge tear, excellent condition; $20–50.

Coca-Cola, dart board; near-mint condition; $40–70.

Coca-Cola, 3-D cardboard cutout display piece; 1948; 17 x 18 inches (hair net is real); near-mint condition; $300–700.

Coca-Cola, 3-D cardboard cutout window display; 1926; 23 x 37 inches; near-mint condition; $1,200–3,000.

Coca-Cola, die-cut cardboard 3-D display piece; 19 x 20 inches; 1948; near-mint condition; $300–600.

Coca-Cola, doll (made by Buddy Lee Company); composition; sent to bottlers to show new uniform; 12 inches; of the two versions—one in

Coca-Cola, 3-D cardboard cutout display piece; 1948; 17 x 18 inches (hair net is real); $300–700. *Collection of Allan Petretti, author of* Petretti's Coca-Cola Collectibles Price Guide. *Photo by Donald Vogt.*

Coca-Cola, 3-D cardboard cutout window display; 1926; 23 x 37 inches; $1,200–3,000. *Collection of Allan Petretti, author of* Petretti's Coca-Cola Collectibles Price Guide. *Photo by Donald Vogt.*

SODA ■ 377

Coca-Cola, die-cut cardboard 3-D display piece; 19 x 20 inches; 1948; $300–600. *Collection of Allan Petretti, author of* Petretti's Coca-Cola Collectibles Price Guide. *Photo by Donald Vogt.*

Coca-Cola, doll (made by Buddy Lee Company); composition; sent to bottlers to show new uniform; 12 inches; of the two versions—one in plastic—composition doll is more desirable; "hat is the key"; 1950; $500–1,000. *Collection of Allan Petretti, author of* Petretti's Coca-Cola Collectibles Price Guide. *Photo by Donald Vogt.*

plastic, composition doll is more desirable; "hat is the key"; 1950; near-mint condition; $500–1,000.

Coca-Cola, doll (Buddy Lee); composition; no tie; some flaking and hairlines but nothing too serious; elastic on hat stretched; rare; excellent condition; $700–1,000.

Coca-Cola, doll (Buddy Lee); plastic; wearing overalls; no hat; near-mint condition; $80–150.

Coca-Cola, Santa doll; Coke bottle in hand; some wear; excellent condition; $80–150.

Coca-Cola, fan; Japanese scene on one side; some pieces out of edge; excellent condition; $50–100.

Coca-Cola, festoon; 1940s; piece of Masonite war plane; near-mint condition; $20–50.

Coca-Cola, fish spinner; nice piece and rare; near-mint condition; $100–250.

Coca-Cola, game set; complete in shipping case; consists of table tennis, bingo, game box full of cards, cribbage, dominoes, checkers, backgammon, scorepads; near-mint condition; $300–650.

Coca-Cola, glasses (8); complete set of 1916–1966 50th anniversary glasses; Somersworth, New Hampshire; paper label; in box, never opened; rare; mint condition; $75–150.

Coca-Cola, glasses (16); in box; near-mint condition; $20–50.

Coca-Cola, glass negative; 8 x 10 inches; used for printing; ca. 1949; "Good With Food"; very unusual piece; rare; near-mint condition; $10–40.

Coca-Cola, golf tee set; mint condition; $5–20.

Coca-Cola, handbook; 1948 advertising; loaded with great color photos; 60–70 pages; near-mint condition; $50–100.

Coca-Cola, ice pick; "Enjoy Coca-Cola"; mint condition; $5–25.

Coca-Cola, advertisements in *Radio News* magazine, 1932; complete magazine; super full-color center advertisement depicting grand opening of Jamestown, New York, plant; also two other Coke advertisements, one with 1915 bottle and one with 1916 bottle; near-mint condition; $20–50.

Coca-Cola, menu board; 1939; nice color; some chips, scratches, and edge rubs; very good condition; $75–175.

Coca-Cola, menu board; ca. 1960s; wood; nice color; excellent condition; $50–100.

Coca-Cola, opener; German; near-mint condition; $10–30.

Coca-Cola, opener; "It's the Real Thing"; mint condition; $1–5.

Coca-Cola, opener; "Serves Hospitality in the Home"; nice piece; mint condition; $20–40.

Coca-Cola, paper sign; 1902; 14 x 20 inches unframed; this example is framed and is extremely rare, perhaps only one in existence (per Allan Petretti); near-mint condition; $3,500–10,000.

Coca-Cola, paper sign; 1903; Hilda Clark; 14 x 20 inches unframed; this piece is framed and is only known one in existence; extremely rare (per Allan Petretti); near-mint condition; $3,500–10,000.

Coca-Cola, paperweight; made of Lucite, "Coke" logo; mint condition; $10–30.

Coca-Cola, pencil; early; wood; stamped in gold; near-mint condition; $5–20.

Coca-Cola, pewter mug; "Enjoy Coca-Cola" appears on body; mint condition; $30–70.

Coca-Cola, photo; depicts early marble drugstore soda fountain with three-spigot dispenser; Coke sign above mirror; Hires (two-girl) sign on backbar; near-mint condition; $20–50.

Coca-Cola, playing cards; 1943; airplane spotter cards; in box; some wear, very good condition; $45–100.

Coca-Cola, playing cards; 1956; shows girl in ice skates on cover; in box; wear on box, excellent condition; $50–100.

Coca-Cola, playing cards; recent deck; full in box; red-and-white logo on cover; mint condition; $5–15.

Coca-Cola, pocket mirror; 1911; some staining on mirror; front is nice, shows woman in large hat; excellent condition; $100–225.

Coca-Cola, postcard; sign on store; Richwood, West Virginia; ca. 1910; excellent condition; $5–20.

Coca-Cola, postcard; sign on roof of pier; Folly Pier, South Carolina; color; near-mint condition; $5–20.

Coca-Cola, postcard; San Francisco, California; small part of a Coke sign; near-mint condition; $1–5.

Coca-Cola, radio; in shape of vending machine; AM-FM; in box; mint condition; $25–60.

Coca-Cola, record; "Buy the World a Coke"; 1971; mint condition; $1–5.

Coca-Cola, record; "A Visit from St. Nick"; 1952; Christmas promotion; near-mint condition; $10–40.

Coca-Cola, serving tray; oval; 1913; woman in large feathered hat, holding glass of Coke in her right hand; real nice color; some rim chips and rubs, spot on hat upper left, excellent condition; $500–750.

Coca-Cola, serving tray; oval; 1914; woman facing right with flowered bonnet that ties under her chin; some wear on face and dress, chips on rim, good condition; $250–400.

Coca-Cola, serving tray; long rectangle; 1916; woman with back to viewer, leaning on table; roses on table; some wear and scratches, rim chips, color good, average condition; $250–400.

Coca-Cola, serving tray, rectangular; 10½ x 13¼ inches; woman in picture hat, voile dress with cummerbund; 1920; nice color; very minor pinhead back dent, rim chips and rim rubs, excellent condition; $600–750.

Coca-Cola, serving tray; oval; woman in light-colored picture hat, voile dress with cummerbund; 1920; slight fading, minor wear, some rim chips/scratches, very good condition; $450–700.

Coca-Cola, serving tray; rectangular; 10½ x 13¼ inches; girl with summer hat holding Coke in right hand; 1922; nice color; very good condition; $330–500.

Coca-Cola, serving tray; rectangular; 10½ x 13¼ inches; 1923; dark-haired woman (bust) with stole over shoulders holding glass of Coke in right hand; super high shine; great color; minor rim chips and scratch, near-mint condition; $500–800.

Coca-Cola, serving tray; rectangular; 10½ x 13¼ inches; 1928; male soda jerk with glasses of Coke in both hands, super color and shine; minor rim chips, minor scratches, excellent condition; $350–505.

Coca-Cola, serving tray; rectangular; 10½ x 13¼ inches; girl sitting with phone in left hand; 1930; great color; some rim rubs and chips, excellent condition; $300–495.

Coca-Cola, serving tray; rectangular; 10½ x 13¼ inches; boy in country clothing, straw hat, dog at feet, bottle of Coke in right hand; 1931; great color; wear spots or rubs on rim, above bottle, and on sandwich boy holds in hand; very good condition; $250–400.

Coca-Cola, serving tray; rectangular; 10½ x 13¼ inches; blond woman in bathing suit seated on chair, left arm behind back, right hand holding bottle of Coke; 1932; great color; some white spots in background, rim chips, very good condition; $250–375.

Coca-Cola, serving tray; rectangular; 10½ x 13¼ inches; 1933; dark-haired woman in bathing suit wearing high heels, sitting on beach wall, and holding a bottle of Coke in right hand; nice color and shine; excellent condition; $300–450.

Coca-Cola, serving tray; rectangular; 10½ x 13¼ inches; Johnny Weismuller and Maureen O'Sullivan in bathing suits, back to back; 1934; outstanding color and shine; some chips on bottom logo, minor light scratches, excellent condition; $700–1,500.

Coca-Cola, serving tray; rectangular; 10½ x 13¼ inches; blonde woman standing, Coke in right hand, left hand on back of chair, folding screen in background; 1935; great color; rim rubs, excellent condition; $250–500.

Coca-Cola, serving tray; rectangular; 10½ x 13¼ inches; 1936; Buvez (French); dark-haired woman with orchid on shoulder, sitting with Coke in right hand; super color; rim rubs, nice condition; $250–500.

Coca-Cola, serving tray; rectangular; 10½ x 13¼ inches; girl in bathing suit, cape over shoulders, running toward viewer with bottles in both hands; 1937; super color and shine; few minor rim rubs, near-mint condition; $250–500.

Coca-Cola, serving tray; rectangular; 10½ x 13¼ inches; dark-haired woman in frothy summer dress and picture hat, sitting with both hands on knees and holding Coke bottle; 1938; great color and shine; scratches and chips, very good condition; $75–150.

Coca-Cola, serving tray; rectangular; 10½ x 13¼ inches; dark-haired woman in bathing suit, sitting on striped diving board and holding Coke bottle in right hand; 1939; outstanding color and high gloss; one rim chip, otherwise mint/near-mint condition; $275–500.

Coca-Cola, serving tray; rectangular; 10½ x 13¼ inches; light-haired woman dressed in "sailing" outfit, sitting on a pier with fishing pole in left hand, Coke bottle in right; 1940; flawless color and shine; minor surface scratches, near-mint condition; $350–550.

Coca-Cola, serving tray; rectangular; 10½ x 13¼ inches; dark-haired woman in skates, sitting on blanket with Coke bottle in right hand; 1941; great color and high-gloss shine; minor rim chips and surface scratches, near-mint condition; $350–500.

Coca-Cola, serving tray; rectangular; 10½ x 13¼ inches; two women— one is dark-haired and in car driver's seat (wears hat), one is blond and is standing beside car door holding glass of Coke in right hand; 1942; great color and shine; rim chips in two spots on car and skirt, very good condition; $100–250.

Coca-Cola, serving tray; rectangular; 10½ x 13¼ inches; blond woman (head only), scarf around neck, hand holding Coke bottle; 1950 (formerly dated 1948—see Allan Petretti's book on Coca-Cola collectibles); super; line across center of tray is manufacturer's flaw; three scratches, rim chips, near-mint condition; $250–350.

Coca-Cola, serving tray; rectangular; 10½ x 13¼ inches; red-haired woman wearing beret, leaning on chin, head and shoulders only; 1953; minor chip, near-mint condition; $50–100.

Coca-Cola, serving tray; rectangular; 10½ x 13¼ inches; dark-haired woman in raincoat, holding striped umbrella in left hand, bottle of Coke in right; 1957; nice color; rim chips and rubs, excellent condition; $100–275.

Coca-Cola, serving tray; rectangular; 10½ x 13¼ inches; hand pouring Coke from bottle into glass that sits on bed of flowers; 1961; rim chips, near-mint condition; $10–25.

Coca-Cola, serving tray; rectangular; 10½ x13¼ inches; 1971 reproduction of 1910 tray; shows girl in large plumed hat; the repro is flat, the original tray has curved edges with a nice of-the-period border around the edges; near-mint condition; $5–10.

Coca-Cola, serving tray; rectangular; 10½ x 13¼ inches; ca. 1970s; Coke Santa reading a book by a fireplace; near-mint condition; $30–50.

Coca-Cola, serving tray; rectangular; 10½ x 13¼ inches; 1972 reproduction of 1913 tray; features woman in large hat, smiling and holding glass of Coke in left hand; near-mint condition; $25–35.

Coca-Cola, serving tray; rectangular; 10½ x 13¼ inches; 1976; depicts the Cotton Bowl of that year; near-mint condition; $5–20.

Coca-Cola, serving tray; rectangular; 10½ x 13¼ inches; 1982; Pembroke plant; shows old truck loaded with cases of Coca-Cola; near-mint condition; $10–25.

Coca-Cola, sheet music; "Rum and Coca-Cola"; Andrews Sisters on cover; near-mint condition; $15–45.

Coca-Cola, pre-1900 sidewalk sign; tin litho; 19 x 27 inches; wood frame; $2,200–6,000. *Collection of Allan Petretti, author of* Petretti's Coca-Cola Collectibles Price Guide. *Photo by Donald Vogt.*

Coca-Cola, tin sign; 1915; bottle; great colors; some scratches and edge rubs, nothing serious, excellent condition; $500–1,000.

Coca-Cola, oval cardboard cutout hanging sign; 1926; 7 x 11 inches; near-mint condition; $200–350.

Coca-Cola, pre-1900 sidewalk sign; tin litho; 19 x 27 inches; wood frame; near-mint condition; $2,200–6,000.

Coca-Cola, cardboard sign; ca. 1920s; depicts flappers and their cars; panoramic two-part sign; each part nicely matted; some wear and fading on red; rarely found together; good condition; $1,000–2,500.

Coca-Cola, tin sign; 1926; 8 x 11 inch oval; woman in bobbed hairstyle offering a bottle of Coke to the viewer; set against the Coca-Cola logo; bright colors; some minor scratches, minor rim bends, excellent condition; $2,500–3,500.

Coca-Cola, cardboard sign; 1930; telephone man; great colors; some edge wear and light minor stains, general wear, very good condition; $300–800.

Coca-Cola, tin sign; 1931; depicts bottle; 6 x 13½ inches; super colors; some scratches and minor edge bend, excellent condition; $300–500.

Coca-Cola, cardboard sign; 1940s; cardboard frame insert display; colorful and very rare; frame has Coca-Cola logo at top; shows seasonal (autumnal) view of woman with Coke (in center of frame); 32 x 61 inches; near-mint condition; $750–1,500.

Coca-Cola, wood sign; 1940s; NRA member; cutout sign; super blue, gold, red colors; excellent condition; $1,000–1,500.

Coca-Cola, cardboard sign; 1950s; brilliant colors; in German; small peeling spot lower right, excellent condition; $100–200.

Coca-Cola, cardboard sign; 1952; Jesse Owens and Alice Coachman; gold wood frame; colorful and rare; crease lower right, general wear, scratches, very good condition; $250–600.

Coca-Cola, cardboard sign; 1952; easel-back Santa; excellent condition; $100–250.

Coca-Cola, porcelain finish sign; 1953; "It's a Natural"; brilliant colors, high-gloss finish; minor edge and surface scratches, never used, near-mint condition; $500–750.

Coca-Cola, tin sign; 1964; 12 x 36 inches; "Things go Better with Coke"; scratches and edge wear, very good condition; $50–100.

Coca-Cola, celluloid sign; 9 inches; hangs; circular; minor scratches, near-mint condition; $100–250.

Coca-Cola, porcelain sign; fountain service; some wear and scratches and big wear spot lower left, good condition; $150–250.

Coca-Cola, porcelain sign; two-sided rack; yellow, red, and white; minor chips and edge wear, minor wear around screw holes, near-mint condition; $300–500.

Coca-Cola, wood six-pack; hand and wings on end; unusual; cardboard hanging separators; printed on inside "The New Consumer Case" trademark; some wear, excellent condition; $150–300.

Coca-Cola, six-pack; 1930s; Christmas; near-mint condition; $75–150.

Coca-Cola, six-pack; 1960s; near-mint condition; $10–30.

Coca-Cola, tap knob; plastic; "Have a Coke"; excellent condition; $5–20.

Coca-Cola, thermometer; wood; early; super color, no fading; minor edge paint chipping, near-mint condition; $800–1,250.

Coca-Cola, thermometer; gold bottle; rough; no tube; good condition; $20–50.

Coca-Cola, spotlight band ticket; 1944; near-mint condition; $10–20.

Coca-Cola, tip tray; 6 inches; round; actress Hilda Clark is portrayed; great color and detail; beautifully framed in gold; highly collectible; one rub spot (small) above hair and very minor rim chips, excellent condition; $1,000–3,500.

Coca-Cola, tip tray; 6 inches; round; Hilda Clark; 1900; great color; nice rim; rare and very collectible; some chipping in a circular area around her and into logo, very good condition; $800–1,200.

Coca-Cola, tip tray; oval; 1907; lettering on tray reads "Drink Coca-Cola" above the image of a woman in Victorian dress raising a glass of Coke; chipping and wear, has been coated to eliminate further damage, color good, good condition; $175–275.

Coca-Cola, tip tray; oval; 1914; woman in bonnet; nice color; minor stain and chip, excellent condition; $100–250.

Coca-Cola, celluloid-and-wood toy plane; original box; rare; box wear, excellent condition; $250–500.

Coca-Cola, toy Ford taxicab; in box; box wear, some scratches and minor dents, excellent condition; $100–250.

Coca-Cola, Marx plastic toy truck; with side doors; original box; rare snub-nose version; decals in nice condition; excellent condition, flaps missing on one end of box; $500–750.

Coca-Cola, Marx tin toy truck; in box; with cases and hand truck decals in great shape; very minor chips, flap off box, near-mint condition; $500–750.

Coca-Cola, Metalcraft toy truck; rubber wheels; in original box; some wear and writing on box; end flaps missing, but nicely filled and shrink-wrapped truck has all bottles, decals; very good condition; $700–1,000.

Coca-Cola, Technofix toy bus terminal; with double-decker bus and key; near-mint condition; $150–250.

Coca-Cola, yo-yo; plastic; mint condition; $1–5.

Coca-Cola, tray; 1922; 10 x 13; girl with summer hat; $350–900. *Collection of Allan Petretti, author of* Petretti's Coca-Cola Collectibles Price Guide. *Photo by Donald Vogt.*

Coca-Cola, serving tray; 9¾ inches; round; Hilda Clark; 1901; 2,000–3,000. *Collection of Allan Petretti, author of* Petretti's Coca-Cola Collectibles Price Guide. *Photo by Donald Vogt.*

Coca-Cola, tray; 1922; 10 x 13 inches; girl with summer hat; near-mint condition; $350–900.

Coca-Cola, serving tray; 9¾ inches; round; Hilda Clark; 1901; near-mint condition; $2,000–3,000.

Coca-Cola, tray; Johnny Weismuller and Maureen O'Sullivan; 1934; 10 x 13 inches; rectangle; near-mint condition; $700–1,500.

Coca-Cola, tray; 10 x 13 inches; medium oval; 1909; Exposition Girl; near-mint condition; $1,200–1,800.

Coca-Cola, tin toy truck; 1960; litho (yellow); Corvair pickup truck; mint in-box condition; $500–1,500.

Coca-Cola, tray; 10 x 13 inches; medium oval; 1909; Exposition Girl; $1,200–1,800. *Collection of Allan Petretti, author of* Petretti's Coca-Cola Collectibles Price Guide. *Photo by Donald Vogt.*

Coca-Cola, tin toy truck; 1960; litho (yellow); Corvair pickup truck; mint in-box condition; $500–1,500. *Collection of Allan Petretti, author of* Petretti's Coca-Cola Collectibles Price Guide. *Photo by Donald Vogt.*

Coca-Cola, circus window display; 1932; rare; few pieces missing; some wear and repair; clown hat and top of Coca-Cola logo on big top repaired, some repair on performers, very good condition; $750–1,000.

Coca-Cola, 3-D cutout window display; 1938; shows teenage couple being handed a Coke on a tray; very colorful; front piece with hand and glasses comes down for 3-D effect; some paper wear on left side and tape repair on back at fold-down crease; rare; very good condition; $750–1,000.

Coca-Cola, window display; 1939; depicts woman turning toward viewer with bottle in hand; colors include metallic gold; bright; never been used; few scratches from handling, couple of marks on woman's back, near-mint condition; $750–1,500.

Coca-Cola, 3-D window display; 1957; rocket Santas; 33 inches; some paper damage at nose of rocket, excellent condition; $100–300.

Coca-Cola, window display; 1948; Santa cutout; full size; super color; folds in half; excellent condition; $300–600.

COTT
Cott, songbook; crease, excellent condition; $1–5.

DAD'S
Dad's Sugar-Free Root Beer, bottle; near-mint condition; $5–20.

DOUBLE COLA
Double Cola, lighter; some wear, good condition; $10–30.

DR PEPPER

In 1885, a Waco, Texas, drugstore clerk named Charles Courtice Alderton created the beverage called Dr Pepper, and for almost forty years the drink remained in Texas. Eventually, a local ginger ale bottler perfected the formula. By the 1920s, the owners finally decided to distribute outside the state, and they sold the drink under the slogan "Drink a Bite to Eat at 10, 2 & 4 o'clock. Dr Pepper—Good for Life!"

In the early days of promoting the soda, a lion was used to advertise Dr Pepper's "vim, vigor and vitality." (And the early name of the sodas contained a period after the "Dr"—the period was dropped in 1950.)

The Dr Pepper company has produced many advertising items to promote its product, such as calendars, bottle openers, signs, watch fobs, plates, matchboxes, posters, thermometers, clocks, and even a bubble gum in 1985 (through the Wm. Wrigley Jr. Co.).

The ad agency Young & Rubicam took over the account in 1978 and developed the "I'm a Pepper, too!" campaign.

The Dr Pepper Collectors Club produces a newsletter that can be obtained by writing to Dr Pepper Collectors Club (10-2-4), c/o Irene Wright, 1614 Ashberry Drive, Austin, Texas 78723. For further information about the company and its products, the Dr Pepper historian/archivist is located at P.O. Box 225086, Dallas, Texas 75265.

DR PEPPER

Dr Pepper, barbecue grill; very unusual piece; minor wear; excellent condition; $30–50.

Dr Pepper, clock; "Good for Life" on glass front; has motor but loose wires; excellent condition; $100–250.

Dr Pepper, clock; octagon; red, black, and white; painted dial with neon tube; 16 inch diameter; ca. 1940; excellent condition; $750–850.

Dr Pepper, fan; 1960 Texas State Fair; excellent condition; $20–50.

Dr Pepper, eraser; "Good for Life"; mint condition; $1–5.

Dr Pepper, flyer; full color; shows advertisement and magazines; near-mint condition; $15–25.

Dr Pepper, clock, octagonal; red, black, and white; painted dial with neon tube; 16 inch diameter; ca. 1940; excellent condition; $750–850. *Collection of and photo by Michael Bruner.*

Dr Pepper, letter opener; plastic; near-mint condition; $5–20.

Dr Pepper, pencil; excellent condition; $1–5.

Dr Pepper, pencil clip; a beauty; mint condition; $5–20.

Dr Pepper, postcard/coupon; worth ten cents; mint condition; $5–20.

Dr Pepper, postcard; depicts six-pack; mint condition; $1–5.

Dr Pepper, radio; in shape of vending machine; screw missing in back; near-mint condition; $100–250.

Dr Pepper, receipts (lot of 2); 1953; mint condition; $1–5.

Dr Pepper, sign; two sides; hangs; creased; excellent condition; $5–20.

Dr Pepper, sign; easel back; colorful; near-mint condition; $50–100.

Dr Pepper, thermometer; name painted in two spots; excellent condition; $50–150.

Dr Pepper, thermometer; tin; scratches, excellent condition; $15–30.

Dr Pepper, treasure contest bill; 1966; shows both sides; mint condition; $1–5.

Dr Pepper, wood pick; near-mint condition; $10–20.

DR. SWETT'S

Dr. Swett's Root Beer, celluloid hanging sign; early; pretty girl holding mug; nice colors; minor edge and corner wear, excellent condition; $300–600.

Dr. Swett's Root Beer, tin sign; curled-corner sign with woman holding mug of this "Great Health Beverage"; 14½ inch square; very good condition, some minor scratching, slight soiling overall; $350–650.

GRAPETTE

Grapette, calendar; 1955; full pad; crease and stains, very good condition; $30–50.

GROSMAN'S ROOT BEER

Grosman's Root Beer, bottle; paper label; excellent condition; $5–10.

HIRES

Charles Elmer Hires, a Philadelphia pharmacist, concocted "Rootbeer" in 1870 after becoming enamored of his neighbor's root tea. After some friendly encouragement, Hires sold his mixture at the 1876 Philadelphia Centennial Exposition, and eventually created a syrup for soda fountains in 1905. For almost fifty years, Hires was sold as a packet of dried flavorings that could be mixed at home, as a liquid concentrate, as a syrup, and in bottles.

Hires advertised his product in many unique ways, including producing mugs with his trademark pointing child, lamps, mirrors, trays, signs, dispensers, trade cards, whistles, thermometers, and many other novelties.

The name varies, but does not help to date the item (i.e., Hires, Hires', Hire's). However, the clothing in which the pointing boy is dressed will help the collector. For example, from 1891 to 1906, the boy wore a dress; from 1907 to 1914, a bathrobe; and from 1915 to 1926, a dinner jacket.

HIRES ROOT BEER

Hires, bottle; early embossment on bottom; cloudy; excellent condition; $5–20.

Hires, bottle stopper; cast iron; near-mint condition; $5–20.

Hires, fountain glass with syrup line; nice early piece; mint condition; $10–30.

Hires, tin dispensers (2); die-cut topped root beer concentrates wall dispensers; blue, red, and white; 5 x 18 x 2 inches; good original condition, general overall soiling, some minor denting; $100–200.

Hires Ginger Champagne, stemmed glass; beautiful; nice early piece; near-mint condition; $40–70.

Hires, knife; ugly kid on one side with mug, "Drink Hires" waiter on reverse; super and early piece; rare; some minor staining, near-mint condition; $200–400.

Hires, mug; pot-bellied version of Mettlach mug with trademarked pointing boy; 4½ x 4½ inches including handle; near-mint condition, minor age glaze crazing and color spotting to background; $75–150.

SODA ■ 391

Hires, mug; Villeroy & Boch stoneware; made in Germany for the Charles E. Hires Company; ca. 1915; average condition; $50–225.

Hires, paper poster; depicts an elaborately dressed female answering the door to a girl selling new, improved Hires Root Beer; 10¼ x 14½ inches excluding mat and frame; excellent condition with bright vivid colors; $500–750.

Hires, serving tray; rectangular; parrot; chips and scratches, very good condition; $20–40.

Hires, paper sign; small; "Say Hires Drink 5 Cents"; excellent condition; $30–60.

Hires, tin sign; nice bright colors; bottle; excellent condition; $50–100.

Hires, embossed tin sign; colorful; minor edge bend, excellent condition; $50–100.

Hires, tin sign; classic image of pointing boy holding mug; 19 x 27 inches excluding frame; very good condition, some general overall scuffing, minor scratching, horizontal scratch above boy's lip, holes along edge; $2,000–4,000.

Hires, reverse glass sign; early 1900s; 4 x 8 inches; near-mint condition; $200–600.

Hires, Mettlach stein; no chips or marks; near-mint condition; $200–300.

Hires, syrup dispenser; classic hourglass ceramic dispenser with orig-

Hires, reverse glass sign; early 1900s; 4 x 8 inches; $200–600. *Collection of Allan Petretti, author of* Petretti's Coca-Cola Collectibles Price Guide. *Photo by Donald Vogt.*

inal pump; 7½ x 14 inches; excellent/near-mint condition, minor age crazing to glaze, slight corrosion to interior shaft of pump, age discoloration to exterior of pump; $300–500.

Hires, Mettlach syrup dispenser; rare Villeroy & Boch syrup dispenser with multiple images of trademarked boy pointing and holding mug; "Drink Hires 5 cents America's Health Drink"; 10½ inch diameter x 20 inches; very good/excellent condition, chip on interior of lid, hairline on inside of footed base, minor discoloration and hairline crazing to glazing of lid; $15,000–28,000.

Hires, thermometer; depicts bottle; porcelain; colorful; excellent condition; $25–75.

Hires, trade card; shows baby with dog; ca. late 1890s; near-mint condition; $5–20.

HOSTER

Hoster Brewing Co., tin sign; drunken monk among beer barrels; 20 x 16 inch oval excluding frame; good/very good condition, slight wear overall, minor scratching; $50–150.

IRONPORT

Ironport, syrup dispenser; rare and desirable; "Drink Ironport, made where the sun shines, You'll Like It, 5 cents"; 15½ x 18½ inches; very good original condition; $1,500–2,000.

LEMON KOLA

Lemon Kola, blotter; very large; colorful; near-mint condition; $10–30.

MISCELLANEOUS

American Soda Book; 260 pages; hardbound; pre-1900s; early photos of soda-making equipment plus recipes for making soda; rare; near-mint condition; $50–100.

Harwich Pharmacy, soda fountain fan; pre-1900; depicts lady sitting at fountain; minor bent corner, excellent condition; $35–75.

Marble soda locker; early 1870s; marble Tuff's soda fountain with ten flavor pumps, including "nectar," "raspberry," "claret," "don't care," and "beer" among others; elaborate German silvered pump facings housed within a pink marble case; approximately 31 x 50 x 20 inches; fair condition, top marble slab missing, some breaks, some marble discoloration, needs assembly, most parts appear present, builder's plate missing; $400–1,000.

MOUNTAIN CLUB
Mountain Club, bottle; paper label; excellent condition; $5–20.

MOXIE
Moxie, bottle; "Nerve Food" blob top; really early; near-mint condition; $20–60.

Moxie, syrup bottle; no cap; near-mint condition; $150–200.

Moxie, cardboard spinner; colorful; some stains and wear in center post, excellent condition; $50–100.

Moxie, ceramic ashtray; Moxie Man in middle; edge is white; very colorful; minor edge wear, excellent condition; $50–125.

Moxie, change tray; girl holding glass with leaved border; 6 inch diameter; good condition, some slight chipping and scratching, general soiling; $150–300.

Moxie, die-cut cardboard displays (5); varied sizes; good condition overall; $50–150.

Moxie, cardboard cutout window display piece; 1918; framed; 20 x 36 inches; near-mint condition; $600–1,000.

Moxie, fountain glass; early; unusual shape; near-mint condition; $70–110.

Moxie, fountain glass with syrup line; near-mint condition; $15–25.

Moxie, postcard; photo of Moxie on store window; excellent condition; $5–20.

Moxie, postcard; signs on front; Whitcomb Summit, Massachusetts; color; near-mint condition; $1–5.

Moxie, postcard; "Weather" card; creased, very good condition; $5–20.

Moxie, sheet music; "Just Make it Moxie for Mine"; "Words by W. Pence Mitchell, Music by Bert Potter"; early; excellent condition; $20–50.

Moxie, sheet music; "Moxie Song"; 1921; Moxie Man on cover; very good condition; $15–25.

Moxie, sign; easel back; cutout; excellent condition; $50–125.

Moxie, tin sign; vertical multicolored image of people running toward bottle of Moxie in the "Hall of Fame"; 19 x 54 inches; very good condition, some minor denting and distortion, scratches, edge holes; $200–400.

Moxie, tip tray; round; depicts a woman in Victorian clothing holding a glass of Moxie; bottom of rim reads "I just love MOXIE don't you"; great color; a beauty; minor rim wear, excellent condition; $150–250.

Moxie, cutout window display; early piece; shows woman in large bonnet trying to wake up sleeping gent; some edge wear, torn and repaired from back, minor touch-up, good condition; $400–800.

NEHI
(*see also* "Royal Crown Cola")
Nehi, blotter; marked "drink NEHI for Health and Happiness too ... in Your Favorite Flavor"; near-mint condition; $5–20.

Nehi, jig square puzzle; mint condition; $5–20.

Nehi, sign; bottle; 15 x 42 inches; super colors; near-mint condition; $50–125.

Nehi, tin sign; "Gas today"; 15 x 42 inches; great color; near-mint condition; $250–500.

NESBITT'S
Nesbitt's, mechanical pencil with bottle; bottle off end; good condition; $15–30.

NUGRAPE
NuGrape, blotter; shows NuGrape figure-eight-shaped bottle; near-mint condition; $5–20.

ORANGE CRUSH
Orange Crush, stand-up cardboard billboard; very colorful; nice piece; near-mint condition; $50–100.

Orange Crush, bottle; embossed; ribbed; near-mint condition; $15–40.

Orange Crush, clock (Regulator); reverse glass lower panel, painted dial, rectangular regulator; 19 x 36 x 6 inches; good condition, case and dial repainted, lower glass appears replaced, has pendulum; $150–300.

Orange Crush, fountain glass; etched; syrup line; near-mint condition; $50–75.

Orange Crush, serving tray; round; depicts bottle cap in middle of tray surrounded by stylized flowers; Mexican; near-mint condition; $25–40.

Orange Crush, tin sign; ca. 1920s; bottle; great color; minor bend, excellent condition; $100–200.

Orange Crush, tin sign; diamond-shaped; "Drink Orange Crush"; minor edge flaking, excellent condition; $20–50.

Orange Crush, syrup dispenser; figural glass dispenser with embossed orange top on black glass "deco" base; 7½ x 16 x 12 inches; good condition, some discoloration to embossed top, repaired crack in base, chip under lid of syrup top; $100–300.

Orange Crush, tattoos; Dogpatch characters; rub-on; mint condition; $5–20.

Orange Crush, thermometer; some wear and paint specks, very good condition; $25–75.

PEPSI-COLA

At only thirty-one years of age, Caleb Bradham concocted his own soft drink, a unique mixture of kola nut extract, vanilla, and rare oils. It was the summer of 1898, and the drink became so popular that customers called it "Brad's Drink," even though Caleb renamed it "Pepsi-Cola." He advertised the drink, business began to grow, and in 1902 Pepsi-Cola Company opened its doors (in the back room of Caleb's pharmacy).

In 1903, the name "Pepsi-Cola" was registered with the U.S. Patent Office and the first advertisement appeared in a local North Carolina newspaper. By 1909, Caleb had made so much money with his new product that he was able to build a spectacular new headquarters building in New Bern, North Carolina. By that time, Pepsi-Cola delivered its product in motor vehicles instead of horse-drawn carts, and 250 bottlers were under contract in twenty-four states. 1909 is also noted as the year Pepsi was first endorsed by a celebrity: automobile race pioneer Barney Oldfield said the drink was a "bully drink—refreshing, invigorating, a fine bracer before a race." His endorsement was repeated in Pepsi's newspaper ads.

Business was good for the company until World War I shortages forced Pepsi-Cola to increase in price because of the rising price of sugar. Caleb purchased large stocks of sugar, but the price dropped by the end of 1920 and, in 1921, the company suffered enormous financial losses due to his bad investment. Bradham hung in for three years, then was forced to return to the pharmacy and put the Pepsi-Cola trademark up for sale. The company was sold five times and had fifteen bad years before Loft, Incorporated, the owner of a large chain of candy stores and soda fountains along the eastern seaboard, acquired 80 percent of the newly formed Pepsi-Cola Company. Within two years, the company earned $1 million. Unfortunately, its success brought them right into the Great Depression.

Instead of decreased sales, Pepsi-Cola increased its sales in 1934 to a landmark level by "selling a twelve-ounce bottle of Pepsi for just a nickel—twice as much as other soft drinks for the same price" (see *The Pepsi-Cola Story*, published by Pepsi-Cola Company, Purchase, New York 10577). In 1935, the operation was moved to Long Island City, New York, where national territorial boundaries were set up for the Pepsi bottler franchise system. During that same year, Companies Pepsi-Cola de Cuba was formed, and a year later Pepsi-Cola Limited of London was established.

Pepsi's advertising scheme included the comic strip characters Pepsi and Pete (from ads in the late 1930s) and the creation of the first jingle to be nationally aired to advertise a product. The jingle made broadcast history, was called "immortal" by *Life* magazine in 1940, was recorded in fifty-five different languages, and was even played in Carnegie Hall. The tune combined the cola's new price (a nickel) with the fact that it "hits the spot," thus was titled "Pepsi-Cola Hits the Spot." Around this time, the Loft company changed its corporate name to Pepsi-Cola Company.

Ads during World War II proclaimed "American energy will win," and Pepsi supported the war effort by operating a USO Canteen in New York City's Time Square so that families could record messages for the men and women overseas. It also used skywriting at that time (the Pepsi Skywriter continues to tour the United States to this day).

After the war, Pepsi-Cola produced new, smaller bottle sizes and began to package the soda in cans (1948). This period of time brought some change to Pepsi with a new president (Alfred Steele) and stronger sales. Steele was responsible for strengthening the bottling system, and his wife, Joan Crawford, is credited with moving the company into the "Sociables" campaign of the 1950s.

Other changes made during the 1950s included the formation of Pepsi-Cola International, Ltd., a division of Pepsi-Cola, in 1954. The straight-sided Pepsi-Cola bottle was replaced by the swirl bottle in 1958. Steele died of a heart attack in 1959 and Joan Crawford was elected to the board of directors.

The 1960s were known as the Pepsi Generation, and slogans such as "You've got a lot to live. Pepsi's got a lot to give"; "Catch that Pepsi Spirit"; and "Have a Pepsi Day" were used in advertising campaigns. In 1963, Donald M. Kendall assumed command of the company and the 12-ounce bottle was upgraded to 16 ounces.

During the 1970s, Pepsi led the way in introducing the soda industry's first one-and-a-half-liter and two-liter bottles. It was also the first company to use polyester plastic bottles. In 1974, it opened its first plant in the USSR after a preliminary trade agreement between the USSR and Pepsi was signed in 1972.

By the early 1980s, Pepsi started using a new slogan and new advertising tactics. "Pepsi. The Choice of a New Generation" ads were well-known for the excitement Michael Jackson and his brothers incited. Lionel Richie followed Jackson as the recognizable face in Pepsi ads. In 1986, Pepsi became the first major sponsor of the Goodwill Games and also reunited with Michael Jackson, forming a long-term agreement for worldwide collaboration.

The company sold only Pepsi-Cola for its first sixty-five years, but in 1963 it developed Diet Pepsi and introduced the product with its "Girl Watchers" campaign—again, the company had a hit song. In 1964, Mountain Dew joined the Pepsi family, then caffeine-free products Pepsi Free and Diet Pepsi Free were produced in the 1980s.

Pepsi-Cola Company merged with Frito-Lay, Inc. in 1965. Other U.S. divisions of the company include Pizza Hut, Taco Bell, Wilson Sporting Goods, Kentucky Fried Chicken, and La Petite Boulangerie (see information about some of these other enterprises under their own headings).

The company continues to expand its selling base throughout the world, having been the first American product to be sold in both Russia and China. Pepsi-Cola is now sold in over 145 countries.

Here's a list of Pepsi-Cola's slogans through the years:

1909–1939	"Delicious and Healthful"
1939–1950	"Twice As Much for a Nickel Too"
1950–1963	"The Light Refreshment"
1953–1961	"Be Sociable"
1961–1963	"Now It's Pepsi for Those Who Think Young"
1963–1967	"Come Alive! You're in the Pepsi Generation"
1967–1969	"Taste that Beats the Others Cold. Pepsi Pours It On"
1969–1973	"You've Got a Lot to Live. Pepsi's Got a Lot to Give"
1973–1975	"Join the Pepsi People Feelin' Free"
1976–1978	"Have a Pepsi Day"
1979–1981	"Catch that Pepsi Spirit"
1981–1982	"Pepsi's Got your Taste for Life"
1983	"Pepsi Now!"
1984–1986	"Pepsi. The Choice of a New Generation"

For further information, or to correspond with other collectors, write to Pepsi-Cola Collectors Club, P.O. Box 1275, Covina, California 91722.

PEPSI-COLA

Pepsi-Cola, baseball cards; 1991; Red Sox; mint condition; $5–20.

Pepsi-Cola, baseball game; fits in vest pocket; 1941; colorful; excellent condition; $20–50.

Pepsi-Cola, beach tray; round; minor scratches, near-mint condition; $20–35.

Pepsi-Cola, blotter; shows blond woman holding tray with Pepsi bottles and glasses; lettering reads "Tempty . . . Tasty"; near-mint condition; $20–50.

Pepsi-Cola, blotter; no picture, lettering reads "Drink Pepsi-Cola Delicious Healthful"; looks early; near-mint condition; $35–75.

Pepsi-Cola, blotter; shows the Pepsi Cops, "Pepsi" and "Pete"; bottle is marked "5 cents" so piece must be ca. 1930s; near-mint condition; $50–100.

Pepsi-Cola, booklet; group insurance; 1966; mint condition; $1–5.

Pepsi-Cola, bottles; six-pack; Desert Storm; July 4, 1991; "Welcome Home"; long neck; near-mint condition; $5–20.

Pepsi-Cola, calendar; 1947; complete; near-mint condition; $75–150.

Pepsi-Cola, carton stuffer; 1965 Miss America game; mint condition; $5–20.

Pepsi-Cola, carton stuffers (lot of 2); Disneyland/Walt Disney World; mint condition; $1–5.

Pepsi-Cola, Christmas card; cartoon; excellent condition; $5–20.

Pepsi-Cola, cigarettes; full pack; sealed; very unusual piece; mint condition; $50–175.

Pepsi-Cola, circus ticket; nice piece; near-mint condition; $5–20.

Pepsi-Cola, clock; plastic with metal base; light-up sign; near-mint condition; $275–425.

Pepsi-Cola, tin coaster/ashtray; scratches, very good condition; $20–50.

Pepsi-Cola, counter display; Pepsi's Norman Rockwell Santa; dancing with Pepsi bottle in hand; 20 inches high; self-standing; cardboard; $45–75.

Pepsi-Cola, dart board; single dot stain and corner off top right; very good condition; $40–70.

Pepsi-Cola, tin desk organizer; early; top embossed "Compliments of The Pepsi-Cola Co., New Bern, NC"; top lifts up; three compartments inside for pen points, etc.; front part holds pen; embossed on front "Drink Pepsi-Cola"; early and unusual; one hinge repaired, some stains and wear; excellent condition; $400–800.

Pepsi-Cola, door handle; minor flaking, excellent condition; $100–250.

Pepsi-Cola, film; six-pack; "3 Thirsty People"; in box; near-mint condition; $10–40.

Pepsi-Cola, clown game; single dot; creased, very good condition; $15–50.

Pepsi-Cola, hand spinner; block letters; 12-ounce bottle; near-mint condition; $20–50.

Pepsi-Cola, kite; excellent condition; $50–100.

Pepsi-Cola, makeup mirror; on stand; nice; unusual piece; excellent condition; $50–100.

Pepsi-Cola, menu board; nice color; some scratches and flaking spots, not serious, excellent condition; $40–100.

Pepsi-Cola, opener; brass; excellent condition; $20–60.

Pepsi-Cola, pin; 1942 Pepsi-Cola softball champs; near-mint condition; $50–100.

Pepsi-Cola, lapel pin; single dot; red, white, and blue enameled; near-mint condition; $50–100.

Pepsi-Cola, playing cards; "Pepsi-Cola Bottling Co., Quincy, Massachusetts"; still in box; tape on box, excellent condition; $50–75.

Pepsi-Cola, salt and pepper set; in box; near-mint condition; $150–300.

Pepsi-Cola, service pin; enameled; Whitehead and Hoag; rare; red, white, and blue inlaid enamel on gold; shows early bottle with diamond label and early script; mint condition; $400–750.

Pepsi-Cola, serving tray; rectangular; 10½ x 13¼ inches; diagonal bottle pictured on center of tray; around the edges are the words "Bigger and Better" on left side and "Coast to Coast" on right side; very colorful; some manufacturer's flaws that look like scratches, near-mint condition; $100–275.

Soda ■ 401

Pepsi-Cola, serving tray; rectangular; 10½ x 13¼ inches; reads "Enjoy Pepsi-Cola Hits the Spot"; light scratches, one bad spot, excellent condition; $50–75.

Pepsi-Cola, serving tray; rectangular; 10½ x 13¼ inches; promotes Everess Sparkling Water (a product of the Pepsi-Cola Company)—"It's Good for You"; scratches, rim chips, very good condition; $25–50.

Pepsi-Cola, serving tray; round; promotes Everess Sparkling Water; striped background; some scratches, excellent condition; $50–75.

Pepsi-Cola, serving tray; rectangular; 10½ x 13¼ inches; bouquet of flowers; near-mint condition; $30–50.

Pepsi-Cola, serving tray; round; depicts Pepsi-Cola bottle cap; Mexico; chips and scratches, good condition; $25–50.

Pepsi-Cola, serving tray; round; 16 inches; 1976; depicts U.S. quarter dated 1776–1976; one flake spot and minor rim dent, very good condition; $10–30.

Pepsi-Cola, serving tray; square; depicts nine bottle tops set in ice with Pepsi logo in middle; minor chips and rubs, excellent condition; $20–30.

Pepsi-Cola, serving tray; square; Mexican; depicts Pepsi bottle cap in center; "Pepsi-Cola" is repeated around border; excellent condition; $50–75.

Pepsi-Cola, tin sign; yellow with black; "Drink Pepsi-Cola"; near-mint condition; $100–250.

Pepsi-Cola, cardboard sign; 1950s; Santa; colorful; near-mint condition; $50–100.

Pepsi-Cola, toy giveaway; punch-out cardboard "Sound Jet"; never used; mint condition; $5–25.

Pepsi-Cola, toy; party pack plastic set; still sealed; mint condition; $10–20.

Pepsi-Cola, wood toy baseball hat; minor wear, near-mint condition; $30–50.

Pepsi-Cola, umbrella; canvas; excellent condition; $100–250.

Pepsi-Cola, watch; plastic; large; near-mint condition; $20–50.

Pepsi-Cola, watch fob; "The American Beverage"; a nice clean piece; near-mint condition; $100–250.

Pepsi-Cola, wristwatch; Waltham; seventeen jewels; scratches and edge wear, works fine, stain on face, excellent condition; $100–250.

PHENIX
Phenix Sparkling Drink, die-cut tin sign; advertises "a delicious sparkling drink for tired nerves"; 19½ x 26¼ inches; good condition; $150–300.

ROBIN HOOD
Robin Hood, bottle; paper label depicts fictional character; excellent condition; $10–30.

ROYAL CROWN COLA

Claude A. Hatcher organized the Union Bottling Works in 1905, selling a ginger ale called Royal Crown, another soft drink called Chero-Cola, and a line of flavors. By 1912, the company had reorganized under the name Chero-Cola Co. and in 1928, changed it once again to the Nehi Corporation.

Royal Crown Cola was introduced in 1933. By 1935, the company had 315 franchised bottlers—310 bottled Chero-Cola and 263 sold flavors under the name Nehi.

One of the first advertising slogans RC used was introduced in 1939 ("Royal Crown Is Tops in Taste") and heard weekly on Robert Ripley's "Believe It or Not" radio show. Through the years, many celebrities would endorse the product, including Joan Bennett, Rita Haworth, Merle Oberon, Dorothy Lamour, Claudette Colbert, Loretta Young, Gene Tierney, Mary Martin, Gary Cooper, Shirley Temple, Rhonda Fleming, Shelley Winters, Bing Crosby, Joan Crawford, Bob Hope, Barbara Stanwyck, Art Linkletter (also on the board of directors), Johnny Unitas, many of the Miss Universe title winners, Nancy Sinatra, Jill Haworth, Twiggy, Lena Horne, Tony Danza, and many others.

Through the years, the RC slogan changed to include the following:

1939–1940	"Royal Crown Is Tops in Taste"
1941	"Best by Taste Test"
1956	"Better Taste Calls for RC!"
1959	"RC—the Fresher Refresher"
1962	"Royal Crown Is Made Fresher to Taste Fresher"

1963	"Go Fresher with RC"
1965	"You'll Flip at the Z-Z-Zip in RC Cola!"
1967	"Escape—Come on Over to RC Cola—The One with the Mad, Mad Taste"
1968–1969	"RC Cola . . . the Comer"
1970	"We Cool off Hot Towns"
1971	"Easy on the Syrup, Easy on the Gas . . . For People Who Can't Stop Drinking Cola"
1972	"The One You Loved Is Back"
1975	"Me and My RC"
1980	"Here's to Fun"
1984	Cola Lovin' Woman, Cola Lovin' Man"
1985	"Some People Go out of Their Way for the Taste of RC"
1988	"Decide for Yourself"
1989	"New Look, Same Great Taste" and "C'mon Say Yes to RC"
1990	"Take the RC Challenge"

The company is recognized for many industry firsts, including being the first to distribute soft drinks nationally in cans (1954); the first to introduce the 16-ounce bottle (1958); the first low-calorie diet cola (Diet-Rite Cola, 1962); the first to introduce the all-aluminum can (1964); the first caffeine-free diet cola (RC100, 1980); the first decaffeinated regular cola (Decaffeinated RC, 1982); the first salt-free diet cola (Diet-Rite Cola, 1983); the first diet cherry cola (Diet Cherry RC Cola, 1985); and the first no-salt, no sodium, caffeine-free flavored soft drink with 100 percent Nutrasweet® (Diet-Rite).

Royal Crown Cola's advertising campaigns began to feature Hollywood endorsements in 1941 and have continued in that vein till today. Several times throughout the history of the company, one particular celebrity was named spokesperson—in 1961, Art Linkletter began his stint as RC spokesperson. He shared TV commercials with a cartoon character introduced in 1965 called "Zippy"; however, Zippy was phased out in favor of other celebrities such as Jill Haworth, Joey Heatherton, and the group Dino, Desi & Billy in 1967. As advertising agencies changed, so did the slogans used by the company.

Diet-Rite Cola had its own celebrity spokespersons, including Twiggy, Lena Horne, and Tony Danza, depending on which advertising agency was handling the account at the time.

The company expanded its product line in the mid-1970s by acquiring Arby's, a fast-food chain specializing in roast beef sandwiches, and in 1984, Royal Crown and all its divisions were acquired by Chesapeake Financial Corporation, a Victor Posner affiliate.

ROYAL CROWN

Royal Crown, bottle lighter; very good condition; $10–20.

Royal Crown Cola, cooler; sliding top; restored to original condition; takes fifteen cents; working; ca. 1950s; $2,200–2,500.

Royal Crown, fan; 1936; colorful; depicts bottles of the soda and price ("5 cents"); near-mint condition; $25–75.

Royal Crown, free bottle card; mint condition; $1–5.

Royal Crown, pencil clip; minor wear, excellent condition; $5–20.

Royal Crown, tin straw dispenser; unusual piece; some pitting and edge wear, knob missing, very good condition; $50–100.

Royal Crown, straws; full box (500); marked "Royal Crown"; very colorful; near-mint condition; $100–250.

SCHUSTER'S

Schuster's Root Beer, mug; minor wear, near-mint condition; $25–75.

7UP (SEVEN-UP)

7Up, ashtray; glass; lettering reads "Fresh Up with Seven-Up. It likes you"; near-mint condition; $10–20.

7Up, bottle; paper label; near-mint condition; $30–60.

7Up, case; cardboard 24-bottle carrier; near-mint condition; $10–25.

7Up, clock; "Real 7Up likes you"; made in U.S.A.; 16 inch square; original as-found condition; $450–600.

7Up, wall clock; Modernistic design (1950s?); works; near-mint condition; $75–200.

7Up, clock; in shape of can; near-mint condition; $5–20.

7Up, child's chair; unusual piece; disassembles; minor wear, excellent condition; $20–50.

7Up, Fresh-up Freddie figure; 9 inches; ca. 1959; vinyl; rare; excellent condition; $300–400.

7Up, mechanical pencil; with bottle; bottle off end; good condition; $10–20.

7Up, mechanical pencil; some wear, excellent conditon; $10–20.

7Up, menu board; Masonite; near-mint condition; $10–30.

7Up, push plate for door; "In case of Emergency, Please Notify"; near-mint condition; $50–100.

7Up, receipts (lot of 3); mint condition; $1–5.

7Up, sign; 1947; two sides; hangs; near-mint condition; $5–20.

7Up, sign; 1948; two sides; hangs; cardboard; excellent condition; $5–20.

7Up, sign; 1948; easel; back cutout; near-mint condition; $10–25.

7Up, sign; 1950; Halloween bottle display; colorful; mint condition; $20–50.

7Up, telephone; 7Up Spot; 12 inches; giveaway; excellent condition; $75–100.

7Up, thermometer; porcelain; still in box; near-mint condition; $50–100.

7Up, Fresh-Up Freddie figure, 9 inches, ca. 1959, vinyl, rare, $300–400; telephone, 7Up Spot, 12 inches, giveaway, $75–100. *Courtesy of Neil and Nancy Berliner. Photo by Donald Vogt.*

SPRITE

Sprite, coupon; 1950s Sprite Boy; mint condition; $1–5.

Sprite, napkin; depicts Sprite Boy; mint condition; $5–20.

Sprite, school package; pencil, blotter, and ruler; mint condition; $20–50.

Sprite, sign; 1948; 10 x 66 inches; two sides; with two 12 inch button signs; wood and Masonite; hangs; reverse side says "Menard's Market"; minor flaking on Sprite Boy decal, excellent condition; $500–800.

Sprite, tip tray; Mexican; reads "Tome Sprite—El Refresco . . . Refresco"; scratch, near-mint condition; $10–20.

SQUIRT

Squirt, business card; 1949; near-mint condition; $10–25.

Squirt, calendar; 1947; complete; very colorful; a real beauty; edge wear, excellent condition; $75–125.

Squirt, countertop display piece; "Just call me Squirt"; with original bottle; 13 inches; composition; ca. 1940s; excellent condition; $400–550.

Squirt, sign; 1949; two sides; cardboard; hangs; depicts Squirt Boy holding a bottle as big as he is; near-mint condition; $15–25.

Squirt, sign; 1955; two sides; cardboard; hangs; lettering says "Switch to Squirt—never an after-thirst"; some wear, excellent condition; $10–40.

Squirt, countertop display piece; "Just call me Squirt"; with original bottle; 13 inches; composition; ca. 1940s; $400–550. *Courtesy of Neil and Nancy Berliner. Photo by Donald Vogt.*

Ward's Crush, dispensers; lime is 13½ inches high, orange is 14½ inches high, and lemon is 13½ inches high; all are ceramic; ca. 1920s; excellent condition; $2,500–3,000 for set of three. *Collection of and photo by Grant Smith.*

SUN CREST
Sun Crest, calendar; 1942; full pad; super colors; very bright; near-mint condition, $50–100.

TRY-ME
Try-Me, blotter; lettering reads "7 Varieties 7 Famous Try-Me Blends"; excellent condition; $5–20.

WARD'S
Ward's Lemon Crush, syrup dispenser; illusive figural-shaped lemon Ward's with original lettered pump; rare; 10 x 7 x 12 inches; excellent/near-mint condition, slight fade to color at bottom, minor color chipping at foot, some light soiling; $800–1,300.

Ward's Lime Crush, syrup dispenser; figural porcelain lime-shaped dispenser, rarest of three Ward's; original pump; 9 x 13 x 7 inches; good/very good condition, old chip to foot, minor overpainting especially around letters and partial areas of base; $100–1,500.

Ward's Crush, dispensers; lime is 13½ inches high; orange is 14½ inches high; lemon is 13½ inches high; all are ceramic; ca. 1920s; excellent condition; $2,500–3,000 for set of three.

WHITE HOUSE
White House Ginger Ale, pen tip and pencil; celluloid; mint condition; $5–7.

WHITE ROCK
The girl kneeling on the rock has perfect measurements, is named after the Greek beauty Psyche, and her butterfly wings convey a state of immortality. She was created by artist Paul

Thumann and was first displayed at the 1893 World's Columbian Exposition in Chicago, but had measurements of a girl of that day (37-27-38)—changes to her measurements were made over the years by the company. White Rock Mineral Springs Company's owners visited the fair, spotted the painting, and felt it symbolized the purity and quality aspects they wanted to use when advertising their product.

In some advertisements, Psyche has moved from her original kneeling position (an ad for White Rock Vodka Mix showed her ready to jump into the water). She has undergone changes to modernize her as well—in 1924, her hairstyle changed; in 1947, she was again updated, had a new hairstyle, lost weight, grew two inches, and had different perfect measurements (35-25-35). In 1960, the figure became less nude, and in the late 1960s, a contest for a three-word slogan for Psyche resulted in "Ah, so pure!"

WHITE ROCK

White Rock, tin advertising signs (4); series of fanciful images promote this water; vivid bright colors on these offset signs; 10¾ x 7½ inches; excellent/near-mint condition, very minor scratching on the edges; $300–600.

White Rock, tin sign; depicts White Rock's logo woman; oldest version known with original frame dated 1881; 17¼ x 17½ inches; very good/excellent condition with vivid colors and fancy original frame; $1,000–2,500.

CHAPTER FORTY-ONE
■ SOUPS ■

BRUNSWICK

Brunswick Soups, paper sign; jovial fellow with large ladle of "Rich and Delicious" soup; 11¼ x 13¼ inches; very good/excellent condition, slight horizontal rub marks, border trimmed; $200–400.

CAMPBELL'S SOUPS

In 1869, Joseph Campbell and Abram Anderson began canning tomatoes, vegetables, jellies, condiments, and mincemeat in Camden, New Jersey. In 1897, Dr. J. T. Dorrance (former president Arthur Dorrance's nephew) began condensing the soup (taking out the water). Dorrance had joined the company in 1892. The company began advertising in 1899, putting up streetcar signs and promoting the red-and-white soup cans. In 1900, the company won the Gold Medallion for excellence at the Paris Exposition, and the medallion has been featured on labels ever since that time. Soon, the Campbell's company was known for buying the first page after the contents page in magazines, and it used color printing as soon as it was available. By 1911, Campbell's was one of the first American companies to market a brand-name food product nationally.

The two chubby-cheeked, round-eyed Campbell's Kids, created by Grayce Gebbie Drayton, first appeared in 1904—the same year that Campbell's Pork & Beans was introduced. In 1905, the company name changed to Joseph Campbell Company.

Over a million souvenir postcards of the no-necks/ears/profiles/names Kids were produced in 1910. The Kids became a staple of Campbell's advertising, and children of the day collected the kids' ads as well as any premium they could get their hands on. Through the years, the red-and-white can, immortalized by pop artist Andy Warhol, has changed very little.

The company began producing Franco-American products after acquiring the New Jersey company in 1915. In 1923, the company was changed to Campbell Soup Company.

Other products made under the Campbell aegis include Campbell's Tomato Juice (1932), V-8 Cocktail Juice (1948), Swanson Frozen Dinners (1955), Pepperidge Farm products (1961), Godiva candies (1974), Mrs. Paul's Kitchens, Inc. products (1982), LeMenu products (1986), and Vlasic Pickles (1978).

Campbell's advertising history includes recipe books, advertising cards, colorful ads (including all of the Campbell's Kids ads), many different types of dolls, and television and radio ads. The Center for Advertising History in Washington, D.C., holds the Campbell Soup Collection, and there is a club for collectors: The International G. G. Drayton Association, 649 Bayview Drive, Akron, OH 44319.

CAMPBELL'S

Campbell's, dolls; made of cloth; approximately 15 inches tall; the pair wear red clothes; near-mint condition; $95–125.

Campbell's, dolls; pair of Campbell's Kids dolls; approximately 8 inches tall; plastic; dressed in red outfits; excellent condition; $80–100.

Campbell's, dolls; the Campbell's Kids pair in Colonial dress; approximately 10 inches tall; rubber; near-mint condition; $150–200 for the pair.

Campbell's, electric can opener; in the shape and design of the Campbell's soup can; ca. 1970s; approximately 8 inches tall; excellent condition; $25–45.

Campbell's, mug; ceramic; ca. 1960s; excellent condition; $8–12.

Campbell's, tin sign; reproduction; depicts Campbell's Kids going to school; 10½ x 16 inches; $15 retail. *Courtesy of Doc Davis/Antique-Alike. Photo by Donald Vogt.*

Campbell's, sign; depicts American flag made up of Campbell's soup cans; 40 x 26 inches; few examples are known because of the controversy the sign raised; manufactured by Standard Advertising Company of Coshocton, Ohio; excellent condition; $65,000–95,000.

Campbell's, tin sign; reproduction; depicts Campbell's Kids going to school; 10½ x 16 inches; $15 retail.

Campbell's, soup mug; plastic; ca. 1980s; excellent condition; $6–10.

Campbell's, thermos; holds approximately 12 fluid ounces; red cap; ca. 1960s; excellent condition; $18–22.

Campbell's, wooden box; approximately 16 x 24 inches; used to ship cases of soup; marked with maker's name and address in Napolean, Ohio; excellent condition; $38–42.

HEINZ

(*see also* "Heinz" in Condiments/Spices chapter)
Heinz Soups, enameled metal sign; two-sided; red, white, and black; very good condition; $300–600.

Heinz Soups, tin sign; depicts Colonial waiter carrying bowl in center of sign and names of soups on both sides of inset; 15½ x 6½ inches; reproduction; $15 retail.

CHAPTER FORTY-TWO
■ STORE FIXTURES ■

BARBER POLES
(*see also* "General Information" in Bits 'n Pieces)
Barber Pole, wooden; figural newel post; 5½ inch diameter x 74 inches; fair/good condition; $200–400.

CASES
Cattaraugus Cutlery; small oak trapezoidal display case for forged cutlery; 18 x 11½ x 4½ inches; very good condition; $150–300.

Country store ribbon case; multiwindowed; missing interior shelving; oak; 23 x 48 x 25½ inches; excellent condition; $300–500.

Sandford's Inc., display case; gold-leafed wood-and-glass store case; 22 x 36 x 9½ inches; very good condition (shelves missing); $400–600.

Display-front store counter; twenty-seven glass-fronted removable display drawers; 120 x 36 x 25½ inches; dark-stained oak; very good condition; $800–1,200.

Glass-and-oak cheese display cabinet; 22 x 20¼ x 22 inches; very good original condition; $250–500.

Glass-fronted display store counter; unusual four-glass-doored display cabinets on multidrawer store counter; 121 x 36 x 25 inches; fair/good condition, some glass broken, original condition, some wear, cracks in wood; $300–700.

Nut and bolt wooden cabinet; octagonal; revolving store case with multiple drawers and porcelain handles; 24 x 44 inches; good condition, original with all drawers; $400–800.

Oak-and-glass display case; 21½ x 13½ x 24 inches; very good original condition; $200–500.

Oak-and-glass display case; small case with the letters "ABE" stenciled in gold leaf; shelved interior; 151 x 19½ x 8 inches; good overall condition; $150–300.

Oak display case; horizontal oak-and-glass raised-pedestal showcase; 72 x 42 x 26 inches; very good original condition, two glass tops missing; $200–400.

Showcase, small and curved; 18½ x 10 x 12 inches; good original condition; $400–600.

COUNTERS
Grain bin and store counter; four curved-glass grain bin displays and raised-panel oak store counter; 90 x 34 x 34 inches; fair original condition, some panels and styles missing, curved glass complete, age cracks; $800–1,200.

DISPLAYS
General grocery tin display; three-dimensional; shows children buying products from the stocked store; shelves contain sample-size cardboard boxes for various products; 22 x 14 x 8 inches when opened; very good condition, minor use wear and soiling; $300–600.

JARS
Barsam Brothers, glass store jar; octagonal; 9 x 12 inches including lid; excellent condition, slight wear; $125–225.

LAMPS
Exit glass lamp; ruby glass exit globe on wall fixture; globe is approximately 5½ inches triangular x 6 inches excluding fixture; excellent condition; $100–225.

REGISTERS
National Brass, cash register; early nickel-over-brass No. 30 register with original marque and complete interior; 8½ x 22 x 15 inches; very good original condition, green overpaint, some keys missing numbers, slight fade to register tabs; $1,000–1,500.

SAFES
Salamander Safes, embossed brass plaque; interesting figural casting, possibly to mount on safes themselves or to wall mount; 7½ x 5¼ x ½ inches; good condition; $75–125.

SCALES
Caille Washington Scale; full-size 1 cent wood and iron-trimmed scale by an early coin-op manufacturer from Detroit; 22 x 76 x 28 inch-

es; good as-found condition, missing cast-iron ornamental faceplate, overpainted with red, missing back; $2,000–5,000.

Howe Scale, paper sign; woman standing on platform scale; printed by "Donaldson Brothers Lith."; ca. 1889; 14½ x 28½ inches excluding mat and frame; good condition, good colors, some horizontal creasing, tears at edges; $250–500.

Mills One-Cent Scale; ornate cast-iron and porcelain platform scale; retains original marque; distributed by American Automatic Sales, New Hampshire; 16 x 69 x 24 inches; good condition; $700–1,200.

SHOWCASE

Countertop showcase with cash drawer; glass and oak; 11¼ x 53¾ x 21½ inches; three showcase compartments; middle compartment is half high with cash drawer below; excellent condition; $250–350.

Slant-front showcase; glass and mahogany; 24 x 75 x 10¼ inches; ca. 1890; countertop size; adjustable shelves; excellent condition; $200–400.

Rolled-front showcase; unusual stained-glass curved-front showcase with vertical display above; 24 x 34½ x 24 inches; very good original condition; $275–475.

SIGNS

Geo. D. Getty/City Drug Store, sign; approximately 3 feet x 30 inches; depicts apothecary mortar and pestle in left-hand corner; ca. 1870s; excellent condition; $10,000–15,000.

SLOT MACHINES

Mills Twenty-Five-Cent Watermelon Hightop; ca. 1940s; slot machine with watermelon feature; two/five payout; 16 x 26 x 16 inches; good condition, original with key and working; $1,000–1,500.

SPOOL CABINETS

Spool cabinet and desk; six-drawer spool cabinet and lift-top leather-inlaid oak desk; 33 x 16 x 23 inches; fair/good condition, original darkened surface, soiling, bracket back missing; $300–600.

STRAW HOLDERS

Glass straw holder; unusual narrow blown-footed straw holder with original insert and lid; includes old straws; near-mint condition, some age discoloration; $200–400.

STORE FIXTURES ■ 415

VENDORS

Mills Postage Stamps, vendor; patriotic motif on this cast-metal-fronted oak case; two-column vendor for 2 cent and 1 cent stamps; ca. 1915; 7 x 22 x 9 inches; excellent original condition, minor paint chips, includes key, original finish to wood; $1,800–2,400.

One-cent Dixie cup dispenser; coin-operated Dixie-Vortex Co. iron-and-glass dispenser; in original condition with keys; 4 x 31 inches; very good condition; $200–400.

One-cent match machine; glass dome and oak-cased vendor with cigar cutter attachment; 11 x 18 x 10 inches; fair/good original condition, cloth fringe over carousel missing, one marquee card missing, wood separations, general wear; $300–600.

CHAPTER FORTY-THREE
■ STORES ■

A & P
(The Great Atlantic & Pacific Tea Company)

In 1859, George Huntington Hartford of Augusta, Maine, headed to New York City to make his fortune. He planned to buy tea by the shipful and sell it at dockside for one third what everyone else was charging. He succeeded immediately and opened a store on Vesey Street in Manhattan, where a Saturday night brass band lured in new clients. Soon, the store began to be recognized as Hartford determined its original goal—to sell food at discount prices. He added coffee to the grocery line, started advertising nationally, then hired Wells Fargo wagons to distribute his wares.

When the first coast-to-coast rail service allowed him the opportunity to sell his products nationally, he began calling his stores "The Great Atlantic and Pacific Tea Co." But the stores were not established on the West Coast until after Hartford's demise in 1917.

A & P

A & P Tea Company, cardboard calendar; 1903; intricate store card displays shopkeeper surrounded by products and patrons; vignettes of people using products; full calendar pad below; approximately 10 x 13¾ inches excluding mat and frame; overall 15¼ x 19 inches; excellent condition, some minor paper loss; $75–150.

A & P, color die-cut card; black boy sitting on basket holding baskets of flowers and a card that says "Compliments of the Great Atlantic & Pacific Tea Co., N.Y."; ca. late 1800s; good condition; $150–200.

A & P, paper sign; depicts early America's rush to work; titled "Ten Minutes for Refreshments"; from the Great Atlantic & Pacific Tea & Coffee Co.; ca. 1886; 32 x 22 inches excluding frame; good/very good condition, some overall age discoloration, foxing, minor water staining and wood staining; $750–1,500.

A & P, slip-top canister; printed by Ginna & Co.; ca. 1880s; depicts grandmotherly-type woman in insert who states "A & P's Teas and Coffees have been my Solace through Life"; 11 x 7 x 7 inches; very good condition; $150–200.

AMERICAN STORES
American Stores, paper calendar; depicts children dressed in Colonial clothes; thirteen-starred flag; 1932 calendar; approximately 12 x 25 inches excluding mat and frame; overall 17½ x 30¾ inches; very good condition; $25–100.

IGA
IGA Stores, porcelain sign; states store name; 17 feet long; good condition; $575–625.

IGA, porcelain sign; in shape of shield with eagle depicted in center; large; very good condition; $50–100.

LORD & TAYLOR
Lord & Taylor, Christmas catalog, 1946; features Christmas tree pop-up inside; excellent condition; $35–45.

MAY COMPANY
May Company, tip tray; 4¼ inches; ca. 1910; depicts beautiful woman advertising "Ohio's Largest Department Store"; near-mint condition; $65–115.

WALGREEN'S
In business since 1901, Walgreen's was founded by Charles R. Walgreen and the company has been controlled by the Walgreen family ever since.

Up until the early 1980s, the stores operated soda fountains as well as pharmacies—by the 1950s, Walgreen's was the largest United States drugstore operation to still have soda fountains. Records prove that Walgreen's sold more ice cream, malts, and sundaes than any retailer. With the advent of fast-food chains, the soda fountains disappeared, but many objects produced to run the fountains are available to collectors.

Walgreen memorabilia includes ice cream products, drugs, golf balls, toys, and many other interesting items. Over 1,800

418 ■ ADVERTISING

Walgreen's, ice cream truck; made as toy for children; manufactured by Mark Toys; steel; 20½ x 7 x 4 inches; white with blue letters; 1950; very good condition; $200–300. *From the collection of and photo by W. Gordon Addington.*

stores are currently operating from coast to coast, and by the year 2000, that total will be over 3,000.

WALGREEN'S

Walgreen's, ice cream truck; made as toy for children; manufactured by Mark Toys; steel; 20½ x 7 x 4 inches; white with blue letters; 1950; very good condition; $200–300.

Walgreen's, Malted Milk backbar sign; hung behind the soda fountain (only one known by collector—though thousands were made); 47 x 25 x 3 inches; malted brown, yellow, red, and cream; weighs 25 pounds; wood with glass; 1935; excellent condition; $400–600.

Walgreen's, Malted Milk can; 25 pounds; used to ship malted mix to soda fountains; 13 x 9½ x 9½ inches; orange, cream, black; inset picture of malted and cookie; 1935; very good condition; $200–300.

Walgreen's, Malted Milk backbar sign; hung behind the soda fountain (only one known by collector—though thousands were made); 47 x 25 x 3 inches; malted brown, yellow, red, and cream; weighs 25 pounds; wood with glass; 1935; excellent condition; $400–600. *From the collection of and photo by W. Gordon Addington.*

Walgreen's, Malted Milk can; 25 pounds; used to ship malted mix to soda fountains; 13 x 9½ x 9½ inches; orange, cream, black; inset picture of malted and cookie; 1935; very good condition; $200–300. *From the collection of and photo by W. Gordon Addington.*

WOOLWORTH'S

Frank Winfield Woolworth, age fifty-nine, announced he had the capital behind him to open a new corporation on November 2, 1912. He would call the company the F. W. Woolworth Company, and all his storefronts would be uniformly painted in scarlet and gold. The corporation was the coming together of a group of stores, some owned by Frank's cousin, Seymour Knox (98 in the United States and Canada); some owned by Frank's younger brother, Charles (15); some owned by Earle Charlton (35 in the United States, 18 in Canada); some owned by Frank Kirby (96); the original (in Watertown, New York), owned by William Moore; and Frank's own 319 stores in the United States and 12 in England.

For all his business sense, F. W. Woolworth did not trust paid advertising. He let the no-nonsense store window signs tell the story and it worked. Under the self-made millionaire's guidance, the Woolworth corporation thrived, turning the rest of the family into millionaires as well. Remember Barbara Hutton, the woman who made news by marrying actor Cary Grant? She was part of the Woolworth family. By the time Hutton divorced Grant in 1945, there were 5,848 Woolworth stores, with yearly sales totaling $477 million. A few husbands later, Barbara Woolworth...Hutton...Grant...died in 1978 and was buried as the last Woolworth heir to be involved with the corporation. The company was then taken over by the Toronto-based conglomerate Branscan Limited.

420 ■ ADVERTISING

Woolworth's, advertisement from *Better Homes and Gardens*, November 1953; depicts Hubley toys for Christmas, $8–10. *Courtesy of Paper Lady/Bernie and Dolores Fee. Photo by Donald Vogt.*

F. W. WOOLWORTH

Woolworth's, advertisement from *Better Homes and Gardens*, November 1953; depicts Hubley Toys for Christmas; $8–10.

F. W. Woolworth, memorabilia (2 pieces); photograph of the Webster, Massachusetts, store in 1915 and the lease for that store, signed by "F. W. Woolworth"; excellent condition; $100–200.

CHAPTER FORTY-FOUR
STOVES

BLACK CAT
Black Cat Stove Polish, bottle; 6 ounces; made by J. L. Prescott Co., Passaic, New Jersey; label has red background, white letters trimmed in black; black cat with red bow around neck; ca. 1920s; excellent condition; $20–25.

BLACK IRON
Black Iron Stove Polish, bottle; 12 ounces; orange-and-black label with stove on label; made by J. L. Prescott, Passaic, New Jersey; ca. 1890s; very good condition; $8–12.

BORN STEEL
Born Steel Range, match safe; picture of range; black, white, and red lettering; ca. 1920s; excellent condition; $175–225.

The Born Steel Range and Mfg. Co., paperweight; ca. 1890–1910; depicts the stove; made in Cleveland, Ohio; 2½ x 4 inches; excellent condition; $50–75.

BUCK'S
Buck's Junior-2, salesman's sample cookstove; unusual configuration on raised legs; includes several miniature utensils, including fry pans and sauce pans; rare; 22 x 23 x 11 inches excluding stovepipe; excellent/near-mint condition; $2,500–3,500.

BUFFALO COOPERATIVE
Buffalo Cooperative Stove Co., paperweight; ca. 1890–1910; for Amherst Stoves and Furnaces; depicts the stove; 2½ x 4 inches; excellent condition; $50–75.

CLIMAX STOVES
Climax Stoves, tray; pictures trademarked flaming warrior standing on pedestal, which reads "The Taplin, Rice-Clerkin Co., Taplin, Ohio"; very good condition, background has some rust spotting and overall chipping; $50–100.

Black Cat Stove Polish, bottle; 6 ounces; made by J. L. Prescott Co., Passaic, New Jersey; label has red background, white letters trimmed in black; black cat with red bow around neck; ca. 1920s; excellent condition; $20–25. *Courtesy of Irreverent Relics. Photo by Donald Vogt.*

Born Steel Range, match safe; picture of range; black, white, and red lettering; ca. 1920s; $175–225. *Courtesy of Marilyn and De Underwood/Tins Again Collectibles. Photo by Donald Vogt.*

The Born Steel Range and Mfg. Co., paperweight; ca. 1890–1910; depicts the stove; made in Cleveland, Ohio; 2½ x 4 inches; $50–75. *From the collection of Stuart Kammerman. Photo by David Kammerman.*

Buffalo Cooperative Stove Co., paperweight; ca. 1890–1910; for Amherst Stoves and Furnaces; depicts the stove; 2½ x 4 inches; $50–75. *From the collection of Stuart Kammerman. Photo by David Kammerman.*

DETROIT STOVE WORKS

Detroit Stove Works, self-framed tin sign; panoramic view of factory for producers of Jewel stoves and ranges; 37¼ x 13 inches; good condition; $100–300.

DOE-WAH-JAK

Doe-Wah-Jak Stove, embossed cardboard sign; unusual vertical full standing image of Indian with peace pipe and beaded logo for Round Oak stove advertisement on this later photo offset issue; 8¼ x 23½ inches; near-mint condition, very minor soiling; $200–400.

GLENWOOD

Glenwood, wood-and-sand sign; large store stove advertisement; raised gold leaf letters on sand-coated tin insert; promotes the "Best Stoves Sold"; 14 feet x 22 x 3 inches; good condition, general wear overall, some splitting to wood due to age; $500–1,000.

HAPPY THOUGHT FOUNDRY CO.

Treasure Stove, tip trays (2); slight color variation to these two complimentary trays picturing a kitchen range; 4¼ inch diameter each; made by Happy Thought Foundry Co., Brantford, Canada; very good/excellent condition, minor overall wear, slight scratching; $75–150.

HOME COMFORT

The Home Comfort line of ranges and stoves was sold by traveling salesmen from the backs of wagons that took them around the country. Obviously, the ranges were too heavy to be carried on the wagons themselves, so the salespeople carried scaled-down samples, much easier to carry—and to sell.

An 1892 advertisement in magazines and newspapers advertised the "latest improved style No. 64."

HOME COMFORT

Home Comfort, advertisement from *Ladies' Home Journal*, November 1906; advertises the Perfection Oil Heater; black and white; excellent condition; $5–10.

INCANDESCENT LIGHT & STOVE CO.

Incandescent Light & Stove Co., tip tray; illustrates interior scene of mother cooking at stove, child playing with blocks on floor behind; 4¼ inch diameter; excellent condition, minor wear and rim chips; $50–100.

Home Comfort, advertisement from *Ladies' Home Journal*, November 1906; advertises the Perfection Oil Heater; black and white; $5–10. *Courtesy of Paper Lady/Bernie and Dolores Fee. Photo by Donald Vogt.*

424 ■ ADVERTISING

Isaac A. Sheppard & Co., paperweight; ca. 1890–1910; company made Paragon furnaces; offices in Philadelphia and Baltimore; 2½ x 4 inches; $50–75. *From the collection of Stuart Kammerman. Photo by David Kammerman.*

ISAAC A. SHEPPARD & CO.

Isaac A. Sheppard & Co., paperweight; ca. 1890–1910; company made Paragon furnaces; offices in Philadelphia and Baltimore; 2½ x 4 inches; excellent condition; $50–75.

JEWEL STOVES

Jewel Stoves, match safes (2); woman cooking with pictured product; duplicate pair of interesting strikers; made by Burrow, Stewert & Milne Co., Hamilton, Canada; 4¼ x 5½ x 1 inch each; very good overall condition; $300–475.

D. MOORE CO.

D. Moore Co., Home Treasure Stoves and Ranges, tip tray; irregular embossed-edge tray picturing woman cooking at kitchen range; made by D. Moore Co.; Hamilton, Ontario, Canada; 6 x 4 inches; good condition, general overall wear, some paint loss to stove highlights, burn spots; $25–75.

D. Moore Co., Treasure Stoves and Ranges, tip tray; oval tray picturing cooking range and base-burner stove flanking factory; D. Moore Co.; Hamilton, Ontario, Canada; 7 x 4 inches; very good condition, some rust spotting primarily to background, slight overall wear; $75–150.

D. Moore Co., Treasure Line Stoves, tip tray; early dual image of woman at fancy cookstove in kitchen and fancy heat stove in parlor, slight variation of interior scenes in comparison to tray below; made by the D. Moore Co.; Hamilton, Ontario, Canada; 7½ x 4¼ inches; very good/excellent condition, minor chipping primarily to edges; $100–200.

NEW EMPIRE

New Empire, paper sign; large poster that reads "New Empire Base Burning Cooking Stove"; 20 x 28 inches excluding mat and frame; early C. H. Crosby lithograph; excellent condition; $800–1,200.

NOON DAY STOVES

Noon Day Stove Polish, paper sign; depicts woman polishing iron stove, dog and baby see reflection, while grandmother and dog owner look on; period objects on mantlepiece and in background; slice of 1870s life; 17 x 21½ inches; excellent condition, minor edge tear, slight overall yellowing due to coated stock aging, minor paper loss in border; $3,500–5,000.

PAT. WOOD BOX STOVE POLISH

Pat. Wood Box Stove Polish, paper label; depicts a man polishing his shoes while woman is polishing the stove—each extols a Pat. Wood Box product; 9¾ x 8¼ inches; very good condition, slight fading, borders trimmed; $125–250.

RISING SUN

Rising Sun Stove Polish, paper sign; colorful lady leaning over railing surrounded by roses with factory in background; 13 x 29¼ inches; very good condition, crisp colors; $500–1,000.

ROYAL STOVES

Royal Stoves, tip tray; embossed bent-rim tip picturing a Royal kitchen range, unusual piece; made by Westman Bros.; Chatham, Ontario, Canada; 3 x 3¾ inches; good condition, damage primarily to right foot and surrounding background at five o'clock of image; $75–150.

SAPOLIN

Sapolin Enamel Stove Paint, tin sign; three-dimensional sign featuring additions to stove top and furnace boiler; 17½ x 24½ inches; good condition, some scratching and chipping; $275–375.

TREASURE LINE

Treasure Line Stoves and Ranges, tin shovel; unusual advertising promotion; with lithographed image of woman cooking at kitchen range ("Home Treasure") next to fancy heat stove ("Art Treasure"); 4 x 9¼ inches; excellent condition, minor scratches, minor soiling; $300–600.

Treasure Line Stoves and Ranges, tin shovel; advertising promotion; with image of fancy cookstove ("Othello Treasure"); 4 x 9¼ inches; very good condition, minor wear primarily to bottom of shovel, slight scratching; $300–500.

UNCLE SAM

Uncle Sam Range, paper sign; depicts a variety of patriotic symbols (Lady Liberty, eagle, the sections of the United States—Dixie, the West, New England); also black man cooking turkey on elaborate stove for this centennial (1876) dinner; printed by Schumacher & Ettlinger Lith. Co.; 20½ x 13¼ inches; excellent condition, borders trimmed, minor corner loss lower left, slight overall soiling; $5,000–10,000.

CHAPTER FORTY-FIVE
■ TEA ■

BAIRD & PETERS
Baird & Peters Tea, figural tin; house-shaped; with glass windows to display contents; unique hinged door opens; rare piece, especially with chimney intact; 9 x 8 x 5¾ inches; good/very good condition overall, some chipping and scratching, minor denting; $200–500.

BANQUET
Banquet Tea, brown ceramic figural pot; lettering reads "A Wonderful Flavor Iced or Hot" on both sides; 9½ x 10 inches; very good overall condition; $100–200.

BEN HUR
Ben Hur Tea, tin; shows Lew Wallace's hero driving a chariot on front; opposite side shows medals; 6¼ x 7 x 7 inches; good condition; $100–300.

CASTLE BLEND
Castle Blend Tea, tins (2); both have multiple images of castles around sides; 6¼ x 7 x 6¼ inches each; good condition, overall general wear, some scratching and chipping; $100–175.

CHOICE FAMILY TEA
Choice Family Tea, store bin; stenciled with flowers and bee; made in Quebec, Canada; 10¼ x 13½ x 10¼ inches; good condition, general wear; $100–200.

CROWN DERBY
Crown Derby, store bin; large stenciled-front store container; 15 x 19½ x 15 inches; fair/good condition, general overall wear; $50–100.

EAGLE ORANGE PEKOE
Eagle Orange Pekoe, tin; ¼ pound; very good condition; $10–15.

FORBES BROTHERS
Forbes Brothers Tea, bin; made in St. Louis; slope front; litho of two horses on lower front; fair/good condition, general soiling and wear overall; $50–100.

Eagle Orange Pekoe, tin; ¼ pound; $10–15. *Courtesy of Bob Taylor. Photo by Donald Yogt.*

GREAT AMERICAN

Great American Tea, can; 2 pounds; early black over red; pictures New York store; 6 inch diameter x 7½ inches; good condition, some minor denting and chipping, overall soiling; $75–150.

HILLSIDE

Hillside Tea, store bin; red, black, and gold; made in Toronto, Canada; 13 x 13¼ x 13 inches; good condition, general overall wear, slight denting; $50–125.

HUDSON'S BAY

Hudson's Bay Tea, tin; "Hudson's Bay Company Tea"; in box form with hinged lift top; lithographed panels depict Upper Fort Garry (1835–1882) and Jack Canuck in the Northwest "today" and the Golden West; 4¼ x 6½ inches; good condition; $45–100.

IMPERIAL BLEND

Imperial Blend Tea, tins (3); ocean liner on all three; made in Hamilton, Brantsford, Woodstock, London, Toronto, and Peterboro; 6¼ x 4½ inches, 6½ x 7¼ x 4 inches, and 6½ x 7 x 6¾ inches; fair/good overall condition, some scratching and chipping, slight rubbing, minor denting; $50–150.

JAPAN

Japan Tea, large paper advertising parasol; Mastiffchop; very good condition; $150–200.

Japan Tea, store bin; early stencil and litho front store bin with lift lid; 13¼ x 16 x 15 inches; good condition, general overall soiling; $100–200.

JAVA

Java, bag; decorated in colorful Oriental style; excellent condition; $3–5.

LIPTON

The face seen on Lipton's packages is actually a sailor—Sir Thomas Lipton, who entered the America's Cup yacht races between 1899 and 1930. His reputation as a tea drinker was celebrated in 1931 when Will Rogers wrote the *New York Times* and suggested the paper's readers pitch in to buy a cup of tea for the "world's most cheerful loser."

Born in Scotland, Lipton came to America to earn his fortune, then returned to Glasgow to open a successful grocery store chain. His tea business began when he sailed to Ceylon in 1891 and purchased every tea plantation available. Instead of putting his tea in traditional teak chests, Lipton packaged it in tins and packages, put his name on his product, and soon became well-known as a purveyor of the popular beverage. He became so famous that Queen Victoria knighted him in 1898.

Lipton's company grew, even after his death in 1931. By 1940, Lipton's began selling dried soup mixes, and in 1952, it introduced the "Flo-Thru" tea bag. One of Arthur Godfrey's listeners was responsible for a new use for Lipton's Onion Soup in the 1950s—the California Dip.

LIPTON

Lipton Tea, paper sign; depicts a Victorian lady with a full tea set in front of her; approximately 36 x 24 inches; very good condition, some dog-eared corners; $175–325.

Lipton Tea, paper sign; depicts can of product at the bottom and women from all over the world in a smokelike question mark; caption reads "Lipton's Teas Famous the World Over/Have *You* Enjoyed Them"; ca. 1901; approximately 20 x 14 inches; full color; $700–1,100.

Lipton Tea, tin; 1 pound; depicts the famous sailor on front; paper label; very good condition; $15–25.

MONARCH

Monarch Tea, tin; 4 ounces; copyright 1923; chromolithographed; excellent condition; $24–34.

NESTEA
(see "Nestlé" in Candy chapter)

OWL CHOP
Owl Chop Teas, tin; unusual; ornate owl motif logo and hinged lid; made in Montreal, Canada; 7 x 9 x 4½ inches; good condition, slight overall fade, minor denting, scratches; $75–125.

ROSE MARIE
Rose Marie Tea, tin; ½ pound; very good condition; $10–15.

SAHIB
Sahib, various sizes in tin and cardboard; ca. 1930; $18–30.

SALADA TEA
One of the best excuses to drink Salada Tea is that there's a fortune in every cup—not money, mind you, but a little piece of philosophy. John W. Colpitts, an adman, had the idea for Salada's folksy tea tag sayings including "To avoid that run-down feeling, cross streets carefully"), but the name of the company came from the name of a small Indian tea garden.

Peter C. Larkin of Canada founded the company in the late 1880s when he packaged Ceylon tea and called it the "Golden Tea Pot Blend" of the Salada Ceylon Tea Company Ltd.

Rose Marie Tea, tin; ½ pound; $10–15. *Courtesy of Bob Taylor. Photo by Donald Vogt.*

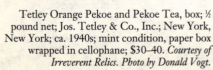

Tetley Orange Pekoe and Pekoe Tea, box; ½ pound net; Jos. Tetley & Co., Inc.; New York, New York; ca. 1940s; mint condition, paper box wrapped in cellophane; $30–40. *Courtesy of Irreverent Relics. Photo by Donald Vogt.*

At first the tea was packaged by hand, but Larkin soon recognized that the process was too slow, so he invented and perfected a semiautomatic tea-packing machine, which he later sold all over the world. When Larkin became Canadian High Commissioner to Britain, his son, Gerald, took over the business.

Shirriff-Horsey bought Salada in 1957 and changed the company name to Salada-Shirriff-Horsey.

SALADA

Salada Tea, door push; ca. 1950s; approximately 34 x 3 inches; excellent condition; $50–75.

Salada Tea, shelf strip and porcelain door push bar; shelf strip ca. 1950s, 14 x 1 inch; excellent condition; $15–25.

SALMON'S

Salmon's Tea, tin; unusual small tin with picture of fish; 2 x ¾ x 2½ inches; good condition; $75–150.

STERLING

Sterling Tea, store bin; offset photos of Quebec landmark inserts on four sides; 8¾ x 11¼ x 8¼ inches; good condition, some chipping, overall wear, slight denting, hinged lid partially lifting; $250–450.

TEA HOUSE TEA

(*see* "McCormick" in Condiments/Spices chapter)

TETLEY

Tetley Orange Pekoe and Pekoe Tea, box; ½ pound net; Jos. Tetley & Co., Inc.; New York, New York; ca. 1940s; mint condition, paper box wrapped in cellophane; $30–40.

UNION PACIFIC

Union Pacific Tea, tin tray; depicts multiple images in border of large bear, little girl, little boy, and snowman, with large image of little girl with pink bow in her hair in the center; 8 inch diameter; very good overall condition; $50–100.

CHAPTER FORTY-SIX
◼ TIMEPIECES ◼

BIG BEN CLOCKS
Big Ben Clocks were originally sold via mail order, but as their popularity grew, the company turned to selling its clocks at retail.

BIG BEN
Big Ben Clock, tin sign; American Art Works; embossed oval picturing clock; 13 x 19 inches; fair condition, some whiting to background, slight fading to color, overall soiling, some scratches; $225–425.

BULOVA
Bulova Clock, sign; advertises "Gerry Jewelers"; 17 inch diameter; good condition; $75–150.

Bulova Watches, paper poster; depicts Santa with Bulova watches on sale at Siegels on "South Side"; "terms as low as 50 cents week"; ca. 1950s; 28 x 11 inches; very good condition; $40–60.

ELGIN
Elgin Watches, clock; advertises "James Jewelry"; no numbers; approximately 15 inch diameter; excellent condition; $125–175.

Elgin's Clock; jeweler's clock from 1920s; neon; clock at bottom, faceted diamond on top; excellent condition; $1,200–1,500.

Elgin, wood sign; lithographed color transfer of Elgin Watch Boy in tattered clothing; lettering reads "My Elgin's All Right"; 15 x 22 inches; very good condition, slight chipping, small scratches primarily in background; small veneer loss at edges; $200–550.

HAMILTON
Hamilton Watch, tin sign; colorful image of small child; 13 x 19 inches; good condition, some denting, rust spotting, chipping overall; $200–300.

TIMEPIECES ■ 433

ILLINOIS
Illinois Watch Co., reverse glass sign; depicts locomotive and tender in gold and black; 1925; 20 x 12 inches excluding frame; excellent condition; $100–250.

Illinois Watches, sign; classic image of railroad engineer with oiling can and Springfield watch; "Always on Time"; 13 x 19 inches; good condition, soiling, some scratches and wear; $400–600.

MISCELLANEOUS
Watches and clocks, wood sign; hand-painted early jeweler's sign; 21 x 13 inches; very good/excellent condition; $25–100.

SOUTH BEND
South Bend Watch, tin sign; pocket watch in ice cube on woodgrain background; 13 x 19 inches; excellent condition, some minor scratches, slight denting; $325–425.

WALTHAM WATCHES
A 1917 advertisement shows the Czar of Russia using a Waltham watch to see whether or not Russia's trains are on time.

WALTHAM
Waltham Chronographs, advertisement from *Keystone* (jeweler's guide), 1916; depicts racetrack; black and white; $12–15.

Waltham Clocks, advertisement from *Review of Reviews*, 1918; full color; depicts couple dressed for formal evening passing grandfather clock at end of staircase; $5–10.

Waltham Chronographs, advertisement from *Keystone* (jeweler's guide), 1916; depicts racetrack; black and white; $12–15. *Courtesy of Paper Lady/Bernie and Dolores Fee. Photo by Donald Vogt.*

434 ■ ADVERTISING

Waltham Clocks, advertisement from *Review of Reviews*, 1918; full color; depicts couple dressed for formal evening passing grandfather clock at end of staircase; $5–10. *Courtesy of Paper Lady/Bernie and Dolores Fee. Photo by Donald Vogt.*

Waltham Watches, advertisement from *Liberty*, 1916; full color; depicts riverside on Charles River; $8–10.

WESTCLOX

Westclox, die-cut cardboard pocket watch display; father and son arriving at work; "Right on the Dot"; display includes three original pocket watches; 29 x 24 inches; very good condition, minor soiling and wrinkling, watches appear working; $75–150.

CHAPTER FORTY-SEVEN
■ TOBACCO ■

GENERAL INFORMATION

After years of producing tobacco-related products, the industry experienced enormous change in the post–World War II years. Television affected the industry with its power as an advertising medium, filter-tip cigarettes were introduced, and the controversial health effects of smoking were recognized.

Obviously, the change in the way Americans look at the tobacco industry will have an effect on what is produced—and the trickle-down theory will be in full force, meaning the items produced *today* will be collectible *tomorrow*.

ABBEY TOBACCO

Abbey Tobacco, upright pocket tin; pictures Gothic cathedrals on both sides; made in Hamilton, Canada; 3 x 3 x ¾ inches; very good/excellent condition, pinpoint spotting, slight scratching, discoloration to lid; $125–175.

ADVANCE AGENT

Advance Agent Cigar, canister; pictures Lindbergh's historical flight; 5 inch diameter x 5 inches; fair condition, slight fade, overall wear with chipping and denting; $25–75.

Advance Agent Cigar, Liberty tin; pictures Lindbergh's flight from New York to Paris; 4½ inch diameter x 5¼ inches; good condition, minor chipping and scuffing, overall general fading; $150–250.

AMERICAN TOBACCO COMPANY

John Ruffin Green of Durham's Station, North Carolina, the enterprising man who processed a variety of "bright tobacco" during the final years of the Civil War, sold his product in small cloth bags decorated with a bull on the side. Green's tobacco was so popular, soldiers contacted him after the war to see if they could continue to purchase it. Bull Durham Tobacco, as Green's product became known, grew even more popular when Green spent over $200,000 on advertising and premiums in the

1880s. By mid-century, his company had become the largest tobacco processor in the world.

Green spent almost a million dollars on advertising his new prefabricated cigarette, yet he still felt the effects of his competitors. Thus, in 1890, five of the cigarette producers joined to become the American Tobacco Company—an unbeatable entity. The American Tobacco Company was one of the most prolific advertisers of the 1890s. One of the mediums the company used was a series of picture cards that were inserted into cigarette packs. In order to get a complete deck of what American called "Sporting Girls," a smoker had to collect and redeem seventy-five premium certificates. James Buchanan Duke ("Buck" Duke) of Durham, North Carolina, was the genius behind the idea.

The company beat all its competitors—even the smallest ones—and angered so many people that the government split it up in 1911. By World War I, the Bull Durham company grew to immense popularity—even to the point where the United States government requested the company's entire output so the government could supply the troops.

The American Tobacco Company then became one of three companies that resulted from the government's intervention—Liggett & Myers and P. Lorillard were the other two companies born of the breakup.

When the R. J. Reynolds company surprised the other tobacco companies by introducing Camel cigarettes, George Washington Hill (head of the American Tobacco Company) retaliated with Lucky Strike cigarettes. He created a bull's-eye package design and the slogan "Lucky Strike, It's Toasted." By 1917, the cigarettes were being sold nationally.

Hill hired Albert J. Lasker, one of the advertising geniuses of that era, to help him advertise the new product. (Surprisingly, women ended up being Luckies' best customers.) Lasker's idea of promoting Luckies included getting celebrity endorsements and assuring potential customers that Luckies were good for them ("No Throat Irritation, No Cough"). He also created so many slogans for the cigarettes that four or five were often injected into one ad or radio commercial. The one most people remember—"Lucky Strike Means Fine Tobacco"—was eventually shortened to simply "L.S.M.F.T." Lasker's unusual way of pushing the product worked. The company eventually passed the competition and was still leading the way in the cigarette industry in 1955.

AMERICAN
American Tobacco Company, paper sign; Wiley image of mustached cowboy smoking a cigar; one of a series of posters with bold advertising in background; 17½ x 25½ inches excluding frame; near-mint condition, colors bright, minor wrinkling to edges, minor edge tears; $200–400.

American Tobacco Company, paper sign; colorful image of equestrian gentleman smoking cigar; one of same series as above entry; 17½ x 25½ inches excluding frame; near-mint condition, minor scratching, some edge tears; $150–300.

American Tobacco Company, paper sign; 1899 version of Uncle Sam smoking Virginia cheroot; one of same series as above entries; 17½ x 25½ inches excluding frame; excellent/near-mint condition, several small edge tears, bright colors; $350–600.

American Tobacco Company, paper sign; colorful image of pubmaster smoking cigar on this 1899 version; one of same series as above entries; 18 x 25½ inches excluding frame; mint condition; $100–200.

AUTOBACCO
Autobacco Tobacco, tin; duster-decked driver; 6¼ x 4½ x 4 inches; good condition, some fade primarily to back, slight color distortion between lid and can, minor scratches; $25–75.

AVALON
Avalon Cigarettes, paper sign; near-mint condition; $5–20.

BELMONT
Belmont Tobacco, upright pocket tin; cube cut with crossed pipes over shield; made in Montreal, Canada; 3 x 4 x 1 inch; good condition, slight spotting of color, slight denting to back, wear to lid; $300–400.

BENEDICT
Benedict Cigars, cigar cutter and match striker; dual-handled; cast iron; 8 x 9 x 5½ inches; very good condition, some discoloration to original plating, minor rusting; $50–150.

BEN HUR
Ben Hur Cigars, sign; paper on cardboard; exciting image of horse-drawn chariots racing at the Roman Coliseum; 31½ x 22 inches excluding

frame; very good condition, several small holes primarily in sky, minor chipping, slight overspotting to surface; $300–500.

Ben Hur Cigars, sign on wood; biblical scene of wise man; 1904; transfer on guartered oak veneer board; 15 x 21 inches; good/very good condition, some minor chipping and scratches due to general wear, minor wrinkling of veneer at left edge; $100–300.

BENSON & HEDGES

Benson & Hedges, desktop clock; promotional; battery operated; ca. 1970s; excellent condition; $5–10.

BETWEEN THE ACTS

Between the Acts Cigar, cardboard trolley sign; 20 x 11 inches excluding frame; good condition, some edge tears; $25–100.

BIGGER HAIR

(*see also* "Nigger Hair")

Bigger Hair Smoking Tobacco, cardboard container; depicts black person with earrings in both ears and in nose (tobacco used to be called "Nigger Hair"); 5¼ x 6¼ inches; very good overall condition with some minor scratching and creasing; $100–200.

BIG WOLF

Big Wolf, label; chromolithographed inner lid cigar box label; "Title and Design owned by the James W. Smith Cigar Co.", ca. 1910s; 10 x 6¼ inches; mint condition; $5–7.

BLACK FOX

Black Fox Cigar, tin; logoed image of seated fox on red background for this rare cigar canister; London & Canada; 5¼ inch diameter x 5¼

Big Wolf, label; chromolithographed inner lid cigar box label; "Title and Design owned by the James W. Smith Cigar Co."; ca. 1910s; 10 x 6¼ inches; $5–7. *Courtesy of Cerebro Lithographs. Photo by Dawn Reno.*

inches; good condition, some denting to body, wear to lid resulting in fade and chipping; $200–400.

BOWL OF ROSES
Bowl of Roses Tobacco, tin; vivid colors with image of gentleman in leisure chair smoking pipe in front of fireplace; 3¼ inch diameter x 4 inches; excellent condition, some minor wear to the cover; $100–150.

BRIAR PIPE
Briar Pipe, store card; depicts black child holding two bags of labeled tobacco; 8 x 11/14 inch; very good condition, some overall wear and soiling; $125–275.

BULL DURHAM
(*see also* "American Tobacco Company")
Bull Durham Tobacco, cardboard sign; large bullfighting scene in original frame; 51½ x 33 inches including frame; good condition, some water staining primarily at bottom, creasing, minor chipping, veneer damage to frame; $400–600.

BULWARK
Bulwark Cut Plug, tin; sailor with telescope; 6¾ x 4 x 1½ inches; good condition, some scratching and appears to have small nail holes in side, paint loss on edges; $75–125.

BURLEY BOY
Burley Boy, upright pocket tin; 3½ x 4 x 1 inch; fair/good condition, overall fade, some spotting and chipping; $200–350.

BUSTER BROWN
Buster Brown Cigar, tin; great comical image on this colorful and desirable tin; 5 inch diameter x 5 inches; fair/good condition, some rust spotting, chipping, minor denting; $500–800.

CALABASH
Calabash Tobacco, embossed upright pocket tin; lettered logo on colorful tin; made in Montreal, Canada; 3½ x 4 x 1¼ inches; good condition, overall wear, some chipping primarily to embossed letters, lid edge, and under flap; $200–300.

CAMEL CIGARETTES
(*see also* "R. J. Reynolds Tobacco Company")

Camels, cardboard box; first one made to hold packages of cigarettes; good condition; $3–8.

Camel Cigarettes, lighter; depicts classic Camel box and contemporary Joe Camel figure; $2–5.

Camel Cigarettes, shower curtain; depicts the contemporary Joe Camel cartoon figure in various "tropical" poses; new; $25–35.

Camel Cigarettes, watch; depicts contemporary Joe Camel cartoon figure lounging on the beach in watch face; new; $25–50.

Camels, sign; advertises cigarettes with familiar camel logo (original dromedary); porcelain; yellow and brown; approximately 15 x 16 inches; very good condition; $60–80.

Camels, thermometer; made of tin; approximately 13 inches long; yellow and brown; excellent condition; $30–50.

Camels, tin; flat fifty; very good condition; $10–15.

CANNON'S
Cannon's Irish, pocket tin; 3½ x 3 inches; very good/excellent condition, some minor wear and some fading in spots; $75–150.

CAPTAIN CORKER
Captain Corker, cigar box label; ca. 1890s; approximately 4½ by 4½ inches; mint condition, "Lithographer George Schlegel, N.Y."; $12–15.

CHESTERFIELD CIGARETTES
(*see also* "Liggett & Myers Tobacco")
Chesterfield, door push plate; tin; green and red; approximately 3 x 8 inches; very good condition; $20–25.

Chesterfield Tobacco, pocket tin; gold and white; very good condition; $10–15.

Chesterfield, tin; flat fifty; green and red; good condition; $10–15.

CIGAR STORE FIGURES
Cigar Store Figure, chief with axe; made of white pine; polychrome wood; ca. 1860; from New York; made by John L. Cromwell (1805–1873); excellent condition; $20,000–25,000.

TOBACCO ■ 441

Cigar Store Figure, chief with axe; made of white pine; polychrome wood; ca. 1860; from New York; made by John L. Cromwell (1805–1873); $20,000–25,000. *From the collection of Mark Goldman. Photo by Lynne S. Goldman.*

Cigar Store Figure, Indian chief; blanket over right shoulder, holds tobacco leaves in left hand; made by Louis Jobin (1845–1908); from Canada; ca. 1875; $25,000–30,000. *From the collection of Mark Goldman. Photo by Lynne S. Goldman.*

Cigar Store Figure, chief; stands with one foot forward; bare-chested; holds tomahawk in right hand down by side; made of pine; ca. 1880; maker unknown; from New England; excellent condition; $25,000–30,000.

Cigar Store Figure, chief; wears blanket over shoulder; left arm folded across belly, right arm down at side (looks like it might have once have held a tomahawk); made of pine; ca. 1860; maker unknown; from New England; very good condition; $15,000–20,000.

Cigar Store Figure, Indian chief; blanket over right shoulder, holds tobacco leaves in left hand; made by Louis Jobin (1845–1908); from Canada; ca. 1875; excellent condition; $25,000–30,000.

Cigar Store Figure, Indian princess; wears short dress, carries tobacco leaves in right hand and lifts cigars in left; made of pine; maker unknown; from New York City; ca. 1860–1870; excellent condition; $30,000–35,000.

Cigar Store Figure, Indian princess; wears long-sleeved dress and blanket over shoulder, tall headdress, holds cigars in right hand; pine; maker unknown; from New York; ca. 1870; excellent condition; $25,000–30,000.

Cigar Store Figure, Indian princess; wears short dress, carries tobacco leaves in right hand and lifts cigars in left; made of pine; maker unknown; from New York City; ca. 1860–1870; $30,000–35,000. *From the collection of Mark Goldman. Photo by Lynne S. Goldman.*

Cigar Store Figure, Indian princess; holds cigars in front of stomach, wears simple shift-like dress, full headdress; pine; maker unknown; from New York city; ca. 1860; $20,000–25,000. *From the collection of Mark Goldman. Photo by Lynne S. Goldman.*

Cigar Store Figure, Indian princess; star in middle of forehead, holds cigars in right hand, wears boots; pine; maker unknown; from New York City; ca. 1850; $25,000–30,000. *From the collection of Mark Goldman. Photo by Lynne S. Goldman.*

Cigar Store Figure, Indian princess; arms missing, wears full headdress; pine; maker unknown; from New York City; ca. 1860; excellent condition; $8,000–10,000.

Cigar Store Figure, Indian princess; holds cigars in front of stomach, wears simple shiftlike dress, full headdress; pine; maker unknown; from New York City; ca. 1860; excellent condition; $20,000–25,000.

Cigar Store Figure, Indian princess; made by William Rush of Philadelphia; ca. 1830; excellent condition; $25,000–30,000.

Cigar Store Figure, Indian princess; star in middle of forehead, holds cigars in right hand, wears boots; pine; maker unknown; from New York City; ca. 1850; excellent condition; $25,000–30,000.

Cigar Store Figure, zinc Indian chief; 6 feet 7 inches tall; holds bow in left hand, arrow in right; wears long pants and blanket over shoulder; ca. 1880; made by "Wm. Demuth and Co., New York City"; $25,000–30,000. *From the collection of Mark Goldman. Photo by Lynne S. Goldman.*

Cigar Store Figures (2), Indian maidens; (left) zinc maiden, holds torchiere, made by "E. Selig, Brooklyn" ca. 1870, $10,000–15,000; (right) pine princess, made by "Wm. Demuth Co., New York City"; ca. 1870, $15,000–20,000. *From the collection of Mark Goldman. Photo by Lynne S. Goldman.*

Cigar Store Figure, Indian princess; holds tobacco leaves aloft in right hand; pine; unknown maker; from New York; ca. 1870; excellent condition; $20,000–23,000.

Cigar Store Figure, Indian chief; 6 feet 7 inches tall; holds bow in left hand, arrow in right; wears long pants and blanket over shoulder; ca. 1880; made by "Wm. Demuth and Co., New York City"; excellent condition; $25,000–30,000.

Cigar Store Figure, zinc Indian maiden, holds torchiere; made by "E. Selig, Brooklyn"; ca. 1870; excellent condition; $10,000–15,000.

Cigar Store Figure, pine Indian princess, made by "Wm. Demuth Co., New York City"; ca. 1870; excellent condition; $15,000–20,000.

CITADEL

Citadel Tobacco, tin; rare; much sought after; multiple-imaged ovoid tin with colorful images of Citadel and soldiers on four sides; interesting piece from Eagle Tobacco Works, Quebec; 4¾ x 6½ x 4 inches; good condition, some slight chipping and scratching, rust spotting; $750–1,250.

CLIMAX
Climax Golden Twins, tin; 1 pound; made by P. Lorillard Co.; golden color; ca. 1890s; very good condition; $8–10.

CONTINENTAL CUBES
Continental Cubes, pocket mirror; girl atop canister of pipe tobacco; 1¾ x 2¾ inches; excellent condition, minor wear to surface; $100–200.

CROSS-CUT CIGARETTES
Cross-Cut Cigarettes, small cardboard box; name of product is written on saw placed diagonally across package; trademarked image of men sawing; includes eight photo insert cards of females; 1½ x 3 x ¼ inch; excellent condition, some staining and creasing; $50–100.

CYCLONE
Cyclone Twister Five Cent Cigars, hanging cardboard sign; full-color lithograph; depicts the cyclone twister ripping through the wilderness; 9 x 11 inches; near-mint condition; $40–50.

DAN PATCH
Dan Patch Tobacco, lunch pail; famous horse and trotter with original woodhandled bail; 7 x 4¼ x 4½ inches; good/very good condition, some minor chipping, slight distortion, minor fade; $250–350.

DICK CUSTER
Dick Custer, label; chromolithographed inner lid cigar box label; "Holds you up"; cowboy pointing pistol; ca. 1900s; 6½ inches; mint condition; $10–12.

Climax Golden Twins, tin; 1 pound; made by P. Lorillard Co.; golden color; ca. 1890s; very good condition; $8–10. *Courtesy of Dawn and Bob Reno. Photo by Donald Vogt.*

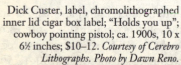

Dick Custer, label, chromolithographed inner lid cigar box label; "Holds you up"; cowboy pointing pistol; ca. 1900s, 10 x 6½ inches; $10–12. *Courtesy of Cerebro Lithographs. Photo by Dawn Reno.*

DOCTOR'S BLEND

Doctor's Blend Tobacco, tin; lid pictures doctor measuring medicines on balance beam; made in Montreal, Canada; 5 x 3 x 3¾ inches; very good/excellent condition, some general minor wear; $50–100.

DUKE

Duke Cigarettes, paper sign; portrait of woman with feathered hat touting Duke Cigarettes as "The Best in the World"; 25 x 33 inches including original frame; very good/excellent condition, some creasing, minor edge discoloration; $300–600.

DUKES

Dukes Tobacco, folding advertising chair; front and back paper label inserts for Dukes Cameo cigarettes; fair condition; $100–200.

DURHAM

Durham Tobacco, paper label; rare; shows woman in sidesaddle on rearing stallion; "The Favorite Durham"; 10 x 22½ inches; excellent condition, minor soiling and trimmed borders; $200–400.

Durham Tobacco, paper sign; colorful depiction of "The Pride of Durham" to the king of Spain and the Conquistadors; approximately 22 x 15½ inches excluding frame; good/very good condition, separation tear in upper right corner, trimmed borders; $200–400.

Durham Tobacco, paper sign; humorous image of schoolmaster and children promoting the clock-packaged product for this smoking tobacco; rare and unusual; 20 x 27½ inches including original banding; early Giles litho; excellent/near-mint condition, some minor creasing; $500–800.

EDGEWORTH

Edgeworth, pocket tin; ca. 1920s; near-mint condition; $10–20.

Edgeworth, tin; ca. 1930s; 6½ inches with knob top; concave shape; very good condition; $25–50.

Edgeworth, tin; ca. 1940s; 5 inches; round canister; excellent condition; $20–40.

Edgeworth, tin; ca. 1950s; 5 inch canister; very good condition; $10–20.

Edgeworth, pocket tin; ca. 1950s; excellent condition; $80–100.

Edgeworth grouping of representative tins; (the company made fifty to sixty tins—these are just a sampling); (rear left) ca. 1940s, 5 inches round canister, excellent condition, $20–40. (rear middle) ca. 1930s, 6½ inches with knob top, concave shape, very good condition, $25–50. (rear right) ca. 1950s, 5 inch canister, very good condition, $10–20.; (middle left) ca. 1920s, pocket tin, near-mint condition, $10–20; (middle center) ca. 1950s, excellent condition, $80–100; (middle right) unusual design, ca. 1950s, excellent condition, $200–250; (front left) flat pocket tin, ca. 1920s, excellent condition, $10–20; (front right) sample size, ca. 1950s, very good condition, $60–90. *Courtesy of Marilyn and De Underwood/Tins Again Collectibles. Photo by Donald Vogt.*

Edgeworth, pocket tin; ca. 1950s; unusual design; excellent condition; $200–250.

Edgeworth, flat pocket tin; ca. 1920s; excellent condition; $10–20.

Edgeworth, tin; sample size; ca. 1950s; very good condition; $60–90.

EGYPTIENNE

Egyptienne Cigarettes, paper sign; depicts girl in bonnet with package of cigarettes on left; original frame; 17½ x 19½ inches overall; very good condition, some wrinkling and soiling; $100–200.

ELECTRIC MIXTURE

Electric Mixture Tobacco, tin; square-edged can with four burlesque women on cover; 4½ x 2¼ x 3¼ inches; fair/good condition, overall wear, chipping; $100–250.

EL MACCO

El Macco Cigars, self-framed tin sign; oval image of pretty girl and tuxedoed man lighting stogie; 20 x 24 inches; good condition, overall chipping, slight fading, some in-painting primarily to rust spots; $150–350.

EL SYMPHONIE

El Symphonie Cigars, tin sign; inverted tray by Shonk for this Havana cigar; advertising pictures composer; 15 x 18 inch oval; very good condition, hairline scratches, minor rubbing; $200–400.

ESKIMO
Eskimo Smoking Tobacco, canister, husky dog in front of igloos in gold on brown can with original slip lid; made in Montreal; 4¼ diameter x 6 inches; good/very good condition, some general wear; $200–400.

EVERY DAY
Every Day Tobacco, tin; round-edge flat pocket on this rare can; 4½ x ¾ x 2¾ inches; very good condition, some chipping and scratches; $300–500.

EXQUISITE MIXTURE
Exquisite Mixture Tobacco, tin; square edge; early Hasker & Marcuse tin; 4½ x 2¼ x 3¼ inches; fair/good condition, chipping overall, minor denting; $800–1,500.

F & M HERBS
F & M Herbs Cigar, paper sign; well-appointed Victorian interior scene of woman surrounded by Eastlake furniture, Oriental rugs, and table full of cigar brands; 1880; Clay & Richmond lithograph; 15½ x 25 inches excluding mat and frame; very good condition, some tears, some minor paper loss; $200–500.

FACTORY SMOKERS
Factory Smokers, cigar humidor and display; metal-cased slant-front cigar counter display; 16¼ x 13 x 8½ inches; fair/good condition; $25–75.

FAST MAIL
Fast Mail, label; depicts Fast Mail train; J. J. Bagley & Co.; 13¾ x 9¼ inches; very good condition, some chipping, some rubbing; $350–650.

FATIMA CIGARETTES
(*see also* "Liggett & Myers Tobacco")

Fatima Cigarettes, framed tin sign; depicts trademark veiled maiden holding package of Turkish cigarettes; 16½ x 22½ inches; fair condition; $100–250.

Fatima Cigarettes, round self-framed tin sign; 19 inches; ca. 1905–1910; depicts the veiled woman trademark; excellent condition; $300–500.

Fatima Turkish Cigarettes, ashtray/match holder; ceramic; 3¼ inches tall; near-mint condition; $50–125.

Fatima Turkish Cigarettes, oval self-framed tin sign; 22¾ x 16½ inches; printed by "The H. D. Beach Co."; ca. 1905–1910; colorful; depicts Fatima endorsing her cigarettes; excellent condition; $700–900.

FOREST & STREAM

Forest & Stream Tobacco, can; fishermen in canoe with dog; 4¼ x 3¾ inches; very good condition, slight scratching and chipping primarily at embossed rim, some denting; $400–600.

Forest & Stream Tobacco, canister; logoed image of man fishing in stream; made by firm in Montreal & Granby, Canada; 5 inch diameter x 6¼ inches including original embossed slip lid; very good/excellent condition, minor wear, slight chipping and scratching, some lid discoloration; $200–300.

Forest & Stream Tobacco, canister; logoed image of man fishing in stream; 4 inch diameter x 5½ inches; original embossed slip lid; very good/excellent condition, slight denting, minor chipping, some lid discoloration; $375–500.

Forest & Stream Tobacco, upright pocket tin; two men and a dog fishing from a canoe on both sides; 3 x 4¼ x 1 inch; good/very good, minor overall wear, slight fade to one side; wear to lid; $400–600.

Forest & Stream Tobacco, upright pocket tins (3); pair with man fishing and other with flying duck; 3¼ x 4 x 1 inch, 3 x 4¼ x 1 inch, and 3 x 4 x 1 inch; good overall condition, some scratching, denting; $100–200.

FORT GARRY

Fort Garry Tobacco, tin; pictures fort at Hudson Bay with Indians in foreground; made in Canada; 4 x 4¼ x 2½ inches; very good condition, minor rust spotting, slight chipping/fading; $100–200.

FOX TROT

Fox Trot Panatelas, tin; rare can with running fox on yellow background; only one known; 4½ inch diameter x 5¾ inches; very good/excellent condition, minor chipping primarily at embossed rim; $600–800.

FRONTIER MIXTURE

Frontier Mixture, tin; small canister with original slip lid and paper label that pictures soldier riding toward small outpost and exhibition medallions pictured on reverse; made by British-American Tobacco Company, Canada; 3 inch diameter x 3¾ inches; good/very good condition, some water staining to label, color fading, minor chipping; $100–200.

GOBBLERS

Gobblers Cigars, tin; rare can picturing full-feathered turkey; 5 inch diameter x 5 inches; fair/good condition, overall slight fade, minor pinpoint spotting, small dents; $300–400.

GOLD HUNTER

Gold Hunter, cigar box label; chromolithographed outer side label; below the hunter's feet: "The independent gold hunter on his way to Klondike"; in red letters below that: "I neither borrow nor lend"; 4½ x 4½ inches; Lithographer George Schlegel, New York; ca. 1890s; mint condition; $25–35.

GREAT WEST

Great West Cut Plug, lunch pail; only Canadian-made lunch box; 7¾ x 4½ x 5 inches; very good condition, minor rust spotting, slight denting, slight color irregularity between lid and sides; $75–150.

GOLD BOND

Gold Bond Tobacco, pocket tin; large bow on pale yellow background; 3¼ x 1 x 4½ inches; good condition, some paint loss and chipping; $75–125.

GRANT'S

Grant's U.S. Tobacco, paper label; graphic Civil War image of General Grant with soldiers in background; rare vertical label; 6¾ x 14¼

Gold Hunter, cigar box label; chromolithographed outer side label; below the hunter's feet: "The independent gold hunter on his way to Klondike"; in red letters below that: "I neither borrow nor lend"; 4½ x 4½ inches; Lithographer George Schlegel, New York; ca. 1890s; $25–35. *Courtesy of Cerebro Lithographs. Photo by Dawn Reno.*

inches; printed by Graphic Company, New York; very good/excellent condition, slightly trimmed, minor edge tears and slight overall soiling; $600–900.

GREAT WEST
Great West Cut Tobacco, pocket mirror; rare and unusual celluloid puzzle mirror; 2¼ inch diameter; near-mint condition; $100–200.

H. B. GARDNER
H. B. Gardner Cigars, tin sign; rare and early Wells & Hope stone lithographed image of Chief Joseph Brant standing among tobacco plants in full dress holding a box of open cigars; reportedly, this Indian chief helped the Canadians repel the Americans at the Battle of Niagara and was honored by having the town of Brantford, Ontario, named after him; 13¾ x 10 inches excluding frame; excellent condition, some minor flaking; $1,000–2,000.

HAVANA CIGARS
Havana Cigar Cutter; oval mirror; "Havana cigars of excellent quality" in border around mirror; 8 x 8½ inches; good overall condition; $200–400.

HENRIETTA
Henrietta cigars, embossed tin sign; depicts fellow at desk holding cigar; 9¼ x 13¼ inches; very good/excellent condition; good sheen, slight overall soiling; $150–300.

HERBE DE LE REINE
Herbe De La Reine Tobacco, tin; pastel colors of gold, pink, and cream on this American Tobacco Company can; 4½ x 2¾ x 3¼ inches; very good condition, minor chipping; $50–150.

HIAWATHA
Hiawatha Tobacco, wood bucket; very early paper-labeled leaf bucket; 13 inch diameter x 12 inches; poor condition; paper loss to label, general age discoloration, separation at slats; $50–100.

Hiawatha Tobacco, tin; pictures Indian with bow on all sides; 5 x 3 x 2 inches; good condition; $75–125.

HONEYSUCKLE
Honeysuckle Tobacco, can; depicts bees and honeysuckle blossoms; made in Montreal, Canada; 5 inch diameter x 4½ inches; fair condition, some denting, chipping and overcoat residue; $100–150.

Irish Singer, chromolithographed outer side cigar box label; approximately 4 by 4½ inches; man has blue eyes, auburn hair, and is wearing green jacket trimmed in red; ca. 1900; $5–7. *Courtesy of Cerebro Lithographs. Photo by Dawn Reno.*

HOPE CHEST

Hope Chest Cigars, tin; paper-labeled can depicts woman dreaming of hope chest; 6 inch diameter x 5¼ inches; fair/good condition, chipping and scratching, some staining and oversoiling to paper label; $50–150.

IRISH SINGER

Irish Singer, chromolithographed outer side cigar box label; approximately 4 by 4½ inches; man has blue eyes, auburn hair, and is wearing green jacket trimmed in red; ca. 1900; mint condition; $5–7.

J. G. DILL'S

J. G. Dill's Best Cut Plug, pocket tin; trademark country woman in vignette on left; ca. 1880s; very good condition; $8–15.

J. J. BAGLEY

J.J. Bagley Tobacco, label; the Orange Blossom brand is aptly depicted with orange-colored bare-chested woman with auburn hair peeking through orange-covered vines; approximately 13½ x 10 inches; printed by Clay and Company; very good/excellent condition, borders trimmed; $250–400.

JACKSON'S

Jackson's Best Tobacco, cardboard sign; Victorian lass holding plug of Jackson's Best while daughter leans over crate of "Sweet Navy" holding Victorian-clad doll; in background is rare advertisement of black boy stealing plug; 18½ x 24½ inches excluding frame; very good condition, color darkening due to age, minor creasing, repaired edge; $1,500–2,500.

Jackson's Tobacco, paper sign; believed to be images of Jackson and Madison; colorful, funny images of the two men carrying plugs of

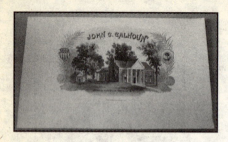

John C. Calhoun, label; chromolithographed inner lid cigar box label; Calhoun Homestead; Abbeville, South Carolina; 10 x 6 inches; ca. 1900s; $17–20. *Courtesy of Cerebro Lithographs. Photo by Dawn Reno.*

"Jackson's best"; 11 x 14 inches; excellent condition, borders trimmed; $600–1,200.

JOHN C. CALHOUN

John C. Calhoun, label, chromolithographed inner lid cigar box label; Calhoun Homestead; Abbeville, South Carolina; 10 x 6 inches; ca. 1900s; mint condition; $17–20.

JOHN RUSKIN

John Ruskin Cigars, cardboard sign; 26 x 19 inches; American Lithograph Co.; excellent condition; $2,000–3,000.

JOHNNIE BIRD

Johnnie Bird Cigars, tray; pictures girl in diaphanous gown for this Maine cigar distributor; 4¼ inch diameter; near-mint condition; $75–150.

J. P. ALLEY'S

J. P. Alley's Hambone Cigars, chromolithographed cigar box label; 7 inches; round; double sided; ca. 1920s; mint condition; $35–45.

J. P. Alley's Hambone, reproduction of old tin depicting African-American pilot in plane; 13¾ x 9½ inches; new/reproduction condition; $12 retail.

J. P. Alley's Hambone Cigars, chromolithographed cigar box label; 7 inches; round; double sided; ca. 1920s; $35–45. *Courtesy of Cerebro Lithographs. Photo by Dawn Reno.*

TOBACCO ■ 453

J. P. Alley's Hambone, reproduction of old tin sign depicting African-American pilot in plane; 13¾ x 9½ inches; new/reproduction condition; $12. *Courtesy of and photo by Castle Antiques & Reproductions.*

Kool Cigarettes, Kool Penguin countertop display piece; ca. 1940s; 14 inches; $300–500. *Courtesy of Neil and Nancy Berliner. Photo by Donald Vogt.*

KEEN KUTTER

Keen Kutter, iron match holder; 7½ inches; all red; reproduction; $14 retail.

KING EDWARD

King Edward Tobacco, upright pocket tin; logoed image of portrait and royalty seal on rare can; made in Montreal, Canada; 3 x 4½ x 1 inch; good condition, some chipping, slight dent (top front); $250–350.

KINNEY

Kinney Bros. Cigarettes, paper sign; unusual poster of intricate Victorian interior scene with people dancing while wearing period costumes; original advertising mat; 36 x 26 inches including mat but excluding frame (although frame appears to be original); near-mint condition, slight overall darkening due to age; $100–300.

KODAK

Kodak Tobacco, tin; factory image on lid; made in Toronto, Canada; 5 x 1½ x 3¾ inches; very good/excellent condition, some chipping primarily to edges of lid, good color sheen; $100–200.

KOOL

Kool Cigarettes, figural lighter; trademarked Kool Penguin with electrical lighter in hat; 4 x 9 x 4 inches; excellent condition, some minor wear to paint; $100–200.

Kool Cigarettes, Kool Penguin countertop display piece; ca. 1940s; 14 inches; excellent condition; $300–500.

LA-ZENDA

La-Zenda Cigars, standing cardboard sign; depicts skywriting plane writing "smoke" in the sky and large depiction of the cigar; 10 x 11 inches; near-mint condition; $40–50.

LEGGAT & BUTLER'S

Leggat & Butler's, label; insert depicts bare-chested woman; trim surrounding insert is floral; grower located in St. Louis; 12 x 9½ inches; very good condition, trimmed borders, minor paper loss on edges and slight soiling; $150–300.

Legatt & Butler's Tiger Brand Tobacco, label; depicts trademark tiger in center insert; printed by A. P. Gast; 11 inches; square; excellent condition, minor soiling; $175–300.

LIGGETT & MYERS TOBACCO

Created as a result of the government's breakup of the American Tobacco Company in 1911, Liggett & Myers produced one of the most popular cigarettes of the pre–World War I years: Fatima. The company put Chesterfield cigarettes on the market around World War I in order to compete with Camel and Lucky Strike cigarettes. The three brands controlled the market until World War II.

Velvet pipe tobacco, another product the company sold, was one of the first to advertise a woman in the same room with a man who was smoking—in fact, the 1912 advertisement began, "I wish I were a man . . ."

See specific brand names for more information.

LOG CABIN

Log Cabin, paper tobacco label; depicts a black man sitting in front of his log cabin and smoking tobacco; 13½ x 8¼ inches; excellent condition, borders trimmed; $600–1,000.

LONDON LIFE

London Life Cigarettes, tin sign; depicts cricket players smoking London Life cigarettes with dapperly dressed spectators; 28 x 38 inches; excellent/near-mint condition, very minor chipping to background by tent edge, slight discoloration to frame, vibrant colors, excellent sheen; $600–1,000.

LONE JACK

Lone Jack Tobacco, paper sign; powerful image of Turk, black man,

Indian, Chinaman, and Caucasian man with dog, all at table smoking pipes of Lone Jack Smoking Tobacco; colorful; 12 x 9½ inches; excellent condition, minor edge trim; $750–1,250.

LONG TOM

Long Tom Tobacco, tin; pictures black man with funny long legs dressed in checkered suit; made in Toronto, Canada; 5 x 2 x 3½ inches; good condition, some denting to lid, minor chipping and scratching overall; $50–125.

LORILLARD TOBACCO

Lorillard was one of the companies created by the governmental breakup of the American Tobacco Company. Its cigarette (Zubelda) was produced to compete with the Turkish imitation (Fatima) made by Liggett & Myers.

Lorillard's outlook on advertising was old-fashioned; it thought its smoking customers would feel a sense of loyalty to Lorillard products.

LORILLARD

Lorillard's Fine Tiger Cut; embossed tin sign; depicts tiger leaping ferociously; marked in lower left corner "2 ounces—5 cents"; 9½ x 13½ inches; minor flakes, very good condition; $400–600.

P. Lorillard Tobacco, paper sign; depicts demure woman being pushed and tugged by cherubs on early crate label for Captive variety of smoking tobacco; ca. 1874; approximately 11½ x 13½ inches excluding mat and frame; overall 19 x 21½ inches; excellent condition; $150–350.

P. Lorillard Tobacco, tin tag display case; glass door and drawer marque classic store case; 34 x 43 x 19 inches; very good condition, split in bottom molding; $1,500–2,000.

LOVE AMONG THE ROSES

Love Among the Roses, label; bare-chested woman bursts forth from bouquets of flowers; extremely colorful; 13½ x 8½ inches; very good condition, slight soiling, trimmed borders; $350–550.

LUCKY STRIKE

("*see also* "American Tobacco Company")

Lucky Strike Tobacco, clock; Roman numerals; mahogany case; red center with company and product name; 15 inch diameter; excellent condition; $350–550.

Lucky Strike Cigarettes, reproduction of old tin sign; features Jean Harlow; "Cream of the Crop"; 13 x 15 inches; new/reproduction condition; $12 retail.

LYALL & BUCHANNAN

Lyall & Buchannan Tobacco, paper sign; one of a series of four firefighting scenes for this tobacco company; approximately 26 x 20 inches including mat but excluding frame; appears the advertising margins are covered by the mat; very good condition, some water staining; $75–150.

MAGNET

Magnet Tobacco, oak clock; "Chew Magnet Fine Cut"; Myers & Cox Company; Dubuque, Iowa; 16 x 36 inches; good condition; $500–750.

MAIL POUCH

Mail Pouch, sign; depicts Indian printed in full color on card stock; die-cut circular top; 34 x 24½ inches; very good color and condition; $75–115.

MALLEY ECLIPSE

Malley Eclipse, 1 cent trade stimulator; early, ornate pressed-oak cigar machine; appears to work; clock wound and two hands spin to indicate winning prize; 11½ x 18¼ x 5½ inches; fair/good original untouched condition, dry wood base split in front, half of award card missing, original back door and money box; $800–1,000.

Lucky Strike Cigarettes, reproduction of old tin sign; features Jean Harlow; "Cream of the Crop"; 13 x 15 inches; new/reproduction condition; $12. *Courtesy of and photo by Castle Antiques & Reproductions.*

Group of chromolithographed outer side cigar box labels; Pony Post, ca. 1900s, approximately 4 by 4½ feet, $5–7: Uncle Sam, ca. 1890s, approximately 4½ by 4½ feet, $15–20; Captain Corker, ca. 1890s, approximately 4½ by 4½ feet; lithographer George Schlegel, New York, $12–15. *Courtesy of Cerebro Lithographs. Photo by Dawn Reno.*

MARINE
Marine Tobacco, tin; portrait of marine on tortoiseshell background; made in Canada; 4¼ x ¾ x 3¼ inches; good/very good condition, some chipping and scratches to lid, general wear to sides resulting in loss of gold overcoat; $100–200.

MARLBORO CIGARETTES
(*see* "Philip Morris")

MASTER MASON
Master Mason Tobacco, upright pocket tin; rare; with well-known image; 3¼ x 4½ inches; good/very good condition, some minor flaking, slight fade; $500–700.

Master Mason Tobacco, upright pocket tin; image of mason squaring a block of tobacco; made in Canada; 3 x 4½ x 1 inch; good condition, minor chipping and rust spotting, in-painting to lid and background, primarily right side; $800–1,200.

MAYO'S
Mayo's Cut Plug, cardboard signs (2); humorous images of gentlemen in open touring car, all smoking pipes with Mayo's Cut Plug Tobacco; 19 x 12 inches each; good/very good condition, both show soiling, some creasing and minor staining; $200–400.

Mayo's Cut Plug, collapsible lunch pail; 7¾ x 4 x 5 inches; original wood-handled bail; excellent condition; $200–400.

Mayo's Cut Plug, collapsible lunch box; blue and gold; collapsed size is 8 x 5 x 3 inches; open size is 7½ x 4½ x 5½ inches; good condition; $175–250.

MELACRINO
Melacrino Cigarettes, self-framed tin sign; display of cigarette packages; 19½ x 15½ inches; very good condition, some overall soiling, gold frame retouched; $100–300.

MISCELLANEOUS
Cast-iron plug cutter; marked "Five Brothers Tobacco Works"; fair condition, some overall rust, still works; $40–75.

Cigar labels; lot of over 150 highly decorative cigar labels; varied sizes; near-mint condition; $100–200.

Counter top display; black man with cigar; 27 inches; ca. 1840–1860s;

458 ■ Advertising

Hanging display; Indian figure; English; 30 inches; made of English oak, early colors; one is in Smithsonian; early 1800s; missing raised arm; $4,000–5,000. *Courtesy of the Marinace Collection. Photo by Donald Vogt.*

Storefront display figure; Indian with headdress, pack of cigars in hand; 60 inches tall; attributed to Robb (carver); ca. 1885–1900; $5,000–7,000. *Courtesy of the Marinace Collection. Photo by Donald Vogt.*

made of southern pine; base not original to piece; good condition; $5,000–7,000.

Countertop display figure; Punch; 44 inches; from the turn of the century; very good condition; $3,000–5,000.

Hanging display; Indian figure; English; 30 inches; made of English oak; early colors; one is in Smithsonian; early 1800s; missing raised arm; very good condition; $4,000–5,000.

Storefront display figure; Indian with headdress, pack of cigars in hand; 60 inches tall; attributed to Robb (carver); ca. 1885–1900; excellent condition; $5,000–7,000.

Storefront display figure; Indian maiden with crossed legs; 64 inches; ca. 1880–1885; made by Thomas V. Brookes; axe is replacement for original spear, good condition; $15,000–20,000.

MODEL

Model Tobacco, tin sign; mustached gentleman with smoking pipe; 34 x 11¼ inches; very good condition, general overall soiling, some wear; $35–75.

MOGUL

Mogul Cigarettes, self-framed tin sign; Arabian smoking this

Egyptian cigarette; 20 x 24 inch oval; fair condition, coverall darkening, some rust, general wear; $75–150.

NEW BACHELOR
New Bachelor, tin sign; one color; photo offset; depicts man dreaming of woman while playing solitaire and smoking cigar; 8 x 11 inches; excellent condition; $50–150.

NIGGER HAIR
Nigger Hair Tobacco, pail; slurious image of black woman with Afro, false eyelashes, and ornamental hoops; 5½ inch diameter x 6½ inches with original slip lid and bail; excellent condition, slight scratches, slight glue residue from tax stamp; $200–400.

NORTH POLE
North Pole Tobacco, lunch pail; flag waver and polar bear; 6 x 6 x 4 inches; good condition, some age darkening, chipping, minor denting; $100–300.

NOSEGAY
Nosegay Tobacco, trade sign; polychrome porcelain-enameled metal; very good condition; $50–150.

OHIO BOYS
Ohio Boys Cigars, tin; oval portraits of three famous political natives—Rutherford B. Hayes, William McKinley, and James A. Garfield; featured on cover of *Tin Type*; 4¼ inch diameter x 6 inches; fair/good condition, some denting, rust spotting; $150–250.

OLD ABE
Old Abe Cigars, tin; paper label with image of Abe Lincoln on front; 5½ inch diameter x 5½ inches; fair condition, some paper loss to label, soiling and tears; $25–75.

OLD CHUM
Old Chum Tobacco, porcelain thermometer, 8 x 38½ inches; excellent condition, minor scratches, some chipping primarily at mounting holes and rolled edge, in working condition, $100–200.

OLD DAD
Old Dad, cardboard sign; small; early; very little graphics, mostly words; excellent condition; $20–30.

OLD GLORY
Old Glory Cigars, can; eagle can with humidor slip lid; 5 inch diameter x 5 inches; good condition, slight fade, minor denting and chipping; $75–150.

OLD KING COLE
Old King Cole Smoking Mixture, tin; illustration by Maxfield Parrish; made by B. Wasserman Co., New York; 4¼ inch diameter x 4¼ inches; very good condition, normal wear; $500–800.

OLIVER & ROBINSON
Oliver & Robinson Cigars, paper label; early clay-coated stock label for this Virginia tobacco; pictures Victorian woman with advertising fan of cherubs in insert; 10½ x 13¼ inches; good condition, some edge tears, borders trimmed; $150–300.

OVERLAND CIGAR
Overland Cigar, advertising art; original layout for factory cigar ad including window with original cigar; 16½ x 12 inches excluding mat and frame; very good condition, deaccessioned from Strawberry Banke; $175–350.

PANIC
Panic Brand, paper label; depicts owl carrying plug of tobacco, gentleman looks on from below; 10½ inches; square; D. H. McAlpin Co.; excellent condition, borders trimmed; $300–500.

PASTIME
Pastime Tobacco, tin; flat burly ginna tin box with multicolored interior litho of jockey and horse jumping rails; 12½ x 9¼ x 4 inches; exterior condition good, overall general fading of color, scratches and dents; interior label in good/very good condition; $250–450.

PATRIOT
Patriot Tobacco, canister; rare lettered black-and-yellow upright can; made in Quebec, Canada; 4½ x 6½ inches; original slip lid; fair/good condition, overall wear, scratching/chipping; $100–225.

PENN
Penn Tobacco Company, embossed tin sign; great image of small child with droopy drawers holding soft pack of "Gold Crumbs" followed

by his favorite cat; "Here Papa is go' cum' bacci!"; exceedingly rare and unusual piece; 9¾ x 13½ inches; fair condition, overall fading, denting, scratching/chipping; $1,000–1,300.

<u>PETE DAILEY</u>

Pete Dailey Cigars, die-cut tin figure; depicts Dailey standing in front of tin of his cigars; Charles Shonk litho; 13 inches tall standing up; very rare (one or two in existence); ca. 1910; near-mint condition; $10,000–12,000.

PHILIP MORRIS

Johnny Roventini, a former bellhop from Brooklyn, was the figure used by Philip Morris for over thirty years to advertise its cigarettes. The bellboy who called "for Philip Morris" was used in advertisements for over a decade before Johnny was discovered. Milton Biow, head of the company's ad department, decided to find a live Johnny in order to do radio advertising for the product. In 1933, Johnny began doing live radio ads for the cigarettes and was a great hit over the next two decades, presenting name brands such as Harry James and making guest appearances on radio shows such as "This Is Your Life."

The early ads for Philip Morris cigarettes claimed "every case of irritation of nose and throat—due to smoking—either cleared up completely, or definitely improved." Philip Morris was responsible for creating one of the "all-time great" advertising campaigns for its product Marlboro Cigarettes. It gave the account to advertising genius Leo Burnett of Chicago in 1954. Burnett changed the packaging to a strong red and white, made it a flip-top box, and used a cowboy to define the product as masculine. Marlboro had one of the longest running modern campaign histories and a highly recognizable advertising theme.

Philip Morris also developed Virginia Slims cigarettes, designed specifically to appeal to the female gender with its slimmer size and attractive, flowered packaging.

When the surgeon general's report that cigarette smoking could endanger your health began appearing on packages, advertising revenues shifted into magazines, newspapers, and other avenues (besides radio and television). One innovative way of keeping this particular cigarette before the public eye was to create the Virginia Slims tennis tournaments.

PHILIP MORRIS

Philip Morris, advertisement from *Life* magazine, 1945; "An Ounce of Prevention . . ."; two colors; excellent condition; $5–6.

Philip Morris, tin sign; depicts cigarette and Philip Morris bellboy; 28 x 10 inches; ca. 1940s; excellent condition; $75–110.

Philip Morris, table lighter; pot metal painted silver; 5 inches; "Occupied Japan"; ca. 1940s; excellent condition; $400–500.

Philip Morris, tin sign; outdoor sign depicting the Philip Morris bellboy in yellow, red, and black; 36 x 15 inches; ca. 1940; good condition, some nicks, bends, and rust; $350–450.

PICKWICK

Pickwick Club Tobacco, tin; rare square-edge tobacco can; 4 x 1¼ x 2½ inches; excellent condition, some chipping, primarily at edges; $375–500.

PICOBAC

Picobac Tobacco, tin sign; large lettered store sign with image of upright pocket tin; 72½ x 36¾ inches including frame; good condition, some touch-up to lettering and background; $50–150.

PIEDMONT

Piedmont Cigarettes, folding wood advertising chair; reads "For

Philip Morris, advertisement from *Life* magazine, 1945; "An Ounce of Prevention . . ."; two colors; $5–6.
Courtesy of Lester Morris. Photo by Donald Vogt.

Philip Morris, table lighter; pot metal painted silver; 5 inches; "Occupied Japan"; ca. 1940s; $400–500.
Courtesy of Neil and Nancy Berliner. Photo by Donald Vogt.

Cigarettes Virginia Tobacco Is the Best"; porcelain insert; fair condition, as found, chair broken, porcelain dirty, edge chipping; $50–100.

Piedmont Cigarettes, folding chair; navy-blue background, white letters; very good condition; $100–200.

Piedmont Cigarettes, porcelain sign; large building sign showing package of products; 30 x 46 inches; good condition, general wear, some in-painting, primarily background and lettering; $75–150.

Piedmont Cigarettes, porcelain sign; a curved sign picturing package of cigarettes; 14 x 16 inches; excellent condition, minor dirt rubs, slight edge wear; $350–500.

PILOT
Pilot Tobacco, can; pictures unusual aircraft, "CF-ARO"; made in Montreal; 5 inch diameter x 4 inches; excellent condition, minor pinpoint spotting; $45–100.

Pilot Tobacco, can; skywriting airplane for 10 cent plug; made in Montreal; 5 inch diameter x 4¼ inches; excellent to near-mint condition, slight chipping; $25–125.

PINCH-HIT
Pinch-Hit Tobacco, reproduction of old tin sign; depicts Babe Ruth holding bats, saying "Chew Pinch-Hit Tobacco"; 11 x 14 inches; new/reproduction condition; $12 retail.

PIPER HEIDSIECK
Piper Heidsieck Tobacco, self-framed tin sign; depicts champagne popping plug and package of chewing tobacco; 14½ x 17¾ inches; good/very good condition, some general rubbing primarily to background black; $350–550.

Pinch-Hit Tobacco, reproduction of old tin sign; depicts Babe Ruth holding bats, saying "Chew Pinch-Hit Tobacco"; 11 x 14 inches; new/reproduction condition; $12. *Courtesy of and photo by Castle Antiques & Reproductions.*

PLAYERS TOBACCO

A painting of a British seaman within a life belt marked "Players Please" was originally used by W. J. Parkes and Company to advertise its Jack's Glory Cut Cavendish Tobacco. John Player bought the painting and registered it as his trademark in 1883. The life belt was added in 1888, and in 1891, the trademark was modified so that the sailor's head faced to the right. It was not the last time changes would be made to the portrait. In 1927, the final portrait was painted by Arthur David McCormick. The sailor's hat now denotes him as being from the boat called *Hero*.

PLAYERS

Players Navy Cut, cigarette tin; trademark sailor in life preserver in center; 1¼ x 3 inches; very good condition; $10–20.

POGUE'S

Pogue's, paper label; early Durham Twist box label with portrait insert; 6½ x 9¾ inches; excellent condition, border appears trimmed; $50–150.

POKER

Poker Tobacco, embossed tin; four gents playing cards; made in Toronto, Canada; 4¼ x 1¼ x 3 inches; good/very good condition, slight chipping and dents; $300–500.

PONY POST

Pony Post, cigar box label; chromolithographed; ca. 1900s; approximately 4 by 4½ inches; mint condition; $5–7.

PRINCE ALBERT

(*see also* "R. J. Reynolds Tobacco Company")

Prince Albert Tobacco and Camel Cigarettes, enamel flange sign; depicts Prince Albert upright tin on one side and package of Camel cigarettes on other; 10½ x 17½ inches; fair/good condition; $150–350.

Prince Albert, cardboard sign; caption reads "Prince Albert/The National Joy Smoke"; ca. 1940s; approximately 12 x 20 inches; excellent condition; $80–110.

Prince Albert, paper sign; 1935; colorful; caption reads "You're Right, No Bite"; depicts man smoking pipe; near-mint condition; $30–50.

Prince Albert, paper sign; 1943; colorful depiction of two different men promoting the taste of their tobacco; near-mint condition; $5–20.

Prince Albert Tobacco, tin sign; rare; white background portrait of Chief Joseph with opened upright pocket tin; 19½ x 25½ inches excluding frame; good/very good condition, slight imperfection to background printing (appears like a whitewash), minor chipping and scratching, slight fading of lettering, minor in-painting of gold enhancements to Indian's costume; $1,500–3,000.

PUCK
Puck Tobacco, can; unusual hockey player motif; cigarette tobacco tin; made in Quebec, Canada; 4 inch diameter x 6½ inches; original slip lid; fair/good condition, overall wear, scratching/chipping; $100–225.

R. A. PATTERSON
R. A. Patterson Tobacco Company, clock; advertises Lucky Strike cigarettes; 14 inch diameter; original excellent condition; $400–600.

R. M. BISHOP
R. M. Bishop & Co., stoneware owl; 13 inches; blue-and-brown glaze; impressed on base: "R. M. Bishop & Co., Fine Cigars, Cincinnati"; excellent condition; $3,700–4,500.

RALEIGH
Raleigh Cigarettes, paper sign; caption reads "Cost No More Than Other Popular Brands"; near-mint condition; $5–20.

REAL TOBACCO
Real Tobacco, cloth banner; depicts man smoking with images of the tobacco products floating around his head; 22½ inches; square; excellent condition; $100–200.

RED DEVIL
Red Devil Tobacco, reproduction of old tin sign; features Nap LaJoie; "Nap LaJoie Chews Red Devil/Ask Him if He Don't"; Queen City Tobacco Co.; Cincinnati, Ohio; 11 x 14 inches; new/reproduction condition; $12 retail.

RED DOT
Red Dot Cigars, sign; cardboard cutout of cigar; original envelope; excellent condition; $75–150.

Red Devil Tobacco, reproduction of old tin sign; features Nap LaJoie; "Nap LaJoie Chews Red Devil/Ask Him if He Don't"; Queen City Tobacco Co., Cincinnati, Ohio; 11 x 14 inches; new/reproduction condition; $12. *Courtesy of and photo by Castle Antiques & Reproductions.*

Red Man, reproduction tin sign; depicts Native American with knife in one hand and package of tobacco in other; 11 x 16½ inches; $15 retail. *Courtesy of Doc Davis/Antique-Alike. Photo by Donald Vogt.*

REDFORD'S NAVY CUT

Redford's Navy Cut Tobacco, paper sign; flagpole-climbing sailor on boldly imaged poster in red, white, and blue; lettering reads "The Finest Tobacco in the World . . . Best & Goes Farthest"; 20 x 30 inches; good condition, paper chipping to edge, some creasing and wrinkling; $75–150.

RED INDIAN

Red Indian Cut Plug, lunch pail; black lettering on red background; image of Indian with full Indian headdress; 7¾ x 5¼ x 4¼ inches; good condition with some chipping and minor paint loss; $800–1,200.

RED MAN

Red Man, reproduction tin sign; depicts Native American with knife in one hand and package of tobacco in other; 11 x 16½ inches; $15 retail.

RED SEAL

Red Seal/Capital/Embassy Cigarettes/Pinhead/Hatamen/Chienmen Cigarettes, advertising calendar; full color with Oriental scene of figures in a garden; Chinese characters; signature and illustrations of the cigarettes mentioned above; 40 x 15 inches; excellent condition; $50–100.

REGAL CUBE

Regal Cube Cut, upright pocket tin; rare; with unique rolled cover and image of two lions; 3¾ x 4 inches; very good condition, shows some wear and minor chipping; $150–250.

REINKEN

Reinken's Havana Cigars, tin sign; profiled portrait of pretty girl with boa and roses in her hair; 13¾ inch diameter; fair/good condition, border has been painted over, some overall rust hazing, general wear; $35–100.

REO

Reo Tobacco, tin; lettered logo encircled by belt; made in Canada; 4 x 4¾ x 2½ inches; good/very good condition, minor dullness of color, minor overall wear; $50–125.

REX'S

Rex's Tobacco, upright pocket tin; 3 x 1 x 4½ inches; good condition, minor paint loss; $35–80.

R. J. REYNOLDS TOBACCO COMPANY

Richard Joshua Reynolds began learning about tobacco at a very young age. His father grew tobacco in southwestern Virginia and sold it throughout the South. After attending college, Richard returned to help his father manage the tobacco factory, often taking wagonloads of chewing tobacco as far as Kentucky and Tennessee to search for customers.

In 1874, he sold his partnership in Rock Spring (the plantation where he was born and raised) and rode south to seek his fortune. He settled in Winston, North Carolina, where he saw an opportunity to continue selling chewing tobacco. He bought a lot and built a two-story structure called "the Little Red Factory," turning out 150,000 pounds of tobacco that first season.

In 1890, the R. J. Reynolds Tobacco Company was incorporated in North Carolina—Richard was president and his brother Will was vice president (another brother, Walter, later joined the firm). Several years later he built Number 256, a factory whose smokestack alone cost more than the whole Little Red Factory building. He used the factory for ten years, quadrupling his production, but outgrew the building and had to put Number 8 into operation in 1901.

Reynolds became one of Winston's most important citizens, helping to establish a savings bank, serving as city commissioner, and even fighting J. P. Morgan's railroad monopoly on the area.

Each plug brand produced by the R. J. Reynolds factory in those early days had a distinctive tag. Some of the brand names included Frog, Mild and Mellow Sun Cured, Old Port, Fat

Back, North America (which used a side view of an Indian as its symbol), Red Rabbit, Red Bird, Old Rip, Big Plug, Big Schooner, Olive Branch (showing a dove with an olive branch in its beak), Acme, Brown's Mule, Speckled Beauty, Wine Sap, and RJR.

The company was the first to learn to age tobacco in the leaf before manufacture, and in 1907 introduced a tobacco using Kentucky burley that became known as Prince Albert tobacco. This was a turning point for Reynolds, because he hired an advertising agency to promote the new product in 1910. Advertisements sold the tobacco that "can't bite your tongue," and a signboard overlooking New York's Union Square heralded "Prince Albert The Nation's Joy Smoke, R. J. Reynolds Tobacco Company, Winston–Salem, N.C." The slogan was later changed to "The International Joy Smoke."

Though Reynolds had cornered the market on tobacco, he still wasn't ready to rest on his laurels. In 1913, he introduced four brands of cigarettes: Reyno, Osman, Red Kamel, and Camel. He wanted the packaging designs to combine simplicity with pictorial possibilities (when a small northern firm also made a Red Kamel brand, Reynolds bought it out) and hired lithographers to create labels. The Richmond lithographers created two labels: "Kamel" and "Camel"—naturally, the latter won out (should you find one of the original "Kamel" designs, consider it rare). Wording on the package and the product's quality were important to Reynolds, thus the famous inscription "Don't look for premiums or coupons, as the cost of the tobaccos blended in Camel Cigarettes prohibits the use of them."

The original Camel pictured on the first package was "a pathetic, one-humped beast with short, pointed ears, two pronged hoofs and a drooping neck" (quote from R. J. Reynolds's hundredth anniversary publication, 1975). After consulting the Encyclopedia Britannica and discussing the camel's dismal looks, Barnum & Bailey's dromedary, Old Joe, was photographed and used as the Camel representative.

Advertising the cigarettes was an expensive project for that era. Reynolds paid the agency $250,000 to introduce Camel cigarettes. The ad campaign started with a series of teaser ads ("The Camels Are Coming!"), until the *Saturday Evening Post* finally printed its first cigarette ad, a two-page Camel spread, in

1914. The ads worked: The company sold 425 million cigarettes that first year, and by 1921, it had sold more than 18 billion. In World War I, the cigarettes were so popular that General Pershing himself appealed to the Reynolds company in Winston-Salem for more Camels to be sent to doughboys overseas. In 1918, Reynolds died. By that point in time, the company employed 10,000 people in 121 buildings in Winston-Salem. He never learned that a comment overheard on a golf course would become one of the most recognizable advertising phrases in the world: "I'd walk a mile for a Camel." In 1921, the slogan was being used on billboards and in ads.

The R. J. Reynolds company moved its quarters into a new twenty-two-story building on the site of the old City Hall in Winston-Salem in April 1929. The building was awarded the best building of the year recognition by the National Association of Architects.

Before the Depression, Camel cigarettes began experiencing some heavy-duty competition from Lucky Strike and Chesterfield. It was time for the advertising companies to do battle, and in 1934 Reynolds's advertising costs amounted to nearly 81 percent of net earnings (figure from Reynolds's hundredth anniversary booklet).

In the early 1930s, cigarette packaging changed. Reynolds developed the first single-piece folding-style cigarette carton and began wrapping Camels in moistureproof cellophane.

Some of the marketing campaigns run by the Reynolds company to promote Camel cigarettes included a nationwide $50,000 contest to answer the question "What significant change has recently been made in the wrapping of the Camel package and what are its advantages to the smoker?" (a million entries flooded the Winston-Salem office and, finally, three winners were chosen); a series of magician's trick books started with the theme "It's Fun to Be Fooled . . . It's More Fun to Know"; the "Try Ten Camels" money-back guarantee; a 3,000-square-foot electric sign overlooking New York City's Times Square from Forty-fourth Street; even radio programs were sponsored by the cigarette ("The Camel Pleasure Hour" and "The All-Star Radio Revue" premiered in 1930; others soon followed).

In 1935, the cigarette war ended with Camels the undeniable winner. Camels were sent at no charge to servicemen overseas during World War II, and President Franklin D. Roosevelt was often photographed with a Camel in the end of his cigarette holder. The cigarette maintained its popularity for quite a while, becoming such a recognizable advertising symbol that, when the company wanted to "fancy up" the package in 1958, smokers protested loudly—so loudly that the manufacturers brought back the original package. The 1958 design omitted the phrase "Turkish and Domestic Blend" and the camel was paler than the original version. When television was introduced, Camel cigarette commercials ran during broadcasts of Madison Square Garden's sports events, and in 1948, when national networks were born, the "Camel News Caravan," featuring John Cameron Swayze, was one of the first national television news programs. During the late 1960s, the company brought back its "I'd walk a mile for a Camel" slogan, boosting sales tremendously.

In March 1954, a new product introduced the American public to filter-tip cigarettes. The cigarette was named Winston, and in the first nine months after its introduction it sold 6.5 billion packs. By 1956, it was the top filter brand, and ten years later it became the best-selling cigarette in the nation. The jingle associated with the cigarette—"Winston tastes good, like a cigarette should"—became the focal point of a phenomenally effective advertising campaign. Grammar experts argued about the correctness of the jingle's language—on television, on radio, and in print. No other advertising slogan had ever gotten so much media attention.

In 1956, after top-secret preparation, Reynolds introduced the first filter-tipped menthol cigarette, Salem. Sales for this cigarette also exceeded all expectations and it soon became one of the world's top-selling brands. Both Winston and Salem were packaged simply. Winston's striking red-and-white design resulted in what is now considered a classic example of packaging. Salem's green pack was "carefully chosen to suggest the green buds of the outdoors" (quote from Reynolds's hundredth anniversary booklet).

Throughout the next couple of decades, the Reynolds company produced new cigarettes and smoking tobacco (i.e. Doral, Vantage, and Camel Filter cigarettes; Carter Hall, Madeira Gold, and Apple smoking tobaccos). One of the fastest growing major brands today, Vantage cigarettes, was first produced in

1970, before cigarette advertising was banned on television and radio.

Today the company sponsors auto racing and rodeo events, major bowling tournaments, and programs for recreational skiers in an attempt to advertise its products, and it continues to broaden its product lines. Reynolds continues to be the industry leader: It is the only company to have three cigarettes in the top ten brands, the top-selling little cigar, the number-one smoking tobacco, and the leading plug chewing tobacco. R. J. Reynolds products are now available in over 140 countries, it has controlling interests in European cigarette manufacturers, and regional headquarters have been established all over the world.

In 1963, Reynolds began exploring a new area—convenience foods and beverages. It has acquired companies, such as Hawaiian Punch fruit drinks, Vermont Maid syrup, Brer Rabbit molasses, My*T*Fine puddings, College Inn products, Davis baking powder, Chun King Oriental food products, Patio Mexican foods, Sunkist citrus products, and many others.

The company's logo remains the initials "RJR." The trademark was registered in 1886 and remained an ornate symbol until 1961, when it was redesigned in an open oval shape. The present logo is a continuous double-line version of the original initials.

See individual brand names for item information.

ROBERT BURNS

Robert Burns Cigars, tin charger; Scottish plaid background with portrait image and cigar box; 24 inch diameter; very good/excellent condition, appears lacquered, darkened overall; $150–300.

ROSEBUD

Rosebud Tobacco, cardboard sign; bold illustrated image of men on dock watching sailing schooners with package of tobacco in foreground; 35¼ x 20¼ inches including frame; very good/excellent condition; $45–100.

ROYAL NAVY

Royal Navy Tobacco, tin; smiling pipe-smoking sailor on can; made in Canada; 3¾ x 5 x 2½ inches; very good condition, minor denting, slight general wear; $35–75.

ST. LAWRENCE TOBACCO

St. Lawrence Tobacco, tin; shows flag; 6 x 2¾ x 4¼ inches; good/very good condition, overall scratches and chips; $175–275.

SANCHEZ & HAYA

Sanchez & Haya Cigars, reverse glass sign; primarily lettered with company name and offices; etched seals in center; 36 x 24 inches excluding frame; good condition, some touch-up to gold and background; $200–400.

SALEM CIGARETTES

(*see* "R. J. Reynolds Tobacco Company")

SATIN

Satin Cigarettes, tin charger; classic depiction of pretty woman in picture hat; 19 inch diameter; good condition, some restoration; $300–600.

Satin Cigarettes, tin charger; bonneted baby with package of product; 19 inch diameter; excellent condition, nice sheen, minor edge chipping, slight scratches; $1,700–2,200.

SEAL OF NORTH CAROLINA

Seal of North Carolina Tobacco, paper poster; strong image of "The Honorable Bardwell Slote" holding aloft a package of the logoed tobacco; 8¼ x 20¼ inches; excellent condition; $200–400.

Seal of North Carolina Plug Cut, tin, 5 x 1 x 3½ inches; American Tobacco Co.; Montreal, Canada; pictures a package of plug cut tobacco; fair/good condition; $500–700.

Seal of North Carolina, wooden box; small unusual plug box with paper labels; 4½ x 1¾ x 3½ inches; very good condition; $50–100.

SENSATION

Sensation Cigar, canister; sensuous, almost translucent, gowned goddess with tobacco leaf overhead; purchased from lithographer's personal collection; very good/excellent condition; uncirculated; $200–500.

Sensation Cut Plug, cardboard sign; bronze man holding back charging dogs; a Lorillard product; approximately 25 x 17 inches excluding frame; good condition, some general wear; $150–250.

SILVER BELL

Silver Bell Tobacco, tin; sides and top picture bannered bell; made in

Toronto, Canada; 3 inch square x 2½ inches; very good condition; minor edge chipping; $75–125.

SIR HAIG
Sir Haig Cigars, canister; depicts silhouetted soldier background; made in Ontario, Canada; 5½ x 5¼ inches; good/very good, minor scuffing and rim chips; $100–250.

SITTING BULL DURHAM
Sitting Bull Durham Tobacco, paper sign; depicts defiant image of Sitting Bull dressed in headdress with his rifle aloft while sitting astride a posed horse; 9½ x 12½ inches; excellent condition; $1,000–2,000.

SOCRATES
Socrates, label; chromolithographed inner lid cigar box label; "Know thyself"; Schlegel Lithographing Co.; New York; 9 x 7 inches; ca. 1910s; mint condition; $7–10.

SPIRIT OF ST. LOUIS
Spirit of St. Louis, label; chromolithographed inner lid cigar box label, Mazer-Gressman Co. Inc., Detroit, Michigan; American Lithographic Co., New York, U.S.A.; 7¾ x 6¼ inches; ca. 1920s; mint condition; $8–10.

STAR AND CRESCENT
Star and Crescent Cigars, canister; lithographed by Tony DeFranco of Lancaster, Pennsylvania; 5½ inch diameter x 5 inches; uncirculated condition, age discoloration; $200–400.

Socrates, label; chromolithographed inner lid cigar box label; "Know thyself"; Schlegel Lithographing Co.; New York; 9 x 7 inches; ca. 1910s; $7–10. *Courtesy of Cerebro Lithographers. Photo by Dawn Reno.*

Spirit of St. Louis, label; chromolithographed inner lid cigar box label; Mazer-Gressman Cigar Co. Inc., Detroit, Michigan; American Lithographic Co., New York, U.S.A.; 7¾ x 6¼ inches; ca. 1920s; $8–10. *Courtesy of Cerebro Lithographs. Photo by Dawn Reno.*

SUMATRA

Sumatra Tobacco, paper sign; appealing girl in red outfit for this "Seed Leaf" tobacco from Philadelphia; 14½ x 20 inches excluding mat and frame; excellent condition, some rubbing and fading to overprinted lettering, some white spotting to underside of glass; $1,000–1,500.

SURE SHOT

Sure Shot, storage bin; depicts Indian with stretched bow; yellow, red, and blue; 15¼ x 7½ x 10¼ inches; very good condition, general soiling, minor scratches and chips; $400–650.

SWEET CAPORAL

Sweet Caporal Tobacco, paper label; soldier with bayonetted rifle on shoulder, burning building in background; 8¾ x 21½ inches; excellent condition, slight overall soiling; $100–200.

TIGER

Tiger, tin; P. Lorillard Co.; paper over tin; large container; ca. early 1900s; very good condition; $80–100.

Tiger Tobacco, tins; in blue (rather than the more common red); lunchbox shape; ca. 1920s; excellent condition; $75–125.

Tiger Tobacco, Lunch pail; red-and-black tiger over wicker design; 8 x 6 x 6½ inches; good condition, as found, some minor chipping and denting; $30–75.

Tiger tin; P. Lorillard Co.; lunchbox style; all tin; ca. early 1900s; very good condition; $60–80.

Tiger Tobacco, tins; in blue (rather than the more common red); lunchbox shape; ca. 1920s; $75–125. *Courtesy of Marilyn and De Underwood/Tins Again Collectibles. Photo by Donald Vogt.*

TONKA

Tonka Tobacco, tin; rare; from the McAlpin Tobacco Co.; Toronto, Canada; picturing soldiers in the field on lid and flowered urn on side; 5 x 3¼ x 3¾ inches; good/very good condition, some denting, minor chips, slight fade to lid; $400–700.

TROUT-LINE

Trout-Line Tobacco, pocket tin; pictures trout fisherman netting fish with fly equipment; 3¼ x 3¾ x 1¼ inches; good condition, minor chipping, general soiling overall; $200–400.

TUXEDO

Tuxedo Tobacco, cardboard sign; depicts sophisticated couple being waited on in restaurant—both the man and woman are smoking; approximately 11½ x 15½ inches excluding mat and frame; very good/excellent condition; $175–350.

TWIN OAKS

Twin Oaks Tobacco, figural tin; embossed; coffin-shaped can with humidor lid; 8¼ x 4½ x 3¾ inches; very good condition, slight dents, minor wear overall; $75–150.

UNCLE SAM

Uncle Sam, cigar box label; chromolithographed; ca. 1890s; approximately 4½ x 4½ inches; mint condition; $15–20.

UNIFORM

Uniform Cut Plug Tobacco, tin; exceedingly rare; one of two known; original tax stamp under paper label with image of U.S. sailor; 4½ inch diameter x 7 inches; good/very good condition, one spot the size of a dime missing in the label, but not part of image; small scratches, pinholes; $400–700.

Uniform Cut Plug Tobacco, tin; logoed image of "Reliable" sailor in wreath; 6 x 3 x 3¾ inches; very good condition, some minor chipping, colors bright; $25–100.

UNION COMMANDER

Union Commander Cut Plug, tin lunch pail; red, gold, and black with image of George Washington; 7 x 4¼ x 4½ inches; fair/good condition, clasp missing; $75–150.

UNION LEADER
Union Leader Tobacco, cream can; eagle on cut plug; 4¼ inch diameter x 9¼ inches; very good condition, minor denting; $200–400.

U.S. MARINE
U.S. Marine Cut Plug, tin lunch pail; nautical images of warship and pipe-smoking sailor in porthole; 7½ x 4½ x 4½ inches; good condition, some chipping and scratching, slight fade and denting; $200–300.

VANITY FAIR
Vanity Fair Cigarettes, paper sign; one-color Major & Knapp image of frog; 8½ x 10½ inches; excellent condition; $100–150.

VELVET PIPE TOBACCO
(see "Liggett & Myers Tobacco")

VIRGINIA SLIMS CIGARETTES
(see "Philip Morris")

WEEK END SPECIAL
Week End Special Cigars, tin; rare paper-labeled can with women riding in open touring car with train in background; featured on cover of *Tin Type*; 4¼ inch diameter x 5¼ inches; fair/good condition; $350–500.

WINNER
Winner Plug Tobacco, lunch pail; colorful image of racing cars; 7¾ x 4¼ x 5 inches; excellent condition, minor chipping, slight scratches; $150–300.

WINSTON CIGARETTES
(see "R. J. Reynolds Tobacco Company")

YANKEE
The Yankee Cigar, cutter and match vendor; ornate cast-iron countertop cutter with original plating; 6 x 7 x 8 inches; very good, working condition; $300–500.

Y-B CIGARS
Y-B Cigars, embossed tin sign; portrait of cigar box holding "La Cubana Havana Cigars"; 13½ x 19½ inches; "Standard Adv. Co."; good condition, some paint chipping; $200–300.

CHAPTER FORTY-EIGHT
TOURIST ATTRACTIONS, TRAVEL

AUSTRALIA

Australia, travel poster; "The Tallest Trees in the British Empire"; Marysville, Victoria; color; signed "Trumpf"; ca. 1930; "for Australian National Travel Assn."; 21 x 13 inches; very good condition; $35–65.

RINGLING BROTHERS & PHINEAS T. BARNUM/BARNUM & BAILEY

P. T. Barnum did everything in a big way—including advertising for his circus engagements. He utilized every bit of white space in every ad, filling them with slanted lines, various typefaces, and woodcuts depicting his special events. Barnum created larger and more imaginative advertising formats rather than to stay within the limits of a dull, half-inch ad that ran every two weeks.

He began as a salesman for patent medicine and used wild displays to attract attention to his products. He also utilized testimonials and endorsements by the dozens, moving product advertising into a new realm—one typified by oversized type and fancy borders. Barnum said, "Advertising is like learning—a little is a dangerous thing. If a man has not the pluck to keep *on* advertising, all the money he has already spent is lost."

BARNUM & BAILEY

Bailey's Circus, paper poster; depicts crowd entering the big top; 20 x 29 inches; ca. late 1800s; good condition, mounted on foamcore, some slight tears and wrinkling; $100–200.

P. T. Barnum's, broadside poster; depicts multiple images of various people and circus animals; 14½ x 21½ inches; good overall condition with some creasing and minor paper loss; $75–125.

Ringling Bros. Barnum & Bailey Circus, brochure; 1934; features Coke advertisement on inside cover; very colorful; near-mint condition; $20–50.

Ringling Brothers Barnum & Bailey Circus, color lithographed poster (2); framed; very good condition; $100–300.

BATTLE OF GETTYSBURG PANORAMA AND MUSEUM

Battle of Gettysburg Panorama and Museum, paper poster; unusual museum promotion for early 1889 museum institution located on Market and Tenth Streets, San Francisco; museum promoted history of Civil War era; 9½ x 14 inches; very good condition, great colors, very small paper loss on bottom right-hand corner; $350–650.

BOSTON MUSEUM

Boston Museum Theater, broadside and poster; 1880; 9 x 25½ inches and 15 x 22 inches, respectively, excluding frames; fair overall condition, some holes and wrinkling, some staining; $125–225.

BUFFALO BILL'S WILD WEST

Buffalo Bill's Wild West, canvas poster; depicts Buffalo Bill on his white horse; marked "Buffalo Bill's Wild West/Sells Floto Circus"; extremely colorful and large; ca. 1913; excellent condition; $1,300–2,000.

CHRISTY BROS.

Christy Bros. Wild Animal Show, poster; colorful panoramic view of all the animals in cages and people who have come to see them; 42 x 28 inches; excellent condition, some minor wear, dry mounted on heavy backing; $250–500.

COLUMBIAN EXPO

Columbian Expo, medal; Chicago Day; excellent condition; $24–30.

EUROPE

European Destination, poster; ca. late 1930s; 24½ x 39 inches; good overall condition with some minor tears; $50–75.

European Destination, poster; Londonderry or Belfast; 24½ x 40 inches; fair overall condition with some tears; $50–100.

European Destination, poster; advertises "P & O Carriers"; 24½ x 40 inches; good overall condition; $15–50.

FLORIDA

Florida, paper store cards; depicts man braving winter winds; reads "Shut the door!/or go to/Florida/Atlantic Coast Line/where you will find warm weather/for tickets, time tables & c. apply at 229 Broadway, N.Y."; approximately 10¾ x 9 inches; good condition; $600–850.

Miami, wood sign; depicts typical Florida ocean scene with palm trees, bay scene in background; 6¼ x 19¾ inches including frame; good/very good condition with some scratches and nail holes; $600–1,000.

GREAT LAKES EXPO
Great Lakes Expo, registration booklet/color envelope; 1936; excellent condition; $20–25.

INDIA
India, travel posters; four-color lithographed; mounted on Masonite; very good condition; $100–200.

INTERNATIONAL GREAT LAKES FLYING BOAT CRUISE
International Great Lakes Flying Boat Cruise, poster; depicts biplane flying above lake where two people are in a canoe; held in Chicago, July 5–8, 1913; some margin soiling; very good condition; $4,000–5,000.

ITALY
Italy, poster; Italia Travel poster; (3); printed by ENIT, the travel bureau of Italy; posters depict scenes by Pizzi and Pizio of Rome, Naples, and Venice; 39 x 26 inches; good condition; $30–50.

JAMAICA
Jamaica, travel poster; "Spend Your Holidays in Jamaica"; color lithograph by Waterlow & Son, Ltd., London; depicts pirate and treasure chest overlooking blue lagoon; 30 x 20 inches; very good condition; $35–75.

JEAN WALTHER CRUISE LINE
Jean Walther Cruise Line, travel poster; no text; color lithograph by Hall, England; 40 x 25 inches; excellent condition; $25–40.

MADISON SQUARE GARDEN
Madison Square Garden Masquerade Ball, paper poster; image for 1880 social event; "tickets $5"; printed by Neuman & Dingoinger Co.; 11 x 14½ inches; good/very good condition, overall soiling, trimmed around edge; $150–350.

MEXICO

Mexico, travel poster; surrealistic image; "Handy—Mysterious—Colorful—Exotic Mexico"; printed for National Railways by Offset-Galas, Mexico; 37 x 28 inches; very good condition; $25–50.

NARRAGANSETT PARK FAIR

Narragansett Park Fair, broadside; colorful early poster of people and animals at this Rhode Island fair; 14½ x 22½ inches excluding frame; fair/good condition, age darkening, some foxing, wrinkles, appears trimmed top and bottom; $50–100.

NEW YORK WORLD'S FAIR

New York World's Fair, posters (5); color lithograph; 1964–1965; excellent condition; $300–500.

New York World's Fair, *Long Island Gazetteer*, 1939; 140 pages; Coney Island section; excellent condition; $22–25.

NORUMBEGA

Norumbega Park, paper poster; colorful multi-vignetted scenes from this turn-of-the-century Boston amusement park showing animals, automobile station, and people canoeing with bison-encircled inset in middle; rare; 22 x 28 inches excluding mat and frame; good condition, minor horizontal tear through word "attractions" on right side; $1,500–2,500.

Norumbega Park, paper sign; lithograph; printed by Forbes Co.; ca. 1910; colorful vignetted display of various attractions at the amusement park located in Newton, Massachusetts (park closed in 1964); 28 x 22 inches; excellent condition; $1,200–1,800.

THE STRATHMORE

The Strathmore, paper sign; an unusual promotion for this Revere, Massachusetts, seaside resort; includes band playing under cupola and bathing beauties in foreground ocean scene; 30 x 24 inches; very good condition, some overall wear, slight fading, some foxing; $250–500.

CHAPTER FORTY-NINE
TOYS, HOBBIES, GAMES, SPORTS

AMERICAN TOY COMPANY
American Toy Company, tin sign; reproduction; depicts American "Drummer Bear" teddy bear; 10 x 16½ inches; $15 retail.

ARCADE CAST IRON TOYS
Arcade Cast Iron Toys, sign; reproduction; depicts kids looking at shelves of toys (including lots of steam shovels, trains, and trucks); 14 x 12 inches; $15 retail.

BRIST GAME
Brist Game, cardboard top and pieces; pictorial box cover shows women and men using this paddle-raquet-type game; comes with paddles and birdies; made in Topeka, Kansas; 19 x 11¼ inches excluding mat and frame; some minor discoloration, very good condition; $175–375.

BRUNSWICK
Brunswick/Balke-Collender Co., cardboard sign; vignettes of the "Billard Experts of the World" superimposed over crossed cues and balls; 36½ x 27 inches excluding frame; overall 40½ x 31 inches; fair/good condition; $350–600.

CANNON BALL VEHICLES
Cannon Ball Vehicles, advertisement from *Hardware Age*, 1926; full-color ad for the company's wagons; excellent condition; $8–10.

CONGRESS
Congress Playing Cards, paper sign; rare advertising for Russell Morgan playing cards showing three pictorial images of women for backs of 1903 cards; 12 x 18 inches excluding frame; near-mint condition; $300–700.

Congress Playing Cards, paper sign; unusual advertisement for pictorial playing card backs; ca. 1903; two views depict women, third depicts men on horseback; 12 x 18 inches excluding frame; near-mint condition; $500–800.

American Toy Company, tin sign; reproduction; depicts American "Drummer Bear" teddy bear; 10 x 16½ inches; $15 retail. *Courtesy of Doc Davis/Antique-Alike. Photo by Donald Vogt.*

Cannon Ball Vehicles, advertisement from *Hardware Age*, 1926; full-color ad for the company's wagons; $8–10. *Courtesy of Paper Lady/Bernie and Dolores Fee. Photo by Donald Vogt.*

Arcade Cast Iron Toys, sign; reproduction; depicts kids looking at shelves of toys (including lots of steam shovels, trains, and trucks); 14 x 12 inches; $15 retail *Courtesy of Doc Davis/Antique-Alike. Photo by Donald Vogt.*

Congress Playing Cards, paper sign; promotes three Dutch-type images for the "Gold Edges" series of pictorial backs; 12 x 18 inches excluding frame; near-mint condition; $650–800.

Congress Playing Cards, paper sign, promotes three Spanish-type images for the "Society Favorites" series; 12 x 18 inches exluding frame; near-mint condition; $650–800.

FISHING

Fishing Tackle, trade sign; depicts large lure; excellent condition; $475–525.

Fishing Tackle, trade sign; two-sided; shows rod hooking boot while fish swim around hook; excellent condition; $375–450.

South Bend Fishing Tackle, die-cut sign; depicts fisherman in center and his catches flying out of the water on each side; five folds; excellent condition; $850–1,000.

GEO. BORGFELDT & CO.

Geo. Borgfeldt & Co., sign; reproduction; depicts Fontaine Fox's Toonerville Trolley mechanical tin toy; 8½ x 11 inches; $15 retail.

HASBRO

Hasbro, advertisement from *Life* magazine, 1954; depicts "Hasbro Guide to America's Top Ten Toys"; features Mr. and Mrs. Potato Head; excellent condition; $10–12.

HORSMAN'S

Horsman's, paper poster; depicts woman shooting bow and arrow with others in background for this manufacturer of archery and lawn tennis equipment; rare; approximately 17½ x 22¼ inches; good condition, poster trimmed into border image and lettering at top, minor edge tears, overall wrinkling and soiling; $800–1,600.

KIDDIE-KAR

Kiddie-Kar Scooters, advertisement from *Ladies' Home Journal*, October 1919; depicts two kids on their scooters; full color; excellent condition; $18–25.

LIGHTNING WHEEL

Lightning Wheel, coaster wagon; child's wood wagon with spoked wheels; marked with maker's name on side; 16½ x 42 x 16 inches; good original condition; overall wear; $300–600.

Hasbro, advertisement from *Life* magazine, 1954; depicts "Hasbro Guide to America's Top Ten Toys"; features Mr. and Mrs. Potato Head; $10–12. *Courtesy of Lester Morris. Photo by Donald Vogt.*

Kiddie-Kar Scooters, advertisement from *Ladies' Home Journal*, October 1919; depicts two kids on their scooters; full color; $18–25. *Courtesy of Paper Lady/Bernie and Dolores Fee. Photo by Donald Vogt.*

MILTON BRADLEY

Milton Bradley advertises strongly so that children will desire its products enough to ask their parents to buy them.

MILTON BRADLEY

Milton Bradley, puzzle box; colorful train wreck; 8¼ x 6½ x 1¼ inches; very good condition, no contents; $125–175.

OTTO SCHMIDT & SONS

Otto Schmidt & Sons Teddy Bear Toy Co., sign; reproduction; depicts jointed teddy; 10 x 14 inches; $15 retail.

PARKER BROS.

(*see also* "General Mills" in Baking Products chapter)

Parker Brothers, advertisement from *McCall's*, 1964; depicts all the games for that year's Christmas gift list; $6–8.

PLANTERS

(*see also* "Planters" in Peanuts and By-Products chapter)

Planters, Little Black Sambo board game; made by Funland Books and Games in New York; 12 x 16 inches; ca. 1940s; very good condition; $50–100.

RADIO FLYER

The Radio Flyer company began in 1917 when a European immigrant began making wood wagons in a one-room shop in Chicago. By 1923, the business had grown so much that the

Parker Brothers, advertisement from *McCall's*, 1964; depicts all the games for that year's Christmas gift list; $6–8. *Courtesy of Lester Morris. Photo by Donald Vogt.*

Liberty Coaster Company was founded. In 1930, the Radio Steel & Manufacturing Company was incorporated and claimed it was the "Largest Manufacturer of Coaster Wagons and Scooters in the World."

In 1933, the Radio Flyer wagon was exhibited at the World's Fair in Chicago. The company erected a 45-foot-tall statue of a boy riding in a gigantic wagon; beneath the wagon, visitors could purchase a hand-held version of the giant wagon for only twenty-five cents.

Today, many versions of the original wagon exist, and the original is even the subject of a movie called *Radio Flyer*. The company changed its name in 1987 to Radio Flyer.

RADIO FLYER

Radio Flyer, advertisement from *Popular Mechanics*, ca. 1940s; black and white; excellent condition; $2–4.

REXALL AND COUNTRY CLUB, BRIDGE WHIST AND FIFTH AVENUE

Rexall and Country Club (smooth finish), Bridge Whist and Fifth Avenue (linen finish) Playing Cards, cardboard sign; rare advertisement promoting four brands of playing cards; depicts woman holding hand of thirteen cards and saying, "Would you like to hold my hand?"; 11 x 14 inches excluding frame; good/very good condition, some spotting primarily at top, minor creases; $700–1,000.

SHAPLEIGH COASTER

Shapleigh Coasters; advertisement from *Hardware Age*, August 5, 1926; advertises the detachable bed coaster; excellent condition; $10–12.

Shapleigh Coasters, advertisement from *Hardware Age*, August 5, 1926; advertises the detachable bed coaster; $10–12. *Courtesy of Paper Lady/Bernie and Dolores Fee. Photo by Donald Vogt.*

Uncle Wiggily, advertisement from *Ladies' Home Journal*, 1929; black and white; "Gifts for the Kiddies"; $20–25. *Courtesy of Lester Morris. Photo by Donald Vogt.*

UNCLE WIGGILY

Uncle Wiggily, advertisement from *Ladies' Home Journal*, 1929; black and white; "Gifts for the Kiddies"; excellent condition; $20–25.

UNIQUE ART MFG. CO.

Unique Art Mfg. Co., tin sign; reproduction; depicts Ham and Sam mechanical toy; patent October 1921; 10½ x 14 inches; $15 retail.

CHAPTER FIFTY
◼ TRANSPORTATION ◼

ALBANY GREASE
Albany Grease, handled tin; no. 3 grease; late 1860s; excellent condition; $30–60.

ATLANTIC MOTOR OIL
Atlantic Motor Oil, cloth banner; unusual large aviation motor oil banner with air-plane-logoed oil cans; rare; 60 x 36 inches; very good condition, darkening due to age and general soiling, some staining; $200–350.

BLUE FLAME
Blue Flame, gasoline globe; glass; 15 inches round; excellent condition; $75–150.

CACTUS
Cactus Tire Boots & Patches; sign; reproduction of old tin sign featuring "Kaktus Kid"; new/reproduction condition; $12 retail.

CADILLAC
Cadillac, sign; reproduction of old tin sign featuring 1930 V-8 Roadster; new/reproduction condition; $12 retail.

CHAMPION SPARK PLUGS
Champion Spark Plugs, cabinet; chromolithographed tin-and-wood display cabinet; very good condition; $100–300.

Champion Spark Plugs, clock; neon around clock face; outside writing lights up; approximately 2½ feet in diameter; ca. 1940s; restored; $500–750.

CHEVROLET
This line of American cars was named after Swiss-French auto racer Louis Chevrolet, but he didn't have anything to do with the company's success. William C. Durant acted as Chevrolet's backer, but he did not use Chevrolet's original designs for big, expensive cars. Instead, he made cars that were

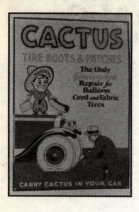

Cactus Tire Boots & Patches, sign; reproduction of old tin sign featuring "Kactus Kid"; new/reproduction condition; $12. *Courtesy of and photo by Castle Antique & Reproductions.*

Cadillac, sign; reproduction of old tin sign featuring 1930 V-8 Roadster; new/reproduction condition; $12. *Courtesy of and photo by Castle Antiques & Reproductions.*

simpler and cheaper, retained the Chevrolet name, and merged the Chevrolet company with another of his businesses: the Little Motor Company.

Durant produced his first car in 1912, then followed that with an economy roadster (the Royal Mail) in 1913. Durant stole the square and parallelogram trademark from a Paris hotel's wallpaper pattern and it has been used ever since.

Advertising has always been an important part of the Chevrolet car industry's success. In a recent year, nearly $71 per car ($150 million) total was spent on advertising. In 1927, an Art and Color Division was introduced in order to concentrate on style and color, and for the first time, the General Motors Company outsold Ford. The next year, Chevrolet was America's number-one choice for a basic car.

In the 1960s, women were used in ads that stated that the powerful cars built for the era attracted the "feminine gender." By the next decade, the powerful car was still popular, but different ways of advertising it had been discovered (the 1970 Chevelle SS 396 advertisement depicted the car tied down by powerful ropes—giving it the look of power even though it hadn't moved an inch).

One of the most collectible classic cars is the Chevrolet Corvette, a two-seater sports car that has undergone major changes in configuration details but still retains the mystique of being one of the fastest and sharpest cars on the road.

CHEVROLET

Chevrolet, advertisement from *Chevy Trucks* magazine, 1939; excellent condition; $15–20.

Chevrolet, advertisement from unknown magazine; depicts 1966 Impala; excellent condition; $10–15.

Chevrolet, advertisement from unknown magazine, 1928; Roadster; excellent condition; $8–10.

Chevrolet, advertisement from unknown magazine, 1965; Corvair; excellent condition; $8–10.

Chevrolet, advertisement from unknown magazine, February 1923; depicts the Utility Coupe; excellent condition; $8–10.

Chevrolet, porcelain sign; used on side of garage; approximately 4 x 3 feet; excellent condition; $100–200.

Chevrolet, trolley sign; for Central Motor Company Limited; early; near-mint condition; $20–50.

CHRYSLER

Chrysler, Mr. Fleet bank; 9 inches tall; rubber; 1973, rare; excellent condition; $250–350.

Chrysler, Mr. Fleet bank; 9 inches tall; rubber; 1973; rare; $250–350. *Courtesy of Neil and Nancy Berliner. Photo by Donald Vogt.*

CONOCO

Conoco, gasoline globe; glass and plastic; 15 inches; round; excellent condition; $75–100.

DIXIE

Dixie, gasoline globe; glass and plastic; 15 inches; round; excellent condition; $75–150.

DODGE

The Dodge brothers, John and Horace, began their association with cars at the turn of the century when they both worked for someone else as mechanics in Niles, Michigan. Their first personally owned business was the Evans & Dodge Bicycle Company, founded in 1897 with Fred S. Evans, a Windsor, Ontario, businessman. The bike the brothers created was of the highest possible quality and was produced for approximately two years before the company was taken over by the National Cycle and Automobile Company, another Canadian firm.

With the $7,500 profit from their company's sale, the brothers started a business in Detroit in 1901, hiring twelve men to build automobile engines for customers such as the Oldsmobile Corporation. The Olds company continued to be a client even after the company was over a year old, ordering 3,000 transmissions in 1902. Soon, the Dodge brothers were one of the largest suppliers in the industry. Their reputation, created by working for Olds, spread, and Henry Ford soon came knocking on their door. Their factory grew, and by 1903, the Dodges employed more than 150 men.

In 1907, a portrait done of the Ford Motor Company's stockholders shows John F. Dodge and H. E. Dodge as part of the group. By 1913, the Dodge brothers ended their relationship with the Ford Motor Company, and in 1914, the first advertisements for the "new Dodge Brothers' car" appeared in newspapers and magazines. During the same year, the Dodge Brothers Motor Car Company was incorporated with $5 million worth of stock.

On each of those early cars, the Dodge Brothers emblem (a turquoise-blue-and-white six pointed star superimposed on a globe) was placed on the radiator. In successive years, production increased from the 1915 total of 45,053 to 1920s 145,000. They competed with the Ford Motor Company quite aggressively.

John Dodge died in January 1920, and Horace was devastated. In December of the same year, Horace died. To this day, their mysterious deaths arouse suspicion that the brothers were murdered because of the rocketlike popularity of their cars (they had risen to number three in sales across the nation).

The company passed through the family, and in 1925, the value of Dodge Brothers was approximately $50 million, though it was sold for about $150 million. The sale took the company out of family hands and into the hands of the investment firm of Dillon Read. After Dillon Read purchased the company, they brought in some truck manufacturers to run the company and the Dodge trucks they created were a great success.

When Dodge couldn't meet its payroll in 1928, the Chrysler Corporation purchased it, a move Chrysler later commented "was one of the soundest acts of my life."

DODGE

Dodge, calendar, illustrated by Maxfield Parrish; "A Calendar of Friendship"; 1927; complete with color cover: Prince Agib from the Arabian Nights; 8 x 5¾ inches; good condition; $95–135.

FISK TIRES

Fisk Tires, clock; electric; wood case; excellent condition, some scratches on face; $50–150.

FORD

The Ford Motor Company entered the business world on June 16, 1903. Henry Ford and eleven associates filed incorporation papers in Michigan, with only $28,000 cash and a whole

Ford Motor Company, brochures; (*a*) with well-known Scottie dog, reads: "The 60 Horsepower 1937 Ford V-8/The Economy Car in the Low-Price Field," opens to black-and-white display of models, 6 x 9 inches, 1937, $25–30; (*b*) Mercury (first year), opens to color display of models, 10 x 6 inches, 1939, $15–20. *Collection of Tim O'Callaghan. Photo by Tim O'Callaghan.*

lot of determination. But work had actually begun more than a decade earlier when Ford began experiments on the internal combustion engine. The first car was completed on June 4, 1896, in Detroit.

Those first cars were named by the letters of the alphabet, nineteen letters being used between 1903 and 1908. The first production car, the two-cylinder Model A, was sold on July 23, 1903, after being assembled at the Mack Avenue plant. Ford later moved to a larger building at Piquette and Beaubien streets, but not before he produced 1,700 cars in the old wagon factory on Mack Avenue. Ford Motor Company went international early in its history, incorporating Ford Motor Company of Canada, Ltd. on August 17, 1904.

In 1908, the first Model T was introduced. It had left-side steering and was the company's first immediate success because of its considerable improvement over all previous models. It should be noted here that some of the first nineteen cars were experimental, never reaching the public. The most successful of those first nineteen was the Model N, a small, light, four-cylinder machine that sold for $500.

After the Model T was introduced, the Ford Motor Company underwent some corporate changes, such as building the first moving automobile assembly line (1913), replacing the

Ford Motor Company, brochures; (*a*) "Ford Times," September 1916, cover is a painting of a landscape, a Ford, and a home or church, 98 pages, 9 x 6 inches, $17–22; (*b*) "Ford Times," September 1976, cover is a painting of a tugboat, 65 pages, 7 x 5 inches, .25–.50. *Collection of Tim O'Callaghan. Photo by Tim O'Callaghan.*

Ford Motor Company, brochure; with well-known slogan "There's a Ford in Your Future"; painting of a hand holding a Ford in a bubble; 20 pages of models in color; 11 x 8½ inches; 1946; $15–20. *Collection of Tim O'Callaghan. Photo by Tim O'Callaghan.*

old wage of $2.34 for a nine-hour day with at $5 daily wage for eight hours, and acquiring the Rouge Plant property (1915). By 1915, the company had built one million cars, and by 1917, it had introduced the first Ford truck as well as the world's first mass-produced tractor.

The company grew rapidly, incorporating the Delaware in 1919, purchasing the Lincoln Motor Company in 1922, and becoming a giant industrial complex with global influence by 1927. Edsel Ford succeeded Henry Ford as president of the company in 1919, and the two men shared the honors of driving the fifteen-millionth Model T off the assembly line on May 26, 1927.

On December 2, 1927, the Model A was introduced to the public and it was a vastly improved car, made in several body styles and a wide variety of colors. The Model A was produced until 1932, when the company discontinued production of all Model A passenger cars and trucks. By that time, 4,813,617 cars had been produced in the United States.

In 1932, the first V-8 Ford car was produced, and it became the favorite of performance-minded Americans. The year after it was introduced, the company built 199 Tri-Motor planes.

The company entered the medium-priced field with its Mercury in 1938, but all car production ceased in 1942 when efforts went toward supporting the war in Europe. The company, now headed by Edsel Ford, produced 8,600 four-engined B-24 "Liberator" bombers, 57,000 aircraft engines, and over 250,000 jeeps, tanks, tank destroyers, and other pieces of war machinery during the next three years.

After the war, the company was in poor financial straits. Edsel Ford had died in 1943 and Henry had resumed the presidency until the war was over, then his oldest grandson, Henry II, became president. He tackled the job of building the company's success all over again. In 1948, production began on the first postwar design, a 1949 Ford.

During the 1950s, several new cars were introduced, such as the Thunderbird (October 22, 1954), the Continental Mark II (October 4, 1955), the Edsel (September 4, 1957), the Galaxie Town Sedan (April 29, 1959), and the Falcon (October 8, 1959). But the most significant event of that decade was when Ford Motor Company common stock was sold to the public for the first time. Today the company has some 287,000 stockholders. The Edsel didn't last very long and the company announced it was dropping the line on November 19, 1959.

Perhaps Ford's greatest decade since the beginning years was the 1960s. The decade began with Henry Ford II being elected chairman of the board (in addition to being president) in 1960. During that same year, the company introduced its new Econoline truck series, including van, pickup, and station wagon bus. In 1961, the Fairlane was introduced, and in 1964, one of America's all-time favorites, the Mustang, a low-priced, four-passenger car, went on the road.

The advertising campaign that announced the Mustang proved historic. Reporters originally viewed the car at the Ford Pavillion at the New York World's Fair, after which they were given Mustangs and a set of road rally instructions that would take them 750 miles to Detroit. Stories were written by all the major newspapers, including simultaneous cover stories in *Time* and *Newsweek*. The company sponsored simultaneous programs on three major television networks and announcement ads were run in more than 2,600 newspapers in approximately 2,200 markets. The results were amazing: In less than two years, one million Mustangs were produced, making it the third-best selling car in the industry.

During the rest of the decade, the company introduced the Mercury Cougar (1966), dedicated the Automotive Safety Research Center and Service Research Center (1967), endured a company-wide strike by UAW (1967), introduced the Continental Mark III (1968) and the Ford Maverick (1969), and reorganized its senior management (1969).

One of the most recognizable men in American business today, Lee Iacocca, was elected president of Ford Motor Company on December 10, 1970, the same year the company introduced its new subcompact car, the Pinto. Three years later, the Mustang II was introduced to the public. Iacocca worked throughout the decade, helped to introduce the Fiesta to the European market in 1976 and a new Fairmont and Zephyr in 1977, but left the company in 1978.

Ford continued to produce new cars and make inroads into other types of industries throughout the 1970s and 1980s, and into the 1990s. For example: In 1979, the company purchased a

25 percent equity in Toyo Kogyo of Japan, which later became Mazda Motor Corporation: it launched the 1981 Ford Escort and Mercury Lynx "World Cars" in 1980; introduced the Ranger pickup truck in 1982; the first Ford Robotics and Automation Applications Consulting Center in Dearborn in 1982; introduced the Tempo, the Topaz, and several new European models in 1983; and even acquired interest in the Carnegie Group, Inc. and Inference Corp., artificial intelligence companies, in 1985. In 1987, the company added the Hertz Corporation to its list of acquisitions, and in 1988, introduced a new sporty specialty car, the Probe. By the end of the decade (1988), worldwide earnings were at an all-time high of $5.3 billion, the highest ever for any automotive company. And the company continues to acquire new companies and break new ground in the automotive industry on a regular basis.

It should be noted that with each new vehicle introduced, each anniversary that has passed, and each "changing of the corporate guard," the Ford Motor Company has produced memorabilia such as fountain pen sets, paperweights, lighters, toys, bookends, special awards, ashtrays, calendars, advertisements, and many other collectible items that aficionados have added to their collections. The items produced are too numerous to name here, but would give collectors enough to gather for quite a few years to come without ever becoming bored.

FORD

Ford, advertising mirror; Ellsworth Harrold Ford-Lincoln, Sacramento, California; Art Deco style; 1936; excellent condition; $50–75.

Ford, advertising mirror; Ford and Fordson; Hughes-Parmer Motor Co., Council Bluffs, Iowa; ca. 1920; excellent condition; $25–45.

Ford, advertising mirrors; Keller Bros., Buffalo Springs, Pennsylvania; three different years—1932, 1934, and 1948; all in good condition; $15–25.

Ford, ashtray; with V-8 motor on pedestal; issued by Universal Credit Company (GMAC for Ford); made of metal; 1940 giveaway to better accounts; rare; excellent condition; $400–600.

Ford, tin bank; "$100 over Book for your Car on a Big 1941

496 ■ ADVERTISING

Ford, advertising mirrors; Keller Bros., Buffalo Springs, Pennsylvania; three different years—(left) 1932, (center) 1934, (right) 1948, all in good condition; $15–25. *Collection of Charles Camara. Photo by Donald Vogt.*

Ford/dealer: Ragon Motor Co., Kenosha, Wisconsin"; excellent condition; $25–75.

Ford, bank; Model T; bronze; ca. 1918; 4 x 2½ x 2½ inches; Van Lopik Motor Sales Co., Coldwater, Michigan; customer giveaway; excellent condition; $150–175.

Ford, banks; the Galpin dogs; set of four; available only from Galpin Ford, Sepulveda, California; ceramic; all four are marked "Ford"; scarce; ca. 1954; excellent condition; $45–65 each.

Ford, book bank; made by H. O. Bell Company; Missoula, Michigan; ca. 1918; excellent condition; $150–175.

Ford, ashtray; with V-8 motor on pedestal; issued by Universal Credit Company (GMAC for Ford); made of metal; 1940 giveaway to better accounts; rare; $400–600. *Collection of Charles Camara. Photo by Donald Vogt.*

Ford, tin bank; "$100 over Book for your Car on a Big 1941 Ford dealer: Ragon Motor Co., Kenosha, Wisconsin"; $25–75. *Collection in Charles Camara. Photo by Donald Vogt.*

Transportation ■ 497

Ford, banks; the Galpin dogs; set of six; available only from Galpin Ford, Sepulveda, California; ceramic; all four are marked "Ford"; scarce; ca. 1954; $45–65 each. *Collection of Charles Camara. Photo by Donald Vogt.*

Ford, clock and pen desk set; November 1936; mahogany; dealer set; one-of-a-kind; original pen not available; excellent condition; $500–750 (all original).

Ford, compacts; dealer giveaways at Christmastime; four or five different styles; 1932, round; 1932, smaller round; $100–300 each; 1937, rare set, compact and cigarette case, mint, $300–500/the set; fiftieth anniversary, 1953, compacts, $75–125 each.

Ford, crystal ball bank; "Save for the new Ford"; ca. 1949; mint condition; $25–50.

Ford, game/advertising mirror; Sonora Motor Co., Sonora, Texas; ca. 1920; excellent condition; $25–45.

Ford, group of toy cars; all made of hard rubber; purchased at five-and-ten stores; made by Sieberling Rubber Company; all made in 1935; delivery van, state body truck, two-door sedan, coupe; excellent condition; $25–35 each.

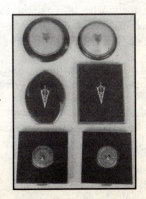

Ford, compacts; dealer giveaways at Christmastime; four different styles; (top, left to right) 1932, round; 1932, smaller round, $100–300 each; (middle) 1937, rare set, compact and cigarette case, mint, $300–500/the set; (bottom) 50th anniversary, 1953, compacts, $75–125 each. *Collection of Charles Camara. Photo by Donald Vogt.*

Ford, group of toy cars; all made of hard rubber; purchased at five-and-ten stores; made by Sieberling Rubber Company; all made in 1935; delivery van, state body truck, two-door sedan, coupe; $25–35 each. *Collection of Charles Camara. Photo by Donald Vogt.*

Ford Motor Company, assortment of pinback buttons; multicolored (From top left) (*a*) "1932 Ford 4 Ford Year," (*b*) "New V-8 Ford," (*c*) lettering over grill: "America's Choice for '34." (From bottom left) (*d*) lettering reads: "Ford," and photo of what appears to be a Ford sedan of 1940's, (*e*) lettering over drawing of a young woman at the wheel: "Take the Wheel . . . Try the new Ford 'Feel'," (*f*) lettering reads: "'Aye and Thrifty too!'" with photo of what appears to be a Scottie dog; ca. 1930s; $15–25 each. *Collection by Tim O'Callaghan. Photo by Tim O'Callaghan.*

Ford, matchbook covers; through the years; all in excellent condition; $5 each (except Model A version, which is approximately $15–20).

Ford, match safe; Hornberger Motor Co., Duquesne, Pennsylvania; ca. 1920; excellent condition; $25–65.

Ford Motor Company, assortment of pinback buttons; multicolored: "1932 Ford 4 Ford Year"; "New V-8 Ford"; lettering over grill "American Choice for '34"; lettering reads "Ford"; also photo of what appears to be a Ford sedan of 1940s, lettering over drawing of a young woman at the wheel: "Take the Wheel . . . Try the new Ford 'Feel'"; lettering reads "Aye and Thrifty too!" with photo of what appears to be a Scottie dog; ca. 1930s; all are in excellent condition; $15–25 each.

Ford Motor Company, brochure; "The New Ford,"; 1931 model; opens to full-color display of models; 9 x 5 inches; very good condition; $30–40.

Ford Motor Company, brochure; "Soy Bean Oil Meal and Soy Bean Oil Flakes"; red and black; 6 x 3 inches; 1923; excellent condition; $5–10.

Ford Motor Company, brochure; "Precision Ford Johansson Gaging [sic] Tools"; black and white; 8 x 5 inches; 1923; very good condition; $10–15.

TRANSPORTATION ■ 499

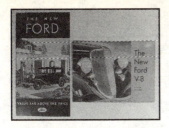

Ford Motor Company, brochures; (*a*) "The New Ford," 1931 model, opens to full-color display of models, 9 x 5 inches, $30–40; (*b*) "The New Ford V-8," 1933 model, opens to display of models, orange and black, 7½ x 5 inches, $20–25. *Collection of Tim O'Callaghan. Photo by Tim O'Callaghan.*

Ford Motor Company, brochures: (*a*) "Precision Ford Johansson Gaging [sic] Tools," black and white, 8 x 5 inches, 1923, $10–15; (*b*) "Soy Bean Oil Meal and Soy Bean Oil Flakes," red and black, 6 x 3 inches, 1923, $5–10. *Collection of Tim O'Callaghan. Photo by Tim O'Callaghan.*

Ford Motor Company, brochure; "The New Ford V-8"; 1933 model; opens to display of models; orange and black; 7½ x 5 inches; excellent condition; $20–25.

Ford Motor Company, brochure; "Visit Ford Airport [Dearborn]"; 4 x 8 inches; 1929; blue and white; good condition; $10–15.

Ford Motor Company, dealer giveaway; Wilken Auto Co., Breckenridge, Minnesota; daily calendar; 6 x 3 inches; 1914; very good condition; $5–10.

Ford Motor Company, flyer; "The Ford Model T"; 7 x 4 inches; folder; inside black with red price, outside red with white lettering; 1910; very good condition; $10–15.

Ford Motor Company, dealer giveaways; (*a*) Wilken Auto Co., Breckenridge, Minnesota, daily calendar, 6 x 3 inches, 1914; (*b*) shopping list, 5 x 3 inches, 1917; $5–10 each. *Collection of Tim O'Callaghan. Photo by Tim O'Callaghan.*

Ford Motor Company, flyer, "The Ford Model T"; 7 x 4 inches; folder; inside black with red price, outside red with white lettering; 1910; $10–15. *Collection of Tim O'Callaghan. Photo by Tim O'Callaghan.*

Ford Motor Company, brochures; (*a*) Ford Tri-Motor all-metal airplane, 8½ x 11 inches, 1930, $50–60; (*b*) "Visit Ford Airport [Dearborn]," 4 x 8 inches, 1929, both blue and white, $10–15. *Collection by Tim O'Callaghan. Photo by Tim O'Callaghan.*

Ford Motor Company, lapel pin; 1 inch; gold on blue enamel; 1909–1912; $35–45. *Collection of Tim O'Callaghan. Photo by Tim O'Callaghan.*

Ford Motor Company, Spanish language flyer; promotes weekly payments; folded; 6 x 4 inches; ca. 1920; $5–10. *Collection of Tim O'Callaghan. Photo by Tim O'Callaghan.*

Ford Motor Company, brochure; Ford Tri-Motor all-metal airplane; 8½ x 11 inches; 1930; very good condition; $50–60.

Ford Motor Company, lapel pin; 1 inch; gold on blue enamel; 1909–1912; very good condition; $35–45.

Ford Motor Company, shopping list; 5 x 3 inches; 1917; very good condition; $5–10.

Ford Motor Company, Spanish language flyer; promotes weekly payments; folded; 6 x 4 inches; ca. 1920; very good condition; $5–10.

Ford, Crystal ball paperweight, "There's a Ford in your Future"; H. R. Sivers; 1949; excellent condition; $40–65.

Ford, paperweight; Detroit Motor Sales Co, Inc.; ca. 1928; very good condition; $50–125.

Ford, paperweight; D. Ford Sullivan; dated September 11, 1922; excellent condition; $50–125.

Ford, paperweight; scalloped edge; W. I. Tupman Co.; "Figueroa & Jefferson" (California?); ca. 1920; excellent condition; $50–125.

Ford, pens and pencils giveaways group; Russell & Turner, Madison, Wisconsin (shows car), 1935; Berlin Motors, Berlin, Wisconsin, 1936; C. M. Combs, Cumberland, Ohio, 1936; Elliot Motor Co., Emporia, Kansas, 1936; Orangeville Sales & Service, Orangeville, Illinois, 1936; Arlington Motor Co., Arlington, Wisconsin, 1939; all in near-mint condition; all $20–35 each.

Ford, perpetual calendar; "The Pearson Co., Kenmore, Ohio"; ca. 1930; good condition; $75–150.

Ford, group of assorted pinbacks; ca. 1915–1953; all in excellent condition; $5–100.

Ford, salt and pepper shakers; World's Fair, 1934; "Century of Progress"; metal; die-cast; excellent condition; $100–300.

Ford, group of assorted tokens; various years; bronze; used to advertise special events; given by dealers to their customers; all near-mint condition; $5–35 each.

Ford, perpetual calendar; "The Pearson Co., Kenmore, Ohio"; ca. 1930; good condition; $75–150. *Collection of Charles Camera. Photo by Donald Vogt.*

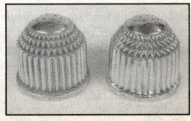

Ford, salt and pepper shakers; World's Fair, 1934; "Century of Progress"; metal; die-cast; $100–300. *Collection of Charles Camera. Photo by Donald Vogt.*

502 ■ ADVERTISING

Ford; upholstery brush, Southwestern Motor Sales, ca. 1936, $12–65; upholstery brush, Zirkle Motor Co., ca. 1920, $12–65; upholstery brush with handle, Dyck Motor Co., Fowler, Kansas, 1929 Christmas greeting (Model A era), $25–60. *Collection of Charles Camera. Photo by Donald Vogt.*

Ford, world paperweights; given out by the company to the public; (from left to right, first row) Cologne, Germany, plant, 1931, $100–300; 1938, $100–300; (second row) Henry Ford medallion, very rare, 1920, $100–300; three heads of Ford, 1953, 50th anniversary, $25–75. *Collection of Charles Camera. Photo by Donald Vogt.*

Ford, toy cars; 1935; on top of original box; from San Diego World's Fair; one is red and one is blue (they were available in five different colors); near-mint condition; $200–400 each.

Ford, upholstery brush with handle; "Dyck Motor Co., Fowler, Kansas"; 1929 Christmas greeting (Model A era); excellent condition; $25–60.

Ford, upholstery brush; Southwestern Motor Sales; ca. 1936; excellent condition; $12–65.

Ford, world paperweights; given out by the company to the public; Cologne, Germany, plant, 1931, $100–300; 1938, $100–300; Henry Ford medallion, very rare, 1920, $100–300; three heads of Ford, 1953, 50th anniversary, all in excellent condition; $25–75.

Ford, World's Fair postcards (set of 10); 1934; excellent condition; $100–125.

Ford, World's Fair souvenir gear shift knobs; 1934 (Century of Progress), 1935 (San Diego), 1935 (Atlantic City), 1936 (Dallas), 1936 (Rotunda), 1937 (Rotunda, mushroom knob), 1939 (New York World's Fair); all in excellent condition; $100–300 each.

FRIGIDTEST ANTIFREEZE
Frigidtest Antifreeze, can; depicts polar bears on icebergs with plane

in background; blue and white; 7¾ x 6½ inches; ca. 1940s; excellent condition; $15–20.

FRY/RED CROWN

Fry/Red Crown Gas Pump; Fry made the pump; Red Crown is the gasoline; approximately 9 feet tall; completely restored; original globe; ca. 1920s; excellent condition; $2,600–3,000.

GENERAL ELECTRIC/MAZDA

(*see also* "General Electric" in Lighting chapter)

General Electric/Mazda Super Auto Lamps, porcelain corner sign; 6 x 6 x 16 inches; blue and white; ca. 1940; very good condition; $300–400.

GENERAL MOTORS

William Crapo Durant became head of the Buick Manufacturing Company in 1904, and by 1907, he had made the company the second largest car manufacturer in the country. With a dream to meet the country's future demand of "a million cars a year," Durant drew together a group of suppliers and producers, then filed incorporation papers for General Motors Company in New Jersey in 1908. In 1909, Buick, Olds, Oakland, and Cadillac had joined General Motors; Chevrolet joined in 1918; and by 1920, more than thirty companies came under the GM umbrella.

GM offered a line that included seven automobiles, a truck company, and other companies that included Harrison Radiator, DELCO, Champion Spark Plug, Dayton Wright Airplane, and Hyatt Roller Bearing.

General Electric/Mazda Super Auto Lamps, porcelain corner sign; 6 x 6 x 16 inches; blue and white; ca. 1940; very good condition, $300–400. *Collection of and photo by Michael Bruner.*

During World War I, GM turned its talents and manufacturing abilities to producing war materials such as trucks, staff cars, tractor V-8 engines, mortar shells, and America's first fully armored car. It also continued to manufacture domestic cars. By the 1920s, the car was firmly established in America, and GM went through a huge expansion. New cars were continually introduced in all lines GM produced. During this period, General Motors opened its first international office in Denmark, on October 25, 1923. By the end of the decade, GM had become the largest automobile manufacturer in Europe. In 1925, GM acquired the Yellow Cab Manufacturing Co., once owned by John Hertz (who would later begin the rent-a-car industry).

During the 1930s, the face of the automobile industry changed almost as much as the face of the country, which had endured a major depression and was now struggling through recovery. The design of the car flowed to the top of the tires rather than resembling the 1920s version of a box on wheels. Radiator hoods and the rear end now blended smoothly with body—the car, as the nation, had become streamlined. GM's 1930 Cadillac sported a V-16 engine, the first car engine to be styled. A classic, it was the first of its kind and the forerunner of a whole generation of V-16s. In 1933, GM exhibited two experimental 600 horsepower 8-cylinder Diesel engines at the Century of Progress World's Fair in Chicago. The exhibit marked the beginning of GM's entry into the locomotive industry.

Throughout the 1930s, GM built 1,462 models exclusively for the Greyhound Bus Lines. These models helped Greyhound become the best-known long-distance bus company in America's history.

World War II interrupted the automobile industry, as it did every other aspect of American life. Once again, GM turned its manufacturing abilities to helping the war effort, this time producing shells, trucks, gun parts, and aircraft engines. But it also continued to produce new cars—in fact, 1940 was Buick's best production year since 1928.

The early 1950s saw Chevrolet's introduction of its popular Corvette (1952). The first run of 319 Corvettes was produced—and hand-assembled—at the company's Flint, Michigan, plant. All were painted Polo White (see also the section on Chevrolet).

The 1950s was a decade of experimentation. Unfortunately, quite a few of the innovations never made it any farther than the splashy Motorama productions that introduced them.

Compact cars came to the fore in the 1960s, when Americans became concerned about fuel economy. GM also produced sports cars like the Corvette, the Camaro, the Firebird, and the Pontiac GTO during that turbulent decade.

Concern with fuel economy heightened in the 1970s and federal involvement with the auto industry further shaped the designs to come. High fuel costs and foreign competition changed the automobile marketplace and started a trend that ran rampant through the 1980s—customers turned to the less expensive, fuel-efficient imports. Sales went down and the corporation experienced its worst yearly sales total since the mid-1970s.

In the 1990s, the company's American outlets are concentrating on building American faith in American products.

GENERAL MOTORS
(*see also* GM's other products and companies, listed individually)
General Motors, Mr. Goodwrench Jim Beam bottle; made by Regal China Corp., 14 inches; ca. 1978; excellent condition; $75–125.

GOODRICH
Goodrich Tires, advertisement from *Saturday Evening Post*, June 1923; advertises Goodrich Heavy-Duty Cord "Best in the Long Run"; two colors; very good condition; $3–5.

General Motors, Mr. Goodwrench Jim Beam bottle; made by Regal China Corp.; 14 inches; ca. 1978; $75–125. *Courtesy of Neil and Nancy Berliner. Photo by Neil Berliner.*

Goodrich Tires; advertisement from *Saturday Evening Post*, June 1923; advertises Goodrich Heavy-Duty Cord "Best in the Long Run"; two colors; very good condition; $3–5. *Courtesy of Past Gas. Photo by Donald Vogt.*

Goodrich, tire repair kit; kit and original tin can holding it; ca. 1915; very good condition; $20–40.

GOODYEAR

In 1839, Charles Goodyear, a Connecticut inventor, spilled a batch of India rubber and sulfur on a hot stove. His accident resulted in the discovery of vulcanized rubber. Though he applied for patents and did some initial business with the United States government, Goodyear had bad luck in establishing his business. He was sued, then tried (and failed) to start his company in France. Sadly, he died in a Paris debtors' prison in 1860, almost thirty years before two brothers from Akron, Ohio, memorialized him.

The actual Goodyear company began in 1898, bought by thirty-eight-year-old Frank Sieberling with $3,500 he borrowed from a brother-in-law. The brothers Frank and Charles Sieberling used Charles Goodyear's process to make bicycle tires. They named the company "The Goodyear Tire & Rubber Company" and used the winged-foot symbol as their trademark after seeing a statue of Mercury on a stairway's newel post in Frank's home.

Production began in 1898 with a line of bicycle and carriage tires, horseshoe pads, and, believe it or not, poker chips. The company produced the world's first rubber tire in 1926. Other firsts include a patent for the tubeless tire in 1903; special pneumatic tires for aircraft, developed in 1909; the first interstate truck fleet (the Wingfoot Express); the first American-made synthetic rubber tire in 1937; the first nylon cord tire in 1947; and the first all-season auto tire, the Tiempo, in 1977.

The company's first recognizable slogan—"More people ride on Goodyear tires than on any other kind"—was adopted in 1916. Its first rubber plantation began operation in Indonesia the same year. It appears that other companies began running rubber plantations before this date and that some (one?) may have used the same Goodyear name, however, *the* Goodyear company did not begin producing rubber outside the United States before the date heretofore mentioned.

Eighteen years after the company began making bicycle tires, it had become the nation's biggest tire manufacturer and had factories all over the world. Ads produced during the second decade of the twentieth century touted Goodyear's winning cord tires, showing them in use during record-setting races such as the Akron-Chicago-Baltimore run, entered by a driver named Barney Oldfield, who was sponsored by carmaker Henry Ford.

During the Depression, Goodyear joined other companies in a desperate attempt to attract new customers with the use of fear in advertising—showing pictures of cars wrecked by a tire blowout and stating that certain Goodyear tires could give owners a modicum of safety.

Today the company makes tires for almost every vehicle—except, ironically, bicycles. Goodyear's product line also includes such a variety of products as automotive belts and hoses, industrial hoses and conveyor belts, polyester for tire cord and bottles, packaging films, polyurethane and composite plastic panels, and shoe soles and heels. The company has one of the most recognizable corporate symbols—and one of the only ones that "flies on its own"—in the Goodyear blimp. Though other companies currently fly blimps, the Goodyear blimp is still the one we see over sports facilities, and even young children know which company it represents. Goodyear has more than eighty production facilities throughout the world and employs approximately 100,000 people. It is the only major publicly held tire-and-rubber company in the United States and ranks second in worldwide sales, first in the United States.

GOODYEAR

Goodyear, advertisement from *Saturday Evening Post*, June 13, 1953; caption reads "True in 1915 . . . still true in 1953"; full color; very good condition; $5–8.

Goodyear, advertisement from *Saturday Evening Post*, June 13, 1953; caption reads "True in 1915 . . . still true in 1953"; full color; very good condition; $5–8. *Courtesy of Past Gas. Photo by Donald Vogt.*

Goodyear, calendar; 1940; full pad; excellent condition; $8–15.

Goodyear, key chain; company name written on tag with familiar Mercury logo; plastic; excellent condition; $6–8.

GULF
Gulf, gas tanks; one Gulftane; ca. 1960s, no globe, $700–800; other Gulf No-Nox, 1964, replaced globe, $795–895. Both in restored condition.

HILLMAN MINX
Hillman Minx Automobile, polychrome porcelain enameled trade sign; very good condition; $400–600.

KORODY-COYLER
Korody-Coyler Corporation, KC piston nodder; 7 inches; ca. early 1970s; excellent condition; $500–600.

LIBERTY
Liberty Gasoline, globe; 1990 reproduction; glass; 14 inch diameter; red, black, and white original was made in 1940s; new/reproduction condition; $50–65.

MARATHON
Marathon Tires, tin sign; depicts family in car going over treacherous road; 22½ x 16½ inches; 1915 copyright; excellent condition; $5,000–6,000.

MICHELIN TIRE CO.
The Michelin Tire Man, also known as Bibendum, has been the company's trademark since 1896. Designed by a cartoonist named Maurice Rossillon, who signed his work O'Galop, Mr. Bib first appeared on a poster with his champagne glass raised, saying "Nunc est bibendum . . . A Votre Sante" ("Now we can drink . . . To Your Health"). Instead of bubbly champagne, the glass held nails, broken glass, and bottles, and across the bottom of the poster was written "The Michelin tire drinks all obstacles."

Bib's image pops up along French roadsides, giving travelers speed limits and other useful information.

MICHELIN
Michelin, ashtray; 5 inches; ca. 1970s; near-mint condition; $75–125.

Transportation ■ 509

Michelin; large figure made for truck hoods, 17½ inches tall, ca. 1970s, also used as a lamp, $100–250; figure in racing car, 3 inches, ca. 1980s, promotional piece, $75–125; figure sitting on truck, 6 inch toy, (possibly a Dinky), ca. 1940–1950s, $250–300; ashtray, 5 inches, ca. 1970s, $75–125; small hood ornament, 8 inches, ca. 1980s, $75–125. *Courtesy of Neil and Nancy Berliner. Photo by Donald Vogt.*

Michelin, figure in racing car; 3 inches; ca. 1980s; promotional piece; excellent condition; $75–125.

Michelin, large figure made for truck hoods; 17½ inches tall; ca. 1970s; also used as a lamp; excellent condition; $100–250.

Michelin, figure sitting on truck; 6 inches; toy, (possibly a Dinky); ca. 1940–1950s; excellent condition; $250–300.

Michelin, small hood ornament; 8 inches; ca. 1980s; excellent condition; $75–125.

MISCELLANEOUS

Four gas pumps; completely restored; Blue Sonoco, approximately 7 feet tall, ca. 1940s; $1,400–1,600; Esso, Sinclair, and Shell are all approximately 6 feet tall, all ca. 1950s, all have replacement globes, all priced at $1,075–1,200 each.

MOBIL

Begun in 1886 as the Vacuum Oil Company, the company became one of the pieces of Rockefeller's oil trust split in 1911 (see the section on Exxon, page 736. In 1931, Vacuum joined with Socony and began selling oil and gasoline products under the Mobil flying red horse symbol. In 1935, the name was charged to Socony-Mobil, and in 1966, to Mobil.

Mobil's trademark, the winged horse, is used for all aspects of Mobil's multibillion-dollar business, refineries, gas stations, bulk plants, trucks, and so on. The trademark, originally used by foreign subsidiaries of Standard Oil of New York (Socony) and the Vacuum Oil Company as early as 1911, became Americanized around 1933.

For a long time, the flying red horse symbol was used alone on Mobil gas station signs, until the company realized the general public was not associating the logo with a particular company. After much discussion, they redesigned the sign to include the company's name as well as the familiar logo.

Mobil supports the Public Broadcasting System. In December 1984, it stopped advertising in the *Wall Street Journal*, but in 1987, the company ended its boycott of the newspaper.

MOBIL

Mobil, globe; glass with metal frame; marked "Standard Kerosene" with flying horse logo; approximately 15 inch diameter; ca. 1930; excellent condition; $500–650.

Mobil, porcelain sign; round Mobil oil Socony-Vacuum sign; depicts flying horse symbol; approximately 24 inch diameter; very good condition; $200–300.

Mobil, porcelain sign; oil; red; approximately 20 x 24 inches; excellent condition; $50–110.

MORAND CUSHION WHEELS

Morand Cushion Wheels, paperweight; made for "Motor Trucks"; ca. 1900–1920; 2½ x 4 inches; excellent condition; $50–65.

OLDSMOBILE

Oldsmobile, sign; marked "Walker & Co., Detroit"; 60 inches across; good/original condition; $800–1,200.

Morand Cushion Wheels, paperweight; made for "Motor Trucks"; ca. 1900–1920; 2½ x 4 inches; $50–65. *From the collection of Stuart Kammerman. Photo by David Kammerman.*

The Peckham Truck Co., paperweight; depicts truck frame; company located in New York; ca. 1900–1920; 2½ x 4 inches; $50–75. *From the collection of Stuart Kammerman. Photo by David Kammerman.*

Phillips Petroleum Company, nodder; 8 inches; man holding gas nozzles rather than guns; ca. 1960s; $300–400. *Courtesy of Neil and Nancy Berliner. Photo by Donald Vogt.*

PECKHAM TRUCK CO.

The Peckham Truck Co., paperweight; depicts truck frame; company located in New York; ca. 1900–1920; 2½ x 4 inches; excellent condition; $50–75.

PHILLIPS PETROLEUM

Phillips Petroleum Company, nodder; 8 inches tall; man holding gas nozzles rather than guns; ca. 1960s; excellent condition; $300–400.

POLARINE

Polarine Motor Oil, can; 5 gallons; pictures people in open touring car, mountains in background; Standard Oil Company product; 9½ inches square x 15 inches; very good/excellent condition, slight overall fade; $400–600.

Polarine Motor Oil, tin can and case; illustration on oil can shows open touring car; accompanied by original standard oil company wooden crate; overall size 10½ x 14½ x 11 inches; very good condition, some fading to can colors; $400–600.

PONTIAC

Pontiac, calendar; nicely matted and framed; dated 1950, December; overall framed size approximately 27 x 37 inches; excellent condition; $175–200.

Pontiac Service, porcelain sign; large two-sided silhouetted Indian logo in red, white, and blue; 41¾ inch diameter; fair/good condition, general wear overall, some fading, in-painting on both sides; $100–200.

POWER G.

Power G., gasoline globe; glass; 15 inches; round; excellent condition; $200–300.

PURE GAS PUMP

Pure Gas Pump; approximately 7 feet tall; completely restored; $1,400–1,800.

RED CROWN

Red Crown, gasoline globe; Standard Oil; glass; 15½ inches tall x 13 inches wide at widest point; average condition; $100–200.

Red Crown, gasoline globe; white milk glass with red lettering; excellent condition; $1,250–1,500.

REX ENCLOSURES AND TOPS

Rex Enclosures and Tops, advertisement from *Saturday Evening Post*, September 13, 1924; depicts a car fitted with a Rex Enclosure; very good condition; $3–5.

SHELL

Shell, advertisement from *Saturday Evening Post*, ca. 1940s; depicts wounded soldier in bed with caption "He's doing all right . . . Thank you."; full color; very good condition; $5–8.

Shell, gas cans; 5 gallons; restored condition; $95–125.

Shell, enamel sign; red and white with Shell logo; approximately 3 feet square; excellent condition; $45–75.

SINCLAIR POWER

Sinclair Power, gasoline globe; glass and plastic; 15 inches; round; excellent condition; $200–300.

SOCONY

Socony, gasoline globe; blue, red, and white metal-banded glass inserted motor gasoline globe; 18 x 20 x 6 inches; good condition, some lifting and background color loss to insert, slight fading of color; $200–300.

STEELCOTE

Steelcote Auto Polish, tins (4); interesting lot of automobile pictured tins with original contents; 2½ x 5 x 1¾ inches each; good/very good condition, some minor scratching and denting, slight discoloration; $25–75.

STUDEBAKER

Studebaker, sign; "Studebaker Authorized Service"; marked "Walker and Company, Detroit"; 45 inches across; excellent condition; $200–400.

SUNOCO

Sunoco, gas pump; approximately 7 feet tall; completely restored; 1940s; original globe; $2,400–2,700.

TEXACO

Joseph Cullinan, a former Standard Oil employee, became partners in 1902 with Arnold Schlaet, an investment banker, to form the Texas Fuel Company. At first, the company's oil ran home lamps, southern planters' sugar boilers, and locomotives. However, when cars came into vogue, Texaco opened a chain of service stations. In 1936, Texaco went international when it joined Standard Oil of California (Chevron).

As did other companies of the era, Texaco made some unfortunate decisions during World War II—selling oil to Francisco Franco, Spain's dictator, shipping oil to Germany, and serving as courier for Germany's peace plan (the one that required England to surrender). Texaco's president, Torkild Rieber, even celebrated Germany's invasion of France, was accused of harboring a Nazi spy, and was finally forced to resign. To erase their negative image, the company began sponsoring Metropolitan Opera broadcasts and expanded into every state.

Today, Texaco is an international corporation, having refineries all over the world.

TEXACO

Texaco, advertisement from *Saturday Evening Post*, December 29, 1923; "All aboard!"; depicts father in raccoon coat herding kids into car; two colors; excellent condition; $3–5.

Texaco, advertisement from *Saturday Evening Post*, October 4, 1952; depicts referee with arms crossed; full color; very good condition; $3–5.

Texaco, advertisement from *Saturday Evening Post*, October 4, 1952; depicts referee with arms crossed; full color; very good condition; $3–5. *Courtesy of Past Gas. Photo by Donald Vogt.*

Texaco Motor Oil, can; made to go under the seat; marked "The Texas Company, Port Arthur, Texas, U.S.A."; side handle; ½ gallon; 5½ x 7½ x 2½ inches; ca. 1920s; very good condition; $200–300.

Texaco, pump; completely restored; approximately 7 feet tall; ca. 1930; $2,000–3,500.

U.S. TIRE

U.S. Tire, clock; lithograph on wood; brass hands; 18 inch diameter; depicts satisfied customer wearing duster cap and goggles; excellent working condition; $4,000–5,000.

VALVOLINE

Valvoline Go Mix Outboard Fuel, gasoline globe; glass and plastic; 15 inches; round; excellent condition; $300–400.

WAYNE TANK & PUMP COMPANY

Wayne Tank & Pump Company, advertisement from *Saturday Evening Post*, 1922; "Building a filling station that pays"; very good condition; $5–8.

WHIZ AUTO TOP DRESSING

Whiz Auto Top Dressing, paper sign; depicts two gnomes applying the dressing to a car; 37 x 12 inches excluding frame; good condition, some creasing and slight paper loss; $300–500.

ZEPHYR

Zephyr, gasoline globe; glass; 15 inches; round; excellent condition; $75–150.

BICYCLES
■ ■ ■

COLUMBIA BICYCLES
Columbia produced the largest number of America's bicycles in the nineteenth century. Its Art Nouveau ads depicting Victorian ladies riding bicycles speak most explicitly about the nation's transition from self-propelled transportation to motorized vehicles.

<u>COLUMBIA BICYCLES</u>
Columbia Bicycles, advertisement from *Ladies' Home Journal*, ca. 1934; depicts family on bicycles; excellent condition; $4–6.

Columbia Bicycles, paper roll down; unusual; illustrates a woman on a three-wheel bicycle; rare; colors are very bright and vivid; 13 x 28 inches; complete with metal hands on both top and bottom; very good condition with minor creasing; $1,500–2,000.

BOATS/SHIPS
■ ■ ■

<u>AMERICAN LINE</u>
American Line, tin letter folder; multicolored die-cut marker; pictures ocean liner under full steam; 12 x 3¼ inches; excellent to near-mint condition with minor superficial wear, slight edge chipping and minor chipping to back; $250–400.

<u>EVINRUDE</u>
Evinrude Outboard Motor, packing crate lid; pictures the motor on lid and includes company information; 43 x 16 inches; very good condition; $25–75.

<u>FALL RIVER LINE</u>
Fall River Line, paper sign; small but powerful image of the *Bristol* steamer running between New York and Boston; interesting night scene; 13 x 10½ inches; very good/excellent condition, margins appear trimmed; $350–650.

<u>GUION LINE</u>
Guion Steamship Line, paper poster; early advertisement by Hatch Litho Co.; pictures the *Arizona*—"The fastest steamer afloat"; 31 x 21 inches; fair condition, overall wrinkling of paper, some image loss due to center fold, borders trimmed; $75–150.

STATE LINE

State Line, paper sign; 1870s Hatch litho; pictures sailor on State Line flagpole with ship in background surrounded by world globes representing ports of call; bannered topography; classic presentation; 21¼ x 14¾ inches; excellent condition, some minor soiling overall, very minor edge trimming; $800–1,200.

BUSES

GREYHOUND

Though Greyhound Dial still makes buses, it also handles airline food, airport luggage and fueling (Dobbs and Carson International), runs a cruise line, and sells products such as Armour Star canned meats, Brillo soap pads, Dial soap, Lunch Bucket microwave meals, Purex detergents, and Boraxo and 20 Mule Team.

The company began by transporting miners over Minnesota's Mesabi Iron Range, something Greyhound's leader, John W. Teets, wanted to forget. Greyhound actually came about as the result of a merger of Carl Eric Wickman's Motor Transit Company with several smaller companies. The largest company became the Greyhound Corporation and used the running dog symbol—at one point, a live Greyhound (Lady Greyhound) was used on promotional tours.

GREYHOUND

Greyhound, advertisement; color photo of family sitting in driveway; "We're a two-car family now!"; excellent condition; $4–7.

Greyhound, advertisement from *Life*, ca. 1954; caption reads "When you want to travel straight through . . ."; excellent condition; $4–7.

Greyhound, advertisement from *Country Gentleman*, October 1939; full color; "Last Call for the Fair"; excellent condition; $4–7.

Greyhound, advertisement from *Life* ca. 1944; depicts army man saying "I fought for this . . . one day I'm going to see and enjoy all of it!"; excellent condition; $4–7.

Greyhound, advertisement from *Saturday Evening Post*, March 5, 1932; full color; excellent condition; $4–7.

TRANSPORTATION ■ 517

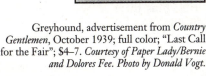

Greyhound, advertisement from *Life*, ca. 1954; caption reads "When you want to travel straight through . . ."; $4–7. *Courtesy of Paper Lady/Bernie and Dolores Fee. Photo by Donald Vogt.*

Greyhound, advertisement from *Country Gentlemen*, October 1939; full color; "Last Call for the Fair"; $4–7. *Courtesy of Paper Lady/Bernie and Dolores Fee. Photo by Donald Vogt.*

MISCELLANEOUS

Bus station, porcelain sign; unusual two-sided porcelain sign in black and white picturing people getting onto a public service bus, with original iron flange holder; 16 inch diameter excluding holder; fair/good condition, chipping in image on both sides, soil staining; $100–300.

MOTOR BUS LINES

Motor Bus Lines of America, advertisement from *Colliers*, 1943; full color; caption reads "Over Highways of Tomorrow"; excellent condition; $4–7.

Motor Bus Lines of America, advertisement from *Collier's*, 1943; full color; caption reads "Over Highways of Tomorrow"; $4–7. *Courtesy of Paper Lady/Bernie and Dolores Fee. Photo by Donald Vogt.*

MOTORCYCLES
###

HARLEY DAVIDSON

Harley Davidson, mug; reads "Happy Birthday to a Monumental American" and shows the Statue of Liberty; box is marked "Harley Davidson Mug"; ca. 1986; mint in-box condition; $20–25.

INDIAN

Indian Motorcycles, sign; reproduction of old tin sign; features 1934 model; new/reproduction condition; $12 retail.

Indian Motorcycles, lot of ephemera; printer proof plates for 1949 interim model and celebrities, plus three showroom banners; very good/excellent condition; $50–200.

MISCELLANEOUS

Tin sign; 16 x 12 inches; depicts man in knickers and golf cap on 'cycle; reproduction; $15 retail.

PLANES
###

AIR FRANCE

Air France, poster; Air France to Japan; lithographed in bright reds, oranges, and yellows with blue and green; printed in Paris by S. A. Courbet; 1962; very good condition; $30–50.

Harley Davidson, mug; reads "Happy Birthday to a Monumental American" and shows the Statue of Liberty; box is marked "Harley Davidson Mug"; ca. 1986; mint in-box condition; $20–25. *Collection of and photo by Iris November.*

Indian Motorcycles, sign; reproduction of old tin sign; features 1934 model; new/reproduction condition; $12. *Courtesy of and photo by Castle Antiques & Reproductions.*

AMERICAN AIRLINES

In the 1940s, American Airlines' advertisements focused on the soldier who needed to be someplace *urgently*. The ads also tended to try to convince the average American that flying was as safe as other types of travel.

During the 1960s, airline advertising appeared to focus on the company's flight personnel, particularly attractive stewardesses. Presumably, if a customer believed that one airline's stews were prettier than another, that would constitute good enough reason to change companies. One ad produced by American Airlines in 1968 asked the reader to look at the attendant sitting seductively in a chair and "Think of Her as Your Mother."

AMERICAN AIRLINES

American Airlines, calendar; 1956; shows plane; excellent condition; $85–100.

American Airlines, poster; designed by Ben Hill for New England Travel; 40 x 30 inches; excellent condition; $25–40.

American Airlines, poster; promotes flights to Mexico; designed by Loweree; 40 x 30 inches; excellent condition; $20–40.

BOEING AIRLINES

I mentioned earlier that an American Airlines 1968 ad asked the reader to think of an attractive attendant as "Your Mother." Less than a decade later (in 1977), advertising's depiction of the American female had changed so much that Boeing's ad for that year depicted a middle-aged female executive poring over business papers while en route home. What a difference a decade makes!

BOEING

Boeing Airlines, advertisement from *Newsweek*, 1946; full color; shows Boeing Stratocruiser; excellent condition; $5–7.

Boeing Airlines, advertisement from *Saturday Evening Post*, 1948; black and white; shows Boeing Stratocruiser; excellent condition; $5–6.

Boeing Airlines, advertisement from *Saturday Evening Post*, 1957; full color; photo of Boeing 707; excellent condition; $6–8.

520 ■ ADVERTISING

Boeing Airlines, advertisement from *Saturday Evening Post*, 1957; full color; photo of Boeing 707; $6–8. *Courtesy of Lester Morris. Photo by Donald Vogt.*

Boeing Airlines, advertisement from *National Geographic*, 1966; full color; depicts pilots' emblems; $5–7. *Courtesy of Lester Morris. Photo by Donald Vogt.*

Boeing Airlines, advertisement from *Fortune* magazine, 1964; shows Boeing Cargo Jet, black-and-white photos of all Boeing's lines (including Pan Am, TWA, Qantas, etc.); excellent condition; $5–7.

Boeing Airlines, advertisement from *National Geographic*, 1966; full color; depicts pilots' emblems; excellent condition; $5–7.

Boeing Airlines, advertisement from *Time* magazine, 1966; black and white; depicts Boeing SST; excellent condition; $3–4.

MISCELLANEOUS

Poster, "The Nation, State and City welcome the world's greatest aviators/Dayton, Ohio/June 17–18, 1909"; depicts Wright brothers in upper corners and their plane in the center; 30½ x 21 inches; good condition, some damage; $5,000–7,500.

PAN AMERICAN

Pan American World Airways, poster; advertises nonstop to Jamaica via Avianca; color lithograph; designed by Adolph Treidler; 40 x 30 inches; excellent condition; $35–70.

SWISS AIRLINES

Swiss Airlines, poster; promotes Mediterranean travel; abstract design; printed in Switzerland; 40 x 25 inches; excellent/very good condition; $20–40.

TWA

TWA Jets, poster; promotes flights to Paris; multicolor Parisian scenes by David Klein; 40 x 25 inches; excellent condition; $25–50.

TRAINS
■■■

AMERICAN LOCOMOTIVE

American Locomotive Company, framed locomotive builder's photograph; steam engine, 4-8-4; Lehigh Valley, New York; very good condition; $150–250.

BOSTON AND MAINE

Boston and Maine, railroad prints (2); framed; black-and-white print of the steam engine *Black Arrow*, and a color print depicting the 4200 diesel freight locomotive designed and built by Electro-Motive Division, General Motors Corporation; very good condition; $75–150.

BOUND BROOK

Bound Brook Root, calendar; early locomotive image on this unusual mechanical calendar; 10½ x 8¾ inches; good condition, missing three of the corner edges, some scratching; $25–75.

BROTHERHOOD OF RAILROAD TRAINMEN

Brotherhood of Railroad Trainmen, posters (2); both posters promote "benevolence, sobriety and industry" for this organization with multiple images; 22 x 28 inches each excluding frames; very good overall condition, minor fading to one poster; $50–150.

CHESAPEAKE & OHIO RAILROAD

L. C. Probert, vice president of the Chesapeake & Ohio Railroad, was responsible for procuring the company's trademark, known as "Chessie." In 1933, Probert saw an etching (titled *The Sleepy Cat*) by Viennese artist Gruenewald in a New York newspaper. He immediately clipped the picture and wanted it included in the advertisement announcing C & O's new air-conditioned sleeper cars. The slogan became "sleep like a kitten in air-conditioned comfort," and the first ad ran in the September 1933 issue of *Fortune*.

CHESAPEAKE AND OHIO

Chesapeake and Ohio Lines, advertisement from *Fortune* magazine, ca. 1930s; excellent condition; $5–8.

Chesapeake and Ohio Lines, tin sign; depicts Chessie the Cat; 15 x 12½ inches; reproduction; $15 retail.

GREAT NORTHERN RAILROAD

Great Northern Railroad, calendar; 1931 July sheet; titled "Yellow Head"; approximately 10 x 22 inches excluding mat and frame; overall 15¼ x 27½ inches; near-mint condition; $75–125.

Great Northern Railroad, calendar sheet; 1928; pictures Little Plume, chief of Blackfeet; approximately 10 x 22 inches excluding mat and frame; near-mint condition; $100–200.

GREAT ROCK ISLAND ROUTE

Great Rock Island Route, paperweight; promotes "Solid Vestibule Trains"; ca. 1910–1930; 2½ inch diameter; excellent condition; $50–75.

HINCKLEY & WILLIAMS WORKS

Hinckley & Williams Works, lithograph for steam locomotive; sign done by the New England Litho Co., Summer Street, Boston; colors are very nice and depict an old steam locomotive with a cowcatcher in front pulling a coal car marked "Hinckley"; much brass-colored work on the train in shades of red, green, and black; matted and nicely framed; overall 32 x 22½ inches; good condition, some water discoloration to the right but does not affect the locomotive, staining; $800–1,200.

Chesapeake and Ohio Lines, tin sign; depicts Chessie the Cat; 15 x 12½ inches; reproduction; $15 retail. *Courtesy of Doc Davis/Antique-Alike. Photo by Donald Vogt.*

Great Rock Island Route, paperweight; promotes "Solid Vestibule Trains"; ca. 1910–1930; 2½ inch diameter; $50–75. *From the collection of Stuart Kammerman. Photo by David Kammerman.*

LAKESHORE AND MICHIGAN RAILROAD

Lakeshore and Michigan Railroad, paper poster; early double-registered image of "The mail carrier of 100 years ago"; shows the Pony Express rider, then below (and triple the size) "The flight of the Fast Mail on the Lake Shore and Michigan Southern RY."; early historic print documented in the *Democratic Art*; ca. 1875; printed by Cosack & Co.; 22½ x 28½ inches excluding mat and frame; excellent condition; $2,500–4,000.

LAWRENCE MACHINE SHOP

Lawrence Machine Shop Locomotive, paper poster; large folio print of 1853 engine and tender printed by S. W. Chandler & Co. Lith., Boston; shop located in Lawrence, Massachusetts; early and rare manufacturer's presentation print; approximately 38½ x 22 inches excluding frame; good condition, residual wood and water staining in background with vertical soil stain; print has been deacidified and partially cleaned; $1,500–2,500.

LOWELL MACHINE SHOP

Lowell Machine Shop, lithograph advertisement; large early lithograph for stem "Locomotives for passengers with outside cylinders built by the Lowell Machine Shop, 1852"; depicts large steam locomotive with cowcatcher in front, labeled on the side "Columbia Lowell Machine Shop 1852"; engine in shades of green, gold, red, and gray; drawn by G. E. Cushing, August 1852; signed by "Tappin & Bradford's Litho., Boston"; 39½ x 26½ inches including frame; good condition, some stain in the background paper, colors intact; $1,500–2,500.

PENNSYLVANIA RAILROAD

Pennsylvania Railroad; dining car bell; brass bell and ringer; reproduction; 7 inches; $19 retail.

Pennsylvania Railroad, dining car bell; brass bell and ringer; reproduction; 7 inches; $19 retail. *Courtesy of Doc Davis/Antique-Alike. Photo by Donald Vogt.*

ROCK ISLAND

Rock Island Railroad, paper timetable; graphic Victorian illustration depicting a woman in a bustled gown reading one of the timetables; dated 1881; 6½ x 10 inches; printed by Kosak & Clark; excellent/near-mint condition, borders trimmed; $100–200.

SOUTHERN FREIGHT

Southern Freight, paper sign; ca. 1870s; promotes freight and passenger line to Savannah, Georgia, the southern locales, including Havana and Nassau on the "City of Macon and City of Savannah"; 13¼ x 21½ inches; excellent condition, borders appear trimmed, slight water staining at bottom, general overall soiling; $1,750–2,500.

TEXAS AND PACIFIC

Texas and Pacific Railway, tin sign; reproduction; depicts Indian maiden rowing birch canoe past autumnal scene; 16 x 12 inches; $15 retail.

UNION PACIFIC RAILROAD

In 1862, an act of Congress created the Union Pacific Railroad. Its job was to meet the Central Pacific Railroad halfway across the United States in order to create the America's first transcontinental railroad. Union Pacific was to start from the East; Central Pacific would begin in Sacramento. The railroad was supposed to raise money from private sources, while the government would pay for each mile the railroad built (in cash as well as land grants). Unfortunately, the project proved a bit intimidating for the railroad, and when Union Pacific hadn't done anything by 1864, Congress doubled the land grants.

In 1865, the project began in earnest, and the two railroads finally met in Promontory, Utah, on May 10, 1869. After the triumphant connection, Union Pacific experienced a quarter century of roller coaster business, complete with bankruptcies and upheavals. Only during Jay Gould's stewardship from 1873 through 1884, and when he reassumed control of the railroad from 1890–1892 (he died in 1892), did the Union Pacific function well.

In 1892, the railroad was auctioned and the top bidder—Kuhn, Loeb & Co.—paid $75 million for it. Edward Henry Harriman, the investor behind the deal, revamped Union

TRANSPORTATION ■ 525

Wood, Taber & Morse's Steam Engine Works, reproduction of old tin sign; features horse-drawn steam engine and vignettes of others; new/reproduction condition; $12. *Courtesy of Castle Antiques & Reproductions.*

Pacific, spending hundreds of millions of dollars on new equipment and lines by the time he died in 1909.

After Harriman's death, his sons, W. Averell and E. Ronald Harriman, and Judge Robert Lovett and his son, Robert Abercrombie Lovett, took over. The Harriman family continued to run the railroad until 1978, with its main office in Omaha, Nebraska.

UNION PACIFIC

Union Pacific, ashtray; square; glass; very good condition; $8–15.

Union Pacific, calendar; 1953; full pad intact; excellent condition; $15–25.

Union Pacific, matchbook; excellent condition; $5–10.

WOOD, TABER & MORSE'S

Wood, Taber & Morse's Steam Engine Works, reproduction of old tin sign; features horse-drawn steam engine and vignettes of others; new/reproduction condition; $12.

■ CONCLUSION: SOME ■ COMPANIES TO WATCH IN THE FUTURE

BIC
■■■

The BIC Corporation started in the United States in 1958, but was founded by a Frenchman named Marcel Bich in 1945. Bich had been the production manager for a French ink manufacturer and bought a factory outside Paris to set up business as the manufacturer and bought a factory outside Paris to set up business as the maker of parts for fountain pens and mechanical lead pencils.

As one of the first manufacturers to purchase presses to work with plastics, and to work with the best Swiss precision machinery available, he set himself up to become the largest pen manufacturer in the world. While Bich's writing instruments parts business began to grow, the development of the ballpoint pen was advancing in both Europe and the United States.

After years of development, Bich introduced his ballpoint pen in 1949 (the first was produced in 1945 by an American named Milton Reynolds); Bich called his pen "BIC," an easy-to-remember version of his own name. He supported the pen with memorable, effective advertising and its sales surpassed even his own expectations. In 1958, he bought out the Waterman Pen Company in Seymour, Connecticut, but realized shortly afterward that he would need much larger and more modern facilities and moved the company to its present site in Milford, Connecticut.

BIC's national television advertising campaign told consumers that this was a ballpoint that would write "first time, every time"—and for only twenty-nine cents! To illustrate this, BIC created a succession of "torture test" commercials in which the BIC Stic was drilled through wallboards, scraped along ice, pounded by flamenco dancers, baked in a fire, and shot from a gun. In addition to its best-selling BIC Stic and BIC Round Stic, the company today offers a complete line of writing instruments, including its Micro Metal and Metal Point Roller, Pencil, Clic, Clic Stic, Four-color Pen, Brite Liner, and Roller.

After establishing itself as the country's largest pen maker, BIC went on to introduce its cigarette lighter in 1973. Today, the BIC lighter is the number-one-selling lighter in America.

BIC chose to advertise the lighter heavily with television commercials and advertisements such as the ones that used the slogan "Flick your Bic®." While the lighter was introduced at $1.49, BIC's efficiency at manufacturing the item soon allowed the company to drop the price to under $1.

In 1985, BIC introduced a second lighter to its line—the Mini BIC Lighter, because it had been so successful in Europe and to help BIC Lighter grow beyond its already dominant share of the market.

Despite enormous competition, BIC introduced its BIC Shaver in the United Stated in 1976. Today, BIC controls more than 20 percent of the total shaver market, which includes traditional shaving systems. In addition to BIC Shaver and BIC Lady Shaver, BIC introduced the BIC Shaver for Sensitive Skin (the first shaver to address this need) in 1985. The BIC Metal Shaver was introduced in October of 1988, followed in 1990 by the BIC Pastel Shaver, designed specifically for women.

In 1981, BIC Corporation recognized the growth in the leisure industry and began a subsidiary called BIC Sport. This company markets BIC sailboards in the United States.

BIC's most recent acquisition (1992) is Wite-Out Products, Inc., the second largest U.S. manufacturer of correction fluid.

EXXON

The company began in 1863 when John D. Rockefeller invested in a Cleveland oil refinery. By 1865, he took control of the business, and in 1870, Standard Oil was born. Rockefeller ran the company aggressively, buying out competitors (even his brother, Frank), and by 1880, refined 95 percent of America's oil.

Rockefeller became so powerful that some states passed antitrust laws, the government sued Standard Oil in 1906, and the Supreme Court declared the company an illegal monopoly in 1911. After that time, Standard split into thirty-four separate companies. Standard Oil of New Jersey eventually became Exxon in 1972. Even though the company had shady dealings with Germany during World War II, it continued to prosper, especially after the war, when Standard began operations in Iran and Saudi Arabia.

A major reconstruction of the company took place in 1986 after the *Exxon Valdez* oil spill, and actually decreased its research-and-development spending from 1985 to 1990.

The company's registered trademark, the Esso oval, was a combination of Standard Oil's initials (SO) and the prefix ES. The trademark is used everywhere except the United States, where a court case precipitated the change to EXXON.

MATTEL

Mattel, the creator of the toy industry's most successful doll ever (Barbie), is also involved in other businesses, such as the Ringling Bros. & Barnum and Bailey Circus (see its listing elsewhere in this volume), Shipstad & Johnson's Ice Follies, and Western Publishing.

Barbie's popularity so overrides anything else Mattel has made that even the number-one toy maker (Hasbro) has not been able to produce any dolls that have even come close to Barbie's phenomenal staying power. She was created in 1959, and more than 500 million versions of the doll have been sold—it is estimated that 90 percent of preteen girls own at least one Barbie. In fact, sales of Barbie dolls and the accompanying products make up half of Mattel's business.

PIZZA HUT

Pizza Hut, the largest pizza restaurant chain in the world, was created by Frank and Dan Carney, two Wichita, Kansas, college students. The brothers borrowed $600 from their mother to purchase secondhand equipment, hire a pizza cook, and open for business. Almost overnight, the tiny restaurant became a success, and within six months, the Carneys opened a second Pizza Hut. At the time Dan was only twenty-five years old and Frank was nineteen.

By 1963, 43 company and franchised Pizza Huts had been opened, and by 1971, the restaurant had become the largest chain in the world, both in sales and in number of restaurants. Today more than 5,000 Pizza Huts are owned by franchisees (the other half are operated by Pizza Hut, Inc.).

Pizza Hut's advertising campaigns have included celebrities such as Martin Mull and Rita Moreno, who eat the pizza and ad-lib before the cameras. The celebrity endorsements plus the introduction of the

Personal Pan Pizza in 1983 have expanded the restaurant's offerings and garnered more of the lunchtime crowd business.

PepsiCo's financial investments in Pizza Hut have helped to double the number of restaurants in the system as of the end of 1985.

TACO BELL

In 1947, Glen Bell, a former marine, bought a hot dog stand in San Bernardino, California, for $400. Business boomed, and in 1952, Bell added hamburgers to the menu, then sold the stand and bought a new one. Pretty soon, he added a second unit, at the same time that McDonald's was getting on its feet.

Knowing that the competition would be stiff, Bell decided to go in a different route with his menu and devised ways to make tacos quickly. The first ones were sold for nineteen cents each and were a big hit.

In 1962, he began Taco Bell and sold forty shares to family members at $100 apiece. The idea worked so well that Bell took the corporation public in 1969 and split the original stocks 30,000 to 1.

In 1975, Glen Bell resigned as chairman of the company, and in 1978, PepsiCo bought Taco Bell.

More than 2,300 Taco Bell restaurants are found in forty-seven states, and six foreign countries and territories. They recently redesigned their logo, their building design decor, and their packaging to compete more completely in the fast service food business industry.

The "Run for the Border" commercials and print advertising of the early 1990s have been one of Taco Bell's more popular ad campaigns.

APPENDIX A
■ LIST OF CONTRIBUTORS ■

AUCTIONEERS

C. E. Guarino
Box 49
Berry Road
Denmark, ME 04022

James D. Julia, Inc.
P.O. Box 830
Fairfield, ME 04937

Nostalgia Publications, Inc.
　Coca-Cola Auctions
21 South Lake Drive
Hackensack, NJ 07601

Anne Trodella, Public Relations
Skinner, Inc.
357 Main Street
Bolton, MA 01740

AUTHORS

Dr. M. Stephen Miller
Six Park Place
New Britain, CT 06052
author of *A Century of Shaker
　Ephemera*

Allan Petretti
Nostalgia Publications
21 South Lake Drive
Hackensack, NJ 07601
author of *Petretti's Coca-Cola
　Collectibles Price Guide*

Estelle Zalkin
7524 West Treasure Drive
Miami Beach, FL 33141-4118
author of *Zalkin's Handbook of
　Thimbles and Sewing Implements*

COLLECTORS

Evelyn Ackerman
P.O. Box 2117
Culver City, CA 90230
Miscellaneous

Gordon Addington
260 East Chestnut, #2801
Chicago, IL 60611
Walgreen's

George Arnold
71 Lloyd Road
Ho-Ho-Kus, NJ 07423
New York City breweriana

Frank Baranco
147 Beech Street
Fords, NJ 08863
Breweriana

Neil and Nancy Berliner
41-61 Kissena Boulevard
Flushing, NY 11355
Advertising figurines

Bette Mae Biggar
P. O. Box 1135
Lake Alfred, FL 33858
General advertising items

Leo J. Bouffard
4801 Van Meter Street
Dayton, OH 45424
Breweriana

Paul E. Brady
32 Hamilton Street
Newton, NJ 07860
New Jersey breweriana

Michael Bruner
6980 Walnut Lake Road
West Bloomfield, MI 48323
Telephone items

Leonard A. Calabrese
3065 Rumsey Drive
Ann Arbor, MI 48105
Planters Peanuts

Charles Camara
P. O. Box 112
Tiverton, RI 02878
Ford memorabilia

Jay Dertinger
837 Seymour Avenue
Linden, NJ 07036
Breweriana

Kristin Duval
Irreverent Relics
1670 Massachusetts Avenue
Arlington, MA
General tins, packages, and bottles

Jim Ed and Jenny Garrett
2915 Observatory Avenue
Cincinnati, OH 45208
Jean advertising

Jay Herbein
625 Carbon Avenue
Harrisburg, PA 17111
Breweriana

Matthew E. Hunt
2281 Forest Hills Drive
Harrisburg, PA 17112
Breweriana

Stuart Kammerman
3262 West Chateau Avenue
Roseberg, OR 97470-2411
Paperweights

Marinace Collection
P.O. Box 774
Melville, NY 11747
General

Dennis McEvoy
48 Valley Way
West Orange, NJ 07052
Breweriana

Eleanor Nelson
3116 Bermuda Village
Advance, NC 27006
Ocean liner memorabilia

Iris November
26601 Bernwood Road
Cleveland, OH 44122
Statue of Liberty items

Tim O'Callaghan
46878 Betty Hill
Plymouth, MI 48170
Ford Motor Company

Mark Oleske
311 River Renaissance
East Rutherford, NJ 07073
Breweriana

Alan E. Paschedag
61 Fairfield Avenue
West Caldwell, NJ 07006
Breweriana

Diana Perry
Perry's Antiques and Collectibles
6 Cascades Drive
Little Rock, AR 72212-3306
Sunshine Biscuits

Joe Radman
4 Maple Drive
Colts Neck, NJ 07722
Breweriana

Grant Smith
408 17th Street
Manhattan Beach, CA 90266
Tobacco and general

Sam Stephens
319 Juniper Street
Warminster, PA 18974
Sharples and Alfa De Laval

Bob Taylor
58 Kentnor Street
Metuchen, NJ 08840
Breweriana

COMPANIES

For more information than what you find within this book, please contact the following companies:

Sam Stephens, Archivist
Alfa-Laval Separation, Inc.
955 Mearns Road
Warminster, PA 18974-0556

Linda Kwong, Public Relations Manager
BIC Corporation
500 Bic Drive
Milford, CT 06460

Mary Sylvia Swerts, Director/Public Relations
Brown Group, Inc.
8400 Maryland Avenue
P.O. Box 29
St. Louis, MO 63166

Archivist
Campbell Soup Company
Campbell Place
Camden, NJ 08103-1799

Archivist
Cadbury Schweppes PLC
1-4 Connaught Place
London W2 2 Ex
England

Archivist
Cracker Barrel Old Country Store, Inc.
P.O. Box 787
Hartmann Drive
Lebanon, TN 37088-0787

Archivist (Cracker Jack and Borden's)
Borden
Public Affairs Department
277 Park Avenue
New York, NY 10172

Archives Department
Coca-Cola Company
P.O. Drawer 1734
Atlanta, GA 30301

Archivist
Cigna Companies
2 Liberty Place, Archives TLP-05
1601 Chestnut Street
P.O. Box 7716
Philadelphia, PA 19192-2057
Chrysler/Plymouth/Dodge/Jeep/Eagle

Ross Roy Communications
100 Bloomfield Hills Parkway
Bloomfield Hills, MI 48304

Archives
Ford Motor Company
The American Road
Dearborn, MI 48121-1899

E. Barry Wegener
Manager/Public Relations
General Mills
P.O. Box 1113
Golden Valley
Minneapolis, MN 55440

Danielle Frizzi
Corporate Public Relations
The Gillette Co.
Prudential Tower Building
Boston, MA 02199

Archives
Goodyear Co.
Akron, OH 44308

APPENDIX A ■ 533

Edwin C. Lehew, Archivist
Heinz, U.S.A.
P.O. Box 57
Pittsburgh, PA 15230-0057

Public Relations
Interco, Inc.
101 South Hanley Road
St. Louis, MO 63105

Public Affairs
Kellogg's
One Kellogg Square
P.O. Box 3599
Battle Creek, MI 49016-3599

Elizabeth Adkins
Archives Manager
Kraft General Foods, Inc.
6350 Kirk Street
Morton Grove, IL 60053

Public Affairs Department
Kentucky Fried Chicken
P.O. Box 32070
Louisville, KT 40232

Public Relations
Maytag Company
1 Dependability Square
Newton, IA 50208

Kimberly Jackson, Representative
Customer Relations
McDonald's Corporation
McDonald's Plaza
Oak Brook, IL 60521

Public Relations
Morton International, Inc.
Morton International Building
100 North Riverside Plaza
Randolph Street at the River
Chicago, IL 60606-1597

Archivist
Miles, Inc.
1 Mellon Center
500 Grant Street
Pittsburgh, PA 15219-2502

Public Relations
United Fresh Fruit and Vegetable
    Association
727 North Washington Street
Alexandria, VA 22314

Archivist
RJR Nabisco
1301 Avenue of the Americas
New York, NY 10019

Bronwyn Overstreet
Consumer Affairs
Pepsi-Cola Co.
12377 Merit Drive
Dallas, TX 75251

Mary Jon Dunham
Public Affairs Division
Procter and Gamble Co.
1 Procter and Gamble Plaza
Cincinnati, OH 45202-3315

Archivist
R. J. Reynolds Tobacco Co.
401 North Main Street
Winston-Salem, NC 27102

Archivist
Radio Flyer, Inc.
6515 West Grand Avenue
Chicago, IL 60684

Archivist
Sears Co.
Sears Tower
Chicago, IL 60684

Archivist
Royal Crown Cola Co.
P.O. Box 41-4210
6917 Collins Avenue
Miami Beach, FL 33141-0210

Gordon Addington, Photography Division
Walgreen's
Corporate Offices
200 Wilmot Road
Deerfield, IL 60015

Archivist
Wendy's International, Inc.
P.O. Box 256
4288 West Dublin Granville Road
Dublin, OH 43017

Suellen Russel, Corporate Affairs
Whirlpool Corp.
Benton Harbor, MI 49022-2692

DEALERS

Biggar's Antiques
140 West Haines Boulevard
Lake Alfred, FL 33850
(813) 956-4853
AND
5576 Peachtree Road
Chamblee, GA 30341
(404) 451-2541
General advertising

Castle Antiques & Reproductions
515 Welwood Avenue
Hawley, PA 18428
(717) 226-8550
Reproduction tin advertising signs

Cerebro Lithographs
David C. Frieberg
P.O. Box 1221
Lancaster, PA 17603
1-800-69-LABEL

Doc Davis Antiques & Collectibles
Antique-Alike
3147 Joppa Road
Baltimore, MD 21234
(410) 668-4319

Flash, The Antique Co.
3186 East Thousand Oaks Boulevard
Thousand Oaks, CA 91362
Breweriana and fruit cake labels

Mark Goldman
House of Oxford Distributors
172 Fifth Avenue
New York, NY 10010
(212) 243-1943

Irreverent Relics
1670 Massachusetts Avenue
Arlington, MA
(617) 646-0370
General

Leo's Quality Cans
4801 Van Meter Street
Dayton, OH 45424
(513) 237-7363
Breweriana

McKee's Collectible Connection
Marvin McKee
RR 1, Box 4345
Thorndike, ME 04986
Antique & Collectible Finder Service
(207) 568-3108

Tim O'Callaghan
46878 Betty Hill
Plymouth, MI 48170
(313) 459-4636
Ford Motor Company advertising

Paper Lady
Dolores and Bernie Fee
16210 Lake Saunders Drive
Tavares, FL 32778
AND
also visit them at their
permanent booth at
Renniger's
Mount Dora, FL
Paper advertising

Past Gas
Walter W. Kostrzewa
308 Willard Street

Cocoa, FL 32922
(407) 636-8590
Gas pump parts and restoration

Tins Again Collectibles
Marilyn and De Underwood
P.O. Box 140
Micanopy, FL 32667

(904) 591-5019
Advertising tins

Yesteryear's Magazines
Lester Morris
1200 North Lake Sybelia Drive
Maitland, FL 32751
(407) 645-1223

APPENDIX B
CLUBS

Beer Can Collectors of America
747 Merus Court
Fenton, MO 63026-2092

Campbell's
The International G. G. Drayton
   Association
649 Bayview Drive
Akron, OH 44319

Candy Bars
The Great American Candy Bar Club
Six Edge Street
Ipswich, MA 01938

Cast Iron Seat Collectors Association
Box 14
Ionia, MO 65335

Cigarette Pack Collectors Association
61 Searle Street
Georgetown, MA 01833

Coca-Cola
The Cola Clan
Route 4, Box 2
Kutztown, PA 19530

John Deere
The John Deere Two Cylinder Club
P.O. Box 3164
Minot, ND 58701

Key Chain Tag Collectors Club
c/o Dr. Edward H. Mills
888 Eighth Avenue
New York, NY 10019

Lighters
The Lighter Collectors International
   Society
829 Rockaway Street
Grover City, CA 93433

Matchcovers
Rathkamp Matchcover Society
c/o John Williams, Secretary
1359 Surrey Road
Vandalia, OH 45347

Motion Pictures Collectibles
   Association
P.O. Box 33433
Raleigh, NC 27606

Oil Products and Ephemera
   Collectors
P.O. Box 25763
Colorado Springs, CO 80936

Painted Label Sodas
POPS (Procurers of Painted Label
   Sodas)
P.O. Box 8154
Houston, TX 76104

Pepsi Cola Collectors Club
P.O. Box 1275
Covina, CA 91722

Planters Peanuts
Peanut Pals (the Associated
   Collectors of Planters Peanut
   Memorabilia)
c/o Leonard A. Calabrese
3065 Rumsey Drive
Ann Arbor, MI 48105

Pop Cans
National Pop Can Collectors
3014 September Drive
Joliet, IL 60453

Radio Premium Collector's Club of
   America
303 Augustus
Excelsior Springs, MO 64024

Rose O'Neill
The International Rose O'Neill Club
Box 668
Bronson, MO 65616

Salt Shakers
The Salt Shaker Collectors Club
2832 Rapidan Trail
Maitland, FL 32751

Sebastians
The Sebastian Miniature Collectors
   Society
321 Central Street
Hudson, MA 01749

Sheet Music
National Sheet Music Society
1597 Fair Park Avenue
Los Angeles, CA 90041

Sleepy Eye
The Old Sleepy Eye Collector Clubs
   of America, Inc.
P.O. Box 12
Monmouth, IL 61462

Statue of Liberty Collectors' Club
c/o Iris November
P.O. Box 535
Chatauqua, NY 14722

Studio Collectors Club
P.O. Box 1566
Apple Valley, CA 92307

Sugar Packets
The Sugar Packet Collectors Club
370 North Main Street
Perkasie, PA 18944

Telephones
Antique Telephone Collectors
   Association
P.O. Box 94
Abilene, KS 67410

Tin Container Collectors Association
P.O. Box 440101
Aurora, CO 80014

Watch Fobs
International Watch Fob Association, Inc.
6613 Elmer Drive
Toledo, OH 43615

Western Films
Old Time Western Film Club
Box 142
Siver City, NC 27344

Wrappers
The Wrapper
309 Iowa Court
Carol Stream, IL 60187

Wristwatch and Lighters
International Wristwatch and Cigarette
   Lighter Club
832 Lexington Avenue
New York, NY 10021

APPENDIX C
■ BIBLIOGRAPHY ■

BOOKS and PERIODICALS
■■■

Alves, Margaret. "Meandering with Meg." *Spoony Scoop Newsletter*, Connecticut, 1992.

Americana magazine. "Ad on the Looking Glass." October 1989.

Anderson, Scott. *Check the Oil*. Wallace-Homestead Book Company, Pennsylvania, 1986.

Antiques Monthly. "Sell it Again, Sam." December 1991.

———. "Repro War." May 1992.

———. "AAA Alert." May 1992.

———. "News/The Nation." 1990–1992.

(The) Antique Trader Weekly. "Stein Tops Seventh Glasses, Mugs and Steins Sale." Dubuque, Iowa, July 29, 1992.

———. "Keep in Touch with Schiffer Books."

Arnold Oren. *What's In a Name: Famous Brand Names*. Julian Messner, New York, 1979.

Art & Antiques. "Sketchbook." July 1992.

Association of National Advertisers, Inc. *The Role of Advertising in America*. Assn. of National Advertisers, Inc.; Washington, D.C., 1988.

Atwan, Robert; McQuade, Donald; and Wright, John W. *Edsels, Luckies & Frigidaires: Advertising the American Way*. Dell Publishing Co., Inc.; New York, 1979.

Bagdale, Susan and Al. "Answers on Antiques." *The Antique Trader Weekly*, Dubuque, Iowa, July 15, 1992.

Baley, George J. *Back Bar Breweriana*. L-W Book Sales, Indiana, 1992.

Barach, Arnold B. *Famous American Trademarks*. Public Affairs Press, Washington, D.C., 1971.

Basori, Tom. "Kansas Collectibles." *Maine Antique Digest*, August 1992.

Bockus, H. William, Jr. *Advertising Graphics*. 2nd ed. Mac Millan Publishing Co., Inc., New York, 1974.

Broekel, Dr. Ray. "The Great American Candy Bar." *Antique & Collecting: Hobbies*, March 1989.

Brough, James. *The Woolworths*. McGraw-Hill Book Co., New York, 1982.

Burrough, Bryan and Helyar, John. *Barbarians at the Gate: The Fall of RJR Nabisco*. Harper & Row, New York, 1990.

Campbell, Hannah. "The Birth of Baker's Chocolate." Fleet Press Corp., New York, 1964.

———. "There's Always Room for Jell-O." Fleet Press Corp., New York, 1964.

———. "The Story of Quaker Oats." Fleet Press Corp., New York, 1964.

Carson, Gerald. *The Old Country Store*. E. P. Dutton & Co., Inc., New York, 1965.

Clark, Eric. *The Want Makers: The World of Advertising/How They Make You Buy*. Viking, New York, 1988.

Clifford, Mary. "Preserving Tradition." *Country Living*, November 1987.

———. "Champions for Breakfast." *Country Living*, February 1988.

Congdon-Martin, Douglas. *America for Sale*. Schiffer Publishing Co., Pennsylvania, 1991.

Country Home. "Colorful Advertising Ephemera." October 1987.

———. "Traveling Salesmen at the Turn of the Century." June 1991.

Country Living. "Matchbook Mania." April 1990.

———. "Store Stuff." January 1991.

———. "For Love of Country." July 1992.

———. "Visit a Country Store." June 1991.

Cray, William C. *Miles: A Centennial History*. Prentice Hall, Inc., New Jersey, 1984.

Curreri, Joe. "The Strasburg Railroad." *The Antique Trader Weekly*, Dubuque, Iowa, April 1992.

Dairy Dialogue. "Golden Record" (Sealtest). No. 3, October 1985.

Davern, Melva. *Salt and Pepper Shakers: Figural and Novelty*. Collector Books, Kentucky, 1985.

Della Femina, Jerry. *From Those Wonderful Folks Who Gave You Pearl Harbor: Front-Line Dispatches from the Advertising War*. Simon & Schuster, New York, 1970.

Detloff, Paul. *Cream Separator News*, vol. 4, September–October 1988 and January–February 1989.

Dodds, William. "Original Model A Ford Ads: An Edsel Success Story." *The Antique Trader Weekly*, Dubuque, Iowa, April 1992.

Dorian, Max. *The Du Ponts: From Gunpowder to Nylon*. Little, Brown and Company, Boston, 1961.

Ferguson, James L. *General Foods Corporation: A Chronicle of Consumer Satisfaction*. The Newcomen Society of the United States, New York, 1985.

Fox, Stephen. *The Mirror Makers: A History of American Advertising and Its Creators*. William Morrow and Company, Inc., New York, 1984.

Friz, Richard. "12th Annual Fair & Exhibition/Ephemera Society of America." *Marine Antique Digest*, July 1992.

———. "A Review of Recent Toy Sales, or What Have You Thrown Out Lately?" *Antique Review*, August 1992.

Gilbert, Anne. *American Illustrator Art*. House of Collectibles, New York, 1991.

———. "Souvenir Spoons Are Still a Bargain Collectible." *Antique Press*, February 16, 1992.

Goodrum, Charles and Dalrymple, Helen. *Advertising in America: The First 200 Years*. Harry N. Abrams, New York, 1990.

Grist, Everett. *Playing Cards Identification & Value Guide*. Collector Books, Schroeder Publishing Co., Kentucky, 1992.

Hake, Ted and King, Russ. *Collectible Pin-Back Buttons 1896–1986*. Wallace-Homestead Book Co., Pennsylvania, 1986.

Hastin, Bud. *Avon Collectibles Price Guide*. Bud Hastin, Missouri, 1991.

Hayes, Joanne L. "Toy Treasures." *Country Living*, March 1990.

Heimann, Robert K. *Tobacco and Americans*. McGraw-Hill Book Company, Inc., New York, 1960.

Hernon, Peter and Ganey, Terry. *Under the Influence: The Unauthorized Story of the Anheuser-Busch Dynasty*. Simon & Schuster, New York, 1991.

Hervey, John. *Cartoon & Promotional Drinking Glasses*. L-W Book Sales, Indiana, 1990.

Holme, Bryan. *Advertising: Reflections of a Century*. Viking Press, New York, 1982.

———. *The Art of Advertising*. Peerage Books, London, 1982.

Hornung, Clarence P. *Handbook of Early Advertising Art*. Dover Publications, Inc., New York, 1947.

Hornung, Clarence P. and Johnson, Fridolf. *200 Years of American Graphic Art: A Retrospective Survey of the Printing Arts and Advertising Since the Colonial Period*. George Braziller, Inc., New York, 1976.

Hothem, Lar. *Country Store Antiques*. Brooks Americana, Inc., Alabama, 1984.

Jailer, Mildred. "From Tupperware to Big Bird: The Challenge of 20th Century Collecting." *Antique Monthly*, April 1991.

———. "Following the Paper Trail." *Antique Monthly*, June 1992.

———. "Toymakers Gebruder Marklin." *Antiques & Collecting: Hobbies*, March 1989.

Jaramillo, Alex. *Cracker Jack Prizes*. Abbeville Press, New York, 1989.

Jones, Edgar R. *Those Were the Good Old Days: A Happy Look at American Advertising, 1880–1950*. Simon & Schuster, New York, 1979.

Kaduck, John M. *Advertising Trade Cards*. Wallace-Homestead Book Co., Iowa, 1976.

Klug, Ray. *Antique Advertising Encyclopedia*. L-W Book Sales, Indiana, 1978.

Kovel, Ralph and Terry. *Kovels' Advertising Collectibles Price List*. Crown Publishers, New York, 1986.

Kraft, Ken and Pat. "A Seedy Business." *Country Living*, May 1991.

Kroll, Pete. "Interest Grows in U. S. Brewery Mugs & Steins." *The Antique Trader Weekly*, Dubuque, Iowa, April 1992.

Krumholz, Phillip. "The Barber Pole: Symbol with a Past and a Future." *Antiques and Collecting: Hobbies*, March 1989.

Larkin, Connie. "Philly 100th Anniversary." *Kraft Ink*, vol. 5, no. 1, 1981.

Latham, Caroline and Agresta, David. *Dodge Dynasty: The Car and the Family That Rocked Detroit*. Harcourt Brace Jovanovich, New York, 1989.

Magnusson, Borje. *The Evolution of the Alfa-Laval Centrifugal Separator*. Alfa-Laval AB, Tumba, Sweden, August 1978.

———. *From Gustaf De Laval's Cream Skimmer to Industrial Processing*. Alfa-Laval AB, Stockholm, Sweden, 1988.

Manns, William. "Spurs Bring Top Dollar at Cowboy Auction." *Antique Press*, February 16, 1992.

Marquette, Arthur F. *The Story of the Quaker Oats Company: Brands, Trademarks and Good Will*. McGraw-Hill, Inc., New York, 1967.

Megson, Frederic and Mary. *American Advertising Postcards/Sets & Series 1890–1920*. Gotham Book Mark & Gallery, Inc., New York, 1985.

Miller, Dr. M. Stephen. *A Century of Shaker Ephemera*. Dr. Stephen Miller, Connecticut, 1988.

Miller, Rex. "Radio Prizes: The Rarest Premiums." *The Antique Trader Weekly*, Dubuque, Iowa, May 20, 1992.

Modern Packaging. "Jell-O." New York, December 1950.

Oberg, Sven and Edsund, Gote. *The Growth of a Global Enterprise: Alfa-Laval 100 Years*. Alfa-Laval AB, Sweden, 1983.

Ogan, Sharon, "St. Petersburg Hosts Outstanding Bottle Show." *The Antique Shoppe*, St. Petersburg, Florida, March 1992.

Oglivy, David. *Confessions of an Advertising Man*. Atheneum, New York, 1963.

Orlando Sentinel. "Bar's Colorful History Just Beneath Surface." Orlando, Florida, August 1992.

Petretti, Allan. *Coca-Cola Collectibles Price Guide*. Nostalgia Publications, New Jersey, 1992.

———. "Coca-Cola Collectibles Q & A." *The Antique Trader Weekly*, Dubuque, Iowa, July 15, 1992.

Ponzani, Michael. "Bottle Basics." *Country Living*, January 1992.

Pope, Daniel. *The Making of Modern Advertising*. Basic Books, Inc. Publishers, New York, 1983.

Reid, Robert. "The Collectibles of A. Lincoln." *The Antique Shoppe*, St. Petersburg, Florida, March 1992.

———. "Gold Dust Twins Still Golden." *Black Ethnic Collectibles*. Silver Springs, Maryland, vol. 4, no. 4, Spring 1991.

———. "The Cards of Cracker Jack." *The Antique Shop*, March 1992.

Rentzer, Robert D. "What's a Cream Separator?" *The Antique Trader Weekly*, Dubuque, Iowa, vol. 26, issue 25, June 1992.

Rice, Berkeley. "Minding the Store." *Countryside*, September 1991.

Richards, Thomas. *The Commodity Culture of Victorian England: Advertising and Spectacle, 1851–1914*. Stanford University Press, Stanford, California, 1990.

Rivera, Betty, "Vintage Paper Collectibles." *Country Living*, September 1988.

Roberts, Bruce and Jones, Ray. *American Country Stores*. The Globe Pequot Press, Connecticut, 1991.

Robinson, Joleen Ashman and Sellers, Kay. *Advertising Dolls Identification and Value Guide*. Collector Books/Schroeder Publishing Co., Kentucky, 1980.

Rowsome, Frank, Jr. *They Laughed When I Sat Down: An Informal History of Advertising in Words and Pictures*. Bonanza Books, New York, 1959.

Smith, Linda Joan. "Dunham's Cocoanut Doll House." *Country Home*, August 1987.

Solis-Cohen, Lita, "Money in your Jeans." *Maine Antique Digest*, April 1992.

———. "Ray Holland's Main Street Auction." *Maine Antique Digest*, September 1992.

Stage, Sarah. *Female Complaints: Lydia Pinkham and the Business of Women's Medicine*. W. W. Norton & Company, New York, 1979.

Stiling, Marjorie. *Famous Brand Names, Emblems and Trademarks*. David & Charles, London, 1980.

Swedberg, Robert W. and Harriet. *Tins 'N Bins*. Wallace-Homestead Book Co., North Carolina, 1985.

Time-Life Books Editors. *The Country Home*. Time-Life Books, New Jersey, 1988.

Tumbusch, Tom. *Radio Premium & Cereal Box Collectibles*. Tomart Publications, Ohio, 1991.

USAir Magazine. "The Avenues of Advertising." November 1990.

Vigoda, Arlene. "Betty's 40 Year Recipe for Success." Published by *USA Today*; supplied by General Mills.

Weiner, Michael A. *The Taster's Guide to Beer: Brews and Breweries of the World*. Collier Books, New York, 1977.

Wildbur, Peter. *International Trademark Design: A Handbook of Marks of Identity*. Van Nostrand Reinhold Company, New York, 1979.

Wood, James Playsted. *The Story of Advertising*. The Ronald Press Company, New York, 1958.

Young, Frank H. *Advertising Layout*. Corici/Friede Publishers, New York, 1928.

Zabriskie, George A. *The Bon Vivant's Companion*. The Doldrums, Ormond Beach, Florida, 1948.

Zalkin, Estelle. *Thimbles & Sewing Implements*. Warman Publishing Co., Willow Grove, Pennsylvania, 1988.

INFORMATION SUPPLIED DIRECTLY BY COMPANIES

Baker's Chocolate
"Baker's Chocolate: A Business That Grew Up with America."

Baker's Coconut
"General Foods Newsletter," vol. 1, no. 12, December 1940, pp. 2–3.

Franklin Baker
General Foods Family Album, 1948.

Walter Baker
General Foods Family Album, 1948.

BIC
1991 Annual Report.

Buster Brown
"The Life & Times of Buster Brown."

Cadbury Schweppes
1991 Annual Report.

Calumet
"35 Years of Service: Calumet Baking Powder." Chicago, 1924.
General Foods Family Album, 1948.

Campbell Soups
Chronology, Campbell Soup Co.
The Campbell Soup Advertising History Collection.
Fortune articles, November 1935.

Chrysler Corporation
"1992 Product Information."
"Marketing/Advertising."
"Chrysler/Plymouth/Dodge."
"Dodge Truck—Jeep/Eagle."
"Furniture Directions."

"Engineering/Design."
Smithsonian article, dated August 1992.

Cigna
Historial background report, Cigna Archives, Philadelphia, March 1992.

Coca-Cola
"A Centennial Sampler," Coca-Cola, Atlanta, Georgia, 1992.
"The Chronicle of Coca-Cola," Coca-Cola, Georgia, 1986.

Cracker Barrel
"Guide to Good Country Cookin'."
1991 Annual Report.
Nashville Banner article, published May 1992.

Ford Motor Company
"An American Legend–1991."
"Historic Dates & Events."
"Ford on the American Road 1896–1991."
"The Mustang Story."
"A Car Is Born."
Ford bibliography.
"An American Legend—1992."
"The Automobile & the Environment '91."
"Ford Is in Your Future."

General Mills
"The Story of Betty Crocker."
Company history.

General Motors
"General Motors: The First 75 Years of Transportation Products," *Automobile Quarterly Publications*, Detroit, Michigan, 1983.

The Gillette Co.
Chronology.

Goodyear
Company history.

Interco, Incorporated
1991 Annual Report.

Jell-O
General Foods Family Album, 1948.

Kellogg's
Company history.

Kentucky Fried Chicken
"Kentucky Fried Chicken to Get New Logo: 'KFC' will reflect Contemporary Product's Image," 1991.
"Today's KFC," 1990.

50th Anniversary, 1980.
"Out of the Bucket," vol. 5, no. 1, January–February 1963; vol. IV, no. 5, June–August 1962; vol. III, no. 2, November 1961; vol. I, issue 4, 1959; vol. I, issue 3, 1959; vol. I, issue 1, 1959.

Kraft
Company history; biography of James Lewis Kraft.

Log Cabin
General Foods Family Album, 1948.

Lydia Pinkham
"Lydia Pinkham: American Legend."

Maxwell House
"Maxwell House Messenger," vol. 19, no. 5, August–September 1972.
General Foods Family Album, 1948.

Maytag
Brief history of company.

Miles, Inc.
Annual Report 1991.

Miracle Whip
"Kraft Ink," vol. 7, no. 2, 1983, pp. 15–17.

Morton Salt
Fact Book, Morton International, 1991.

Oscar Mayer & Co.
"Links with the Past: A History of Oscar Mayer & Co.," 1979.

Pepsi-Cola
"The Pepsi-Cola Story."

Procter & Gamble
"Memorable Years in P & G History."

Radio Flyer
Craftsman Classics, Radio Flyer, Illinois, 1992.

RJR Nabisco
1991 Annual Report.
R. J. Reynolds Tobacco Co.

Royal Crown Cola
Company history.

Sears
"Sears Yesterday & Today."

United Fresh Fruit & Vegetable Association
History.

Velveeta
 "Kraft Ink," vol. 12, no. 2, 1988, pp 10–11.
 "Velveeta—60 Years of Cookin' Good."

Wendy's
 Company history.

Whirlpool
 Company history.

■ INDEX ■

A & P (The Great Atlantic & Pacific Tea Company) 416-417
A & W Root Beer 365
Abbey Tobacco 435
Abbott's Angostura 255
Acme 468
Acorn 314
Adams Gum 199
Adams Taylor & Co. 240
Addressograph 297
Adorn hair spray 332
Adriance Buckeye Farm Machinery 176
Ads 2, 5, 22-23, 31-32, 34, 41, 60, 64, 65, 70, 72, 74, 75, 76, 77, 78, 79, 82, 83, 84, 85, 88, 89, 90, 91, 92, 93, 94, 95, 96, 97, 99, 100, 101, 103, 106, 107, 115, 122, 134, 136, 137, 138, 158, 159, 161, 163, 168, 169, 170, 171, 181, 184, 189, 190, 199, 212, 213, 214, 215, 216, 219, 220, 225, 226, 227, 231, 232, 235, 247, 248, 252, 253, 254, 255, 257, 273, 277, 278, 279, 289, 295, 296, 324, 325-326, 333-334, 357, 358, 372-373, 395, 396, 409, 410, 420, 423, 433-434, 436, 460, 461, 462, 477, 481, 483, 484, 485-486, 489, 490, 494, 505, 507, 512, 513, 514, 515, 516, 517, 519-520, 521-522, 523, 527, 528
Advance Agent Cigar 435
Advertising cards 36, 55, 162, 165, 190, 345, 410, 436
Advertising firms 278
Aetna Insurance 223
Air France 518
Alabama Power Company 238
Alba 154
Albany Grease 487
Ale Containers 53
Alfa De Laval 154-157
Alka-Seltzer 255, 267-268
All-Bran 87
Allenburys 64
Almanacs 6, 155, 193, 255, 262, 372
American Ace Coffee 118
American Airlines 519
American Biscuit 140
American Exchange National Bank 283
American Express Co. 283
American Line 515
American Locomotive Company 521
American Red Cross 196
American Safety Razor Company 328
American Shoe Polish Co. 353
American Steel Farm Fences 176
American Stores 417
(American Telephone & Telegraph Co.) AT&T 125-126
American Tobacco Company 435-437, 439, 454-455, 465
American Toy Company 481
Amerikorn—The Nation's Breakfast Food 83
Anami 209
Anchor Brewing 40
Anheuser-Busch 1, 40-42, 60
Animal Crackers 140, 141
Ann Pillsbury 33
A. Overholt Rye 240
A. P. Little 297
Apollinaris Table Water 301
Apothecary globe 271
Apothecary jars 260
Apple Smoking Tobacco 470
Arby's 404
Arcade Cast Iron Toys 481
Arm & Hammer 20
Armed Forces 196
Armour and Company 251-252
Armour Star 516
Armstrong Mfg. Co. 283
Army 197
Arrow Beer 42
Arrow Shirts 103-104
Art plates 41, 115
Ashtrays 237, 373, 393, 399, 404, 448, 495, 508, 525
Aspir-Mint 267
Atlantic Motor Oil 487
Auburn Wagon Co. 176
Ault & Wiborg, Inc. 323
Aunt Jemima 11, 14, 20-22

548 ■ ADVERTISING

Aurora Coffee 118
Australia 477
Autobacco Tobacco 437
Automatic Tap & Faucet Co. Ltd., The 394
Automotive items 487-514
AutoStrop Safety Razor Company 330
Avalon Cigarettes 437
Avon Club Coffee 118
Ayer's 255-256
Ayer's Hair Vigor 209

B

B & M Milling & Elevator Co., The 36
Babcock Printing Press Mfg. Co., The 394
Baby items 278-279
Baby Ruth 64-65, 199
Bactine 256, 270
Badger's Pony 288
Bagdad Coffee 118
Baird & Peters 427
Baker's Chocolate 114
Baker's Cocoa 12, 114-115
Baker's Coconut 22-23
Ballantine Beer 42-43
Baltimore Telegram 126
Bancroft, Milton 198
Band-Aid 209, 256-257
Banks 44, 80, 94, 200, 317, 335, 338, 342, 352, 373, 489, 496, 497
Banners 107, 108, 109, 110, 113, 207, 373, 465, 487
Banquet Brand 136, 427
Bar 58
Barbeque grill 388
Barber poles 7, 576
Barbie 528
Barbour's Salted Peanuts 314
Barbour's Thread 344
Barb wire 279
Barclay, McLelland 195
Barker's Horse and Cattle Powder 15
Barnum & Bailey 477-478
Barry Peanuts 314
Barsam Brothers 413
Bartel's Malt Extract 43
Bartel's Brewery 43
Bartholomay Beer 43
Baseball 12, 67, 373, 398
Bathtub card 373
Batteries 279
Battle of Gettysburg Panorama and Museum 478
Bauer & Black 257-258

Bayer AG 271
Bayer Aspirin 258
Beard Cinnamon 131
Beatles 306
Beaver Brand Peanut Butter 314
Bee Brand 136
Beecham's Pills 258
Beech-Nut 65, 199, 258
Beefeater Gin 240
"Before the White Man Came" 303
Belding Thread 344
Bells 523
Belle of Kentucky Whiskey 240
Bell Telephone 125
Belmont Tobacco 437
Benedict Cigars 437
Bengal Gin 240
Ben-Hur Horse Blankets 15
Ben-Hur Cigars 437-438
Ben Hur Tea 427
Benson & Hedges 438
Berghoff Brewing Co. 43
Bernard Fisher Whiskey 241
Berry, Chuck 307
Best Foods 132
Betty Crocker 14, 26-31
Between the Acts Cigar 438
BIC Corporation 526-527
Big Ben Clocks 432
Big Brother & The Holding Company 306
Bigger Hair Smoking Tobacco 438
Big Plug 468
Big Schooner 468
Big Wolf 438
Billboards 351, 377, 394
Billings-Chapin 309
Billy Beer 43
Bilow 43
Bingo board 373
Bins 12, 25, 76, 261, 315, 474
Birds Eye 161, 181
"Birth of a Nation, The" 304
Bisquick 27-28
Bit-O-Honey 65, 78
Bixby's Shoe Polish 350
Black & White Scotch 240
Black Cat Shoe Polish 350
Black Cat Stove Polish 421
Black Fox Cigar 438-439
Black Iron Stove Polish 421
Blood Purifier 266
Blotters 7, 37, 55, 236, 366, 373, 392, 394, 399, 407

INDEX ■ 549

Blue Bird Marshmallows 65
Blue Flame 487
Blue Jeans 104
"Blue Jeans" 308
Blue Moon Silk Stockings 104
Blumers Shirt Waist Starch 95
Board of Elections 196
Bob's Big Boy 335
Bobbi home permanent 332
Boeing Airlines 519-520
Bold 360
Bommer Spring Hinges 283
Bon Ami 95
Bone Eagle & Co. 259
Bonnie-B Hair Net 209
Bond Bread 37
Bookends 495
Booklets 356, 399, 479
Books 156, 166, 211, 266, 279, 358, 373-374, 392, 410
Borax 95
Boraxo 516
Borden, Inc. 67, 157-158, 169
Born Steel Range 421
Boschee's and Green's 259
Bossie's Best Brand Butter 158
Boston Belting Company 284, 296
Boston Candy Company 79
Boston Garter 104
Boston and Maine Railroad 521
Boston Museum Theater 478
Boston Sunday Globe 293
Bottles 7, 50, 51, 131, 132, 133, 162, 193, 219, 240, 244, 260, 266, 274, 291, 326, 349, 368, 370-371, 374, 387, 389, 393, 395, 396, 397, 399, 403, 404, 421, 505
Bottle caps 44
Bottle opener 374, 388
Bottle stoppers 390
Bound Brook 521
Bowes Peanut Butter 314
Bowl of Roses Tobacco 439
Boxes 10, 16, 22, 27, 65, 72, 78, 83, 87, 95, 99, 100, 101, 105, 112, 114, 140, 158, 162, 164, 167, 180, 181, 182, 190, 193, 194, 203, 210, 219, 222, 271, 274, 277, 290, 292, 318-319, 337, 353, 355, 364, 411, 431, 440, 444, 457, 472, 481
Boyce 344
Brach's Fine Candies 65
Bracker, M. Leone 196
Branscan Limited 419
Brassieres 111

Braun AG 333
Brer Rabbit 471
Brewing trays 42
Briar Pipe 439
Brickmore Easy Shave Cream 209-210
Bricks 279
Bright & Early 372
Brillo 516
Brist Game 481
Broadsides 112, 196, 307-308, 477, 478, 480
Brochures 6, 447, 498-500
Broder 197
Brook Thread 344
Brooks & Co. 309
Brooks Glace & Soft Cotton 344
Brookside Vinegar 131
Brotherhood of Railroad Trainmen 521
Brownie Laundry Wax 95
Brown's Mule 468
Breweriana 1, 2
Brownies Log Cabin 140
Brown Shoe Co. 350
Brunswick/Balke-Collender Co. 481
Brunswick Soups 409
"Brush, King of Wizards" 307
Buckets 450
Buckeye Root Beer 365
Buck's 421
Budweiser Beer 41, 43-44
Buffalo Bill's Wild West 478
Buffalo Brewing Co. 44
Buffalo Cooperative Stove Co. 421
Bugs Bunny 269
Buick Manufacturing Company 503
Bull Durham 436, 439
Bulova 432
Bulwark Cut Plug 439
Bunker Hill Brewery 44
Bunnies Salted Peanuts 314
Burger King 34
Burgermeister Beer 44
Burlap sacks 188
Burley Boy 439
Burma-Shave 210-211
Burt's Fine Shoes 350
Busch 41
Busch Beer 45
Business cards 406
Buster Brown 350-352, 439
"Bus Stop" 303
Butterfly Match 292
Butter Nut Bread 37
Butter-Nut Coffee 372

Butternut 66, 73
Buttons 307

C

Cabinets 131, 173, 174, 175, 344, 345, 346, 347, 348, 349, 412
"Cabin in the Sky" 303
Cactus Tire Boots & Patches 487
Cadillac 487, 503
Caille Washington Scale 413-414
Cake Mixes 30
Calabash Tobacco 439
Calendars 7, 25, 46, 55, 63, 166, 190, 206, 208, 223, 224, 225, 236, 263, 267, 309, 367, 375, 388, 389, 399, 406, 407, 416, 417, 491, 495, 501, 508, 511, 519, 522, 525
California Interstate Telephone Company 125
California Perfume 211
California Raisins 14, 181-182
Calumet Baking Powder Company 23-24
Calvert Extra 241, 248
Camel Cigarettes 436, 439-440, 454, 468-470
Cameras 279-282
Campbell Coffee 118
Campbell's Soups 409-411
Campbell's Varnish 309
Canada Dry 365
Canada Nut Co. 315, 322
Candy bar wrappers 8, 64, 65
Canisters 417, 447, 448-449, 460, 472, 473
Canned goods 282-283
Cannonball Adderly 307
Cannon Ball Vehicles 481
Cannon's Irish 440
Cans 8, 9, 24, 43, 46, 47, 50, 51, 52, 53, 54, 58, 99, 118, 119, 120, 121, 123, 183, 217, 258, 282, 290, 292, 315, 317, 322, 353, 365, 375, 403, 410, 418, 428, 448, 450, 460, 463, 465, 502-503, 511, 512, 514
Cape Cod Cranberries 182
Caps 112
Captain Corker 440
Cardboard cutout 203
Cards (*see also* Advertising cards and Trade cards) 156, 416
Carnation 78, 158, 199
Carnegie Group, Inc. 495
Carter Hall 470
Carter's 297
Carter White Lead 309
Cartons 124, 367, 369

Carton stuffer 375, 399
"Casablanca" 304
Cases 404, 412, 413
Case Tractors 176
Castle Blend Coffee 118
Castle Blend Tea 427
Catalog 107, 167, 283, 417
Cattaraugus Cutlery 412
Cat-Tex Soles 352-353
Cawy Bottling Co. 365
Cel 85
Celluloid Corsets 104
Centilivre Tonic 259
Central Motor Company 489
Centrum 269
Ceramics 71
Ceresota 24
Chadwick's 344
Chairs 375, 405, 445, 462-463
Chalkware 58
Champion King Bull Dog Collar 15
Champion Spark Plugs 487, 503
Change tray 43
Charger 242, 471, 472
Chase & Sanborn 11, 78, 118-119, 120
Chase's Ice Cream 159
Cheek & Norton 122
Cheek & Sons 122
Cheek, Norton & Neal 122
Cheek-Neal Company 122
Cheer 360
Cheerios 27, 83
Cherry Blossoms 366
Cherry Smash 387
Chesapeake and Ohio Lines 521-522
Chesapeake & Ohio Railroad 521-522
Chevalier's Hair Restorer 211
Cheez Whiz 160
Chesterfield Cigarettes 440, 454
Chevrolet 487-489, 503
Chicago Tailoring Co. 345
Chief Two Moon Bitter Oil 259
China 352
Chipso 359
Chiquita Bananas 182
Chloraseptic 361
Chock's 269
Choice Family Tea 427
Christian Feigenspan Brewing Co. 47
Christmas cards 375, 399
Christmas ornament 44
Christy Bros. Wild Animal Show 478
Christy, Howard Chandler 195, 196, 198

INDEX ■ 551

Chrysler Corporation 489, 491
Chunky 66, 78
Chun King 471
Cigarette Lighter 527
Cigarettes (*see also* Tobacco) 8, 14, 82, 399, 435
Cigars (*see also* Tobacco) 8
Cigar cutter 450, 476
Cigar store figures 440-443
Circus Club Mallows Candy 66
Circus ticket 399
Citadel Tobacco 443
City of New York Insurance 223
Civil War 196
C.J. Fell & Brother Spice Co. 131
Clabber's 24
Clark, Hilda 371, 372
Clark Spool Cotton 345
Clark's 199-200, 315, 345-346
Clayton's Dog Remedies 15
Clausen Beer 45
Clearasil 361
Cleo Cola 366
Cleveland Faucet Co. 294-295
Clicquot Club 366
Climax Golden Twins 444
Climax Stoves 421
Clocks 19, 23, 38, 134, 164, 214, 237, 261, 273, 279, 290, 294, 327, 339, 350, 352-353, 367, 375-376, 388, 395, 399, 404, 432, 438, 455, 456, 465, 487, 491, 497, 514
Clothing 376
Club Manhattan Cocktails 241
Clyde Porcelain Steel 234
Coasters 52, 59, 113, 399
Coats & Clark's 346
Cobak Co. 37
Coca-Cola 366-387, 477
Coffee bin 120
Coffee grinder 120
Colgate and Co. 15
Colgate-Palmolive 211-213
Collars 112
College Inn 471
Collier's 293
Colman's Mustard 131
Columbia Bicycles 515
Columbia Bikes 515
Columbia Brewing Co. 45
Columbia Herp C. Hair Tonic 213
Columbia Yarns 346
Columbian Expo 478
Colt 204

Combs 68
Comfort Powder 213
Comic books 306
Compacts 497
Companies/Corporations (miscellaneous) 283-287
ConAgra, Inc. 251
Condor Coffee 119
Congress Playing Cards 481-482
Connecticut General Fire Insurance 223
Connecticut Mutual Insurance 223
Conoco 490
Construction companies 287
Container 162, 222, 246, 306, 353, 438, 474
Continental Cubes 444
Continental Insurance 223
Cook, Everett and Pennell 259
Cookies 21
Cooler Keg Tap Knob 56
Coolers 369, 404
Coors 45-46
Copper-Kleen 270
Corbin, Sons & Co. 131-132
Corn Products Refining Co. 132
Corsets 111-112
Corticelli Spool 347
Cosmair 78
Cott 387
Counter displays 116, 236, 240, 256, 296, 334, 376, 399, 406, 453, 457-458
Counters 412, 413
Coupons 262, 368, 406
C.R. Thomas Eclectric Oil 259
Cracker Jack 66-69
Cracker Jack prizes 67-69
Crackle! 88
Cream City Flour 25
Cream of Wheat 83-85, 141
Cream separator 156
Crest 213, 360-361
Cricket 333
Crisco 25, 359
Cromwell, John L. 440
Cross-Cut Cigarettes 444
Crown Beer 46
Crown Derby 427
Crown Royal 241, 248
Cups 43, 62, 341
Curlox Hair Net 213
Curtains 287
Curtiss Candy Company 64
Cushing Medical Supply Co. 260
Cutouts 376

Cutter's 270
Cyclone 444

D
D. Moore Co. 424-425
Dactylis Talc Powder 213
Dad's Sugar Free Root Beer 387
Daft Bros. 177
Daisy 333
Dalley's Prime Coffee 119
Dan Patch 444
Darby's Swan Tolu 260
Darkie/Darlie Toothpaste 213-214
Dart & Kraft, Inc. 161
Dart boards 376, 399
Dart Indistries, Inc. 161
Dash 360
Daukes Ale 46
Dauntless Coffee 119
Daval Gum 200
David's Prize Soap 355
Davis Baking Powder 25
Davis' Pain Killer 260
Dayton Wright Airplane 503
Deep Magic Skin Conditioner 332
Deering 177
Defender Brand Tomatoes 183
Defense Plant 197
Defiance 315
DeKalb Corn 183
Delco 503
Demuth, William 443
Derby Paint 309-310
Desk organizers 399-400
Detmer Woolen 105
Detroit Stove Works 422
Devil Dogs 169
Devoe Oil 291
Devoe Varnish 310
DeVry Cameras and Projectors 279
Dewar's Whiskey 241
Dial, Greyhound 516
Diamond Dyes 173-174, 264, 272
Diamond Gloss Starch 96
Diamond Match 292
Diamond Spring Brewery, Inc. 50
Diamond State Brewery 46
Dick Custer 444
Diddley, Bo 306
Diehl Brewing Co. 46
Diet Cherry RC Cola 403
Diet Pepsi 397-398
Diet Rite Cola 403
Dietz 200

Dingman's Soap 355
Dining car bell 523
Dippity-do Setting Gel 332
Disney, Walt 287,
Dispensers 32, 163, 289, 314, 327, 365, 367, 370, 387, 390, 391-392, 395, 404, 407
Display cabinets/cases 124, 128, 201, 209, 222, 257, 258, 263, 272, 334, 347, 354, 455
Displays 37, 58, 65, 76, 77, 78, 88, 95, 99, 100, 104, 105, 108, 110, 111, 112, 114, 124, 128, 131, 169, 172, 175, 199, 200, 201, 202, 203, 207, 208, 213, 222, 236, 245, 256, 257, 258, 266, 272, 291, 292, 294-295, 309, 317, 318-319, 327, 352, 353-354, 363, 374, 376, 387, 393, 394, 413, 434, 447, 457-458
Dixie 490
Dixie Boy Flashlight Crackers 288
Dixie Boy Vegetable Seeds 189
Dixie-Narco 231
Djer-Kiss 214
D.M. Ferry & Co. 189
Dobler Brewing Co. 46
Doctor's Blend Tobacco 445
Dodge 490-491
Doelger's Beer 46
Doe-Wah-Jak Stove 422
Dolls 21, 68, 84, 85, 90, 110, 128, 181, 182, 237, 251, 252, 253, 273, 278, 335, 340, 342, 343, 352, 362, 376-377, 410
Domino's Pizza 335
Donruss Baseball Cards and Gum 69, 72
Door handle 400
Door push 38, 405, 431, 440
Doors 307
Doral 470
Double Cola 387
Dover Egg Beater 229
Drake Bakeries 169
D.R. Brown's Patent Baby Tender 289
Dr. Daniels 15-16
Dr. DeWitt's Remedies 260
Dr. Frost's Medicinal 260
Dr. Jaeger's Woolens 105
Dr. Lynas Extracts 260
Dr. Morse's Indian Root Pills 260
Dr Pepper 373, 387-389
Dr. Pierce's Medicinal 261
Dr. Price's 132
Dr. Scholl's 261
Dr. Shoop's Restorative 261
Dr. Swett's 261, 389
Dr. Thomson's Sarsaparilla Cure 261
Douglass & Sons 261

Drako Coffee 119-120
Dramamine 361
Drayton, Grayce Gebbit 409
Dread-Not 327
Drugs (*see also* Medicine) 417
Drum Major Marshmallows 69
D. S. Brown Toilet Soaps 355
Duchess Trousers 105
Duke Cigarettes 445
Duke's Pharmacy 261
Dukes Tobacco 445
Dunlap's Seeds 189
DuPont 204-205
Duquesne Can-o-Beer 46
Duracell 161
Durham Tobacco 445
Dutch Boy Paints 310-311
Dutch Cleanser 96
Duz 360
D.W. Hoegg Canned Goods 282

E
E & J Burke Ale 44-45
Eagle Brand Dry Cleaner 353
Eagle Orange Pekoe 427
Earthquake 306
Eastman-Kodak 280-282
Economy Whiskey 242
Eddie Bauer, Inc. 31
Edelweiss Beer 46
Edgeworth 445-446
Edison Mazda 236-237
Edison, Thomas 237
Educator Crackers 140
Efdelit, S. A. 332
Egg-O-See Cereal Company 85
Egyptienne Cigarettes 446
"Eight Bells" 307
Elastilite Varnish 311
Electric-Lustre-Starch 96
Electric Mixture Tobacco 446
Electric Storage Battery Co., The 286
Elgin 432
Elijah's Manna 92
Elkhorn 160
El Macco Cigars 446
El Symphonie Cigars 446-447
Emmerling's Beer 47
Empire Brewing Co. 47
Empress Chocolates 69
Encore Beer 47, 60
Engines 287
Enterprise Brewing Company 47
Enterprise Coffee 120

Era 360
Erasers 388
Eric Burdon and the Animals 306
Eriksen 298
Eskimo Smoking Tobacco 447
Espell Perfumes 214
Eureka Spool 347
Europe 478
Evans & Dodge Bicycle Company 490
Ever-Ready 214, 327
Every Day Tobacco 447
Evinrude Outboard Motor 515
Excelsior 311
Exeter Lily 183
Exxon 527-528
Exquisite Mixture 447

F
Fab Flakes 96-97
F & M Herbs Cigar 447
F.S. Webster Co., Inc. 298
Factory Smokers 447
Fairbanks Soap Company, N.K. 97-98, 355
Fairy Soap 97-98, 99, 355
Fall River Line 515
Fanny Farmer Easter Candies 69
Fans 38, 99, 277, 377, 388, 392, 404
Fanta 372
Farina 33, 85
Fast food 9
Fast Mail 447
Fat Back 468
Fatima Cigarettes 447-448, 454, 455
Fehr's Tonic 262
Feigenspan's Ale 47
Feigenspan Breweries 47
Ferris Corsets 105
Ferris Waists 105-106
Ferry Seeds (*see also* D. M. Ferry & Co.) 189
Festoons 367, 377
Fidelio Brewery 47
Fig Newtons 141
Figural costume 319
Figural display 111, 241, 320, 324, 353
Figurals 162, 319, 427
Figures/Figurines 9, 71, 90, 110, 128, 157, 159, 182, 184, 232, 236, 238, 275, 311, 317, 335, 341, 405, 461, 509
Film 400
Finck's Overalls 106
Firecrackers 288
Fire extinguishers 288
Fire kegs 288

"Fireman, The" 304
Firkins 186
First National Stores 168
Fishing 482
Fish spinner 377
Fisk Tires 491
Five Alive 372
Five Crown (5 Crown) 248
Five Roses Flour 25
Flagg, James Montgomery 195, 198
Flair pens 332
Flaroma Coffee 120
Flaked Rice 85
Fleer's 200
Fleischmann's Yeast 25
Flintstones 269, 306
Florida 478-479
Florida Water 301
Flour sacks 35
Flyers 6, 389, 499
Foam scrapers 52
"Fogg's Ferry" 308
Food preservation 288
F.O. Pierce 279
Forbes Brothers Tea 427
Ford Motor Company 491-502
Forest & Stream, 293, 402, 448
Fork 62
Fort Garry Tobacco 448
Fort Pitt Coffee 120
Foster Hose 106
Fox Trot Panatelas 448
Franklin Baker Co. 25
Franklin Ribbon & Carbon Co. 298
Frog 467
Frontier Mixture 448-449
Franco-American 409
Franklin Mills Flour 25
Frank Miller's Blacking 353
Freezers 367
French's potatoes 34
Fresca 372
Fresh-Up Freddie 405
Friedman 242
Frigidtest Antifreeze 502
Frito-Lay 398
Frontenac Beer 48
Fruit 9, 14
Fruit Doodles 169
Fruits of California 183
Fry & Sons, J. S. 69
Fry/Red Crown Gas Pump 503
Fry's Cocoa 115
Fuel 288

Fulton's Ice Cream Parlor 159

G
Gaines 16
Gaming Machine 317
Games (*see also* Toys) 81, 244, 320, 340, 370, 377, 400, 497
Gasoline globes 487, 490, 508, 510, 512, 514
Gas pumps 509, 513
Gem Damaskeene Razor 327
General Electric 236-238
General Electric/Mazda Super Auto Lamps 503
General Foods Company 11, 114, 122, 159, 181, 270, 291
General Mills 26-31, 72, 83, 94, 252, 484
General Motors 488, 503-505
Geo. Borgfeldt & Co. 483
Geo. Ehret's Brewery 48
Gerber Baby Foods 278
Gibbs Plows 178
Giblin's Liniment 262
"GI Blues" 304
Gibson's Lozenges 262
Gillette Company 326, 327-334
Ginsberg, Allen 305
Giveaways 237, 269, 499
Glamour Puss 134
Glass 7
Glasses (drinking) 9, 59, 243, 305, 335, 337, 340, 341-342, 365, 367, 377-378, 390, 393, 395
Glass negative 378
Glass shade 42
Gleem Toothpaste 214, 360
Glenlivet 242, 248
Glenwood 423
Glidden Steel Barb Wire 279
Globe Dyes 174
Glorex Cleanser 98-99
Gloves 6
Glue 289
Gobblers Cigars 449
Godiva candies 410
Gold Bond Tobacco 450
Gold Dust 97-98, 99-100
Gold Dust Twins 97-98
Goldey Bros. Inc. 214
Gold Hunter 449
Gold Medal 12, 26-32
Gold Medal Beer 48
Gold Seal 242, 288
Gold Soap 355
Golden Fleece 347

Golden Grains Coffee 120
Goldenrod Beer 48
Golden Rod Coffee 120
Golf 378, 417
"Gone With the Wind" 304
Goobers 69, 78
Goodman Chemical Co. 215
Good 'N Plenty 69, 73
Goodrich Tires 505-506
Good Roads Farm Machinery 178
Goodyear 506-508
Gorton's 30-31, 169, 252
Grant's U. S. Tobacco 450
Grape-Nuts 11, 85, 91
Grapette 389
Grateful Dead 306
Great American Tea 428
Great Lakes Expo 479
Great Northern Railroad 522
Great Rock Island Route 522
Great West Cut Plug 449
Green Giant 34
Green River Whiskey 242
Green's Medicinal 262
Greenway's Ales 48
Gregory, Dick 305
Greyhound Bus Lines 504
Greyhound Dial 516
Griffith & Boyd Co. 189
Grommes Ullrich 37
Grosman's Root Beer 389
Guion Line 515
Gulf 508
Gum (chewing) 9, 69, 375
Gum wrappers 199, 200, 201
Gunpowder 204-206

H

H. B. Gardner Cigar 450
H. H. Kohlsaat & Company 37
H. M. Storms Co. 298
H. McWilliams & Co. 293
H. Waterbury & Sons, Co. 293
Haagen-Dazs 34
Haberdashery 289
Hall's Hair Renewer 215
Hamilton 432
Hamm 49
Hampden Ale-Beer 49
Hampden Brewing Co. 49
Handbills 6
Handbook 378
Hand puppets 342
Hand spinners 400

Handy Dyes 174
Hanes Hosiery 106
Hangers 47, 58
Hapgood's Wooden Wagon 178
Happy Thought Foundry Co. 423
Hardwick Stove Company 230, 231
Harley Davidson 518
Harrison Radiator 503
Hartford Insurance 224-225
Hartley Grain Co. 178
Hartz 16-17
Harvard Ale 49
Harvard Brewing Co. 49
Hasbro 483
Hathaway Shirts 106-107
Hats 107, 111, 112
Havana Cigar Cutter 450
Hawaiian Punch 291, 471
Hawley & Hazel 212
Hayden, Hayden 196
Hazard's Dyes 174
Hazelton, B. 197
Hazelton's High Pressure Chemical Fire Keg 288
Head & Chest 361
Head & Shoulders Shampoo 361
Heads Up 332
Heath Bars 70, 72
Heath Brothers 72
Heating 289
Hecker's Buckwheat 32
Heil-Quaker Home Systems, Inc. 234
Heinz 133-135, 185, 253, 254, 411
Hellman Bock Beer 49
Hellman Brewing Co. 49
Henrietta Cigars 450
Henry and Johnson Liniment 262
Hensler's Light Beer 50
Herbe De La Reine 450
Hercules Powder 206
Hershey's 8, 12, 70-71, 317
Hertz Corporation 495, 504
Heywood-Wakefield 278
Hiawatha Tobacco 450
Hi-C 372
Hilla Coffee 120
Hillman Minx 508
Hills Bros. 78, 119, 120
Hills & Sons Coffee 120
Hillside Tea 428
Hilton's Boots 353
Hinckley & Williams Works 522
Hinds Honey & Almond Cream 215-216
Hingham Mutual Fire Insurance 225

Hires Root Beer 390-392
Hoadley's Gum 200
Hohner Harmonicas 292
Holders 61
Holidays 13
Holihan's Ale 50
Hollywood Brands 71
Holsum 37
Holton Band Instruments 293
Home Comfort Stoves 423
Honey Comb 85-86
Honeysuckle Tobacco 450
Hood ornaments 509
Hood's 262-263
Hoover 230, 231
Hopalong Cassidy 306
Hope Chest Cigar 451
Horlick's Wood 302
Horsman's 483
Hosiery 106, 108, 111
Hoster Brewing Co. 50, 392
Hostetter's Bitters 263
Hot fudge 289
Hotpoint 237
Household furniture 289-290
Household Sewing Machine 347
Household spray 290
Howdy Doody 306
Howe Scale 414
Hoyt's 30, 71, 216
H. P. Hood 159
Hudson's Bay Tea 428
Humidor 447
Humphrey's 17, 263
Hunting/Fishing 290
Hunt's Health Pills and Liver Cure 263
Hunter Baltimore Rye 243
Hurd's Washing Mixture 100
Hyatt Roller Bearing 503
Hy-Quality 120

I
I.G.A. 417
Ice cream 159, 160, 162-163, 164, 167
Ice cream scoop 163
Ice cream wrappers 306
Ice pick 378
Icy Hot 361
Illinois Watch Co. 433
Illustrators 195, 196, 197, 198
Imperial Ale 50
Imperial Blend Tea 428
Imperial Cough Drops 263

Incandescent Light & Stove Co. 423
Independent Lock Company 291
Independent Telephone 127
India 479
Indian Motorcycles 518
Infallible Smokeless Shotgun Powder 206
Inference Corp. 495
"Inquirer, The" 307
Instamatic 280
International Great Lakes Flying Boat
 Cruise 479
International Stock Food 17
Irish Singer 451
Iron City Beer 50
Iron Glue 136
Ironport 392
Isaac S. Sheppard & Co. 424
Italy 479
"I Thought She Loved Me" 304
Ivory Soap 356, 357, 359
I.W. Harper 242-243
Izaak Walton League of America 290
Izod 31

J
J. G. Dill's Best Cut Plug 451
J. I. Case Threshing Machine Co. 178
J.J. Bagley Tobacco 451
J. L. Taylor 107
J. M. Paul 290
J. P. Alley's Hambone Cigars 452
J. Pettibone 249
J. R. Leeson & Co. 347
J. S. Fry & Sons 69
J. W. M. Field's Whiskey 245
Jack Daniel's Whiskey 243
"Jack-Harkaway" 307
"Jack-O-V-Cudgel" 307
Jackson's Best Tobacco 451-452
Jamaica 479
James E. Pepper Whiskey 243
James Hanley Brewing Co. 243
Jantzen 107
Japan Tea 428
Jars 193, 202, 211, 276, 290, 317, 318,
 320-321, 375, 413
Jas. E. Pepper 245
Java 429
Jean Walther Cruise Line 479
Jefferson Airplane 306
Jell-O 11, 161, 169-172
Jenn-Air Corp. 230, 231
Jersey Coffee 12

"Jetson's—The Movie" 304
Jewelry *(see also* Timepieces section) 290-291
Jewel Stoves 424
Jim Beam 244, 505
Jobin, Louis 441
John C. Calhoun 452
John Deere 177
John Hancock 223-224
John Jamison & Son Whiskey 244
John Ruskin Cigars 452
Johnnie Bird Cigar 452
Johnnie Walker 244-245
Johnson & Johnson 256-257
Johnson's Baby Powder 216
Johnson's Instant Hot Fudge 289
Jolly Rancher 71
Jos. Linz & Bro. 290
Jos. Fleming & Son 264
Joseph Schlitz Brewing Company 60
Jones Brewing Company 51
Juices 291
Juicy Fruit 201

K

Kalamazoo 178-179
Kandy Kake 64
Katy the Kangaroo 88
Keen Kutter 453
Kegs 131
Kellogg Telephone 127
Kellogg's 11, 86-90
Kendall's 17
Kennedy's Medicine 264
Kenner Products 31
Kentucky Fried Chicken 335-339, 398
Kentucky Whiskey 245
Key chain 508
Keys/Locks 291
Khush-Amadi Talcum Powder 216
"Kid, The" 304
Kiddie-Kar 483
Kidney-Wort 173, 264
Kiltie 183
King, B.B. 306
King Cobra Beer 51
King Cobra malt liquor 41
King Cole Coffee 121
King Edward Tobacco 453
King, Hamilton 371
King Pelican 183
King's Beer 51
King's Cadets 183

Kinney Bros. Cigarettes 453
Kis-Me Gum 201
KitchenAid 234
Kites 400
Klein's Cough Drops 264
Knickerbocker Beer 51
Knickerbocker grouping 51
Knives 390
Knox Hats 107
Knox Knit Hosiery 108
Knox Unflavored Gelatin 172
Kodak 280-282
Kodak Tobacco 453
Kool Cigarettes 453
Korody Coyler 508
Kraft Chocolate Fudgies 72
Kraft General Foods 159-161, 163, 164, 168, 169, 184, 252, 291
Krueger 51
Krystal Hamburgers 335
Kuppenheimer 108

L

LA Beer 41, 51
Labels 9, 70, 184, 185, 186, 191, 266, 425, 440, 445, 447, 449, 450, 451, 452, 454, 455, 457, 460, 464, 475
Lactated Food 173
Laflin & Rand 206
Lakeshore and Michigan Railroad 523
Lake Shore Seed Co. 189-190
Lamp Oils 291
Lamps 254, 311, 339, 367, 390, 413
Lamp shades 125, 159
Lancome 78
Lander 217
Landseer, Sir Edwin 224
La Petite Boulangerie 398
Larson's Spearmint Gum 201
Lash's Bitters 264
Lautz Soap 356
Lavine Soap 356
Lawrence Machine Shop 523
La-Zenda Cigars 454
Leaf, Inc. 66, 69, 71, 72-73
Leary, Timothy 305
Ledger marker 222
Lee Lewis Ice Cream 161
Lee Riders 108
Leggat & Butler's 454
Leggett & Platt 284
LeMenu 410
Lemon Kola 392

558 ■ ADVERTISING

Lennox Heating 289
LePage's Liquid Glue 289
Letterhead 287
Letter openers 389
Letters 166-167
Levi Strauss & Co. Museum 109
Levi's 108-111
Lewis Shoemaker 353
Leyendecker, J.C. 195, 197
Libby's 184
Liberty Coaster Company 485
Liberty Gasoline 508
Liberty National Life 225
Lids 515
Lifebuoy Soap 356
Lifesavers 74
Liggett & Myers 436, 447, 454, 455
Lighters 318, 321, 387, 404, 440, 453, 462, 495
Light fixture 236, 337
Light 'n Lively 160
Lightning Wheel 483
Lilt Home Permanents 217, 360
Lily of the Valley Coffee 121
Lily White 100
Lincoln Club Coffee 121
Lincoln Motor Company
Lindsay & McCutcheon 493
Lion Coffee 121
Lipton 115, 429
Lisk Wash Boiler 100
Listerated Gum 201
Lithographs 60, 91, 126, 183, 199, 208, 522
Little Motor Company 488
Little's Brilliant 298
Littleton Creamery Company 161
Lobby cards 303, 304
Loft, Inc. 396
Log Cabin 161, 291-292, 454
Lillipop scale 76
London Life Cigarettes 454
Lone Jack Tobacco 454-455
Long Beach National Bank, The 286
Long Tom Tobacco 455
Lord & Taylor 417
L'Oreal 78, 217
Lorie 217
Lorillard 436, 444, 455, 474
Louis Brand Peanut Butter 315
Love Among the Roses 455
Lowell Machine Shop 523
Lower Canada Maple Syrup 292
Lowney's Cocoa 116
Lucky Strike 290, 436, 454, 455-456

Luden's Cough Drops 264
Lunch Bucket 516
Lutted's Cough Drops 265
Luzianne 11, 121
Lyall & Buchannan Tobacco 456
Lydia Pinkham 265-266
Lysol 100

M

Macbeth-Evans Glass Company 284
MacKinnon Pens 324
MacLaren's 316
M & M/Mars 74-75
Madeira Gold 470
Madison Square Garden 479
Magic Chef 231
Magic Moment 332
Magic Yeast 32
Magnet Tobacco 456
Mahoney Whiskey 245
Mail Pouch 456
Malley Eclipse 456
"Maltese Falcon, The" 304
Mandeville & King 190
Mansfield Pepsin Gum 201
Manson Campbell 18
Maple syrup 291-292
Marathon Tires 508
Marine Tobacco 457
Marlboro Cigarettes 457, 461
Mar-O-Bar 74
Mars/Marsettes Candies 75
Marvo Beauty Laboratories 222
Marx toys 385
Maryland Club Coffee 372
Mason's Essence of Beef 252
Massachusetts Bonding and Insurance 225
Mastercraft Industries Corporation 234
Master Mason Tobacco 457
Masury's Color 312
Matchbooks 10, 55, 498, 525
Matchboxes 388
Matches 292, 335, 337
Match holders 24, 176, 309, 311, 453
Match safes 24, 157, 167, 201, 246, 421, 424, 498
Mathieu Syrup 266
Mattel 528
Maxwell House 119, 121-122
May Company 417
Mayo's 295, 457
Maypo 90
Mazda (lighting) 236
Mazda (autos) 495

Maytag 229-232
M. B. Cook Co., The 301
McCormick 136, 431
McCormick, Arthur David 464
McCormick's Jersey Cream 162
McCormick Reaper 179
McCullough's Leap Rye Whiskey 245
McDonald's 1, 14, 339-343
McKesson's Baby Powder 217
McMenamin & Co. 253
McSorley's Famous Lager Beer 51
Meadow-Sweet Peanut Butter 316
Mechanical card 201
Mechanical display 38
Medal 478
Medicinal herb industry 193
Medicine 2, 7, 10, 13
Melacrino Cigarettes 457
Melanie 307
Mello Mints 75
Mello Yello 372
Mellow Fruit Gum 201
Melrose Marshmallows 75
Mennen's 217-218
Menu board 378, 400, 405
Merit Separator Co. 162
Merita Bread 37-38
Merrick's 347-348
Metamucil 361
MGM (Metro-Goldwyn-Mayer) 303
Mexico 480
Michelin Tire Co. 508-509
Michelob Beer 41, 51
Mickey Mouse Animal Crackers 140
Middlesex Mutual Fire Insurance 225-226
Mild and Mellow Sun Cured 467
Miles Laboratories 102, 256, 266-271
Milk Bone Dog Biscuits 141
Milk Duds 72, 75
Milkshake 73, 75
Milky Way 75, 76
Millais, Sir John E. 357
Miller 51, 60, 298-299
Millins Taystee Lemon Flavored Dessert 172
Mills 414, 415
Milton Bradley 484
Minard's Liniment 271
Mink 333
Minute Maid Corporation 372
Miracle Whip 137, 160, 161
Mirador Perfume Co. 219
Mirrors 10, 16, 57, 68, 167, 313, 367, 379, 390, 400, 444, 450, 495, 497

Mi-Te Good Bread 38
Mittag & Volger 299
Mobil 14, 509-510
Model Tobacco 458
Modox 271
Moerlein's Beer 52
Mogul Cigarettes 458-459
Monadnock Coffee 122
Monarch 76, 116, 282-283, 429
Monet 31
Monkey Brand 356
Monk's Brew 91
Monogram 237
Monticello Distilling Company 245
Moonlight Mellos 76-77
Morand Cushion Wheels 510
Morning Cheer 185
Morningstar Farms 271
Morton Salt 11, 137-139
Moses Cough Drops 272
Motorcycles 518
Mother Hubbard Energy 91
Mountain Club 393
Mountain Dew 398
Mountain States Tel. & Tel. Co. 126
Movie card 304
Movies 9, 11, 13, 27
Moxie 393
Mr. Control 232
Mrs. Dinsmore's Cough Drops 272
Mrs. Paul's Kitchens, Inc. 410
Mugs 269, 335, 340, 365, 379, 390, 404, 410, 411, 518
Muhammad Ali and Joe Frazier Fight 307
Munsing Wear 111
Munyon's Homoeopathic 272
Murphy Hatter 111
Murray's Superior Hair Dressing Pomade 219
Musical instruments 292-293
Mutual Life of New York Insurance 226
Myadec 269
My Favorite Chocolate Chewing Gum 201
My*T*Fine puddings 471

N
N. K. Fairbanks Soap Company 97-98
N. T. Swezey's Son & Co. 32
Nabisco 83, 84, 140-142, 153, 169, 316, 338
"Nanook of the North" 304
Napkins 406
Narragansett Beer 52
Narragansett Park Fair 480
Nash's Coffee 123

560 ■ ADVERTISING

National Biscuit Company 141
National Bohemian Pale Beer 53
National Brass 413
National Cycle and Automobile Company 490
National Dairy Products Corporation 159, 160, 164
National Hay Rake 179
National Insurance 226
National Lead Company 310
National Mazda Lamps 236
National Mints and Gum 77
National Park Bank 285
Natural Light Beer 41, 53
Nature's Remedy 272
Navy 197-198
Necco Wafers 77
Needle case 344
Nehi 394, 402
Nelson, Willie 307
Nescafé 78, 123
Nestea 430
Nestlé 12, 66, 69, 77-78, 116, 118, 120, 123, 158, 217, 430
Nerve and Liver Pills 266
Nervine 266
Nesbitt's 394
Netting 293
New Bachelor 459
New Empire 425
New England Fertilizer 190
New Home Sewing Machine 348
Newman Brothers, Inc. 53
Newspapers/Magazines 293, 337, 351, 357, 358, 378, 423, 461, 494
New York Biscuit 140
New York Enamel Paint Company 312
New York Life Insurance 226
New York World's Fair 480
Niagara Fire Insurance 226
Nigger Hair Tobacco 459
Nine-Lives (9-Lives) 134
Nineteen Hundred Washer Company 233-234
Nizo 333
Nodders 283, 335, 339, 508, 511
Noon Day Stoves 425
Nordica, Lillian 371
Norge 231
North America 468
North Pole Tobacco 459
Norumbega Park 480
Norwich Aspirin 361
Nosegay Tobacco 459

NuChief 185
NuGrape 394
Nysis Talcum Powder 219

O

Occident 32
O-Cedar 100
O'Doul's Non-Alcoholic Beer 41, 53
O.V.G. Whiskey 247
O'Henry! 78
Ohio Boys Cigars 459
Oglive's Flour 33
Ohio Associated Telephone Co. 126
Old Abe Cigar 459
Old Boston Brewery 53
Old Chum Tobacco 459
Old City Peanut Butter 316
Old Copper Snapper 53
Old Crow 246
Old Dad 459
Old Dutch Carbon & Ribbon Co. 299
Old Dutch Cleanser 96, 100-101
Old German Premium Beer 53-54
Old Glory Cigars 460
Old Grist Mill Dog Bread 38
Old Judson 246
Old King Cole 460
Old Log Cabin 246
Old Milwaukee Beer 54, 60
Old Overholt Whiskey 246
Old Port 467
Old Rip 468
Old Schenley Whiskey 246
Oldsmobile Corporation 490, 503, 510
Old Town 300
Olive Branch 468
Oliver Plows 179
Oliver & Robinson Cigars 460
One-A-Day Vitamins 268-269
Openers 378, 400, 410
Opticians 290
Optician's devices 271
Orange Crush 394-395
Ore-Ida 134
Ore-Ida Frozen Potatoes 185
Oreo Cookies 141, 142
Oscar Mayer 159, 252-253
Osman 468
Ossipee Valley Tel & Tel 126
Our Jewel Coffee 123
Outboard Fuel 514
"Outlaw, The" 305
Otto Schmidt & Sons 484
Overland Cigar 460

Owl Chop Teas 430
Oxydol 11, 360
Oysterette Crackers 141, 142
Oysters 293

P
P.K. Wilson & Son 287
P. Lorillard 436, 444, 474
P.N. Corsets 111
Pabst Blue Ribbon Beer 54
Pabst Brewing Company 54-56
Pacific Grain Co. 179
Packages 334
Packing crate lid 515
Page & Shaw 78
Pails 80, 118, 314, 315, 316, 322-323, 449, 457, 459, 466, 475, 476
Paine's Celery Compound 173, 272
Paintings 82
Pal Double Edge Blades 334
Palmolive 356
Pamphlets 55, 100, 114, 255, 266
Panama 306
Pan American World Airways 520
Pan-Dandy Bread 38
Panic Brand 460
Paper 293
Paper cutout 135
Paper dolls 267, 352
Paper Mate Company 332
Paperweights 35, 53, 81, 135, 161, 178-179, 238, 240, 243, 247, 252, 264, 283-284, 285-287, 288, 293, 347, 378, 421, 424, 495, 500-501, 502, 510, 511, 522
Papillon Cure 272
Pard Dog Food 19
Parkay 160
Parker Brothers 31, 484
Parker Pens 324-325
Parrish, Maxfield 170-171, 214, 236, 254, 491
Parrot Peanut Butter 316
Pasta 293
Pastime Tobacco 460
Patches 60
Patio Mexican foods 471
Patriot Tobacco 460
Patterson Preserving Co. 288
Pat. Wood Box Stove Polish 425
Paul Jones Whiskey 247
Pay Day 72, 78
Peacock Ink 325
Peanut butter 9
Peanut butter warmer 323

Pearl Milling Company 20
Pears' Soap 357-358
Peckham Trust Co. 511
Peek Frean's Biscuits 142
Peerless Dyes 174-175
Pencil clips 389, 404
Pencils (*see also* Pens) 239, 379, 389, 394, 405, 526
Pennsylvania Railroad 523
Penn Tobacco Company 460-471
Pens 495, 497, 501, 526
Pepperidge Farms 410
PepsiCo 338
Pepsi-Cola 395-402
Pepto-Bismol 272-273, 361
Perfection Dyes 175
Perfume vendor 219
Perry Davis' Pain Killer 273
Pest control 294
Pete Dailey Cigars 461
Peter Paul Mounds 78
Pettengill Company 192
Peter Rabbit Peanut Butter 316
Peters 207
Pettijohn's Breakfast Food 91
Pez 78
Pfaff's Lager 56
Phenix Cheese 163, 402
P.H. Hamburger Co. 247
Philadelphia Brand Cream Cheese 160, 161, 163
Philadelphia Old Stock 57
Philip Morris 122, 161, 457, 461-462
Phillips Petroleum 511
Phoenix Sewing Machine 348
Photos 379, 420, 421
Pickwick Ale 57
Pickwick Club Tobacco 462
Picobac Tobacco 462
Piecrust Mix 30
Piedmont Cigarettes 462-463
Piel Bros. Beer 57
Pillsbury 33-34
Pilot-Knob Coffee 123
Pilot Tobacco 463
Pinbacks 167, 342, 498, 501
Pinch-Hit Tobacco 463
Pins 135, 400, 500
Piper Heidsieck 463
"Pirates of Penzance, The" 307
Pitchers 21
Pizza Hut 397, 528-529
Plaques 62
Planters Peanuts 141, 316-322, 484

562 ■ ADVERTISING

Plates 10, 44, 61, 263, 388
Players Tobacco 464
Playing cards 367, 370, 379, 400, 481-482, 485
Playtex 279
Plug cutters 457
Plumbing 294-295
Plume & Atwood 238
Pogue's 464
Poker Tobacco 464
Poland Water 301
Polar 73, 78
Polarine Motor Oil 511
Polly Peachtree Hair Dressing 219
Pompeian Massage Cream 219
Pond's Creams 220
Pontiac 511-512
Pony Post 464
Pop! 88
Poppin' Fresh Doughboy 33
Popsicles 295
Porter's Liniment Salve 273
Poser 95
Post 91-92
Postcards 55, 56, 60, 157, 167, 306, 379, 389, 393, 409
Posters 5, 10-11, 12, 17, 24, 37, 42, 45, 49, 52, 55, 96, 100, 101, 104, 109, 119, 139, 169, 176, 179, 180, 187, 189, 190, 196, 197, 198, 207, 216, 234, 248, 249, 262, 276, 282, 293, 303, 304-305, 306, 307-308, 310, 326, 344, 355, 358, 359, 367, 371, 388, 391, 432, 472, 477, 478, 479-480, 483, 515, 519, 520-521, 523
Post Toasties 92
Postum 23, 92, 169, 181
Pot and pan scraper 167
Power G. 512
Powerpoint 332
Prell Shampoo 220, 360
Premier Beer 57
Premiums 253, 266, 330, 435
Premium Saltines 141, 142
Presley, Elvis 306
Preston Cocoa 111
Primley's California Fruit Gum 201-202
Primo Beer 57, 60
Primrose Ice Cream 164
Prince Albert Tobacco 464-465, 468
Procter & Gamble 1, 101, 213, 214, 217, 220, 221, 272, 356, 358-362
Program book 304, 306
Prom home permanent 331
Process Gas Range 232

Providence Insurance 226
Prudential Insurance 226-227
Puck Tobacco 465
Puffed Wheat 92
Pulver Gum 202
Pulver's Cocoa 116
Pump 514
Punky Special Beer 57
Pure Gas Pump 512
Pure Gold 185
Purex 516
Purity Ice Cream 164
Putnam Dyes 175
Putnam Horseshoe Nails 19
Puzzles 84, 90, 251, 262, 312, 340, 484
Pynx 233

Q

Quaker Oats Company 1, 11, 20-22, 35, 92-93
Quaker Oats 12, 91
Quaker Puffed Wheat 93
Queen City Tobacco Co. 465
Queen Hair Dressing 220
Quest Mfg. Co. 300
Quicksilver Messenger Service 306
Quik 78, 116
Quincy Brand Allspice 139
Quisp 94

R

R. A. Patterson 465
RC100 Cola 403
R & G Corsets 112
R & H Adams Netting 293
R. J. Reynolds 25, 106, 186, 338, 436, 439, 464, 467-471, 476
R. M. Bishop & Co. 465
Racks 162
Radio Coffee 123
Radio Flyer 484-485
Radio Premiums 11
Radios 379, 389
Radio Steel & Manufacturing Company 485
Radway's Medicinal 273
Raid 294
RainBlo 73
RainBlo Gum Balls 78
Rainier Beer 57-58
Raisinets 78
Raleigh Cigarettes 465
Ralston Purina 94
Ramblin' Root Beer 372
Ram's Head Ale 58

Rawleigh's 220-221, 273
RCA 128-129, 234, 237
Real Tobacco 465
Reamer 187
Receipts 389, 405
Recipes 27-28, 171, 410
Records 379
Reddy Kilowatt 238-239
Red Bird 468
Red Crown 512
Red Devil Tobacco 465
Red Dot Cigars 465
Red Feather Peanut Butter 322
Redford's Navy Cut Tobacco 466
Red Indian Cut Plug 466
Red Kamel 468
Red Lobster Inns, 31, 343
Red Man 466
Red Rabbit 468
Red Seal 466
Red Top Flour 35
Red Wolf Coffee 123
Reed's Tonic 273-274
Reel Man Talcum Powder 221
Regal Boots 353
Regal Cube Cut 466
Registers 413
Reid's Stout 58
Reinken Havana Cigars 467
Reliable 136
Relio Brand Jar Rubbers 290
Remington 207
Remington Typewriters 300-301
Reo Tobacco 467
Reproductions 11-12, 39, 71, 82, 525
Restorative Nervine 266
Reunion cups 62
Rexall and Country Club; Bridge Whist and Fifth Avenue 485
Rex Enclosures and Tops 512
Rex's Tobacco 467
Reyno 468
Rheingold 58
Rheingold Scotch Ale 58
Rice Krispies 87
Rice's Seeds 190-191
Richardson Vicks, Inc. 361
Ricoh 333
Ring Dings 169
Ringed Licorice 79
Ringling Brothers & Phineas T. Barnum 477-478, 528
Rising Sun Stove Polish 425
RJR 468

Roasters 314
Robert Burns Cigars 471
Robert Griffin Co. 285
Robeson Razor 334
Robin Hood 402
Rocket 81
Rock Island 524
Rockwell, Norman 92, 195, 197, 198, 218, 371
Roessle Brewery Co. 58
Roll downs 515
Rolling Rock Premium Beer 58
Rolls Razor 334
Roly Poly 295
Roper 234
Rosebud Tobacco 471
Rose Marie Tea 430
Royal Baking Powder 35
Royal Crown Cola 373, 394, 402-404
Royal Navy Tobacco 471
Royal Society 348
Royal Stoves 425
Rubber goods 296
Rubin, Jerry 305
Rubsam & Horrmann Brewing Co. 58
Rugs 254, 352
Rulers 159
Runkel Brothers Cocoa & Chocolates 116
Ruppert Knickerbocker 58-59
Rush, William 442

S
St. Charles Evaporated Cream 164
St. Charles Manufacturing 234
St. Jacob's Oil 276
St. Lawrence Tobacco 472
St. Louis Beef 253
Saddle and trunk makers 296
Safes 413
Sahib 430
Salada Tea 430-431
Salamander Safes 413
Salem Cigarettes 470, 472
Salesman's samples 139, 296, 421
Salmon's Tea 431
Salt and pepper shakers 42, 60, 237-238, 289, 335, 400, 501
Samoset Chocolates 79
Samples 266
Samsung 237
Sanchez & Haya Cigars 472
Sandford's Inc. 412
Sandwich Manufacturing Company 179
Sanford's Gingers 139
Sanford's Inks 325

Sanatogen 274
Santa Claus Soap 362-363
Santana 307
Sapolin 312, 425-426
Satin Cigarettes 472
Sawyer Farms Butter 164
Sawyer's Crystal Blue Dyes 175
Sawyer's Slickers 112
Scales 76, 413-414
"Scarlet Empress, The" 305
Schenck's Medicinal 274-275
Schlitz Beer 59-60
Schlitz Brewing Co. 54, 59-61
Schlitz Malt Liquor 60
Schmidt's Beer 61
School package 406
Schrafft's 79-80
Schuster's 404
Scope Mouthwash 221, 361
Scraper holder 61
Sea Foam 35
Seagram's 241, 242, 247-248
Seal of Kentucky Whiskey 248
Seal of North Carolina Tobacco 472
Sealtest 161, 164
Sears, Roebuck and Co. 233-234
Sebastian Miniatures 171
Seed packages 189, 190, 191-193, 194
Seeger Refrigerator Co. 234
Seitz Brewing Co. 61
Selig, E. 443
Selox 360
Sensation Cigar/Cut Plug 472
Sen-Sen Gum 202
Seven Crown (7 Crown) 248
Seven-Eleven (7-11) Ice Cream 164
Seven-Up (7Up) 373, 404-405
"Seven Year Itch, The" 305
Sewing kit 165, 370
Shackamaxon Worsted Co. 285
Shakers 35, 186, 191-194, 275
Shapleigh Coaster 485
Sharples Separator Co. 165-167
Sharp's Toffee 80
Shaving 7
Shaw's Malt 275
Sheet music 382, 393-394
Shelf 163
Shelf strip 431
Shell 512
Sherwin-Williams 312
Ship 'n Shore 31
Shipstad & Johnson's Ice Follies 528
Shirts 107, 112

Shoe Lace Service Station 353-354
Shoes 5, 12
Shonk, Chas. W. 278
Shopping list 500
Short's Skotchemint Chewing Gum 202
Shot glass porcelain holder 247
Shovels 426
Showcases 414
Shower curtain 440
Sifters 25
Signs 9, 12, 15, 18, 19, 22, 25, 32, 33, 34, 35,
   36, 37, 38, 39, 40, 42-43, 44-45, 46, 47, 48,
   49, 50, 51, 52, 53, 54, 56, 57, 58, 60, 63, 74,
   79, 80, 85, 93, 96, 100, 104, 105-106, 107,
   108, 110, 111, 112-113, 114, 115, 116, 117,
   119, 120, 121, 125-126, 127, 129-130, 131,
   135, 154, 157, 158, 159, 161, 164, 167,
   172, 174, 175, 176-177, 178-179, 183, 185,
   189, 190, 196, 197, 200, 201-202, 205,
   206-207, 208, 209, 210, 216, 221, 223, 225,
   226, 229, 240, 241-243, 244, 245, 246, 247,
   248-250, 253, 255, 256, 258, 259, 260-261,
   262, 263, 264, 272, 273, 274-275, 277, 279,
   282, 283, 285, 288, 289-290, 293, 294, 295,
   296-297, 309, 312-313, 321, 324, 326, 334,
   337, 339, 344, 345, 346, 347, 348-349, 350,
   354, 355, 356, 362-363 367, 378, 383-384,
   388, 389, 390, 391, 394, 395, 401, 405,
   406, 408, 409, 411, 414, 416, 417, 418,
   422-423, 425-426, 429, 432-433, 437-438,
   439, 440, 445, 447, 448, 449, 450, 451-452,
   462, 463, 464-465, 466, 467, 471, 472, 474,
   475, 479, 480, 481, 482, 483, 486, 487,
   489, 508, 510, 512, 513, 514, 515, 516,
   517, 518, 522, 524, 525
Silas King Dry Goods 112
Silver Bell Tobacco 472-473
Silver Dust 97-98, 101
Silver-Kleen 270
Silver Medal 136
Silver Twins 98
Similac 275
Sinclair Power 512
Singer Sewing Machine 348-349
Singer's Gravel 19
"Si Perkins/or The Girl I Left Behind
   Me" 307
Sir Haig Cigar 473
Sitting Bull Durham Tobacco 473
Six packs 384
Skippy Premium 134
Sleepy Eye Flour 36
Slippery Elm Lozenges 275
Slot machines 414

Index — 565

Smiling Sam 322
Smith Brothers 276
Smith & Wesson Revolvers 207-208
Snacks 296
Snap! 88
Snickers 74, 80
"Snow White and the Seven Dwarfs" 304
Snow White Flour 36
Snowboy Washing Powder 101
Soap 95
Society King 354
Society Rye 248
Socony 512
Socony-Mobil 509
Socrates 473
Soda bottles (*see also* Bottles) 2, 50
Soda fountain 417
Soda locker 392-393
Soft & Dri 332
Softasilk 29
Solar Tipped Shoes 354
Songbook 56, 387
"Son of the Shiek, The" 305
Sons of Champlin 306
S.O.S. Soap Pads 102, 270
South Bend Fishing Tackle 482
South Bend Watch 433
Southern Enriched Bread 38
Southern Freight 524
Souvenirs 317, 502
Sozodont Tooth Powder 221
Speckled Beauty 468
Spilter's Buttermilk Talcum Powder 221
Spinner 393
Spirit of St. Louis 473
Spool cabinet/chest (*see also* Display cabinets/cases) 344, 345, 346, 347-348, 349, 414
Spoons 13, 62
Sports 13, 41
Sprite 372, 406
Squaw Brand 186
Squire's Pig 253
Squirt 406
Squirrel Peanut Butter 322
Staggs-Bilt Homes 283
Stag Trousers 112
"Stampede, The" 305
Standard Brands 119, 316
Standard Oil 509, 527, 528
Standard Sewing Machine 349
Standard Varnish Works 312
Star and Crescent Cigar 473
StarKist 134, 253-254

Star Soap 363
Statues 311, 317, 321
Steak 'n Ale 34, 343
Steak-umm 134, 254
Stegmaier Brewing Co. 48, 61
Steins 42, 44, 45, 51, 56, 62, 391
Steelcote Auto Polish 513
Sterling Drug 215
Sterling Pepsin Gum 202
Sterling Tea 431
Stix Bar 73
Stollwerck 80, 116
Stone Hill Wine 248-249
Stoneware 296, 465
Store bins 427, 428, 431
Store card 114, 255, 353, 439, 478-479
Store display figure 240, 352
Story 39, 85
"Strathmore, The" 480
Straws 404
Straw holders 414
String holder 311
Stroh's Beer 61-62
Stuart Bros. Company 285
Studebaker 513
Suchard Cocoa and Chocolate 116
Sumatra Tobacco 474
Sun Crest 407
Sundblom, Haddon 371
Sun dial 68
Sun Garter 112
Sunkist 186-187, 471
Sunny Brook Whiskey 249
Sunoco 513
Sunshine Biscuit Company 2, 142-153
Supreme Peanut Butter 322-323
Sure Shot 474
Swansdown Coffee 123
Swanson Frozen Dinners 410
Sweet Caporal 474
Sweetheart Soap 363
Swift's Premium 254
Swift's Pride Washing Powder 102
Swiss Airlines 520
Switzer 72
Switzer Licorice 72-73, 80
Sykes Comfort Powder 221-222
Syrup 297
Syrup of Figs 187

T
T.S. Townsend Creamery Co. 167
Tab 372
Taco Bell 398, 529

Tanlac 277
Taster's Choice 78, 123
Tape measures 237
Tap knobs 50, 51, 57, 58, 60, 63, 384
"Tarzan and His Mate" 304
Tattoos 395
Taylor's Homemade Peanut Butter 323
Teachenor-Bartberger Engraving Co. 285
Tea House Tea 136, 431
Tea pots 427
Teddy Bear Peanut Butter 323
Telephones 291, 294, 343, 405
Television 269-270
Terre Haute Brewing Co. 62
Tetley 431
Tetlows Face Powder 222
Texaco 513-514
Texas and Pacific Railway 524
The Automatic Tap & Faucet Co. Ltd. 285
The Babcock Printing Press Mfg. Co. 286
Theragran 269
Thermometers 16, 24, 56, 266, 309, 384-385, 388, 389, 390, 392, 395, 440, 459
Thimbles 18, 111, 297
Thomas Bread 38
Thomas' Inks 325
Thomas-Houston Electric Company 237
Thomas Mills & Bro. Ice Cream 167
Thompson & Taylor Spice Co. 36
Tide 101, 360
Tiffany Studios 283
Tiger 474
Timetable 524
Timken Roller Bearing Co. 287
Tin clip 278
Tin letter folder 223, 226
Tins 2, 6, 12, 15, 16-17, 18, 32, 35, 64, 65, 66, 69, 71, 75, 76-77, 80, 82, 98-99, 114, 115, 116, 119, 120, 122, 131, 136, 140, 141, 142, 143-153, 172, 199, 200, 205, 209, 212-213, 214, 215, 216, 217, 218-219, 220-222, 259, 260, 262, 263, 264, 272, 273, 277, 292, 293, 314, 315, 318, 322, 427, 428, 429, 430, 431, 437, 439, 440, 443-444, 445-446, 447, 448-449, 450, 451, 453, 455, 457, 459, 460, 464, 466, 467, 471-473, 474, 475, 476, 487, 513, 515
Tip trays 44, 59, 61, 115, 116, 128, 162, 203, 242, 245, 271, 364, 385, 393, 394, 406, 417, 423, 424-425
Tire repair kit 506
Tobacco 2, 8, 9, 12, 106
Tokens 501
Tom Sawyer Apparel for Real Boys 112

Toni Company 331
Tonka Tobacco 475
Tony the Tiger 87
Tootsie Roll 80-81
Tops 68
Towle's Log Cabin Syrup 292
Town Talk Caps 112
Toys 68, 116, 159, 317, 340, 385, 401, 418, 495, 497, 502
Trade cards 13, 21, 84, 158, 252, 258, 262, 266, 345, 358, 390, 392
Trademarks 14, 21, 26-31, 41, 70, 81-82, 83-84, 91, 92-93, 96, 97-98, 103, 266, 276, 278, 310, 312, 328-329, 337, 350, 359, 365, 471, 506, 509, 521
Transworld Airlines 521
Trays 42, 43, 44, 45, 46, 47, 48, 49, 51, 52, 54, 57, 61, 62, 63, 68, 94,164, 245, 367, 379-382, 386, 390, 391, 395, 399, 400-401, 421, 431, 452
Treasure Line Stoves and Ranges 426
Triners Bitter Wine 249
Trommer's Beer 62
Trout-Line Tobacco 475
Try-Me 407
Tubular Cream Separators 167
Tuffy 270
Tumblers 60
Tums 277
Tupperware 233
Turkish Dyes 175
Tuxedo Tobacco 475
TWA (TransWorld Airlines) 521
Twenty Mule Team 516
Twin Oaks Tobacco 475
Typewriters and Supplies 297-301
Typewriter ribbons 297-301

U
Umbrellas 401
UMC 208
Uncle Ben's Rice 75
Uncle John's Maple Syrup 292
Uncle Sam Peanut Warner 323
Uncle Sam's Nerve and Bone Liniment 136
Uncle Sam Ranges 426
Uncle Sam Tobacco 475
"Uncle Tom's Cabin" 305
Uncle Wiggily 486
Uneeda Biscuit 141, 153
Uniform Cut Plug Tobacco 475
Union Beer 62
Union Central Life 288

Union Commander Cut Plug 475
Union Leader Tobacco 476
Union Pacific Railroad 524-525
Union Pacific Tea 431
Union Razor 334
Unique Art Mfg. Co. 486
United Fresh Fruit and Vegetable
  Association 182, 187-188
United Nations 197
United States Banking 140-141
United States Fuel Administration 197
United States Tire 514
Upholstery brush 502
Upton Machine Co. 233
U.S. Ammunition 208
U.S. Marine Cut Plug 476
U.S. Typewriter Ribbon Mfg. Co. 301
Utica Club 62

V
V-8 Coctail Juice 410
Vacuum Oil Company 509
"Vagrants, The" 307
Valley Farm's Ice Cream 167
Valley Forge Beer 63
Valvoline 514
Van Houten's Cocoa 117
Vanity Fair Cigarettes 476
Vantage 470
Vaseline 222
Vegetables 9
Velveeta 161, 168
Velvet Coffee 123
Velvet Pipe Tobacco 454, 476
Vending Machines 77, 80, 200, 201, 322,
  325, 456
Vendor 200, 415
Vermont Maid Syrup 471
Vermont Mutual Fire Insurance 228
Veteran Brand 124
Vicks 277, 361
Victor Berliner Gram-o-phone Co. 128
Victor Macaroni 293
Victor Talking Machine Co. 127-128
Victory Lozenges 277
Vindex Shirts 112
Virginia Slim Cigarettes 461, 476
"Virginian, The" 305
Vitos 33
Vlasic Pickles 410
Vogue 293
Vroman Foods 31
V. Schoenecker Boot & Shoe Co. 354
Vulcan 334

VX Beer 63

W
W. G. Dean & Son 81
W. J. Parkes and Company 464
W. W. W. Ring 291
Walgreen's 418
Walker & Co. 510
Walko Tablets 180
Walla-Walla Gum 202
Wall plaque 62
Wall pocket 177
Waltham 433-434
War Bonds 197
Ward's Cake 172
Ward's Collars 112-113
Ward's Crush 407
War Eagle Fuel Co. 288
Warhol, Andy 409
Warner Lambert 72
Washburn Crosby Company 26
Washington's Coffee 124
Watches 304, 321-322, 401-402, 440
Watch fobs 388, 402
Water 301
Waterman Pens 325-326
Watertown Steam Engine Co. 287
Watkins 139
Watkins Baking Powder 36
Watney's Ale 63
Wayne Tank & Pump Company 514
Wayne's 188
W.B. Fonda 287
Wedding Bell Coffee 124
Week End Special Cigar 476
Weight Watchers 134
Welcome Soap 363
Wells and Hope Distillers 249
Wells Co. 294
Wells Fargo 416
Wells Shoes 354
Welsh Rabbit Biscuit 153
Westclox 434
West Electric Hair Curlers 222
West End Brewing Company 63
West Hair Net 222
Western Publishing 528
Western Union 129-130
Wheaties 27, 94
Whirlpool 233-235
White House Ginger Ale 407
White Rain 331, 332
White Rock 407-408
White Rose 36

White Seal Pure Rye 249
White Sewing Machine 349
White Star Rye 249
White Swan Coffee 124
White Swan Peanut Butter 323
Whitman's 81-82
Whittemore's Bon Ton Boot Polish 354
Whiz Auto Top Dressing 514
Who 307
Whole-Sum Mints 82
Whoppers 72, 82
Wilbur, Lawrence 196
Wild West Soap 364
William Elliot/First National Stores 168
William G. Lord Insurance 228
Willimantic 349
Wilson Sporting goods 398
Wilson Whiskey 249-250
Winchester Potatoes 188
Winchester 208
Winsor Coconut 139
Wine Coca 277
Wine Sap 468
Wingfoot Express 506
"Wings" 305
Winner Plug Tobacco 476
Winston Cigarettes 470, 476
Winter Hill 291
Wisconsin Telephone Company 126
Witol's Vampire Shampoo 222
"Wizard of Oz, The" 305
Wonder Bread 39
Wood 302
Wood-Lac Enameloid 313

Wood pick 389
Wood, Taber & Morse 180, 525
Woodlawn Mills 354
Woolsey's Varnishes 313
Woolworth's 419-420
Worcester Salt 139
World, The 293
World War I 5, 195-198, 329, 396, 436, 454, 504
World War II 195-198, 230, 337, 397, 454
Wrangler 113
Wright & Taylor Whiskey 250
Wright's 277
Wrigley's 202-203
Wyeth, N.C. 371
Wyler's 82

Y

Yankee Cake Co. 169
Yankee Cigar 476
Yankee Doodles 169
Y-B Cigars 476
Yellow Cab Manufacturing Co. 504
Yoplait 30
York Steak House Systems 31, 343

Z

Zang Brewing 63
Zeno gum 201
Zephyr 514
Zeppelin Bread 39
Zero 73, 82
Zingo 82
Zubelda Cigarettes 455